THE PASTRY CHEF

THE PASTRY CHEF

William J. Sultan
Consultant
Tamarac, Florida

AVI PUBLISHING COMPANY, INC. WESTPORT, CONNECTICUT

Photographs, including cover, by Constance Brown

*Courtesy of John J. Bowen, Dean and Director, and
Robert M. Nograd, Curriculum Director and Dean of Faculty,
Culinary Arts Division, Johnson & Wales College,
Providence, Rhode Island*

Library of Congress Cataloging in Publication Data

Sultan, William J.
　　The pastry chef.

　　Bibliography: p.
　　Includes index.
　　1. Pastry. 2. Quantity cookery. I. Title.
TX773.S924　1983　　　　641.8′65　　83—21481

ISBN 0-87055-422-0

Printed in the United States of America

2 3 4 5　　0 9 8 7 6

Contents

4 Doughnut Varieties   117

5 Variety Pies   139

6 Puff Paste and Choux Paste Products   191

7 Variety Cakes—Gateaux   231

8 Dough Conditioners and Softeners   323

9 Prepared Mixes   343

14 Variety Tarts (Flans), Fruit Cakes (Cobblers), and Strudel   551

15 Variety Cheese Cakes and Specialties   579

16 Frozen Desserts   601

17 Cake Decorating and Finishing   635

Appendix   646

Preface

The Pastry Chef is a comprehensive reference resource for the baker and pastry chef. It has evolved from an earlier, successful two-volume book, *Modern Pastry Chef*.

Changing times and eating habits, nutritional awareness, food selection, and food preparation and service produced a need for organized production systems and efficient service. Prepared mixes, fillings, and quick-frozen bread products, all of which are now quite common in mass-feeding and quick-feeding operations as well as in many hotels, restaurants and institutional feeding establishments, reduce the preparatory work of the pastry chef.

The feeding of large groups in institutions such as schools requires rapid preparation and service of baked goods with careful attention to quality and appearance. The use of microwave ovens, convection heating equipment, quick-defrost equipment, and food service equipment, supplement the work of the pastry chef.

This book contains information on prepared mixes and formularies for the preparation of prepared mixes. Facts and information about dough additives and emulsifiers are supplemented with new formularies and dough mixing methods. New products, and formularies for these products, have been added to keep the book current with new product development. For pastry chefs and bakers who are producing bakery foods at elevations of 2000 feet or more above seal level, an appendix explaining necessary procedures is included.

Not only has equipment been streamlined, but tasks once done by the baker chef, the pastry chef, and the decoration and ice cream or frozen dessert chef are now combined under the supervision and direction of a single, skilled pastry chef. This text has been prepared to help the pastry chef and his assistant. Included are suggestions for the use of prepared and supplementary products that will be of direct assistance to the pastry chef. The recipes, formulas, and methods of production cover all baked products, desserts, and pastry supplements included on the menus of most dining establishments from luxury gourmet to the fast service operation.

Recipes and formulas are constructed to serve approximately 100 diners. There will be variable yields due to variables in portion control and method of service; any adjustment can be made by the pastry chef. Every recipe is easily divided to obtain smaller yields. A homemaker may not wish to make 10 ten-inch cakes, so he or she could divide the recipe by five for instance, and make two ten-inch cakes. You can do the same for cookies. You may not want 100 cookies, so divide the recipe in half to obtain 50 cookies. Or, make the cookie dough for the full recipe and freeze whatever portion of the dough you do not wish to use immediately.

September 1983   WILLIAM SULTAN

Related AVI Books

PRACTICAL BAKING
  Revised 3rd Edition   *Sultan*

PRACTICAL BAKING MANUAL
  Sultan

COOKIE AND CRACKER TECHNOLOGY
  2nd Edition   *Matz and Matz*

ENERGY MANAGEMENT IN FOODSERVICE
  Unklesbay and Unklesbay

FOOD PRODUCTS FORMULARY
  VOL. 1, 2nd Edition, MEATS, POULTRY, FISH AND SHELLFISH
    Long, Komarick, and Tressler
  VOL. 2, CEREALS, BAKED GOODS, DAIRY AND EGG PRODUCTS
    Tressler and Sultan
  VOL. 3, FRUIT, VEGETABLE AND NUT PRODUCTS
    Tressler and Woodroof
  VOL. 4, FABRICATED FOODS
    Inglett and Inglett

HANDBOOK OF SUGARS
  2nd Edition   *Pancoast and Junk*

MENU PLANNING
  2nd Edition   *Eckstein*

L. J. MINOR FOODSERVICE STANDARDS SERIES
  VOL. 1 NUTRITIONAL STANDARDS   *Minor*
  VOL. 2 SANITATION, SAFETY AND ENVIRONMENTAL STANDARDS   *Minor*

PRACTICAL MEAT CUTTING AND MERCHANDISING
  VOL. 1, 2nd Edition BEEF   *Fabbricante and Sultan*
  VOL. 2,   PORK, LAMB, AND VEAL   *Fabbricante and Sultan*

QUALITY CONTROL IN FOODSERVICE
  Revised Edition   *Thorner and Manning*

QUANTITY COOKING
  Mario

1

Specialty Quick Breads

The term "specialty" here refers to the special qualities and varieties of quick breads prepared by the skilled pastry chef. The high quality of the ingredients and the special attention given to serving the quick breads are important factors that enhance basic as well as sophisticated menus. Quick breads also permit feeding large groups within short time periods. Many restaurants and finer dining rooms are known for the hot or warm quick breads served before menu selections are made. The aromas are appealing to the diner and frequently stimulate the diner's appetite.

There are many uses for the variety of hot breads and quick breads served at meals and at snack periods. The breakfast served with a variety of biscuits, muffins, cornsticks, scones, and similar quick bread varieties is usually filling and quite satisfying. This is especially noteworthy among the younger patrons at schools and colleges. The use of muffins and similar quick breads for between-meal snacks is equally popular and satisfying. The freshly made biscuit is often used for shortcake desserts. Strawberry deep-dish shortcake, served with a tender biscuit base and top, garnished with whipped cream, is an old-fashioned delicacy. The tender biscuit is an important factor. The same tender biscuit may be used as a dumpling, or as the base for a hot, creamed dish such as chicken à la king. The pastry chef and the chef are the principals in planning the supportive quick breads that supplement the menu dishes.

The recipes that follow are somewhat richer and just a little more costly than the quick bread recipes used for commercial production. The improved quality and variety account for the slight increase in cost. However, the cost is minor when compared to the cost of other food items on

1

the menu. For example, biscuits are often made without the use of eggs, but when eggs are used they provide added nutrition, increased volume, tenderness, and improved keeping qualities. The use of a small amount of egg yolk in the recipe will further improve the quality of biscuits. Biscuit varieties are also enhanced by the use of different fillings and by altering the shapes.

Quick breads are often baked, cooled, and then immediately frozen for later use. This applies to all types of quick breads. It is important that the quick breads be stored so that the wrapping may be removed quickly for defrosting. Microwave, infrared, and convection ovens are used extensively for quick defrosting and heating of quick breads. In many instances, metal trays and wrappings must be removed before inserting the breads into the microwave ovens. The directions must be strictly adhered to when using such equipment.

As indicated in the preface, recipes will be presented so that they meet the requirements for feeding approximately 100 people. Adjustment for increased needs may be made easily. The size of the biscuit or muffin will actually determine the count. For example, the 2½-in. round biscuit is standard although the small 1½-in. variety may be served, especially when biscuits are mixed with other quick breads in a basket.

Biscuits

Flour
Pastry flour, called for in many biscuit recipes, is somewhat stronger than the average cake flour in that it contains a slightly larger amount of gluten-forming proteins. It will make a tender biscuit but may also cause spreading and loss of shape. The use of a blend of bread flour, which is strong in gluten-forming proteins, and cake flour, which supplies a softening effect due to its finer starch particles, provides a favorable balance. If a very strong patent bread flour is used, containing approximately 13 to 14% protein, then the proportion of cake flour should be increased and the amount of bread flour reduced slightly. Because of periodic variations in the flour, judgment will have to be used when making adjustments. For example, you may find the dough becoming tougher or stiffer when mixed in the final stages without any decrease in the liquid used in the recipe. This is a sure indication that the bread flour is stronger. You may also find a sticky effect and excessive spread during baking of the biscuits. This may indicate that the flour is weaker and there should be a slight increase made in the amount of bread flour. With experience in making biscuits, the pastry chef and chef will quickly respond to changes in biscuit doughs and make the necessary adjustments to obtain quality biscuits.

Types of Fat
A good quality all-purpose vegetable shortening will provide excellent results. Of course, butter will increase the flavor, but it is expensive when used alone. Butter may be blended with equal parts of shortening or

margarine. Since the percentage of fat used for biscuits is not very great (often less than 15% based on the total weight of the flour) many chefs will use all butter for their biscuits. The fat for the flaky type of biscuit should be given careful consideration because these biscuits require a slightly higher percentage of fat. For example, it is suggested that the fat content in the recipe for home-style biscuits be increased by at least 50% to 1 lb 2 oz to provide the desired flakiness. The fat to be cut in or rubbed in with the flour should be firmer than that used for the blended method of mixing. It is common practice for chefs to use shortening in the dough and then brush the tops of the biscuits before and after baking with melted butter to provide the butter flavor.

Mixing Biscuit Dough

Fluffy cake-type biscuits use a blending and creaming method of mixing. Flaky-type biscuits use a cutting in or rubbing together of fat and flour to create lumps. The addition of the liquid to the flaky biscuit dough and minimal final mixing must be done carefully to prevent overmixing and resulting toughness. The flaky-type dough should be mixed just enough to moisten the flour and form a dough. The dough should be slightly lumpy and sticky. The home-style biscuit requires complete mixing to hydrate the flour and form a developed dough. This method is also used for the combination-type biscuit to ensure complete hydration and distribution of the yeast. One's own judgment is used to avoid overmixing, with the resulting tough dough.

Leavening of Biscuits

Most biscuits are leavened by the action of baking powder. The baking powder should be sifted and blended with the flour to ensure thorough distribution. This is especially important with the flaky dough where mixing is minimal. Baking soda is used for baking soda biscuits which tend to spread and flatten during baking because of the quick-acting and spreading effect of the baking soda. Some biscuits, such as Irish soda bread and scones, require a blend of baking soda and cream of tartar. Baking soda is best added to the dough by dissolving it first in part of the liquid; the solution is easily distributed and lumps of soda are avoided. When yeast is added in conjunction with baking powder, the yeast is dissolved in part of the liquid and then added in solution after the flour and baking powder have been slightly mixed. It is important to use baking powder and baking soda that is fresh and has been kept in a tightly closed container. Leavening agents do lose part of their strength when exposed to air and humidity. It is also important to use fresh yeast of good quality to ensure a vigorous and continuous fermenting action.

Panning and Washing the Tops of Biscuits

Biscuits that are widely spaced on pans tend to dry out during baking. Biscuits should be placed about ½ in. apart for regular size and ¼ in. apart for the smaller sizes. It is beneficial for the biscuits to touch slightly during baking so that they are softer when baked. It is advisable to place the biscuits on parchment paper baking sheets. It is more sanitary than greasing the pans. Brushing the tops of the biscuits with egg wash (a blend of two-thirds egg and one-third water) produces a shiny brown crust when baked. Biscuits may also be brushed with melted fat, butter, margarine, or a blend of milk and some fat to produce a dull, homemade effect. Some pastry chefs will moisten the tops of the biscuits lightly with water and then dust the tops with cake flour for variety. These biscuits are often termed white mountain biscuits and are served with other hot breads and quick breads.

Scrap Biscuit Dough
There should be very little if any scrap dough left. After the first rolling of the dough, and the second, the scrap dough remaining from the round cut-out biscuits should be formed into a rectangular shape and allowed to relax. This dough can then be rolled out and cut into small square or triangular (scone) shapes. These biscuits should be allowed to relax longer than others before baking because they will be slightly tougher due to the overworking.

Baking Biscuits
Biscuits should be baked at a higher temperature than other types of quick breads. Because they do not contain as much sugar as other quick breads, they take longer to brown. Because they are leavened largely by the action of the baking powder, a higher oven temperature will cause a more rapid action on the part of the chemical leavening agent with resulting volume. A cooler baking temperature will result in lower volume and drier baked biscuits because they remain in the oven longer to form a desirable crust color. The recommended oven temperature is 425–435°F. Judgment must be used because ovens vary.

Biscuit Specialties
Judgment and imagination will enable the chef and pastry chef to find many uses as well as to make great varieties of biscuits from the basic home-style biscuit dough. For example, approximately 8 oz of grated cheddar cheese may be blended with flour and mixed in with the dough to provide a tasty cheese flavor. Bacon bits (4 oz) may be added to the flour with a slight increase in the salt content for the special bacon-

1.1
Cut out the biscuits

flavored biscuit. Celery (1 oz of celery flakes) may be added in the final stages of mixing for this biscuit specialty. Garlic powder (½ to 1 oz, depending upon the strength and quality) may be added for specialty biscuits. These biscuits may be used for appetizing hot dishes and especially for the popular small pizzas. The chef can find many more uses for desserts and hot dishes.

Home-Style Biscuits

Ingredients	lb	oz	Mixing procedure
Sugar		10	Scale and measure accurately. Blend to-
Salt		1	gether to a smooth consistency
Skim milk powder		6	
Shortening, butter, or margarine		12	
Clover honey		4	
Eggs (part yolks optional)		12	Add in two stages and blend in well
Water (cool)	3		Stir in lightly
Bread flour	3	12	Sift together. Add and mix to a smooth
Cake flour	1	12	dough
Baking powder		4¼	

1. Flour the work table with bread flour.
2. Form the dough into a rectangle.
3. Roll out the dough about ½ in. thick.
4. Relax dough for a few minutes and cut out biscuits with round cutter (Fig. 1.1).
5. Place biscuits on parchment paper-lined or lightly greased baking pan. Space the biscuits about ½ in. apart (Fig. 1.2).
6. Roll scrap dough again and cut out. Remaining scrap dough can be rolled and cut into square shapes.
7. Brush tops of biscuits with egg wash, milk, or butter and margarine before baking.
8. Relax biscuits 10 min and bake at 425°F.

Yield: Approx. 100 2-in. biscuits

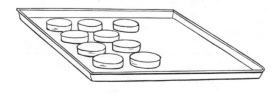

1.2
Space the biscuits on a pan

Flaky-Type Biscuits

For these biscuits, increase the shortening content of the home-style biscuit recipe to 1 lb 8 oz. The blend of shortening, butter, and margarine
will depend upon the chef and pastry chef.

1. Sift flour and baking powder together. Place in a mixing bowl with
    the shortening and rub together until small lumps of fat and flour
    are formed. If mixing in a machine, use slow speed and avoid form-
    ing a paste. The lumps formed will create flakiness.
2. Dissolve the skim milk powder, sugar, and salt in the water. Add the
    eggs and honey to the water and mix together.
3. Pour the solution into the flour-fat combination and mix slowly until
    the liquid is absorbed and a sticky, lumpy dough is formed. If mix-
    ing by hand, form a hollow in the center of the fat-flour combina-
    tion, add the liquid, and fold over gently to form the sticky dough.
4. It is advisable to chill the dough before rolling to avoid the extra
    stickiness.
5. Place the dough on a well floured work table and follow the same
    procedure for making the biscuits as you would when using the
    home-style biscuit method of mixing.

Note: Do not overmix the liquid with the fat and flour, as this will cause
gluten development in the flour with resulting toughness.

Raisin Biscuits   Soak 1–2 lb of raisins for about 10 min in cool water.
Drain raisins and fold into the dough gently during the final mixing stages
of the dough.

Combination Biscuits   (*Yeast–baking powder*)

Ingredients	lb	oz	Mixing procedure
Yeast (variable)		4–8	Dissolve and place to one side
Water (lukewarm)	1		
Sugar	1		Blend together to a smooth paste
Salt		1½	
Skim milk powder		6	
Shortening, marga-		12	
rine, or butter,			
Eggs (yolks		12	Add in 2 stages and blend in
optional)			
Water	2		Stir in
Bread flour	4		Sift together. Add to the above and stir
Cake flour	1	8	slightly. Add yeast solution and mix to a
Baking powder		2	smooth dough

Regular Biscuits

1. Cover the dough and place in a warm place to relax and rise until it feels gassy.
2. For the regular round or square-shaped biscuits, place the dough on a floured work table and follow the same procedure for the making of home-style biscuits (Figs. 1.1 and 1.2)
3. Space the biscuits ½ in. apart on pans. Allow biscuits to rise until they feel soft and gassy to the touch. Bake at 425°F. The biscuits will touch slightly as they bake. Biscuits are considered baked when they spring back gently to the touch and have the proper crust color. Do not overbake.

Yield: Approx. 100 2-in. biscuits

Cinnamon Biscuits

1. Place the relaxed dough on the flour dusted work table and divide into two or three equal pieces. Shape each piece into a rectangular shape and allow to relax 10 min.
2. Roll out the dough evenly, about ¼ in. thick. (Fig. 1.3)

1.3
Roll out the dough ¼ in. thick

3. Remove excess flour from surface of the dough with a brush. Brush the dough with melted butter or margarine and sprinkle the surface with cinnamon sugar (1 oz cinnamon blended well with 2 lb of granulated sugar). Raisins may be sprinkled on as well. (Fig. 1.4)

1.4
Brush dough with oil or melted fat and sprinkle with raisins, cake crumbs, and cinnamon sugar

4.   Roll up the dough into a tight roll and seal the edge. (Fig. 1.5)
5.   Cut slices of the rolled up dough ½ to three-quarters in. thick and place on parchment paper or greased baking pan. Space them 1 in. apart. Flatten slightly with the palms of the hands and brush tops with egg wash or melted butter or margarine. (Figs. 1.6–1.8)

1.5
Roll dough up tightly; seal the edge

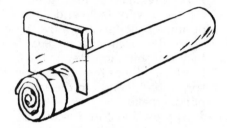

1.6
Brush top of roll with oil or melted fat and cut into even pieces with a scraper

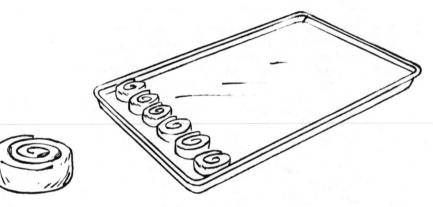

1.7
Cinnamon biscuit

1.8
Place on pans six down and nine across (more if biscuits weigh less), flatten lightly, and brush with egg wash

Cinnamon Muffin Biscuits

1.   The roll of dough (as in Fig. 1.5) should be about 1½ in. in diameter. Cut the slices 1 in. thick and place them into greased muffin tins.
2.   Allow the biscuits to relax in a warm place (proof box, if available) until they rise or spread and feel soft and gassy.
3.   Bake at 415–425°F. Do not overbake. These biscuits may be brushed or dabbed with simple icing when cool.

Muffins

The pastry chef and chef are aware of the great values that are present when serving warm or hot muffins and quick breads. Breakfast and luncheon menus often feature these baked items as a part of the home-made or baked-on-premises approach. Muffins, like biscuits, have many varieties. A variety can often be prepared from a basic muffin batter. Specialty and health-type muffins require separate recipes. They will be presented in this chapter and will be sufficient to serve approximately 100 patrons or diners.

Special Ingredients

Muffin variations are dependent upon the special ingredients that are added to make the differences or varieties. For example, raisin muffins and blueberry muffins merely require the addition of prepared raisins or blueberries in required amounts to the basic muffin batter. It is important that fruits and other specialty ingredients be prepared properly. For example, raisins may be very dry and must be presoaked to return moisture to them; and blueberries should be washed in cold water to remove foreign matter before being added to the batter. These ingredients are folded into the batter in the final stages of mixing.

Special Flours

Cereals and grains such as cornmeal, whole wheat flour, and bran make for additional varieties. It is important to remember that these special grains contain the total components of the grain, including the outside husk or bran. They may also include the fatty portion of the germ, such as wheat germ. This wheat germ portion may be added to increase the nutritional value, and the muffin or hot bread may be termed a "health muffin or bread." These ingredients are dry and branny rather than soft and starchy like a good cake flour. Therefore, when bran flour or corn-meal is added to a muffin batter the consistency of the batter will tend to thicken as it stands; the rate of liquid absorption is slower than with ordinary flour. You will find that muffin and hot bread batters have a soft consistency for that reason. In addition, the softness is due to the large percentage of liquid which also produces a moist muffin.

Mixing Muffin Batters

The term "cream" will be present in most instructions for mixing. This refers to the absorption of air and the creation of more air cells in the mixing process. This is especially evident in the mixing of dry ingredients with shortening or other fats, such as butter or margarine, in the first stages of mixing. The batter turns from a blended paste consistency to one of light softness. The air cells formed and incorporated into the batter are responsible for approximately one-third of the leavening of the muffins and hot breads, as well as the development of an even cell structure with smooth grain and texture. The flour is mixed into the batter only until the batter is smooth. It is not developed, for that would cause the gluten-forming proteins in the flour to form a tough, stretchy consistency causing tunnels in the muffins as well as a loss of volume. Additional emphasis will be placed upon mixing with each recipe. Some recipes, such as corn muffins, will have the liquid added in two stages to avoid lumping the cornmeal and improper mixing.

Quality

Many chefs and pastry chefs will use butter and egg yolks in their recipes. Of course, the taste and quality will be improved but the expense will increase as well. Since most muffins are smeared with additional butter, jams, and other sweet preparations, the fine flavor of the muffin is often overshadowed. This is a judgment to be made by the pastry chef. It is important to note that muffins can be prebaked and then frozen. The muffins are then reheated by placing them in muffin tins back in the oven. The heat of the oven is first absorbed by the metal of the pan and then gradually transferred to the muffin. If necessary, the muffins can be covered with tinfoil or another pan to prevent a dark crust from forming. If defrosting and reheating or warming is done in a microwave or similar oven, the muffins can be placed on a tray and placed in the oven for the specified time. Timing is crucial to avoid drying out the muffins when reheating.

Baking Muffins and Hot Breads

Since muffins are small units they should be baked at temperatures which will cause them to bake quickly without drying out. It must be remembered that some muffins are richer in sugar and fat content than others. Richer muffins are baked at lower temperatures. Large units, such as banana bread, are baked at lower temperatures because of the size of the loaf. Ovens that bake with strong bottom heat may require the chef to place the tins on double pans to avoid dark crust formation on the bottom. Muffins baked in greased muffin tins (without paper liners) should be removed from the tins while still warm to avoid condensation and gumminess while they are cooling. The muffins may be replaced in the tins after they have cooled to avoid drying out or rapid staling and also to permit quick reheating while the muffins are in the pans.

Steam is often injected into the oven when baking muffins. The moist steam prevents rapid crust formation on the muffin tops and reduces the possibility of cracking or peak formation. The steam allows for the formation of a smooth, rounded top, with a slight ridge around the edge of the muffin. While this is not essential for the homemade appearance, a small amount of moist steam should be injected into the oven before placing the muffins into it. The steam should be allowed to continue until the muffins have risen and begun to set. This should be done only if the oven, called an indirect-fired oven, has a steam injection system.

Size and Shape of Muffins and Hot Breads

Muffin tins vary in size and shape. There are the small size for the delicate 1-in. diameter muffins, as well as the larger 3-in. types. Naturally the size of the muffin tin will affect the yield from the batter, as will the addition of fruits, raisins, nuts, and other ingredients to the basic batter.

This is also true of hot quick breads baked in loaf pans. These pans will vary from the narrow small pans to the regular pans used for baking bread. There are square muffin tins as well as square pans for hot breads such as Southern corn bread.

Use of Prepared Mixes

There are many prepared mixes available to the chef. They will save time because the ingredients do not have to be scaled in dry form. Only liquid need be added. The mixes provide an average quality muffin, although many pastry chefs will add extras to batters to enrich them. Extras may be in the form of added eggs and yolks, melted butter, and milk. These adjustments require care to prevent the formula balance from being so changed as to yield poor results.

Basic Plain Muffins

Ingredients	lb	oz	Mixing procedure
Sugar	2	4	Cream these ingredients until soft and
Salt		1	smooth. Scrape sides of the machine kettle
Skim milk powder		5	to ensure complete blend of all ingredients
Corn syrup or glucose		4	
Shortening	1	8	
Eggs (part yolks)	1	4	Add the eggs in three stages and cream well after each addition
Water (cool)	2	4	Add and stir in slightly
Vanilla		1	
Cake flour	4	2	Sift together and add to the above. Mix
Baking powder		3	until smooth

1. The small size muffin tins (1-in. diameter) are usually greased with a soft shortening and brush. Larger muffins, either plain or filled varieties, may be baked in greased muffin pans or in paper-lined pans. Most muffins are baked in greased tins (Figs. 1.9 through 1.11).
2. Drop the muffin batter out by hand or with a scoop. For the corn-sticks, grease the tins and use the special finger-shaped scoop. The tins should be slightly more than half full.
3. Bake the muffins at 385–390°F. Plain muffins are baked without steam. Muffins that have a golden brown crust color and spring back gently to the touch are considered done.

Yield: Approximately 100 1-in. muffins

Raisin Muffins Raisins (2 lb, variable) are added to the batter during the final stages of mixing. The raisins should be presoaked for about 10 min in cool water to absorb moisture and to plump the raisins. This will

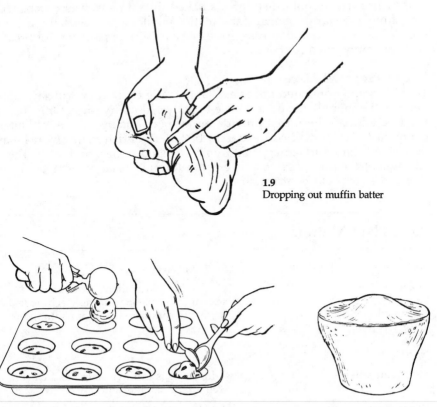

1.9
Dropping out muffin batter

1.10
Muffin mix may be deposited with a scoop
or spoon

1.11
Baked muffin

add moisture to the baked muffin, keep the muffin tender, and improve keeping qualities. Raisins that are unusually dry should be soaked for a longer period.

Blueberry Muffins Blueberries (2 to 3 pints, variable) of fresh, firm quality should be added to the batter and mixed in lightly after the batter is almost completely mixed. Blueberries should be rinsed in cold water and foreign matter removed before adding. Mix the batter at slow speed if mixing on the machine. This will avoid bruising and breaking the berries; if this happens, the batter will be discolored and the internal appearance will be grayish rather than golden yellow with whole blueberries throughout. These muffins are usually baked in paper-lined pans.

Date-Nut Muffins Pitted dates (1 lb) and walnuts (1 lb) are added to the batter in the final stages of mixing. Use a French knife dipped in cool water to chop through the dates. The nuts should also be chopped into small pieces. Blend the dates and nuts by tossing them gently together and then add to the batter by sprinkling over the batter while mixing at slow speed. This will avoid formation of large chunks of dates and nuts. These muffins are usually baked in paper cups.

Jelly or Jam Muffins These muffins may represent some specialty of the house. Jam, jelly, preserve, marmalade, or other spread specialty may be used. Fill the paper-lined muffin tins about ¼ full with batter. Drop about one teaspoon of filling into each muffin tin. Fill the tins slightly more than half full with batter so that the jam or other filling is covered. For identification of the filling variety used, place a drop of jam or filling on top of the batter before baking. This filling will spread during baking and will provide a homemade appearance. These muffins may be lightly dusted with confectioners sugar after they have been baked.

Bacon Muffins Dehydrated bacon bits or imitation bacon bits (4 oz, variable) are folded into the batter after it is mixed. Be sure to distribute the bits evenly. (Leftover bacon may be crisped and then finely chopped before adding to the batter.)

Corn Muffins

Ingredients	lb	oz	Mixing procedure
Sugar	1	8	Cream these ingredients together until soft
Salt		1	and smooth. Scrape sides and bottom of
Skim milk powder		6	mixing kettle several times during cream-
Shortening	1	4	ing
Corn syrup or glucose		4	
Eggs (part yolks)	1	8	Add in three stages and cream well after each addition
Water (cool)	2	4	Stir in gently
Vanilla (optional)		1	
Yellow cornmeal	1	2	Sift the flour and baking powder together.
Cake flour	3	12	Blend with the cornmeal. Add and mix
Baking powder		3½	until flour is absorbed
Water (cool)	1		Add and mix to a smooth batter

Reminder: The water is added in two stages to avoid lumping of the cornmeal. This will happen when all the water is added at one time. To eliminate the lumps, additional mixing will be required. This may cause the batter to toughen.

1. Grease the muffin tins well.
2. Drop the batter into the muffin tins by hand or with a scoop (Figs. 1.9 through 1.11).
3. Fill the tins half full.
4. Bake the muffins at 400°F if baking without steam in the oven. If baking with steam, set the oven temperature at 410°F. Inject mild

wet steam into the oven about 2 min before placing the muffins into the oven. Keep the steam on until the muffins have fully risen in the oven, then shut it off and allow the muffins to complete baking.
Yield: 100–125

Cornsticks Be sure the individual form tins are greased well. A blend of 3 lb of shortening and 1 lb of cake flour may be used. Be sure the greasing mix is soft. It may be necessary to add some vegetable oil and further soften the greasing preparation. The cornstick tins should be half full and the batter distributed evenly. The finger scoop is best suited to drop the batter into the tins.

Southern Corn Bread Bake in the regular baking sheets or in special baking pans that are square and about 1¼ in. high. These pans should be greased well and then dusted lightly with bread flour. Be sure to remove excess flour by tipping the pan. It is also good practice to line the pans with parchment paper instead of dusting with flour. If the pan liner is used, the corn bread must be removed by turning over onto another pan or board to remove the paper before cutting. The baked corn bread may be returned to the original pan in which it was baked for later reheating or warming. Fill the pans slightly more than half full. Bake at 390°F. It is best to cut the Southern corn bread with a sharp knife while the corn bread is still warm. Serving requires that the exposed cut sides of the corn bread slices be covered with a serving cloth or napkin to retain the heat and prevent excessive drying.

Whole Wheat Muffins

Ingredients	lb	oz	Mixing procedure
Sugar	1	8	Cream all ingredients together until soft
Salt		1	and smooth. Scrape sides and bottom of
Skim milk powder		6	kettle for even distribution
Shortening	1	4	
Molasses		8	
Cinnamon		¼	
Eggs	1	4	Add in three stages and cream in well after each addition
Water	2		Dissolve the soda in the water and add to
Baking soda		¾	the above. Stir in slightly
Bread flour	1	2	Sift these ingredients together. Add and
Cake flour	1		mix until the flour is absorbed
Whole wheat flour	1	4	
Baking powder		2½	
Water	1		Add and mix smooth
Raisins (presoaked) (optional)	2		Add and mix in lightly

1. Grease the muffin tins well. This will prevent the raisins that are in contact with the tins from sticking.
2. Fill the tins slightly more than half full. Use a scoop or drop out by hand.
3. A mild amount of steam may be injected into the oven before placing the muffins into the oven, but these muffins are usually baked without the steam in the oven. Bake at 400°F. Smaller muffins should be baked at a slightly higher temperature.
4. Muffins (all muffins baked without paper liners) should be removed from the pans while still warm. This will avoid excessive condensation. The muffins may be replaced in the tins after they have cooled.
5. Whole wheat muffin batter may also be baked as a hot bread. The batter may be placed into square pans as for Southern corn bread or into loaf pans and baked as a hot bread. Breads are baked at lower temperatures depending upon the size and thickness of the loaf.

Yield: 100 muffins

Bran "Health" Muffins

Ingredients	lb	oz	Mixing procedure
Light brown sugar	1	6	Blend ingredients together to a smooth
Salt		1	paste
Skim milk powder		8	
Shortening	1		
Molasses (unsulfured) (½ quart)	1	8	Add the molasses in three stages and cream well after each addition
Eggs		12	Add in two stages and cream in
Water (cool)	3		Dissolve the soda in the water and stir in
Baking soda		1½	lightly
Bread flour	2		Sift flours and baking powder together.
Cake flour	1		(Be sure to return the large bran flakes to
Bran flour	1	4	the flour blend.) Add and mix in lightly
Baking powder		1	until flour is completely absorbed
Water (cool)	1		Add to the above and mix smooth
Raisins (optional) presoaked	2		Fold in when batter is almost completely mixed

1. Use greased round or square muffin pans.
2. Fill the tins slightly more than half full. The tops of the muffins may be sprinkled lightly with bran flakes before baking.
3. Bake at 385–390°F.

Yield: 100–125 muffins (pan size variable)

Note: For "health and nutrition" variables, 1 lb of rolled oats and 2 oz of wheat germ may be added to replace the bran flour. This batter will thicken if allowed to stand.

Orange Muffins

Ingredients	lb	oz	Mixing procedure
Sugar	2	4	Cream all ingredients together until soft
Salt		1	and smooth
Skim milk powder		5	
Shortening and butter	1	8	
Corn syrup or glucose		4	
Eggs (part yolks)	1	4	Add in three stages and cream well after each addition
Orange juice (fresh or frozen reconstituted)	1		Blend the liquids together. Add and stir in lightly
Rind of 3 oranges (or orange flavoring)		½	
Water (cool)	1	4	
Vanilla		1	
Cake flour	4		Sift, add, and mix smooth
Baking powder		3	

1. Greased muffin tins or paper-lined pans may be used.
2. A pastry bag and large plain tube may be used to fill the small size muffin pans. A scoop may be used to fill the regular muffin tins.
3. Bake these muffins at 380°F.
4. The batter may be placed in loaf or square pans and baked as a hot bread. Bake these hot breads at a lower temperature depending upon the height or thickness of the pan.

Yield: 100–125

Note: The rind of the orange refers to the thin, outside skin of the orange which contains the natural oils and flavors. Do not use the white, internal pulp.

Quick Breads, Scones, and Popovers

There is a decided advantage in preparing and serving hot breads or quick breads. They provide variety in appearance from regular muffins. They also vary in composition. Longer shelf-life or keeping quality is an important matter. Since the loaf is a larger unit than a muffin and is baked in paper-lined pans, it tends to stay fresher for a longer period of time. Like muffins, hot breads can be baked and then chilled or frozen for later service. In fact, when cool or cold, the quick breads may be sliced thinner without crumbling than when fresh.

Quick breads are baked in a variety of loaf pans. The variables may go from the extreme of the large loaf pan to the more desirable narrow loaf pan, about 2 in. high. These breads may also be baked in the more shallow square pans, as for Southern corn bread, and cut into delicate squares or finger shapes for service while they are hot or warm. Because of the exposure of the sides of the slices and squares, quick breads should be placed in the serving tray and covered with a napkin or cloth to prevent rapid drying.

For banana bread it is best to use fully ripe bananas. These bananas have maximum sweetness and flavor. The bananas supply almost all the liquid, other than from the eggs, in the batter. Do not allow the bananas to remain exposed for a long period after they have been peeled; they oxidize and turn brown. That would cause the baked bread to have a darker or browner color rather than yellow flecked with slight traces of brown.

Popovers are a very popular hot bread and are served in fine dining establishments. Like muffins, popovers may be baked in small or large muffin pans. While the special iron pans are best suited for popovers because of heat retention, the usual muffin pans may be used very effectively. The characteristics of well made popovers are: a thin shell similar to a cream puff choux paste shell, crispness when baked, hollowness and ability to separate or tear easily for eating.

Popovers are leavened by the conversion of the moisture in the batter to steam during the early stages of baking, and by the natural expansion of the eggs in the batter. The structure of the popover is provided by the gluten-forming proteins present in the bread flour. The batter is very thin and is poured into the muffin tins after it has been thoroughly mixed.

Banana Bread

Ingredients	lb	oz	Mixing procedure
Sugar	1		Blend the ingredients together until soft
Brown sugar		12	and smooth
Salt		1	
Skim milk powder		2	
Shortening		14	
Eggs (part yolks)	1	8	Add in three stages and cream in well after each addition
Ripe mashed bananas	3		Add and stir in well
Vanilla		½	
Water		4	Dissolve the soda in the water. Add and
Baking soda		½	stir in lightly
Bread flour	1	8	Sift together and add. Mix to a smooth
Cake flour	2	2	consistency
Baking powder		1½	

1. Pans may be greased and dusted with flour (Fig. 1.12) or they may be lined with a parchment loaf pan liner (Fig. 1.13).
2. Fill the pans approximately half full.
3. Bake at 360°F until the loaf springs back gently to the touch. Larger loaves require longer baking at a lower temperature. (Fig. 1.14).

Yield: 100–150 slices

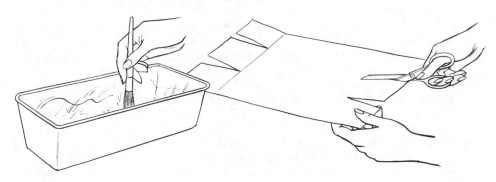

1.12
Grease pan and dust with flour

1.13a.
Cut liner paper to fit the loaf pan

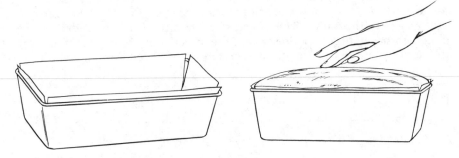

1.13b.
Insert paper liner evenly into the loaf pan

1.14
When baked, the loaf springs back to the touch

Banana Nut Bread Add 1 lb chopped walnuts or pecans to the banana bread recipe. Select the nuts carefully and avoid rancid or old nuts. Fold the nuts in gently during the final stages of mixing. When slicing the baked loaf, use a sharp knife to avoid tearing the slices because of the nut pieces.

Prune Bread Substitute 3 lb strained, cooked prunes for the bananas. Be sure to include the prune juice to supply the necessary liquid for the flour. If the batter feels rather stiff, soften by adding milk. The batter should have the same consistency as the plain muffin or basic muffin batter.

If the hot breads are baked in shallow square or regular baking pans, line the bottom of the pans with parchment paper. This will prevent sticking and burning of the fruit pieces such as the skin particles of prunes.

Other Quick Bread Variables Use the basic banana bread recipe substituting other cooked, strained fruits for the bananas. Be sure to include the juices that accumulate when straining or mashing the cooked fruits. Where chopped nuts are called for, use medium sized pieces or chunks. Do not use ground nuts.

Irish Health Bread and Scones

Ingredients	lb	oz	Mixing procedure
Sugar	1	2	Mix together to a smooth consistency
Salt		1½	
Skim milk powder		8	
Shortening, butter, or margarine	1		
Potato flour		2	
Soya flour		3	
Clover honey		6	
Baking soda		2	
Eggs (yolks optional)	1		Add in three stages and blend in
Water (cool)	4		Add and stir in gently
Bread flour	5		Sift flour and cream of tartar together. Add
Cake flour	1	12	and mix to a smooth dough
Cream of tartar		2½	

Raisins (2 lb) may be added to the dough during final mixing.

1. Place the dough on a floured work table and scale into 8-oz pieces. Round up the pieces into smooth round shapes and place on parchment paper-lined pans or greased baking pans. Allow the units to relax and then flatten with the hands to a thickness of ½ in. Egg wash and then cut three-quarters of the way down as a cross and form four sections.
2. The dough may be formed into a rectangular shape and relaxed 10 min. Roll dough out ½ in. thick. Cut into triangular shapes with a pastry wheel for scones. Place triangular sections on pans and egg wash.
3. Bake at 415–425°F (Figs. 1.15 and 1.16).

Yield: Approx. 100–150 scones

1.15
Old-fashioned, round-shaped loaves

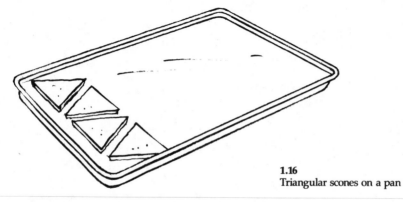

1.16
Triangular scones on a pan

Popovers

Ingredients	lb	oz	Mixing procedure
Bread flour	2	8	Sift the dry ingredients together to blend
Salt		1	well. Place on machine with wire whip
Skim milk powder		12	
Eggs (slightly beaten)	2		Combine these ingredients thoroughly. Add gradually to the above at slow speed
Water (lukewarm)	5		until all the liquid is blended in well. Mix
Melted shortening		6	the batter at high speed for about 4–5 min until the batter is smooth and partially aerated

1. If regular iron popover pans are available, heat them before greasing well. The grease will melt and require a slight brushing again before filling. The heat of the pans will keep the batter mildly warm and allow a more rapid expansion of the batter during the first stages of baking. Regular muffin pans may be used and prepared like the iron pans. It is suggested that the two center slots in the muffin tin be

left empty so that the expanding popovers may rise without baking into each other. This allows for 10 muffins in a 12-slot tin.

2. Fill the tins half full. Use a pitcher.
3. The oven temperature for the first stages of baking should be 450°F. Bake for about 20 min at that temperature until the popovers have risen and expanded fully and have started to develop a light brown crust color. Lower the oven temperature to 375°F and allow the popovers to bake for an additional 15 min. This will crisp the exterior of the popover as well as remove any excess moisture. Popovers removed from the oven too soon will collapse because the crust cannot retain its shape.
4. Allow the popovers to cool until they feel slightly warm and then lift from the pans. Allow them to cool further and return them to the pans for later reheating. Popovers may be covered and frozen. They may be quickly defrosted and warmed in radar or microwave ovens just before serving.

Yield: 100–125 popovers

Squash-Zucchini Quick Bread

There are a variety of squashes that may be used for this type of quick bread. The summer squashes such as Italian or zucchini or hookneck squashes may be used. The winter squashes known as hubbard and acorn squashes may also be used. The baked quick breads vary in the color due to the color variables of the different squashes. The zucchini has been the most popular. The consistency of the batter also varies with the moisture content and pulp starchiness of the squash varieties. The individual batter consistency will have to be judged.

Zucchini is prepared by washing, removing the ends or stems, cutting or slicing lengthwise, and removing the seeds from the center. It is then ground through a coarse grinder or finely chopped. The liquid and pulp are used in the weight of the formulary indicating squash.

Ingredients	lb	oz	Mixing procedure
Sugar	4		Sift all dry ingredients together to blend
Brown sugar	2	8	well
Salt		1	
Nonfat dry milk		3	
Baking soda		1¼	
Baking powder		2	
Cinnamon		½	
Nutmeg		¼	
Bread flour	4	12	
Cake flour	1		
Prepared zucchini or crookneck squash	8		Blend together and add to the dry ingredients. Blend in well
Eggs	2	8	

	lb	oz	
Vegetable oil	2	8	
Chopped nuts (walnut or pecan pieces)	1	12	Add and blend in well
Raisins (optional)	1	8	

Deposit the batter into paper-lined loaf pans. Fill slightly more than half full. Bake at approximately 370°F. Baked loaves are checked for proper bake by gently touching the center of the loaf. The baked loaf should spring back to the touch. The size and depth of the loaf pan will determine baking temperature and length of baking time. The batter may also be deposited into paper-lined muffin pans and baked as muffins. For multiple and rapid feeding, the batter may be baked in large sheet pans, cut into serving portions and served warm from the pan.

Note: Squash may be prepared while in season and frozen for later use.

Date Nut Quick Bread

Ingredients	lb	oz	Mixing procedure
Sugar	4		Blend together to a smooth paste
Salt		¾	
Shortening (emulsified)		12	
Emulsifier (glyceride)		1	
Baking soda		1	
Baking powder		1	
Cream of tartar		½	
Eggs		10	
Molasses		8	
Date paste or coarse pitted dates [1]	2	8	Add to the above and blend in well
Water	2	8	
Vanilla		1	
Bread flour		12	Sift together. Add and mix smooth
Cake flour	2	10	
Water	1	4	Add and mix smooth
Pecan pieces	1		

1. Deposit the batter into paper-lined loaf pans and fill slightly more than half full.
2. Bake at 355–360°F. If aluminum foil pans are used, place the loaf pan on sheet pans and bake to avoid excessive bottom heat.
3. The top of the batter may be garnished with pieces of date and pecan halves before baking.

[1] The date paste will blend in smoothly with other ingredients; coarse, pitted dates will be visible in the baked loaf.

2

Specialty Breads and Rolls

Today's pastry chef is usually skilled and knowledgeable in the production of a variety of specialty yeast-raised products that span the areas of specialty hard-type bread products and the varieties made from sweet yeast dough products. This is important in that many restaurants, hotels, institutions, and fast food operators serve specialty bakery products produced on the premises. These specialties are usually supplemented with bakery products ordered from commercial or retail bakeries. While the availability of frozen dough units, frozen baked products, and the equipment to defrost and heat or bake these units are a part of most feeding operations, the homemade specialties of bakery foods are an attraction and a well advertised part of the menu. In fact, many of these house specialties are the creations of the skilled pastry chef. The following are some examples of specialties in the area of bread and rolls and related bakery foods:

1. Special white bread that is firm, more nutritious in terms of natural ingredients, and lends itself well to the production of French toast (grilled or deep fat fried), melba toast, tea sandwiches, grilled sandwiches, and so forth.
2. Mini-loaves made from naturally enriched Italian and French bread doughs. Units of dough or baked breads are frozen for use when required.
3. Enriched loaves of bread (mini-size) of the "natural" types and known as the specialty of the house.
4. Twisted egg breads and banquet rolls (special catering).
5. Hard-type roll specialties for hero or submarine sandwiches (schools, institutions, fast food specialties, and so forth).

6. Pizza dough for variety pizzas (refrigerated and frozen units).
7. Bread sticks of various spices and flavors.

These are some examples of current, popular bakery products that play an important part in the menus of restaurants, fast food franchises, hotels, schools, and institutions. The recipes that follow are special in that they contain added grains and ingredients to increase the nutritional values as well as provide the characteristics associated with specialty bakery foods. Some of the formulas can be used for the production of a number of bakery products from the same dough. The pastry chef will expand the varieties with use and experiment. The production of the varieties from each of the formulas will be explained. Each of the recipes will be able to feed approximately 100 persons and increasing production requirements will be simplified for the pastry chef.

The pastry chef is usually limited in the amount of space for production and service; one of the reasons for using the straight dough method of mixing is to eliminate the need for equipment to hold sponge doughs. It will also reduce the amount of time for dough conditioning. Most yeast dough formulas in this unit will follow the straight dough method of mixing. Where a sponge dough method is usually required, the suggestion will be made for the use of prepared dry sour cultures. These may be used for such products as sourdough bread, sour rye bread, rye breads of varying types, and products usually made with the sponge and dough method of mixing. The factors affecting and controlling the conditioning of the dough and the proofing of the made-up units will be explained with each of the doughs and the products made.

Specialty White Breads and Rolls

Specialty White Bread

Ingredients	lb	oz	Mixing procedure
Yeast (variable)		8–12	Dissolve the yeast and set aside
Water	1		
Sugar		6	Stir together well to dissolve the dry in-
Salt		3	gredients and blend ingredients
Skim milk powder		6	
Soy flour (defatted) (optional) [1]		4	
Butter or margarine		4	
Eggs (part yolks)		8	
Water	4		
Bread flour	10		Sift and add the flour. Stir slightly and
Vegetable shortening		4	add the yeast solution. Mix to a dough. Add the shortening and develop the dough

[1]The soy flour will provide added nutritional value and improve the grain, texture, and keeping quality of the bread. It will also improve the toasting qualities.

2.1
Flatten to eliminate gas and air pockets

2.2
Fold one end of dough to center

2.3
Fold opposite end over first fold

2.4
Roll up snugly and seal the edge tightly

2.5
Cleaned and greased bread pan

2.6
Molded unit of dough placed in the pan

1. Dough temperature 78–80°F.
2. First rise approximately 1½ to 2 hr.
3. Punch the dough and allow the dough to rise again. (Placing the dough in a warm, moist environment will increase the rate of fermentation due to the increased activity of the yeast under such conditions. Keep the dough covered during this period to prevent crust formation.
4. Scale the dough into units for the bread or rolls and round up. The weight of the units will vary with the types of bread to be made and the size of the rolls.
5. Allow the scaled and rounded units to relax about 15–20 min (preliminary proofing) and then shape the loaves of bread. The roll units are divided in the press machine (roll divider and rounder, if available) and made up into a variety of rolls. (Fig. 2.1 through 2.6 illus-

trate makeup or shaping of bread and panning the units.)

6.   If there is a delay in the makeup of the bread and rolls, the rounded units of dough should be placed in the retarder to slow the rate of conditioning and prevent the dough from aging.

Yield: 8 large pullman loaves; 16 one-pound loaves; 32 mini-loaves (8 oz each); 200–250 small rolls

General Uses: French toast (grilled or deep fat fried), cinnamon toast, melba toast (thin slice), variety sandwiches.

Large Pullman or Sandwich Breads   Usually these are scaled 2 lb or more depending upon the size of the pan. Pullman pans have covers, so that the dough rises almost to the top of the cover before baking and then flattens against the cover during baking to form a square-shaped loaf of sandwich bread.

Regular Pan Breads (Open Top)   Place in regular bread pans for the usual 1 lb loaf. Use 18 oz of dough for each 1 lb loaf.

Mini-Loaves   Place in special small pans and use about 8 oz of dough before baking. Pans are lightly greased.

Homemade Varieties   These may be made by washing the tops of breads lightly with water and dusting lightly with cake flour or rye flour before placing the breads in the oven. These loaves are usually called white mountain loaves. The tops of the loaves may be cut lengthwise through the center before baking and then brushed lightly with melted butter for the butter crust type of bread. (Figs. 2.7 through 2.10.)

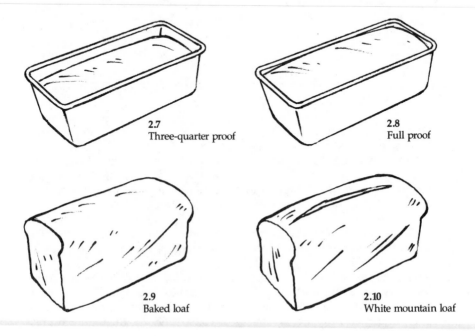

2.7
Three-quarter proof

2.8
Full proof

2.9
Baked loaf

2.10
White mountain loaf

Twisted Breads Twisting the strands of dough (divide the scaled units of dough into two pieces and twist them together) will provide a different shape. It will also provide a firmer structure for proofing and baking, as well as improved grain and texture.

Small Round Loaves These may be made in layer pans. They may be mini-loaves. Four pieces of dough each weighing 2 oz are rounded and then placed in the pan (aluminum foil pans may be used for individual table service) and baked with a cloverleaf effect.

Variety Rolls For variety rolls, scale the dough into units or dough presses. Weights may vary from 2½ to 4 lb. These presses are divided into 36 equal pieces in the divider. If a divider is not available, units of dough may be scaled 1¼ to 1½ oz for individual rolls.

Shaping or Molding Variety Breads and Rolls

Except for the larger restaurants, institutions, and multi-unit feeding establishments, most pastry chefs will make the various bakery products and foods by hand. However, where a steady production of variety breads and rolls is required, consideration should be given to the use of automated equipment. For example, a dough divider for rolls is essential for a number of uses other than just roll making. Other yeast-raised products may be divided on it. Rounding equipment is useful also. It rounds up the units of divided dough and makes them ready for panning. There are compact units for bread making. These are rounders and molders and sheeters. This equipment will speed the production of variety breads. Some have a full setup that includes proofing equipment. Automation or semiautomated production can be very helpful.

Proofing and Baking Variety Breads and Rolls

Homemade type breads and breads that are richer in formulation are closer in grain, smoother textured, and firmer. These characteristics are partly due to the fact that these breads are not given maximum proof before baking. These breads are usually given slightly more than three-quarters proof and then baked. Actually, the sense of touch rather than the fullness of the pan will determine the degree of proof. At three-quarters proof the bread or rolls will spring back softly and with some degree of firmness when touched. *Do not try to fill a pan with too little dough.* Trying to stretch the dough by overproofing will cause the loaf to collapse either before or during baking.

Final cutting or sectioning of the top of the bread is best done at the three-quarters proof stage when the dough and gluten strength are sufficiently firm to withstand the washing with water or other wash and the cutting with a razor or Vienna knife. At full proof, the gluten has been fully extended and may not be able to withstand the washing and cutting.

Breads are usually baked with a mild amount of steam in the oven.

Hard-type breads such as French, Italian, sour rye, and so forth, require a greater amount of steam for a longer period. If a steam generator oven attachment is unavailable, then it is good practice to brush the tops of the loaves with water and spray the oven chamber with a fine mist from a spray bottle filled with water before placing the breads into the oven. The steam created will have a softening effect on the outer crust of the bread or rolls and allow for greater oven spring (rapid rise during the first few minutes of baking) and a thinner crust formation. It will also provide a crisp crust in hard-type breads and rolls. Pan bread types should be baked at 410°F. Leaner, hard-type breads require a higher temperature. Richer breads (containing higher percentages of sugar, shortening, butter, eggs, syrups,) will require a slower bake at a lower temperature. Large loaves will require a longer baking period and should also be baked at a lower temperature. The pastry chef must make judgments regarding each variety.

Breads are considered baked when they produce a hollow sound when tapped. Of course, breads should also have a desirable crust color. If ovens do not bake evenly, breads must be shifted after they have set and are in the final stages of baking. Oven temperatures may have to be lowered for breads that develop a crust color rapidly. The average 1 lb loaf of white bread takes about 30–35 min to bake. The richer, old-fashioned types require a longer baking period. Baking out too quickly will generally cause the sides of the bread to collapse or shrink.

Breads should be removed from the pans soon after they are removed from the oven. This will avoid "sweating" in the pans. Breads should be cooled before they are refrigerated or placed in the freezer. It is quite common to have the mini-breads, bread specialties, and rolls baked in advance of the busy time of the day or the weekend. These breads are usually frozen and then placed in microwave ovens for quick defrost and heating before serving. If the microwave oven is not used, the frozen breads and rolls must be removed from the freezer and placed in the refrigerator to defrost 12 to 24 hr in advance. The units are then placed in the oven for reheating for a few minutes. In this process, the pastry chef would do well to bake the units to the just done stage to avoid excessive drying out during reheating. It is also advisable to reheat with a small amount of steam in the oven to avoid drying out. A simple trick is to cover the breads with a moist cloth and then place the breads and rolls into the oven to freshen them.

Roll varieties are increased by washing the tops of the rolls with egg wash for shiny, brown crust color, or with melted butter or milk for the homemade effect. The rolls may also be garnished with poppy seeds or sesame seeds for variety.

Egg Breads, Banquet and Soft Rolls

Egg Breads and Banquet Rolls

Ingredients	lb	oz	Mixing procedure
Yeast (variable)		6	Dissolve the yeast and set aside
Water	1		
Sugar		12	Stir well to dissolve the dry ingredients
Salt		2½	and blend all ingredients
Vegetable oil		12	
Egg yolks	1		
Water	3		
Bread flour (high gluten)	9		Sift and add the flour. Stir slightly and add the yeast. Develop dough well

1. Dough temperature: approximately 78–80°F. It is advisable to use cool water for making the dough.
2. First rise approximately 1½ to 2 hr.
3. Punch the dough and allow the dough to relax about ½ hr. (As a reminder, using warm water and placing the dough in a warm place such as the steam box, will increase the rate of fermentation and a more rapid conditioning of the dough.)
4. Take the dough to the bench as soon as it has relaxed after punching. The dough should be slightly on the young side (not fully conditioned) because it does take longer to make up the braided breads and variety twisted rolls than it does to make up ordinary pan breads or rolls that are simply rounded.
5. The dough is rich in egg yolks and will have greater volume. Thus, units should be scaled at a lesser weight than pan bread dough units. For example, the average pan for a 1 lb loaf of pan bread will require no more than 15 oz of dough. This is 3 oz less than that used for pan bread. The richness of the dough and its ability to withstand more proof will result in greater volume by weight. This holds true for the scaling for mini-loaves and for the variety of twist-banquet rolls. A scaler-rounder should be used if available. When scaling and rounding by hand, be sure to round up well and then cover the units to prevent crust formation.
6. At this point, it may be advisable to brush the rounded units with vegetable oil and place the units in the refrigerator (retarder) if the twisted breads and/or rolls are to be made up later.
7. The units may also be covered well and placed in the freezer for an extended period. Frozen doughs should be transferred to the retarder for slow defrosting. They may also be left at shop temperature for a quicker defrost. Be careful to avoid crust formation on uncovered dough.

Yield: 15 egg bread loaves (section or braided); 30 mini-loaves; 200 variety twist rolls.

Note: This dough is quite stiff in consistency. The final stages of dough development should be done at slow speed to avoid excessive friction and a high dough temperature.

General Uses: Braided breads, mini-loaf specialty, display loaf, variety rolls, French toast specialty, individual 3-twist rolls.

Makeup of Braided Egg Breads

Refer to Figs. 2.11 through 2.16 for guidance in braiding the units and twisting the doughs. The following varieties may be made:

1. Three-twist bread may be used for the pan-type egg bread loaf. A 4-twist will also be popular. Scale the units 15 oz for the average pan loaf. This will yield a high loaf.
2. The 4- and 5-twist breads are usually baked on large baking pans. The 4-twist can be made in tapered form or in long, straight form. The 5-braid will usually have a small 3-braid on top (equal to one strip divided into 3 smaller pieces).
3. The 6-braid is usually a larger loaf. These are specialty loaves for special occasions. The 5-braid with a 3-braid top is also used for special occasions and parties.
4. The oval loaf with a single strip across the top is usually used for the mini-loaf variety in addition to the 3- and 4-twist mini-loaves.
5. The snail-shaped loaf is a holiday specialty and is usually made with raisins in the dough. Some specialties will require the addition of dried mixed fruit in addition to the raisins.
6. The section loaf is made by dividing the unit into 6 or 8 sections and shaping into small strips. The strips are then placed together into the pan.

Making Braided Breads

1. The dough is rich in egg yolk, sugar, and vegetable oil, resulting in greater volume after baking. Scale the units to meet the size of the pans. The average 1-lb bread pan will require 14–15 oz of dough. A lesser amount will yield a lower loaf. It may be necessary to experiment with special loaf pans, especially with mini-loaf pans. Some pans may require as little as 6 oz of dough. Individual braided breads baked on sheet pans may vary in weight and in the shape desired.

2. The sheeter can be used for making the beginning strips of dough for the braided breads. Most breads require that the strips be tapered slightly at the ends. This will produce a tapered loaf, the characteristic of the braided egg bread. Straight dough strips will yield a straight-shaped loaf. This is a specialty for the small slice or cocktail egg bread slice. When strips are taken from the sheeter, it will be necessary to make the final taper by rolling the ends with the palms of the hands. Strips shaped by hand are formed into a taper while rolling the strip of dough

3. Rye flour is usually used for dusting purposes when forming the tapered dough strips and braiding the breads. The rye flour is soft and

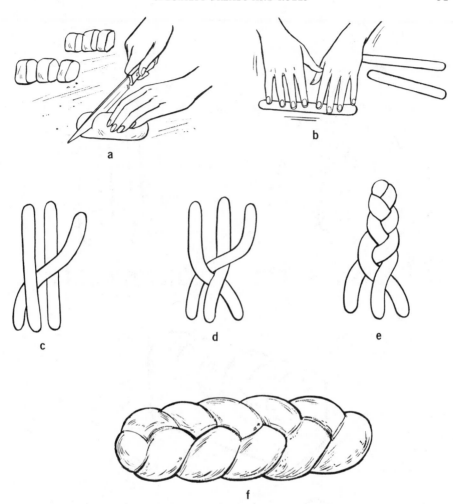

2.11
Three-braid bread. a. Use 3 pieces of dough or one larger piece divided into 3 equal pieces; b. Roll each piece of dough into a strip of even thickness 5 to 6 in. long; c. Place 3 strips next to each other in a vertical position. Take the strip on the right and fold it over the middle strip and under the strip on the left; d. Place the strip on the left under the center strips and pull the end gently to the right. Return to the outside strip and fold it over into the center, forming the braid; e. Fold the braid over when half the strips are braided; continue to braid as before. Be sure to start with the strip furthest away from the center; f. A three-braid roll.

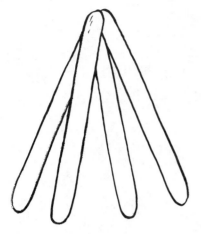

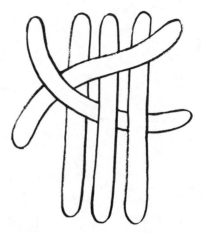

2.12
Four strips of dough for the four-twist bread.
Start braiding from the top

2.13
Five strips of dough for the 5-twist bread.
Separate the strips in the center and start the
braid with no. 5 and then no. 1

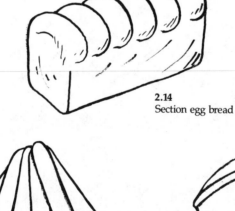

2.14
Section egg bread

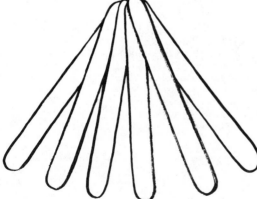

2.16
Oval-shaped egg bread with thin
strip of dough across the top

2.15
Six-twist egg braid

will prevent the dough from drying or crusting rapidly. It also helps to separate the strips of dough during proofing and baking. It avoids the blending of strips of dough into each other during baking (when this happens, it is called "blind strips"). Since the dough is stiff, little dusting flour is rquired. Some bakers and pastry chefs will brush the surface of the work bench with a little vegetable oil to keep the dough from sticking and to separate the dough strips when braiding.

4. When forming the strips of dough to be braided, be sure to remove large air pockets from the strip. If left, the pockets will expand during proof and baking creating large holes in the loaf. They also tend to form blisters on the crust and break and shred after baking. Use the heel of the palm to press down on the dough strip to obtain a tight strip of dough.

5. Dust the strips of dough lightly with rye flour before beginning to braid the strips. This will keep the strips apart and distinguishable. Be sure that the strips of dough are equal in length and of equal firmness. Soft or gassy strips will stretch during braiding while firm strips will not.

6. Use a snug braid without stretching the strips of dough. Stretching the strips in the braiding will often cause the breads to curve or curl. This will result in an uneven loaf.

The following roll varieties may be made (see Figs. 2.17 through 2.25):

1. The single-knot roll
2. The double-knot roll
3. The figure-8 roll
4. The snail shape roll
5. The owl-eye roll
6. The cross roll
7. The 3-twist roll

Bread pans for loaves should be lightly greased or brushed with vegetable oil. Breads and rolls baked on sheet pans should be placed on lightly greased or parchment-paper lined pans. Spacing on sheet pans is very important. Allowance must be made for expansion and greater volume of these units. Breads and rolls should not be allowed to bake into each other. This will cause a change in shape and symmetry.

Proofing and Baking Egg Breads and Banquet Rolls

Egg breads are usually egg washed (fresh whole eggs will provide a brown shine and luster to the baked loaves) before the loaves are placed into loaf pans or placed on sheet pans. This will avoid possible dripping of the egg wash and sticking of the breads to the bottom or sides of the pans. The breads and rolls are usually washed lightly a second time when they have reached three-quarter proof. At this time, the breads and rolls are garnished with seeds, if desired. The seeds most popular are poppy seeds and sesame seeds.

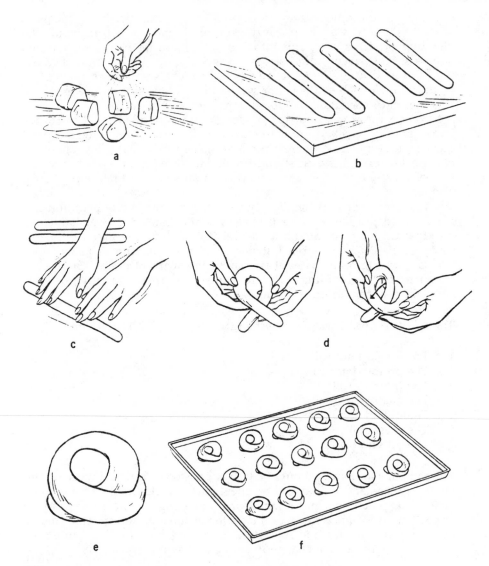

2.17
Single-knot rolls. a. Dust pressed out dough pieces with flour; b. Roll
dough pieces into 6-in. strips; c. Relax strips and roll a little longer; d.
Form a loop. Pull one end through the loop; e. A single-knot roll; f.
Place on a sheet pan 5 x 7 in.

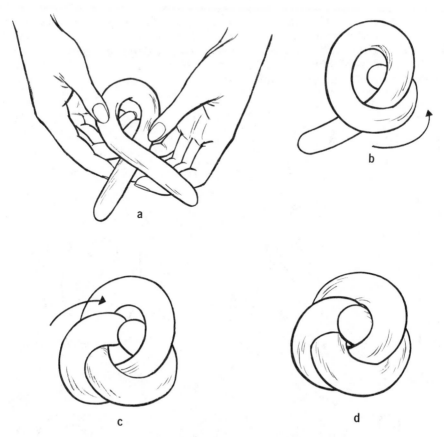

2.18
Double-knot rolls. a. Roll out and cross over; b. Pull one end through the
loop; c. Pull one end under and up through the center of the loop. Pull
the other end over and through the center; d. A double-knot roll.

Egg breads and rolls are given slightly more than three-quarter proof.
The dough will spring back lightly to the touch but will still have a firmness to the feel. This is due to the fact that this is a stiff dough. Avoid
full proof or overproof to prevent the units from collapsing or flattening
during baking. The strips and twists will also tend to run into each other
causing a "blind" appearance. A three-quarter proof will allow for a good
oven spring (rapid rise during the first minutes of baking) and maximum
expansion during baking—the result of the expansion of the air pockets,
release of moisture in the form of steam during early baking, further
activity of the yeast cells until the thermal death point is reached (140°F),
and the natural expansion of the egg yolks.

Egg breads and banquet rolls are usually baked at a lower oven temperature. Larger egg breads are baked at 350°F, smaller units are baked
at 360°F. The breads are considered baked when they produce a hollow

sound when tapped, and a dry, crisp crust. The temperature may be increased in the final stages of baking to obtain a browner crust color. Banquet egg rolls are baked at approximately 385–390°F. Smaller rolls may be baked at a higher temperature to avoid excessive drying. Cool the breads and rolls before freezing.

2.19
Braided figure-8 rolls. a. Roll each strip out about 8 in. long. Keep the strip in a vertical position; b. Form a loop so that the strip looks like a "6"; c. Pull the top edge through the loop to form the shape of a lasso; d. Twist the bottom part of the lasso loop to the left so that the figure "8" is formed; e. Pull the loose end through the bottom loop of the "8"; f. The braided figure-8 roll.

2.20
Roll out straight strip of dough with palms of hands

2.21
Taper strip gently at each end

2.22
Snail roll. Tuck the end under the roll

2.23
Owl-eye roll

2.24
Cross roll. Use the figure-8 roll which is folded in half and the pinched ends placed under the roll

2.25
Braiding the three-twist roll

Specialty Soft Rolls

Ingredients	lb	oz	Mixing procedure
Yeast (variable)		8	Dissolve the yeast and set aside
Water	2		
Sugar		12	Blend together to a uniform consistency
Salt		2½	
Skim milk powder		6	
Soy flour (defatted) (optional)[1]		4	
Wheat germ (optional)[1]		4	
Honey (clover)		4	
Butter or margarine		8	
Shortening		6	
Eggs (part yolks)	1		Add in two stages and blend in
Water	3		Add and stir in
Bread flour	8	12	Sift, add, and stir slightly. Add the yeast and develop the dough

1. Dough temperature: Approximately 78–80°F.
2. First rise approximately 1½ hr. Punch and allow the dough to rise a second time. Do not punch a second time.
3. To test the dough for punching, insert the fingers up to the palm of the hand into the risen dough. If the dough starts to fall back slowly, it is time to punch the dough. *Do not wait for the dough to start to fall back by itself before punching.*
4. Scale the dough into presses. The weight of the press will determine the size of the roll. The suggested weight for each press for average size rolls is 2 lb 12 oz. Larger rolls will require an increased weight of the press. This may be necessary for special hamburger and frankfurter rolls.
5. Allow the presses of dough to relax for about 15 min (preliminary proofing) before dividing. The divider rounder is used for round hamburger rolls. The sheeter is usually used for forming the strips for frankfurter rolls and for rolling the units out for variety twist rolls. If this equipment is not available, the rolls are shaped by hand.

Yield: Approx. 216 rolls (6 press-2 lb/12 oz each)

General Uses: Hamburger rolls, frankfurter rolls, yeast-raised muffin varieties, butter roll specialties, twisted roll varieties

---

[1]The soy flour and wheat germ will increase the nutritional value of the rolls through the increase in protein. The soy flour will also contribute to improved texture and softness. If these grains are not used, increase the flour slightly.

Frankfurter and Hamburger Rolls Refer to Figs. 2.26 through 2.29 for shaping frankfurter and hamburger rolls. Use the special pans for each if they are available. Be sure to have enough dough to fill the pan shapes in order to get a full size roll when baked. These rolls may be made and baked on regular sheet pans.

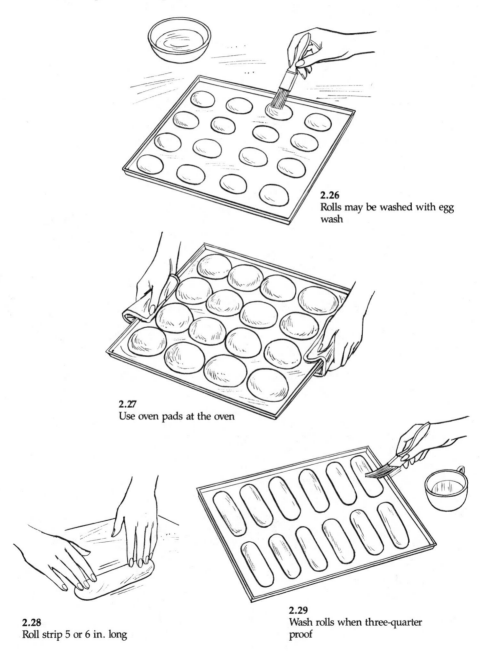

2.26
Rolls may be washed with egg wash

2.27
Use oven pads at the oven

2.28
Roll strip 5 or 6 in. long

2.29
Wash rolls when three-quarter proof

Parker House Rolls   These rolls are made by dividing the presses on the dough divider. The pieces of dough may be rounded and relaxed before rolling out. The units may be rolled out as they are separated without rounding. Refer to Figs. 2.30 through 2.35 for makeup procedures.

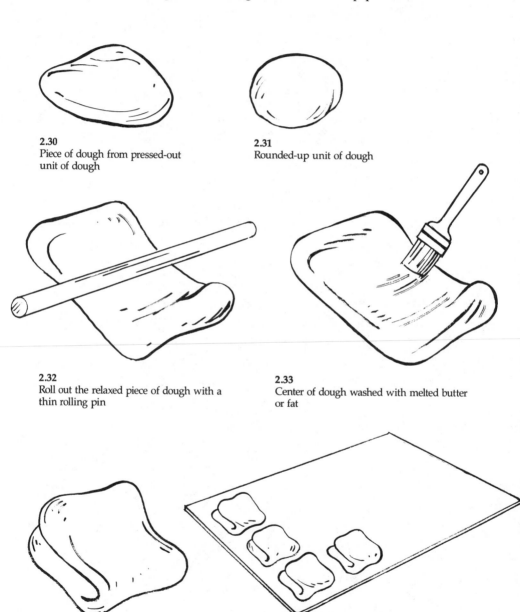

2.30
Piece of dough from pressed-out
unit of dough

2.31
Rounded-up unit of dough

2.32
Roll out the relaxed piece of dough with a
thin rolling pin

2.33
Center of dough washed with melted butter
or fat

2.34
End folded over end

2.35
Rolls placed on sheet pan

Cloverleaf Rolls These are usually made by dividing the units of dough that have been divided in the dough divider into 3 equal parts. These parts are rounded and the 3 rounded sections are placed into the muffin pan sections. Refer to Figs. 2.36 through 2.40 for makeup procedures.

2.36
Rolled-out strip of dough cut into three parts

2.37
Rounded-up pieces of dough

2.38
Place 3 rounded units in each cup

2.39
Rolls at almost full proof

2.40
A cloverleaf roll

Note: A docker may be used to divide the single rounded piece of dough into 3 sections. It will make 3 distinct cuts or separations when pressed into the rounded dough unit. The size of the muffin pan will determine the size or amount of dough to be scaled into the presses.

Butterflake Rolls   These are made by layering sections of rolled out dough that have been brushed with melted fat or butter. The dough may be cut into strips and the strips placed in layers over each other. The rolled out dough may be folded into flat sections one over the other similar to the makeup of cinnamon rolls. These rolls are cut into individual units by hand. Care should be used when cutting so that rolls are all of equal size. The size of the muffin pan will determine the amount of dough required for each unit (Figs. 2.41 through 2.45).

2.41
Brush dough with melted fat

2.42
Cut dough into equal strips 1½ in. wide and stack the strips 5 or 6 high

2.43
Cut pieces about 1½ in. wide

2.44
Place in pans cut side up

2.45
Butterflake roll

Factors in Soft Roll Production

The makeup of soft roll varieties requires considerable time and handling of the dough. During the makeup on the bench, the dough continues to ferment. Therefore, it is better to take the dough to the bench before it is fully conditioned. The dough should be slightly on the young side. For rolls made up with automatic equipment, the makeup time will be shorter and the dough should be fully conditioned.

The specialty soft rolls should be given three-quarter proof and brushed with melted butter or margarine or washed with egg wash. At this point in the proofing, the rolls can withstand brushing better than at full proof. The washed rolls may then be returned to the proof box for additional proof. Give the rolls slightly less than full proof before baking. The richness of the dough (butter, shortening, eggs, yolks) will provide for excellent volume. Avoid maximum proof to prevent possible collapse and loss of volume.

Rolls may be shaped into a variety of twist rolls similar to those made from the egg bread dough. These rolls may be washed with egg wash for the shiny, brown crust color. They may be washed with melted fat or butter for the homemade effect. Rolls that are to be retarded for later baking or placed in the freezer without baking, should be given little proof. It is advisable to wash these rolls once before retarding. Melted butter or fat or egg wash may be used. Rolls for the freezer should be well wrapped to avoid deposit of ice crystals and frost on the rolls. To defrost these rolls, place the rolls into the retarder overnight. They may be left at shop temperature for several hours to defrost. **Do not place frozen or partially frozen rolls into the proof box.** Be sure the centers of the rolls are defrosted. Soft rolls that are baked and then frozen may be quickly defrosted and heated in a microwave oven. Since the timing can vary with different types of equipment, check the instructions for the equipment used. Frozen, baked rolls may also be quickly defrosted and heated by placing them into muffin pans or on sheet pans and placing them into the oven for a few minutes. The rolls may be covered with a damp or moist cloth to avoid excessive drying of the outside crust. These rolls may also be brushed lightly with melted butter after reheating.

The proofed rolls are baked at 400°F. Larger rolls may be baked at a slightly lower temperature. Rolls that are to be quick frozen may be baked at a slightly higher temperature for a quicker bake in order to maintain maximum moisture and freshness. When baking hamburger and frankfurter rolls, it is advisable to inject a small amount of steam into the oven before loading and during the first few minutes of baking. This will give a more tender crust and slightly larger volume. Where the oven does not have steam injection equipment, the oven shelves may be sprayed lightly with water to form steam before placing the rolls in the oven. In addition to having the desirable crust color, the soft rolls will spring back gently to the touch when baked. It may be necessary to shift pans during baking if the oven heat is not distributed evenly. Do not shift pans until the rolls have risen and set to avoid possible collapse of the rolls. Rolls that have been brushed with melted butter or fat should be washed lightly with butter when removed from the oven. This will improve the flavor. This is often the practice with Parker House rolls, cloverleaf rolls, and butterflake rolls.

Specialty Breads and Pizza

Cinnamon-Raisin Tea Loaf

Ingredients	lb	oz	Mixture procedure
Yeast (variable)		10	Dissolve the yeast and set aside
Water	1	8	
Sugar		12	Blend all ingredients together to a smooth
Salt		2½	consistency
Skim milk powder		6	
Soy flour (defatted)[1]		4	
Potato flour[1]		4	
Honey (clover)		4	
Butter		12	
Egg yolks		8	Add the yolks and water and stir in
Water	3	8	
Bread flour (variable)[2]	9		Sift and add the flour. Stir slightly and add the yeast solution. Develop the
Raisins (variable) presoak and drain the raisins	2		dough. Add the raisins in the final stage of dough development

1. Dough temperature: 78–80°F.
2. First rise and punch about 1½ to 2 hr; second rise: approximately 45 min.
3. Take the dough to the bench without a second punch. The dough will be fully conditioned during the makeup period.
4. Scale the units of dough approximately 15 oz to 1 lb for the regular 1-lb white pan bread size. For the mini-loaves, scale the dough units approximately 8 oz. Mini-loaf pans may vary in size and the dough will have to be varied accordingly. Some mini-loaves for this bread specialty may weigh as little as 7 oz when baked.
5. Shape the scaled dough units into rectangular shape and allow to relax for about 15 min. Roll out the units of dough about ¼ in. thick and wash the surface of the dough with egg wash or water. (Fig. 2.46)
6. Sprinkle the surface with additional raisins if desired, and sprinkle well with cinnamon sugar. A stronger concentrate of cinnamon sugar may be used. (Fig. 2.47)
7. Roll up the units into a tight roll and seal the ends. Place into greased loaf pans with the closed seam at the bottom center of the pan. The units may then be stippled or docked with a large fork to prevent

[1] The soy flour and potato flour enrich the dough. They may be omitted.
[2] A medium strong bread flour should be used (a hard spring and hard winter wheat may be blended).

2.46
Roll out the dough ¼ in. thick

2.47
Sprinkle with additional cinnamon sugar

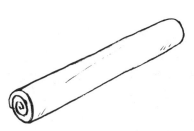

2.48
Roll the dough up tightly and seal edge

2.49
Molded unit of dough placed in the pan

the formation of large air pockets during proofing and baking. (Fig. 2.48 and 2.49)

8. The dough may also be scaled into units weighing 8 to 9 lb and formed into a rectangle. After relaxing the dough, it is rolled out and filled as for making cinnamon rolls. Instead of cutting small slices, large cuts are made weighing about 1 lb for the larger units and 8 oz for the mini-loaves. These units are then placed into the greased pans. These are also docked.

9. The breads are to be given a slow proof so that proofing in the center is equal to that of the dough on the outside of the loaf. Give the units slightly more than three-quarter proof. The tops may be brushed with melted butter before baking for a dull finish, or the tops may be washed with egg wash for a shiny, brown crust color.

10. The larger units are baked at a lower temperature (360°F). Smaller units are baked at a higher temperature (370°F). The loaves will spring back to the touch when pressed gently in the center.

11. The egg washed loaves may be washed with a syrup glaze while hot. These loaves may also be striped with a fondant icing when cool. Loaves brushed with melted butter may be brushed with melted butter once again when they have almost cooled. These loaves are then dipped into a blend of cinnamon sugar.

12. Units that are to be frozen after baking should not be washed with either a syrup glaze or butter before placing into the freezer. The units are to be wrapped in a freezer wrap. Upon defrosting and reheating, the units are then finished with either the syrup and icing or the butter and cinnamon sugar. Pastry chefs who use this loaf for a dry cinnamon toast will not finish the tops at all.
13. The mini-loaves may be served in either form and sliced at the table. Most larger loaves are chilled and then sliced into thin slices while chilled. Chilling makes slicing easier and keeps the raisins from falling out.

Yield: Approx. 20 loaves scaled 15 oz, or 40 mini-loaves scaled 7½ oz
Uses: Specialty bread, mini-loaf, cinnamon-raisin toast, specialty tea sandwiches

Granola Bread

Granola bread is one of the more recent bread specialties to become popular because of its enrichment through the use of a variety of natural grains. A number of pastry chefs are producing this loaf as a house specialty. Some are purchasing the bread. Eating establishments that specialize in "natural" foods serve this bread. The pastry chef, or the baker he may supervise, probably uses the prepared granola flour mix. This makes mixing the dough quite simple. Some prefer to prepare their own blend of grains and cereals. The following formula for granola bread is standard and yields a bread of excellent quality.

Granola Bread

Ingredients	lb	oz	Mixture procedure
Yeast (variable)		8	Dissolve the yeast and set aside
Water	1	8	
Brown sugar		6	Blend the dry ingredients and water well
Salt		3	to dissolve the dry ingredients and hy-
Skim milk powder		6	drate the grains. About 6 min of mixing at
Soy flour (defatted)		4	slow speed will be necessary
Rolled oats		9	
Pumpernickel flour		8	
Potato flour		4	
Yellow cornmeal		6	
Honey		3	
Molasses (dark)		4	
Water	4		
Butter or margarine		7	
Whole wheat flour (stone ground preferred)	1	2	Add the flour and yeast and develop to a smooth dough
Bread flour (high gluten)		6	

Raisins (optional) presoak and drain	2	Add the raisins in the final stages of mixing

1. Dough temperature: 78–80°F.
2. First rise and punch about 1½ to 2 hr; second rise: 45 min; take to bench.
3. The dough should be somewhat softer than the old-fashioned white pan bread. The whole grains and bran will absorb moisture from the dough as the dough is being conditioned (fermented).
4. Scale the units 18 oz for the average pan bread size. For a larger slice from a higher loaf, scale the dough at 20 oz. Mini-loaves will vary from 8–10 oz depending upon the size of the pan.
5. Make up the breads as for regular pan bread loaves. Give these loaves no more than three-quarter proof and wash with water. The tops of the loaves may be sprinkled with rolled oats and bran flakes for variety.
6. Give the units a bit more proof and bake at 400°F. If there is a steam attachment to the oven, inject a mild amount of steam or the oven chamber may be sprayed with water before placing the bread into the oven. Bread units may be brushed lightly with water before placing them into the oven.
7. These loaves will take longer to bake than white bread. The regular loaf will take about 45 min to bake through thoroughly. The mini-loaves will take approximately 25 to 30 min depending upon their size.
8. The loaves will have a closer grain and mildly rough texture due to the bran and whole grains. It is best to chill these loaves and slice them while cold in order to get a fine, thin slice.

Yield: Approx. 14 loaves scaled 18 oz of dough or 28 mini-loaves scaled at 9 oz of dough.

Sourdough Bread

Sourdough breads have attained wide acceptance and popularity. Because of the special flavor and taste developed through the use of aged sourdough, these breads require extensive care and attention. Most of these breads are purchased commercially in a frozen state to be defrosted, warmed, and served. There are prepared sourdough dry cultures available which eliminate the preparation of sourdough "freshings" to develop the lactic and acetic acids necessary for the special flavor. The pastry chef simply follows the instructions provided by the producer of the sourdough culture. For the pastry chef who may wish to prepare a milder type of French sourdough loaf, the following formula and freshings procedures are presented.

Preparation of the First Sourdough

Ingredients	lb	oz	Mixing procedure
Yeast (variable)		12	Dissolve the yeast. Add the flour and mix
Water	3		to a dough. Allow the dough to rise and
Bread flour	4		fall back by itself. Do not punch
Second sourdough or freshing			
Water	3		Add water to the above and mix well to break up the sponge
Bread flour	4		Add the flour and mix to a dough. Allow the dough to rise and fall

1. Do not punch the dough. It must rise and fall back by itself. The aging increases the development of the required acidity.
2. After the second freshing has matured, remove approximately 12 lb of the sourdough to use as a base for the final dough.
3. The remaining sourdough is refrigerated or frozen to start a freshing again. This process is continuous where daily production of sourdough bread is made.

Final Dough Preparation

Ingredients	lb	oz	Mixing procedure
Conditioned sourdough	12		Add to the sourdough and mix to dissolve
Sugar		6	the dry ingredients and break up the sourdough.
Salt		5	
Malt (nondiastatic)		6	
Water	2		
Yeast (variable)		8	Dissolve and set aside
Water	2		
Bread flour	9		Add the flour and stir slightly. Add the
Shortening		4	yeast and mix in. Add the shortening and develop to a smooth dough. Do Not Overmix

1. Dough temperature: Approximately 80°F.
2. Allow dough to rise well (45 min to 1 hr)
3. Scale the dough into 8-oz units for demi-loaves. Scale 12–14 oz for the larger loaves.
4. The units are rounded and relaxed for about 15 min. Shape the breads as for Italian or French bread. The units may also be shaped as round loaves.

5. Give the units three-quarter proof and brush lightly with water. The tops of the long loaves may be cut down the center or sliced diagonally across.
6. Give the loaves a bit more proof and then bake with a mild amount of steam in the oven at 425°F. If there is no steam injection into the oven, wash the tops of the loaves with water before placing into the oven. The oven chamber should be sprayed with water from a spray type bottle to form steam.
7. Breads should be baked crisp as for French bread. The units are frozen when cool, and then defrosted and warmed before service.

French Bread, Mini-Loaves, and Rolls

French breads and rolls are provided by commercial bakers to restaurants, institutions, schools, and other eating establishments. However, the pastry chef and baker may *not* have these products available and may have to produce them. The following is a standard formula for French bread and rolls which can be used for crisp French bread loaves, French rolls for special sandwiches, mini-French bread loaves, and garlic and variety spice flavored breads.

French Bread Dough

Ingredients	lb	oz	Mixing procedure
Yeast (variable)		6	Dissolve the yeast and set aside
Water	1		
Sugar		2	Stir together to dissolve the dry ingredi-
Salt		2	ents
Malt		2	
Water	3		
Bread flour (high gluten)	7		Add the flour and stir slightly. Add the yeast and mix to a dough. Add the short-
Shortening		2	ening and develop

1. Dough temperature: 78–80°F.
2. First rise and punch approximately 2 hr; second rise and second punch approximately 1 hr. Allow to relax and take to the bench.
3. Scale the units as desired. Round up and allow to relax 15 min. Shape the units into long loaves and place on cornmeal dusted pans or peels. Use peels if the bread is to bake on the hearth.
4. Give the units three-quarter proof and wash lightly with water. The breads are then cut diagonally and allowed to proof to almost full proof. (Figs. 2.50–2.52.)
5. The mini-loaves are shaped the same as the longer loaves. They are placed on sheet pans and may be baked as for French rolls.
6. The size of French rolls will determine the weight of the presses of dough. The rolls are shaped as for the French bread. The rolls are also cut across the top at three-quarter proof.

2.50
French bread proofed, washed, and cut

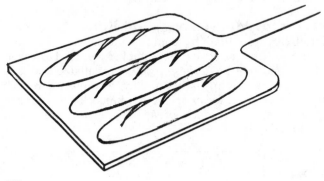

2.51
French breads placed on dusted peel for
loading into oven

2.52
French roll proofed and cut

7. The bread and rolls are baked in a hot, 425°F oven. The oven should be filled with steam before loading. A fine spray from a bottle will be helpful in promoting the desired crisp crust on the bread. It will also help to create the proper break and shred where the cuts have been made in the loaf. The breads will have a hollow sound when tapped when they are fully baked. The loaves will also have a crisp crust.

8. The breads may be brushed lightly with a starch-water solution when removed from the oven. Loaves and rolls to be frozen must be cooled and then freezer-wrapped before freezing. These units may be defrosted quickly and reheated by placing the units in a microwave oven. The breads may be covered with a moist covering and placed in the regular oven to defrost and reheat.

Yield: 16 loaves at 12 oz; 32 mini-loaves; approx. 150 rolls

Italian Bread and Pizza Dough

Pizza, heros, submarines, and other specialities that are covered, supported, or enrobed by bread dough are now a major part of the fast food business. The pastry chef is involved since many of these dough and bread specialties are not always available. While frozen doughs, breads, and rolls can be purchased from the commercial baker, they may not meet the special requirements of the chef or pastry chef. For example, the chef may wish a fresh dough for the pizza varieties he is making. The mini-loaves may be of a special size for a special service. The submarine or hero sandwiches may require a special size for the sandwich contents and the service.

Italian Bread Dough

Ingredients	lb	oz	Mixing procedure
Yeast (variable)		4	Dissolve the yeast and set aside
Water	1		
Salt		2	Mix to dissolve the salt and the malt
Malt syrup		2	
Water	3		
Bread flour (high gluten)	6	12	Add the flour and stir. Add the yeast and mix to a dough. Add the shortening and
Shortening		2	develop the dough

1. Dough temperature: 77–79°F.
2. First rise and punch about 1½ to 2 hr. Second rise and punch 45 min to 1 hr. Relax dough for 15 to 20 min and take to bench.
3. Scale the units into the desired weights. Round up the units and allow them to relax for 15 to 20 min.
4. Shape the units into long, tapered bread loaves as for French bread (Fig. 2.53). Round loaves may be made. The sheeter may be used for shaping the loaves of bread and the special rolls.
5. For the pizza, determine the size with the chef. Large units will require larger amounts of dough. Smaller units for small group service may require less. The thickness of the base will also determine the weight of the dough. The rounded units of pizza may be placed in the retarder or the freezer for later use. Some pastry chefs will roll the dough out into a circle about ¼ to ½ in. thick. They will complete the rolling or stretching of the pizza dough at the time of

2.53
Baked Italian loaf of bread

makeup. This will speed up the stretching of the dough. The rolled out units may be placed in layers separated by parchment paper and then frozen. They separate easily when defrosted.

6. The shaped bread is given about three-quarter proof and then brushed lightly with water and cut across the top diagonally. Allow the breads to get slightly more proof and bake with steam in the oven as for the French bread.

7. Italian breads and rolls are baked at 425–430°F. Bread and special rolls are usually baked on the hearth. If baked on sheet pans, the pans should be dusted with cornmeal. If placed on peels for peeling on to the hearth, the peels should be dusted with cornmeal.

Yield: 15 loaves at 12 oz; 30 loaves at 6 oz (mini); 45 special rolls at 3 oz
Uses: Italian loaves (long or round shaped), mini-loaves, special sandwich loaves, pizza dough bottoms for pizza pie

Enriched Italian Wheat Bread

With the current emphasis on the use of natural grains, many schools, colleges, and institutions are increasing the nutritional values of the bread they purchase or bake on the premises. The pizza dough, hero rolls, and other baked dough specialties may be made from the following formula:

Italian Wheat Bread Dough

Ingredients	lb	oz	Mixing procedure
Yeast (variable)		8	Dissolve the yeast and set aside
Water	2		
Sourdough culture (dry) (optional)		2	Mix these ingredients at slow speed for about 5 min to soften the grain and bran and to dissolve dry ingredients
Malt		3	
Soy flour (defatted)		4	
Bran flour		6	
Wheat germ (toasted)		3	
Wheat gluten		4	
Whole wheat grains (presoaked and optional)		8	
Water	6	8	
Salt		4	
Whole wheat flour (stone ground)	3		Add the flour and mix slightly. Add the yeast and mix to a dough. Add the shortening and develop the dough. Mix at slow speed to develop
Bread flour (high gluten)	10		
Shortening		4	

1. Dough temperature: 78–80°F.
2. First rise and punch about 2 hr. Second rise about 1 hr. Take to bench. Scale and make up as for regular Italian bread.

3. The pizza made from this dough requires more careful handling. It should be stretched slowly and should not be stretched as thin as the regular Italian bread dough. The whole grains and the coarse bran may cause the dough to tear. Keep the pizza base dough slightly thicker.

4. For the hero or submarine sandwich rolls, scale the presses between 5 and 6 lb per press. Each roll will be almost 3 oz.

5. If using the sheeter to mold the strips for rolls and for the bread, open the roller space slightly to prevent tearing the dough. The dough may be tightened in the final hand shaping to taper the ends if desired.

6. The mini-breads may be made the same size. Because of the whole and coarse grains, the units should be given slightly less than full proof. This will prevent tearing during the final stages of proofing and baking. The units are to be washed and cut as for regular bread made from the Italian bread dough.

7. Round breads may be placed in aluminum foil pans and proofed and baked in the pans. Some restaurants will bake the round loaves in small pie pans. The units are also cut when three-quarter proof. The units are sprinkled with bran after washing. Sesame seeds or caraway seeds may be applied for variety. After baking, the loaves may be sliced almost three-quarters through and the insides brushed with garlic butter or other spice blended with the butter for variety.

Pizza [1]

At one time, pizza was sold only through pizzerias. Today, with its increasing popularity, it is sold also through restaurants, grocery stores, bars, and bakeries.

Pizza is a food of many variations. We will limit our discussion to some of the major differences.

Most people classify pizzas by the variations in crust. For instance, there are thick crust pizzas and thin crust pizzas; round pizzas and square; rich (high shortening content) dough and lean dough. Typically, the thick crust or deep pan pizza is known as the Sicilian pizza and the thin crust pizza is called the Neapolitan pizza.

The basic pizza crust is a lean bread dough made from high-gluten flour, water, sugar, salt, shortening, and yeast. The last four ingredients are generally less than 4% each. However, in recent years, many pizza bakers have been experimenting with additional ingredients and have also been increasing the sugar/shortening content for a richer dough.

Different methods can be utilized for rolling out the crust. Of course, the basic method is by hand pressing, slapping, and spinning the dough from a ball shape to the round thin crust or skin, as it is sometimes called. For uniformity in dough thickness, a rolling pin can be used. If exact uniformity is desired, a dough roller or sheeter is necessary. The dough can be scaled and rounded into balls several hours in advance of

[1] Source: John D. Correll, President, Pizzutis, Inc., Canton, Mich.

rolling or it can be held in a large batch. With the large batch method, pieces of dough are cut from the batch, run through a sheeter, and then cut to the shape of the pan immediately prior to baking.

Traditionally, a pizza was made on a wooden peel and then slid onto a stone hearth, or the oven deck. Cornmeal, sprinkled on the peel prior to laying down the dough, allowed the baker to slide the pizza from the peel onto the deck. Today many bakers have eliminated the use of corn-meal. In its place the baker uses a pan, screen, or silicone-treated paper.

The sauce is made from tomato sauce, paste, or puree, or a combina-tion thereof. Typical spices for pizza sauce are oregano, basil, fennel, thyme, black pepper, white or red pepper, garlic, and onion. Some pizza bakers simmer the sauce with the spices.

The traditional cheese for pizza is mozzarella. However, bakers fre-quently blend in other cheeses such as Muenster, brick, and Monterey Jack.

Most anything can go on top of pizza. Some of the common toppings are pepperoni or pizza sausage, ham, fresh pork sausage (Italian sau-sage), mushrooms, onions, green peppers, hamburger, olives, bacon, and anchovies.

Thin crust pizzas are usually baked at 550°F; thick crust at about 450°F. Generally, a pizza is considered done when the bottom crust is a golden-brown color.

Pizza   (*Lean dough*)

Ingredients	lb	oz
High-gluten bread flour	10	
Warm water, 80°F	6	
Salt		2½
Sugar		2½
Yeast, granulated		8
Vegetable oil		2½

1. Dissolve the sugar and yeast in the warm water. Let the yeast bloom (10–20 min).
2. Add vegetable oil and salt to the water mixture.
3. Add flour to the mixture and mix/knead for 10 min at low speed. If necessary, add additional flour at the end of mixing to increase the dough's firmness. When lifted, the finished dough should just barely pull away from the sides of the bowl.
4. Bench rest 15 min.
5. Divide and round into balls. To prevent crusting, brush with oil. Use:
    10-oz ball for 12-in. round pizza
    13-oz ball for 14-in. round pizza
    18-oz ball for 16-in. round pizza

Pizza Sauce

For each No. 10 can of tomato sauce use:

Ingredients	oz
Salt	1 (1½ tbsp)
Granulated sugar	½ (2 tsp)
Ground black pepper	¼ (1 tbsp)
Whole basil	1/20 (2–2½ tsp)
Whole oregano	1/20 (2–2½ tsp)
Garlic powder	½ (1½ tbsp)
Ground romano	⅓ (1½ tbsp)

1. Mix together all ingredients. For a thicker sauce, add tomato paste.
2. Use sauce in the following portions:
    For 12-in. round pizza: 3 oz
    For 14-in. round pizza: 4½ oz
    For 16-in. round pizza: 6 oz
3. Add ground or shredded mozzarella cheese in the following proportions:
    For 12-in. round pizza: 4 oz
    For 14-in. round pizza: 5½ oz
    For 16-in. round pizza: 7½ oz

Crisp Crusted Rolls

The Kaiser roll, crescent roll, salt stick, water roll, oval shape, onion roll, and other varieties, are the introduction to a meal in many restaurants and hotel dining rooms. These rolls are usually small and are often placed in a basket with some of the specialty breads. Such an introduction to a meal is impressive and usually received very favorably by the diners. Of course, the hard roll varieties are often purchased from a local commercial bakery, but there are times when these are not available and the pastry chef may produce them. The following formula is standard for restaurants and hotels. The formula may be reduced in egg content with a slight change in crispness and interior texture.

This dough is also used for enrobing small cocktail frankfurters and other meatlike fillings for baking and serving hot.

Crisp Crusted Roll Dough

Ingredients	lb	oz	Mixing procedure
Yeast (variable)		6	Dissolve the yeast and set aside
Water	1		
Sugar		7	Stir well to dissolve the dry ingredients
Salt		2¼	and blend all ingredients
Malt		3	
Egg yolks		4	
Egg whites		6	
Water	3		
Bread flour	8	8	Add and stir the flour. Add the yeast and
Shortening		8	mix to a dough. Add the shortening and develop to a smooth dough

1. Dough temperature: 78–80°F.
2. First rise and punch about 2 hr. Second rise about 1 hr. Take to bench without punching a second time. The dough will be fully conditioned during the period it takes to scale, round, and make up the presses of dough.

Yield: 5 press at 3½ lb per press

Kaiser Rolls Scale the dough into presses of desired weight. Small rolls will be about 3 lb per press. If the rolls are shaped by hand, refer to Figs. 2.54 through 2.58 for makeup guidance. Most Kaiser rolls are now made by machine with a die shape forming the relaxed and rounded units of dough as they are placed in the machine.

The stamped-out or hand-shaped rolls are turned face down on cloth covers placed in roll boxes. The cloths may be placed on sheet pans. The rolls may be placed on pans that are filled with a layer of poppy seeds and allowed to proof. The rolls are given almost full proof and then peeled into the oven. The rolls are turned face up so that the cuts or folds may open during baking. The rolls may also be baked on regular sheet pans.

2.54
Place thumb in center of dough and fold over a small section

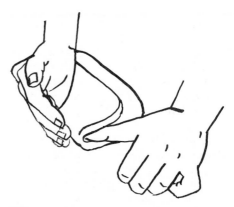

2.55
Make a crease in the fold by hitting the dough with the side of the hand

2.56
Repeat the folds four times and tuck the fifth fold into space occupied by thumb

2.57
Finished Kaiser roll

2.58
Turn roll upside down in a roll box lined with a canvas cloth or with poppy seeds

Baking hard rolls requires the use of steam in the oven for best results. The steam creates a moist film over the top surface of the dough as well as the sides of the roll and allows the roll to expand fully before the crust dries in the oven. The folds or cuts in the Kaiser roll and other hard-type rolls have a chance to open fully with proper break and shred. The moist steam also helps to form a crisp crust that is not too thick. The egg whites in the dough will also help to provide the crispness desired in hard rolls.

If steam injection is not available for the oven, brush the tops of the rolls lightly with water before placing them into the oven. The oven chamber should be filled with steam before placing the rolls into the oven. The steam is allowed to continue for 2 min and then shut off. The chamber of the oven may be sprayed with a moist spray of water from a spray bottle. The chamber can be sprayed again after the rolls have been placed in the oven.

Club Rolls   Scale the dough into units weighing about 1 lb. Round up and allow the dough to relax for 15 min. Shape the dough into a long strip about 36 in. long and about ½ to three-quarters in. in diameter. Allow the strips of dough to relax 10 min and then cut into rolls about 4 in. long. Place the rolls on parchment paper-lined pans or plain pans dusted with cornmeal (Figs. 2.59 and 2.60). Space the rolls about 1½ in. apart. Give the rolls three-quarter proof and then wash lightly. The rolls may be cut through the center and then given full proof. Bake the same as Kaiser rolls.

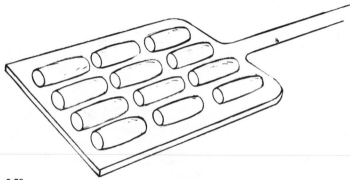

2.59
Place strips in cornmeal-dusted roll box.
When half proof, cut in 4-in. strips. Allow
three-quarter proof and cut across top

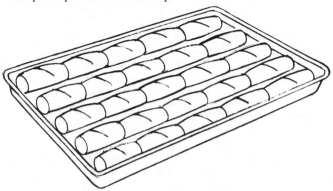

2.60
Proofed rolls placed on parchment paper-
lined pans to be peeled onto the hearth of
the oven

2.62
Crescent roll

2.61
Salt stick

Crescent Rolls and Salt Stick Rolls Scale the dough into presses of de-sired weight. For the average size, scale the units 3 lb 4 oz to 8 oz. Relax the presses and divide. Roll out the pieces of dough about 5 to 6 in. in length. Send them through the sheeter-moulder for larger quantities. Stretch the relaxed units slightly and then roll up with the palm of one hand while holding the other end in order to form a tight roll. By press-ing down firmly with the palm of the hand while rolling, the roll may be longer and thinner. Some sheeter-molders may have the attachment for rolling the dough into a salt stick or crescent shape. The longer shapes are curved slightly to form a crescent shape. The rolls which are shorter and thicker in the center are usually made into salt sticks. The rolls are lined up on the bench after shaping and washed with water. They are then sprinkled with either poppy seeds or sesame seeds. Salt sticks are garnished with caraway seeds and coarse salt. The rolls are placed on pans and given almost full proof. Bake with steam as for the Kaiser rolls. (Figs. 2.61 and 2.62)

Water Rolls These are a popular variety of hard rolls and are made up quickly (Figs. 2.63 through 2.69). Scale the dough into presses weighing 3 lb to 3 lb 8 oz. Round up the presses of dough and relax about 15 min. Press out and round up the units of dough. Give the rounded units half proof. Press the centers of the units down with a small rolling pin and then turn the rolls over as for Kaiser rolls. The rolls may be placed in cloth-lined boxes with the cloth pulled up to keep the rolls from spread-ing during proof. The rolls may be placed on pans with a cloth. Give the rolls almost full proof and place on cornmeal dusted peels to peel onto

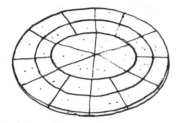

2.63
Press out the units of dough into 36 equal pieces

2.64
Round up pieces of pressed-out dough

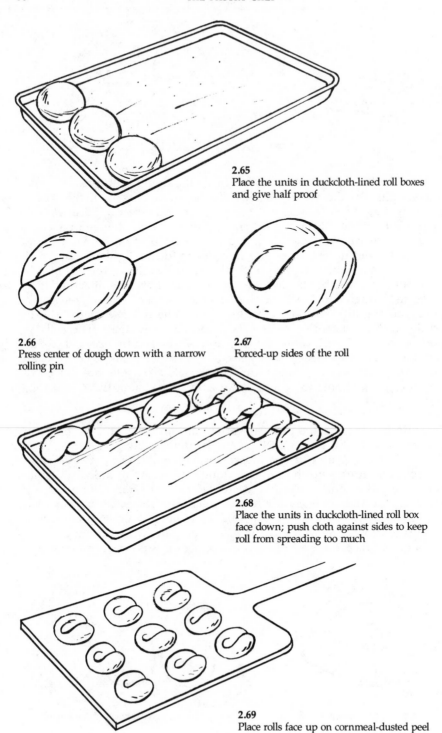

2.65
Place the units in duckcloth-lined roll boxes and give half proof

2.66
Press center of dough down with a narrow rolling pin

2.67
Forced-up sides of the roll

2.68
Place the units in duckcloth-lined roll box face down; push cloth against sides to keep roll from spreading too much

2.69
Place rolls face up on cornmeal-dusted peel

the hearth of the oven. The rolls may be placed on parchment paper-lined pans or lightly greased pans and baked. Bake with steam.

Oval and Round Rolls   These are made simply by pressing out the re-laxed presses of dough and rounding up the units. A divider-rounder will do this automatically. For the oval-shaped rolls, the rounded units are relaxed and then shaped into an oval or slightly tapered roll by press-ing down with the palm cupped and pressing gently toward the ends. Sending the units through the molder-sheeter will shape them into a short, thick strip. They are then slightly tapered by hand to form an oval shape. The round and oval rolls are given three-quarter proof and then cut through the centers before baking. Bake the rolls with steam. These rolls may be baked directly on the hearth of the oven or on sheet pans.

Onion Rolls   These are made by rounding the units of dough and then allowing them to relax. The units are then dipped into the onion prepa-ration and rolled out with the onion side facing the bench. A little oil on the bench will prevent the dough from sticking. Roll the dough about 4 in. in diameter. Place the rolls on sheet pans and give three-quarter proof. Press the center of the roll gently to form a slight depression. More on-ions may be added to the center of the roll at this time. Onion rolls may also be made by rolling the divided units out to about 4 in. in length. Dip the dough into the onion preparation and then fold over twice form-ing two layers or folds of onions. Place these rolls on pans and flatten gently with the palms of the hands. Give the rolls almost full proof and brush the tops with water. Additional onions and poppy seeds may be added at this time. Bake as for Kaiser rolls. (Fig. 2.70.)

Dried, chopped onions are usually used. The onions are soaked in just enough water to soften and reconstitute them. Drain any excess water. For each 4 oz of dehydrated onions, add the following after excess water has been drained: Vegetable oil (2 oz), salt (¼ oz), poppy seeds (1 oz). Mix well and use as required. Keep covered when not in use. Refrigerate in a covered receptacle.

Bread Stick Specialties

Bread sticks are made in various sizes, thicknesses, and flavors. They are flavored with garlic, others with celery, sage, and even saffron. They

2.70
Cross-section of onion roll

may be garnished with salt, sesame seeds, caraway seeds, and other seeds and condiments. The following formula is enriched with various grains.

Wheat Bread Stick Dough

Ingredients	lb	oz	Mixing procedure
Yeast (variable)		6	Dissolve the yeast and set aside
Water	1		
Sugar		2	Mix ingredients at slow speed for 4 to 5
Salt		2¼	min to soften the grains and dissolve the
Skim milk powder		2	dry ingredients
Soy flour (defatted)		2	
Bran flour		2	
Wheat germ		2	
Wheat gluten		1½	
Malt		2	
Water	4	8	
Whole wheat flour	2		Add the flour and stir slightly. Add the
Bread flour	6	8	yeast and mix to a dough. Add the butter
Butter (soft)	1		and margarine and develop to a smooth
Margarine or short-	1		dough. Mix at slow speed to avoid a high
ening			dough temperature.

1. Dough temperature: 80–82°F.
2. First rise and punch about 1½ to 2 hr. Second rise about 45 min. Take to bench.
3. Scale the dough into 3 lb presses and round up. Allow the presses of dough to relax about 20 min and divide into units (36 per press). The units may be hand-scaled at about 1 oz each.
4. Roll out the units of dough about 14 in. in length. For shorter bread sticks, cut the strip in half and make two pieces out of each strip of dough. Thicker bread sticks should be rolled out shorter. Little flour is needed for dusting because this is a stiff dough. Units that are sent through sheeter will require very little dusting flour.
5. Units should be slightly moist. This will enable the seeds used for garnish to stick. If the dough strips are dry, moisten the hands slightly when rolling.
6. The strips may also be placed onto a sheet pan containing seeds and rolled in the seeds. Place the sticks on sheet pans and space about 1 in. apart. Give the sticks three-quarter proof and bake in a moderate oven 380–385°F. Thicker sticks will take longer to bake. The sticks should be dry and crisp after baking.

Note: Spices and flavorings are usually added in a solution form with the water. Avoid excessive use of spices and flavorings. All or some of the special grains such as wheat germ, wheat gluten, and bran flour may be left out. The amount of whole wheat may be reduced. Replace the amount removed with an equal amount of bread flour. If the dough is too stiff, add a little water. Check the dough consistency before the dough is fully developed.

3

Sweet Yeast-Raised
Dough Products

The experienced and skilled pastry chef adjusts his formulas and methods of production to meet specific needs. For example, a quick breakfast sweet roll will not be as rich as the miniature Danish pastries served as the finale to a more luxurious breakfast. The coffee break Danish or Babka (grandmother's loaf) will be richer than the breakfast crumb bun. There will be variations in institutional feeding, fast food operations, and hotel and restaurant menus that apply to the sweet yeast-raised bakery products. The modern pastry chef is also governed by the cost factors of meal production. Very often the sweet roll or bun may be the major factor in the breakfast service. It may require a more enriched product as well as one larger in unit size. This will also be controlled by the individuals to be served. The first-grade school child will require somewhat less than the college student. These are the judgments to be made by the pastry chef.

Sweet yeast-raised doughs and the products made from them may be categorized as follows:

1. The basic sweet yeast dough used for buns and sweet rolls. These doughs will vary in richness and quality depending upon requirements.
2. The rich sweet yeast dough used for the production of Babka, coffee cakes, filled coffee cake strips (stongen), Russian coffee cake, and so forth.
3. Danish pastry and roll-in type sweet yeast doughs that will vary in richness based upon the butter and other fats rolled into the dough.

4. Frozen yeast-raised doughs, usually a remix of fermented sweet yeast doughs that include leftover and scrap dough. This dough is usually placed in the retarder for a day to condition. Very often the dough is scaled and shaped into large units (about 4–5-lb pieces) and then placed in the freezer for future use.

The amount and types of ingredients used for making the doughs play important roles in determining the quality of the baked product. Sweet yeast-raised doughs have higher percentages of sugar. The sugar provides sweetness, has a tenderizing effect, and also increases the keeping quality of the product. The shortening, butter, or margarine provide the degree of richness and tenderness required. They also are responsible for the tender flakiness of the product when rolled into the dough. The amount of fat rolled in and the method of rolling in are important. The increased use of eggs, with emphasis upon the use of egg yolks, adds to the lightness and volume of the product. The additional nutrition provided by the eggs and other ingredients are important factors. The addition of soy flour, wheat germ, wheat gluten, and other grains in limited proportions will add to the protein enrichment qualities of the product. These are often indistinguishable when added in limited amounts. Such sweet yeast rolls and buns are now quite popular in feeding school children.

Sweet yeast doughs require added yeast for conditioning. Extra rich coffee cake doughs are often made with the sponge and dough method. The sponge serves as the preliminary base for fermenting the dough. After the sponge has risen, the final dough is made. The yeast has had an opportunity to develop in the sponge dough and the final dough is now easily conditioned by the action of the yeast in the conditioned sponge dough. Doughs made with the straight dough method will require added yeast to leaven the richer dough.

The fillings and toppings used for sweet yeast dough products are of special importance. The experienced pastry chef can often enrich a sweet yeast dough by skillfully using fillings and toppings that will replace the lack of butter and eggs and sugar. Very often the sweetness and variety of the filling and the quality of the spices and flavors will provide the taste that is appealing without the added cost of ingredient enrichment. The wise use of toppings and variety of toppings will have a decided influence on the product. Too often, the rich ingredient qualities of butter and eggs are overshadowed by the fillings and toppings. A selected group of popular fillings and toppings will be provided before the dough formulas are presented. This will act as a reference for the pastry chef in deciding the method of production for a particular type of sweet yeast product.

Eye appeal is the first factor in the selection of the sweet yeast dough product. Naturally, neatness and workmanship are important. Automated icing equipment will provide uniformity of icing application. The prepared syrup wash and hand-applied icing will do equally well and may have a better taste. The pastry chef will do well to use quality materials for the topping and the final finishing of the baked products.

Basic Fillings and Toppings

The pastry chef uses cinnamon in two forms—the natural stick and ground cinnamon. Ground cinnamon is used for cinnamon sugar. The amount of cinnamon to use is very important. It will depend upon the type of product and the quality of the cinnamon. Quality cinnamon containing more of the natural oil of the bark is most desired. The delicious flavor of cinnamon is evident when a fine grade is used. Although synthetic cinnamon flavoring in powdered form may be purchased, there is a decidedly inferior flavor.

The average cinnamon sugar is a blend of the following:

Ingredients	lb	oz	Mixing procedure
Fine granulated sugar	2	8	Blend well to distribute the cinnamon evenly
Cinnamon (ground)		1	

Blending cinnamon sugar is important. In haste, bakers will mix the cinnamon and sugar at random producing uneven distribution—some parts of the cinnamon sugar will be stronger than others. This may cause a bitter taste where the cinnamon is very strong or concentrated.

The type of bakery product made will also determine the amount of cinnamon to be used. Most yeast-raised sweet goods have a cinnamon-flavored filling or topping. Very often both are used. For example, a cinnamon-crumb cake, in loaf or strip form, will have a cinnamon-based filling and a streusel (crumb) topping that also contains a mild amount of cinnamon. Cinnamon tea loaves will require a stronger flavor of cinnamon. These loaves are often dipped in cinnamon sugar after they are baked to increase the cinnamon flavor. Judgment is to be used.

Streusel-Crumb Topping

Ingredients	lb	oz	Mixing procedure
Almond or macaroon paste		12	Mix well to a smooth blend
Egg whites		4	
Brown sugar (dark)	1		Add to the above and blend well to a smooth consistency
Granulated sugar	1		
Salt		1/2	
Butter or margarine	2		
Cinnamon		1	
Vanilla		1/2	
Cake flour	2		Sift and add to the above. Rub together with the palms of the hands or at slow speed to form medium large lumps
Bread flour	2		

Note: Toasted chopped filberts or almonds may be added to the above after the lumps of topping have been formed. It is good practice to mix the topping and then refrigerate it to firm up the batter. The topping is then rubbed through a coarse sieve to obtain uniform lumps. If butter is used, it is advisable to keep the topping refrigerated when not in use. If the topping should feel dry or powdery after mixing, add a small amount of melted fat or butter and rub in lightly. If the topping is too moist, add some bread flour and rub in lightly.

Yield: Sufficient to cover approx. 200 individual crumb buns
Uses: Topping for small sweet rolls and buns, topping for larger coffee cakes, topping for fruit tarts and cakes, garnish for large-type cookies, garnish and topping for puff pastry specialties

---

Almond Filling

Ingredients	lb	oz	Mixing procedure
Almond paste, macaroon paste, or kernel paste (a blend of each may be used	4		Blend together to a smooth consistency
Egg whites		12	
Sugar	5		Add to the above and cream in until soft
Salt		½	and smooth
Butter or margarine	2		
Shortening	2		
Cinnamon		1	
Water	2		Add the water and stir in. Add the cake
Cake crumbs (variable)	6		crumbs and mix to a smooth consistency

Uses: For Special Coffee Cakes and Danish
Note: The crumbs used may be obtained from a variety of leftovers and stale cakes and sweet yeast goods. The crumbs should be sifted after they have been ground at slow speed on the mixing machine. The crumbs should be of medium fine granulation to avoid lumping when added to the filling. If the crumbs are stale and dry, they will require more water to moisten them to obtain a filling that can be easily smeared. Richer crumbs, those obtained from cakes high in sugar and fat content, will not absorb quite as well as dry crumbs made from a lean product. It may be necessary to add more crumbs to absorb the water. Toasted chopped nuts may be added to supplement the cake crumbs. Mixed, diced fruits and raisins may be added for variety and enrichment. This filling should be refrigerated when not in use.

Cheese Filling

Ingredients	lb	oz	Mixing procedure
Baker's cheese	5		Blend the cheese, flour and cornstarch to-
Cake flour		8	gether
Cornstarch		4	
Sugar	1	8	Add to the cheese and blend at slow speed
Salt		1	until smooth
Skim milk powder		4	
Butter or margarine	1		
Shortening		6	
Eggs (part yolks)	1	4	
Vanilla		1	Add the flavors and stir in. Add the water
Rind of 1 fresh lemon or lemon flavor		½	gradually while mixing at slow speed. Check the consistency for dropping out or smearing
Cold water (variable)	1		
Raisins (optional)	1	8	

Yield: Sufficient for 200 medium sized Danish pastry cheese pockets
Uses: Sweet rolls, buns (cheese filled), Danish pastry, large coffee cake strips, Danish and puff pastry strudel
Note: Baker's cheese will vary in quality from time to time. This means that the cheese will vary in its ability to absorb and retain water. Cheese of good quality will readily absorb the water and may require additional water or milk.

If cottage cheese is to be used, blend the cottage cheese with 4 oz of cornstarch and then grind or force through a fine strainer. It is then ready to be mixed as though it were baker's cheese. Whey that may come out with the ground cottage cheese should be returned with the cheese when mixing into cheese filling.

Cream Cheese Filling

Ingredients	lb	oz	Mixing procedure
Cream cheese	3		Blend the cheese, starch and cake flour to-
Cornstarch		4	gether. Add the remaining ingredients and
Cake flour		3	blend smooth. Mix at slow speed
Sugar		14	
Salt		½	
Butter (soft)		6	
Rind of 2 lemons			
Egg yolks	1		
Sour cream		8	Add and blend in

For additional lightness and chiffon-like effect, whip:

Egg whites	10	Whip to a wet peak and fold gently into
Sugar	2	the above

Raisins may be added if desired. The amount is optional. Refrigerate before using. This will make handling easier.

Uses: Cheese pastry specialties, cheese strudel

For Almond-Chocolate Smear For Danish and coffee cake specialties add 12 oz to 1 lb of melted chocolate liquor (bitter chocolate) to the almond smear and mix in well while the chocolate is in a liquid form.

Many pastry chefs will smear melted sweet chocolate over the surface of the dough after it has first been washed with melted butter. They will then cover the chocolate with almond smear or sprinkle with cake crumbs, nuts, and cinnamon sugar.

Cinnamon Crumb Filling

Cinnamon crumb filling is a dry type of filling for sweet rolls, buns, Danish coffee cakes, and crumb specialties. As indicated previously, leftover cakes and sweet yeast dough products are used for the preparation of crumbs for fillings and toppings. These cakes *should not contain fruits, custards, or other soft fillings* which may turn sour or rancid. This is a method for pastry chefs to use leftovers for making quality baked products. The crumbs are rich in sugar, butter, shortening, milk, eggs, and can be made into a very tasty filling. With the addition of sugar and cinnamon, and melted butter or margarine, the crumbs are further enriched. The amount of sugar, fat, and spice will depend upon the type of cakes and other products used. Lean products, such as ordinary sweet rolls, soft rolls without seeds, are not very rich and will require additional sugar and fat to enrich them. The pastry chef will use his sense of taste to determine the amounts to be added.

In most cases, the pastry chef will try to have a blend of products. For example, he will not use a spice cake only to be ground into crumbs because of the darkness of the crumb and the predominant flavor of the molasses. Neither will he use an all chocolate cake. A combination of dry leftovers will result in a desirable blend of color and flavor. Many pastry chefs will add toasted, ground filberts, almonds, cashews, and other nuts to the crumbs and have a special blend of crumbs and nuts. This will be on hand all the time to be used for filling many of the yeast-raised sweet dough products. In some instances, additional butter (melted) will be added to further soften and enrich the crumbs for special cakes. For example, the cinnamon crumb stick, the Russian coffee cake, cinnamon-nut-crumb topping on cakes, are some of the products that will have added butter in the crumbs.

Prepared Toppings and Fillings

Toppings and fillings are usually purchased by the pastry chef in the prepared form. It is time saving and more economical to purchase these items rather than to make them. For example, poppy filling, fig jam or fig filling, lemon filling, and so forth are best purchased from a quality supplier of bakery supplies. Of course, the pastry chef can still prepare his own fillings if desired. Such fillings and toppings as custard, fruits, and similar types are usually available because they are used for so many other products. The custard used for filling eclairs and cream puffs can very well be used for garnishing the tops of sweet rolls and Danish pastry. The fruit fillings used for pies can also be used for the same purpose.

The use of cold process thickeners has now made these filling and topping preparations easy to prepare. The pastry chef will simply follow the instructions as provided by the manufacturer. For large volume production and fast food service, these prepared mixes and thickeners are excellent. The more specialized pastry chef in the hotel and restuarant may still prefer to cook his or her own fillings and topping specialties.

Sweet Roll and Danish Glaze

Ingredients	lb	oz	Mixing procedure
Granulated sugar	5		Bring to a boil and continue to boil for ap-
Corn syrup or glucose		8	proximately 2 min. Stir well to be sure sugar is dissolved before the boiling point
Water	4		is reached
Apricot coating	1		
Orange and lemon quarters (1 full orange and lemon)			

Use this syrup wash on sweet rolls and Danish while it is still hot.

Coconut Topping

Ingredients	lb	oz	Mixing procedure
Sugar	2	2	Blend the dry ingredients together
Salt		1/4	
Skim milk powder		4	
Cake flour		8	
Macaroon coconut (unsweetened)	4		
Melted butter		8	Add the butter and the eggs and blend in
Eggs	1		
Water (variable)	1		Add and mix smooth
Vanilla		1	

Allow the batter to stand for a short while. This will allow for a thickening effect caused by absorption of liquid by the cocoanuts. A sweetened cocoanut will cause the mix to become softer because a syrupy condition will form as the sugar on the cocoanut dissolves. Pastry chefs will often mix some yellow cake batter or cupcake mix into the batter to provide a firmer consistency and easier spread. It will also make for greater volume when the topping bakes. This topping may be used for coffee cakes, Danish rings, sweet rolls, and large Danish twists.

Honey Bun and Pecan Roll Glaze

Ingredients	lb	oz	Mixing procedure
Brown sugar	2		Blend the sugar, salt, and shortening to-
Salt		¼	gether well. Add the honey and mix to a
Shortening	1	8	smooth consistency. Add the water and
Honey	1		blend in
Water (variable)		4	
Pecans (variable) as desired in each muffin tin			

Grease the muffin tins well with the pecan glaze. Be sure the glaze is applied more heavily at the bottom of the muffin pan. After the pans have been greased, sprinkle chopped pecans over the bottom of the pans before placing the units of dough into the pans. The baked units are to be turned over as soon as the pecan rolls or honey buns are baked. Soak the pans immediately to soften and remove the baked-in glaze that adheres to the sides of the pans.

Icing for Sweet Rolls and Buns

Ingredients	lb	oz	Mixing procedure
Confectioners sugar	10		Sift the sugar. Dissolve the gelatin in part
Glucose or corn syrup		6	of the water. Combine all ingredients and mix to a smooth consistency. Place in a
Hot water (variable)	2		warm water bain marie to warm
Vanilla		1	
Gelatin (optional)		½	

If the sweet rolls and buns are to be exposed for some time to warmth and moisture, it is best to add the gelatin. It will prevent the icing from softening and running. Additional sugar may be added for a thicker icing. Icing to be striped on the units should be of medium soft consistency. The icing should be about 110–115°F when applied. If the icing is too thick, it may be thinned down by adding a small amount of simple syrup to it. This icing may be used for sweet rolls and buns, for Danish pastry, large sweet roll strips, and puff pastry varieties.

Variety Sweet Rolls or Buns

Basic Sweet Yeast Dough

Ingredients	lb	oz	Mixing procedure
Yeast (variable)		12	Dissolve the yeast and set aside
Water	2		
Sugar	1	10	Blend all ingredients in this stage to a
Salt		2¼	smooth consistency
Skim milk powder		8	
Defatted soy flour (optional) [1]		4	
Wheat germ [1]		4	
Butter or margarine	1		
Shortening		12	
Honey		4	
Eggs (part yolks)	1	8	Add in 2 stages and blend
Water	2		Add the water, flavoring, spices and stir
Vanilla		1	lightly
Spices (mace, etc.) optional		½	
Cake flour [2]	1	8	Sift the flour and add. Stir lightly and add
Bread flour [2]	6	8	the yeast. Develop to a smooth dough

1. Dough temperature: 78–80°F.
2. First rise approximately 2 hr. (Increased yeast and warmer dough temperature will speed up the rate of dough conditioning.)
3. Punch or fold the dough and allow dough to relax for ½ hr. It is better to keep the dough slightly on the young side (not fully conditioned) since it does take considerable time to make up the sweet roll and bun varieties.
4. Scale the dough into presses if the varieties require the dough to be pressed out into uniform pieces on the dough divider. For varieties to be made from doughs that are rolled out and filled on the bench, or rolled out through the dough sheeter, scale the dough pieces into 4, 5, or 6 lb units and form into a rectangular shape. After rounding or shaping the scaled dough, allow the dough to relax for 15 to 20 min (preliminary proofing). At this point, many pastry chefs prefer to retard the dough units for later makeup or makeup the following morning. This is especially important where refrigeration space is limited and madeup units cannot be stored.

[1] The soy and wheat germ will increase the nutritional value.
[2] A selected short patent flour may be used in place of the cake and bread flours.

Yield: Approx. 216 buns or sweet rolls weighing approx. 1¼ oz (dough); 6 press scaled at 2 lb 14 oz per press
Uses: Sweet roll varieties, leaner Danish varieties, snack and coffee break buns, fruit and nut varieties for economy desserts, enrichment buns.

Crumb Buns (Streusel Rolls)   Press out the scaled dough presses on the dough divider. Do not round up the units of dough. Allow units to relax 5 min and stretch each piece about 4 in. long and 2 in. wide. Place on a greased sheet pan or greased parchment paper-lined pan. Space the units of dough about ¼ in. apart (8 down and 7 across; Figs. 3.1 and 3.2) and flatten. Egg wash the buns and sprinkle well with streusel (crumb) topping. Be sure the lumps of topping are even. Allow some of the topping to fall between the units of dough. This will enable the buns to be separated easily after baking. Allow the buns to get slightly more than three-quarter proof before baking. Additional topping may be added at this time by sprinkling vacant areas of dough lightly with topping. Bake these buns at 400°F. The topping should have a golden brown, nut-like appearance and the buns should spring back softly to the touch when baked. Crumb buns are usually dusted with confectioners sugar after they have cooled and are ready to be served.

Cinnamon Buns or Cinnamon Sweet Rolls   When baked close together and then separated from each other, they are usually called buns. When these buns are spaced separately and baked as individual units they are often termed Danish cinnamon rolls.

Roll out the rectangular shaped dough to an even thickness of about ¼ in. Brush the surface with melted butter or margarine. Sprinkle with

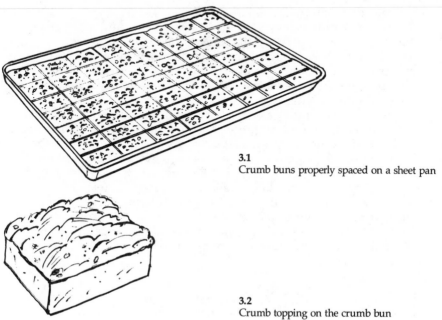

3.1
Crumb buns properly spaced on a sheet pan

3.2
Crumb topping on the crumb bun

prepared cake crumbs, raisins, and cinnamon sugar. Roll in the filling with the rolling pin. Roll up the dough into a tight roll and seal the edge tightly with the heel of the hand. Brush the top of the roll with melted butter and then cut into even slices. Place on a sheet pan close together (approximately 6 down and 9 across) and then flatten. Egg wash and give three-quarter proof. (Figs. 3.3 through 3.7.)

Egg wash the cinnamon buns again and return to the proof box for a short time. The buns will now be in close touch with each other. Bake the buns at 390–400°F. The buns will be baked into each other and will spring back gently to the touch. Wash with warm syrup glaze as soon as removed from the oven. Ice the tops with warm simple icing when the buns are just mildly warm.

3.3
Roll out the dough ¼ in. thick

3.4
Brush dough with oil or melted fat and sprinkle with raisins, cake crumbs, and cinnamon sugar

3.5
Roll dough up tightly and seal edge

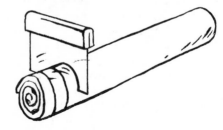

3.6
Brush top of roll with oil or melted fat and cut into even pieces with a scraper

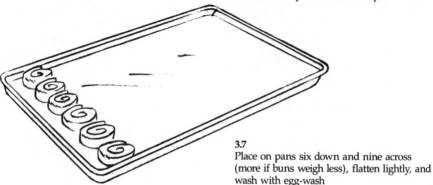

3.7
Place on pans six down and nine across (more if buns weigh less), flatten lightly, and wash with egg-wash

3.8
Dough dipped in crumb
filling

3.9
Crumbs sticking to dough

3.10
Fold over one side

Note: The cinnamon buns will be easily separated because the top surface of the dough was brushed with melted butter or fat before the buns
were cut and placed next to each other on the pan. The melted fat makes
possible the ease in separation of the buns.

Cinnamon Stick Buns   These buns allow the pastry chef to use up any
excess or leftover stale cakes or sweet yeast products. The crumbs are to
be softened or moistened with melted butter. Additional cinnamon sugar
may be added. The feel of the crumbs should be such that the crumbs
will stick to the dough when the dough is pressed into the crumbs.
Toasted ground filberts or cashews may be added to the crumbs.

Divide the dough presses in the dough divider. Brush the tops of the
units with melted butter or fat. Separate the units of dough. Allow them
to relax about 10 min before shaping into sticks.

Form the crumbs into a pile on one part of the work bench. Dip each
unit of dough into the crumbs so that crumbs stick to the dough. Fold
the dough over to form 2 layers of crumb filling and shape into a stick
shape that is slightly tapered. (Figs. 3.8 through 3.10.) Place the sticks on
parchment paper-lined pans. Flatten the sticks so that they almost touch
each other (8 × 7) on a pan. Give the sticks a little more than three-
quarter proof. Sprinkle the tops of the sticks with additional crumbs and
cinnamon sugar. Bake at 390°F. The center sticks should spring back
lightly to the touch when baked. Dust the cinnamon sticks with confectioners sugar after they have cooled.

Note: The cinnamon sticks may be cooled and then frozen. Cover with
freezer wrap to prevent frost and crystallization from forming on the surface. Defrosting may take place by leaving the units at room temperature,
or placing in the retarder overnight. Separate sections may be placed in
microwave ovens for 2 or 3 min for quick defrost and reheating. Dust
with confectioners sugar before serving.

Butterfly Buns   Roll out the dough as for cinnamon buns, but longer
and narrower. Fill as for cinnamon buns and roll up into a tight roll and
seal. The roll of dough should be about 2 in. thick. With a bench scraper
or knife cut slices weighing about 1¼ oz. Press down the centers of each
slice with a narrow rolling pin. This will cause the sides to flare out
giving the appearance of butterfly wings. Place the units on pans and

3.11
Roll out ¼ in. thick in long, narrow shape

3.12
Wash and sprinkle as for cinnamon buns

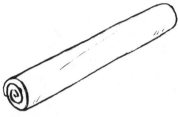

3.13
Roll up tightly and seal

3.14
Cut in equal pieces

3.15
Press down in center with a thin rolling pin

space about 1 in. apart. Egg wash and give the units three-quarter proof. Egg wash lightly again. At this point, sliced nuts, jam or jelly, or other garnish may be placed in the center of the bun. Give the buns slightly less than full proof and bake at 400°F (Figs. 3.11 through 3.15).

The buns or sweet rolls should be light brown in crust color and spring back gently to the touch. Wash the baked buns with warm syrup wash as soon as removed from the oven. Ice the buns with a criss-cross design of simple icing when cool. If the buns are to be retarded or frozen, allow them to cool and then wrap the pans for the freezer. Defrost and reheat in a microwave oven or by placing in a moderate baking oven for a few minutes. Be sure to wash the buns with hot syrup after defrosting and heating. Ice the buns when cool.

Variety Twist Buns   These are buns that may be filled with a variety of fillings. For example, the rolled out dough first may be brushed lightly with melted butter and covered with a soft almond smear. A softened jam or jelly may be used as a smear. The butter smear may be used as a base to hold the filling. The filling is then sprinkled with cake crumbs, cinnamon sugar, and chopped nuts. The type of filling may often determine the name of the sweet roll. For example, some pastry chefs will call them variety almond twist. In fast food and institution service they may be termed Danish twists.

Roll out the dough as for cinnamon buns. Brush with melted butter and smear and fill as desired. Roll in the filling lightly with a rolling pin. The dough may now be folded in half or given three folds. Cut the dough into strips weighing about 1¼ to 1½ oz. Twist the units of dough so that several twists are made (Figs. 3.16 through 3.21) and a twisted circular bun is formed. The strips of dough may be rolled out 8 to 10 in. in length and twisted into a variety of shapes as for Danish pastry. These varieties will be discussed in the Danish pastry section.

Place the units on parchment paper-lined pans and space them about 1 in. apart. Flatten lightly with the palms of the hands, then egg wash. Give the units three-quarter proof and egg wash again. The units are then garnished with nuts, sugar, jam, jelly, or other fillings. Give the units a little more proof, until they spring back lightly when touched gently, and bake at 390–400°F. Wash with warm or hot syrup as soon as the units are removed from the oven. When cool, ice with simple icing. Follow the same procedure for freezing and defrosting as for butterfly buns.

Cheese and Fruit-Filled Buns   The pastry chef often uses the filled bun or sweet roll to round out a breakfast which may not be quite filling. These buns are often used for coffee breaks and snacks. In fact they may replace Danish pastry since they will appeal to younger consumers because of the added fillings and sweetness. A display of cheese-filled, fruit-filled, prune and jam-filled, and custard-type fillings placed on a cafeteria counter or in a dessert section will almost always bring a good response. The pastry chef will determine whether it is better to purchase prepared fillings or prepare the fillings. This may depend upon volume and production time as well as cost. Certain fillings, such as prune, are best purchased. Fruit fillings may be stretched by increasing the amount of liquid and starch in the preparation. The quality of the product and the cost are the important considerations.

Sweet rolls are made in a round-filled form. Others may be made in an open pocket form. Some may call for enclosing the filling in a rolled out piece of dough by pinching the ends of the dough together and then

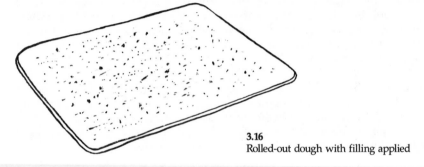

3.16
Rolled-out dough with filling applied

3.17
Folded dough

3.18
Flatten lightly with the rolling pin

3.19
Cut strips with pastry wheel

3.20
Twist in direction of arrows

3.21
Form into a snail shape

placing them in a muffin pan. Finally, others may be twisted into snail and similar forms and filled after the buns have reached almost three-quarter proof. This unit will stress the most popular of the filled buns, namely, the round-filled type and the open pocket variety.

Round-Filled Buns—Makeup Procedure Scale the conditioned dough into presses of desired weight. The average will be approximately 2 lb 12 oz. to 3 lb. Allow the presses to relax for about 10 to 15 min and then divide and round the units. Allow the rounded units to relax after placing on a sheet pan spaced about five down and seven or eight across. Flatten the centers of the rounded units with a round weight or the

3.22
Flatten center of proofed bun with a 1-lb
weight or similar object

3.23
Egg-wash buns and fill centers

handle of a pastry wheel. (Fig. 3.22) The fingers may be used. Do not depress the dough so that the center is broken. Egg wash the units and then fill with cheese filling (see formula) or other filling (Fig. 3.23). Do not overfill to avoid running out of the filling during baking. Give these units three-quarter proof and check to see if there is enough filling or equal amounts of filling in each. Do not overproof since this may cause the sides to collapse and the filling will run out. Wash with warm or hot syrup wash after the buns are baked. Be careful to avoid smearing the soft fruit fillings when washing with syrup. These buns are usually iced with a heavier simple icing after they have cooled and are ready to be served. When freezing these buns, be sure to cover well with a freezer wrap to avoid frost or crystallization on the fruit fillings. Defrost and heat as for butterfly buns.

Open Pocket Filled Buns Scale the dough into presses and allow to relax. Press out the dough and separate the units. Sprinkle lightly with dusting flour and allow to relax about 10 min. Roll out the units into oblongs about 4 in. long and about 2½ in. wide. Several units may be lined up and rolled out at one time. Line up the units close to each other on the bench. Drop the filling into the center of each unit of dough (Fig. 3.24). A scoop or spoon may also be used to control the amount of filling. A pastry bag is usually used for custard-type fillings. Fold one corner of the dough over the filling. Fold the opposite corner over the dough and seal with the thumb. (Fig. 3.25). Line the units or pockets on the bench

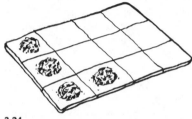

3.24
Roll pressed-out pieces of dough into oblongs
or squares. Deposit filling in center

3.25
Fold end of one side over the filling. Fold
other end over and seal

and wash with egg wash. Place on parchment paper-lined pans and space about 1 in. apart. Give these units about three-quarter proof before baking. Overproofing will cause the dough to flatten and the filling may tend to run even before baking. Overproofed sweet rolls that are filled will flatten during baking. The units may be washed when at three-quarter proof with egg wash and then garnished with nuts, sugar, or other topping. Bake these units and the round-filled units at 400°F. Wash with syrup as soon as the units are removed from the oven. Stripe the simple icing across the buns when they have cooled.

Another method of making these pocket-type buns is to scale units of dough about 4 to 5 lb and form into a rectangular shape. Allow the dough units to relax for about 20 min before rolling out into ¼ in. thick rectangle. Allow the rolled dough to relax about 5 min and then cut into squares with a pastry wheel (single wheel or multiple wheel). The squares are about 4 in. square. Deposit the filling in the center of each square in equal amounts. Fold the end of the square over the filling. Take the diagonally opposite end and fold over the dough and seal well with the thumb. Handle these buns as you did the round-filled variety.

Bow Tie or Necktie Sweet Rolls or Buns   These sweet rolls may be made with a variety of fillings and toppings. For example, they may be filled with an almond smear and crumbs and cinnamon sugar. A jam or jelly filling may be used. The tops of the buns may be topped with streusel (crumb) topping, coconut topping, sugar and nuts, and others. These combinations will allow for greater variety while using the same basic dough and makeup procedure.

Scale the conditioned dough into 4- or 5-lb pieces and form into long rectangular shape. Allow the dough strips to relax about 15 min. They may be retarded or frozen at this point for later makeup. Roll out the dough to about ¼ in. thickness and only about 9 in. wide and quite long. Check for even thickness. Brush the top of the dough with melted butter and apply the desired filling. Roll in the filling lightly. Fold the dough over twice so that 2 layers of filled dough are formed (double-decker sandwich). Roll the dough slightly and then cut into slices after washing with butter or egg wash and applying the desired topping (Fig. 3.26). The slices should be about 1½ to 2 in. wide. Twist each slice so that a bow tie shape is formed. It requires a double twist to have the topping showing on both sides of the bow tie. (Fig. 3.27.) It is advisable

3.26
Slice of filled dough cut from the dough

3.27
Twist in center to form the bow tie

to roll the topping in slightly before cutting the slices and twisting. This will avoid losing some of the topping when twisting and shaping the buns. Place the buns on parchment paper-lined pans and space about 1 in. apart. Give these buns slightly more than three-quarter proof and then bake at 400°F. Buns that have a nut topping may be washed with warm syrup glaze or wash. Those that have a streusel or coconut topping are usually striped with simple icing when cool. These sweet rolls are also dusted with confectioners sugar in place of the icing. Units that have been frozen or chilled in the retarder should be reheated and then iced or dusted with confectioners sugar.

Honey Buns and Pecan Rolls   These sweet rolls are usually made from a Danish pastry dough or rolled-in basic sweet yeast dough. However, since the basic dough is quite rich, it can be used for the makeup of these varieties. They are baked in muffin tins that have been lined with a special glaze (see honey bun glaze). The honey buns can be made with chopped walnuts while the pecan rolls use chopped or whole pecans. The muffin pans are usually prepared in advance. Be sure to have the bottoms of the pans well greased. The chopped nuts are deposited at the center bottom of each muffin tin.

Pecan rolls can be made up as for cinnamon buns by dipping each slice of dough into a pan filled with chopped pecans and cinnamon sugar and placing on sheet pans about 1½ in. apart. Give slightly more than three-quarter proof and bake at 400°F.

Scale and shape the units of conditioned dough as for cinnamon buns. Allow the dough to relax about 15 min before rolling out. These units may be retarded or frozen at this point. These doughs may be rolled out and made up at a later time. Roll out the relaxed dough about ¼ in. thick. Brush the surface with melted butter and then apply the filling of chopped nuts, cake crumbs, and cinnamon sugar. Roll up into a tight roll and seal with the palm of the hand. The roll of dough should be about 2 in. in diameter (Fig. 3.28). Cut slices weighing about 1½ to 2 oz (the size of the muffin tin will determine the size). Place the slices on sheet pans or into the prepared muffin pans and press each slice in gently (Figs.

3.28
Rolled-up, filled dough cut for cinnamon buns

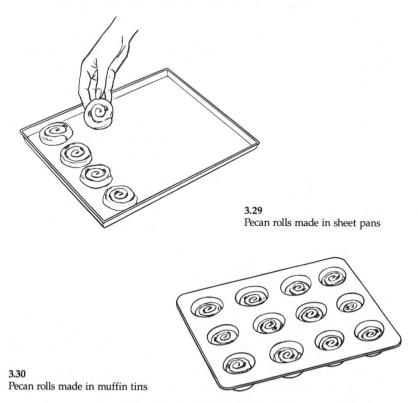

3.29
Pecan rolls made in sheet pans

3.30
Pecan rolls made in muffin tins

3.29, 3.30). Give the units almost full proof. They will spring back lightly when touched gently. Bake at 385°F. They are considered baked when they spring back to the touch. The honey buns and pecan rolls must be turned over as soon as they are taken from the oven. Turn them over on a clean sheet pan. Allow the rolls to cool slightly before picking them up. The glaze will form a natural shine. Nuts that stick to the pan may be removed with a spoon and placed on the bun while still hot. If the rolls tend to stick because of delay in removing from the pans, place the pans in the oven for 1 min and then turn over immediately. Tap the pan to release the buns if necessary. Use enough glaze in the pans to avoid sticking. (See Figs. 3.28 through 3.30.)

Rolled-In Basic Sweet Yeast Dough

Because of the high cost for Danish pastry dough and other rich doughs, the basic sweet yeast dough is often put through a roll-in process after it has been partially conditioned. The dough is allowed to rise and then scaled into units weighing from 4 to 8 lb. The units are formed into rectangular shapes and allowed to relax by placing in the retarder until the dough is chilled. The dough is then rolled out about ½ in. thick and a fat or combination of fats is rolled in. The rule is 2 oz of fat for each pound of dough to be rolled in. Thus, an 8-lb piece of dough will have 1 lb of butter, or combination of butter and other fats, rolled in. The dough is folded in 3 parts so that two layers of fat and 3 layers of dough are formed. This dough is then rolled out two more times (some prefer 3 rolls) giving a three-fold turn after each rolling. The dough is placed in the retarder between rolls to relax and remain chilled. This will also keep the rolled-in fat chilled and make each successive roll easy to handle. Larger bakeshops and institutional pastry chefs will use the roller sheeter to roll out the units of dough.

The rolled-in sweet yeast dough can replace the dough used for making Danish products. Use it for the makeup of large coffee rings and strips of filled sweet yeast dough. These rings and strips are later cut into portions and slices for service.

Sweet rolls and buns of a slightly richer variety resemble Danish pastry. This is a form of cost control and yet produces a product of good quality. All previous sweet rolls may be made from this dough, particularly those made from large strips of dough rolled out.

Danish Pastry

Danish pastries are basic to most food establishments. Their popularity is related to the richness of the product, the many varieties, the ease of handling and serving, the ready acceptance by the public for coffee breaks, and the nourishment provided at other refreshment periods. The pastry chef takes special pride in the Danish pastries made and served. In many food establishments, the role of Danish pastry surpasses all other types of cakes and desserts. Many restaurants are frequented and known for the Danish pastry and other types of sweet yeast products baked. Danish of high quality is judged by the volume, flakiness, variety, and taste and flavor. These factors are controlled by the ingredients used and the manner in which the doughs are made. Danish is a rich dough that is rolled for the formation of layers of fat and dough.

The following factors are to be given careful consideration:

1. Yeast is the basic leavening agent. A high-quality yeast should be used because the Danish doughs are usually retarded for as much as 36 hr before makeup. The yeast must be such that its strength and leavening qualities are not weakened. Danish doughs are very often frozen. The pastry chef will want to be sure that the yeast will resume its fermenting and leavening activity after defrost and makeup. The amount of yeast to use will depend upon production needs and production techniques. Danish is a dough rich in sugar, fat, and eggs, and will require more yeast to leaven it than that required for a lean dough.

2. Sugar will vary from one formula to another. Some pastry chefs prefer a lesser amount (10 to 12 oz per quart of dough). Others prefer a higher amount. The formula presented will use 1 lb of sugar per quart (equal to 11.8% based on the weight of the flour). This is a moderate amount. It will provide sufficient sweetness for the total amount of dough and will provide a measure of tenderness and improved keeping quality.

3. The butter and other fats used are very important. They not only provide tenderness, excellent keeping quality, and richness, but also make possible the formation of layers of fat and dough which account for the flaky characteristic of Danish pastries. Some pastry chefs will use as much as 3 lb of sweet butter to be rolled into each quart of dough (2 lb of milk used for the dough). This is rather rich and costly. Others will use considerably less. In fact, they may not use butter at all but substitute a fat compounded of margarine, shortening, and other fats. Cost is usually the controlling factor. The lack of butter is usually covered by the use of sweet fillings, glaze, toppings, and icing on Danish. Quality Danish pastries are only washed or glazed with syrup. They are seldom iced with an icing such as fondant or simple icing. A blend of sweet butter and margarine with some hydrogenated shortening is often used. This blend of roll-in fats is chilled before using to make rolling in easier. The formula that follows will use a moderate amount of roll-in fat and butter in the dough.

4. Eggs play an important part in Danish dough and in the baked pastry. Eggs provide nutritional value, improve taste, make for increased volume with the use of egg yolks, provide attractive color, and add to the richness and keeping quality of the product. The yolk of the egg contains lecithin which acts as an emulsifier and an extender. The average amount used is 1 lb of eggs and yolks mixed for each quart of dough. Some pastry chefs will use egg yolks only for added enrichment and volume.

5. Because of the richness of Danish pastry dough, a flour of sufficient strength must be used to support the added fats and other ingredients during the mixing of the dough and the conditioning of the dough. It is especially important to have a flour with a high-quality gluten strength to allow for the rolling in process. A weak flour will tend to tear when rolled several times as required in the making of Danish dough. However, it is equally important not to have an extra strong flour which will be difficult to roll and be difficult to roll out when making the Danish pastries. A blend of high gluten flour mellowed with a small percentage of cake flour is used in the formula. The cake flour will have a moderating and softening effect upon the high gluten bread flour.

Danish Pastry Dough

Ingredients	lb	oz	Mixing procedure
Yeast (variable)		8	Dissolve the yeast and set aside
Water	1		
Sugar	2		Mix these ingredients to a soft, smooth
Salt		2¼	consistency
Skim milk powder		8	
Butter or	1		
margarine			
Ground cardamom		¼	
(or coffee cake			
flavoring)			
Eggs (part yolks)	2		Add in 3 stages and blend in
Vanilla		1	Add and stir in
Water	3		
Bread flour (high	7		Sift and add the flour. Stir slightly, add
gluten)			the yeast and develop to a smooth dough
Cake flour	1	8	

Form the dough into a smooth rectangular shape on the bench and allow the dough to relax for 10 min. The dough may be placed in the refrigerator to chill and relax before rolling. This will make rolling the dough easier when sending the dough through the sheeter. (Figs. 3.31 through 3.34.)

Yield: Approx. 180 2-oz units

Roll-in Fat

Butter	2		Blend the fats together and chill to
Margarine	2		firm, plastic consistency

1. The roll-in fat should be slightly firmer than the dough.
2. Chill the dough before rolling in the fat. This makes rolling easier.
3. Distribute the fat over two-thirds of the dough and fold the remaining third of the dough over one-half of the fatty portion. Fold once again to form two layers of fat encompassed in three layers of dough. Roll the dough out to about ½ in. thickness and make a four-fold turn. Do this by first removing the excess dusting flour and then folding each end to the center. This will form two layers on each side. Fold one section over the other and and four layers will be formed. Be sure to check the bench for sufficient dusting flour when rolling to prevent the dough from sticking to the bench. (Figs. 3.31 through 3.34.)
4. Three such rolls of four folds each should be given. Some pastry chefs will give the dough four such rolls. The rolls of fat and dough will provide for the flakiness.

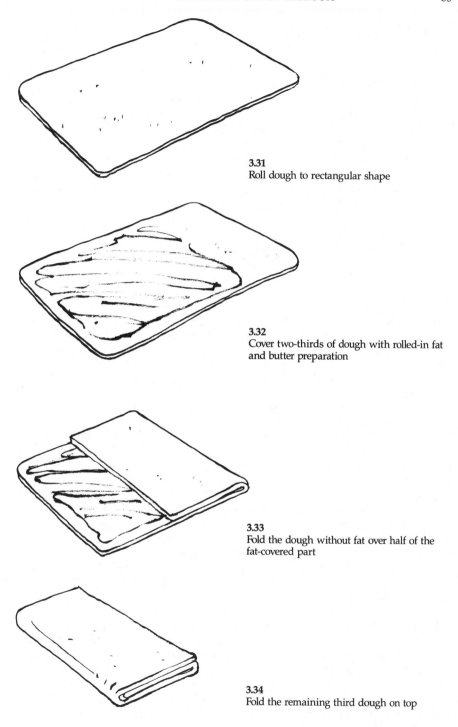

3.31
Roll dough to rectangular shape

3.32
Cover two-thirds of dough with rolled-in fat
and butter preparation

3.33
Fold the dough without fat over half of the
fat-covered part

3.34
Fold the remaining third dough on top

5. It is important to refrigerate the dough between rolls to keep the fat and dough chilled. This prevents the fat from softening and leaking out during the rolling in process.
6. The dough, when given the final roll-in, should be brushed free of flour and covered with a thin film of vegetable oil before placing into the retarder. This will help prevent formation of a heavy crust on the dough. The dough should be covered with a cloth or parchment paper as well. If the dough is to be placed in the freezer, it is advisable to wrap the dough in freezer wrap to avoid formation of ice crystals on the dough as well as preventing excessive crusting.

Roll-in fat blends are usually prepared in advance and kept in a separate container under refrigeration. This may be done in large amounts to avoid the necessity of preparing the blend for the daily preparation of Danish dough. It is especially valuable when large amounts of dough are prepared at one time and stored in the freezer for later makeup. Many pastry chefs will do this to meet the requirements for advance special orders and the added needs for weekend and party service.

Leavening of Danish Pastry
The yeast will function in Danish dough as it does in other yeast-raised doughs. Danish units are proofed, usually three-fourths proof, and then baked. The oven spring takes place as for other yeast-raised products, due to expansion of the gas in the cells and the further activity of the yeast during the first few minutes of baking. The layers of fat and dough formed provide for the flakiness as well as added leavening. The moisture present in the butter, margarine, and the dough will be free when the fats dissolve and the heat penetrates the dough. Part of this moisture is evaporated in the form of steam. The pressure of this steam has a lifting or leavening effect. The expansion of the eggs, especially the egg yolks, during baking contributes to the leavening and increased volume of the Danish pastries.

Freezing and Defrosting of Danish Doughs and Madeup Units
As indicated, Danish doughs should be placed in the freezer after the final roll. Some pastry chefs will allow the doughs to relax in the retarder for an hour or two before placing them in the freezer to allow the dough to become partially conditioned and handle easier when defrosted for makeup. It is a matter of opinion that the dough is being partially conditioned during the rolling-in process. Doughs should be freezer-wrapped to prevent crustation and ice crystal deposit formation.

Madeup Danish units should be placed on pans close together to conserve space. The units need not be egg washed; they should be covered or freezer wrapped. These units are separated when removed from the freezer and spaced on pans for defrosting and later baking. Forced air defrosting is used in larger plants. Smaller producers will defrost by placing the units in the retarder overnight or leave at shop temperature for several hours. The pastry chef will check to see that there are no ice crystals in the center of the units before placing them in the proofer.

Danish that is baked and then frozen should also be wrapped for the freezer. These units can be defrosted quickly in microwave ovens or in conventional ovens at a moderate temperature. When defrosted and heated the Danish units are washed with a hot glaze.

Closed Danish Pockets All points of the square-shaped closed Danish pockets are diagonally folded over each other. Roll out the dough about ⅛ to ¼ in. thick in a rectangular shape. Trim the uneven edges of dough. Cut the dough into even squares (the desired size will determine the size of the square). The average will be about 4 in. square. Deposit the cheese filling in the center of the dough square. Fold the diagonally opposite ends of the dough over each other. Stretch the dough ends a bit before folding.

This will form an open pocket. Fold the other two ends and this will form a closed pocket. (See Fig. 3.35 through 3.37). It may be necessary to stretch the dough to square off uneven units to form the square shape. Press the points of the dough to prevent the ends from opening during proof and baking. Place the madeup units close to each other on the bench and flatten slightly. Wash the units with egg wash and then place on parchment paper-lined sheet pans. Space the units about 1 in. apart. Larger units will require additional space to keep them from baking into each other. Give the Danish pockets about three quarter proof and then egg wash a second time. The units may be garnished with sliced almonds or toasted chopped nuts. Units filled with fillings other than cheese are usually garnished with sugar or crumb topping to identify them. Bake at 390°F. Wash with hot syrup or glaze after baking.

Variety Open Pocket Danish Pastries The open pockets are similar in makeup to the open pocket sweet rolls. The conditioned Danish dough

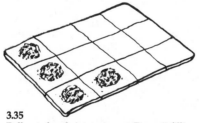

3.35
Roll out dough into squares. Deposit filling in the center

3.36
Fold end of one side over the filling. Fold other end over and seal

3.37
Fold open pocket ends over each other to form a closed square

is rolled out into a rectangular shape about ¼ in. thick. Small units should be rolled out thinner. The pockets are cut after the dough has relaxed a few minutes on the bench to avoid shrinkage of the dough units after cutting. Deposit the filling in the center of the square of dough.

Fruit fillings and other soft fillings should be thickened slightly more than for pies to keep the filling from running too much. It will make shaping and handling the units easier during makeup, and it will also keep the filling from running during proof and baking.

Fold the diagonal end of one corner over the center of the filling and press the point or edge of the dough down. Stretch the diagonally opposite end of the dough slightly and fold over to the other side and press down firmly to seal. Place the units close to each other in straight lines and egg wash the tops. Place on pans lined with parchment paper or greased well. Give the units three-quarter proof and egg wash a second time. Be careful not to smear the filling. Garnish the top with nuts, sugar, or other topping. Bake at 390°F. Wash with syrup glaze as soon as removed from the oven. Be careful not to smear the filling.

Danish Cinnamon Whirls (Snecks) and Pecan Rolls   The makeup for these varieties is similar to that of cinnamon buns or sweet rolls. The conditioned Danish dough is rolled out into a rectangular shape about ¼ in. thick. The dough is brushed with melted butter and then smeared with a desired filling—usually, an almond smear or cake crumbs, nuts, and cinnamon sugar. A chocolate smear may be used for specialty filled Danish products. The filling is rolled in slightly with a rolling pin and the dough rolled up into a tight roll. The thickness of the roll is determined by the size of the Danish desired. The slices cut are about ½ in. thick. The end piece is stretched slightly and then placed under the unit when placing on the pan. The sliced units may be dipped into a pan filled with cinnamon sugar before panning. Others may be dipped into chopped pecans before panning. Space the units about 1½ in. apart on the pan. Larger units will require more space. Units that are not dipped before panning are egg washed and then given about three-quarter proof. The units are washed a second time and then garnished with sliced almonds, streusel, or they are filled with a fruit filling. Before adding the filling, make a depression in the center of the unit to contain the filling and prevent it from running during baking. Bake the units at 390–400°F (depending upon the size). Wash gently with syrup glaze after baking. Pecan rolls are iced with a simple icing. (See Figs. 3.38 through 3.41.)

Japanese Rolls (Made from Danish Dough)   Similar to honey buns these rolls are made from basic sweet yeast dough. Roll out the conditioned Danish dough into a rectangular shape. Brush with melted butter and sprinkle with cake crumbs, cinnamon sugar, and chopped nuts. Roll up into a tight roll and seal. Cut into slices about 1 in. thick. The size of the muffin pan will determine the size and weight of the unit of dough to be cut. The muffin pans are to be greased well or they may be lined with a cupcake liner. Place the units into the muffin pans and give them approximately three-quarter proof. Egg wash the tops and give slightly more

3.38
Roll out the dough ¼ in. thick

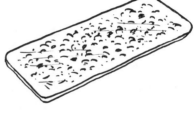

3.39
Brush dough with oil or melted fat and
sprinkle with raisins, cake crumbs, and
cinnamon sugar

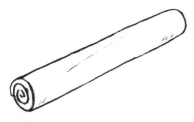

3.40
Roll dough up tightly and seal the edge

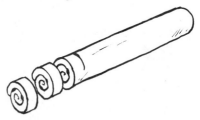

3.41
Brush the top of the roll with oil or melted
fat and cut into even pieces

proof. Bake at 390°F. The units should rise above the top of the pan if
the units fill at least half the pan when first placed in the pan before
proof. The baked units are washed with a syrup glaze while hot. They
may be iced with a simple icing swirl or butter cream piping after they
have cooled.

Honey Buns, Pecan-Nut Rolls, Orange Pecan Rolls These units may
also be made from Danish pastry dough. Prepare the muffin pans with
the special pan dressing as for honey buns and pecan rolls. Be sure the
muffin pans are at least half-filled with dough before proofing. Miniature
pecan rolls are made from Danish pastry dough. These are baked in the
special, small muffin pans used for tea roll specialties. It is advisable to
bake these specialties on double pans to prevent too dark a crust color
from forming at the bottom since the bottoms become the tops when
removed from the pans (Fig. 3.42).

3.42
Pecan rolls made in muffin tins

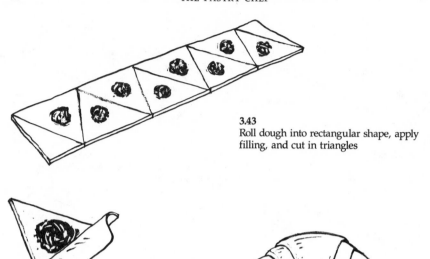

3.43
Roll dough into rectangular shape, apply filling, and cut in triangles

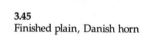

3.44
Roll base of triangle toward the point. Keep roll tight

3.45
Finished plain, Danish horn

Danish Butter Horns and Crescents Roll out the conditioned Danish dough into a rectangular shape about ¼ in. thick. Remove excess flour and then brush the top of the dough with melted butter. A variety of fillings may be applied. The most common are cake crumbs, toasted nuts, and cinnamon sugar. Roll the filling in lightly. With the pastry wheel, divide the dough into triangular shapes. The average unit will be about 6 in. long from point to bottom and about 3 in. wide at the base. For butter horns, roll up the units by starting at the base and rolling to the point. It is advisable to stretch the dough slightly while rolling to form a tighter roll. Be sure the point is at the bottom center of the horn formed. For the crescent shape, cut the center base with a knife or bench scraper about 1 in. deep. Spread the base and then roll up. This will form a longer and narrower roll than the butter horn. These horns are turned into a crescent or half moon shape when placed on the pans. Place the horns next to each other on the bench and egg wash. The butter horns are washed with melted butter. Place the units on pans and give them three-quarter proof. Wash the egg washed units again and garnish with sliced almonds or chopped nuts. The butter horns may be brushed lightly with melted butter again. Bake the horns at 385–390°F. The egg washed units are brushed with syrup glaze after baking. The butter horns are usually dusted with confectioners sugar before serving. (See Figs. 3.43 through 3.50.)

Danish Twist Fancies A variety of twisted shapes are made from the Danish dough. These are then garnished with a variety of fruit and cus-

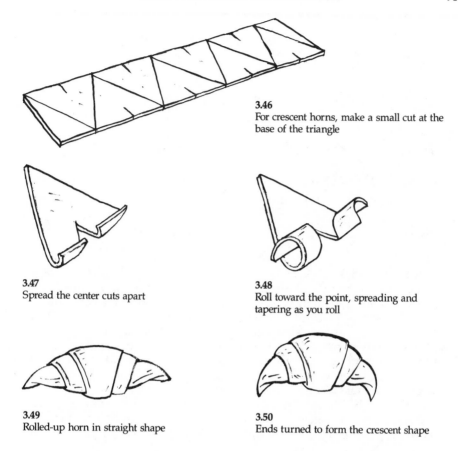

3.46
For crescent horns, make a small cut at the base of the triangle

3.47
Spread the center cuts apart

3.48
Roll toward the point, spreading and tapering as you roll

3.49
Rolled-up horn in straight shape

3.50
Ends turned to form the crescent shape

tard type fillings. The filling in the dough may also be varied. The pastry chef usually makes a great variety of these twist units for display. Roll out the dough into a long, rectangular shape (approximately 12 in. wide at most) and about ¼ in. thick. Remove the excess flour and brush the top of the dough with melted butter. Apply a specialty filling (almond, chocolate, cinnamon sugar, and so forth) over half of the dough surface. Fold the other half to form a sandwich. Roll the dough slightly to make the filling stick. Cut into strips about ½ in. wide and about 6 to 7 in. long. The strips are then rolled out and twisted in the palms of the hands and formed into the following shapes: Snails, figure "8," eyeglass ovals (Figs. 3.51 through 3.55).

Place the twist Danish varieties on parchment paper-lined sheet pans. Brush the tops with egg wash and then give the units three-quarter proof. Wash the units again with egg wash and then garnish with a variety of fruit fillings or custard. The custard is usually piped on with a pastry bag. Give the units slightly more proof and bake at 390°F. Smaller units should be baked at a slightly higher temperature. Wash the units with hot syrup glaze as they are removed from the oven. Be careful not to smear the toppings and garnish when glazing.

3.51
Twist the strip

3.52
Make up into snails by curling

Danish Pastry Sticks (Spirals)   These Danish sticks are spiral and may be made with a variety of fillings. The most popular are those filled with cinnamon sugar and nuts. Pastry chefs will often use a chocolate filling for contrast between the golden yellow of the dough and the dark filling. The spirals may vary in size depending on the occasion and service. Because of their shape, the spirals are often used for tea and snack service as well as coffee breaks. Pastry chefs often use this variety to use up any Danish scrap dough that may be left over. It is rolled in with the large piece of dough and is covered with the filling.

Place the Danish dough on a floured part of the bench. Flatten slightly with the rolling pin. Leftover Danish scrap dough should be spread over the entire surface of the dough and pressed in with the rolling pin. Roll

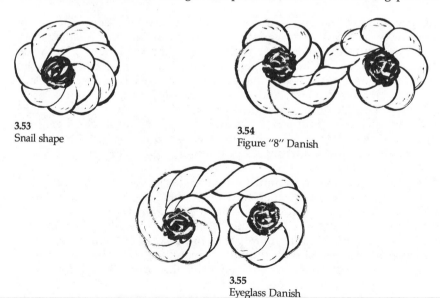

3.53
Snail shape

3.54
Figure "8" Danish

3.55
Eyeglass Danish

out the dough about ¼ in. thick. Brush the surface with melted butter and smear the filling base over the surface. Sprinkle with nuts, cake crumbs, and cinnamon sugar. Roll in the filling gently with the rolling pin. Allow the dough to relax a few minutes and then cut the dough into long strips about 1 to 1½ in. wide. The wider strips are used for larger units. Start at the end of the strip and roll tightly until about ½ in. thick. Turn the roll at an angle and roll tightly until about ½ in. thick. Turn the roll at an angle and roll tightly to about 4 to 6 in. in length. Shorter and narrower sticks may be made to serve with Danish miniatures. (See Figs. 3.56 through 3.58.)

Be sure the sticks are rolled in tightly. To test, hold up a spiral stick at one end. If it does not unravel, it is well made. Line up the sticks next to each other on the bench and flatten with the palms of the hands. Egg wash the sticks and then place on parchment paper-lined pans. Space them about 1 in. apart. Give the sticks three-quarter proof and egg wash a second time. Garnish the tops with chopped nuts. Bake at 390°–400°F. Smaller units are baked at slightly higher temperatures, larger units at slightly lower temperatures. Wash the units with a hot syrup glaze as soon as they are removed from the oven.

Danish Stars or Pinwheels These are similar to closed pockets when made, but the filling varieties are placed in the center and on the outside rather than inside. The dough is rolled out as for Danish pockets. Allow the rolled out dough to relax for a few minutes before cutting out the squares. This will prevent the squares from shrinking (gluten relaxation). Fold each corner of the square of dough into the center and press the end in firmly. It is also advisable to depress the centers with an object like a

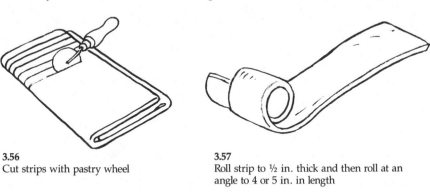

3.56
Cut strips with pastry wheel

3.57
Roll strip to ½ in. thick and then roll at an angle to 4 or 5 in. in length

3.58
Danish pastry stick completed

one pound weight dipped in flour. This will cause the folds of dough to flange out slightly. Egg wash the units and give them three-quarter proof. Depress the centers slightly again to provide a bed for the variety of fillings. Give the units slightly more proof and bake at 385°–390°F. Wash carefully with syrup glaze after baking. Be careful not to smear the filling. Pastry chefs will often add fresh filling to the centers after baking.

Small Danish Rings   These rings are another form of twisted-type Danish. Following the same procedure as for making the Danish twist varieties, cut the units into strips about 6 in. long and about three-quarter in. wide. Roll out the twist about 9 in. in length. Form into a circle and seal the ends. Keep the folded ends under the closed seal. Place on a parchment paper-lined pan and press down gently. Space the units about 1½ in. apart. Egg wash the rings and give them three-quarter proof. Egg wash a second time and garnish with chopped nuts or sliced almonds. Give the units a little more proof and bake at 390°–400°F. Wash with warm or hot syrup glaze as soon as removed from the oven. (Figs. 3.59 through 3.62.)

Larger Coffee Rings   Many restaurants, cafeterias, and other dining establishments have a large retail sales or takeout department. The pastry chef will often have a large variety of regular size Danish and larger units. Popular among these are the coffee rings, filled rings, Danish strips, and variety filled strips. These are often merchandised by weight per pound rather than sold at a unit price. For the larger cinnamon-nut filled coffee rings, the dough is rolled out about ½ in. thick and then brushed with melted butter. Apply the filling or smear desired and sprinkle with raisins, chopped nuts, cake crumbs, and cinnamon sugar. Fold the dough over to form a sandwich effect and roll in gently with the rolling pin. Depending upon the size of the coffee ring, scale the units accordingly. Most large size coffee rings are usually scaled 10 to 12 oz when filled. The strips of dough are twisted and the ring shape formed. Pastry chefs will often roll the ends into a taper form and then twist the ends around each other to form a twist effect. The ends are placed at the bottom of the ring. Normally, six coffee rings are placed on a sheet pan. The rings are egg washed and given three-quarter proof. They are washed a second time and garnished with chopped nuts or sliced almonds. The rings are then given slightly more proof and baked at 385°F. These rings are baked longer and at a lower temperature than are the small rings. Wash the rings with hot syrup glaze when removed from the oven. The rings may be striped or iced with fondant icing when cool.

Braided Rings   After the strips have been cut to size, divide the strip into 3 narrower strips and twist these as for a small ring. Line the 3 strips up and braid them into a 3 braid. Stretch the braid to about 16 to 18 in. in length and then seal the ends. The braided rings are egg washed and then given half proof. The rings are then egg washed again and garnished with a coconut topping, streusel crumb topping, custard topping, and others which may be spread easily over the top. The units are

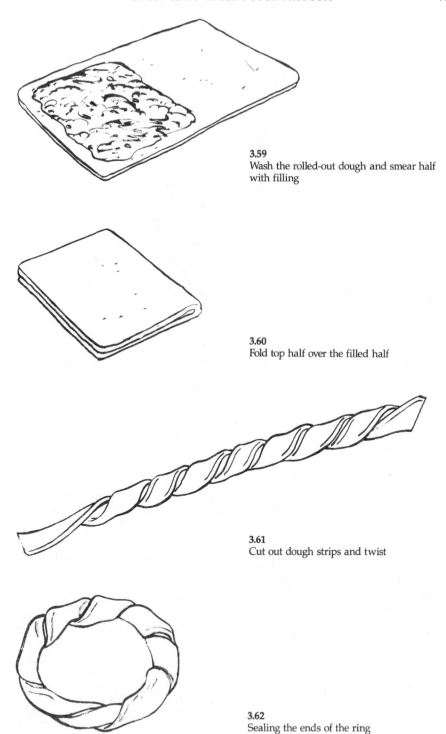

3.59
Wash the rolled-out dough and smear half
with filling

3.60
Fold top half over the filled half

3.61
Cut out dough strips and twist

3.62
Sealing the ends of the ring

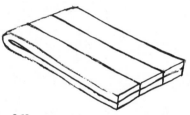

3.63
Scaled dough cut in three equal strips

3.64
Braiding the three strips

3.65
Braided strip to be shaped into ring

given slightly less than full proof and baked at 380°–385°F. The units are then washed with hot or warm syrup glaze. Streusel topping rings are not washed with syrup after baking. They are usually dusted lightly with confectioners sugar. (See Figs. 3.63 through 3.65.)

Cheese-Filled Rings Scale pieces of Danish dough approximately 8 oz each. Roll out the units about 5 in. wide and about 10 to 12 in. long. For cheese-filled rings brush the dough with melted butter. Sprinkle the dough lightly with cake crumbs and cinnamon sugar. Place a strip of cheese filling across the center of the dough (Fig. 3.66). Fold the top over the cheese filling and to the edge of the bottom of the dough and seal tightly (Fig. 3.67). Stretch the sealed unit and form into a ring shape. The top of the ring may be cut with a scissor and the cuts spaced evenly. Egg wash the rings and place on pans (4 to a sheet pan to allow for spread during proofing and baking). The units are egg washed and given three-quarter proof. They are washed a second time and usually garnished with streusel crumb topping. Bake the units at 385°F. These rings are usually dusted with confectioners sugar when cool.

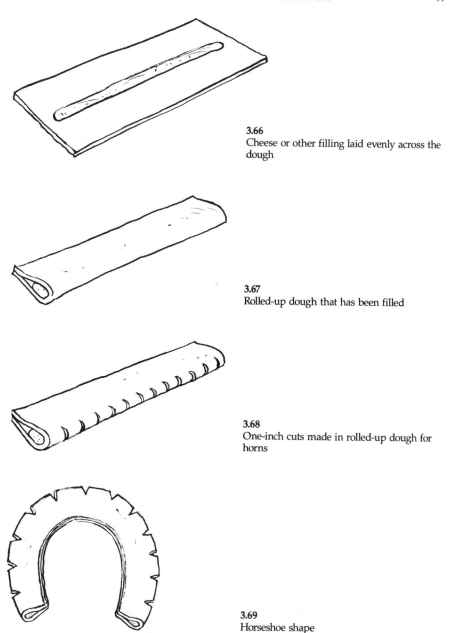

3.66
Cheese or other filling laid evenly across the dough

3.67
Rolled-up dough that has been filled

3.68
One-inch cuts made in rolled-up dough for horns

3.69
Horseshoe shape

For large cheese horns make cuts in the edges of the dough after the strip has been folded and sealed (Fig. 3.68). Form into a horn shape (the cuts will spread slightly when the dough is shaped into a horn) and place on pans (Fig. 3.69). These units are also garnished with streusel crumb topping and dusted with confectioners sugar when they have cooled.

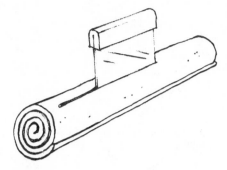

3.70
Rolled-up dough cut through for almond
ring

3.71
Almond ring opened up

Danish Almond Sunburst Ring   The dough is filled with almond filling, nuts, cake crumbs, and cinnamon sugar after it has been rolled out. Roll up the dough so that it is about 8 in. long and about 1½ in. in diameter (Fig. 3.70). Cut through the center with a bench scraper and open the ring. Turn the ring so that cuts or layers of dough and filling are exposed (Fig. 3.71).

Danish Palm Leaf Strip   Prepare the same as for the Danish almond sunburst ring. Place the strip on the pan after it has been rolled up and sealed. With a scissors, make cuts about 1 in. deep at an angle on alternate sides of the strip. Lay each of the cuts back to form the shape of a cut leaf. These strips are given three-quarter proof and then egg washed. The tops are garnished with sliced almonds. The units are given almost full proof and then baked at 390°F. The units are washed with hot syrup glaze and then iced with fondant stripes when cool. (Figs. 3.72 and 3.73.)

Specialty Fruit-Filled Danish Rings   Roll the dough out as for a cheese-filled ring. Place a heavier strip of crumbs in the center of the rolled out dough. Place the desired fruit filling over the crumbs in an even strip. Fold the dough over the fruit and seal the edges well. Be sure the seam

3.72
Cuts made in the strip with scissors

3.73
Palm leaf strip

is at the bottom to prevent the seam from opening during proofing and baking. The tops of the strips may be cut with a scissors. These rings or horn shapes are usually garnished with a crumb topping after they have been proofed. Bake at 385°F and dust with confectioners sugar when cool. If they have been egg washed and not garnished, these rings are washed with hot syrup glaze when baked and striped with fondant when cool.

Large Danish Strip Varieties Much like the larger rings, large Danish strips use a larger piece of dough. The pastry chef will scale units of dough about 2 to 3 lb depending upon whether the strip will be the length or the width of the pan (18 to 20 in.) or the full length of the pan (about 24 to 26 in.). The thickness of the strip will also determine the amount of dough to be used. The type of fillings used are many and varied. For example, the usual butter, chopped nuts, cake crumbs, cinnamon sugar, and raisin filling may be used. An almond filling is quite popular. Pastry chefs will often combine an almond smear with a smear of melted sweet chocolate as a variety. The usual poppy seed (Mohn) filling is often made. When apples or other fruits are used, the strip is often called Danish strudel. The strips are usually given no more than three-quarter proof before baking. This will tend to prevent the strips from flattening excessively during baking. Because these are large units filled with a soft filling, the strips are baked at a lower temperature (370°F) and baked well. Underbaking will cause the strips to settle after baking. These strips are usually served by slicing into narrower strips about 1½ to 2 in. wide. They are also sold at a scaled per pound price.

Miniature Danish Pastries These Danish varieties are very popular and the experienced pastry chef will always have a supply in the freezer ready to be defrosted and baked. He may also have them in a baked frozen state for quick defrost and warming in the microwave or conventional baking oven. Many of the better hotels will serve miniature Danish as a breakfast dessert. They will also maintain a supply for between-meal snacks or coffee breaks. Very often miniature Danish pastries are mixed with an assortment of cookies and petits fours. Cheese, prune, jam, and apricot-filled miniatures are usually made in open pocket form. The dough is rolled out about ⅛ in. thick. The dough is allowed to relax and then cut into squares about 1½ to 2 in. square. The filling is deposited with a pastry bag. Cheese filling may be rolled out in flour and then cut into small sections which are then placed in the center of each square. The pockets are closed on one side as for regular open pocket Danish. The units are placed close together on the bench and egg washed. They are placed on parchment paper-lined pans and spaced about ½ in. apart. The units are given a second light egg wash and baked at 400–410°F. The units may be garnished with chopped nuts and sugar before baking. After baking, the units are washed with hot syrup glaze.

The filled miniature Danish may be made faster by rolling out the dough and then cutting long strips about 3 in. wide. The filling is then bagged into the center of the strip and the top of the strip of dough folded over the filling. The dough is sealed and the seam folded into the bottom center of the strip. The strips are then cut with a bench scraper or a pastry wheel into long strips the length of the pan and then into small sections about 1 in. long. The units are then egg washed, proofed, and baked. The long strips are washed with hot syrup after baking and then cut through again as for miniature Danish strudel.

Miniature cinnamon horns are made very much like the regular Danish butter horns. The dough is rolled out about ¼ in. thick and filled with almond and chocolate smear if desired, followed by a generous sprinkling of chopped nuts, raisins (optional), cake crumbs, and cinnamon sugar. The filling is rolled in lightly with the rolling pin. The dough is then cut into strips about 4 in. wide and into small triangles about 1½ in. at the base. Each is rolled up tightly and placed next to each other on the bench. The units are then flattened slightly with the palms of the hands and egg washed. They are proofed and baked as other miniatures. Those washed with melted butter instead of egg wash are usually garnished with streusel crumb topping and dusted with confectioners sugar when baked and cooled.

The miniature cinnamon snacks are made as the regular Danish snacks are made. The strips are rolled up into smaller rolls about 1 in. in diameter. The units are then sliced about ½ in. thick and placed on pans. These units are egg washed and then given half proof. At this point, the centers may be depressed slightly with the fingers and filled with apricot or other quality jams. These units are given almost full proof and then baked at 410°F. They are washed with hot syrup glaze when removed from the oven.

Brioche

Brioche is a reflection of quality and luxurious dining. Originated in France, it is very rich in egg content, providing a light, crisp-crusted, tender bakery specialty. The addition of melted butter and margarine adds to the richness and tenderness of brioche. Because of its richness, brioche lends itself well to freezing, and the product has a prolonged shelf life after defrosting and reheating. The dough is usually made with a sponge and dough mixing method, due to the added richness and the need for high amounts of yeast to leaven the dough. If a straight dough mixing method were to be used, the added yeast might leave a yeasty odor and flavor. The use of a conditioned sponge dough will avoid the use of excessive amounts of yeast.

Brioche Dough

Ingredients	lb	oz	Mixing procedure
Yeast (variable)		12	Dissolve the yeast in the water and milk
Water (lukewarm)	3		powder. Add the flour and mix well to
Skim milk powder		6	form the sponge dough. Allow the sponge
Bread flour	4	8	dough to rise and then start to fall back
			slightly

Sugar	1	6	Add these ingredients to the conditioned
Salt		2¼	sponge dough and mix well to dissolve the
Egg yolks	2		dry ingredients and to break up and dis-
Whole eggs		8	tribute the sponge dough
Rind of 2 lemons			
Vanilla		1	
Bread flour	4		Add the flour and stir or mix in lightly.
Melted butter	1		Add the melted butter and margarine and
Margarine (melted)	1		mix until the dough is smooth and pulls
			away smoothly from the sides of the mix-
			ing kettle

1. Temperature out of machine 84–86°F. Allow dough to rise and take to the bench.
2. It is advisable to scale the dough into presses (weight of the press of dough will depend upon the size of the tart or muffin pans in which the brioche will be baked). Place the presses in the retarder to chill before makeup. This will make handling the units easier.
3. Press out the dough presses in the dough divider and round up the units. Press down with the outside of the palm to cause a small piece of the dough to extrude. Roll this slightly to cause the small piece of dough to stand out without removing it from the ball of the dough. (It may be necessary to remove a small piece of dough and round it up separately. The small ball of dough is placed into the center of the rounded ball after a depression is made in the unit of rounded dough.) Wash the top of the unit with a blend of egg wash and egg yolks for a shiny, brown crust color. Place the rounded units into scalloped tart pans that have been greased. The size of the pan will vary with the type of service and time of day (meal service). Brioche may be placed into muffin pans but the shape will vary. The beauty of brioche is enhanced when baked in a scalloped tart pan. Allow the units to obtain three-quarter proof and wash again with egg yolk and egg wash blend. Allow the brioche to rise to almost full proof and then bake at 375°–380°F. The brioche should feel crisp when baked and should spring back quite firmly to the touch. Quick baking at high temperatures will cause the brioche to shrink and soften. Brioche is usually baked on double pans, especially when using tart or muffin pans. This precaution will avoid the possible formation of a dark crust color at the bottom of the baked unit. (See Figs. 3.74 through 3.76.)

3.74
Force out small portion

3.75
Place smaller unit on larger

3.76
Place unit into greased tart pan

Brioche that is to be frozen should be wrapped well in freezer wrap before placing in the freezer to avoid drying and crusting during the initial stages of blast freezing. It will also avoid the deposit of frost on the surface of the product. Defrosting and reheating may be done in a microwave oven or in the regular baking oven. A partial defrost at room temperature before placing in the oven is advantageous to avoid the possibility of ice crystals remaining in the center of the brioche. It will also allow the oven heat to fully penetrate the brioche during the reheating period. Serve the brioche as soon as defrosted and heated.

Croissants

The croissant or French butter horn is similar to the horns made from a rich Danish pastry dough. The croissant is not filled with any special filling nor is the dough as rich in sugar content. Pastry chefs should have croissants as part of the menu in conjunction with brioche and other specialties. The quality and cost of croissants may be controlled by the degree of richness. For example, the amount of egg yolks and the butter content may be decreased slightly. In some instances, pastry chefs will use a blend of sweet butter and margarine for roll-in purposes. The flakiness of the product depends, in good part, on the amount of fat rolled in as well as the method of rolling in. Like Danish pastry, the fat must be chilled a bit so that it is firmer than the dough. The dough should be placed in the retarder between rolls to maintain the firmness of the fat and to relax the dough.

Croissant Dough

Ingredients	lb	oz	Mixing procedure
Yeast (variable)		6	Dissolve the yeast and set aside
Water	1	8	
Sugar		8	Blend the ingredients together well
Salt		2	
Skim milk powder		8	
Shortening		8	
Eggs (half yolks)	1		
Water	1	8	Add and stir in
Bread flour	6	4	Add the flour and stir slightly. Add the yeast and mix to a smooth dough

Place the dough on the bench and form into a rectangular shape. The dough may be placed in the retarder to relax for 15 to 20 min. This will make rolling or sheeting the dough easier.

Roll-in Fat Ingredients

Ingredients	lb	oz	Mixing procedure
Butter	2		Blend the fats together and chill so that it
Margarine	2		is firmer than the dough

Roll the fat into the dough as for Danish pastry. Three rolls may be given instead of four. Pastry chefs will vary their approach.

Follow the same makeup procedure as for Danish horns. The dough is brushed with melted butter and then cut into triangular shapes as for Danish horns. No filling is used. The units or triangles of dough are rolled up and placed close together on the bench. They are flattened slightly and brushed lightly with melted butter. The croissants are given three-quarter proof and baked at 375°–380°F. The croissants should feel quite springy to the touch and be flaky when baked. (Figs. 3.77 through 3.79.)

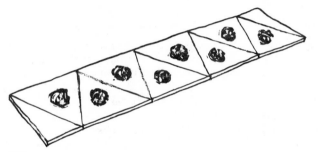

3.77
Roll dough into rectangular shape, and cut in triangles

3.78
Roll base of triangle toward point. Keep roll tight

3.79
Finished croissant

Rich Coffee Cakes

A sponge dough method is used for rich coffee cake dough because of its richness. The high percentage of sugar, fat, and eggs will require additional yeast to leaven the dough. A sponge dough acts as a starter where the yeast grows and the final dough is leavened fully without the need for excessive yeast. This dough can be used for variety coffee cake loaves (Babka), specialty filled strips, Russian coffee cake, stollen, round whirls, kugelhof, savarin, or baba au rhum.

Rich Coffee Cake Dough

Ingredients	lb	oz	Mixing procedure
Sponge			
Water	2	12	Dissolve the yeast in the water. Add the
Yeast (variable)		12	sour cream and milk powder. Add the
Sour cream	1	(1 pint)	flour and mix to smooth dough. Allow the
Skim milk powder		6	dough to rise and start to settle
Bread flour	3	8	
Final Dough			
Sugar	2		Add to the sponge and mix well to dis-
Salt		2	solve and distribute the ingredients and to
Ground cardamom		¼	break up the sponge dough
Coffee cake flavor- ing		1	
Vanilla		1	
Eggs	1		
Egg yolks	1	8	
Bread flour	4		Add and mix to a dough
Melted butter	2		Add the melted fats in a steady stream
Melted margarine	1		while the mixer is running at slow speed. Mix to a smooth consistency

1. The coffee cake dough will be of medium soft consistency. Allow the dough to rise well and take to the bench.
2. Scale the units into desired weights. The average bread pan will require about 14 oz of dough. Larger pullman pans will require 2 to 2½ lb.
3. Scaled units are shaped into rectangular form and allowed to relax before makeup. At this point, units may be placed in the retarder for later makeup or placed in the freezer for delayed makeup. Chilling the units slightly before makeup also allows for easier handling and filling of the dough.

Yield: Approx. 22 loaves the size of the average pan loaf of bread.

Coffee Cake Loaves (Babka or Grandmother's Loaf) Roll out the pieces of dough into rectangular shape. Fill with desired fillings. Most popular fillings are almond, chocolate, and butter nut. Fillings are covered with chopped nuts, cake crumbs, raisins, and cinnamon sugar. It is best to brush the rolled dough with melted butter before applying the filling. Roll up the units as for a cinnamon bun strip. Seal the ends carefully and roll out about 16 in. in length. The units are then twisted by folding the dough strip over and over. Others may be shaped into a figure "8." Still others are shaped like a loaf of bread and placed directly into the pans. The pans are usually lined with parchment paper loaf cake liners. The tops of the loaves are then brushed with melted butter and sprinkled with streusel (crumb) topping. Others may be sprinkled with chopped nuts and cinnamon sugar. (Figs. 3.80 through 3.83.)

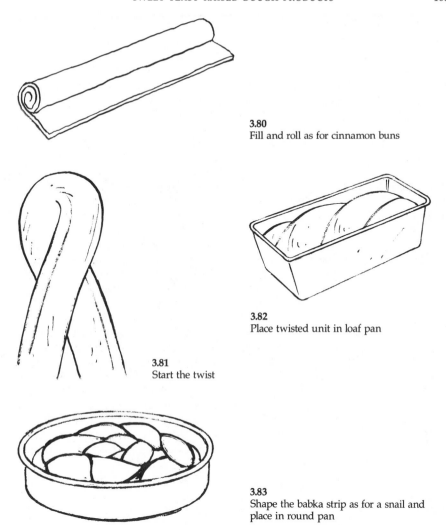

3.80
Fill and roll as for cinnamon buns

3.81
Start the twist

3.82
Place twisted unit in loaf pan

3.83
Shape the babka strip as for a snail and
place in round pan

The units are proofed slowly. A rapid proofing may cause the dough to expand at the surface while the inner part of the loaf may not have proof. A soft, sticky appearance does not mean the entire loaf has proofed. The dough should almost fill the pan to the very top when given a slow proof and it should spring back gently to the touch. Bake the loaves at 350°F. The units will rise well above the sides of the pan. A slow bake is necessary to prevent the units from falling back or the sides from collapsing, as well as preventing a raw, gumminess in the center of the loaf.

The pastry chef in better restaurants will make these loaves regularly. The loaves are sliced into portions and served. The many different fillings allow for greater variety in name and choice. These units are very popular in bakeshops and in restaurants that merchandise directly to the public.

Variety Filled Strips Strips made from coffee cake dough will have greater stability in terms of structure and will retain shape without flattening as much as those made from Danish pastry dough. The selection of fillings and fruits may be varied with the change in menu. It is advisable to thicken the fruit fillings a little more than that used for pies or fruit cobblers. A coffee cake strudel may also be made from these same strips with the use of cheese, apple, and pineapple fillings.

Round Shaped Whirls or Babka These are made from the same dough. The units are scaled according to the size of the pans. Fill as for the long loaves and roll out and twist as for a coffee ring. Form the strip into a spiral or snail shape and place into round layer pans or aluminum foil pans. The tops are brushed with melted butter and garnished with streusel (crumb) topping.

Seven Sister or Crown Coffee Cakes These are made in round pans. Similar fillings are used and may be varied. The units of scaled dough (weight according to pan size) are rolled and filled as for the regular loaves. Roll up the dough as for a pan bread. Cut the strip into seven equal pieces and place a cut into the center of a well greased layer pan or an aluminum foil pan. Surround the center cut with the other 6 cuts to form the shape of a crown. Egg wash and give the units three-fourths proof. The tops are washed again and may be garnished with chopped nuts and sugar. The centers of each section may be garnished with a spiral of jam or custard. Bake these at 360°F. Larger units are baked at a lower temperature. (Figs. 3.85 and 3.86.) The cakes are washed with an apricot coating glaze or hot syrup glaze when removed from the oven. Units baked in aluminum foil pans are sold over the counter as such. Some restaurants will serve the entire unit (to be cut into eight portions) for special groups. Large units are cut into wedges similar to a high layer cake and

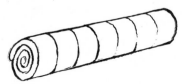

3.84
Cut in seven pieces

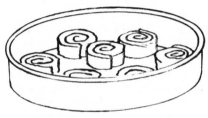
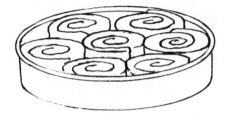

3.85
Place in greased layer pan, egg-wash, give
three-quarter proof, garnish, and bake

served. These units may be frozen before or after baking. To defrost un-baked units, place in the retarder overnight or leave at room temperature for 4 to 6 hr before placing in the proof box. Frozen baked units should be treated as regular frozen coffee cakes made in loaf shape.

Russian Coffee Cake   This is a large cake that is usually baked in a pan of sheet cake size whose sides are approximately 3–4 in. high. It may also be baked in a regular sheet pan. For the regular sheet cake pan, it will be necessary to use approximately 7 to 8 lb of conditioned coffee cake dough. The deeper pan will require approximately 8–9 lb of dough. Remove about 1½ lb of dough from the larger unit of dough and form into a rectangular shape. Do the same for the remaining larger piece of dough. Allow the units of dough to relax on the bench or in the retarder. The pan to be used should be greased well. Roll out the smaller piece of dough so that it is the size of the bottom of the pan. The dough will be very thin. Fold over 2 or 3 times and place in the pan. Unroll the dough and stretch it at the same time so that the entire bottom of the pan is covered. This is a bottom for the cake. The bottom may be sprinkled with cake crumbs, chopped nuts, and cinnamon sugar. Place the pan to one side. Roll out the larger piece of dough about ¼ in. thick. Brush with melted butter and sprinkle with chopped nuts, cake crumbs, cin-namon sugar. The filling is a matter of choice; some pastry chefs prefer to use an almond smear. Roll the dough into strips about 1 in. thick. Seal the ends of the roll. There should be about 5 or 6 such strips. Place the strips into the pan. Cut off excess length and start another strip. After all strips are panned, flatten with the palms of the hands. Make 1 in. cuts through the strips about half way through. (Figs. 3.86 through 3.91.) The tops of the strips are brushed with melted butter and sprinkled with chopped nuts and cinnamon sugar. Allow the cake to get slightly more than three-fourths proof before baking. Additional nuts and sugar may be added to the top of the cake if the topping is sparse. Bake at 350°F. until the cake is golden brown and the center of the cake springs back gently to the touch. Allow the cake to cool before removing from the pan and cutting into portions. Pastry chefs often cut large squares which are placed on cake display dishes. These are cut as required. The lower cakes baked in sheet pans are usually cut into small squares and served as a snack cake for coffee breaks, teas, and so forth. They are served in con-junction with miniature Danish as well.

Stollen   These are coffee cake specialties that are made for the Christmas and Easter holidays. The coffee cake dough may well be used. In the final stages of mixing, diced glazed fruits, raisins, walnuts, and other nut meats are added to the dough. For the recipe provided, the following may be added to the final mixing stages:

Ingredients	lb	oz
Raisins	3	
Whole or half glazed cherries	1	8
Diced mixed fruits	1	8
Walnut meats, chopped pecans	2	

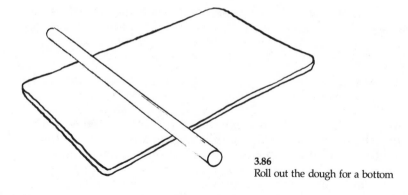

3.86
Roll out the dough for a bottom

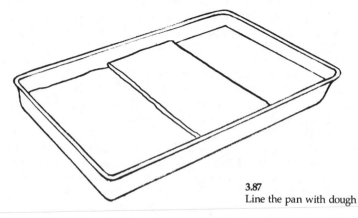

3.87
Line the pan with dough

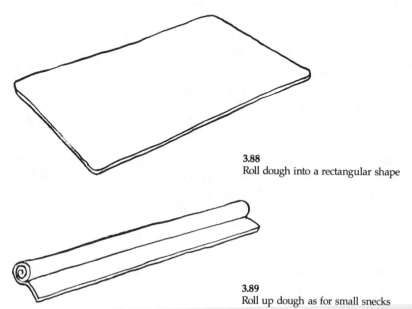

3.88
Roll dough into a rectangular shape

3.89
Roll up dough as for small snecks

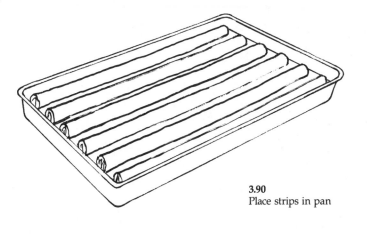

3.90
Place strips in pan

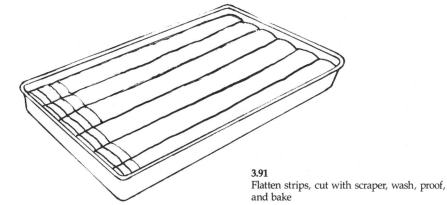

3.91
Flatten strips, cut with scraper, wash, proof,
and bake

Stollen are usually scaled about 12 oz to 1 lb each. The units are rounded
and allowed to relax. They may be placed in the retarder to firm up and
make handling easier. Remove from the retarder and roll out into an oval
shape about 10 in. long. Brush the surface of the dough with melted
butter. Fold over to form two layers as for a Parker House roll. Roll in
well with a rolling pin so that edges expand a bit higher than the rest of
the stollen. Brush the tops of the stollen with melted butter and place on
sheet pans. Smaller sizes are arranged 6 to a pan. Large units are arranged 4 to a sheet pan. Allow the units to get slightly more than three-
quarter proof and bake at 370°F. These units must be baked well in order
to prevent flattening due to the weight of the fruits and nuts. The baked
stollen are brushed lightly after baking with melted butter and then
dipped in mild cinnamon sugar. The stollen may be left to cool and then
dusted with confectioners sugar. The stollen are sliced into strips for service. A single stollen may be served to an entire group at a table for self
service. (Figs. 3.92 through 3.94.)

3.92
Roll relaxed dough to an oval shape

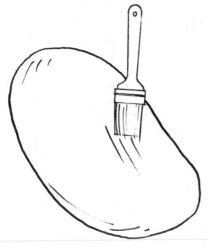

3.93
Wash center with melted butter

3.94
Fold one end over the other, flatten as for Parker House roll, proof, and bake. Dust with powdered sugar when baked

Hot Cross Buns or Breads While they may be rather rich and expensive, these hot cross rolls or breads are house specialities during the holiday season. They may be made from the same dough from which the stollen were prepared. Of course, the rolls and breads may also be made from the basic sweet roll dough by simply adding the raisins, fruits, and nuts in the final stages of mixing that dough. Even here, cost will control the amount and variety of fruits and nuts to be added.

Scale the dough into presses of about 3 lb. Larger rolls will require larger presses. Relax the presses for about 15 min and then press out. Round up the units (use the divider-rounder if available) and place on sheet pans spaced about 1½ in. apart. Flatten the buns well and then make cuts in the form of a cross about half way through the bun. Egg wash the hot cross buns and given them about three-quarter proof. Egg wash the buns again and allow slightly less than full proof. Bake the buns at 390°F. until brown and the centers spring back gently to the

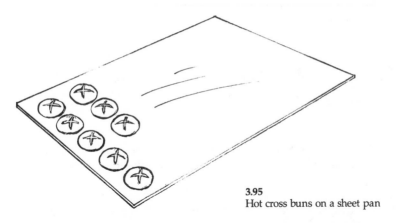

3.95
Hot cross buns on a sheet pan

touch. These rolls will bake into each other slightly. For a closer bake, space the rolls closer together on the pan. The rolls are washed with hot syrup glaze as soon as they are removed from the oven. Allow the buns to cool and then apply a cross design of fondant or thick simple icing across the buns. If the buns are spaced evenly, the lines of icing may be simply bagged out and done quickly. Allow the units to remain together until ready to serve. If the buns are to be served to a large group at one time or in delayed intervals, ice the buns in advance and then cut through with a knife to make separation easier. (Fig. 3.95.)

Hot cross breads are usually scaled about 14 oz each and rounded up. The units are placed on a sheet pan (about 6 to a pan) and then egg washed. Give the units a slow proof to almost full proof. Wash the tops again with egg wash and bake at 350–360°F. The large units require a slow bake to prevent settling after baking. Wash the breads with hot syrup glaze after removal from the oven. Allow them to cool and then ice with fondant. A flat ribbon effect is advisable and a fudge-type white icing may be used. Pastry chefs may serve an entire hot cross bread to each table for a special service. The breads may then be cut at the table by the diners.

Kugelhof Cake This is a rich coffee cake variety that is baked in special scalloped tube pans, often called "Turk-head pans." Tube pans will vary in size and the pastry chef must scale the amount of dough in accordance with the pan size. Grease the pans well with softened butter and shortening and then dip into sliced almonds. Sprinkle some additional almonds at the bottom of the pan. These cakes are turned over after baking and the bottom of the pan becomes the top of the cake. The average angel cake pan requires approximately 8 to 10 oz of conditioned coffee cake dough.

The scaled units of dough are shaped into oval or rectangular shapes. Allow the units to relax 10 to 15 min. Roll out and fill with a layer of melted butter, cake crumbs, toasted chopped nuts, cinnamon sugar. For variety, an almond or chocolate smear may be used. Roll up the dough

3.96
Place softened babka dough in greased turk-head or angel cake pan, one-third full

into a tight roll and twist lightly as for a coffee ring. Form into a ring and seal the ends. Place into the prepared pans and be sure the center tube of the pan is well greased. Give three-quarter proof or slightly more. Bake at 365–370°F. Remove from the pans while the cakes are still quite warm. Allow the cakes to cool and dust with confectioners sugar. The larger cakes are baked at a lower temperature. These cakes are sliced into portions and then served. Kugelhof cake may also be made from a rich pound cake or French coffee cake mix. This is a cake type rather than yeast-raised variety (Fig. 3.96).

Savarins and Baba au Rhum Cakes   These cakes are made from a yeast-raised dough that is similar to that used for brioche. However, the dough is much softer and can almost be poured into the angel cake pans. The softness is due to the high percentage of eggs and egg yolks. The rich coffee cake dough, the basic sweet yeast dough, or the dough for brioche may be used. The most preferable dough is that used for brioche because of its high percentage of eggs and yolks and lesser amount of sugar. If any of the other doughs are used, it will be necessary to soften them with the addition of whole eggs or egg yolks. (Add 2 to 4 oz of eggs to each pound of conditioned dough.) The dough should be quite soft. This is best done when the dough has been conditioned and is ready to be scaled. Return the conditioned dough to the mixer and add the eggs slowly while mixing.

The dough should be smooth when mixing is completed. The pans should be greased well with special attention to greasing the center tube. Fill the pans about ⅓ to slightly less than half full. This dough will have greater volume than coffee cakes because of the high percentage of eggs. Give the units sufficient proof to fill the pans about three-quarters. Handle the pans very gently to prevent collapse. Bake at 360–370°F. Bake thoroughly. The baked units should have a crisp crust and a firm and porous interior because later they will be dipped in a hot rum syrup and then glazed. The baked units are removed from the pans while still hot. Allow the units to cool thoroughly or even chill before dipping. This makes dipping easier and there is less chance of breakage. The baked units are often kept well wrapped in the refrigerator and/or the freezer for special orders.

Rum Syrup

Ingredients	lb	oz	Mixing procedure
Water	3		Bring to a boil and allow to boil for about
Sugar	4	8	2 min. Remove any foam from the syrup
1 sliced orange			with a skimmer. Remove from fire
Corn syrup or glucose		4	
Rum or	1 pint		Add the rum or rum flavoring and stir in.
rum flavoring		1	Remove the orange slices before dipping. Use while hot

1. Dip the cooled or chilled cakes into the hot syrup. Use a skimmer or place the cakes on a screen and put into the hot syrup. Turn the cakes gently with a wooden spoon. Allow the cakes to absorb the syrup (about 1 min at most) and remove.
2. Place on a screen over a pan and allow the cakes to drain well.
3. Glaze the cakes with hot apricot jam. The top may be garnished with glazed cherries flanked by slices of citron and almonds halves. (Fig. 3.97.)

Individual units may be made by depositing the dough into small molds about 3 in. in diameter. These are filled about ⅓ full, proofed until about three-quarters full, and then baked. They are dipped individually.

For Savarin Chantilly slice the small savarins in half. Fill with diced fruits that have been dipped in kirsch and cover. The tops are decorated with whipped cream. Large savarins may be filled with a fine custard and then decorated with whipped cream. These are called savarin á la creme.

3.97
Quickly dip baked cakes in hot rum syrup and place on icing screen to drain

Bienenstich   This continental-style pastry originally from Germany is a rich coffee cake. The basic sweet yeast dough may be used. The bienenstich is made in round layer cake pans. The size of the pans may vary from 6 in. to 12 in. The finished cake is served in wedges as layer cake. Smaller units are often merchandised in restaurants as a part of the takeout service. The average 10 in. layer pan will require approximately 12 to 14 oz of dough. The pastry chef is guided by the desired height of the cake. Naturally, the higher cake will require more dough. However, since this cake is filled after baking, the baked units are usually 1½ to 2 in. high after baking.

Scale the units of dough in accordance with the pan size and round up. Allow the units to rest about 15 min. The layer pans are greased well. Round parchment paper liners may be placed at the bottom of the pan as for a layer cake. Be sure the sides of the pan are greased well. Roll out the dough evenly and place in the pans. Flatten slightly and even out any irregularity in thickness. It is advisable to puncture the dough with a fork at this time. This will help to prevent large air pockets from forming during proofing and baking. It is advisable to chill the units while preparing the topping. It will make smearing the topping on the surface of the dough easier.

Bienenstich Topping

Ingredients	lb	oz	Mixing procedure
Sugar		12	Place the sugar, honey, and butter in a
Honey	1		saucepan and heat over a low flame until
Butter		14	fluid and melted. Add the almonds
Sliced almonds	1	4	

Stirring constantly, continue to cook until the topping thickens slightly and takes on a golden brown color. Have the chilled dough in the pans ready. Remove the topping from the fire and spread evenly over the top of the dough with a spatula or soft bowl knife blade. Try to avoid getting the topping on the sides of the pan. This may burn and cause sticking after baking. It may be advisable to keep the topping in a double boiler if a number of cakes are to be covered. Otherwise, the topping will thicken and make application difficult.

Allow the cakes to proof until almost double in size. A gentle touch on the side of the dough will show a soft return of the dough to the touch. Thicker doughs will fill the pan about to the top. The pan sides are usually about 1½ to 2 in. high. Bake at 375°F. A 10-in. cake will take about 40 min to bake depending upon the thickness of the dough. Allow the topping and the cake to cool before removing from the pan. Run a knife between the cake and the pan if the cake should stick to the sides of the pan.

After the cake has cooled and then been chilled, the cake is cut in half and filled with a fine custard filling. Pastry chefs often fill the centers with custard cream and then pipe a border of whipped cream around the edges of the cake. Bienenstich lends itself well to freezing. The cakes must be wrapped well to prevent frost from settling on the cake and creating a stickiness in the topping. When defrosting and reheating, the microwave oven is best since the topping is not exposed to oven heat. When rewarming in the oven, the topping will soften slightly and firm up again. The cakes are then cut and filled.

Hungarian Cheese Strips

This cheese cake specialty is made in strip form rather than as a large sheet cake or layer cake. Strips of prebaked short dough are required to support the cheese filling and the fruit filling. A special cheese filling is prepared that is of thicker consistency than pan-baked cheese cakes. Fruit filling is optional. The top of the cheese strip is covered with a strip of coffee cake dough, Babka dough, or Danish pastry dough. Some pastry chefs may use a thin sheet of puff pastry dough. The choice is optional. The top dough covering is cut with a scissors for design and effect.

Hungarian Cheese Strip Filling

Ingredients	lb	oz	Mixing procedure
Bakers cheese	6		Blend the cheese and other ingredients
Cream cheese	4		until smooth.
Sugar	3		
Salt		1	
Bread flour		10	
Cake flour		8	
Butter(soft)	1		
Egg yolks	1	8	Add the eggs in 3 stages and blend
Whole eggs	2		smooth.
Raisins (presoaked)	2		Add to the above and blend in. Use slow
Vanilla (variable)		1½	speed for mixing. Chill the filling before
Rind of 2 fresh		½	using for easier handling.
lemons or lemon			
flavor			

Roll out the short dough about ¼ in. thick and about the width of a regular sheet pan. Cut the dough into strips about 4 in. wide. Place the strips on a sheet pan and space about 2 in. apart. There are about five strips to a regular sheet pan. Bake the short dough strips lightly.

Allow the short dough strips to cool. If fruit filling such as pineapple, blueberry, cherry, are to be used, spread the fruit filling on top of the dough strip about ¼ in. thick and about 1 in. wide in the center of the dough. Roll the chilled cheese filling in some dusting flour to form a strip about 1½ in. in diameter and almost the same length as the dough strip. Place the cheese filling gently over the fruit filling.

Roll out a rectangular-shaped piece of fermented or conditioned coffee cake dough, babka dough, Danish pastry dough, or puff pastry dough, about the length and width of a regular sheet pan. Yeast-raised dough should be about ¼ in. thick. The puff pastry dough should be thinner. Allow the dough to relax for about 6 min and then cut into strips about 5 in. wide or slightly wider.

Brush the edges of the baked short dough strips with egg wash. Avoid smearing the fruit filling if it is used. Place the cut strips of coffee cake or other dough strips over the cheese filling and press the edges into the egg washed edges of the bottom short dough crust. The covering dough strip may be stretched, if necessary to cover the cheese filling to the very edge of the bottom crust. With a scissors make 1 in. cuts about 1 in. apart in the top crust or dough covering. Egg wash the top dough and allow the dough to relax (yeast-raised dough covering will rise slightly) for about ½ hour.

Bake the strips at 365–370°F., until the top crust is baked through and has browned. Wash with apricot glaze or regular syrup wash upon removal from the oven. When cool, the tops may be striped with fondant icing or sweet roll icing.

Cut into slices for individual service or larger units for scaled-unit merchandising.

4

Doughnut Varieties

The pastry chef is fully aware of the growth in the production of variety doughnuts. In fact, it is reflected in the growth and expansion of doughnut shops and in the increased consumption of variety doughnuts. As a result, most pastry chefs in institutions, schools, and multi-feeding establishments include variety doughnuts in their menus. The doughnut has a special place in breakfast menus, as a snack item, coffee-break food, dessert specialty, and for special occasions and holidays.

Prepared doughnut mixes are popular with bakers and pastry chefs and are used extensively for doughnut production. They are the basic support for most of the specialty doughnut shops. They provide a large measure of product control, uniformity, and economy by saving time in scaling and storing raw materials and in mixing doughs and batters. With a little training, doughnut production using prepared mixes may be assigned to assistants. When a large volume of doughnuts is required, the pastry chef can provide direct supervision. The prepared mixes serve as a base for production. The skilled and knowledgeable pastry chef may further enrich the prepared mix for a better quality product. This is usually accomplished by adding enriching ingredients such as eggs, egg yolks, milk, and nutritive grains and flours, and making the required adjustments in the formula.

Many pastry chefs prefer to use their own formulas and recipes for the production of variety doughnuts. This may be necessary where availability of prepared doughnut mixes is lacking or the quality of the mixes does not meet the standards of the pastry chef. Through the use of start-to-finish formulas ("scratch" production), the pastry chef is able to control cost and quality, as well as increase doughnut varieties. The special doughnuts also have those characteristics which enable the pastry chef to finish them for specialty desserts. The formulas for a variety of doughnuts presented in this section are specifically constructed for the pastry chef who will produce variety doughnuts and doughnut-type desserts from start to finish.

Yeast-Raised Doughnuts   Leavened primarily through the action of yeast and the resulting conditioning of the dough (fermentation), these doughnuts enable the pastry chef to produce a wider variety of doughnuts and to finish them for a variety of desserts. Production procedures and finishing will accompany each formula.

Chemically Leavened Dougnuts   This term refers to the cake-type, mass produced doughnuts as well as to the hand-made, bench-type of cruller leavened primarily with chemical leavening agents. Variety is largely controlled by the variety of formulas, shapes, sizes, color, flavoring, and finish of the doughnuts. These characteristics will be discussed further with each of the formulas and varieties to be made.

Combination Doughnuts   Made from a dough that is leavened by both yeast activity and chemical leavening, this variety permits a more rapid dough development and conditioning, and provides a combination of doughnut characteristics resembling both the light, yeast-raised doughnut varieties and the tender and short cake-type doughnut.

French Crullers   These are made from choux paste or a formula similar to that for eclair and cream puff shells. The leavening is primarily due to expansion provided by the large percentage of eggs in the batter. Pastry chefs often supplement the leavening with a small amount of chemical leavening, particularly when milk or water is added to the mix to replace some of the eggs. In prepared mixes for French crullers, dried eggs (both egg yolks and whole eggs) are used. These are supplemented with additional chemical leavening.

Enriched or Natural-Type Doughnuts   These doughnuts contain additional protein-and vitamin-bearing grains and flours in addition to other enriching ingredients. They are used extensively for supplementing the diets of children in institutional and school feeding programs. Additional synthetic vitamins are often added to further enrich the food values of these doughnuts. Several formulas for these doughnuts and their production will be presented.

The Frying Fat

Doughnuts and other fried products are changed from a raw dough or batter to a well-risen, structured, and edible state by cooking in heated frying fat. The transfer of heat, as in a baking chamber, must be controlled. In addition, the doughnut absorbs (interior) and adsorbs (surface) a small percentage of the frying fat during the frying process. It is understandable that the type of frying fat used for doughnut production is very important. A preconditioned vegetable shortening specifically manufactured for frying purposes is best. It tends to avoid the flashy or rapid crust color formation on doughnuts being fried in fresh frying fat. However, many pastry chefs use a regular hydrogenated shortening with excellent results.

The shortening or frying fat should be bland and without foreign odor. The frying temperature of the fat should be in the range of 365–385°F depending upon the doughnut or other product to be fried. For example, yeast-raised doughnuts are usually fried at 380–385°F, while cake-type doughnuts are fried at 375–380°F. Other doughnut varieties may be fried at a lower temperature depending upon the contents or formulation of the batter or dough. Frying fat should be strained regularly to eliminate foreign matter and prevent premature breakdown of the frying fat. Many pastry chefs will strain the fat after each frying. The turnover or addition of fresh fat is regulated by the volume of production and care of the frying fat. Special note is made of the absorption of odors and flavors when frying doughnuts. The frying fat for doughnuts should not be used for frying other foods that have distinct odors or flavors, or that may leave a residue of particles that will be caramelized into discoloring specks which will attach themselves to the frying doughnuts. The frying process and maintenance of the quality of the frying fat also depend upon the type of frying equipment. Large volume production may require automated or semi-automated equipment. This will be explained with the formulas and production procedures.

Yeast-Raised Doughnut Varieties

The dough for these doughnuts is leaner or less rich than the doughs used for sweet rolls and buns or coffee cakes. This is necessary because a dough rich in sugar and fat will tend to absorb more fat in frying, form a dark crust color when fried at required temperatures, and tend to lose shape or shrink after frying. The final taste and flavor of most doughnuts is developed by the type of fillings and toppings used in the finishing of the doughnuts.

Yeast-Raised Doughnut Dough

Ingredients	lb	oz	Mixing procedure
Yeast (variable)		12	Dissolve the yeast and set aside
Water	2		
Sugar	1		Blend these ingredients to a soft, smooth
Salt		2	consistency
Skim milk powder		8	
Defatted soy flour (optional)		4	
Potato flour (optional)		6	
Shortening	1		

Egg yolks		8	Add the eggs in 2 stages and blend in well
Whole eggs		8	
Water	2		Add the water and flavorings and mix
Vanilla		1½	lightly
Lemon flavor		½	
Bread flour	7		Sift the flour. Add and mix lightly. Add
(variable)			the yeast solution and develop to a smooth dough

1. Dough temperature: 78–80°F (keep dough on cool side).
2. First rise and punch approximately 1½ hr.
3. Allow dough to relax 20 to 30 min and take to bench.
4. Scale the dough into presses weighing approximately 3 to 3½ lb. The presses are used for producing the Bismarcks (round-filled), bow tie doughnuts, and twist variety.
5. For the production of the Pershings (cinnamon roll), ring-type, and Long John doughnuts, scale the dough into 6-lb pieces and form into a smooth, rectangular shape.
6. Allow the presses and pieces of dough to relax for about 15 or 20 min before placing in dough divider, or rolling on bench, or sending through the sheeter.
7. If large volume production is required, pastry chefs will often retard some of the presses and dough pieces to avoid overfermentation of the doughs. This practice is also used for dough units that are to be relaxed and made up at a later time.

Yield: Approx. 100–150 servings

Bismarcks These are round filled doughnuts, commonly known as jelly doughnuts. (Fig. 4.1.) The following procedure for makeup is to be employed:

1. Press out the presses and round up the individual dough pieces into balls. The divider-rounder, if there is one, will do this. Place the units directly on frying screens or on cloths for proofing. Give the units three-quarter proof. If the units are proofed on cloths, transfer them gently to the frying screens when three-quarter proof. *Be sure the frying fat is ready* (380–385°F). Check the frying thermometer. Have the long wooden frying and turning sticks ready for turning the doughnuts.

2. Carefully lower the screens with the doughnuts (spaced about 2 in. apart to allow for expansion during frying) into the frying fat. Be careful not to cause splashing. There may be some large air pockets or blister formation on some of the doughnuts. These are to be punctured carefully with the point of the doughnut-turning sticks if they are very large. If

4.1
Jelly doughnuts draining on absorbent paper

allowed to remain, they will later peel from the crust. Check the crust color of the doughnuts before turning. They should be golden brown and take from 45 sec to 1 min to fry on each side.

3.   Turn the doughnuts quickly without splashing. This is best done by tilting the doughnut on the side and turning it over. At this point, many pastry chefs will place another screen over the doughnuts to depress them a bit more into the frying fat. This will reduce or eliminate entirely the circle of white dough around the center of the doughnut. Where automatic frying equipmnent is used for large scale production, the doughnuts travel on belts and chain belts and are automatically deposited into the frying fat and turned automatically as they travel through the frying fat.

4.   Remove the fried doughnuts from the frying fat. It is advisable to allow the doughnuts to drain for a few seconds to remove excess frying fat from the surface. The doughnuts are deposited gently on screens to drain. Pastry chefs will often deposit the doughnuts on absorbent sheets of paper for drainage of fat. The drained doughnuts are placed on pans with or without the screens for cooling and finishing.

Methods of Finishing Bismarcks   Bismarcks are filled with jelly when they have cooled. Pastry chefs may place the unfilled doughnuts in the refrigerator to chill and firm up to make handling easier. A variety of jams and jellies may be pumped into the center of the Bismarcks. The jelly or jam should be smoothed before placing into the jelly pump. Some of these pumps will fill two doughnuts at a time. Automatic fillers are used for large-scale production. The Bismarcks are inserted about half-way into the nozzle of the jelly pump. The pressure should be even so that equal amounts of jelly are pumped into each doughnut. Release the pump handle before removing the doughnut to prevent the jelly from running or leaking out. (Do not thin the jelly down unless it is too stiff.) Custard filling may be used. Bismarcks may be chilled and then cut about three-quarters through or cut completely in half and filled with French custard, Bavarian cream, or whipped cream. The filling is bagged out with a pastry bag. Formulas for the custard, Bavarian cream, and the whipped cream will be found in the section for the production of eclairs and cream puffs and other choux paste desserts.

Jams and jellies are usually purchased in ready-to-use form—usually large cans or number 10 cans. Prepared jelly powders that make excellent jelly fillings are available. One must add sugar and water, and boil. Bismarcks, when filled with jelly or jam, are usually finished by dusting with confectioners sugar or rolling in plain or cinnamon sugar. Custard or cream-filled varieties are usually dusted lightly.

Pershings   These may be classified as deep-fat fried cinnamon bun-type doughnuts. They are made from the yeast-raised doughnut dough and the procedure for makeup is much the same as for cinnamon buns. The conditioned doughnut dough is scaled into 4; 6; or 8-lb pieces and formed into a smooth rectangular shape. The units of dough are relaxed for about 20 min and then rolled out on the bench or sent through the dough sheeter to form a rectangular dough about ¼ in. thick. The dough is brushed lightly with water or milk. *Do not use melted fat or oil* since the dough will tend to separate and absorb more frying fat than necessary when fried. Sprinkle the surface of the dough with cinnamon sugar and then roll up into a snug or tight roll. Be sure the end of the roll is well sealed. This will avoid opening during frying and the formation of uneven shapes. Cut the roll into cuts or slices about ½ to three-quarters in. thick and place on screens or cloths for proof. (Figs. 4.2 through 4.4). Give the units three-quarters proof before frying. If placed on cloths to proof, pick the units up gently and place on the frying screens. Fry at 380°F. After turning the Pershings, cover with another frying screen to submerge the units and avoid formation of a white edge around the fried unit. Allow the units to drain slightly before placing on screens to complete draining. Allow the Pershings to cool slightly and then dip into doughnut glaze while still hot. Be sure the Pershings are completely covered with glaze before returning to the screens for draining and drying. The following is a recommended formula for the glaze which is often called *honey dip*.

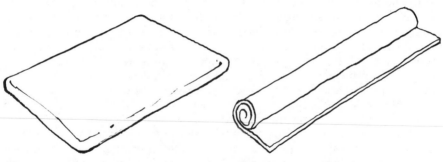

4.2
Roll out dough and brush with water or milk. Sprinkle lightly with cinnamon sugar

4.3
Roll dough up tightly and seal edge

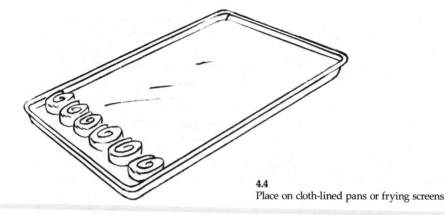

4.4
Place on cloth-lined pans or frying screens

Doughnut Glaze (*Honey Dip*)

Ingredients	lb	oz	Mixing procedure
Gelatin		1	Soak gelatin in water for ½ to 1 hr
Water (cool)		8	
Confectionery sugar	7		Add 8 oz of hot water from the amount
Vanilla		½	listed below to dissolve the gelatin. Sift
Honey (clover)		8	the sugar and blend with the other ingre-
Glycerin (optional)		3	dients. Add the gelatin solution and mix
Salt		pinch	smooth
Cream of tartar		¼	
Hot water	1	14	

1. Do not overmix the glaze as this may cause formation of a froth or foam, and the glaze will lose its clarity.
2. Be sure to keep the glaze warm in a double boiler if large amounts of Pershings or other doughnuts are to be dipped.
3. Cover the entire top surface of the Pershings before returning to the screens for draining and drying.
4. Pastry chefs may also dip the Pershings or ice the centers with a fondant icing. The flavors may be changed and the color of the icing may be changed, as for maple or coffee. The Pershings may then be sprinkled with chopped nuts or other attractive garnish. Be sure the fondant icing is warm (115–120°F) when applied.

Ring Doughnuts Usually made from yeast-raised doughnut dough, they may also be made from the combination doughnut dough described later in this unit. Most pastry chefs will follow the usual procedure of scaling the conditioned dough into large sections of 6 lb or more. The units are then shaped into smooth, rectangular form and allowed to relax for about 20 min or placed in the retarder for later makeup. The relaxed dough is then rolled out or sheeted to about ½ in. thickness. The sheeted or rolled-out dough is allowed to relax for about 5 min before cutting out the doughnuts. This will avoid shrinkage of the doughnuts after cutting them out. Space the cuts as closely as possible to avoid excessive dough scraps. (Fig. 4.5.) Be sure the dough is of even thickness for uniformity of size.

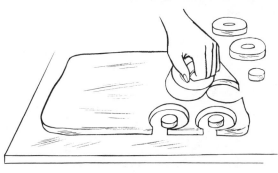

4.5
Cut out doughnuts with cutter

4.6
Shaping a ring doughnut as a bagel

The size of the doughnut cutter (usually 3 in. in diameter) will determine the size of the doughnut. The cut doughnuts are placed on screens or cloths for proofing. Doughnut centers, if fried and sold as miniatures, are placed on separate cloths. Allow the doughnuts to get approximately three-quarters proof and then fry at 385°F. Lift the doughnuts proofed on cloths carefully to avoid collapse or indentations. Space the doughnuts about 1 in. apart on the screens to allow for expansion in frying. Turn the doughnuts and then place a screen over them to submerge them a little more and to reduce the white outer crust on the sides of the ring doughnuts. The scrap dough is folded in with fresh dough and allowed to relax. It is rolled again and allowed to relax for a longer period before cutting out the doughnuts. The reworked dough will have a toughened gluten structure and will require a longer resting period to avoid shrinkage after cutting.

In order to avoid use of scrap dough and shrinkage of ring doughnuts, pastry chefs may scale the scrap dough together into dough presses and then press out the dough for units that are to be rolled out and then made into twist doughnuts. Others may roll out the dough units into even strips and then shape them into a ring as a bagel. (Fig. 4.6.) This eliminates all scrap and center pieces. With skill and speed, the bagel-shaped doughnuts may be made as quickly as others.

When large production of doughnuts is required, the doughnut doughs are placed into hoppers where they are extruded under pressure or through a vacuum system and deposited directly onto the moving chain belt. The belts travel a short distance into a microwave-heated tunnel and doughnuts are proofed in a few minutes before being dropped onto the belt moving through the hot fat.

4.7
Glazed or iced doughnuts
drain on a grate

Ring doughnuts are finished by dipping into honey glaze while hot or very warm. This allows the glaze to dry properly and avoids excessive absorption of the glaze. The doughnuts are also finished with a variety of fondant icings and garnished with a variety of nuts and crunches. The fondant icings should be warm and the doughnuts cool when being dipped. The garnish is applied while the icing is still moist so that the garnish will stick when the icing dries. (Fig. 4.7.)

Bow Tie Doughnuts The conditioned dough is scaled into presses and then rounded. The dough presses are relaxed for about 15 to 20 min and then pressed out. Do not round the units of dough. The units are separated and dusted lightly with flour to avoid sticking. Each of the units is picked up and stretched slightly. With the index finger and thumb a hole is made in the center of the unit of dough. One end of the dough unit is then pulled through the hole, forming a bow tie. (Figs. 4.8 through 4.10.)

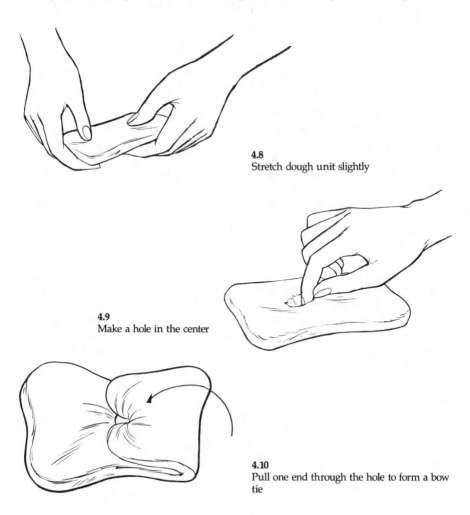

4.8
Stretch dough unit slightly

4.9
Make a hole in the center

4.10
Pull one end through the hole to form a bow tie

The units are then placed on screens or cloths and given three-quarter proof. Units may be stretched to an even thickness of ½ in. Fry the units in prepared frying fat at a temperature of 385°F. To reduce the amount of white crust surface on the sides of the doughnuts, submerge them after they have been turned by placing a frying screen on them. The drained doughnuts may then be finished when cooled or while slightly warm. The usual method of finishing is to roll the doughnuts in granulated sugar or cinnamon sugar. Many pastry chefs may dust the cool doughnuts with confectioners sugar. In addition, a small amount of jelly or jam may be bagged into the center of the depression of the doughnut. This provides a color display as well as adding to the variety and taste of the doughnut.

Twist Doughnuts Made from yeast-raised doughnut dough, or from chemically leavened cruller dough, twist doughnuts are attractive in shape and form and add to the variety of doughnuts. The units made from the yeast-raised doughnut dough are made as follows.

1. Scale the dough into presses and then allow the dough presses to relax for 15 to 20 min. Press out the relaxed dough presses and separate the units. Dust the units lightly with flour to keep them from sticking to each other.
2. Each of the units is rolled out either on the bench or sent through the dough strip shaper of the sheeter to form strands of dough of equal thickness and about 6 in. long. With the palms of the hands, the strips are rolled slightly longer and twisted so that 3 or 4 twists are made. The ends are then sealed tightly to avoid opening during frying. (Figs. 4.11 through 4.14.)
3. Place the units on screens or cloths and give them three-quarter proof. Proofing for yeast-raised and combination-type doughnuts should be slow and with a low humidity. This allows for a slight skin or crust formation to make handling the proofed doughnuts easier, without moist stickiness.
4. Fry the units as the other doughnuts. It is advisable to place a frying screen over the turned doughnuts to prevent them from turning once again and completely frying the entire surface of the twisted doughnuts. These doughnuts are finished by rolling in granulated sugar or cinnamon sugar after they have cooled to a mildly warm state. The units may be finished when cool by dusting lightly with confectioners sugar.

Long John Doughnuts These made from the yeast-raised dough are different from those made from the chemically raised doughs. The conditioned dough is scaled into large units and shaped into smooth, rectangular shapes. The dough units are relaxed for about 20 minutes before rolling out on the bench or sending through the sheeter. The dough should be rolled evenly to about ½ in. thickness. The rolled dough is relaxed for about 5 min and then cut with a pastry wheel into rectangular

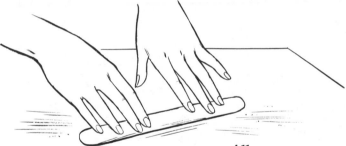

4.11
Roll unit of dough about 6 in. long

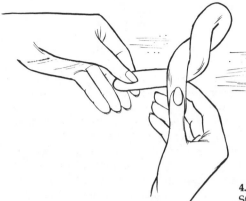

4.12
Start from center and make 3 or 4 twists

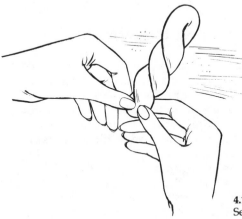

4.13
Seal the ends of the strip

4.14
Twist cruller

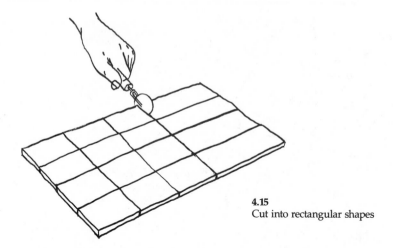

4.15
Cut into rectangular shapes

shapes about 3½–4 in. long and about 1½ in. wide (Fig. 4.15). It is important to have the rolled dough completely relaxed before cutting to avoid shrinkage when the units are cut. Place the units directly on wire, frying screens or cloths. Proof the units to about slightly more than three-quarter proof and fry at 385°F. Place a screen over the turned doughnuts and complete the frying. When cool, these units may be filled with a jam or jelly as for Bismarcks. Fill from both sides, if necessary, in order to get a thin stream of filling. A custard filling may be used as for an eclair. Chill the units to make handling and filling easier. The units may then be iced with a fondant or fudge icing. The units may also be split and filled with a Bavarian custard filling or with whipped cream.

Chemically Leavened Doughnuts

Prepared mixes for chemically leavened doughnuts are widely used by most pastry chefs. They have the values of economy, control, and uniformity of product, and ease in production. There are a number of different companies that produce these mixes, and there are some fundamental variables in the quality of the doughnut. As previously indicated, pastry chefs will enrich some of the mixes and make adjustments in formulation to enrich or further economize. However, there are many pastry chefs who wish to prepare these doughnut varieties from the beginning to the final finishing. There are others who make comparisons between the "scratch" (self-scaled and made) and the products of prepared mixes and then decide. Still others feel that the variety of these doughnuts is limited and wish to enrich and vary the types of doughnuts. The following formulas are for the pastry chefs who wish to produce the doughnuts with special formulas and who may wish to further adjust these formulas to meet consumer specifications.

Special mention is made of doughnuts that are enriched with added proteins present in special grains and flours. Such flours as defatted soy flour, bran, whole wheat and potato flour not only add the natural proteins, but also improve texture, extend freshness, and improve eating qualities of the doughnuts. Soy flour is commonly used in most formulas. In commercial and prepared mixes, the additives for softness, shelf-life, moisture retention, and other qualities are chemical. In addition synthetic vitamins are added to the prepared mixes. These are benefits to be considered. The blend of flavorings and spice is controlled by the pastry chef when using his own formulas.

Cake Doughnuts

Ingredients	lb	oz	Mixing procedure
Sugar	1	8	Blend all the ingredients with part of the
Salt		1¼	eggs to a smooth consistency. Add the re-
Skim milk powder		4	maining eggs and blend in well
Soy flour (defatted)		2	
Nutmeg		¼	
Shortening		5	
Whole eggs		8	
Egg yolks		8	
Water (variable)	2	8	Add the water and flavorings and mix
Vanilla		1	lightly
Lemon flavoring		¼	
Cake flour	3	8	Sift the flours and baking powder. Add
Bread flour	1	8	and mix to a smooth batter
Baking powder		3	

1. Check the consistency of the batter in the final stages of mixing. If the batter feels too stiff, add additional liquid. If too soft or runny, add additional cake flour. The variables in the type and quality of the flours will have a decided effect on batter consistency. The consistency should be that of a medium soft dough or firm batter to allow the doughnuts to be dropped out in equal amounts and of equal thickness to form round, even doughnuts.
2. Allow the batter to rest approximately 5 min before depositing into the doughnut hopper. This period will allow the batter to firm slightly as well as soften the texture for an even, clean cut as the doughnuts are deposited.
3. For the hand dropper, be sure to apply equal pressure to the lever or handle. For the round circle hand dropper, keep the movement even and consistent to avoid uneven doughnut dropping. For the automatic equipment, be sure the extrusion pressure is even.
4. The usual frying temperature for these doughnuts may vary from 380° to 385°F. Check the amount (depth) of frying fat, cleanliness, and additional fat required before frying the doughnuts.
5. For doughnuts that are to be made up on the bench in a dough form, increase the bread flour by 8 oz and the cake flour by 4 oz. The medium dough should be slightly chilled for ease in rolling out and

cutting. These doughnuts will have a more open grain and will not be quite as tender as the regular cake doughnuts.

6. After the doughnuts have been removed from the fying fat and drained and cooled, the doughnuts may be finished in the following manner:

    a.   Left plain for immediate serving.

    b.   Rolled in cinnamon sugar (remove excess sugar). Select a good quality brand of cinnamon and mix according to consumer preference.

    c.   Completely sugar coated by rolling in the following blends:

	lb	oz
Confectioners sugar	8	8
Cornstarch	1	8

For very moist conditions: Use 8 lb dextrose and 2 lb starch.

These doughnuts may also be iced with fondant icing or fudge icing. A chocolate cookie dip (quick drying) may also be used.

Yield: Approx. 100 doughnuts

Uses: Breakfast item, snack food, coffee breaks, specialty item (parties)

Whole Wheat Cake Doughnuts

Ingredients	lb	oz	Mixing procedure
Sugar		14	Blend all the ingredients together with
Salt		1	part of the eggs to form a smooth consis-
Skim milk powder		4	tency
Cinnamon		¼	
Nutmeg		¼	
Soy flour (defatted)[1]		2	
Bran flour[1]		2	
Molasses		4	
Shortening		5	
Baking soda		¼	
Egg yolks		8	Add the remaining eggs and blend in
Whole eggs		4	
Water (variable)	2	8	Add half the water and mix lightly
Vanilla (optional)		½	
Whole wheat flour	1		Sift the flours and baking powder. Add
Cake flour	1	10	and mix lightly. Add the remaining water
Bread flour		8	and mix to a smooth consistency. *Avoid*
Baking powder		2½	*overmixing*

---

[1]The soy flour and bran flour will enrich the protein content and provide for a softer texture. They may be eliminated. If so, add an additional 4 oz of cake flour.

1. Check the consistency of the batter in the final stages of mixing. Adjust if necessary. The batter will tend to firm up slightly as it stands. Rest the batter for 5 min before placing into hopper.
2. The bran flour will provide for a nut-like flavor after the doughnuts are fried. Finely ground and toasted nuts (approximately 4–6 oz) will further improve taste and provide for greater variety.
3. In view of the brown color of the batter, it may be difficult to determine the proper crust color when frying the doughnuts. The frying time should be about 45 sec on each side. It is advisable to check the interior of the first doughnuts for proper frying. Fry at 380°F.
4. For doughnuts that are to be made up on the bench in a dough form, add an additional 8 oz of cake flour and 4–6 oz of bread flour. The medium dough may be refrigerated for a while to firm it up to make it easier to roll or send through the sheeter.
5. Cut out the doughnuts about three-eighths to ½ in. thick. The centers may be fried separately or may be returned to the dough and worked in for the next roll.
6. Allow the dough to relax for 10 min after working over. The automatic extruders or cutters in the hopper may have to be adjusted to allow for the bran and nut particles. For hand droppers this may not be necessary.
7. The doughnuts may be finished in the following manner:
    a. Left plain and served immediately.
    b. Rolled in plain granulated sugar or a blend of cinnamon sugar.
    c. Completely coated with a confectioners sugar blend (see suggested blend listed with plain cake doughnuts). A blend of dextrose and cornstarch may also be used.

Yield: Approx. 100 servings

Chocolate Cake Doughnuts

Ingredients	lb	oz	Mixing procedure
Sugar	1	4	Blend all ingredients with part of the eggs
Salt		1	to a smooth consistency
Skim milk powder		4	
Soy flour (defatted)		3	
Shortening		7	
Egg yolks		6	Add remaining eggs and mix smooth
Whole eggs		8	
Water (variable)	2	8	Dissolve the baking soda in the water.
Baking soda		½	Add the flavorings. Add half the liquid to
Vanilla		1	the above and mix slightly
Chocolate flavoring		½	
Cake flour	3		Sift the flours and cocoa and baking powder together. Add alternately with the remaining water and mix to smooth batter
Bread flour	1		
Cocoa		5	
Baking powder		2	

1. Check the consistency of the batter before completing the final stage of mixing. It may be necessary to add or delete liquid. The batter will tend to firm up or stiffen after mixing. The cocoa will tend to absorb more liquid.

2. Allow the batter to rest for about 5 min before placing it into the hopper for depositing the doughnuts into the hot fat. Large batters may have to be mixed lightly again if not dropped out within a reasonable time (30 min).

3. To substitute chocolate for the cocoa powder, use 8 oz of melted chocolate liquor (bitter chocolate). Add the melted chocolate immediately after blending in the eggs. The chocolate will add a slight increase in the fat because of the cocoa butter present. A more flavorful and tender doughnut should result.

4. For bench-type or roll and cut out doughnuts, add 8 oz of cake flour and 4 oz of bread flour to thicken the batter to a medium soft dough. The dough may be chilled before using to make rolling or sheeting easier.

5. The doughnut balls may be fried as a doughnut specialty. Pastry chefs may combine the yellow cake doughnut balls with the chocolate balls and serve a variety for delicate snacks. These are usually lightly dusted with confectioners sugar.

6. Fry the chocolate doughnuts in frying fat at a temperature of 380°F. Because of the color of the batter, it may be difficult to determine proper crust color and sufficient frying for doneness. The first doughnuts should be fried for approximately 45 sec on each side and then checked for proper completion. It is important to check whether the interior is fully done.

7. After the doughnuts have been drained and cooled, they may be finished in the following manner:
    a. Left plain and dusted lightly with confectioners sugar when served.
    b. Iced with chocolate fudge icing or other colorful fudge-type icings applied with a spatula. A variety of garnishes may be applied immediately after icing.
    c. Pastry chefs will often dip the doughnuts in a special, quick drying, chocolate cookie dip.

Yield: 100 servings

These doughnuts are leavened by yeast and baking powder and the resulting doughnut has the characteristics of the yeast-raised and chemically leavened doughnuts. There is the light, open structure of the yeast-raised doughnut and the tenderness of the cake-type doughnut. There is a decided advantage in making this type of doughnut in that the conditioning period is shortened and makeup is more rapid. In addition, the same varieties of doughnuts can be made from this dough.

Combination Doughnuts

Ingredients	lb	oz	Mixing procedure
Yeast (variable)		4–6	Dissolve the yeast and set aside
Water	1		
Sugar		6	Blend all ingredients to a soft, smooth
Salt		1½	consistency
Skim milk powder		6	
Soy flour (optional)[1]		3	
Wheat germ (optional)[1]		2	
Nutmeg		½	
Shortening	1	2	
Honey (clover)		4	
Eggs (part yolks)	1		Add in 3 stages and blend
Water	2	4	Add to the above and mix lightly
Vanilla		1	
Lemon flavoring		½	
Cake flour	2	4	Sift the flours and baking powder. Add
Bread flour	4		mix lightly, add yeast solution and de-
Baking powder		1½	velop to a smooth dough

1. Check the consistency of the dough before final development. The dough should be almost the same consistency as the yeast-raised doughnut dough. Some pastry chefs prefer the dough to be a bit softer. Judgment by the pastry chef is necessary. The strength of the flour will also have an effect on the dough consistency.
2. Allow the dough to relax for about 30 min. Yeast activity will soften and slightly expand the dough.
3. For units that are to be made from the rolled or sheeted dough (Bismarcks, ring, and Long John doughnuts) the dough is scaled into 6 to 8 lb units and formed into rectangular shape. These units are relaxed for about 15 min and sheeted or rolled. The units may also be retarded at this point for later makeup. Pastry chefs find the dough easier to handle when retarded and more completely relaxed.

Yield: Approx. 140, depending upon size

Makeup of Ring Doughnuts, Long Johns, and Bismarcks Roll or sheet the dough to about ⅜ to ½ in. thick. Allow the sheeted dough to relax for a few minutes to avoid shrinkage when the doughnuts are cut out. The centers of the ring doughnuts may be fried separately and served as a special menu item. The ring doughnuts are to be given half proof (will

---

[1]The soy flour and wheat germ will enrich the protein content of the doughnuts. The soy flour will also help to promote a more tender grain and texture. They may be left out, if desired.

be gassy but spring back firmly to the touch), and fried at 380–385°F. The scrap dough and centers of the ring doughnuts may be worked into fresh dough and then rolled again. The scrap dough may also be scaled into presses of dough and made up into other doughnut varieties. The Long Johns are made as they would from the usual yeast-raised doughnut dough. Give the units only ½ proof before frying. The baking powder will provide additional leavening. The Bismarcks can be made up differently than they were from the yeast-raised doughnut dough. In this case, the rolled or sheeted dough should be about ½ in. thick and then cut out with a plain, round cutter varying in size from 2–3 in. The size will depend upon the preference of the pastry chef. Naturally, a tea or snack size will be smaller than the larger coffee break size. Give the Bismarcks slightly more than ½ proof and then place gently on the screens. The Bismarcks made this way will have a slightly flatter appearance but will be uniform in roundness. They will also have a straighter side. Submerge the doughnuts after they have been turned by placing a frying screen on them. This will reduce the dough whiteness on the sides of the doughnut.

Makeup of Twist and Bow Tie Doughnuts   Scale the dough into presses varying in weight from 2½–3¼ lb. The size of the doughnut desired will determine the weight of the press. Shape these doughnuts the same way they were shaped from the yeast-raised doughnut dough. Place the doughnuts directly on frying screens or dusted cloths for proof. Give the doughnuts ½ proof and fry. Be sure the twist doughnuts are firmly sealed at the ends to prevent separation or unraveling during frying. It is advisable to place a screen over the twist doughnuts after they have been turned. It will prevent the twist doughnuts from turning over during frying. All doughnuts may be finished as they were when made from the yeast-raised dough.

These are a popular breakfast item and often play an important role in the breakfast menu, especially for schools and institutions. Crullers may be enriched with added grains for additional protein content. The cruller dough lends itself well to the production of a variety of sizes and shapes of fried goods.

Old Fashioned Crullers

Ingredients	lb	oz	Mixing procedure
Conditioned (fermented) sweet roll or coffee cake dough (optional)	1		Blend all ingredients together well to form a smooth consistency
Sugar		12	
Salt		1	

Skim milk powder		3	
Soy flour (defatted)		4	
Honey (clover)		8	
Shortening		½	
Nutmeg		12	
Eggs (part yolks)			
Water (variable)	2	4	Add and mix lightly
Vanilla		1	
Lemon flavoring		½	
Cake flour	1	12	Sift the flour and baking powder together.
Bread flour	2	4	Add to the above and mix to a smooth
Baking powder		3	dough

1. The conditioned sweet roll or coffee cake dough provides a sponge dough base which adds to the volume of the cruller. It also provides a slightly firmer texture and ease in makeup.
2. A yeast-raised roll dough may be used. A slight increase in sugar and shortening would be advisable (2 oz of each) to replace the lack of richness in the dough.
3. If no fermented dough is used, increase the cake flour by 4–6 oz to firm the dough slightly.
4. The dough may be chilled before rolling or sheeting. The dough may also be scaled into presses (approximately 3 lb per press) and retarded for later makeup.
5. The same variety of doughnuts may be made from this cruller dough as from the yeast-raised doughnut dough, except for the Bismarcks or jelly-filled doughnuts.

Yield: Approx. 100 servings

Ring Doughnuts   These are rolled out to about three-eighths in. thickness and the doughnuts cut out of the dough. The centers may be fried as a separate specialty and served when cool with a light dusting of confectioners sugar. The fried doughnuts may be finished the same as those made from the yeast-raised doughnut dough, or the cake-type doughnuts.

Twist Doughnuts, Long Johns, Bow Ties   These are made from presses of cruller dough. The weight of the press is determined by the size desired. The presses are relaxed for about 15 min and then divided. The units are rolled out by hand or formed into bow ties as they are made from the yeast-raised doughnut dough. The Long Johns made from the cruller dough are made by rolling each unit of dough to a length of 5–6 in. and of even thickness.

Allow the varieties to relax for about 10 to 15 min before frying at 380–385°F. Fry on each side for 50 sec. Many pastry chefs prepare the crullers in advance and place them in the retarder in a raw state for frying in the early morning. Most of the crullers, when freshly fried, are rolled or dusted with confectioners sugar before serving.

French Crullers

French crullers are fried products that are made from a choux paste or eclair and cream puff batter. The crullers are actually round and resemble the ring or cake-type doughnut. They are primarily leavened by the expansion of the eggs in the batter and the steam released during the frying process. They are also leavened by the baking powder or the ammonium bicarbonate which may be added to leaven the additional water or milk used to replace some of the eggs. These special crullers are rich in eggs and fat and have the special flavor imparted by the eggs. The French cruller has a moist, tender inner structure while being quite open in grain and porous. They are special in terms of fried goods. Their popularity is evident by the growth of the prepared mixes presently available for the production of French crullers. It is advantageous to use the prepared mixes for these products because they save time and may be more economical for large scale production as well as smaller quantities.

French Crullers

Ingredients	lb	oz	Mixing procedure
Water	3		Bring to a rolling boil and continue to boil
Salt		½	until the shortening is dissolved
Shortening	1	8	
Bread flour	2		Sift and add the flour in a steady stream stirring constantly until all flour is absorbed and mix draws away from sides and bottom of bowl or pot. Remove from heat and allow to cool. Place into mixer and run at slow speed until the batter is about 140°F.
Eggs	3		Add the eggs a little at a time. Scrape the sides of the bowl regularly.
Water or milk (variable)		8–12	If the batter is too stiff or firm, add a little liquid to the desired consistency
Baking powder (variable)		½–¾	

1. The batter should be similar to a thick gravy. When bagged or deposited directly into the hot fat, the lines or grooves made by the grooved die or pastry tube should not run together but remain distinct during the entire frying process.
2. The amount of water or milk added will determine the amount of leavening to use. If ammonium bicarbonate is used, use ¼ oz for each 8–10 oz of liquid. Dissolve the ammonium bicarbonate in the liquid.
3. Fry the crullers as soon as possible with this type of chemical leavening. Baking powder has greater leavening tolerance and delay in frying is not extremely important.

4. Deposit the batter into the hoppers when ready and the frying fat is at a temperature of 370–375°F. The cooler frying fat is necessary because the French cruller takes longer to fry through. The eggs expand and require complete structural drying or cooking.

5. A rapid crust color formation will cause rapid turning and removal. If the structure is not completely set, the cruller will collapse and be raw and gummy on the inside. A slow frying process is necessary. Since the flour batter is precooked, there is less absorption of grease or fat while the leavening effect takes place. Each side should be fried approximately 3 min. Smaller and thinner crullers require less time. It is advisable to check the first fried French crullers for timing and proper fry.

6. It is important to have the dies clean and clear of foreign matter for a clear cut grooved design. The hopper should be about 4–6 in. from the frying fat so that there is no loss in shape when dropped.

7. If French crullers are not to be dropped out by hand or automatic dropper, they should be bagged out with a pastry bag and tube on well greased, heavy brown paper. Fill the pastry bag carefully. Use a French tube or star tube (number 5 suggested) to form the rings.

8. Bag out about 1 in. apart on greased papers that are about 18 in. square or rectangular. Be sure each cruller is of equal thickness and size.

9. Deposit the crullers in the frying fat by holding the ends of the paper and gently lowering into the hot fat. When completely flat the crullers will be released when the grease on the paper melts. Remove the paper and drain. Use the sheets of paper again. Turn the crullers gently to avoid marring the design made by the die or pastry tube. (Figs. 4.16 through 4.18.)

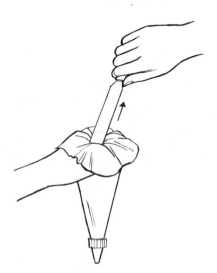

4.16
Filling the pastry bag

4.17
Divide the pastry bag in half

4.18
Space French crullers evenly on greased,
heavy paper and dip into hot fat

10.   When drained and cooled, the doughnuts are finished by dipping
      just the tops in warm fondant icing. A variety of colors and flavor-
      ings may be used. The most popular is vanilla icing.
Yield: Approx. 100

Sugar Coating for Doughnuts

Ingredients	lb	oz	Mixing procedure
Corn sugar or dextrose sugar (powdered) or confectioners sugar	10		Sift either of the sugars with the corn starch several times. Use either corn sugar or confectioners sugar. Do not use both. Add the shortening, if used, and blend in well to form a moist coating.
Corn starch	2		
Emulsified shortening (optional)	1		

This coating is usually used for cake-type doughnuts. However, the coating may be used for yeast-raised and cruller type doughnuts as well.
Doughnuts should be rolled in the sugar coating when cool. For special
occasions, the sugar coating may be colored in light or pastel shades of
pink, green, yellow, and so forth, to suit the occasion.

Sugar coating should be covered when not in use. Leftover coating
may be sifted in with fresh coating.

5

Variety Pies

Pies are often the specialty dessert of the restaurant or other dining establishment. The pastry chef is the person most often responsible for the popularity of this "house specialty." These specialties are limited to a select group of pies for which the restaurant may be well known. However, the skilled pastry chef is capable of making a variety of pies so that dessert menus are often very impressive. The quality of the pie is the important factor and this, of course, is based on the knowledge and ability of the pastry chef. The finest fruits and other ingredients may not always result in an excellent pie if they are not handled properly. This is true of the pie crust which encases the filling, the actual filling, and the proper baking and service of the pie. Each of these factors will be discussed in this chapter.

Pie crust doughs will vary to meet the requirements of the type of pie to be made. For example, the crust for a fruit-filled pie or the cover for a hot casserole dish should be different from the crust used for a baked custard pie. This applies to the variations in crusts used for precooked, chiffon-type pies as well as the fried pies. While the basic ingredients used to make most pie doughs are similar, the amounts used and the methods of mixing the doughs will vary. These factors influence the type of crust made and the resulting crust when the pie is baked.

Basic Ingredients For Pie Crusts

Pastry Flour
A pastry flour milled from a soft winter wheat is the primary flour used for pie crust dough. It does not have the amount and quality of gluten-

forming proteins present in bread flours but is slightly stronger than a fine, soft, cake flour. It is important that the toughening effect of gluten development is avoided when mixing pie crust dough. Bread flour will tend to absorb liquid rapidly and will produce a tough stringy effect when mixed. Cake flour is too soft and will not fully support the high percentage of fat in the dough and may tend to crumble when baked. The pastry flour is the in-between flour. Very often the pastry chef will prepare a blend of flours to obtain a good pastry flour; he may blend 30% bread flour with 70% cake flour. It may also be that the pastry flour is too strong or too weak. In that instance, the pastry chef will make the necessary adjustments with the blending of other flours with the pastry flour. It is important to have the right flour or flour blend for pie crust doughs. Sift the flours to remove lumps before mixing.

Shortening or Other Fats

A short, tender pie crust is very important to the consumer. The initial insertion of the fork into the crust is the first indication of a well-made pie. While the filling is the principal part of the pie and provides the flavor, it may not overshadow the effects of a tough or improperly made crust. In fact, a leftover pie crust is often an indication of a tough or poor quality. When mixed in properly, the shortening or other fat supplies the tenderness or shortness qualities to the crust. Most pie crusts are rich in fat content. The basic crust for most fruit-filled pies contains approximately 75% fat. The fat may be composed of all hydrogenated shortening or a blend of butter and other fats. A bland shortening of good quality, plasticity, and good melting point is most desirable. The use of butter is quite expensive and its flavoring qualities may be overshadowed by the filling of the pie. Lard is favored by many chefs, but it has a distinguishing flavor that may not be desirable with bland fillings. However, pastry chefs may insist on using butter. If so, then no more than 25% butter with shortening is recommended. If salted butter is used, slightly decrease the amount of salt in the formula.

Cold Water or Other Liquids

Water and other liquids make possible the formation of the pie crust dough. The flour is moistened and changed to a sticky, adhering mass containing fats and other ingredients. Cold or chilled water should be used to maintain the firmness and plasticity of the shortening and other fats. Dry ingredients such as sugar, salt, and milk powder are usually dissolved in the water before mixing. The amount of water will vary with the formula and the method of mixing. For example, flaky pie crust dough will require slighly less water than a mealy type of pie crust.

Salt

Salt is used to provide taste in the pie crust dough. A lack of salt will leave the dough with a flat taste. The salt also enhances the flavor of the filling. The contrast with the sweetness of the filling makes the filling more flavorful. Salt is best dissolved in the water before adding.

Skim Milk Powder

Skim milk powder is often used in pie crust doughs to increase the richness and nutritional value. It will also provide a deeper crust color when the pie is baked. The milk powder should be dissolved in the water before adding for maximum distribution in the dough.

Sugars and Syrups

Sugars and syrups are often added to pie crust doughs to increase the sweetness of the crust and to provide for a deeper crust color and more rapid formation of the crust color during baking. However, syrups will tend to absorb and retain mositure and may cause the baked crust to become soft and soggy if kept for extended periods after baking. Normally, about 3% sugar or other sweeteners are used in pie crust doughs and the sweeteners are dissolved in the water before adding to the dough.

Types of Pie Crust

There has recently been a trend to more nutritious types of pie crusts through the use of bran flour, whole wheat flour, wheat germ, and defatted soy flour. These are used in small amounts and are blended with the flour before mixing. The use of these flours and grains will require an increase in the amount of water used because of their high absorption qualities. These ingredients will also require a minimum of mixing to avoid toughness through gluten development. These protein-bearing grains are advantageously used when preparing a graham cracker crust so that their identity is not obvious to the consumer.

There are several different types of pie crust. These may be categorized as follows:

1. The flaky pie crust.
2. The mealy pie crust.
3. The long flake pie crust.
4. Pie crust for soft-filled pies (custard, pumpkin, etc.).
5. Prebaked pie shell or crust dough (custard, chiffon, meringue, and so forth).
6. Combination crust (mixture of pie dough and short dough).

Each of these pie crust doughs, with formulas and mixing procedures, will be explained below.

Fruit-Filled and Other Two-Crust Pies

The flaky, mealy, or long flake pie crust dough may be used for these pies. The flaky pie crust will provide a flaky tenderness. The mealy pie crust has the shortening blended with the flour in fine lumps before the addition of the liquid and other dry ingredients. This will make a short dough. The long flake pie crust dough is made by the formation of larger lumps of fat covered with the flour and mixed lightly. The large fat lumps are rolled in twice after the dough has been placed on the bench. This will reduce the lumps to long, thin flakes of fat which will provide the added flakiness to the baked pie crust.

Basic Pie Crust Dough

For the preparation of flaky, mealy, or long flake pie crust dough.

Ingredients	lb	oz	Mixing procedure
Pastry flour	10		Sift the flour. Add the shortening and rub
Hydrogenated shortening	7	8	together to form small lumps of fat covered with a coating of flour.
Cold water (variable)	3	8	Dissolve the dry ingredients in the water. Add to the above and mix lightly until the
Skim milk powder		2	water is absorbed. Do not overmix.
Salt		3	
Sugar		4	

Refrigerate the dough for several hours or overnight before using. This will enable the dough to mellow and the shortening to chill, making handling and rolling easier.

Mealy Pie Crust Dough Rub the shortening and flour together until fine lumps of fat and flour are formed. Do not cream the shortening and flour together. The amount of water or liquid may be reduced by 4–6 oz to avoid excessive dough wetness or stickiness. This is due to the fact that greater exposure of the flour makes absorption of the moisture rapid. Chill before using.

Long Flake Pie Crust Dough Made from the same formula as for the basic pie crust dough, the shortening is rubbed to form larger lumps about the size of a lima bean covered with flour. The liquid is added and folded in gently, only enough to absorb the moisture so a sticky dough is formed. Many pastry chefs will refrigerate the dough and use it as it is. Others may roll the dough out on the bench twice, giving a three-fold turn after each roll. This will roll out the lumps of fat to a thinner sheet. When not rolled out in this manner, the crust will be rolled when making the pie tops and bottoms. At this time, however, the lumps may be too thick and not well distributed which might cause the fat lumps to melt and produce holes in the crust. If this happens in the bottom crust, the filling will leak and stick to the bottom of the tin. Rolling the dough on the bench in advance of dividing and rolling the crust will ensure thinner lumps with resulting maximum flakiness.

When mixing larger amounts of pie crust dough in the mixing machine, use slow speed to avoid blending or creaming the fat and flour. Use a dough hook or flat beater to avoid overmixing the dough. Check the dough in the final stage for possible addition of water or a slight amount of pastry flour.

Apple Pie

Apple pie is the most popular of pies. It is often the specialty of the house. The "home-made" or "old-fashioned" character is often stressed. The pastry chef skilled in pie making will maintain a consistent uniformity of pie crust and pie filling. Apple pie fillings may include fresh apples, a combination of canned apples and fresh apples or canned apples alone, or frozen or chilled, cured apples. The following are recipes for the preparation of the fillings for apple pie:

Fresh or Frozen Apple Pie Filling

A firm, hard apple, with a mild degree of acidity or tartness is best used (Rome Beauty, Stayman, Jonathan, Spy). The apples are peeled, cored, and sliced into cubes. The size of the slices will depend upon the size of the apple. The frozen cured apples are also firm. They are cured to prevent discoloration.

Ingredients	lb	oz	Mixing procedure
Fresh apples (peeled and cored, or fresh frozen)	16		Mix the apples and sugar and allow to stand for 2 or 3 hr. Drain the apple juice and set aside
Sugar (variable, depending upon tartness and taste)	3		
Cinnamon		1	
			Place drained apples in prepared pie pans which have been covered with a bottom crust. Drained apple juice is cooked into a thickened syrup and added to apples after pies are baked.
Apple pie syrup (per qt)	2	8	Bring to a boil
Cornstarch		2	Dissolve the starch in half of the juice and
Tapioca flour		1¼	set aside
Sugar (variable)	1	8	
Remaining juice (approx.)	1	4	
Cinnamon (additional)		¼	Boil the sugar and salt with the juice. If more juice is present, increase the corn-
Salt		¼	starch
Juice and rind of one lemon (optional			

Add the dissolved starch and tapioca flour in a slow, steady stream to the boiling syrup, stirring constantly. Allow the syrup to thicken and start to boil. Remove from the fire and add the cinnamon and lemon. The syrup remains hot or warm until the pies are baked. The syrup is added to the pie by way of a funnel through the hole made in the top crust. This method avoids excessive steaming of the apples with undue shrinkage of the apple slices during baking. The high type of apple pie is made in this fashion for a home-made appearance.

Yield: 15 10-in. pies

Canned Apple Pie Filling

A solid pack canned apple is best used for pies. The apples should not be broken pieces nor should they be packed in syrup. A firm slice of apple is important. Avoid the use of applesauce as a blend with the apples.

Ingredients	lb	oz	Mixing procedure
Cornstarch		6	Dissolve the starch and tapioca flour in the
Tapioca flour		3	water and set aside
Water	1	8	
Sugar	1	8	Boil the water and sugar. Add the starch
Water	4	8	solution in a steady stream stirring con-
Salt		¼	stantly. Return to a boil
Sugar	2	4	Add and cook until clear and thick. Remove from the fire
Canned Apples (3 No. 10 cans)			Add the apples, cinnamon, and lemon and stir or fold in gently
Cinnamon (variable)		1	
Rind and juice of 1 lemon (optional)			

Place the filling into a clean, shallow pan and allow to cool before placing into pies. The filling may be refrigerated if not used immediately. Pastry chefs will often mix canned apple filling with fresh apples or fresh frozen apples to maintain an even filling texture and make the pie easier to cut and serve. This will require an increase in the sugar to sweeten the fresh apples. The extra sugar may be added with the juice drained from the fresh or frozen apples and cooked with the thickened base used for the canned apples. The pastry chef will use his judgment when a blend of apples is used.

Cold Process Starches and Fillings   A cold process starch or thickener is a starch that has been precooked or pregelatinized so that the starch will swell and thicken fruit fillings when mixed with cold water or fruit juices. No cooking is necessary. These are advantageous for the pastry chef who requires fruit pies in large volume. The pregelatinized starch is usually blended with the sugar and other dry ingredients and dissolved in the water and or fruit juice. These precooked starches are particularly useful when using frozen fruits packed in cans with added water and fruit. It is advisable to carefully follow the instructions provided by the manufacturer when using these precooked starches.

Making Apple and Other Two-Crusted Pies

1. It is important to have the basic pie crust chilled and the dough conditioned through resting in the refrigerator. Many pastry chefs will scale the dough into units for the size of the pies they make. For a 9-in. pie, approximately 9 oz of pie crust dough will be sufficient to cover the bottom of the pie. The top crust is thinner and covers less area than the bottom crust and should be scaled approx. 7 oz. These scaled units of dough are gently shaped into a round shape without overmixing the dough.

2. Grease the pie pans lightly to avoid sticking if the fruit filling runs out during baking. It will make releasing the slices of pie easier also.

3. Roll out the units of pie dough for bottoms on a flour-dusted cloth. Use bread flour for dusting. The cloth permits easier rolling of the dough without excessive use of dusting flour. The bottom crust should be an even ⅛ in. thick. Try to keep the dough in a round shape and just large enough to cover the bottom and side of the pie pan. A small amount of crust should extend over the lip of the pie pan. Measure the first one or two bottom crusts in the pan and then the others can be rolled with almost identical proportions. Place the bottom crust into the pie pan and be sure the entire pan is covered. If the dough is tender and hard to handle, fold the rolled out dough in half and place in the pie pan so that half the pan is covered and then unfold the other half to cover the rest of the pie pan. (Figs. 5.1 and 5.2).

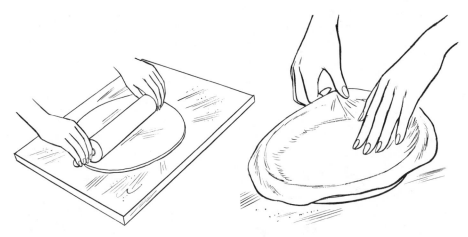

5.1
Rolled-out dough for bottom crust of pie

5.2
Cover bottom of pie pan with crust

5.3
Wash outside edge of bottom crust

4. When all the pans have been covered with a bottom crust, brush the edges around the rim of the pan with water or egg wash solution (Fig. 5.3). This will cause the top crust to stick to the bottom crust and help to keep the fruit filling from running out of the pie.
5. Fill the pie with apple filling. Fresh or fresh-frozen apples may be piled higher than the rim of the pie. In fact, many pastry chefs will pile the apples into a mound so that the baked crust will remain higher than the top of the pie pan rim. If canned apple filling is used, or if a blend of canned and fresh apples is used, fill the pie to the level of the top rim of the pie. Each pie pan should be filled equally (Fig. 5.4). You might wish to weigh or measure the amount of filling to be put into each pie pan.
6. Roll out the top pie crust units. They should be thinner than the bottom crust. Do not use scrap pie crust dough for the tops or even blend scrap dough with fresh for the pie tops or covers. The scrap dough will often cause the crust to shrink during baking and pull away from the edges of the pie. Be sure the crust is round and large enough to cover the entire pie. To cover all the fresh apples piled high, a larger amount of dough is needed.

5.4
Fill the pies evenly

5.5
Top crust rolled out and hole made in center

7. Cut a round hole in the center of the pie crust top with a 1-in. cookie cutter (Fig. 5.5). This will allow release and evaporation of steam during baking and allow the pie to be filled with syrup after baking. For canned apple pie filling, slits or cuts may be made in the crust with a scraper or knife since these pies do not require a syrup filling after baking. Place the top crust on the pie in the same manner in which the bottom crust was placed in the pie pan.
8. Crimp or seal the edges of the pie firmly with the fingers or a fork. Pie-making equipment will automatically do this (Fig. 5.6).
9. Cut the excess scrap dough from the edges of the pie and place to one side. The first scrap dough is usually blended or folded gently with fresh pie crust dough and used for pie bottoms again.
10. Remove the excess flour from the top crust and brush the tops of the pie with milk or melted butter or margarine for a dull, home-made effect. Egg wash is used to obtain a shiny brown crust color (Fig. 5.7).
11. Apple and other fruit-filled pies are baked at a higher oven temperature than are many other baked products. Apple pies are usually baked at 425–435°F. Pie crust dough has little sugar and is very thin. In addition, the fruit filling keeps the crust moist. Thus, a higher baking temperature is required to properly bake the pie crust, especially the bottom crust supporting the fruit filling.

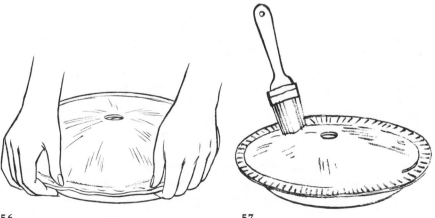

5.6
Seal edge of pie firmly

5.7
Pie is washed before baking

Some pastry chefs will sprinkle light cake crumbs on the bottom crust of the pie before adding the fruit filling. The cake crumbs will absorb part of the moisture of the filling and allow the crust to bake through thoroughly and avoid the sogginess of a raw bottom crust. Pies are to be baked only long enough to bake the crust and soften firm, fresh fruits. Overbaking will cause the fruit filling to boil and fillings may tend to boil out the sides of the pie even if the pie edges are sealed carefully. Very often a fruit filling with a high sugar content will break through or crack the top crust of the pie if baked at a lower oven temperature. Larger pies (10- or 12-in. pies) are often shifted in the oven after baking for 15 or 20 min. This will expose the bottom crust of the pie to fresh over heat and ensure a proper bake. Pies are tested for doneness by gently shaking the pie after the top crust has sufficient color. If the pie moves freely in the pan it is a sign the bottom crust is baked through. Pastry chefs usually are familiar with the baking characteristics of the oven and know when the pies and other products are fully baked. Remove the pies carefully from the oven. Avoid tilting baked pies as this may cause the fruit filling to run out.

Pineapple Pie Filling

Ingredients	lb	oz	Mixing procedure
Crushed pineapple (unsweetened) (3 No. 10 cans)			Place the fruit contents into a fine collander and drain the juice. Place drained fruit aside. Place the juice, sugar, and syrup on
Sugar	3		the fire and bring to a boil
Drained juice or a blend of juice and water	6		
Corn syrup (optional)		12	
Drained juice and water	1	8	Dissolve the starch and tapioca flour in the water. Add to the boiling syrup in a
Cornstarch		12	steady stream, stirring constantly. Boil
Tapioca flour		3	again
Sugar (variable)	2	8	Add the sugar and boil again. Be sure the
Yellow coloring (optional)	(few drops)		mixture is clear. Remove from the fire and add the drained, crushed pineapple
Rind and juice of 1 lemon (optional)			

1. Unsweetened pineapple is usually in fine, crushed form and requires more sugar. Crushed pineapple or pineapple pieces packed in light syrup will need a lesser amount of sugar. Judgment must be used.

2. Use the drained syrup to cook with additional water to form the thickened base for the fruit.
3. Some pastry chefs will add pineapple chunks or leftover sliced pineapple to the filling. This will enrich the fruit qualities of the pie.
4. Pineapple that is lacking in color, usually the crushed variety that is more economical to use, may require a few drops of yellow coloring to make it more appealing. The corn syrup will improve the luster of the fruit filling.

Yield: Approx. 15 10-in. pies

Canned Cherry Pie Filling

Cherries used for canning and pie making are the sour-pitted variety that have a high degree of acidity. Starch or some other thickening agent must be added to bind the fruit base and prevent excessive "leaking" or "bleeding" after the pie is baked. A blend of cornstarch and tapioca flour is recommended. The sour pitted cherries do not have the same degree of color or redness as do the other sweet fresh cherries. Pie cherries are usually packed in water rather than syrup. This means that the filling will require additional sugar for sweetening. To restore the natural look or redness to the cherries, a few drops of red coloring are added to the cooked stock or base before folding in the cherries which have been drained. This will avoid excessive mixing after the cherries have been added to the cooked base.

Ingredients	lb	oz	Mixing procedure
Canned, sour-pitted cherries packed in water (3 No. 10 cans)			Drain the water or juice from the cherries. Dissolve the starch in the juice or water and set aside
Canned juice or water	2		
Cornstarch		10½	
Tapioca flour		3	
Juice and water	5		Dissolve the sugar in the juice and bring
Sugar	3		to a boil
			Add the dissolved starch solution in a slow steady stream, stirring constantly and boil again.
Sugar	3		Add the sugar and boil again. Add the
Red coloring	(few drops)		coloring and lemon juice and mix in well
Juice of 2 fresh lemons			

Remove the cooked filling from the fire and gently fold in the drained cherries. Allow the filling to cool before using.

Yield: 15 9-in. pies

Frozen Cherry Pie Filling

Frozen, canned cherries and other frozen, canned fruits used for pies, are packed in 30-lb cans. They may also be purchased in 10-lb containers. The cherries may be weighed separately for exactness in dividing the cherries to be cooked. Frozen, canned cherries are usually packed in water or a light syrup, with coloring and cherry flavoring added. This means that additional sugar and syrup will be added to the stock or filling base.

Ingredients	lb	oz	Mixing procedure
Frozen cherries, packed in water or light syrup (½ of 30-lb. can)			Drain defrosted cherries and set aside
Drained juice and water	2		Dissolve the starch and tapioca flour in the juice and water
Cornstarch		12	
Tapioca flour		2	
Drained juice and water	4		Boil the juice, sugar, and syrup. Add the dissolved starch in a slow, steady stream and boil again
Corn syrup	1		
Sugar	1	8	
Sugar	3		Add the sugar and stir in well

Remove from the fire and gently fold in the drained cherries. If a cold process starch is used and the filling is not cooked, follow the instructions listed on the precooked starch package for amounts to use and the procedure to follow.

Yield: Approx. 15 9-in. pies

Blueberry Pie Filling

Canned blueberries are packed in water. Very often huckleberries may be packed as blueberries. The huckleberry closely resembles the blueberry although it is slightly smaller, somewhat darker in color, and has some seeds which are noticeable in pies. However, the berries are interchangeable and make excellent pies. The blueberries should be drained carefully and all the water or juice used to prepare the fruit stock or base for the pie filling. Additional water is added if there is not enough juice in the can.

Ingredients	lb	oz	Mixing procedure
Drained water and juice	2		Dissolve the starch and tapioca flour in the juice and water
Cornstarch		10	
Tapioca flour		3	

Juice and water	5	8	Dissolve the sugar in the juice. Bring to a
Sugar	2		boil. Add the starch solution in a slow,
Corn syrup		12	steady stream, stirring constantly. Bring to a boil once again
Sugar	2	12	Add the sugar and mix in well. Remove from fire
Drained blueberries			Add the blueberries and cinnamon and
Cinnamon (op- tional)		¼	stir in gently

Yield: Approx. 15 9-in. pies
Note: The tapioca flour will provide an added sheen and mild flow consistency to the filling. It has a gelatinous effect rather than a short, binding effect. However, cornstarch may be substituted. The cinnamon is optional. Cinnamon will add to the flavor of the filling.

Frozen Blueberry Pie Filling

Frozen blueberries are packed in cans that vary in weight. For the larger production needs, 30-lb cans are used. The blueberries are defrosted by leaving the cans at room temperature or by placing the cans in warm water baths for quicker defrosting. Frozen blueberries are usually packed with some sugar and syrup added. The sweetening must be taken into consideration when cooking the fruit. Be sure to drain the blueberries well by allowing for a complete defrost. Partially defrosted berries will release the ice crystals and moisture after being added to the cooked hot base causing a thin or watery fruit filling.

Ingredients	lb	oz	Mixing procedure
Frozen blueberries, ½ of 30-lb can			Drain all the fruit. Measure half of the water and syrup pack. Scale half the fruit and return to the other half of the water and syrup. Refrigerate unused half
Water and syrup	2		Dissolve the starch and tapioca flour in the
Cornstarch		12	juice and water
Tapioca flour		3	
Juice and water (variable)	4		Bring the sugar and juice to a boil. Add the starch solution in a steady stream and
Sugar	2	8	boil again. Cook until thick and clear. Remove from fire and add sugar and cinna-
Sugar (variable, depending upon the sugar content in the can when packed)			mon and lemon. Stir in well. Pour the cooked stock over the berries and fold in gently. The berries may be deposited on top of the filling and then stirred
Cinnamon		¼	
Juice of 1 lemon (optional)			

Yield: 12 9-in. pies

Strawberry Pie Filling

Fresh strawberries in season make excellent pies. Pastry chefs will often advise the purchase of strawberries at a reasonable price during the season. The fresh strawberries, if overripe or slightly blemished, will be used in the filling base. The ripe, fresh strawberries will be added to the filling after cooking the base. Pastry chefs will also blend frozen strawberries with fresh strawberries for a richer fruit filling. The fresh strawberries also improve the appearance and taste of the pie filling.

Fresh Strawberry Pie Filling

Ingredients	lb	oz	Mixing procedure
Fresh strawberries (use soft or blemished)	(3 quarts)		Stir the strawberries, sugar and corn syrup with the water. Place on the fire and boil. Stir to prevent scorching
Sugar	3		
Water	4		
Red coloring	(few drops)		
Corn syrup		12	
Water	2		Dissolve the starch and tapioca flour and add to the above in a steady stream stirring well. Boil until thick and clear
Cornstarch		9	
Tapioca flour		3	
Sugar (variable, depends on quality and taste of the strawberries)	1	4	Add the sugar and lemon juice and stir well to dissolve
Lemon juice (2 lemons)			
Strawberries (fresh)	(3 quarts)		Fold gently into the above

Additional red coloring may be added at this time and stirred in carefully. Avoid excessive redness and dark tinges of color. Be sure the strawberries have been hulled carefully and washed before use.
Yield: Approx. 12 9-in. pies

Frozen Strawberry Pie Filling

Ingredients	lb	oz	Mixing procedure
10-lb can frozen strawberries (whole or halves)			
Drained juice and water	1	8	Dissolve the starch and tapioca flour and set aside
Cornstarch		6	
Tapioca flour		2	

Juice and water	3		Boil the juice and sugar and corn syrup.
Sugar (variable, depends on sugar content of the canned berries	2		Stir well. Add the starch solution in a steady stream and boil until thick and clear. Be sure to stir constantly. Pour the filling base over the berries and stir in
Corn syrup		8	gently. Add the lemon juice and the color-
Drained berries			ing and stir in gently
Juice of 1 lemon			
Red coloring (variable)	(few drops)		

To further enrich the fruit filling (increase the fruit content) pastry chefs will often fold in sliced, fresh strawberries. This will also improve the natural, fruit-like appearance of the pie as well as improve the taste. A strawberry flavoring may be used to strengthen the flavor of berries that may be somewhat starchy and flat. The use of increased lemon juice will improve the tartness of the fruit. The increased acidity of the lemon juice may require a slight increase in starch to balance the effect of increased acidity.

Yield: Approx. 8 8-in. pies

Canned Peach Pie Filling

Canned pie peaches are sliced and in a water pack, sometimes called a solid pack. These peaches are usually broken pieces or slices with slight blemishes. They may be packed in a light syrup. If so, the sugar content of the peach pie filling must be adjusted for sweetness. There will be variations in the color of the slices and it will be necessary to add some yellow coloring to the fruit filling base when it is cooked to provide a better color uniformity.

Ingredients	lb	oz	Mixing procedure
Juice and water[1]	2		Dissolve the starch and tapioca flour in the
Cornstarch		9	juice and water. Set aside
Tapioca flour		3	
Juice and water	4		Dissolve the sugar, salt in the juice and
Sugar (variable)	3		water and boil. Add the starch solution in
Salt		¼	a steady stream and boil until thick and clear. Stir constantly
Sugar	2		Add the sugar and coloring and stir in
Yellow coloring (as needed)	(few drops)		well. Pour over the fruit and stir in gently
Drained peaches			

Additional coloring may be added at this time. If the filling is somewhat flat or lacking in tartness, add the juice of one or two lemons to the

---

[1]Drain the juice and add enough water to meet the needs of the recipe.

filling. Pastry chefs may add additional slices of fresh or canned fruits (peaches) to improve the appearance of the pie filling. Leftover peach halves or slices may be cut into chunks and added.

Yield: Approx. 12 9-in. pies

Canned Apricot Pie Filling

Canned apricots are packed in halves or slices and are usually packed in water. There is a solid pack that contains very little water or syrup. The syrup present is essentially the natural juice of the apricot. Canned apricots are to be cooked the same way as canned peaches. If canned apricots of a better quality are used (those packed in light syrup) allowance should be made for the sugar content of the syrup.

Yield: Approx. 12 9-in. pies

Canned Frozen Apricot Pie Filling

Ingredients	lb	oz	Mixing procedure
Frozen apricots, 10-lb can			
Juice and water	1		Dissolve the starch and tapioca flour in the
Cornstarch		5	water. Set aside
Tapioca flour		1½	
Sugar (variable)	1	8	Boil the sugar, salt, and juice. Add the
Salt	(pinch)		starch solution in a steady stream and
Juice and water	2	8	boil. Stir constantly
Sugar	1		Add the sugar, lemon juice, and coloring
Juice of 1 lemon			and stir in well. Add the drained fruits
Yellow coloring	(few drops)		and fold in gently
Drained apricots			

If fancy apricots packed in syrup are to be added, it is advisable to drain and then cook the syrup with the drained water and syrup from the cans. The drained, fancy apricots are then added after the filling base has been cooked.

Yield: Approx. 8 to 9 8-in. pies

Apricot Prune Pie Filling

Dried prunes are used as a blend with apricots to make this pie filling. The dried prunes are soaked or steeped in boiling water to soften. The prunes are then pitted and blended with apricot filling. Stewed prunes are often used. These prunes are drained and folded in with apricots when the base is cooked. The prune juice may be added with the juice and water to be used for the filling base for the apricots and cooked together. This will make a slightly darker filling base. The percentage of prunes to apricots used will vary with the preference of the chef. Some will use approximately 60% apricots and 40% prunes. Others may use an equal amount of each type of fruit. Adjustment will have to be made in the sugar content of the pie filling. If California prunes are used, then little or no sugar is required because these prunes are naturally sweet. If Oregon prunes are used, additional sugar will be necessary to remove the tartness of these prunes, if this is desired.

If dried apricots are used in conjunction with dried prunes, the apricots are soaked and then boiled in the water in which they are soaked. The first soaking water may be eliminated if the apricots are washed first. For each pound of apricots (dried) that are to be soaked and cooked add 3–4 lb of water. Simmer the apricots until most of the water has been absorbed and the apricots plumped. Add 2 lb of sugar and boil at low heat for about 10 min. Thicken slightly with a small amount of cornstarch dissolved in water. The plumped and pitted prunes are then gently mixed in with the apricots. Pastry chefs will often add a small amount of better quality canned apricots to the filling for improved appearance and taste.

Making and Baking Fruit-Filled Pies

Different fruit-filled pies will require particular attention both in makeup and in baking. For example, a cherry pie should be handled quite differently from an apple pie. Apples, because of the natural pectin content, will not run during baking. That is, the filling and the apples are bound or thickened by the natural pectin in the fruit as well as by the starch in the filling base. Cherries, especially the sour-pitted variety used for pie filling, are more acid in content and require a larger amount of sugar to sweeten the filling. The acidity and the high sugar content will cause the fruit filling to expand during baking. This is true for other fruits that are of higher acid content and have higher percentages of sugar in them. Thus, while apple pies may be filled to the very top of the pie pan, and fresh apple or frozen apple pies are filled above the level of the pan, cherry pies, blueberry pies, and similar fruit pies are filled to less than the rim of the pie pan. The fruit will expand during baking and the filling will tend to run out of the edges of the pie or break through the top crust of the pie and run out of the cracks in the pie crust.

As indicated previously, pies should be baked in a hot oven. This will allow for the bottom and top crusts to be baked before the filling reaches an internal boiling temperature. Baking in a cooler oven will allow the internal temperature of the filling to reach the boiling point before the pie crusts are fully baked and have reached a desired crust color. Note is made of the fact that fillings which have less than 50% fruit as compared with liquid and sugar base will tend to spread or run much more than the richer (more fruit) fruit fillings. Fruit fillings that have not been thickened sufficiently, either through a lack of thickeners used or improper cooking of the filling, will be thin and tend to run and expand during baking.

Lemon Pie Filling   (For two-crust pie)

Lemon pie filling may be purchased in prepared form. You need only place the pie filling in the pie bottom and cover the filling with a pie crust top. Many pastry chefs prefer to prepare their own lemon pie filling. It enables them to control the taste and quality. Fresh lemons or dried lemon powder may be used. Frozen lemon concentrate is another source of basic lemon juice. For added lemon flavor, the rind of fresh lemon is added to the prepared filling. If the lemon powder is used, follow the instructions provided on the package. There are powders of varying strengths and directions for use will vary.

Ingredients	lb	oz	Mixing procedure
Water	6		Dissolve the sugar and salt in the water
Sugar	3	12	and bring to a boil
Salt		¼	
Juice of 12 fresh lemons (vary with size of lemons)[1]		12	Dissolve the cornstarch in the water. Add the egg yolks and whip in slightly. Add a small portion of the boiling solution gradually to the egg-starch solution and whip
Water	3		in slightly. Add the starch solution to the
Cornstarch (variable)[2]	1		boiling sugar-lemon syrup in a steady stream
Egg yolks	1		
Rind of 4 lemons			Allow to boil until thick and clear, stirring
Butter		8	constantly with a wire whisk. Remove from the fire and add the lemon rind and butter. Stir briskly until the butter is dissolved and thoroughly distributed.

1. The lemon pie filling is the same as a custard filling. It is precooked and ready to eat. However, placing the filling in a two-crusted pie means that the filling will be exposed to heat once again during the baking. Therefore, the pie should be baked at a high temperature so that the crust is baked more rapidly than that of a fruit pie. This will prevent the lemon filling from boiling out during baking. In fact, pastry chefs will chill the lemon filling before filling the pie.
2. The top crust of the pie should be slightly thinner than fruit pie tops for a more rapid bake. The top crust should be vented to allow for the escape of steam or moisture evaporation during baking. The baking temperature for lemon pies is approximately 450°F. The pies should be shifted slightly during baking to ensure a proper bake of the bottom crust. Some pastry chefs will use a partially or lightly baked bottom crust for lemon pies. This will ensure a complete baking of the bottom crust and will require a shorter baking time.

[1]Lemon concentrate should be diluted before use.
[2]If more eggs are used, especially whole eggs, less starch is required to thicken the lemon filling. The eggs are a binder. Allow the filling to cool before using.

3.   The lemon pie filling should be of medium soft consistency when cooked. The filling will thicken slightly during the baking process. Lemon pie should have a slight spreading effect or softness when served.

Yield: Approx. 10 9-in. pies

Mincemeat Pie Filling   *(For two-crust pie)*

The pastry chef will probably purchase prepared mincemeat filling for pies rather than spend time, labor, and a high cost for the preparation of his or her own mincemeat. Since this type of pie is usually served during the Thanksgiving and Christmas seasons, the large quantity required is usually purchased. However, pastry chefs will add additional ingredients to the mincemeat before making the pies. For example, additional fruits (dried) that have been soaked in brandy may be added. Chopped nuts or nutmeats may be added as well. For those who wish to prepare their own mincemeat, the following recipe is provided:

Ingredients	lb	oz	Mixing procedure
Dried, sweet fruit peel	5		Soak the fruits in a syrup of rum and some brandy for a period of 12–24 hr. The amount of brandy will vary with cost and quality. A syrup cooked with brown sugar is best
Raisins	5		
Currants	4		
Chopped fresh apples (drained canned apples may be used)	5		
Beef suet (variable)	8–10		Grind the suet through a medium fine grinder

Mix all ingredients together well for thorough distribution. If nutmeats are to be added, they should be added last. The nutmeat will provide a resemblance of suet in the filling. Many of the less costly mincemeat fillings that are purchased do not have any suet in them. Since mincemeat is rather thick and requires little cooking during the actual baking of the pie, pastry chefs may use a prebaked or partially baked pie bottom for the pies. This will reduce the baking time. Bake the mincemeat pies at 435–440°F.

Yield: 12 9-in. pies

Rhubarb Pie Filling

Although not a fruit but the stem of a plant, rhubarb is often included in listings of variety fruits. The natural juice present in these stems is quite acid and tart. The rhubarb used for pie filling is canned rather than fresh. The grades of rhubarb will vary from fancy, packed in heavy syrup, to standard grade packed in water. The standard grade is most often used by pastry chefs for making rhubarb pie.

Ingredients	lb	oz	Mixing procedure
3 No. 10 cans of standard rhubarb packed in water			Drain the rhubarb and add enough water to the juice for 3 quarts (6 lb). Dissolve the starch in the water and set aside
Juice and water	2		
Cornstarch		9	
Tapioca flour		3	
Water	4		Dissolve the sugar and bring to a boil. Add the starch solution in a steady stream and boil again
Sugar	3		
Sugar	3		Add the sugar and lemon juice and mix in well. Remove from fire and add the drained rhubarb. Fold in carefully
Juice and rind of 2 lemons			
Nutmeg (optional)		1/8	

If fresh rhubarb is used for the filling, use approximately 15 lb of rhubarb cut into small lengths of about 2–3 in. long. Add the rhubarb after the sugar and water have been boiled and thickened with the starch and tapioca flour. Boil this mixture for about 3 min.

Yield: Approx. 15 9-in. pies

Raisin Pie Filling

Seedless raisins should be used for pie filling. The raisins should be allowed to soak in order to reabsorb moisture and insure the natural plumpness. The water used for soaking may be used in the preparation of the pie filling. This will help retain the natural sugar and flavor of the raisins. Raisins should be washed well before being soaked. The amount of time for soaking raisins will depend upon their freshness. Raisins dried out because of age will require a longer soaking period. Raisins should be fully plumped before cooking.

Ingredients	lb	oz	Mixing procedure
Raisins (presoaked)	10		Cook 1/2 with the water
Water (use the water in which the raisins were soaked. Add more if necessary)	10		Bring all of these ingredients with 1/2 of the presoaked raisins to a boil. Stir well while cooking
Sugar	3	4	
Salt		1/4	
Shortening or butter	1	2	
Lemon juice (variable)		8	
Corn syrup or glucose	1	8	

Corn starch (variable)	1	Dissolve the starch in the water. Add to the above in a steady stream, stirring constantly, and boil
Water (cool)	3	

Remaining presoaked raisins (about 5 lbs)	Add to the above and continue to boil for about 1 min.

Rind of 3 fresh lemons (optional)
Cinnamon (optional and variable)

Allow the pie filling to cool before adding to the pie shells. If the percentage of raisins is increased, the amount of starch used to thicken the pie filling may be reduced slightly.

Open-Faced Pies

Single Crust Fruit Pies

Open-faced pies are made without the full cover of a pie crust top. A special top may be used for a lattice effect. Other pies may be baked with a crumb (streusel) topping. Still others may be finished with a fresh fruit top and then garnished with a special glaze or apricot coating. Lattice-top pies are made by rolling out a piece of chilled pie crust dough into a rectangular shape about ⅛ in. thick and about 12 in. wide. With a knife or pastry wheel cut the pie dough into strips about ½ in. wide (Fig. 5.8). Wash the rim of the bottom crust of the pie. Place the strips of dough, spaced evenly, in a criss-cross fashion across the top of the pie. They may be placed in a diagonal manner to form diamond-shaped spaces between the strips of dough. The strips may be brushed with egg wash or melted butter or margarine before placing on top of the fruit filling. This will avoid smearing the fruit filling if the strips are brushed after being placed on the pie. (Fig. 5.9.) For crumb-topped pies, such as apple crumb or blueberry crumb, sprinkle the tops of the pies with streusel-crumb topping. This is the topping used for crumb buns and coffee cakes. Crumb-topped pies are usually dusted with confectioners sugar when cool and then served.

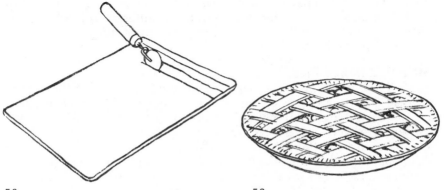

5.8
Cutting strips for lattice-top pies

5.9
Lattice-top pie

Open-faced fruit pies are usually garnished after baking with sliced or whole fresh fruits. For example, fresh or canned peaches may be used to garnish a peach pie. Fresh strawberries are commonly used to garnish or cover the top of a strawberry pie. These fruits are glazed to promote a luster as well as to prevent discoloration of the fruit due to oxidation. The glaze sweetens, colors, covers, and protects the fresh fruit. It also holds the fresh fruit in place when the pie or fruit cake is cut for service. Canned apricot coating or glaze is used as the base for the glaze. The coating is boiled with a blend of simple syrup or glucose in equal amounts. This will dilute the apricot coating and make a tender covering. Additional coloring may be added to enhance the appearance of the fruit. Red coloring is added for the strawberries. A few drops of yellow coloring is added to the glaze for peach or apricot fruits. The glaze is boiled and then applied while hot. When the glaze cools it firms up, but it remains tender to cut and does not drag along with the knife.

Neutral Fruit Glaze

Ingredients	lb	oz	Mixing procedure
Sugar	5		Dissolve the sugar and bring to a boil
Water	4		
Corn syrup or glucose		8	
Water	1		Dissolve the starch in the water. Add to
Cornstarch		7	the above with the lemon juice and boil
Lemon juice (optional)		2	again, stirring constantly. Add coloring as required and use while hot

Soft-Filled Pies

Soft-filled pies have two major categories. The first concerns itself with custard-type fillings which have to be baked in a pie shell until the filling sets as a cooked pudding. During the baking period, the pie shell is also baked. The second category includes the custards, chiffons, and other fillings that are precooked and then poured or deposited into prebaked pie shells. Each of these categories requires a different approach to pie production both in the type of pie crust and in the preparation of the filling and the topping.

Soft-Filled Baked Pies

The shell or bottom for these pies is leaner in fat content than the regular pie crust. This is necessary to support the soft filling and yet bake through. Rich pie crust doughs will not bake through and have a tendency to fall apart when served. The pie bottom for the soft-filled pie contains about 35% fat based upon the total weight of the flour.

The dough is medium soft. It may be scaled into units weighing approximately 10–12 oz for the 9-in. pie pan. The units of scaled pie dough may be chilled before using. If a pie shell machine is used, be sure the doughs are not overly chilled and thus resist the formation of the shell by the die. Check the sides of the pie shell (upper rim of the pie pan) for evenly ridged edges.

Pie Crust for Soft-Filled Pies

Ingredients	lb	oz	Mixing procedure
Sugar		5	Sift all the dry ingredients together to
Salt		2	blend well. Add the shortening and blend
Skim milk powder		4	in well to a smooth consistency. Do not
Pastry flour	7	8	cream
Shortening	2	8	
Water (variable)	3		Add the water and mix to a smooth dough

1. Roll out the units of dough on a floured cloth. Be sure the dough will cover the bottom and the sides of the pie pan. It is advisable to have the pie pan lightly greased with melted shortening.
2. Fold the dough in half. Pick up and cover half the pie pan. Unfold the remainder over the rest of the pie pan.
3. It is advisable to further thin the bottom center of the crust. This is done by taking a rounded piece of dough and dipping it into bread flour. Pat the bottom crust with the dough toward the sides of the pie pan. Do not make the dough too thin. (Fig. 5.10.)
4. Press the sides of the pie pan so that the dough is forced to the very rim. Do not form any holes by pressing too hard.
5. The dough at the sides of the pan should now extend about ½ in. above the rim of the pan.
6. Flute the edges of the dough with the fingers to form a scalloped design. (Fig. 5.11.)
7. The formed pie shells are usually allowed to stand for a period. This will cause a mild crust formation on the surface of the dough. The light crust does help to prevent the soft filling from seeping through causing a soggy and raw bottom crust after baking. It is quite common for pastry chefs to place a liner with beans in the pie shells and bake them until half baked. After the shells have cooled, the beans

5.10
Thin the bottom by tapping with ball of dough

5.11
Flute the edge with the fingers

5.12
Filling the pie shells

are removed and the filling is added. This will ensure a thorough bake. For large-scale production, the pastry chef will make the shells by machine and bake the pies directly in the raw dough. (Fig. 5.12.)
Yield: Approx. 15–18 9-in. pies

Baked Custard Pie Filling

Ingredients	lb	oz	Mixing procedure
Sugar	2	8	Blend dry ingredients together
Salt		½	
Skim milk powder	1		
Cornstarch		3	
Whole eggs (shell eggs preferred)[1]	2	8	Whip the eggs with a wire whip to blend well. Add to the above
Water		8	Add the water and vanilla in a steady
Vanilla		2	stream and blend in. The melted butter is
Butter (melted)[1]		6	added just before filling the pies

1. The oven temperature should be approximately 440–450°F. Place the pie shell in the oven and then fill each shell using a long handled dipper. Fill the pies to the edge of the pie pan.
2. After the pies have been filled and have started to form a crust fill the pies to the very top with added custard.

---

[1]Whole eggs will blend in better than frozen eggs and there will be less chance of the formation of egg particles in the baked custard. Egg yolks may be used to replace the need for cornstarch or other thickening agent. This will also increase the cost of the pie. The melted butter is not a required ingredient but will enrich the pie. Pastry chefs who make custard pies with cost limitations should use only eggs and milk and light cream to make the pies. The melted butter will add richness found in the cream. Allow the prepared custard mix to stand for about ½ to 1 hr. This will allow the starch to absorb some of the liquid and to bind properly during baking. Stir the mix well before filling the pies.

5.13
Distribute coconut over pie bottom

3. The pies should be allowed to form a light brown crust. The oven temperature may be reduced to about 390°F, after the pies have been in the oven for approximately 20 min. The pies are considered baked when they have a mild shimmer and feel slightly firm to the touch. Pastry chefs will insert a pointed knife into the pie. If the blade comes out clean, the pie filling is baked.

Yield: Approx. 12 9-in. pies

Coconut Custard Pie Sprinkle the bottom of the pie with shredded (a medium shred is preferred) coconut before filling the pies. Avoid sweetened coconut, or the coconut may burn when exposed to heat at the top of the pie. (Fig. 5.13.)

Pumpkin Pie Filling

Most pastry chefs use canned pumpkin rather than prepare the filling from fresh pumpkin. The time and effort required to cook (steam) and then strain fresh pumpkin makes it rather expensive. The quality of the pumpkin pie can be improved through the addition of eggs, milk, and melted butter. The pumpkin serves as the base. Canned pumpkin is very satisfactory for making quality pumpkin pie. The choice and amount of spices used are equally important. A mild blend of a selected spice mix or careful blend of selected spices is necessary. The pie shells are prepared the same as for custard pies.

Ingredients	lb	oz	Mixing procedure
Brown sugar	1	4	Blend all dry ingredients together
Granulated sugar	2	12	
Salt		¾	
Skim milk powder	1	8	
Cornstarch		8	
Tapioca flour		2	

Cinnamon (variable)	1		
Nutmeg	½		
Eggs	3		Whip the eggs slightly. Add to the above and blend well
Corn syrup or glucose	1	8	Add the corn syrup and pumpkin and blend in well. Add the water in 3 or 4 stages and blend in well
Pumpkin (2 No. 10 cans)			
Water (variable)	12		

1. The amount of water to be added depends upon the quality of the canned pumpkin. The pack may contain more water and this will reduce the absorption. A solid pulp will absorb more liquid.
2. The amount of thickening will also have a decided effect upon the filling consistency. Allow the filling to stand for at least 1 hr before filling the pies. This will allow for maximum absorption of liquid by the pumpkin and for partial absorption by the starch or other thickeners. An increase in the amount of eggs will tend to have a slight thickening effect and will also require a reduction in the amount of starch used.
3. Pastry chefs may wish to add melted butter or margarine to the filling before pouring into the pie shells. If this is done, approximately 12 oz–1 lb of melted butter may be added to the above.
4. Pastry chefs may also prepare the filling in advance and store the filling in the refrigerator overnight and use it as required. The filling should be stirred well before filling the pies. This will properly blend in the starch and thoroughly dissolve and distribute the sugar and spices which may settle to the bottom if not used for an extended period.
5. Fill the pie shells after they have been placed in the oven and proceed as for the custard pies. Bake at 435°F. Reduce the temperature to 390°F during the final stages of baking. Avoid overbaking. This is usually the cause for the separation of the sugar and syrup and the formation of a syrupy solution on top of the pie.

Yield: Approx. 15–18 9-in. pies

Cheese Pies and Cheese Pie Fillings

The same pie crust dough is used for the shells as for the custard and pumpkin pies. The cheese filling is basically similar to a custard-type filling. It will have slightly more consistency because of the absorption of moisture by the cheese. These pies are made primarily with bakers' cheese. Some pastry chefs will vary the formula and use half cream cheese. They may also fold in beaten egg whites into the basic cheese batter to form a lighter type of cheese filling. Where the chiffon type of cheese filling is used, the pie shells are prebaked or lightly baked before the cheese filling is added. The following recipe presents a more economic type of cheese pie.

Cheese Pie Filling

Ingredients	lb	oz	Mixing procedure
Bakers' cheese	10		Blend the cheese and flour together. Set
Cake flour	1		aside
Sugar	4		Blend the sugar, salt, milk powder, and
Salt		2	shortening together. Add the cheese and
Skim milk powder	1	8	blend in at slow speed
Butter or shortening	1		
Eggs (part yolks)	2		Add the eggs in 3 stages and blend in. Scrape the sides of the mixing machine kettle
Vanilla		2	Add the vanilla and lemon rind. Add the
Rind of 2 lemons			water in 4 stages and mix at slow speed
Water (variable)	4–5 lbs.		

1. The consistency of the filling should be that of a medium thick gravy. It may be necessary to hold back part of the water or add additional water. This will depend upon the quality or dryness of the cheese. A firm, dry bakers' cheese will absorb and retain more water. This is a decided advantage in increasing yield and controlling costs.

2. Variations in cheese pies may be made with the addition of fruit fillings. The very popular pineapple-cheese pie is made by lining the center of the pie crust with pineapple before filling the pie. Pastry chefs may also cover the top of the baked pie after it has cooled with pineapple filling or other fruit filling. Slices of pineapple (canned) may also be spaced for each serving and the top of the pie glazed with a fruit glaze or apricot coating.

3. Cheese pies made with the regular soft-filled, baked pie crust are baked in a rather hot oven (425°F) with the pies placed directly on the hearth or shelf of the oven. If the cheese pies are made in pre-baked or partially baked pie shells, the pies are usually baked on double pans. The high oven temperature will form a crust over the cheese quickly; this will cause the top of the pie to rise in the oven without excessive cracking.

4. The pie is baked until it has formed a light brown ridge or crust around the edge of the pie. The center of the pie us usually very light. The pie is considered baked when it springs back gently to the touch. The center should not be firm (this will indicate excessive baking). The pies will be about 1/2–1 in. above the edge of the pie crust rim. The filling will settle to the level of the pie rim as the pie cools.

5. If cream cheese (approx. 50%) is blended with the bakers' cheese, the filling will be slightly firmer when baked.

6. During baking, it is advisable to shift pies that have been lined with fruit filling to ensure a well baked bottom pie crust.

Yield: Approx. 15 9-in. pies

For the lighter, chiffon-type cheese pie, a recipe using beaten egg whites is used. The bakers' cheese may be blended with cream cheese or the filling may be made entirely with bakers' cheese. This is matter of cost. It is also advisable to use prebaked shells made from the special pie shell dough used for precooked custard-type pies. The shells are baked and then placed into the pie pans for filling. The pies are baked at a lower baking temperature.

Chiffon Cheese Pie Filling

Ingredients	lb	oz	Mixing procedure
Sugar	2	8	Mix on second speed until soft and
Salt		1½	smooth. It is not necessary to cream light
Skim milk powder		8	
Butter	1		
Shortening	1	4	
Egg yolks	1		Add the yolks and part of the whole eggs
Eggs	2		to the above and blend in well
Bakers' cheese	4		Blend the cheese and flour together. Add
Cream cheese	3		the remaining eggs and blend in. Add to
Cake flour		8	the above and mix smooth at slow speed
Bread flour		4	
Water (variable)	3		Add the flavorings. Add the water in 4
Vanilla		1½	stages and blend in. Use slow speed
Rind of 3 lemons			
Egg whites	2	4	Whip to wet peak and fold lightly into the
Sugar	1	4	above

1. The filling before the addition of the beaten egg whites should be that of a thick gravy. Hold back on the water slightly if the cheese filling should not be able to readily absorb it.
2. The quality of bakers' cheese will vary even when purchased from the same distributor. Bakers' cheese that has been frozen may tend to release part of the moisture content when defrosted. It may not absorb as much water as fresh bakers' cheese.
3. The quality of the cream cheese contributes to the absorption as well. Cream cheese that has a large percentage of gum or other binders may not hold as much liquid either. Judgment must be used.
4. Deposit the cheese filling into the baked pie shells as soon as the egg whites have been folded in. A delay will cause a loss in some of the chiffon qualities of the baked pie due to the decrease of some air cells formed in the whipped egg whites.
5. Fill the pie shells to the very edge of the rim. For the fruit-filled pies, spread the desired fruit filling in the bottom center of the pie. The filling will tend to spread during baking.
6. Bake the pies in pans that have been filled with water so that at least ½–1 in. of water will cover the bottom of the pie pan. This will

prevent the bottom crust from becoming overbaked or burned. Remember the pie shell has already been baked. Bake the pies at 415–420°F until the pies have risen about 1 in. above the rim of the pie pan.

7. Reduce the temperature to approximately 385–390°F. The pies will tend to brown evenly over the entire surface of the pie. There will also be a slight cracking in some places. The cracks will come together as the pie cools and recedes slightly in the pan after baking. These pies may also be garnished on top with a fruit filling and glazed after they have cooled.

Yield: Approx. 15–18 9 in. pies

Pecan Pie Filling

Pecan pie filling is a soft filling that is rich in sugar and syrup. The syrup content will vary from corn syrup to honey or even a light molasses. There may be a blend of these syrups or each syrup may be used singly. This will depend upon the formula, since formulas for pecan pies have many sources. Most of these are from the southern areas of the country. Basically, most recipes are similar in content and the variations are not extreme. Of importance is the type and quality of the pecans used for the pie. In most instances the pecan halves or large pieces are deposited on the bottom of the unbaked or partially baked pie shell before the filling is placed in the pie. The top of the filling is usually garnished with pecan halves before the pie is baked.

Ingredients	lb	oz	Mixing procedure
Light corn syrup	12		Combine the syrup and sugar with water.
Honey (clover)	2	8	Use the wire whip on the mixing machine
Water	12		at slow speed to dissolve and blend all in-
Sugar	4	8	gredients
Salt		2	
Cake flour	2	14	Sift the flour and blend in
Eggs	4		Whip eggs slightly to combine the yolk
Vanilla		2	and white. Add with the flavorings to the
Cinnamon		¼	above in 3 or 4 stages and whip at slow
Melted butter	1		speed. Add the melted butter and blend in
			at slow speed. Do not whip the batter to
			aerate it

1. As previously indicated, an unbaked pie shell or a prebaked (lightly baked) pie shell may be used. Where the shell is unbaked, it is advisable to sprinkle pecan halves or large pieces on the bottom crust. This will help to avoid sogginess since the nuts will tend to absorb some of the moisture. When baked pie shells are used, the pecan halves are liberally sprinkled over the top of the pie filling before baking.

2. Fill the pies almost to the very rim of the pie shell. Bake at 350°–365°F until the pie is set. Larger and deeper pies will require a lower baking temperature for a longer period of time. It is important to remember that the filling is rich in sugar content and will rapidly form a dark crust color if baked at high temperature.
3. It may be advisable to bake the pies that have prebaked pie shells on double pans to avoid excessive browning of the pie crust. An oven with a sharp bottom heat will certainly require baking on double pans.
4. The pies are considered baked when they have a moderate firmness in the center to indicate that the filling has set, when a knife inserted into the pie comes out clean. The pecan pies should not be over-baked (this will cause cracking and seepage or "bleeding" of the syrup). A film of syrup often forms on the top, and often on the bottom of the pie, due to separation of the syrup from the body of the pie.

Yield: Approx. 15 9-inch. pies

Sweet Potato Pie

Canned sweet potatoes are usually used for these pies. Mashed sweet potatoes will blend in readily with the pie filling. Canned potatoes that are whole or partially mashed should be mashed. Fresh sweet potatoes that are boiled with jackets should be mashed after the jackets or skins are removed. It is advisable to taste the mashed sweet potatoes for sweetness. Where the taste is flat or lacking in sugar, a slight adjustment should be made in the formulary.

Ingredients	lb	oz	Mixing procedure
Sugar	2	8	Sift and blend all dry ingredients
Salt		3/4	
Cinnamon (variable)		1/2	
Nutmeg		1/8	
Ginger		1/8	
Cake flour		2	
Corn starch		4	
Nonfat dry milk	1		
Eggs	4		Add the eggs and blend in well in two stages
Molasses	1		Add and blend in well
Mashed sweet potatoes	10		Add and blend in well
Water (variable)	8		Add in 3 or 4 stages and blend in well
Melted butter or margarine		8	Add and blend in

Note: The consistency of the filling should be that of a gravy. This will thicken as the filling stands for a period of about one hour. Starchy, soft sweet potatoes will absorb more liquid. Fibrous and coarse sweet potatoes will not absorb as much. Use judgement when adding the liquid.

The pie crust normally used for a soft-filled pie, such as pumpkin pie, is used to make the shells for the sweet potato pies. Allow the pie crust shells to dry slightly before filling. Allow the sweet potato pie filling to rest for about one hour before pouring into the pie crust. The pie filling may be stored in the refrigerator for later use. **Be sure to stir the pie filling well before filling the pies.** Fill the pie shells almost to the top. Bake the pies at 390–400°F. The center of the pie should feel slightly firm or set before removing from the oven.

Shoo-Fly Pie

The pie filling should be deposited in lightly prebaked pie shells. The usual prebaked pie shell dough may be used. A combination pie crust dough composed of equal parts of regular pie crust and short dough that have been mixed together may be used.

Ingredients	lb	oz	Mixing procedure
Sugar	1		Blend these ingredients well until soft and
Salt		½	smooth
Brown sugar	1	4	
Butter or margarine	1		
Shortening	1	4	
Baking soda		1	
Cinnamon		¼	
Eggs	2		Add in 3 stages and blend in well after each addition
Molasses	2	8	Add in 3 stages and blend to a smooth
Honey or corn syrup (Pancake syrup may be used)	2		consistency
Water	2	8	Add the starch gradually to the water and
Precooked corn starch (Regular corn starch dissolved in part of the water and added to the boiling water and cooked to a gel may be used.)		3	stir well. The water should be in gel form. Add to the above and stir in
Cake flour	3	12	Sift the flour and mix into the above. Mix until smooth.

Fill the prebaked pie shells (lightly baked) three-quarters' full. Sprinkle the top of the pie with streussel topping that has been blended with chopped nuts. Bake at 360°F. The center of the pie should feel slightly firm.

Prebaked Pie Shells

Pie fillings that are precooked and deposited into shells are ready to be finished and served. This means that the pie shell must also be cooked or baked and be ready for consumption without further baking. There are several types of doughs that are used for making the prebaked pie shells. Pastry chefs who make the shells individually, as required, will use their own special dough or a combination of doughs to give them the desired dough characteristics. Where large numbers of pie shells are required for mass feeding, the shells are usually made by a pie shell-making machine. The doughs must be tailored to meet the pressures of the dies and the heat application. This is an automated system of production. The formulas that follow are those which have been tested and are applicable to all forms of pie shell dough and the making of prebaked pie shells. The dough should be chilled before using. The dough may be divided and scaled into units for each pie. Weights will vary with the size and depth of the pie pan. The average thickness of a shell for a 9-in. pie will require approximately 12 oz of dough. The units may be shaped into round form ready for rolling.

Special Prebaked Pie Shell Dough

Ingredients	lb	oz	Mixing procedure
Sugar	2	10	Blend these ingredients to a soft, smooth
Salt		3	consistency
Skim milk powder		6	
Corn syrup or glucose		8	
Hydrogenated shortening	5		
Eggs	1	4	Add the eggs in 2 stages and blend in well
Water	2	4	Add the water and vanilla and stir in
Vanilla		2	gently
Bread flour	2		Sift the flours. Add and mix to a smooth
Cake flour	6	4	dough. Use slow speed

1. Adjust the dies and plates for the pie shell-forming machine. Test the first shells for evenness of thickness and finish of rim. Adjust the dies and temperature plates if cracking of the crust occurs.
2. For hand-made shells, proceed as follows. Roll the scaled or measured dough units on a floured cloth. This will reduce the amount

of dusting flour required and avoid sticking. Roll out the dough to slightly less than ¼ in. thickness. Be sure the dough will cover the bottom and the sides of an inverted pie pan.

3. Grease the back of the pie pan lightly to prevent sticking even though the dough is rich in fat content. Lift the dough gently and place over the bottom and sides of the pie pan. Cover the dough with another pie pan of the same size. Trim the excess dough from the edges. Press the top pie pan down gently. This will ensure a flat surface on the baked pie shell. Remove the top pan and stipple or puncture the dough with a docker or fork. This will eliminate the possibility of blister or large pocket formation in the baked pie shell. Work the scrap dough in with fresh dough and scale additional units. (Figs. 5.14 through 5.17.)

3. Place the pie pans with the shells on baking sheet pans and bake at 400–410°F. Check the shells for proper bake by lifting the top pie pan. For complete bake on both sides, the top pan may be removed for good top heat and crust formation. The pans may be inverted to get complete baking on the inside of the crust.

4. Allow the baked shells to cool before removing from the pans. The baked shells may be stored in pie pans or special pie liners for later use. Most pastry chefs will keep a reserve of these shells ready for use. Fillings may be cooked quickly in an emergency.

Yield: Approx. 20–24 9-in. pie shells

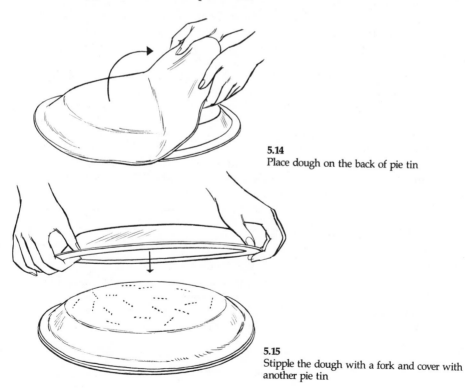

5.14
Place dough on the back of pie tin

5.15
Stipple the dough with a fork and cover with another pie tin

5.16
Trim excess dough

5.17
Bananas are placed in the custard, evenly
spaced

Short dough or sugar dough is often used to make the baked bottoms for large fruit cakes or cobbler-type cakes filled with cooked fruit fillings. The fillings are the same as those used for regular fruit-filled pies. This dough is also used for prebaked bottoms for cheese cakes and other cakes that require a short dough bottom to support the body or filling of the cake. For the smaller type fruit cakes (6–8 in. pans) the fruit cake bottom is not prebaked. However, this dough is often used in conjunction with pie crust dough for making prebaked pie shells. Pastry chefs will often hold the first scrap pie crust dough left over from making fruit pies to blend with the short dough in equal proportions. The doughs are blended in the mixing machine until smooth and evenly distributed. If stiffness or a slight toughness exists, a small amount of melted butter or shortening is added to increase the shortness of the dough. This maintains the short, cookie-like effect of the baked shell.

Short Dough or Sugar Dough

Ingredients	lb	oz	Mixing procedure
Sugar	6		Dissolve the sugar and other dry ingredi-
Salt		2	ents in the liquid. Scrape the sides and
Skim milk powder		3	bottom of the kettle to remove sugar and
Corn syrup		8	other particles sticking to the sides
Eggs	1	6	
Vanilla		1½	
Rind of 3 lemons			
Water	1	4	

Shortening	8	Add and mix to break up the shortening into small lumps
Cake flour	6	Sift the flours. Add and mix until a dough
Bread flour	6	is formed. Do not overmix to develop gluten

1. This dough does not have to be developed until completely smooth. The dough is usually worked smooth on the bench when being rolled. The same applies to sending the dough through the sheeter for rolling out for cake bottoms or for cut-out type cookies.
2. Refrigerate the dough to firm up the shortening before rolling. This will decrease the amount of dusting flour needed for rolling or sheeting. It is also advisable to roll the dough on a cloth if rolling is done by hand.

Combination Dough for Prebaked Pie Shells   Combine equal amounts of pie crust dough with an equal amount of short dough. Mix smooth, refrigerate, and then roll out for pie shells. For specialty shells for special pies and for contrast in taste as well as appearance, melted chocolate (bitter or semisweet chocolate is preferred) is added to the combination dough when mixing. This will produce a chocolate colored dough with the flavor of chocolate. Pie shells may be made from this dough for contrasting color for cream-filled pies and other specialties. Pastry chefs will also make cream rolls from this chocolate combination dough by rolling the dough around the cream stick rolls. The chocolate shells are to be baked carefully for proper bake. Avoid overbaking since this creates a bitter taste. A chocolate fudge base may be used to color the dough and create the chocolate flavor.

Graham Cracker Pie Shells

Graham cracker pie shell dough is often used for pie specialties. It may be used for cream-filled pies as well as cold process cheese pies and cakes. The shells may be baked briefly and then used. They may also be chilled without baking and then used.

Ingredients	lb	oz	Mixing procedure
Ground graham crackers	5		Combine all ingredients in the mixing machine or large mixing bowl to form a mild
Cake flour		12	paste effect. Mix at slow speed. Grease the
Sugar (brown sugar may be used)	1		pie pans and press the graham crust to the
Melted butter	1		sides evenly
Margarine (melted)	1		
Melted shortening	1		

1. Be sure the crust is of even thickness throughout the pie pan.
2. Bake in a moderate oven for about 8–10 min or chill before using.
Yield: Approx. 12 9-in. pies

Precooked Pie Fillings and Fried Pies

The creativity of the pastry chef is often challenged by the need to control costs, particularly in large-scale food service institutions such as schools, colleges, hospitals, and other institutions where mass feeding is the practice. For the pastry chef in hotels and fine restaurants, as well as those in specialty catering service, cost is usually subservient to quality. À la carte menus indicate the cost of specialty desserts. For the cost-controlled pastry chef, the use of prepared pie filling mixes is perhaps the best answer. The fillings are quickly prepared, price- or portion-controlled, and uniform in the results obtained under controlled conditions.

Pastry chefs will often use the prepared pie filling bases and supplement the filling with additional ingredients. For example, a basic custard cream filling may be enriched with added melted butter and flavoring. The pastry chef may chiffon the custard with whipped egg whites. He may add whipping topping rather than heavy cream to the basic custard for Bavarian specialties and other specialty desserts. Very often custard desserts are used for pie fillings—chocolate pudding powders and vanilla custard bases, and lemon custards. These are good products and may be used extensively. In addition, prepared pie and pudding bases are now made with pregelatinized starches and other thickeners. They provide fillings for pies and other desserts which may be frozen without separation or curdling when defrosted. They enable the pastry chef to prepare the fillings in advance for later use. The recipes for fillings presented are those which reflect the skill and knowledge of the pastry chef.

Basic Custard Cream Filling

This filling may be used for vanilla cream pies as well as a variety of others, for cream puffs, eclairs, and even for the finishing of napoleons.

Ingredients	lb	oz	Cooking procedure
Sugar	4		Dissolve the dry ingredients in the water.
Salt		1	Place on the fire (medium flame) and bring
Skim milk powder	2		to a low boil stirring with a wire whip
Water (cool)	12		
Cornstarch	1	4	Dissolve the cornstarch in the water
Water (cool)	4		
Eggs	4		Whip the eggs slightly and add to the
Butter	1		starch solution. Blend in well. Add ap-
Vanilla		2	proximately ½ quart of the hot milk to the
			egg-starch solution. Add the egg-starch
			solution to the hot milk in a slow steady
			stream and return to a boil, stirring con-
			stantly. When thickened and smooth, re-
			move from the fire. Add the butter and
			vanilla and stir with a wire whip until the
			butter is completely dissolved

1. Pour the custard directly into the baked pie shells and allow to cool before finishing.
2. If the basic custard is to be used for finishing other pastries such as Boston cream pie or eclairs, the custard should be poured into clean and water-moistened pans, such as deep baking pans. The moist bottom and sides will keep the custard from sticking to the pan. Sprinkle the top of the hot cream filling with granulated sugar. The sugar will melt and form a protective syrup film which will prevent crust formation. The custard should also be covered with a parchment paper liner.
3. The use of skim milk powder eliminates the use of a double boiler for there is less chance of scorching the milk when stirred from time to time. A stainless steel cooking bowl is useful. Of course, steam cooking large batches in large steam cookers is best.
4. The addition of butter after the custard has been thickened will accentuate the richness present with the use of fresh whole milk.
5. The increased use of eggs and egg yolks will add to the richness and binding of the cream custard. This will require a lesser amount of cornstarch and other thickeners.
6. If the custard is stored in the refrigerator for later use, the chill will have a thickening effect upon the custard. It is best to mix the custard until smooth before using.

Yield: 12 9-in. pies

Coffee Pastry Cream Add approximately 8–12 tablespoons of freeze dried coffee crystals to the water and stir well to dissolve. The degree of coffee color and taste may be adjusted as desired. A coffee and mocha flavoring may be added for color contrast and flavor.

Chocolate Pastry Cream Melt approximately 8 oz of bitter chocolate and 8 oz of semisweet chocolate in a double boiler. Add immediately after the custard has been removed from the fire and stir in. The chocolate will be fully distributed when the melted butter and flavoring are being mixed into the custard cream. It may be necessary to reduce the amount of cornstarch by approximately 3–4 oz because of thickening properties of the chocolate. A chocolate pudding mix may be used for chocolate cream pie. A special chocolate cream custard will be listed for use.

Praline and Chocolate Chip Cream This may be made by folding in approximately 1 lb of praline paste (made by heating in a saucepan 1 lb of granulated sugar and 1 lb of hazel nuts until the sugar turns a light brown). Allow the paste to cool on a marble or stainless steel table and then grind or send through a fine chopper. Many pastry chefs are now using a variety of prepared crunches of various flavors and colors. Chocolate crunchies or chocolate chips or bits may be folded into the cream custard before filling the pies. There are a number of variety of crunchies which are particularly good for specialty use and garnishes. Pour into baked pie shells while hot.

Coconut Cream　Add approximately 1 lb of lightly toasted, macaroon coconut to the cooked cream. Stir in well to distribute and pour into the baked pie shells. Pastry chefs will often sprinkle some of the coconut on the bottom of the baked pie shell before filling the shells. Toasted coconut may also be used as a garnish.

Rum or Liqueur Flavored Custard Creams　These are made by adding approximately 4–8 oz of rum or liqueur to the custard or pastry cream. The rum may be supplemented with a rum flavoring. Additional cornstarch (approximately 2–3 oz) will be necessary to compensate for the softening effect of the rum or liqueur upon the cream. The liqueur or rum should be blended in at the time the butter is added.

Finishing Custard Cream Pies
The use of fruits and fruit fillings to finish custard cream pies is quite popular with many pastry chefs. The fresh fruits (such as bananas and strawberries), cherry filling, and others are popular.

Banana Cream Pie　Fresh, ripe bananas are sliced crosswise and placed into the custard cream after the pie has been half filled. The pie is then filled with custard so that the sliced bananas are covered. Bananas may be sliced lengthwise in halves or quarters, depending upon their size, and placed on top of the pie. The banana slices may be brushed with apricot coating and syrup before placing on the pies to prevent discoloration due to oxidation. The pies are then covered and decorated with whipped cream or a blend of whipped cream and whipped topping. Cost limitations may restrict the pastry chef to the use of whipped topping alone or the use of a stabilizer to extend the use of the whipped cream through the addition of more milk. (Figs. 5.18 through 5.20.)

Whipping Heavy Cream
Heavy cream containing approximately 36–40 percent butterfat should be used. The cream should be allowed to stand about 2 or 3 days to age. This makes for greater volume in whipping as well as stability when milk is added. A good, heavy cream that has been properly aged and carefully whipped should yield approximately three times its original volume. The use of stabilizers and milk will increase that volume substantially. The cream should be very cold, but not frozen. The utensils and mixing machine kettle and beater should be clean and chilled, especially in warm weather or under rather warm kitchen conditions.

5.18
Cross-section of banana cream pie

5.19
Decorating top of pie with whipped cream

5.20
Cover pie with meringue and make a spiral design

Whipping Cream and Cream Blends

Ingredients	lb	oz	Mixing procedure
Heavy cream (aged)		(3 qt)	Pour the cream into the chilled bowl or
Chilled milk	1	8	mixer. Rinse the cream containers with the
Fine granulated or confectioners sugar		12	chilled milk and add to the cream
Vanilla (variable)		1	

1. Whip the cream at medium speed until it forms a light froth. Add the sugar in a slow, steady stream while the machine is running and whip to a soft peak.
2. Add the vanilla and whip until the cream forms a medium peak (it will tend to fold slightly when picked up very much like a soft meringue).

3. Overwhipping will cause the cream to separate or bleed. Continued whipping will result in complete separation and the formation of butter.
4. The whipped cream should be kept chilled if not immediately used.
Yield: 12–15 9-in. pies

Whipped Cream Blends   An equal amount of whipped topping (there are many varieties that are purchased in 10 lb or 30 lb containers) may be blended with the cream. Since the toppings contain stabilizers and whip firmly, it is advisable to whip the topping first to a soft peak and then add the cream, milk, and sugar, and whip to the medium peak. Some pastry chefs prefer to whip the topping separately and combine both the topping and the cream after they have been individually whipped. One then has control of the percentage of the blend.

A meringue or marshmallow topping may be folded into the whipped cream to extend it. In warm weather this is done especially to maintain the body of the cream and prevent bleeding or separation. A meringue containing a stabilizer such as gelatin should be used to blend with the whipped cream. An Italian meringue is well suited

Italian Meringue

Ingredients	lb	oz	Mixing procedure
Gelatin		1½	Dissolve the gelatin in the water and set
Water	1		aside
Water	1		Combine the sugar and water in a sauce-
Granulated sugar	2	8	pan and boil to approximately 240–242°F
Egg whites	1	12	Whip the egg whites to a froth. Add the
Sugar		10	sugar gradually while whipping and whip to a soft peak. Add the hot syrup in a slow, steady stream and whip to a medium stiff peak. Add the dissolved gelatin and whip until medium firm and the meringue is cool. Fold into the whipped cream and dress out and finish the pies

Yield: Enough for 3 qt of whipped heavy cream

The taste of the cream will be affected if large quantities of meringue are blended with it. If a marshmallow powder preparation is used, follow the instructions supplied by the manufacturer.

The custard cream pies are finished in homemade fashion by placing the whipped cream on top of the pie and then finishing with a few swirls or decorations made with a bowl knife. A pastry bag or tube may be used to make a variety of designs and borders. Wet the canvas bag, if one is used, with cold water before filling with cream.

When using fresh fruits or fruit fillings to finish the custard cream pies, the fresh fruit should be washed and drained. The fruit filling should be cold. The chilled custard in the pie shell should be covered with a thin layer of sponge or chiffon cake. A high-ratio yellow layer cake may be used. The size of the cake layer should be sufficient to cover the top of the custard filling. Cut into slices aobut ¼ in. thick and place firmly on top of the custard. If fresh strawberries are used, first brush the top of the cake slice with a strawberry or currant jam or jelly. Set the whole or sliced strawberries neatly over the cake. The jam or jelly will hold the fruit in place. Brush the tops of the berries with a hot glaze of apricot coating and syrup that has been colored a light red. Allow the glaze to cool and then pipe a border of whipped cream around the edge.

Where fruit fillings are used, the prepared or cooked filling is spread over the top of the cake slice to about ¼–½ in. thickness. If fresh fruits such as blueberries or pineapple slices or chunks are to be used, a thinner film may be used to hold the fruits in place. The fresh blueberries may be sprinkled liberally over the top and then pressed gently into the filling. Dust lightly with confectioners sugar when served.

Canned slices of pineapple may be used to form designs across the tops of the pineapple filling and arranged for proper slicing and portion service. The sliced pineapple is glazed with a light syrup glaze blended with apricot coating. A little yellow coloring may be added to the hot glaze. A border of whipped cream may be piped around the edge of the pie if desired. The outer edge may also be firmed with some light sponge cake or yellow cake crumbs which have been lightly toasted.

Chocolate Pie Filling

Chocolate pie fillings can be prepared in several different ways. Each method has its own special advantages and also varies with cost. For example, chocolate pudding preparations may be used. The prepared powder is cooked per instructions and the filling poured into the pre-baked pie shells. Pastry chefs may use a recipe that calls for eggs, yolks, and butter. There are excellent inexpensive chocolate pie fillings that are made without eggs, and will result in a good tasting, smooth-textured filling.

Chocolate Pie Filling   (No eggs)

Ingredients	lb	oz	Cooking procedure
Water	10		Dissolve the sugar and milk powder in the
Sugar	3	6	water and bring to a slow boil, stirring
Salt		½	frequently
Skim milk powder		12	
Water	4		Sift the cocoa. Dissolve the starch and co-
Cocoa (dark)		11	coa in the water. Add about ½ quart of
Cornstarch		14	the hot milk to the starch solution, stirring constantly. Add the starch-cocoa solution to the boiling milk in a slow, steady stream and boil again until thick
Butter		10	Add butter and vanilla and stir well until
Vanilla (variable)		2	the butter is melted and well distributed

Pour the filling into the pie shells and allow to cool before using. Finish the tops with whipped cream or cover with meringue and brown in the oven as for lemon meringue pie.

Yield: Approx. 15 9-in. pies

Meringue-Topped Pies

Meringues are composed primarily of egg whites and granulated sugar, and usually contain a binding agent such as tapioca flour or cornstarch. There are a number of egg white stabilizers in powder form, which act as binders and prevent "weeping" of the egg whites after the meringue has been baked. The stabilizers also enable the pastry chef to obtain greater volume from the egg whites as the meringue is being prepared.

The kettle or bowl as well as the wire whip (hand or machine whip) must be clean and free of grease in order to whip the egg whites to maximum volume without collapsing. The egg white stabilizer contains additional albumen and helps prevent the egg whites from falling back. The suggestions and instructions for use of the dried egg white powder and stabilizers should be followed carefully. Meringues for pies are whipped to a medium dry peak (when touched with a finger, the egg whites will remain in a peak form).

Meringue Topping for Pies

Ingredients	lb	oz	Mixing procedure
Egg whites	3		Whip the egg whites to a light froth. Sift the sugar and starch or tapioca flour together. Add to the whipping egg whites in a slow, steady stream while the machine whips continuously
Granulated sugar (variable)	4		
Egg white stabilizer (follow instructions on container)			
Tapioca flour or cornstarch		2	

Check the consistency of the whipping egg whites. If the peaks are shiny and tend to fall over slowly, this is known as a wet peak. Mix slightly longer and the peaks will firm up and the shiny appearance of the egg whites will turn to a slightly dull color.

Yield: Approx. cover for 12–15 9-in. pies

Lemon Meringue Pies Lemon meringue pies are the most popular of the meringue-topped pies. The lemon filling used for lemon pies (two-crusted pies) may be used to fill the prebaked pie shells. For large volume and cost-controlled service pastry chefs will use commercially prepared lemon fillings. Some pastry chefs will chiffon the pies by adding whipped egg whites to the filling. The whites are added to the regular filling and will cook themselves as soon as the filling has been thickened and removed from the heat. The whipped egg whites will lighten the structure of the lemon filling and provide a light chiffon effect.

Lemon Chiffon Pie Filling

Ingredients	lb	oz	Cooking procedure
Water	6		Dissolve the sugar and salt in the water
Sugar	2	4	and juice, and bring to a boil
Salt		½	
Lemon juice (fresh, or reconstituted frozen)	1		(Follow instructions of the manufacturer if dried lemon powder is used.)
Water	2		Dissolve the starch and flour in the water.
Cornstarch		12	Add the egg yolks and whip in lightly.
Tapioca flour		1	Add about 1 lb of boiling syrup to the
Egg yolks	1	2	yolk-starch solution in a slow stream, stir-
Rind of 3 lemons			ring constantly. Add the starch-yolk solu-
Few drops of yellow coloring, if desired			tion to the boiling syrup in a steady stream, stirring constantly
Butter		6	

Bring to a boil until the filling thickens and has a clear luster to it. Add the butter and mix in well so that the butter is dissolved and distributed. Add the lemon rind and coloring with the butter and be sure they are well distributed throughout the filling.

	lb	oz	
Egg whites	2	8	Whip the whites to a froth. Add the sugar
Sugar	1	8	in a slow, steady stream and whip to a wet peak

Fold the whipped egg whites gently into the hot filling with a hand wire whip and be sure the egg whites are distributed evenly. Pour the lemon chiffon filling into the prebaked pie shells and allow the filling to cool before covering with a meringue topping. The filled pie shells may be chilled after the filling has cooled and then covered with whipped cream or whipped topping as for vanilla cream pies.

1. The meringue may be applied to the pie tops with a spatula or pastry knife. The amount of meringue and height of the meringue will depend upon the finish desired. (Fig. 5.20.)
2. The meringue may also be deposited into a pastry bag with either a plain tube or star or French tube, and the meringue bagged out into a variety of designs. Pastry chefs may make a rosette border design and garnish the top of each rosette with a large dot of lemon filling.
3. The meringue topping is dusted lightly with confectioners sugar before baking. The sugar will caramelize lightly and accentuate the edges and designs made on the meringue topping after baking.
4. Bake the meringue at 410–420°F. Allow about 10 min to bake the average 9-in. pie. Pies with a higher or thicker meringue topping require longer baking than the flat and shallow topping.

5. It is important to bake the meringue thoroughly so that the structure of the protein in the egg whites (albumen) is completely set. If baked too rapidly, the meringue will shrink and then "weep" (release the moisture) when the meringue cools on the pie.
6. A thin piece of sponge or yellow cake placed over the filling before putting the meringue on the pie will absorb any syrup which may be released from the meringue.

Yield: 15 9-in. pies.

Open fruit pies may be finished with a meringue topping. The fruit pies are cooled, additional fruits may be placed over the top, and then covered with a thin layer of sponge or yellow cake. The meringue is then placed over the cake covering and baked. The cake covering or slice provides a separation of fruit and meringue. It also provides a solid base for the meringue to avoid the formation of a syrup film between the fruit and meringue which could cause the topping to slide from the surface of the fruit as the pie is cut and served. The use of meringue is certainly less costly than the use of heavy whipping cream and it is an advantage to the pastry chef who is confined to portion control costs.

Fruit Chiffon Pies

Fruit chiffon fillings are made by adding whipped egg whites, gelatin, and sometimes whipped cream to the cooked fruit filling. Fruit flavored chiffon pies are also made from a prepared, flavored gelatin dessert powder to which fruits and fruit juices may be added. There are many variables and several formulas for these chiffon-type pies are presented. The creative pastry chef may further diversify the variety of pies.

Orange Chiffon Pie

Ingredients	lb	oz	Cooking procedure
Sugar	3	8	Dissolve the sugar and salt in the water
Salt		¼	and juice and bring to a boil
Butter		10	
Water	5		
Orange juice (fresh or remixed con- crate)	2		
Lemon juice (fresh or frozen or concentrate)		10	If powdered or crystalline orange and lemon are used, refer to the instructions provided by the manufacturer.
Water	2		Dissolve the cornstarch in the water. Whip
Cornstarch	1	3	the yolks and eggs slightly and add to the
Egg yolks		12	starch solution. Gradually add about 1 pint
Whole eggs		8	of the hot syrup to the starch-egg solution
Rind of 3 fresh oranges			and whip in. Add the starch solution to the boiling syrup in a steady stream, stir-

Rind of 2 fresh lemons			ring constantly and bring to a boil. Boil until the filling thickens and is smooth and clear. Stir in the fresh orange and lemon rind
Egg whites	1	4	Whip the whites to a soft froth. Add the
Granulated sugar	1	12	sugar gradually and whip to a wet peak

Fold the egg whites gently into the cooked filling. Be sure the whites are evenly distributed. Fill the pie shells with the hot filling and allow to cool. When cool, the pies may be covered with whipped cream or a blend of whipped cream and whipped topping. Other blends may also be used. Garnish with slices of fresh orange.
Yield: Approx. 10–12 9-in. pies

Strawberry Chiffon Filling

Ingredients	lb	oz	Cooking procedure
Fresh strawberries	(3 quarts)		Bruised and crushed berries may be used for the cooking base
Sugar	2		The strawberries should be cleaned,
Salt	(pinch)		hulled, and cut into small pieces. Bring the
Water	4		fruit, sugar, water, and lemon juice to a
Red coloring (variable)	(few drops)		boil
Lemon juice		4	
Water	2		Dissolve the starch. Add to the boiling
Cornstarch		8	fruit syrup in a steady stream and boil to a clear, thick filling. Add more coloring at this point if necessary
Fresh sliced or crushed strawberries	(2 quarts)		Place the strawberries, sugar and egg whites in the mixing machine and whip until thick. Add the dissolved gelatin and
Granulated sugar	2		blend at medium speed until thick. Fold
Egg whites	2		into the hot strawberry filling and mix un-
Gelatin		2	til thoroughly distributed. Pour into the
Water (warm)		8	prebaked pie shells
			The base for this filling may be made with prepared strawberry flavored gelatin dessert (commercial size packages, about 1½ lb per package). Follow the instructions on the package.

Pies may be filled above the rim and finished with a homemade effect using a spatula. The tops may be decorated with whipped cream and fresh strawberries glazed with red colored apricot glaze or heated currant jelly. The whipped part of the recipe may be folded into the gelatin dessert when it is cooled and about to jell firmly.
Yield: Approx. 12–14 9-in. pies

Pumpkin Chiffon Pie Filling

Ingredients	lb	oz	Cooking procedure
Canned pumpkin	(2 No. 10 cans)		Blend the sugar and other dry ingredients.
Sugar (brown)	2		Add to the pumpkin filling and mix in
Granulated sugar	2	8	well
Salt		1/2	
Cinnamon		1	
Nutmeg		1/4	
Ginger		1/4	
Egg yolks	2		Whip the yolks to a smooth consistency and blend into the pumpkin mixture
			Place the entire mixture in a double boiler or steam-jacketed cooker and cook until the filling thickens.
Gelatin		5	Dissolve the gelatin in the water. Add to
Water (warm)	2	8	the thickened pumpkin filling and mix in well

Allow the pumpkin filling to cool until warm before folding in the beaten egg whites. The egg whites will not maintain the lightness and air cells may collapse with continued mixing if added to the hot filling.

| Egg whites | 3 | | Whip the whites to a froth. Add the sugar |
| Sugar | 1 | 12 | gradually and whip to a wet peak. Fold into the cooled pumpkin filling. Be sure the beaten whites are distributed evenly |

Fill the prebaked pie shells and refrigerate. The tops of the pies may be finished with a whipped cream topping, or combination whipped cream and whipped topping.
Yield: Approx. 15 9-in. pies

Apple Chiffon Pie Filling
Solid pack canned apples may be used in place of applesauce. The apples are chopped finely and then used for the filling. Applesauce that contains a high percentage of moisture will require additional thickening in the form of starch or other thickener.

Apple Chiffon Pie Filling

Ingredients	lb	oz	Mixing procedure
Applesauce (or chopped canned apples)	(2 No. 10 cans)		Mix all the ingredients together until well blended. Place on the fire and bring to a boil. Stir well to prevent scorching
Sugar	1	8	
Brown sugar	2		

Ingredients	lb	oz	Cooking procedure
Lemon juice		2	
Salt		½	
Cinnamon		1	
Nutmeg (optional)		½	
Skim milk powder		8	
Water	3		
Water		8	Dissolve the starch in the water. Add the
Cornstarch		3	yolks and blend in. Add to the boiling ap-
Egg yolks	1	8	plesauce and boil again, stirring constantly
Water (warm)	2		Add the dissolved gelatin and stir in well.
Gelatin		6	Allow the filling to cool

The apple filling will cool faster if spread over stainless steel baking pans. When cool, return the apple filling to a large bowl.

Ingredients	lb	oz	Cooking procedure
Egg whites	3		Whip the whites to a froth. Add the sugar
Granulated sugar	1	4	gradually and whip to a wet peak. Fold the whipped egg whites into the cool apple filling. Fill the prebaked shells

Yield: Approx. 15 9-in. pies

Cherry Chiffon Pie Filling

Ingredients	lb	oz	Cooking procedure
Cherries [1] (2 No-10 cans sour-pitted, water packed)			Drain the juice from the cherries and set aside. Chop the cherries into fine pieces for easy distribution in the filling
Sugar	4		Bring the chopped cherries, sugar, and
Juice and water (drained)	3		water to a boil
Lemon juice		2	
Water or juice	2		Dissolve the starch in the water. Add to
Cornstarch		10	the boiling cherries in a steady stream, and boil, stirring constantly. Cook until thick and clear
Water or juice	1		Dissolve the gelatin in the water. Add to
Gelatin (unflavored)		5	the fruit filling. Stir in well. Allow the filling to cool. When cool, return the filling to a large bowl
Egg whites	3	8	Whip the whites to a froth. Add the sugar
Sugar	2		gradually and whip to a wet peak. Fold beaten whites into cooled fruit filling

Deposit into baked shells. Chill and finish or decorate with whipped cream.
Yield: Approx. 15 9-in. pies

[1] Frozen cherries may also be used, but reduce the amount of sugar and coloring.

Whipped Cream Pie Fillings (Bavarians)

The whipped cream pie fillings are a form of chiffon pie filling. Whipped cream is added to the cool vanilla cream base which is also thickened with the addition of dissolved gelatin. In the formulas or recipes to follow, a neutral unflavored gelatin powder is required. The gelatin must be completely dissolved in order to be distributed evenly throughout the basic cream filling.

Basic Custard Cream Filling for Bavarians

Ingredients	lb	oz	Cooking procedure
Sugar	2		Dissolve the sugar and milk powder in the
Salt		½	water. Bring to a boil. Stir to prevent
Skim milk powder	1		scorching
Water	6		
Cornstarch		8	Dissolve the starch in the water. Whip the
Water	2		eggs slightly and whip into the starch.
Egg yolks	1		Add about 1 cup of hot milk to the starch
Whole eggs	1		and whip in. Add the starch solution to
			the boiling milk and sugar in a steady
			stream, stirring constantly. Boil until thick
			and clear
Butter		10	Add the butter and vanilla and mix until
Vanilla (variable)		1	smooth. Dissolve the gelatin in the water
Gelatin		5	and stir into the custard. Pour the custard
Water	1		into clean, wet baking sheet pans and
			sprinkle lightly with granulated sugar. Allow the filling to cool in the refrigerator.
			Place a parchment paper liner over the
			custard to prevent crust formation.
Heavy whipping cream	(2 quarts)		Whip the cream to a froth with the milk
			used to rinse the cream containers. Gradually add the sugar and stabilizer and whip
Cold, fresh milk	1		the cream to a medium soft peak. Fold the
Whipped cream stabilizer (if available)		1	whipped cream gently into the cooled basic custard cream
Sugar		6	
Egg	1	8	Whip the egg whites to a froth. Add the
Sugar		12	sugar and whip to a wet peak. Fold the
			whipped egg whites into the custard
			cream soon after the whipped cream has
			been gently folded in. Blend in carefully
			and evenly

Deposit the filling into prebaked pie shells. Fill the pies above the rim and round out the tops with a spatula. Chill the pies and finish with whipped cream if desired

Yield: Approx. 12 9-in. pies

Note: A graham cracker crust may be used for variety.

Nesselrode Cream Pie   Add approximately 2 lb of prepared nesselrode fruit filling to the basic Bavarian cream filling. Additional rum flavoring may be added. To prepare nesselrode fruit filling, mix 1 lb of chopped, glazed cherries, 8 oz of diced citron, 4 oz of sugared orange peel (or an equal amount of mixed, dried, diced fruits) with a rum-flavored syrup and soak for about 4 hr. Drain the fruit well and fold into the basic Bavarian cream with the whipped cream. The top of the pie is covered with whipped cream and then garnished with chocolate swirls or pieces of shaved chocolate. To make the chocolate swirls, place chopped sweet chocolate into a pan and place in a double boiler of hot water. Mix the chocolate constantly until it is completely melted. Do not permit the chocolate to go beyond 86°F. Overheating will cause it to lose its luster and take on a gray appearance often called chocolate "bloom." If the chocolate is a little too soft add a little melted cocoa butter to thin it down. Pour the chocolate on a marble bench or table top and spread with a spatula to a thin layer. With the edge of the spatula blade scrape forward and the chocolate will form swirls as it curls up. If the chocolate cools too much, it will not curl and will have to be warmed again. Large swirls may be used for French pastries or chopped up for smaller chocolate shavings as for the top of the nesselrode pie.

Coconut Bavarian Cream Pie   This is made by adding 1½ lb of lightly toasted macaroon coconut to the Bavarian cream filling immediately after the filling has cooled and before folding in the whipped cream. The bottom of the pie shells may also be sprinkled lightly with toasted coconut. After the pies have been filled and chilled, cover with whipped cream and sprinkle the top of the cream with added toasted coconut. The edges of the pie may also be garnished with the toasted coconut.

Mocha Bavarian Cream Pie   Dissolve 2 oz of coffee crystals (a lesser amount may be used if a mocha flavoring and coloring are added) in the water when cooking the basic custard cream. Cover the tops of the pies with whipped cream and sprinkle the top with chocolate shavings. Fruits may be used to produce a greater variety of the Bavarian-type pies. Fresh fruits are often used to garnish the tops of the pies while canned fruits and cooked fruit fillings are often blended in with the cream filling.

Pineapple Bavarian Pie or Peach Bavarian Pie   These are made by chopping the larger pieces of canned fruits into smaller pieces and then folding the drained fruit into the basic filling when it has cooled and before folding in the whipped cream. A small amount of the cooked fruit pie filling may be deposited on the bottom of the baked pie shell before adding the basic cream filling. The chilled pies may then be covered with a layer of sponge cake or yellow layer cake about ¼ in. thick. The cake may be brushed with an apricot syrup to which a rum flavoring or liqueur has been added (optional). The pineapple slices or canned peach slices are then placed on the cake. The fruits are brushed with apricot glaze that has been colored slightly. The edge of the pie may have a whipped cream border piped around the edge. Toasted sliced almonds may also be used to garnish the edge of the pie.

Fried Pies

Fried pies are actually small units shaped in a semicircle or in a triangular form as a turnover. When pies are made with a round cutter varying in size from 3½–5 in. in diameter, there is a round bottom with a round top that have been carefully crimped together. The edges for all fried pies must be closed well to avoid opening during frying. The dough for the fried pies contains much less shortening or other fats than regular baked pies. This will avoid a crumbling crust during frying, releasing the filling. Pies are fried at a lower temperature than other fried goods such as doughnuts. The frying temperature of the fat or fried pies is usually 370°F. The pies are usually submerged in the hot fat and fried for about 4–5 min. The following pie crust for fried pies contains a small percentage of glucose or corn syrup to promote better crust color and to maintain crust tenderness after frying.

Pie Crust Dough for Fried Pies

Ingredients	lb	oz	Mixing procedure
Pastry flour or 75% cake flour and 25% bread flour blend	10		Rub the flour and shortening together to a small lump consistency. Use slow speed
Hydrogenated shortening	4	12	
Cold water (variable)	4		Dissolve the salt and glucose in the water and add to the above. Mix lightly to a
Salt		3	smooth dough
Glucose		6	

Allow the dough to mellow (condition) in the refrigerator for several hours. This will keep the fat firm and make rolling or sheeting the dough easier.

1. The fillings for these pies are thicker than regular baked pie fillings. Use an additional 2 oz of cornstarch for each of the pie fillings listed (recipes) for the regular baked pies. This practice applies to the use of canned fruits or frozen, fresh fruits packed in cans.
2. The pie crust dough for the fried pies is rolled out in a rectangular shape about ⅛ in. thick (Fig. 5.21). Dust with bread flour.
3. For automated and machine made pies, the dusting flour will vary with the equipment. The automatic equipment will function so that round, half-moon shapes are made, or pie bottoms and separate pie tops will be placed and crimped over the fillings.
4. For the bench made, the doughs are rolled out as above and the pie bottom and tops are cut out with a hand cutter 4 in. in diameter (Fig. 5.22). The dough may be cut larger if desired. If a pastry wheel is used, the dough is cut into squares of about 4–5 in. (Fig. 5.23).
5. The special filling is deposited in the center of the round cut-out bottoms or the squares (Fig. 5.24).

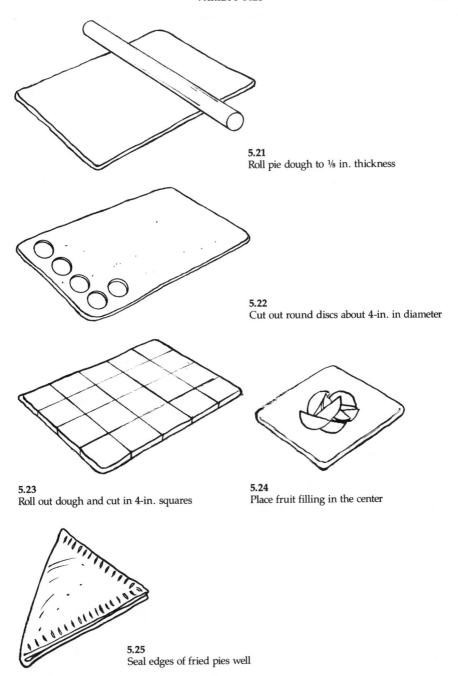

5.21
Roll pie dough to ⅛ in. thickness

5.22
Cut out round discs about 4-in. in diameter

5.23
Roll out dough and cut in 4-in. squares

5.24
Place fruit filling in the center

5.25
Seal edges of fried pies well

6.   The edges of the bottom crust are brushed with water. Fold the round
     half edges over and seal well. The squares may be folded into a rec-
     tangle or formed into a triangle shape. (Fig. 5.25).

7. Place the pies on a screen or griddle and deposit into the prepared hot fat. The pies may be turned when necessary to ensure proper frying and crust color.
8. The fried pies may be dusted with confectioners sugar when cool and served. They may be dipped in cinnamon sugar (apple variety) or they may be glazed with a hot glaze after frying.

Yield: Approx. 100–120 4-in. pies

6

Puff Paste and Choux Paste Products

Puff pastry dough has a wide variety of uses in the preparation of many desserts. Puff pastry products are light, airy, flaky, and tender. Napoleons and fruit-filled turnovers are two popular varieties. The dough, because of its special qualities, is used for many specialty products that contain other types of fillings and spices. The famous patty shell is simply puff pastry in one of its many variations. The baked patty shell is often used for hot meat, fish, or chicken dishes, as well as a wide variety of fruit and special fillings. The tiny pastry shells are used for special hors d'oeuvres with a wide variety of fillings.

Puff pastry dough, as well as the unbaked and baked products, can be refrigerated or frozen for lengthy periods. The pastry chef can prepare the products in advance and keep them on hand for use when needed. It is possible for the pastry chef or chef who wishes to purchase the ready prepared puff pastry dough to do so. These come in sheets and need only be defrosted and rolled and made up into desired products. There are the commercially prepared products, such as turnovers and patty shells, that are sold in a ready-to-bake form. These are defrosted lightly and baked. Of course, these prepared products are more costly than preparing the dough yourself. Most pastry chefs prefer to prepare their own doughs and thereby control quality, cost, and production.

There are two methods for preparing puff pastry dough, both of which apply to the rolling-in of the fat into the dough. In either case, the fat must be rolled into the dough, or the flour-fat lumps, similar to the long flake pie crust dough, are rolled-in to create the necessary layers of fat and dough. The success of the baked puff pastry is dependent upon the technique and method of preparing the dough and rolling-in the fat. There are basic ingredients used to make the dough and a selection of fats to be rolled-in. Each of the ingredients requires some explanation regarding its use and the relative importance of proper selection.

Bread Flour

The flour used for puff pastry dough must have a good quality gluten of sufficient quantity, like that in a good bread flour. Since the dough must be rolled extensively and the dough must sustain and retain the layers of fat formed in rolling, the strong flour is important. Some pastry chefs will modify a very strong bread flour with the addition of a small quantity of short patent flour (similar in character to a family or all-purpose flour).

Fat

The fat used is most often butter, margarine, a blend of butter and margarine, puff paste (a form of oleomargarine of higher melting point, or oleo-stearin) and hydrogenated shortening blended with either of the moisture-containing fats mentioned. The moisture in the fat contributes much to the leavening of the puff pastry products since there is no chemical or organic leavening agent used in the preparation of puff pastry dough. The matter of expense, quality, and unit portion control will determine the type of fats the pastry chef will use. Where quality is the most important factor, most pastry chefs will use a large percentage of butter with a blend of a harder type fat.

Salt

Salt is used primarily for the addition of taste, and to complement the flavors of other ingredients and fillings used in the dough as well as in the final product. Some formulas for puff pastry contain little or no salt since there is the opinion that the dough should be neutral. However, salt is important and contributes to the conditioning and mellowing of the dough after it has been rolled-in.

Eggs

Eggs are optional. The formula presented for the dough will contain eggs. They provide additional protein and increased food value, greater volume in baking, and add a mild color to the dough. When eggs are used in the dough, the amount of water used should be reduced based upon 75% of the weight of the eggs.

Acid Ingredient

Most pastry chefs will use lemon juice (the juice of three lemons is average) in the dough. Others will use cream of tartar or table vinegar. Each of the ingredients mentioned is an acid whose purpose is to relax the gluten in the dough more rapidly than would the natural acidity of the dough. In other words, it makes rolling-in the fat easier and quicker.

Excellent puff pastry is made without the use of acids. In addition, the use of acids will reduce the resting or relaxing periods required for madeup units before they are baked. The lower pH (increased acidity) mellows the gluten faster.

Water

The water used for the dough should be cold. In the summer, many pastry chefs use ice water, as they would for pie crust doughs, in order to keep the butter and other fats in a more solid form to make rolling-in the fat and handling the dough easier. Note that the dough is refrigerated between rolls while the dough is relaxing.

Fat Roll-in

Rolling-in the fat requires a special explanation. As previously mentioned there are two methods. The French method requires the full development of the dough first. There may be a small percentage of fat worked in with the dough to provide smooth extensibility for the gluten development. The dough is formed into a round shape and allowed to relax. The dough is then cut across the top to about half its depth and the four ends opened as a pocket. The roll-in fat is placed in the center of the dough and the four ends or flaps are used to cover the fat and the dough. Thus, all the fat is placed in one piece into the dough. The dough is then formed into a rectangular shape and rolled. The more conventional French method is to form the dough into a rectangular shape soon after mixing, allowing the dough to relax for 10 minutes. The dough is rolled out and the fat spotted over two-thirds of the dough. Then the dough is folded over the fat into a three layer effect. This will be further explained at the time of formula mixing. This method has the advantage of having the fat distributed more equitably and uniformly.

In the Scottish method, the flour and fat are rubbed together into medium large lumps and then hollowed out in the center. The eggs, if used, water, and other ingredients are poured into the center and the dough lightly tossed as for long flake pie crust dough. The sticky, lumpy dough is then placed on the bench and rolled-in several times. It is during the rolling-in of the fat and flour lumps that the gluten is developed. This method requires extensive use of flour in the initial stages of rolling and increase in the absorption of flour. This may lead to toughness and may not allow for complete distribution and layering of the fat and flour.

The leavening of puff pastry requires some explanation since no chemical or organic leavening is used. It will also indicate the importance of the rolling-in of the fat properly. The fat used for rolling contains a percentage of moisture such as that found in butter, margarine, oleo-stearin, puff paste, and others. The fat is rolled into the dough at least four times so that several hundred layers of fat and dough are formed. When the made up puff paste units are baked, the layers of fat and dough are raised or lifted by the partial evaporation of the moisture present in the melted fat as well as the moisture present in the dough. The pressure of the moisture or steam to escape creates this separation and upward, leavening effect. This creates the layered flakiness of the product. If eggs are used, the natural expansion of the eggs will also add to the leavening effect. Most puff pastry products are stippled or punctured with either a fork or roller stippler to make the necessary small holes in the dough. Through these holes, part of the steam created in baking will escape. Without these escape holes, large pockets are formed which later break and cause defects and handling or serving problems.

It is equally important to note that the units are rested for periods of ½ hour or longer, depending upon the type and size of the product. During this period, the gluten is relaxed in the dough. This enables the layers of dough to expand; it is the pressure of the escaping steam that creates the upward expansion of the layers of fat and dough. Should the dough units not be relaxed, the products or units will tend to shrink because the gluten does not expand in unison with the expansion rate of the escaping steam. There will also be a partial release of some of the fat in the layers, causing a greasy effect on the baking pan and the product.

Baking Puff Pastry Products

Because of the richness of the dough and the many layers of fat and dough, the puff pastry products are baked at moderate temperatures to allow for thorough and complete bake. One of the most common faults of puff pastry is that it collapses and/or shrinks after baking. Visualize the regular patty shell approximately 1½ to 2½ in. high that is not baked through properly. The centers will be raw or soggy and the sides will tend to collapse. Most units of regular portion size are baked at approximately 400°F during the initial period and then the temperature is reduced to about 375°F, or less, for the slower final baking. The structure of the gluten must be firmly set to support all the layers of fat and dough. In addition, rapid baking will cause an uneven rate of moisture conversion to steam around the bottom and top, as well as the sides of the unit. This will cause the center to shrink and a dark crust color to form too quickly. Pastry chefs will often cover puff pastry units with a greased parchment paper liner to avoid too rapid or too dark crust color. This is especially effective when the products are brushed with an egg wash before baking.

Units that have been made with scrap puff pastry dough, pieces of dough removed or trimmed from freshly rolled out dough, will require a longer prebake resting period in order to relax the somewhat toughened gluten in the dough. These units will also require a longer baking period at a lower baking temperature to avoid excessive shrinkage and possible loss of fat. Some products such as the rolled up pastry horns (mohn kipful) made with a poppy seed filling and napoleon sheets are representative of the puff pastry products in which the used or scrap dough is incorporated and rolled again.

Puff Pastry Products

Puff Pastry Dough

Ingredients	lb	oz	Mixing procedure
Bread flour	6		Sift the flour and cream of tartar and salt.
Cream of tartar [1]		2½	Blend in the shortening slightly. Add the
Salt		½	eggs and water and develop into a smooth
Shortening or but-ter		6	dough at medium speed
Eggs	1		
Water (variable)	4		

Place the dough on a floured portion of the bench and form into a rectangular shape. Cover the dough with a cloth and allow to relax for about 15 to 20 min. The dough should be medium soft consistency.

Roll-In Fat Preparation

Butter (firm)	4		Mix the butter at slow speed with the
Puff paste	3		flour until the butter is of a smooth,
Bread flour	1		plastic consistency. Blend in lightly with the puff paste

1. Roll out the relaxed dough on the bench to approximately ½ in. thickness, keeping a rectangular shape. Check the bench for enough flour to keep the dough from sticking. The sheeter, if one is available, can be used for rolling the dough. Remove the excess flour from the top surface of the dough with a bench brush.
2. Divide the dough into three equal sections. Dot the roll-in fat preparation in equal pieces over two-thirds of the dough, spacing the pieces evenly.
3. Fold the blank (without fat) section over one-third of the dough. Remove the excess flour from the folded section of the dough. Fold the other third of the dough covered with fat over the top of the dough, forming three layers of dough and two layers of fat. Seal the edges of the dough. (Figs. 6.1 through 6.4.)
4. Turn the dough into the long rectangular shape and roll out or send through the sheeter until an even ½ in. thick. Check the edges to keep the fat from running out.
5. Check the bench for sufficient dusting flour to keep the dough from sticking. Remove the excess flour and now fold the outside quarters of the dough into the center so that the edges of the dough meet.

---

[1] The juice of three lemons or 4 oz of table vinegar may be used in place of the cream of tartar. It may be necessary to increase the flour if either of these liquids is used.

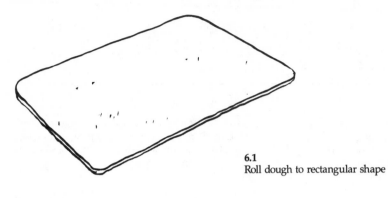

6.1
Roll dough to rectangular shape

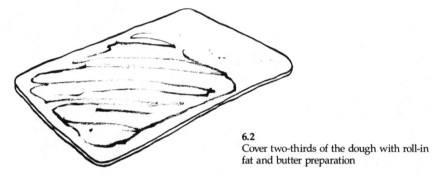

6.2
Cover two-thirds of the dough with roll-in
fat and butter preparation

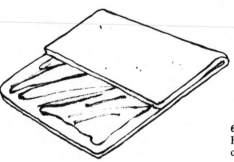

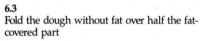

6.3
Fold the dough without fat over half the fat-
covered part

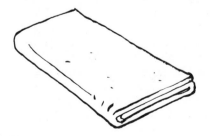

6.4
Fold the remaining ⅓ dough on top

6. Remove the excess dusting flour and now fold the outside section of one over the other to form four layers of fat and dough.

7. Refrigerate the dough for about 15–20 min and roll again. Fold in four sections again and relax in the refrigerator. Repeat this procedure two more times (four times in all).

8. After the final roll, remove the excess flour from the dough top and place the dough on a sheet pan. Brush the top of the dough lightly with vegetable oil and cover with a parchment paper pan liner. This will reduce the formation of a crust on the top surface of the dough. The bottom of the pan may be lined with a parchment paper liner or a floured cloth.

9. Refrigerate the dough for 12–24 hr to mellow or relax the gluten in the dough before using. This preconditioning of the dough will make handling and rolling the dough easier and will result in maximum volume of the product when baked.

10. The dough may also be placed in the freezer for an extended period. The high fat content makes the dough suitable for freezing. The dough should be kept wrapped in a poly wrap or freezer wrap to prevent crustation of the dough resulting from freezer circulation of air. It will also prevent partial dehydration due to evaporation loss. Keep the freezer temperature at 0°F or lower. Defrosting of the dough should take place slowly. The dough should be placed in the refrigerator for 24–36 hr for slow defrost to avoid breakdown of any of the fat and dough layers.

11. When rolling out the dough or sheeting, the dough should be handled without excessive pressure or force. For example, the rolling pin should have even pressure. Pounding on the dough will break or rupture some of the layers formed. The dough should be allowed to relax a bit while rolling. After the desired thickness has been reached allow the dough to rest or relax before cutting or dividing with a pastry wheel or knife. This will avoid shrinkage of the cut units of dough as in the cutting of the squares for the makeup of fruit-filled turnovers.

Yield: Approx. 100–120 units (turnovers) depending upon size of the unit
Uses: Pastries, fruit-filled desserts, French-type pastries, patty shells, hors d'oeuvres.

Patty Shells

Patty shells have many uses in food preparation and service. The pastry chef is responsible for their production. Because of their extensive use for many dishes and desserts, the shell made from the puff pastry dough is very important. For example, chicken á la king or a Newburg dish may be served on a patty shell. The tenderness of the patty shell, the height of the shell, and the ability to hold the hot filling are factors which contribute to the success of the dish. In addition, small patty shells are often used for a wide variety of hors d'oeuvres. The pastry chef uses the patty shells for many desserts that contain a variety of fillings. They make an excellent base from which the dessert may be developed to the final touches.

Patty shells may be made by two methods. One is to use a single cut-out patty. The other, is to use two cut-outs that are placed on top of each other before baking. The single dough shell is made by cutting out the round shell discs from a piece of rolled out puff pastry dough about ⅜ in. thick. The size of the round cutter will vary with the needs and specifications of the chef. Sizes may vary from the small 1 in. used for hors d'oeuvres to the large 3 in. used for more basic dishes and servings. The dough should be of even thickness throughout to ensure uniform sizes and even patty shells. The rolled out dough is stippled with a roller-docker or punctured with a fork. Space the punctures about 1 in. apart. Cut out the dough discs as close together as possible to avoid excessive scrap dough. Allow the cut discs to remain on the bench or table. Using a round cutter about half the size of the cut discs, cut into the center with the smaller cutter about halfway through. Avoid cutting all the way through. The center cuts will be removed after the patty shell is baked. Place the shells on pans lined with parchment paper and allow the shells to relax for about ½ hr before baking. The patty shells are usually washed with egg wash before baking to provide for a brown, shiny crust color. Bake the shells at 400–410°F. It is advisable to place a greased parchment paper pan liner over the tops of the shells after the first few minutes of baking. This will allow the patty shells to rise evenly. The oven temperature should be reduced during the final stages of baking to ensure a dry crispness in the center as well as the outside of the patty shell. The centers of the baked shells are removed with a small paring knife after the patty shells have cooled. The removed centers are often used as a garnish and should be kept intact. If not used, they may be saved for crumbling or chopping into small particles to be used as a garnish for other puff pastry products.

Patty shells made with two discs are completed as follows (Figs. 6.5 through 6.8):

1. Roll out the dough to about ⅛ in. thick. Check for even dough thickness.
2. Cut out the number of bottom shells desired. Cut out an equal number of top discs. With a smaller cutter, cut out the centers of the top discs.
3. Place the bottoms on parchment paper lined baking pans and brush them with water or egg wash.
4. Place the tops evenly over the bottom shells. Egg wash the tops if a shiny brown crust is desired. Allow the shells to relax and bake as the single shells.
5. Patty shells used for desserts may be filled with different fruit fillings, cream custard fillings, and other filling specialties. The tops of the shells may be garnished with a rosette of whipped cream and a slice of fresh fruit or berries. Chopped pistachio nuts or toasted almonds are often used as a garnish. The centers may also be filled with a special ice cream and covered with a sauce of a selection depending upon the creativity of the pastry chef. Fruit sauces that are hot or warm are often used.

6.5
Roll out dough ⅛ in. thick
and cut out

6.6
Bottoms are whole. Tops have centers cut out

6.7
Tops are placed on egg-washed bottoms

6.8
Baked patty shells

Note: The cut-out centers may be baked separately and used to garnish the tops of the patty shells after the filling has been deposited into the shells at the time of serving.

Napoleons (Mille Feuilles)

Napoleons are a very popular puff pastry dessert. They may be finished with a variety of fillings or filling combinations. The tops may also be garnished in a variety of finishes. Thus, the basic sheets are very important. The tenderness and flakiness of the baked puff pastry often determines the quality and success of the dessert. The pastry sheets are baked in regular baking sheet pans. It takes approximately 2 lb 4 oz of fresh puff pastry dough, evenly rolled out, to fill a sheet pan. The dough is rolled to an even thickness and then stippled or docked with a roller, or punctured with a fork before placing onto sheet pans that have been moistened lightly with water. The dough should be slightly longer and wider than the sheet pan. There is usually a bit of shrinkage during baking and the dough is pressed against the sides of the pan to allow for this. Allow the dough to rest about 1 hr before baking. Bake the sheets at 370°F for a slow even bake that will not cause too dark a crust color to form. The baked sheets may be stored if not used immediately. (Figs. 6.9 through 6.11.)

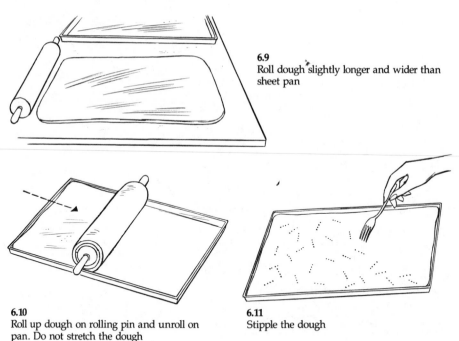

6.9
Roll dough slightly longer and wider than sheet pan

6.10
Roll up dough on rolling pin and unroll on pan. Do not stretch the dough

6.11
Stipple the dough

Finishing Napoleons

The ends or thick edges of the baked puff pastry sheets are trimmed to level the sheets. The trimmings are usually chopped and used for garnishing and finishing. Place the three sheets, or a single sheet cut into three even sections, over each other to check the evenness of sizes. The edges may be trimmed again. The broken or uneven sheet may be used as the center filling sheet.

1. Fill the first sheet, placed on a cake board or the back of a pan, with cream custard filling. The basic filling for cream pies may be used. A Bavarian cream may also be used, or the pastry chef may use a layer of vanilla and a layer of chocolate cream filling for variety.

2. Place the second sheet or section over the filling and press down gently. A pan may be used to press down evenly over the entire sheet. Fill the second sheet with a layer of selected cream or custard filling.

3. Place the top sheet over the filling so that the bottom and smooth surface of the sheet is facing up. Press the top sheet down evenly over the filling. Check all the sides for evenness. Trim any excess where necessary.

4. The top sheet may be covered with a thin layer of cream custard and then sprinkled with finely chopped puff pastry trimmings. The trimmings may be blended with lightly toasted, chopped almonds or filberts.

5. The napoleons are then cut to the desired size for service. The tops are dusted lightly with confectioners sugar after the portions have been cut.

6. The top sheet may be covered with a warm fondant icing and then lines of chocolate or fudge icing may be drawn across (evenly spaced) the fondant icing. While the chocolate is still warm and soft, a spatula or knife is used to cut across the lines to provide a cross-hatched effect.

7. The top sheet may be covered with a Bavarian cream topping and garnished. Whipped cream may be used to cover the top sheet and then a variety of designs (pear shapes and rosettes) may be used to finish each serving as for French pastry. (Figs. 6.12 through 6.14.)

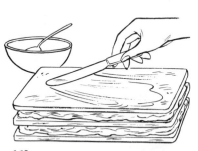

6.12
Assemble the sheets with a filling

6.13
Stripe fondant-iced top sheet with chocolate fudge or fondant

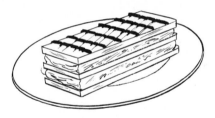

6.14
A Napoleon slice or single serving

Palm Leaves (Palmiers)

Puff pastry dough combined with granulated sugar when rolled out is the basis for this simple pastry. The following procedure is employed when making palm leaves:

1. Roll a piece of fresh puff pastry dough on a bench dusted with granulated sugar. Dust the top of the dough with sugar as well. Roll into a rectangular shape about ¼ in. thick.
2. The dough should be about 12 in. in width. Sprinkle the surface of the dough lightly with sugar and roll in gently.
3. Make a mark dividing the dough in half. Fold the dough three times toward the center. Start from the top and then the bottom. You should have three layers on each side. Fold one layer over the other to form six layers with one side open.
4. Check the thickness of the dough strip. Even out where necessary. Cut ½ in. slices and place on lightly greased pans with the flat cross-section facing up. Open the base slightly at the bottom.
5. Allow the units to relax for about 20 min and bake at 390°F. The bottom will caramelize first. Turn over for equal browning of the top. (Figs. 6.15 through 6.17.).

The palm leaves are usually washed with a syrup glaze as soon as they are removed from the oven. The smooth-surfaced side is washed. The glazed surface may be garnished with chopped pistacio nuts while the syrup glaze is warm and the palm leaves still hot. The palm leaves are often made in miniature form and served with cookies. The dough is rolled smaller and about ⅛ in. thick. Care should be used when baking the miniatures because they will bake faster.

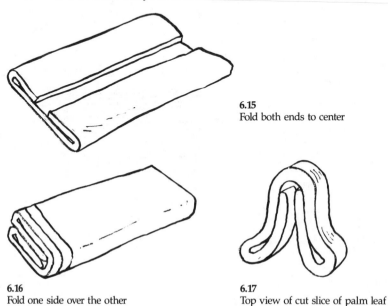

6.15
Fold both ends to center

6.16
Fold one side over the other

6.17
Top view of cut slice of palm leaf

Puff Pastry Butterflies (Papillons)

Butterflies are made in much the same way as the palm leaves. The dough is rolled out into a rectangular shape and of an even thickness of about ¼ in. Check the dough for evenness. Be sure there is sufficient sugar to prevent sticking. Sprinkle the top of the dough with sugar and roll-in gently before cutting the dough. Cut the dough into strips that may vary in size depending upon the portion. The average size of the strip is usually 3½–4 in. wide. Place four strips one on top of the other. Be sure they are equal. Press the center of the top layer down with a rolling pin to make the strips stick to each other. Cut into slices about ½ in. thick. Give each slice a single twist in the center, forming a butterfly effect. Place on a lightly greased baking pan, allowing sufficient space for spreading. Bake the butterflies at 400°F. When the bottoms have browned, turn them over so that the tops may be browned evenly. Very often, both sides may bake and caramelize equally. The butterflies may be left plain and served in this manner. They may also be washed with hot syrup glaze and garnished with chopped nuts. The butterflies may also be made in miniature form and served with cookies.

Turnovers (Chaussons)

Turnovers may be considered the most popular dessert item made from puff pastry dough. This is evident by the frozen turnovers now available on a consumer basis as well as on a commercial basis. The frozen turnovers need only be baked when bought already made. Most pastry chefs will make their own turnovers because they can control the quality, size, type of filling, and cost. Variety is largely dependent upon the fillings used and the type of fruit fillings available at specific times of the year. Turnovers may be made in several shapes. There are the very popular triangular, half-moon, and rectangular forms. The procedures for making each variety are almost identical. For the triangular shaped turnover, roll the dough into a rectangle about ⅛ in. thick. Allow the dough to relax a few minutes and then cut into squares 4–5 in. square. Miniature turnovers are made by cutting the squares into 2 in. size. A pastry wheel (single or set of wheels) or a knife may be used to cut the squares. Brush the edges of the squares of dough with egg wash or water. Deposit the fruit filling in the center of the dough square. Fold the corner of one side of the square diagonally across to the other to form a triangular shape. Seal the ends well with the fingers or a fork. (Figs. 6.18 through 6.20.)

Place the turnovers on a parchment paper-lined sheet pan allowing space for spread and lift during baking. Stipple or puncture the top of the turnover to allow for the escape of steam (moisture from the fruit filling) during baking. Allow the turnovers to relax for 30 min before baking. The turnovers may be washed with egg wash for a shiny brown crust color. Bake at 390–400°F. Reduce the oven temperature to 370°F during the final stages of baking. The turnovers should be crisp and flaky when properly baked. It is customary to wash the baked turnovers with a hot syrup glaze upon removal from the oven. This will provide a luster to the crust. The turnovers are usually iced with a warm fondant icing after they have cooled.

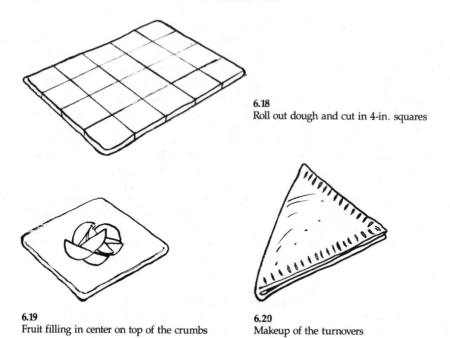

6.18
Roll out dough and cut in 4-in. squares

6.19
Fruit filling in center on top of the crumbs

6.20
Makeup of the turnovers

Some pastry chefs prefer to make the chaussons in a half-moon shape. This is slightly more time consuming and does make for considerable scrap puff pastry dough. These turnovers are made by cutting out round circles of dough after the puff pastry dough has been rolled out. The size of each circle of dough may vary from 4–6 in. in diameter depending upon the size of the turnover or portion required. Remove the scrap dough around each circle of dough and then wash the edges of the dough circle. Place the fruit filling at a point about one-third of the circle so that the upper part may be folded over it without spreading the fruit filling too much. This will form a half-moon shape. Seal the ends carefully, stipple or puncture, egg wash if desired, and proceed as for the triangular shapes.

The rectangular shapes, or finger shapes, are made as are the triangular turnovers. When folding the shapes, they are folded in a square form. The complete edge of one side is folded to the edge of the other side of the square of dough and the ends sealed and the outer edges sealed as well. It now looks like half a square. Fold the seam under the center part of the rectangle and place on a sheet pan. The tops are stippled or punctured and then egg washed. Some pastry chefs will cut thin strips of dough the length of the rectangle and criss-cross two strips across each rectangle. The strips are egg washed. Bake and finish these rectangular turnovers as the others.

Pastry chefs will not always wash the turnovers and similar puff pastry products with egg wash. They will first bake the turnovers. Then they will remove them from the oven and dust the tops with confectioners sugar and return the turnovers to the oven for glazing—the sugar melts and then quickly caramelizes in the oven.

Fruit fillings are often added after the unfilled turnover has been baked. The dough is rolled and cut as for regular turnovers. Pastry chefs may brush the edges of the dough with melted butter or vegetable oil and then lightly fold the ends over as though the turnover was filled. The turnovers are baked and will rise even lighter than those with the fruit filling. There is no restriction on the bottom crust because there is no filling and the expansion will be greater. After the turnovers have cooled, they are easily opened and spread apart. The filling is deposited so that it is in the center and shows out of the sides. Fresh berries and other fruits are often added to the cooked fillings. The turnovers are then dusted with confectioners sugar and served.

Fruit fillings for turnovers should be slightly thicker than the fillings used for pies. The filling will have less tendency to run out or force itself out of the sides of the turnovers during baking. In addition, large fruit pieces should be chopped into smaller pieces. Smaller fruit chunks will make handling easier and avoid the possibility of tearing the puff pastry dough when it is folded and sealed. Thin fruit fillings will tend to spread when deposited. If they reach the edges, the filling will prevent proper sealing. Adding some sponge cake or other light cake crumbs to the filling will bind it.

Puff Pastry Fruit Charlottes or Fruit Baskets

There are a number of variables in the finishing of these basic puff pastry desserts. A variety of fruits and fillings may be used for these charlottes and fruit-filled pastry baskets.

1. Roll the dough out to about ¼ in. thick into a rectangular shape.
2. Cut the dough into 3–4 in. squares. With a round object depress the center of each square. Do not force a hole to be formed. Dip the object used to make the depression in flour to prevent sticking.
3. Place the squares on a parchment paper-lined pan and space about 1 in. apart. The squares may be brushed with egg wash. Deposit the desired fruit filling in the center depression (Fig. 6.21).

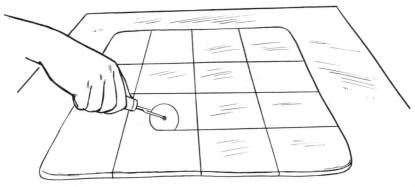

6.21
Cut dough into squares of desired size

4. Relax the units for about 30 min and bake at 400°F until almost baked.
    Reduce the temperature to 375°F during the final stages of baking.

The pastry chef may add additional fruit filling or fresh fruits to the center of the square when baked. A variety of fruits may be used: peaches,
apricots, strawberries, blueberries, pineapple, and so forth. The fruits
are then glazed with a hot apricot coating glaze. When cool, the charlotte
is decorated with a border of whipped cream. A star or No. 5 French
tube is used. A meringue topping may be bagged around the edge in a
high border. The fruit charlottes are then dusted lightly with confectioners sugar and returned to the oven for rapid browning. Additional fruits
may then be placed in the center. The entire fruit filling may be covered
with meringue in a charlotte form and then returned to the oven for
browning. To make the fruit baskets, strips of puff pastry dough about
½ in. wide and ¼ in. thick are criss-crossed diagonally across the tops
of the squares after the filling has been deposited in the centers (Fig.
6.22). The squares are then baked and glazed with a syrup glaze upon
removal from the oven.

Apple Dumplings

Apple dumplings are made with fresh, whole apples that have been
peeled and cored. The pastry chef may order the apples in this form from
a large produce supplier if used in large quantities. A small, firm apple
should be used and the apples peeled and cored just before using. The
size of the apple will determine the amount of dough required to cover
the entire apple.

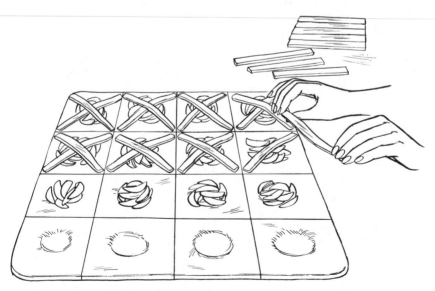

6.22
After filling the square centers, place two
strips of dough diagonally across top

1. Roll out the dough as for apple turnovers. Be sure the dough is of even thickness (⅛ in.).
2. Divide the dough into squares (about 5 in., depending upon size of apple).
3. Brush the edges of each square with water. Sprinkle some light cake crumbs in the center of the square before placing the apples in the center. The cake crumbs will absorb some of the syrup formed and make handling easier.
4. Place the apple in the center of the square and fill the open space (core removed) with a blend of cinnamon sugar. Raisins may also be used, if desired.
5. Lift each corner of the dough square to the top and fold each corner over the other as lifted.
6. Roll out a piece of puff pastry dough to about ⅛ in. thickness. Cut out 1½ in. round discs and place them on top of the dough corners to seal them.
7. Brush the tops of the dumplings with egg wash. (Figs. 6.23 through 6.25.)

6.23
Divide the dough into 5-in. squares

6.24
Place the peeled and cored apple on square
of dough. Fill center with cinnamon sugar

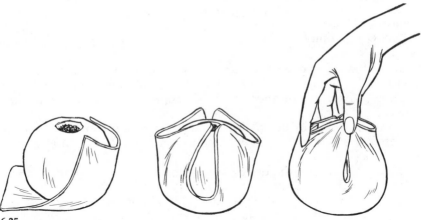

6.25
Enrobe the apple with the dough ends and
seal together

Be sure to seal the sides of the dough surrounding the apple as well. Bake the dumplings on parchment paper-lined sheet pans, spaced about 2 in. apart to allow for settling and slight spreading of the dumplings during baking. Bake at 390°F until the crust is brown and quite crisp. Check the bottoms for proper bake. The bottoms are usually quite soft and may require additional baking. The dumplings may be brushed with a syrup glaze upon removal from the oven. The dumplings are usually kept warm before serving and are served in deep dishes with additional cinnamon sugar syrup added. Dumplings may be refrigerated after they have cooled and then quickly reheated for service. Microwave reheating may be used.

Puff Pastry Pinwheels or Stars

The pinwheel made from puff pastry dough provides the pastry chef with additional variety to enhance the menu or the display of desserts. The number of fillings that may be used to garnish the pinwheels further expands the variety. In addition, the pinwheels are made up quickly and can be refrigerated or frozen for final baking and finishing.

1. Roll out the dough into a rectangular shape about ⅛ in. thick. Remove excess flour.
2. Allow the rolled out dough to relax for about 5 min and then cut into 4–5 in. squares. A pastry wheel (single or multiple) is used. Be sure the squares are even and equal. This will affect the final shape of the pinwheel.
3. From the center out (do not cut through the very center) cut to the point of each corner of the square. You will have 4 cuts. A pastry wheel will serve nicely for making the cuts.
4. Grasp the cut corner on the right and fold a point into the center. Do this with all the corners (all four). This will form the shape of a pinwheel or star. (Figs. 6.26 through 6.28.)

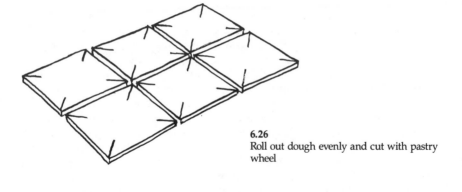

6.26
Roll out dough evenly and cut with pastry wheel

6.27
Fold alternate points to the center and press down gently to make the border

6.28
Finished pin wheel

5. Place the pinwheels on a parchment paper-lined sheet pan and space about 1 in. apart. Depress the centers of the pinwheels so that the points will not rise or peak too much during baking.

Pastry chefs often brush the pinwheels lightly with water and dip them in coarse granulated sugar or crystal sugar. The pinwheels are baked with just the sugar and served that way. An assortment of fruit fillings may be placed in the centers before baking. Additional fruit filling or fresh fruit slices may be used to garnish the pinwheels after baking. Allow the madeup unit to rest for about 30 min before baking. Bake at 390°F until crisp. Be careful not to overbake the edges of the pinwheels. The pinwheels may be baked plain, without garnish or filling. After baking they may be depressed in the center while still hot and the filling applied at that time. Pinwheels baked with fillings in the center are glazed with a hot syrup glaze as soon as they are removed from the oven.

Puff Pastry Ovals (Semelles)

The term semelles refers to shoe soles since this pastry has that appearance in terms of its shape. The pastry ovals provide further opportunities for the pastry chef to make a variety of puff pastries.

Roll out the puff pastry dough to about ¼ in. thickness or slightly thicker. With a round cookie cutter, varying in size from 2–4 in. (the size of the cutter will be based upon the portion size of the baked unit), cut out round dough circles and place to one side. Remove the scrap dough. Clean the work bench. Use granulated sugar for rolling. Dip each dough circle in the sugar and roll out to an even thinness. The 3-in. circle should be rolled out with a small rolling pin to an oval shape about 5 in. long. Use additional sugar to prevent sticking. Place the ovals on parchment paper-lined sheet pans and space about 1 in. apart. Allow the ovals to relax for about 30 min and bake at 410°F until the sugar begins to caramelize to light brown. The door of the oven may be opened and the ovals allowed to bake through thoroughly if they are not sufficiently crisp at the time the sugar caramelizes. It is important to roll the units evenly so that the thickness of the oval is even and will bake evenly. It is obvious that an uneven thickness will result in uneven baking and appearance.

The ovals may be varied by rolling them in streusel topping, chopped nuts mixed with sliced almonds, a combination of cinnamon sugar and nuts, and other toppings. Those rolled in streusel or crumb topping are usually garnished with a fruit filling in the center and then dusted with confectioners sugar before serving.

Puff Pastry Cream Rolls

Cream rolls are quite popular and very impressive as a dessert. The centers are usually filled with whipped cream but other fillings may be used. A blend of cream custard with a light buttercream may be used. A marshmallow filling may also be used in very warm weather or where large volume is often hindred by a lack of sufficient refrigeration. Cream rolls are made on special, metal cream roll sticks. These are tapered metal forms that are about 6 in. long. They may also come in the old-fashioned cornucopia form. The cream roll forms must be clean and well greased before use.

1. Roll out the dough into a rectangular shape about ⅛ in. thick. Check the dough for even thickness. Remove the excess flour from the top surface. Cut strips of dough about 1 in. wide. Brush the strips lightly with water or with diluted egg wash. Grasp the cream roll form at the wide end and lift the strip of dough so that the dry bottom of the strip of dough faces the end of the narrow part of the stick.
2. Make a complete turn of the stick so that a circle of dough covers the edge of the stick.
3. Continue to turn the stick while winding the dough at a 45° angle. The wash or water will cause the winds of dough to stick. Continue to wind almost to the top of the stick and then press the strip of dough gently and tear or cut the dough.
4. Dip the cream roll into granulated sugar and place on a parchment paper-lined sheet pan. The cream rolls may be left plain and dusted with confectioners after finishing. (Figs. 6.29 and 6.30.)

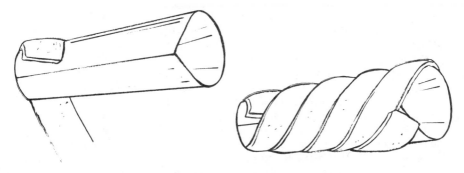

6.29
Roll strip of dough on tube with washed side up

6.30
Rolled-up cream roll

5. Allow the cream rolls to relax for at least ½ hr before baking. This will prevent tearing the strips of dough that have been stretched thin while winding the dough around the stick. It will also prevent shrinkage during baking. Bake at 390–400°F. The cream rolls should have a golden brown crust color. Avoid dark caramelization of the sugar during baking. It will take approximately 30 min for the cream rolls to bake through. The oven temperature may be reduced during the final stages of baking. Remove the cream rolls from the sticks while still hot or warm. If the interior is a bit white or not completely crisp, the cream rolls may be returned to the oven for a few more minutes for additional crisping or baking. The baked cream rolls may be wrapped and placed in the refrigerator for later finishing. Wrapping is suggested for prevention of moisture absorption.

Cream rolls are usually filled with whipped cream or whipped topping. A blend of whipped cream and topping may be used. A pastry bag and star tube are used to fill the cream rolls. It is advisable to fill one half of the roll from each end to be sure the entire cream roll is filled. The ends of the roll may be dipped in chopped pistachio nuts, chopped toasted almonds or other garnish, such as chocolate bits or variety crunchies. Cream rolls may be dusted with confectioners sugar before serving.

A chocolate cream roll may be made in the form of a special pastry. A blend of pie crust dough and sugar or short dough, in equal amounts, is made with the addition of chocolate liqueur or fudge base. Use sufficient chocolate to provide a chocolate color to the dough and to the baked roll. The dough is rolled to about ⅛ in. thickness. Remove excess flour. Cut into rectangular shapes about 6 in. long and 3 in. wide. Place the greased cream roll stick in the center of each piece of dough. Fold the dough around the stick. Moisten the edge of the dough with water and complete the roll. Cut the excess dough from the tapered edge. The roll may be dipped into sugar or chopped nuts. Most pastry chefs prefer to leave the chocolate rolls plain, or to dip them in soft, melted sweet chocolate after they have cooled. A chocolate fudge icing may also be used. The fudge icing may be combed with a fine-edged plastic comb or metal comb to provide a bark-like apppearance. The chocolate cream rolls are filled the same as the regular cream rolls. The chocolate appearance provides variety as well as attractive appearance.

Puff Pastry Pretzels

The pretzels are a delicacy since they may be made with a variety of fillings and made into miniatures as well as any desired serving size. In addition, scrap dough may be used with fresh puff pastry dough to make the pretzels. Open the fresh dough and neatly space out the scrap dough so that it is evenly distributed. Fold the fresh dough top over the scrap and roll the dough slightly with the rolling pin.

1. Roll the dough into a rectangular shape about ¼ in. thick. Check for even thickness. Remove excess flour from the top.
2. Spread the entire surface of the dough with a smooth jam or jelly filling. An almond smear may be used and the smear covered lightly with a melted sweet chocolate. Sprinkle the top of the filling with toasted chopped nuts, cake crumbs, and cinnamon sugar. Fold the dough in half and roll gently with the rolling pin. This will ensure that the filling sticks.
3. Cut the dough into strips about ½ in. wide. Use a pastry wheel or French knife. The strip may be cut in half if smaller pretzels are required.

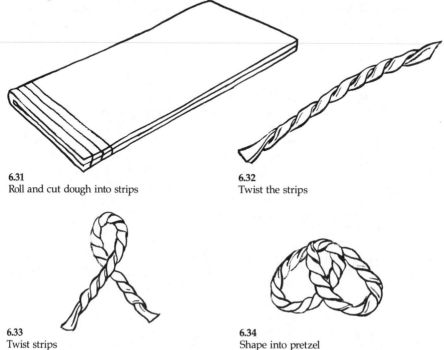

6.31
Roll and cut dough into strips

6.32
Twist the strips

6.33
Twist strips

6.34
Shape into pretzel

4. Twist each strip to form a smooth spiral effect. Use a little dusting flour if the strips tend to stick to the bench or table.
5. Cross the ends of the strips over each other and then gently press the ends into the round base of the oval of dough formed. (Fig. 6.31 through 6.34.)
6. Dip the pretzels into granulated sugar and place them on parchment paper-lined sheet pans. Allow the pretzels to relax for about 20 min (longer if scrap dough was used to make the pretzels). Bake the pretzels at 385–390°F until the pretzels are crisp and dry.

A blend of puff pastry dough and chocolate sugar or short dough may be used to make the pretzels. This will have a cookie effect and may be used to make the miniature pretzels. These are attractive when mixed in with a cookie platter.

After the puff pastry dough has been rolled out as for the regular pretzels, roll out chocolate sugar or short dough to almost the same length and half the width of the puff pastry dough. Smear the puff pastry dough with a thin layer of smooth jam or jelly. Roll up the chocolate short dough on a rolling pin and unroll over the puff pastry dough. Fold the top half of the puff pastry dough over the chocolate short dough. Roll-in gently with a rolling pin. Make up the chocolate-filled doughs as for the regular pretzels.

Almond Nut Slice

The almond nut slice is a very useful form of puff pastry. It may be made in a twisted bow tie form with just the sliced almonds or it may be made as a puffed pastry stick which is later finished in a variety of pastry forms. If left plain and twisted it is often known as *sacristains*. To make the sacristains or twisted almond nut slice, roll out the puff pastry dough to ¼ in. thickness and in a rectangular shape. Trim the edges of the dough with a pastry wheel and remove excess flour from the top surface. Brush the top of the dough with egg wash and sprinkle liberally with sliced almonds. Some pastry chefs will also sprinkle the sliced almonds with cinnamon sugar because there is no sweetening in the dough itself.

The sacristains are cut into rectangular strips varying in size. Usually the strips are about 5 in. long and about 1¼ in. wide. After rolling the sliced nuts lightly with the rolling pin, cut the slices with a pastry wheel. Place the fingers of one hand on the strip if the dough should tend to stick to the wheel, and lift. For smaller sacristains cut the strips smaller. Lift each cut strip and twist it 3 or 4 times depending on the length of the strip. Do not twist too tightly. The sacristain should have an open twist appearance when baked. Allow the units to relax after placing on parchment paper-lined pans. They may also be placed on moistened pans and pressed gently so that the strip does not tend to shrink while on the pan. When sugar is sprinkled on the tops, it is best to use parchment paper liners to prevent sticking to the pan with partial caramelization during baking. Bake the sacristains at 420–430°F until crisp with a golden brown crust color. It is advisable to remove the sacristains from the pans while they are still warm.

When the puff pastry almond nut slice is to be used for a pastry, the procedure for making the slices is changed slightly. The dough is rolled just a little thicker and then the entire rolled out dough is stippled or docked with a roller docker or fork. Allow the dough to relax for a few minutes and then egg wash. Sprinkle the top of the dough with sliced almonds, chopped nuts, and sugar. Roll the topping in gently with the rolling pin. Cut the dough into slices about 5 in. long and 1½ in. wide. Place the units on parchment paper-lined pans and relax for at least 30 min. Baking the slices as soon as they are panned will cause shrinkage.

Note: If scrap dough is rolled in with fresh dough, roll the dough slightly thicker and allow the dough units to rest for 1 hr before baking. This will avoid shrinkage.

Bake the slices at 400°F for about 15 min and then reduce the oven temperature to 375°F for a slow, crisp bake and to develop a light brown crust color. The baked units are cooled before they are further prepared for variety finishing. The baked units may also be prepared in advance and kept in the refrigerator or freezer to be used as required.

Finishing the Puff Pastry Almond Slices
Cut the slices in half as evenly as possible. Place the nut-covered tops to one side on a pan. Align the bottoms close together on another pan. Some pastry chefs prefer to place the bottom and top alongside each other. Fill the bottom slices with a strip of custard cream bagged out with a plain tube. Bag out whipped cream on top or along side the custard cream with a star tube. Gently place the tops over the filled bottoms and press down lightly. Dust the tops lightly with confectioners sugar before serving. Fruit fillings may be used.

Puff Pastry Strudel
Pastry chefs often make a strudel type of pastry from puff pastry dough. It is different, attractive, and allows for a greater variety of desserts. The variations are in the fillings used. For example, one can use a blend of fresh apples and canned apples, or any other fruit fillings that have been prepared slightly thicker than usual to keep them from running too much. A special cheese filling is equally popular for this type of pastry.

Since the strudel strips will be the approximate width of the average sheet pan, the dough should be rolled out to about the same width. The length will depend upon the amount of dough and the work space for rolling.

1. Roll the dough into a rectangular form about ¼ in. thick. Check for evenness in rolling the dough.
2. Remove the uneven edges with a pastry wheel. Cut the strips into widths of about 4 in. Brush the edges of the strips with water or egg wash. Place the cut strips on the baking pans spaced about 2 in. apart before filling the strips (Fig. 6.35).

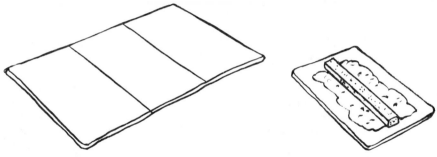

6.35
Rolled out and cut dough for pastry strudel bottoms

6.36
Filled pastry strudel

3. Deposit fruit or other filling in the center of the dough strip, being sure the filling does not run over or cover the edges of the strip (Fig. 6.36).

    Note: It may be advisable to place a strip of light sponge cake or yellow cake crumbs in the center of the strip. The crumbs will hold the fruit filling in place and will also absorb the moisture during the baking.

4. Roll out a similar amount of dough for the tops of the strudel strips. The dough is rolled about ⅛ in. thick and as wide as the sheet pans. Cut the dough into 6 in. wide strips in order to cover the filling and reach the edges of the bottom strip (Fig. 6.37).

5. Fold each strip in half to form a 3 in. width. With a knife or bench scraper make cuts about 1 in. long and spaced about 1 in. apart. Unfold the strip with the cuts (Fig. 6.38).

6. Place the cut tops over the fruit-filled bottoms and seal the edges. The cut spaces will open slightly (Fig. 6.39).

7. Egg wash the top of the strips and allow the strips to stand for about 30 min before baking. The strips may be egg washed again for a browner and more lustrous finish when baked. The tops may also

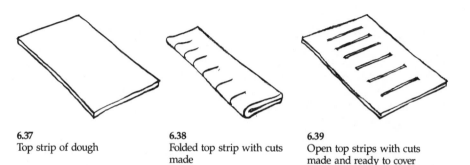

6.37
Top strip of dough

6.38
Folded top strip with cuts made

6.39
Open top strips with cuts made and ready to cover the filled bottoms

be washed only once and then garnished with sliced almonds or toasted chopped nuts before baking. Bake the strips at 400°F until crisp. The temperature may be lowered in the final stages of baking to ensure a well baked bottom crust.

The strips that are baked plain are usually striped with a fondant icing. The strips are cut into portions. The size of each slice will depend upon the nature of the service and the number of portions desired. The average slice is 1½ in. in width. It is advisable to have the dessert slightly warm before serving. The slices may be heated before serving. Fruit fillings such as cherry, blueberry, pineapple, and others should be cooked thicker. If the regular pie filling consistency is used, it is advisable to mix some light cake crumbs in with the fruit to absorb some of the liquid of the filling. This will tighten the filling and prevent excessive running during baking as well as during the makeup of the strudel.

For cheese puff pastry strudel, a special cheese filling is used. The filling is usually made from bakers' cheese or a blend of bakers' cheese and cream cheese. The matter of cost is always present and an excellent cheese strudel filling may be made with bakers' cheese.

Cheese Strudel Filling

Ingredients	lb	oz	Mixing procedure
Bakers' cheese [1]	7	8	Mix these ingredients together at slow
Cake flour		12	speed until uniformly blended
Sugar	2	4	
Salt		1½	
Butter (soft)		12	
Whole eggs	1		Add the eggs in 3 stages and blend in well
Egg yolks	1	4	
Vanilla		1½	Add the raisins and flavorings and blend
Rind of 3 fresh lemons			in well; do not overmix
Raisins (variable) (presoak the raisins)	2		

For the puff pastry cheese strudel roll out the dough as for the fruit-filled variety. The cheese filling should be rolled out into strips before placing on the dough bottom. It is advisable to roll cheese in some bread flour to form the strips and to prevent the cheese filling from sticking to the bench or table. A strip of pineapple filling may be bagged out or placed alongside the strip of cheese filling for a pineapple-cheese variety. **Yield:** Approx. 100–120 servings

[1]Pastry chefs may replace half of the bakers' cheese with cream cheese. It may be necessary to increase the eggs slightly or add some milk if the cheese is of good quality and absorbs more liquid. It is advisable to refrigerate the cheese filling before using.

Puff Pastry Cheese Puffs

These are individual cheese-filled puffs that are rectangular in shape, although they may be made in round form. Roll out the dough into a rectangular shape about ⅛ in. thick. Allow the dough to relax slightly and then cut into strips about 4 in. wide. Wash the edges of the strips of dough with water or egg wash.

Roll out the chilled cheese filling on bread flour into strips about 1 in. in diameter. Sprinkle the center of each of the dough strips with light cake crumbs and cinnamon sugar. Place the strips of cheese filling on the crumbs in an even strip. Fold the edge of the dough strip over the cheese filling to the other dough edge and seal well with the fingers. Fold the dough strip over so that the seam formed is now at the bottom center of the strip. Press the strips down gently. With a thin rolling pin, press down into the strip at about 3–4 in. intervals. Do not press all the way through but enough to press the dough down well. Cut the depressions with a knife or pastry wheel. Place the units on a parchment paper-lined sheet pan.

The individual units are stippled or docked with a fork or knife. A small scissors may be used to make 2 or 3 small cuts in the center of each cheese puff. Brush the tops of the puffs with melted butter and then allow the puffs to rest for about 30 min before baking. Bake the puffs at 400°F for the first 20 min and then reduce the temperature to 375°F. This will allow the puffs to bake crisply and the bottoms to be well baked. The puffs are usually served warm and are dusted with confectioners sugar at the time of serving. (Figs. 6.40 through 6.45.)

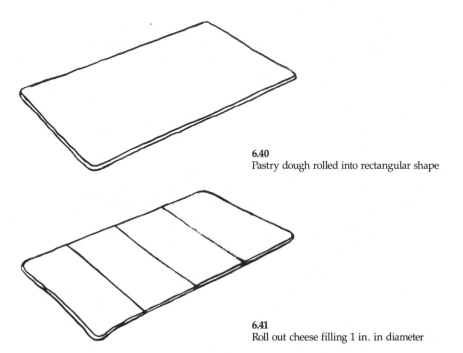

6.40
Pastry dough rolled into rectangular shape

6.41
Roll out cheese filling 1 in. in diameter

6.42
Place cheese on pastry dough

6.43
Roll up and seal the edge

6.44
Make depressions with thin rolling pin at 4
in. spaces and cut through with pastry
wheel

6.45
Stipple unit and wash with butter. Top may
be sprinkled with struesel or other topping

The cheese puffs may be made with pineapple and cheese. This is done by piping a line of pineapple filling alongside the cheese filling before folding the edges over to seal the long strips. Be sure the edges are moistened before sealing. The pineapple-cheese combination will spread much more during baking than the cheese filling alone. A cherry-cheese filling may be used as well. The cherry filling will have to be thickened with more cornstarch when cooked for this purpose. Regular cherry filling may be mixed with some light colored cake crumbs to thicken, or lightly blend the thickened cherry filling with the cheese filling for a marbling effect.

Puff Pastry Horns

Puff pastry horns provide the pastry chef with a means of using leftover scrap dough from other puff pastry varieties. This is also an opportunity to use a variety of jam, jelly, poppy seed, and similar types of smooth, soft fillings. Since the horns are made by rolling up the dough, any firmness or toughness in the dough is eliminated by the softening and flavoring effect of the variety of fillings. Some pastry chefs may make the longer and thinner type of horn and shape them into a half-moon or croissant shape. The size and shape of the horns are dependent upon the pastry chef and the type of service. In addition, when made small, the puff pastry horns can be mixed with other types of miniatures and served as tea cakes.

1. If scrap dough is to be used in conjunction with fresh puff pastry
    dough, place the scrap dough into the center of the fresh dough in a
    single layer so that scrap dough is spread evenly. Cover the scrap
    dough with the opened cover of the fresh puff pastry dough. Flatten
    slightly with the hands and then roll with the rolling pin. Allow the
    dough to relax for about 30 min before rolling it out for makeup.
    Pastry chefs will often prepare the mixed dough in advance and keep
    it in the refrigerator, for this dough may be used for other pastries.
2. Roll out the dough into a rectangular shape about ¼ in. thick. Check
    for uniform thickness. (Figs. 6.46 through 6.49.)

6.46
Roll dough into rectangular shape. Spread
poopy seed filling or other filling over half
the dough

6.47
Fold filled dough in half

6.48
Roll out the dough gently

6.49
Cut into triangles and roll into horns as for
Danish

3. Remove excess flour and spread the top surface with a soft, smooth jam, jelly, poppy seed, or other filling.
4. Sprinkle half the dough lengthwise with toasted chopped nuts, cake crumbs, and cinnamon sugar.
5. Cover the filling with the top half of the dough and seal the edges. Roll the dough lengthwise gently to make the filling stick to the layers of dough.
6. If the width of the dough is about 12 in. wide, cut it in half horizontally so that two 6-in. wide sections are formed.
7. Cut the dough into triangular shapes with the base about 3–4 in. wide. Roll up into horn shapes by starting at the base and rolling up to the point. Do not stretch the dough while rolling up the horn. For the crescent-shaped horn, spread the bottom or base by making a 1-in. cut at the base and then spreading the horn shape as you roll. Place the point at the bottom center.
8. Line up the horns on the table and flatten slightly. Place on a parchment paper-lined baking pan and space about 1 in. apart.

The puff pastry horns should be allowed to rest for about 1 hr before baking at 385°F. The horns should be baked for a longer period so that the centers may expand properly and be baked through with the same crispness as the outer layers of the horn. The baked horns are brushed with hot apricot syrup or a blend of boiled honey and apricot syrup. Bring the honey to a soft boil before blending with apricot coating syrup. The honey may also be used alone. The horns may be garnished with chopped nuts or pistachio nuts while the honey is hot. The nuts will stick to the surface of the horns as the boiled honey cools.

Poppy seed as well as prune fillings may be purchased in a ready-to-use state. It is time consuming and quite an effort to prepare the poppy seed filling. The steamed poppy seeds must be ground to eliminate the coarse, granular feeling. Pastry chefs will often improve the quality of the prepared and purchased poppy filling by adding honey, chopped nuts, jam, and cake crumbs to extend the filling. The degree of "stretching" the filling in this manner depends upon the pastry chef and price concerns.

Poppy Seed Filling

Ingredients	lb	oz	Mixing procedure
Poppy seeds	4		Wash the poppy seeds to remove any foreign matter
Water		6	
			Cook at moderate heat (constant simmer) stirring periodically until most of the water is boiled away and the poppy seeds feel soft. Add additional water if poppy seeds are not quite soft enough. Grind the poppy seeds to form a paste-like puree.

Sugar	1	4	Add these ingredients to the cooled poppy
Cinnamon		½	seeds and mix smooth
Honey (clover)	1	4	
Rind of 1 lemon and 1 orange			

To soften and to extend the filling, additional jam, jelly, or syrup may be added. The pastry chef may also add chopped or ground nuts and cake crumbs.

Yield: Approx. 120 large units (filled horns or triangles)

Cheese Straws or Sticks

Several types of cheese may be used to make the cheese straws or sticks. Parmesan or Swiss cheese may be used since they are hard cheeses that do not run or spread excessively during baking. Be sure to grate the cheese finely.

Cheese Straws

Roll out the dough about ⅛ in. thick into a rectangular shape. Remove excess flour and brush the surface lightly with water. Sprinkle the grated cheese over the surface of the dough. A light dusting or sprinkle of paprika may be used for color and added flavor. Fold one edge of the dough to the other and seal the edges. Roll in the dough gently so that the dough is about the same thickness or slightly more than the ⅛ in. Cut the dough into strips one-half to three-quarters in. wide. It may be advisable to chill the dough for about 1 hr before cutting the strips with a pastry wheel in order to obtain a smooth cut or slice. Divide the strips into the desired size. The strips may be twisted into a spiral the width of the baking pan. Moisten the baking pan with water and remove the excess water. Place the strips on the pan and space about ½ in. apart. Press the ends of the strip against the edge of the pan to keep the strips from shrinking or unravelling. Refrigerate the strips for about 1 or 2 hr and then bake at 390°F until light brown and crisp.

Cheese Sticks

Roll the dough out to about ¼ in. thickness and then brush lightly with water or egg wash. Sprinkle the surface of the dough with grated cheese and a light sprinkling of paprika. Allow the dough to relax and then cut into rectangular slices about 4 in. long and 1 in. wide. The sticks may be cut smaller if they are to be used as part of a display or hors d'oeuvres. Some pastry chefs will save the last two rolls of the rolling-in process to sprinkle the grated cheese into the dough and then roll the last two rolls with the cheese rolled into the dough. This will provide a richer cheese flavor in the cheese sticks. Bake the sticks at 400°F until golden brown and crisp. The cheese sticks may be stored in the refrigerator or freezer and then be reheated before serving. This will crisp the sticks and freshen the flavor.

Puffed Apple Strip (Bande Aux Pommes)

This puff pastry dessert may be made with apple filling or sauce as well as other types of fruit fillings. Upon completion, the long strips are cut into slices and served.

Roll out the puff pastry dough into a rectangular shape about the width of the baking sheet pan. Trim the edges and allow the dough to relax for about 10 min. Cut strips of dough about 4 in. wide. The thickness of the dough should be about ¼ in. Lift the strips and place them upon the sheet pan and space them about 1½ in. apart. Cut strips of dough about ½ in. wide and the length or the width of the pan. These strips will be used as a border to hold the filling. Wash the edges of the strips and place the narrow strips along the edges to form a complete border around the sides and ends of each of the strips. Be sure there are no open spaces.

Fill the center of the strip with a thin layer of cooked apple filling in which the sliced apples or frozen apple slices have been chopped finely. A smooth applesauce may also be used. If the applesauce is too thin, thicken by adding some light cake crumbs or by blending some applesauce with a thickened apple filling. Over the filling place slices of fresh or frozen apples that have been cut thinly. Overlay the apple slices so that one half of each apple slice is covered by another. Bake the strips at 365°F until crisp. The strips are baked slowly to ensure a proper bake of the bottom crust and to avoid sogginess. After the strips have been baked brush the tops with boiled apricot coating applied hot. The coating will firm up slightly when cool. Slice into desired slices for individual servings.

The strips may be made with a variety of fruit fillings. Pineapple strips may be made by filling the dough center with cooked pineapple and placing slices (half slices or quarter slices), spaced evenly, over the top of the filling. Bake as for the apple strips, and glaze with a blend of apricot and syrup glaze that has been colored lightly with a few drops of yellow coloring. The heavy syrup of the pineapple slices may be thickened with some cornstarch when cooked and added with the apricot glaze. A glazed whole or half cherry may be placed on each portion when cut.

Blueberry strips may be made by sprinkling the blueberry filling with some fresh blueberries before baking. After baking, the strips are brushed lightly with apricot glaze and sprinkled with fresh blueberries. When cool, the strips are cut into portions and dusted lightly with confectioners sugar before serving.

For peach strips, fill the center with peach filling. Place slices of fresh peaches spaced closely together across the top of the filling. Bake and brush with apricot coating after baking.

Cream Puff and Eclair Pastries

The shells made from cream puff paste, commonly called choux paste, serve as the base for a great variety of pastries and desserts. In some instances, the desserts are classified as French pastries. In addition, the cream puff shells or oval-shaped shells are used for many dishes other than desserts. For example, the chef may prefer to use a cream puff shell for a hot appetizer or main dish such as chicken á la king rather than a patty shell made from puff pastry dough. In fact, it is much quicker to make the cream puff shells than to prepare the dough for puff pastry and then make up the patty shells. In any event, the shells are usually made by the pastry chef.

There are variations in the formulas or recipes for the makeup of the cream puff shells. Some pastry chefs use butter, or a blend of butter and shortening in the first stage of preparation (cooking of the basic paste). Others use milk in place of water to cook the paste. Both of these factors add to the cost of the shells. The milk and butter will tend to create a darker crust color in the shell. The milk may also tend to cause the shell crust to be slightly thicker and may cause a slight shrinkage after the shells have been stored for a day or so.

The cream puff and eclair shells are leavened by the action of the eggs that expand in the heat of the oven. The evaporating steam, from moisture released in baking, causes expansion. With a chemical leavening agent (usually ammonium bicarbonate, although baking powder may be used with a lesser rate of gassing during baking) additional leavening is provided by the carbon dioxide gas released. The quality shell is usually leavened only by means of eggs. When cost is a factor, pastry chefs will often add water or milk to soften the batter. The shells are hollow and very light because the flour has been precooked and the starch particles have been gelatinized with the protein in the flour. The eggs are blended with the paste formed in cooking rather than being fully absorbed by the flour, thus forming the full body and structure of a cake. The gelatinized protein expands with the eggs and the steam during baking, with light strands of protein providing a hollow interior with structure formation.

Cream puff shells are baked in a rather hot oven during the first stages of baking. The baking temperature is approximately 425°F. It is then reduced to 385°F after the shells have risen and the structure has set. The final baking at reduced temperature allows the shell to become crisp and firm while maintaining a light crust color. This is especially necessary when milk is used to prepare the paste. Shells that are not completely baked will tend to shrink. If baked too rapidly, they may collapse completely when removed from the oven.

Eclair and Cream Puff Paste

Ingredients	lb	oz	Mixing procedure
Water	3		Bring to a rolling boil and continue to boil
Salt		½	until the shortening is dissolved
Shortening	1	8	
Bread flour	2		Sift the flour. Add in a steady stream, stirring briskly until all the flour has been added and mixed in

		Continue to stir until the paste moves cleanly away from the sides of the cooking bowl or kettle. Remove from the fire and deposit the paste into the mixing machine kettle and allow to cool to about 140°F.
Eggs (variable)[1]	3	Add the eggs a little at a time and blend in while mixing at slow or medium speed
		Scrape the sides of the mixing kettle with a spatula periodically to be sure the batter is evenly and smoothly mixed. This will cool the batter down and the eggs will be readily absorbed.
Water or milk (optional)	8–12	Dissolve the ammonium bicarbonate in the water or milk and add last
Ammonium bi- carbonate	$\frac{1}{8}$–$\frac{1}{4}$	

The paste is of medium soft consistency, slightly firmer than that made for French crullers. It will not run or spread when bagged out.

The size of the shells for cream puffs and eclairs will depend upon the service and the portion control factors. It will also vary with the type of dessert. The shells are bagged out in paste form with a pastry bag and a plain tube. A parchment paper-lined pan will prevent excessive spreading as well as keep the shells from sticking to the pan. If the paper pan-liners are not used, clean pans that are very lightly wiped with a greased cloth are used.

Cream puff and eclair shells will expand to 3 or 4 times the original size of the paste. When bagging out the shells, allow at least 2 in. between each cream puff shell for the regular full size (3 in. diameter). Smaller puffs will require less space. The eclairs should be about 1½ in. apart for the regular size. (Figs. 6.50 through 6.54.)

To test the shells for proper bake, tap the shell lightly with a finger. There should be a hollow sound and the shell should feel crisp. Baked shells that have cooled may be covered and stored in the refrigerator or the freezer. Most pastry chefs will keep a reserve stock of shells for future or immediate use.

Note: It is important not to bake small and large units, for instance, the ovals and the goosenecks for swan pastries, on the same pan.

Yield: Approx. 120 shells

Cream Puffs

Cream puff varieties may be increased by the creativity of the pastry chef. The usual cream puffs are filled with cream custard filling using a pump. Where large volume production is involved, the paste for the shells

---

[1]The amount of eggs will be affected by the type of flour used. It is important to use a good quality bread flour with a high gluten content to sustain the liquid and the eggs a provide for maximum expansion during baking. A strong flour will require a larger amount of eggs to soften the paste to the desired consistency. A thick paste will result in poor volume and a thick shell crust.

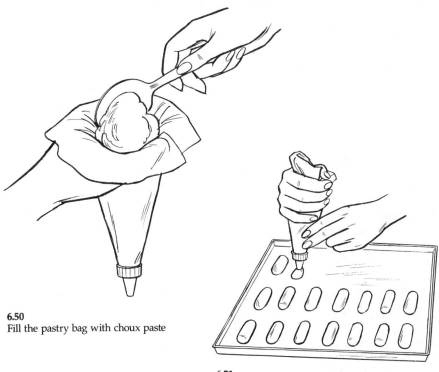

6.50
Fill the pastry bag with choux paste

6.51
Bag out the eclairs evenly

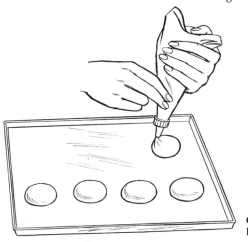

6.52
Bag out cream puffs evenly

is dropped onto pans with an automatic dropper, filling a complete pan at one time. The baked shells are filled with multi-spigots from a pump containing the cream custard filling. As previously indicated, prepared custard cream powders may be used. These custards will also freeze well without separation or weeping when defrosted and served. The filled

6.53
Cream-filled eclair

6.54
Cream-filled cream puff

shells are then dipped into a fondant type of icing for finishing of the tops. Cream puffs may also be dusted with confectioners sugar and served.

Whipped Cream Puff or Choux Chantilly

Cut the top of the baked cream puff shell about ⅓ of the way down from the top. Line up the cut shells on pans with the cut shells adjacent to the shell tops. Fill the shells with whipped cream (refer to the recipes formerly given in the section on Bavarian-type pies) so that the cream is in a spiral form about 1 in. above the top of the bottom shell. Replace the top of the shell lightly and dust the cream puffs with confectioners sugar before serving. These filled shells may be made in advance and kept under refrigeration for later service. Variations may be made with the use of chocolate cream in place of the vanilla custard cream.

Coffee Cream Puffs

For coffee cream puffs fill the shells with a coffee flavored custard cream. If a basic vanilla cream that is chilled is to be used, prepare a concentrate of instant coffee in a little hot water. Allow to cool and blend in with the custard cream. Dip the filled cream puffs into coffee flavored and colored fondant icing. Be sure the fondant is mildly warm and of a consistency that will flow just a little after it has been applied. A rosette of whipped cream may be placed on top and garnished with a pecan or walnut half.

Cream Puff Divorson

Cream Puff Divorson (half and half) is made by filling the shells which have been bagged out in an oval form rather than a complete round form, with a praline cream filling. (Fig. 6.55.) The praline paste may be purchased or made by the pastry chef. To make the paste, brown 2 lb of sugar in a saucepan over a low flame. Stir in 2 lb of chopped, toasted hazelnuts and almonds. Caramelize to a light golden brown color and pour onto a marble table section or a clean pan and allow to cool. Break up the praline by rolling with a rolling pin. The small pieces may then

6.55
Oval-round cream puff shell

6.56
Oval finger-shaped shell

be ground fine. The praline paste is blended into the vanilla cream custard. Cover the top of the oval shell with half vanilla and half chocolate fondant icing. When the icing has almost set or dried, garnish the top with pecan or walnut halves or chopped pistachio nuts.

Vienna Cream Puffs (Pains á la Meque)
Bag the shells out in an oval-finger shape with a plain tube. Control the pressure so that the center is thicker than the ends, very much like a pointed eclair. (Fig. 6.56.) Bake them at 390°F so that the ends do not get very dark. Fill the shells when cool. The shells may be garnished with sliced almonds before baking. It is advisable to brush the shells lightly with egg wash before baking, then apply the sliced almonds. Chopped nuts or large nut pieces may be used. The baked shells are cut in half and filled with whipped cream. Pastry chefs may fill the bottom half with cream custard first and then bag the whipped cream on top in a spiral form with a star tube. Replace the tops lightly and dust with confectioners sugar before serving.

Pineapple Cream Puff (Cream Puff Caribbean)
Cut the baked cream puff shell in half. Fill the bottom half with pineapple filling and garnish the top of the pineapple with a high spiral of whipped cream. Use a star tube for this. Replace the shell and garnish the top with stripes of melted sweet chocolate. The top may also be garnished with whipped cream and a slice of pineapple.

Cherry Cream Puff (Cream Puff Montmorency)
Cut the baked cream puff shell in half. Fill the lower half with cherry pie filling and garnish with a high spiral of whipped cream. Replace the top half and garnish with whipped cream and a glazed cherry. The whipped cream may also be striped with sweet chocolate.

Cream Puff Swans
Bag out the shells in an oval-round form and bake. On a separate pan bag out the swan necks and beaks in the shape of a question mark. Start with a small oval for the beak and then a thinner question mark for the neck. Point the beak slightly with a paper bag filled with choux paste. Use a small plain tube to make the necks. Bake the necks separate from the base shells. Cut the tops from the oval shells and then cut the tops in half to form a pair of wings. Fill the bottom shell with a pineapple filling or another fruit filling. Cover the filling with whipped cream to the top of the shell. Insert the halves at a 45° angle to form the wings. A little whipped cream may be inserted under each wing for additional support. The baked necks may have a dot of chocolate or chocolate pip-

6.57
Wings from top

6.58
Swan neck and beak

ing gel for the eye. Insert the neck at the front in an upright position. Dust the swan with confectioners sugar before serving. (Figs. 6.57–6.58.)

Mushroom Puffs (Religieuses)

This pastry requires a regular cream puff shell and a miniature cream puff shell about 1 in. in diameter when baked. Bake these shells on separate pans. Fill each of the baked shells with cream custard. A chocolate cream custard may be used for the miniature shell. Ice the larger cream puff shell with a coffee or maple fondant icing. Ice the miniature cream puff with chocolate fondant so that the top and most of the sides are covered. Place the miniatures on a screen so that the extra fondant may drip into a pan. Bag a fine ring or border of coffee or chocolate buttercream around the top of the larger cream puff shell. Place the miniature cream puff in the center of the buttercream ring to form a crown or mushroom effect.

Polkas

Polkas are pastries made with a combination of sugar or short dough as a base with a ring of choux paste around the border. Cut out rings or short dough about 3–3½ in. in diameter and about ¼ in. thick. Be sure all the cut-out discs are of equal thickness. Place on a parchment paper-lined sheet pan and space about 1 in. apart. With a plain tube, bag out a ring of choux paste around the edge of the short dough discs about three-eighths in. high. Wash the choux paste border lightly with egg wash. Bake the shells and paste at 375–380°F until the choux paste is crisp and golden brown. Do not underbake because the choux paste border will shrink or collapse. The parchment paper liner will keep the short dough bottom from overbaking. If the oven has a strong bottom heat, bake on double pans. When the shells have cooled, fill the centers with cream custard. Dust lightly with confectioners sugar. Place a small mound of granulated sugar in the center and burn the sugar lightly with a hot iron. A variation may be made in the type of custard filling placed in the center. The center may also be filled with a fruit filling and the filling covered with a meringue top and quickly browned in the oven after dusting with confectioners sugar.

Saint Honorés

Saint Honorés are made the same way as the polkas are made except for the manner in which they are finished. After baking, dip the circle of baked choux paste in chocolate fondant icing. A chocolate cookie dip may be used. Allow the icing or cookie dip to dry and then fill the centers with whipped cream. The top is usually garnished with a glazed cherry.

Eclairs

Eclairs may be made similarly and using the same procedures for making the variety of cream puffs. The size of the eclair is important. For example, larger eclairs may be required to be filled from both ends. Pressure on the pump handle of the filling equipment must be steady, for even distribution of the filling. Shells that are very dry and crisp may tend to break or shred when the pump injector is stuck into the shell. If this happens, cover the shells in a single layer with a damp, moistened cloth. This will soften the shells so that they can be filled. Some pastry chefs will place the dry shells in a steam-filled proof box for awhile. This technique is much faster and will restore the moisture quicker.

Chocolate eclairs are filled with vanilla cream custard and then dipped in warm chocolate fondant. When the fondant has dried, the tops are striped with thin lines of chocolate fondant. The tops of the eclairs may be garnished with chopped pistachio nuts.

Eclair Chantilly

The size of the eclair shell is based upon the size of the finished dessert or an established portion control procedure. The choux paste is usually bagged out 4–5 in. in length and about ½ to three-quarters in. in width. Equal size and shape is important. A plain tube is used. The shells are baked at 425°F until they are crisp. The cooled eclair shells are dipped in warm, chocolate fondant. The fondant is allowed to dry and then the tops are cut carefully and separated from the bottom shell. The bottom shell is filled with a high layer of whipped cream. A spiral effect made with a star tube is effective and impressive. The tops of chocolate-iced shells are replaced gently. Some pastry chefs will garnish the tops with a thin border of spiralled whipped cream down the center and sprinkle with chocolate shavings or chopped pistachio nuts.

Mocha or Coffee Eclairs

Mocha or coffee eclairs are made by filling the eclairs with a coffee flavored cream custard and the tops are iced with a mocha fondant icing. The tops may also be striped with mocha or chocolate fondant. A rosette of whipped cream with a half walnut or pecan may be used as an additional garnish.

French Rings

French rings are baked rather than fried as for French crullers. The rings may be iced with a variety of warm fondant icings and served in this manner. The iced rings may also be sliced in half and filled with a border of whipped cream and the top replaced as for a Chantilly type of dessert. The baked, plain rings may also be filled as for St. Honorés and placed on dishes. The centers may then be filled with a cream custard and garnished with a glazed cherry.

Eclair Miniatures

Miniature cream puffs and eclairs are often used for special pastry platters in conjunction with a variety of petits fours and cookies or tea cakes. These are filled with cream custard and dusted with confectioners sugar. Eclair miniatures may be iced with a variety of fondant icings. Miniatures are usually bagged out so that the cream puffs are about the size of golf balls when baked. The eclairs are about 2 in. by three-quarters in. when baked. These are to be filled carefully to avoid cracking the shells with excessive filling.

An attractive pastry may be made with the round miniatures by filling them with cream and dipping them in hot caramel icing. A warm fudge type of icing that dries quickly may also be used. The cream puffs are arranged in a cone or pyramid shape. This is usually done by arranging them in a mold that has been very lightly oiled until the miniature puffs have dried after dipping. The mold is turned over on a platter and the pyramid is formed. This is usually called Croque-en-Bouche.

Soup Garnish Puffs (Profiteroles)

These puffs, often called soup nuts, are used by chefs to garnish consommes and special soups. The soup nuts are made from the same choux paste used for the cream puffs and eclairs. The batter is made softer with the use of additional eggs. Added salt and pepper provides the desired flavor. The soup nuts are bagged out with a pastry bag and a small plain tube about ⅛ to ¼ in. diameter at the tip. The drops are made on clean pans or parchment paper-lined pans. Space the drops about ¼ in. apart on the pan. The softened batter will make the dropping out easy and rapid. Bake the soup nuts at 400°F until golden brown and crisp. These are stored in sealed cans for use as required.

7

Variety Cakes—Gateaux

Pastry chefs in finer dining establishments will always produce a variety of Continental style pastries. This distinguishes the pastry chef from the baker of ordinary, mass-produced cakes and pastries for large-scale feeding at a more rapid pace. However, the versatile pastry chef may find it necessary at times to follow the techniques and methods of mass-production, particularly when large groups of people are fed at special functions. Caterers cannot cope with special gateaux requiring unusually large amounts of production time and space. Thus, the pastry chef may have to be flexible in his approach depending upon circumstances.

In recent years, there has been a tremendous growth in the production and use of prepared mixes. These prepared mixes are used extensively for large institutional feeding. There are distinct benefits to be derived from their use. For example, uniformity of product, cost control, and ease in preparation are factors to be considered by the pastry chef who supervises a number of assistants in large-scale production. It is no easy matter to prepare desserts in the Continental manner for several thousand meals in a day or at one sitting. The pastry chef will avail himself of quick operational methods and methods that lend themselves to advance preparation and quick freezing of desserts. For the average diner, the cakes or gateaux made from prepared mixes are readily acceptable, especially when the pastry chef finishes the cakes with special icings and decorations that are neat and attractive.

This section presents basic recipes and cake formulas that are related to fast, multiple feeding operations as well as those that require the skill and care of the contemporary pastry chef catering to the needs of the more relaxed and more expensive dining establishments. There is always the need to shift from one method of production to the other in changing situations. Pastry chefs will combine the use of the prepared mixes for cakes as they do for prepared mixes for doughs, prepared puff pastry sheets and strudel dough leaves. There are many preparations available. Their use is limited only by the judgment of the chef and the pastry chef.

For the pastry chef who will make all his cakes and gateaux from scratch, the recipes and methods of mixing and baking will be presented in the categories of the types of cakes themselves. For example, sponge-type cakes will be presented in the section devoted to cakes that are made with the whipping method of mixing. Others will be presented under other methods of mixing. The basic cake mixing methods are: (1) the whipping or foam method, (2) the creaming method, (3) the blending method, and (4) the combination of the whipping and creaming methods. The factors of importance related to each method of mixing will be stressed. The proper scaling, handling, selection, and mixing of the basic ingredients will be explained. Brief emphasis will be placed upon cost factors and equipment related to the production of the various cakes. Variables will be explained in the context of the methods of mixing and production so that the pastry chef may make decisions that best apply to the particular situation.

Whipped or Foam-Type Cakes

Whipped or foam-type cakes are primarily leavened by the addition of whipped eggs, egg yolks, and egg whites to incorporate air cells. The expansion of these cells during baking, the natural expansion of the eggs in the presence of the heat of the oven, the action of the chemical leavening if used, and the natural release of steam in the form of moisture evaporation are the sources of leavening which produce the light, delicate grain and texture of sponge-type cakes. The preparation of the eggs and the type of eggs are important. Whole eggs, yolks, and egg whites are largely purchased in a frozen state in 10- or 30-lb cans. These eggs require less storage space and are reasonably uniform in quality. There is less waste in the use of these eggs than in the use of shell eggs which have to be broken before use. However, some pastry chefs have a decided preference for fresh shell eggs over frozen eggs. It is a matter of individual choice.

Whole eggs or yolks are whipped to greater volume and at a faster rate when the eggs have been properly defrosted and are at room temperature. It is also advisable to warm the eggs or egg yolks with part or all of the sugar before whipping. This must be done carefully by placing the eggs and sugar in a warm water bath or double boiler and stirring constantly to avoid partial cooking of the egg or coagulation of the albumen in the egg white. The warming has a softening effect upon the natural fat present in the egg yolk (lecithin) and makes for a more rapid absorption of air and formation of air cells with increased volume. This technique is especially effective when large quantities of egg yolks are used.

Equipment must be grease free when whipping eggs for sponge-type cakes. Fat or grease will cause a breakdown of the aeration by forming an oily film through the egg structure and causing collapse. Eggs and sugar are considered fully whipped when the foam forms a thick consistency that adheres to the wire whip of the machine and the lines or creases formed do not readily close as in an underwhipped batch. The consistency and thickness are greater where egg yolks are used in larger amounts. Whipping of the eggs may begin at high speed but a medium mixing speed is best after the eggs and sugar have started to foam. Very rapid mixing when the eggs have aerated may cause a reduction in the size and quantity of the air cells with a subsequent reduction in the volume of the cakes. Pastry chefs may also include a small amount of glucose or corn syrup with the eggs and sugar. The syrup will provide additional aeration as well as better keeping qualities in the baked cake. In the case of specialty sponge cakes, such as a honey sponge, the honey is often whipped together with the eggs.

Pastry chefs may wish to add hot water to the sponge mix to economize. This requires fewer eggs and the use of a chemical leavening such as baking powder. When the eggs have aerated part of the hot water is added in a slow stream for easy absorption. The heat of the water will tend to soften the yolk of the egg, allowing for ready absorption of the water and a further increase in the volume of the whipped eggs and sugar. The remainder of the water is added after the eggs have been removed from the mixer and just before the flour is added. In the case of hot milk and butter, or the addition of either hot milk or butter, these ingredients are folded into the batter after the flour has been sifted and folded in. Flavorings are usually combined with the water or milk and then lightly folded in. It is not advisable to add flavoring with the eggs and whip. Many flavorings contain oils of emulsion or the natural oils present in the rind of the fruit. These oils may have a tendency to cause a loss of aeration and even collapse of the whipping eggs.

Because of the delicate structure of the sponge or chiffon-type cake, a soft cake flour is used, a quality cake flour with fine starch particles that have good absorbing and retention qualities, as well as a low gluten content. Good quality is necessary for the supplemental formation of the structure of the cake. The eggs do not provide the total protein for the cake structure. This is done in conjunction with the cake flour. The cake flour should be sifted for aeration and removal of any foreign matter. It is usually sifted with other dry ingredients to be added. Other dry ingredients may be cocoa powder and baking powder. Where baking soda is used, it is advisable to dissolve the baking soda in part of the water and add with the liquid. The flour is added in a slow steady stream and is folded in by hand in many instances, or it may be added into the machine and mixed by the machine for large, commercial production. Chemical emulsifiers must be used to maintain aeration and avoid collapse during machine mixing. The flour is folded in until it is fully hydrated.

Hot milk or melted butter or other fats are added after the flour. The fatty liquid and milk are added in parts or in a slow, steady stream while the light mixing or folding is done continuously until all the melted fat and milk is absorbed and evenly distributed throughout the batter.

Whipped or foam-type cake batters should be deposited into prepared baking pans and baked as soon as the batter has been mixed. If allowed to stand for a period of time without baking, the air cells formed in the cake batter during mixing will tend to lose some of the whipped-in air. Air cells will also collapse with increased standing time. Delay in baking will result in a loss in cake volume with a negative effect upon the grain and texture of the cake after baking. The oven temperature for the cakes should be set and ready for baking, and the pans should be prepared and waiting.

Pans for sponge cakes are usually greased and lined with a parchment paper liner to meet the size and shape of the pan. Round pan liners of various sizes, as well as regular sheet pan liners, are available from purveyors. If pan liners are not available, the pans should be greased well and then dusted with bread flour. The bread flour will act as a buffer to keep the sponge batter from sticking to the sides of the pan. Pans for angel cakes are usually clean and then moistened with water. These are tube-shaped pans and the angel cake batter will adhere to the sides during baking. The cakes will free themselves when they are turned over after baking and start to cool. The mild contraction after cooling and the short tap of the pan against the table or bench will release the sides of the cake from the pan. It is advisable to draw the edges of the cakes away from the pan before tapping the pan to release the cake. For the chiffon-type cakes, the tube-type pans are left dry and the cakes will free themselves very much like the angel cakes. For regular layer cakes or sheet cakes, the pans are usually lined with a parchment paper liner which is removed when the cakes have been turned over and cooled.

Pans should be filled slightly more than half full. Sponge cakes will often double in size when baked depending on the type of batter and the amount of eggs used. Sponge cakes, depending upon the size and richness of the cake and the recipe variations, are baked at temperatures from 350–380°F. The smaller and thinner cakes are baked at higher temperatures. Larger and thicker cakes require a longer baking period at a lower temperature. For example, a sheet cake about 1 in. thick requires a higher baking temperature and a shorter baking period than does a 12-in. layer cake about 2½–3 in. high. The pastry chef usually tests the cakes for proper bake by gently touching the cake in the center after it has risen and set, and the crust color has taken on a golden brown color. If the center of the cake springs back gently to the touch, it is considered baked. When properly baked chiffon-type cakes will have greater springiness because of the whipped egg whites that have been folded into the batter. Cakes that are not fully baked will have a tendency to shrink and even fall back in the center. Sponge cakes should not be moved during the early stages of baking to avoid possible collapse of the liquid or soft structure which has not been sufficiently set.

Immediately after removal from the oven, sponge and other foam-type cakes are usually turned over on parchment paper-lined pans that may be dusted with granulated sugar. Some pastry chefs prefer to turn the cakes on cloths that have been lightly dusted with flour. Turning the cakes allows them to form an even top and releases the cakes from the bottom of the pan. Regular large sponge cakes and specialty cakes such as almond sponge are not often turned because of their firmer interior structure.

Sponge Cakes

Basic Sponge Cake

Ingredients	lb	oz	Mixing procedure
Sugar	3		Warm the eggs in a warm water bath to
Salt		½	about 105°F (mildly warm). Stir constantly
Whole eggs	2		while warming to prevent coagulation.
Egg yolks	2		Whip the eggs and sugar to a thick consis-
Glucose or		6	tency. Add the water and whip in
corn syrup			
Hot water		8	
Rind of 1 lemon			Fold in the flavoring gently. Remove from
Lemon flavoring		½	mixing machine
Cake flour	3	4	Sift the flour and baking powder. Add in a
Baking powder		½	steady stream and fold in gently

The flour is often folded in by hand for large batters. An overhand motion is used with the palm of the hand in a semi-cupped position folding over from the bottom of the mixing kettle to the top. The flour is added in a steady stream during the folding in process. This makes for ready absorption of the flour without the formation of lumps of flour which would require added mixing and a loss of some of the air cells. Deposit the batter into prepared pans. This batter may be used for sponge cake sheets, jelly rolls, layer cakes, and other specialty forms. The cakes may be refrigerated or placed in the freezer after baking for future use.
Yield: Approx. 4 full sheet pans, 1 in. high

Chocolate Sponge Cake

Ingredients	lb	oz	Mixing procedure
Sugar	2	4	Warm the eggs and sugar as for regular
Salt		¼	sponge cake. Whip until light and thick
Egg yolks	1	8	
Eggs	1	8	
Glucose or		5	
corn syrup			
Hot water		4	Add the water and whip in
Baking soda		¼	Dissolve the baking soda in the water and
Vanilla		1	vanilla. Fold into the above gently
Cold water		8	

Cake flour	2	4	Sift the flour, cocoa, and baking powder
Cocoa		6	together. Fold into the above until all the
Baking powder		½	flour and cocoa is absorbed

Deposit the batter into pans that have been prepared in advance. Sheet cakes are baked at 380°F. Layer cakes are baked at 365–370°F. These sponge cakes or sheets may be used for a variety of pastries and other desserts. Sheets may be placed together with whipped cream and cut into a variety of shapes. The individual shapes are then garnished with a whipped cream design bagged out with a pastry bag and tube.

Sheets may be sandwiched with a buttercream or other icing and refrigerated or frozen for use as required. Finishing will depend upon the pastry chef. Suggestions for French and other pastries will follow. Layer cakes may be treated as required or may be combined with plain sponge layers for combination-type layer pastries.

Pastry chefs are often required to control the per unit costs of desserts, particularly when feeding large groups, as in schools or large institutions. Sponge cakes are high in egg content and yet they are desired in spite of the high cost of eggs. Of course, there are times when the egg market fluctuates and eggs are cheaper. For the more economical sponge cake of good quality, the following recipe is recommended:

Yield: Approx. 3 sheet cakes, ⅜ in. high

Economical Sponge Cake

Ingredients	lb	oz	Mixing procedure
Sugar	4	4	Whip the eggs and sugar and corn syrup
Salt		½	to a thick consistency
Glucose or corn syrup		8	
Eggs	4		
Hot water	1	8	Add the hot water to the whipped eggs in 3 stages and whip on second speed until thick
Water		8	Fold into the above gently
Vanilla		1	
Rind of 2 lemons and juice			
Bread flour	1	6	Sift the flours and baking powder and
Cake flour	2	12	milk powder. Fold into the above until absorbed
Skim milk powder		4	sorbed
Baking powder		2¼	
Vegetable oil		12	Fold gently into the above, adding the oil in a slow steady stream

Deposit the batter into prepared pans. Bake as for the regular sponge cake.

Milk and Butter Sponge

Ingredients	lb	oz	Mixing procedure
Sugar	3	8	Warm the eggs and sugar in hot water
Salt		½	bath stirring constantly. When warm,
Eggs	2		place in the machine and whip until thick
Egg yolks	1		
Cake flour	3	5	Sift the flour and baking powder. Fold
Baking powder		2	into the above
Milk [1]	1	8	Break the butter into small pieces and heat
Butter or margarine		12	with the milk. Add the vanilla. Add to the
Vanilla		2	above in 3 or 4 stages and fold in gently. Do not overmix

This sponge cake batter requires the addition of hot milk and melted butter in the final stages of mixing. The butter may be dissolved in the heating milk. The hot milk and butter are added in stages and poured in at the side of a large mixing bowl after the flour has been folded in. The heat of the milk and butter will tend to soften the batter. The batter will tend to become somewhat thicker as it cools.

This batter may be used for sheet cakes and layer cakes. Because of the added milk and butter, the cakes will retain their freshness for a long period. The cakes may be frozen for later use.
Yield: Approx. 4 sheets, 1 in. thick

Genoise Sponge Cake (Butter Sponge)

This cake is often used for large layer cakes as well as special loaf-type cakes. Warm butter enriches the taste and flavor and extends the keeping quality. The butter must be in liquid form for even distribution.

Ingredients	lb	oz	Mixing procedure
Sugar	3		Warm the eggs and sugar in a warm water
Salt		½	bath. Whip until thick and light
Whole Eggs	2	8	
Egg yolks	2		
Rind of 1 lemon			Fold in the rind gently
Cake flour	3		Sift the flour and fold in gently
Melted butter		12	Fold the butter in gently

Deposit the batter into prepared pans. Sheet cakes are baked at 385°F. Deeper or thicker layer cakes or loaves are baked at 365°F.
Yield: Approx. 4 sheet pans, 1 in. thick

[1] If milk powder is used, dissolve in cool water before heating with the butter

Almond Sponge Cake

Almond paste or macaroon paste provides the special taste for the almond sponge cake. The almond paste is combined with eggs to form a soft paste which is then whipped in with the eggs and sugar. The paste is gradually added to eggs that are almost completely whipped and the whipping continues on second speed for further aeration.

Ingredients	lb	oz	Mixing procedure
Almond or macaroon paste	3		Add the eggs to the almond paste very gradually and mix to a soft, smooth paste.
Eggs	2		Remove from the kettle
Sugar	4		Warm the eggs and sugar. Whip to a thick
Salt		½	peak. Add the almond paste gradually to
Whole eggs	2		the whipped eggs and whip at medium
Egg yolks	2		speed
Cake flour	3	10	Sift the flour and fold into the above

Deposit the batter into prepared pans. The pans are usually lined with parchment paper liners. Deep pans and layer cakes are baked at 345°F. Sheet pans and shallow layers are baked at 360°F. The cakes should spring back to the touch when properly baked. The almond sponge cakes may be served plain, dusted with confectioners sugar before serving, or used for other French pastries and desserts.

Yield: 2 deep baking pans 18 × 24 × 4, or 4 sheet pans

Nut Sponge Cake

Ingredients	lb	oz	Mixing procedure
Almond or macaroon paste	1	8	Add the eggs to the almond paste gradually and mix to a soft, smooth paste
Eggs	1	8	
Sugar	4		Warm the eggs and sugar and whip to a
Salt		½	thick peak. Add the almond paste gradually and whip on second speed until thick.
Eggs	2		
Egg yolks	2	8	Sift the flour. Blend in the nuts. Fold into
Toasted filberts (ground)	2		the eggs
Cake flour	3	8	

The nuts may be varied by using ground or finely chopped walnuts. The nut sponge is used for many types of Continental pastries because of its delicate flavor. It is often made into sheets to be finished for French pastries. Loaf cakes and large sheet pans are cut into regular or cubed slices for special service with other types of loaf cakes. Bake the cakes as the almond sponge cake.

Yield: Same as for Almond Sponge cake

Honey Sponge Cake

A light clover honey is suggested for use to maintain the desired yellow honey color of the grain of the cake. The cake will remain moist and very spongy because of the honey whipped with the eggs.

Ingredients	lb	oz	Mixing procedure
Sugar	1	12	Warm the eggs, sugar, and honey in a
Salt		¼	warm water bath to about 108°F. Whip un-
Honey (clover)	1	8	til thick. Use medium speed in the final
(½ quart)			stages of whipping
Eggs	2	4	
Egg yolks	2		
Cake flour	3	6	Sift the flour and fold in gently. Add the
Melted butter		12	melted butter and fold in gently

Deposit the batter into prepared pans that have been greased and lined with parchment paper liners. Loaf pans are usually lined at the bottom and sides with full pan liners. Bake the deeper pans or loaves at 350°F. Sheet cakes may be baked at 365–370°F. The honey will tend to create a deeper crust color and a higher oven temperature will tend to cause a deep brown crust color. Loaves and large, deep pan cakes are usually sliced and served with other cake varieties.

Yield: Approx. 4 sheet pans, 1 in. high

Royal Sponge Cake

This is a special type of sponge cake that contains a variety of dried mixed fruits and chopped nuts or nut pieces.

Ingredients	lb	oz	Mixing procedure
Sugar	3		Warm the sugar and yolks slightly and
Salt		½	whip to a thick consistency
Egg yolks	4	8	
Cake flour	3		Sift the flours together. Break the butter
Bread flour	1	8	into pieces and then chop finely into the
Chilled butter	1	8	flour. Fold in the flour and butter
Walnut pieces	1		Fold the nuts and fruits lightly into the
Pecan pieces	1		above. It is advisable to dust the nuts and
Chopped filberts	1		fruits lightly with bread flour before fold-
Coarsely chopped	2	8	ing in
glazed cherries			
and diced fruits			
Egg whites	3		Whip the egg whites and sugar to a me-
Sugar	1	8	dium soft peak and fold into the above

Deposit the batter into prepared paper-lined pans. Deep pans, loaf pans, and higher layer cake pans are used for this cake. Bake at 350–360°F. These cakes are sliced and served when baked. They may be dusted with confectioners sugar before serving.
Yield: Approx. 2 large sheet pans, 3 in. high

French Sponge Cake

The French sponge cake is prepared in a manner similar to the Royal sponge cake. The yolks and part of the sugar, and the egg whites and remaining sugar, are whipped separately, and then combined. This provides for a very light, spongy, and delicate cake. Pastry chefs will often use this type of cake for the whipped cream layers and delicate sponge cake based desserts. A lemon or orange fruit flavoring is most often used. The flavoring is particularly derived from the outside rind of the lemon or orange containing the natural fruit oils and flavors.

Ingredients	lb	oz	Mixing procedure
Sugar	2	4	Warm the egg yolks and sugar and whip
Salt		¼	to a light and thick consistency
Yolks	2	4	
Rind of 2 lemons			Fold into the above. Sift and fold gently
Cake flour	3	4	into the above
Egg whites	3		Whip the egg whites and sugar to a me-
Sugar	1	4	dium peak. Fold into the above gently

Deposit the batter lightly into the pans. Gently shake the pans to level. When depositing in sheet pans, deposit the batter in equal amounts over the entire pan so that a minimum of smearing with the spatula is required to distribute the batter evenly over the pans. Excessive smearing may cause a loss of some of the air cells. Bake the thicker pans at 350°F. Shallower pans or sheet cakes are baked at 370°F. The cakes will feel springy to the touch when properly baked.
Yield: Approx. 4 sheet cakes, 1 in. high

Chocolate Sponge Roll (Swiss Roll)

This type of cake must be softer and more flexible than regular sponge cake varieties because the sheet cakes are thin and must be rolled when cool, rather than when warm or hot as for the regular sponge-type jelly roll. The sheets made from this batter may also be used for chocolate seven-layer pastries. It is of equal importance that the batter be spread quickly and evenly over the pans after mixing. This requires a somewhat softer batter that flows easily when moved with the spatula.

Ingredients	lb	oz	Mixing procedure
Sugar	3	6	Warm the eggs and sugar and whip to a
Salt		½	medium thick consistency with the glucose
Glucose or corn syrup		8	
Eggs	1	8	
Egg yolks	1	8	
Water	1	8	Dissolve the baking soda in the water and
Sugar		6	vanilla with the remaining sugar. Fold
Baking soda		1¼	gently into the above
Vanilla		2	
Cake flour	2	10	Sift the flour and cocoa and fold gently
Cocoa		9	into the above

Deposit the batter onto prepared sheet pans lined with parchment paper liners. It is advisable to divide the batter over the seven pans equally before spreading the batter with the spatula. Spread evenly to avoid unequal thicknesses in the baked sheet. If this happens, the rolls or seven-layer sheets will be uneven when rolled up or put together.

Bake the sheet cakes at 400°F. These are thin sheets and will bake quickly. Therefore, a hotter oven temperature is advisable to prevent drying out the sheet cakes. The sheets should have a just tender feel and spring back lightly when touched. The sheets will continue to bake or dry for the first moments out of the oven. These sheets may be allowed to cool before rolling or putting together for chocolate seven-layer cake. Pastry chefs often fill the Swiss rolls and layer cakes with the desired filling (buttercream) and refrigerate or freeze the cakes and pastries for finishing as required.

Yield: Approx. 7 sheets

Seven-Layer Sponge Cake

Ingredients	lb	oz	Mixing procedure
Sugar	3		Warm the eggs, sugar, and corn syrup to
Salt		½	approximately 105°F. Whip to a light and
Glucose or corn syrup		6	thick consistency
Whole eggs	3		
Egg yolks	3		
Cake flour	3	2	Sift the flour and fold gently into the above

Deposit the batter onto the prepared sheet pans lined with parchment paper liners. Spread the batter quickly and evenly over the pans. Bake at 400°F as soon as the sheets are filled. Be careful not to overbake. The sheets continue to bake or dry when removed from the oven. The sheets are assembled when cool by sandwiching with desired cream-type icings and fillings. The basic cake is then refrigerated or frozen for final finishing at a later time.

Yield: Approx. 7 thin sheet cakes

Angel Food Cakes

Angel food cakes are foam-type cakes that are aerated and leavened primarily with the use of whipped egg whites. Since the egg whites are the primary ingredient, it is important to stress the use of egg whites that are of excellent quality. The egg whites should be of firm body and not overaged. They should be odorless and have an albumen gel that shows good body when poured. The mixing kettle and the beater must be clean and free from grease when whipping egg whites. When whipping egg whites for angel food cake, the eggs are whipped to a wet peak. The peaks formed in whipping will tend to bend over softly. This will enable the flour, cornstarch if used, and the remaining sugar to be folded into the beaten egg whites without added mixing. A dry peak as for a meringue will make folding in the flour difficult. It will lead to overmixing with the subsequent release and breakdown of some of the cells formed in whipping, resulting in poor volume and a close, rubbery texture.

Most recipes for angel food cakes have equal amounts of egg whites and sugar. The weight of the flour and other starchy ingredients are approximately one-third the weight of the sugar or the egg whites. The sugar is partially whipped in with the egg whites, so that about 50% of the remaining sugar is blended with the flour and folded in when the egg whites have been whipped. Adding all the sugar to the egg whites will create a concentrated and heavy syrup formation which will be difficult for the egg whites to lift and to aerate. Many pastry chefs will use a fine granulated sugar to whip with the egg whites and use confectioners sugar to blend with the flour in the final stages of mixing. The confectioners sugar will cause a closer grain in the baked cake. Where cocoa is used for a chocolate angel food cake a reduction in the amount of flour is necessary to allow for the absorption properties of the cocoa powder. In addition, a small amount of water may be used to have a moistening effect on the cocoa. Increasing the amount of egg whites slightly compensates for the absorptive qualities of the cocoa powder.

Pans for angel food cakes are tubular shaped. They are usually slightly tapered from the top to the bottom outside of the pan. The inside tube is straight and equal in circumference. Pans are cleaned and often left moist. The moistness of the pan will cause the sugar in the mix (now in syrup form) to aid the rise of the cake batter before the heat of the oven fully gelatinizes the albumen in the egg whites and the starch-gluten formation in the flour. The moistness, after drying, will cause better adhesion of the risen cake to the sides of the pan. Angel cakes, because of the high sugar content, are baked at lower baking temperatures than other foam-type cakes. The temperature variation may be from 325°F for large, deep cakes to 355°F for smaller cakes. It is quite common to bake the angel food cakes on double pans (the tube pans placed on baking sheets) to avoid formation of a dark or thick bottom crust. Cakes that are properly baked will spring back with a spongy firmness. The top crust will have a slight, erratic crust cracking.

Angel food cakes are turned over when removed from the oven. They remain in that position until the cakes have cooled. The inverted position allows the bottom crust to detach itself from the bottom of the pan easily when tapped because of the moisture formation and mild "sweating" that takes place during cooling. This is a form of condensation. It is advisable to draw the edges of the cake slightly away from the sides of the pan before tapping the pan gently to remove the cakes. The outside crust of the cake will adhere to the inside of the pan when the cakes are removed. Pans should be soaked and washed immediately after the cakes are removed. To repeat, *the mixing kettle and the beater must be clean and free from grease when whipping egg whites.* Since the angel food cakes are light and delicate they are finished in a similar manner by the pastry chef. The angel cake may be brushed or covered lightly with a warm apricot coating or slightly thinned jam or jelly and then have a thin fondant icing poured over the top and sides. A light marshmallow type of icing is used to cover the cake and long shred coconut may be sprinkled over it. A very light boiled type of buttercream may be used for finishing the cake or it may be lightly dusted with confectioners sugar.

Angel Food Cake

Ingredients	lb	oz	Mixing procedure
Egg whites	6		Kettle and beater must be clean and free
Fine granulated sugar	3		from grease. Whip the egg whites to a froth. Sift the sugar, salt, and cream of tar-
Salt		½	tar, and add to the egg whites in a slow,
Cream of tartar[1]		1¼	steady stream. Whip to a soft, wet peak.
Vanilla		1	Fold in the flavoring lightly
Almond flavoring (optional)[2]		½	
Cake flour	2	4	Sift the flour and sugar together and fold
Fine granulated sugar	3		gently into the above. Do not overmix

Deposit the batter into the prepared angel cake pans. Bake at 340°F. Fill the pans about two-thirds full.

Yield: Approx. 8 or 9 large tube cakes, 100 servings

[1]The cream of tartar is not an absolute necessity. The acid formed when the cream of tartar is dissolved in the egg whites has a softening effect on the protein (albumen) of the egg whites and makes for greater absorption of air cells. This increases the volume. The cream of tartar also has a whitening effect on the interior crumb of the cake.

[2]The almond flavoring is optional. Other flavorings may be used. For example, an orange and lemon angel food cake may be made with the addition of 4 oz of orange juice and the rind of 2 oranges and 1 lemon after the egg whites have been whipped. The lemon angel cake may be made with the addition of 3 oz of lemon juice and the rind of 3 fresh lemons. Where the natural fruit juices are used, the cream of tartar is reduced to ½ oz. The natural acidity of the fruit juices will neutralize some of the alkalinity of the egg whites. Fruit flavored angel food cakes are usually finished with a light, fruit flavored marshmallow or buttercream and garnished with small slices of fruit or jam.

Chocolate Angel Food Cake

Ingredients	lb	oz	Mixing procedure
Egg Whites	6		Whip in the same manner as for the white
Fine granulated sugar	3		angel food cake. Remove from the machine and fold in the baking soda dissolved in
Salt		½	the water and vanilla
Cream of tartar		1	
Cool water		8	
Baking soda		¼	
Vanilla		1	
Cake flour	1	10	Sift the flour, cocoa, and sugar together
Cocoa		12	and fold gently into the whipped egg
Fine granulated sugar	3		whites

Deposit the batter into prepared angel food cake pans. Fill about two-thirds to three-quarters full. Tap the pans gently on the bench to eliminate any air pockets. Bake the cakes at 355°F. Bake smaller cakes at 365°F. Check for proper bake carefully. The chocolate crust may be misleading and a gentle touch in the center of the cake is necessary to see if the cake springs back to the touch. Large cakes will take about 50 min to bake.

The cream of tartar is reduced slightly because the cocoa has a natural acidity. In fact, a small amount of baking soda is used to neutralize some of the acidity in the cocoa and provide some additional leavening. The baking soda will also improve the color of the crumb after baking. The chocolate angel food cakes are finished with a light chocolate buttercream or a thin chocolate fondant icing.

Yield: Approx. 8 or 9 large tube cakes, 100 servings

Nonpareil Angel Food Cake   This is made by cutting a chocolate angel food cake or chocolate sponge cake into small cubes. The cubes are then gently folded into the batter immediately after the flour and sugar have been folded in. The cubes will have a checkerboard effect. The cakes may be finished by coating the top and sides with a half vanilla and half chocolate buttercream or marshmallow icing. The top and sides may also be garnished with chocolate shavings or sprinkles.

Note: For large-scale production of angel food cakes it may be advisable to use prepared angel cake mixes. These mixes usually contain egg white stabilizers which ensure a good volume and less chance of cake collapse during the mixing and baking.

Angel Food Fruit Nut Cake

Limited amounts of fruits and nuts may be added to an angel food cake mix. The delicate structure of the cake batter provides a limited capacity to support fruits and nuts.

Ingredients	lb	oz	Mixing procedure

To the regular white angel food cake batter. Add the following:

Ingredients	lb	oz	Mixing procedure
Glazed cherries		8	Chop the fruits into small pieces. Do not
Dried, glazed citron		4	make a fine paste. Chop the pecans or
Melon rind		4	walnuts. Dust the fruits and nuts lightly
Glazed pineapple		8	with bread flour and then sift to remove
Pecans or walnuts		10	the excess flour. Fold the fruits and nuts
			into the batter lightly

The coating of flour will cause the chopped fruits and nuts to stick to the batter where deposited. The adhesiveness should remain and prevent all the fruits and nuts from sinking to the bottom, although there may be a tendency for some of the fruits to sink. However, the bottom of the angel cake becomes the top after baking. The top of the baked cake may be brushed with a light apricot coating that has been well heated, and then sprinkled with finely chopped glazed fruits and nuts. A thin white fondant icing may then be poured over the top of the cake to form a thin icing glaze. Serve the cake in slices when the icing has dried. A light marshmallow or boiled icing may be used for the tops, which are then garnished with dried, glazed, diced mixed fruits.

Chiffon Cakes

Chiffon cakes may be categorized as very light and fluffy sponge-type cakes. In fact, they resemble the French type of sponge cake except for the fact that the egg yolks are not whipped. They are rich in egg content with the increased nutritional value supplied by the added protein in the egg whites. Caloric values are supplemented by the use of fine vegetable oil in addition to the other ingredients. Chiffon cakes are not difficult to prepare if the procedures for mixing the ingredients are followed carefully. There are two stages of mixing. One requires the proper blending of the yolks with ingredients other than the egg whites. The stage that follows requires that the egg whites be whipped to a medium peak, slightly stiffer than for angel food cake, and then carefully folded into the egg yolk batter. Pastry chefs preparing large batches of chiffon cake mix will generally add the egg yolk preparation to the whipped whites gradually and let the machine fold in the batter at slow speed. Check the bottom of the kettle to see that the yolk batter is properly blended in.

Since the egg yolks are mixed in with part of the sugar, cake flour, and vegetable oil in a blended form rather than whipped form, baking powder and other chemical leavening agents are used to supplement the leavening effect of the beaten egg whites. The vegetable oil provides the added enrichment of a liquid fat. Melted, hard fats such as butter, margarine, or vegetable shortening will not yield good results in chiffon cakes. They tend to return to a solid or semisolid state when cool, thereby preventing even distribution. There are variables in the different chiffon cakes that may be made depending upon the type of cake. A basic chiffon cake may be used for several varieties simply by adding fruit juices and natural fruit rind, replacing some of the water with the natural fruit juices.

Chiffon cakes, while originally made in angel cake pan forms, are used extensively for sheet cakes, layer cakes, and loaf cakes. These cake forms lend themselves to the preparation of many types of pastries. Jelly rolls, seven-layer cakes, and a variety of other desserts are made with a chiffon cake as a base. This cake stays fresh longer because of the added vegetable oil and the high percentage of sugar and liquid. The baked cakes refrigerate well and may be frozen for extended periods without losing their quality. Pans for the chiffon cakes are usually clean and just lined with a parchment paper liner. Tube-type cakes are left dry and treated as angel food cakes when baked. Most pastry chefs and bakers will turn over the layer cakes and loaf cakes immediately after baking to ensure an even top surface and to prevent the possibility of shrinkage or partial settling in the center.

As for the angel cakes, the egg whites for chiffon cakes should be of good quality since they do provide for a goodly portion of the leavening. Canned egg whites are the major source for most pastry chefs. Egg whites that are cool and close to room temperature will whip to a maximum volume. Frozen egg whites should be defrosted at room temperature by being left to stand overnight. They may also be defrosted in a cool water bath or tank with a slow flow of cool water. Avoid the use of hot or very warm water since a high temperature might tend to coagulate the protein in the egg whites. Cream of tartar is also used when whipping the egg whites for the same reasons that it is used when whipping the egg whites for angel food cake.

Basic Chiffon Cake

Ingredients	lb	oz	Mixing procedure
Cake flour	3	8	Sift and blend the dry ingredients to-
Sugar	2	5	gether. Place in the mixing machine
Salt		1	
Baking powder		2½	
Egg yolks	2		Combine the yolks and the oil
Vegetable oil	2		Add to the above in 3 stages and blend in
Water	2	4	well. A paddle or wire whip may be used.
Vanilla		1	Use slow speed to avoid aerating the eggs.
Lemon or orange flavoring		½	Scrape the sides of the kettle after each addition. Mix to a smooth consistency and pour into a mixing bowl
Egg whites	3		Whip the whites to a froth. Add the sugar
Sugar	2	5	and cream of tartar in a steady stream and
Cream of tartar		½	whip to a medium peak. Fold gently into the above. Do not overmix. Be sure the egg whites are thoroughly distributed. Deposit into prepared pans

The batter may be used for jelly roll sheets baked in sheet pans, layer cakes of various sizes and depth, angel cake forms, loaf cakes, and other specialty cakes. The size and thickness of the cake will determine the baking temperature. Since the recipe is high in sugar content, the cakes are baked at moderate oven temperatures. Sheet cakes and jelly rolls are baked at 385°F. Layer cakes and large cakes are baked at 350–360°F. Chiffon cakes baked in very large, deep pans are baked at 340–350°F.

The chiffon cakes will rise quite rapidly and with large volume due to the expanding air cells created in the whipped egg whites, the natural expansion of the eggs in the presence of the heat of the oven, and the action of the chemical leavening agents (baking powder or baking soda, or both). However, the cakes must be allowed to bake through well to ensure full coagulation of the eggs and development of the protein structure provided by the protein in the eggs and the gluten present in the flour. Chiffon cakes should have a firm, springy feel when fully baked. The usual soft and tender spring may not be sufficient. The cakes may tend to shrink and settle if not sufficiently baked. To repeat, layer cakes and large cakes are turned over on parchment paper or cloths dusted with granulated sugar upon removal from the oven. Sheet cakes and sheets for jelly rolls and other filled pastry rolls may be left in the pans without being turned over.

Yield: Approx. 5 sheets, 1 in. thick

Orange Chiffon Cake

Ingredients	lb	oz	Mixing procedure
Cake flour	3	6	Sift and blend the dry ingredients. Place
Sugar	2	5	on machine
Salt		1	
Baking powder		2¾	
Vegetable oil	1	12	Blend the liquids together with the flavor-
Egg yolks	1	12	ing. Add to the above in 3 stages and
Water	1	12	blend in well. A paddle or wire whip may
Orange juice		14	be used. Do not aerate
Rind of 3 oranges and 1 lemon			
Vanilla		1	
Egg whites	3	8	Whip the whites to a froth. Gradually add
Sugar	2	5	the sugar and cream of tartar and whip to
Cream of tartar		1	a medium peak. Fold gently into the egg yolk batter

For large batters that are machine mixed completely, the egg yolk batter is added to the beaten egg whites in a steady stream until completely blended in. Check the bottom of the kettle to see if all the yolk batter is evenly distributed with whites. Fresh orange juice or reconstituted frozen juice may be used. If orange powder or crystals are used, follow the instructions for reconstitution. Deposit the batter into prepared pans and bake as for the basic chiffon cake.

Yield: Approx. 5 sheets, about 1 in. thick

Chocolate Chiffon Cake

Ingredients	lb	oz	Mixing procedure
Cake flour	3	8	Sift the dry ingredients together to blend
Baking powder		1¼	well. Place in the mixing machine or large
Baking soda		½	bowl
Salt		1	
Sugar	3		
Cocoa		8	
Egg yolks	1	12	Add the ingredients in the order listed.
Vegetable oil	1	12	Scrape the sides of the kettle after each ad-
Water	2	8	dition. Mix to a smooth batter
Vanilla		1½	
Orange flavoring (optional)		½	
Egg whites	3	8	Whip the whites to a froth. Add the sugar
Sugar	2		and cream of tartar in a slow, steady
Cream of tartar		1	stream and whip to a medium peak

Fold into the yolk batter gently. Be sure the egg whites are evenly distributed. Deposit the batter into prepared pans. Bake as for regular, basic chiffon cakes.

Yield: Approx. 5 sheets, about 1 in. thick

Marble Chiffon Cake

The basic chiffon (yellow) cake may be striped through gently with melted sweet chocolate after all the egg whites have been folded in. It is advisable to pour the melted chocolate over the top surface of the batter in large circles. It is only necessary to turn the batter over from the bottom 3 or 4 times and then deposit it onto the prepared pans for a marble effect. This may also be done by preparing the basic yellow chiffon batter and the chocolate chiffon batter. The tube or layer pans may then be filled partially with yellow batter followed by a second layer of chocolate batter, and then covered with another layer of yellow batter. The procedure may be reversed so that there are two layers of chocolate batter and a center layer of yellow batter. The chocolate chiffon batter may also be striped with melted sweet chocolate for a marble effect. It is important not to have the chocolate overheated or it will tend to melt some of the sugar in the batter and create a settling effect with the formation of large holes in the body of the baked cake. Chocolate that is cool and quite thick may tend to form large lumps which may settle to the bottom of the cake during baking, since the delicate structure of the cake cannot support the large pieces of chocolate.

Fruit-Filled Chiffon Cakes

The fruit-filled chiffon cakes are made with a chiffon cake batter that is thicker in consistency and firmer in body when baked. This is necessary to support the fruit fillings that are dropped or placed at intervals over the cake. The fruit-filled cakes are baked in sheet pans or smaller round or rectangular layer cake type pans. In order to support the fruit and keep it from sticking to the bottom of the pan, a thin sugar dough or short dough bottom is placed in the pan and prebaked. This cookie dough will provide the support for the fruit and also provide for variety in appearance and taste. Refer to the recipe for the sugar or short dough. The pastry chef normally keeps this dough on hand ready for use.

The dough is rolled out on a floured cloth to about ⅛ in. thick. It is then rolled up on a thin rolling pin at least the width of the sheet pan and then unrolled directly into the sheet pan. The dough is then checked for equal thickness, and stippled or punctured with a fork or stippler. Bake the short dough to a light, golden color and remove from the oven and allow to cool before filling.

For the batter for the fruit chiffon cake use the regular, basic chiffon cake recipe with the following changes:

1. Reduce the water from 1 lb to 8 oz
2. Increase the amount of egg yolks to 2 lb 8 oz
3. Decrease the egg whites from 3 lb to 2 lb

There is an increase in the egg yolks which will provide more body and a decrease in the liquid (water and egg whites). Pastry chefs will use this recipe adjustment for larger chiffon cakes baked in deep pans. They will also use this recipe adjustment for cakes that may contain chocolate chips or bits, or chopped nuts.

When the chiffon batter has been prepared, deposit the batter into the pans with the prebaked short dough bottom. Fill the pans about three-quarters full. A variety of cooked pie fillings (canned or prepared by the pastry chef) may be spaced over the pan at regular intervals about 2 in. apart. The pastry chef may wish to make a tutti frutti type of cake by using apple, pineapple, cherry, blueberry, and other fruit fillings spaced throughout the sheet pan. The cake is baked as soon as the fruit fillings have been placed. The large clumps of fruit will show through the indentations made in the top of the cake. The chiffon batter will bake with a greater degree of firmness and will feel quite solid to the touch as compared with the regular chiffon or sponge cake. The cakes are cut into portions and shapes and served. They may be dusted lightly with confectioners sugar. The individual portions may also be garnished with a rosette of whipped cream and the center filled with some of the fruit filling or a slice of the fruit.

When chocolate chips or chopped nuts are used for a chocolate chip chiffon or a nut-praline chiffon, the chocolate chips and the nuts are folded in gently after the yolks and whipped egg whites have been combined. These cakes do not require baked bottoms when baked in sheet pans. A parchment paper liner at the bottom will be enough. These cakes may also be made in tube pans as for angel cake. They may also be baked in layer cake pans and then finished for special cakes or pastries as determined by the pastry chef.

Chiffon Carrot Cake

Use fresh carrots, coarsely ground, together with the juice. The larger late carrots are better for this cake than the Spring carrots. They have a better color, better taste, and more body pulp. Since carrots contain approximately 88.2 percent moisture, there is no water added to the formula other than the natural moisture present in the eggs.

Ingredients	lb	oz	Mixing procedure
Sugar	4	4	Sift the dry ingredients together. Place
Salt		1	into the mixing bowl or machine
Cake flour	3	8	
Cinnamon (variable)		½	
Baking powder		½	
Baking soda		1	
Vegetable oil	3		Add the oil and eggs and blend in well
Egg yolks	2	8	
Raw carrots (medium ground)	5		Add the carrots and blend in well in slow speed
Egg whites	1	12	Whip to a medium peak as for regular
Cream of tartar		¼	chiffon cake and fold into the above
Sugar		12	

Layer cake pans or loaf cake or angel food cake pans may be used. Prepare the pans as for regular chiffon cakes. Paper liners may be used in the case of the loaf cakes. It may be advisable to moisten these pans with a little water before adding the batter. Fill the pans about two-thirds full and bake at 360–370°F. Larger units are baked at lower temperatures. The center of the cake should spring back firmly to the touch when baked. Cakes should be turned over in their pans when removed from the oven. This will prevent the center of the cake from settling. When almost cool, cakes are removed from the pans.

A fudge icing or buttercream icing may be used to finish the layer cakes. A few drops of yellow color are added to the icings. If desired, some shredded carrot pieces may be added to the icing for effect. Loaf and angel type cakes may be dusted with confectioners sugar.

The Creaming Method of Mixing

The term creaming applies to the ability of a fat (shortening, butter, margarine, lard, and so forth) to absorb and retain air cells during the mixing process. Most cakes were originally made with a shortening that was not emulsified. Regular hydrogenated shortening was found to be most effective for the creaming method of mixing. Pastry chefs soon adopted methods and recipes that would incorporate hydrogenated shortening with butter or margarine and other fats. They found that blending equal amounts of butter with hydrogenated shortening and then creaming these fats with sugar or flour would result in more volume and lighter cakes. This was due to the ability of the shortening to absorb and retain more air cells than regular butter or margarine.

There are several factors which affect the creaming method of mixing. The temperature of the fats is important. For example, a hard butter will not cream easily nor absorb air cells readily. Pastry chefs will soften the butter and then blend with the shortening. Many chefs will prepare a blend of equal parts of butter and shortening and have it ready for use when scaling the fat for various cake recipes requiring the creaming method of mixing. Because of the added volume derived from creaming the shortening alone or in a blend with butter, pastry chefs will often use less butter and thereby reduce costs. Creaming for maximum air cell formation and absorption is best accomplished at medium speed. The sugar and fats are first blended to a medium soft, uniform state. By added mixing on second speed or moderate speed, air cells are absorbed and the batter becomes lighter. The eggs are added in slow stages allowing for the emulsification of the moisture present in the eggs. The natural lecithin of the egg yolk covers the surface of the air cells, allowing for retention of the cell and the further absorption of additional cells. The batter becomes lighter and softer when all the eggs have been creamed in properly.

When large percentages of eggs and/or milk are to be creamed into a batter, as for pound cakes, the pastry chef will often add a small percentage of flour with the sugar and shortening. The flour will tend to absorb some of the liquid present in the eggs and other fluid ingredients, and prevent curdling. Curdling is the breakdown of the water-in-fat emulsion to a fat-in-water solution. The air cells are depleted and many of the cells containing the air are broken. When this happens, there is a loss of volume as well as a close, dense grain, and a very moist or soggy condition in the baked cake. In the final stages of the creaming method of mixing the remaining milk or other liquids are added alternately with the flour. This procedure allows the flour to absorb some of the liquid and prevents the curdling effect. The flour and leavening are added last and mixed until the batter is smooth and complete hydration of the flour takes place. Where a bread flour is used in conjunction with cake flour, as in the case of fruit pound cakes, the mixing of the flour in the final stages of mixing must be done carefully and at slower speed. This is to avoid overmixing and development of the gluten in the flour causing toughness in the batter and resulting cake.

During creaming, the batter is leavened by the air cells formed and retained. The air cells expand during baking and have a leavening effect, as well as having a distinct effect upon the formation of the grain and structure of the cake. Additional leavening is provided by the chemical leavening, the natural expansion of the eggs in the batter, and the formation of steam which is partially released during the baking process. An equal balance of all the factors in creamed cake batters is important for proper cake making. There are literally hundreds of recipes for various types of cakes made with the creaming method of mixing. The recipes that follow all use the creaming method and are selected for their popularity and the many uses for the production of a wide variety of cakes and pastries. Most pastry chefs have a basic library or recipe collection which they gather with experience and use, and they will use these consistently. They will add additional recipes or replace former recipes with new ones as they find these to provide better results and greater varieties.

Pound Cake (Creaming Method)

Ingredients	lb	oz	Mixing procedure
Sugar	6		Sift the dry ingredients together. If the al-
Salt		1½	mond paste is used, soften it to a smooth
Nonfat dry milk		2	paste with a small amount of the eggs be-
Cake flour		8	fore adding. Add the butter and shorten-
Butter	2	8	ing, and cream well until soft and light.
Regular shortening (hydrogenated)	2	8	Scrape the sides of the mixing kettle often
Almond paste or macaroon paste (optional)		12	
Egg yolks	3		Add the eggs in 4 or 5 stages and cream in
Whole eggs	3		well after each addition. Scrape the sides of the kettle
Water		8	Add the water alternately with the flour
Vanilla		1	and baking powder. Mix until smooth
Cake flour	3		
Bread flour	2	12	
Baking powder		½	

Deposit the batter onto sheet pans that have been greased on the sides and lined with parchment paper liners. Layer cakes are prepared the same way. If no parchment paper liners are available, grease and dust the layer pans with bread flour. Unlined pans should be baked on double pans to avoid formation of a heavy brown crust on the bottom of the cake. Loaf pound cakes should be baked in special loaf pan liners. Bake the loaf cakes and deeper layer cakes at 345–350°F. Sheet pans are baked at 360–365°F.

Cakes made from the pound cake are often used for wedding cakes, special occasion cakes, and for the production of variety petits fours. The cake has a fine, close grain and smooth texture when made properly. The loaf cakes may be made into marble-type cakes by striping chocolate mixture through the cake. Use the same preparation as for the high ratio pound cake. Melted sweet chocolate may also be carefully folded into the batter which is then gently deposited into the loaf pans.

For yellow pound cake with nuts and fruits, it is advisable to increase the bread flour to 3 lb 8 oz and reduce the cake flour to 2 lb 4 oz in the final stage of the recipe. As much as 5 or more pounds of raisins and other mixed, dried fruits may be added to the mix. This may be supplemented with 2 lb of walnut pieces. The fruits and nuts should be dusted lightly with bread flour and sifted to remove the excess flour before adding to the cake batter. The flour on the fruits and nuts will tend to support them during the early stages of baking, when the batter becomes more fluid and prevents the fruits and nuts from settling to the bottom of the cake. These cakes should be baked at a slightly lower temperature and for a slightly longer period.

Yield: 4 to 5 sheet cakes. Pound cake loaves will vary with the size of the pan

Cupcakes

Pastry chefs will often use the high ratio type of cake batter to make cupcakes and cupcake style pastries. There are many varieties of desserts to be made from cupcakes. The following is a basic batter that is economical and has sufficient body to be handled quickly by the assistants to the pastry chef. In addition, the batter may be used for several cake varieties other than cupcakes.

Golden Cupcakes (Creaming Method)

Ingredients	lb	oz	Mixing procedure
Sugar	3		Cream the ingredients in this stage until soft and light. Scrape the sides and bottom of the mixing kettle often
Salt		1	
Nonfat dry milk		5	
Butter or margarine	1		
Regular shortening (hydrogenated)	1	2	
Corn syrup or glucose		4	
Whole eggs	1	8	Add the eggs in 4 stages and cream well after each addition
Egg yolks		8	
Water	2		Add ⅓ of the water and ⅓ of the sifted flour and baking powder alternately until all have been incorporated. Scrape the sides and bottom of the kettle and mix smooth
Vanilla		1	
Rind of 2 lemons (optional)			
Cake flour	4	8	
Baking powder		3	

Deposit the batter into muffin pans lined with cupcake liners. For pastry specialties such as Metropolitans, the muffin pans are greased well and may be lightly dusted with bread flour. Remove excess flour. Deposit the cupcakes into the cupcake pans. Fill each cup slightly more than half full. Bake the cupcakes at 380°F until they are golden brown and spring back lightly to the touch.
Yield: Approx. 140

Finishing Cupcakes

As a breakfast item, pastry chefs may use this cake mix for a special muffin. The cupcakes are sprinkled with streusel topping before baking and then dusted lightly with confectioners sugar when mildly cool and ready for service.

Iced Cupcakes   A fondant icing is best used for the plain top icing of various colors and flavors. Warm the icing in a double boiler until mildly warm. Dip the tops of the cupcakes in the icing and then lift quickly and remove the excess with a finger or the blade of a spatula (Figs. 7.1 and 7.2). It is advisable to start with a vanilla fondant and then remove parts of the fondant into a separate pot for other light-colored (yellow, pink, pale green) icing for variety cupcakes. All leftover colored fondant may then be combined and made into a chocolate fondant icing for the cupcakes. If icings are too stiff, add some simple syrup and warm the fondant. If the fondant is too soft and runny, add some confectioners sugar.

Fudge-Iced or Buttercream-Iced Cupcakes   Prepare the basic vanilla fudge icing which may be used for vanilla-iced cupcakes and then made into a variety of other colors and flavors. The remaining fudge leftovers may then be combined with a chocolate fudge icing. This applies as well to the cupcakes finished with a variety of buttercream finishes. The fudge or buttercream may be applied with a spatula and given a swirl with the

7.1
Dip the top of the cupcake in the warm icing

7.2
Wipe off excess icing by running forefinger along edge of the cupcake

7.3
Finishing cupcakes with a spatula

7.4
Finishing cupcakes with a pastry bag and tube

tip of the spatula or knife. A pastry bag and star or French tube may be used to bag out the design on the top of the cupcake (Figs. 7.3 and 7.4). Rosettes or complete circles may be formed on top of the cupcake. The iced cupcakes are usually garnished with a nut piece, chopped nuts, or cocoanut for the pink and vanilla-iced cupcakes. The centers of the buttercream or fudge rings on the cupcakes may be garnished with fondant icing or with jam or jelly. The icing edges of the cupcake may be garnished with a fine border of chopped nuts, chocolate sprinkles, or variety crunchies. The tops of the cupcakes may be finished with a spiral of marshmallow icing of different colors for special occasions.

Metropolitans   These are a form of cupcake specialty that may be classified as a type of French pastry. They lend themselves well to a variety of finishes and the types of icing and garnishes that may be used. These are very popular with younger groups of diners. They are very attractive because of the colors used in the icings and final touches of finish.

Metropolitans are baked in muffin pans that have been greased well and then dusted with a fine dusting of bread flour. The pans are filled slightly more than half full and baked at 375°F. They should have a smooth, even top when baked since the top is turned over and becomes the bottom when finished. The cooled cakes are first covered on the sides with a smooth, fine jam or jelly. A buttercream icing may be used. The sides are garnished with fine or medium shred coconut or chopped nuts. Chocolate sprinkles or crunchies may be used for variety. The tops are encircled with a medium star or French tube and pastry bag using buttercream of various colors and flavors. This will depend upon the judgment of the pastry chef. The centers are then filled with a jelly or jam. A fudge icing may also be used for the centers. Glacéd cupcakes may be made from the basic cupcakes by placing them on icing grates and cov-

7.5
Holding cupcakes to apply jelly

7.6
Rolling them in coconut

7.7
Using the pastry bag to make the border

7.8
Finished metropolitan with jelly center

ering them with a variety of fondant icings. The centers may first be decorated with a rosette of buttercream and chilled (Figs. 7.5 through 7.8).

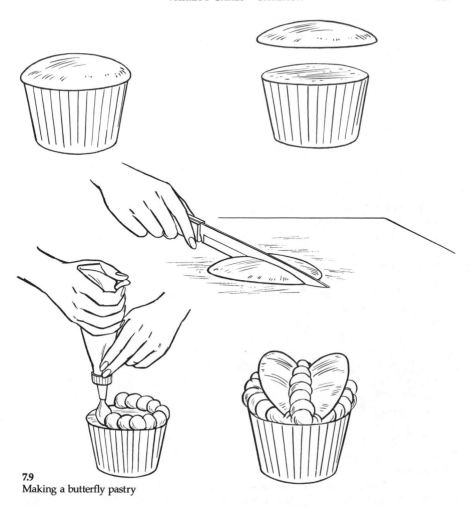

7.9
Making a butterfly pastry

Butterfly Cupcake Pastries   These pastries may be made from a variety of cupcake recipes. They may be finished in butterfly form with the use of variety buttercream. They are often finished with whipped cream or marshmallow icing. Cut the tops of the cupcakes (slightly larger by filling the pans with a little more batter) at the point where the paper liner ends at the top. Line the tops up next to each other in straight lines. When all are cut, cut the tops neatly in half with a French knife. With a pastry bag and tube (French or star tube) bag a circle around the edge of the cupcake. The circle of buttercream or whipped cream should be about ½ in. thick. Dust the cut tops lightly with confectioners sugar and then insert each half at a 45° angle into the circle of icing or cream to form the wing effect. Fill the center at the base of the wings with a full spiral of buttercream or whipped cream. The center may be garnished with a glazed cherry, chopped pistachio nuts, chocolate sprinkles, or other popular garnish (Fig. 7.9).

7.10
Mushroom (cream-filled) cupcake

Mushroom Cupcakes and Pastries   Fill the top of the cupcake with a ring of buttercream or whipped cream. Then fill the centers with a variety of cream pastry or fruit fillings. Replace the top and dust with confectioners sugar or decorate with a rosette of buttercream or whipped cream. Garnish with a glazed cherry (Fig. 7.10).

Black and White Drops (Medallions)   These are actually large cookie-type cakes or medallions that are bagged out on parchment paper-lined sheet pans. The golden cupcake batter has to be thickened so that the cakes do not spread too much and become too thin and brittle. Increase the cake flour to 5 lb 4 oz to thicken the batter. Bag out the drops about 2½ in. in diameter and about one-half to three-quarters in. high. Be sure to have all the drops of even size and spaced about 2 in. apart on the pan to allow for spread during baking.

The cooled drops for the medallions are turned over with the flat side up. Cover half the drop cake with an even cover of white fondant icing (Fig. 7.11). When all have been iced with white fondant return to the first one, which has probably dried, and ice the other half evenly with chocolate fondant icing (Fig. 7.12).

Note: As another breakfast item, pastry chefs may mix the batter with raisins and bag out. Bake the drops at approximately 390–400°F. They should be golden brown and the centers should spring back gently to the touch. Those filled with raisins may be sprinkled or garnished with a few raisins before baking. They are served soon after they are baked with other breakfast items.

7.11
Apply white fondant over half the cake

7.12
Apply chocolate icing over the other half

French Coffee Cake

This cake is usually made in large deep pans with various fillings and toppings. When baked, it is cut into portions and served in slice form. The mix can also be used for smaller layer and loaf cakes with a variety of toppings.

Basic French Coffee Cake

Ingredients	lb	oz	Mixing procedure
Almond or macaroon paste	1		Mix the almond paste and eggs to form a smooth, soft paste
Eggs		4	
Sugar	6		Add these ingredients and cream well.
Salt		1	Scrape the sides of the kettle to ensure
Nonfat dry milk		4	proper mixing of all ingredients
Cake flour		8	
Butter	2		
Regular shortening (hydrogenated)	2		
Egg yolks	2		Add the eggs in 4 or 5 stages and cream
Whole eggs	3	12	well after each addition. Scrape sides of the kettle
Water	2		Sift the flour and baking powder. Add the
Vanilla		2	water and vanilla alternately with the flour
Cake flour	6	4	and baking powder. Mix to a smooth con-
Baking powder		2	sistency

Deposit the batter into large, deep pans that have been greased and lined with a parchment paper liner. The top of the cake may be sprinkled with chopped nuts and cinnamon sugar or plain, granulated sugar. Bake at 345–350°F. Bake on a double pan if the oven has a strong bottom heat.
Yield: Two large pans 18 × 24, 3 to 4 in. deep.

Breakfast Item Deposit the batter into regular sheet pans that have been greased on the sides and lined with parchment paper on the bottom. Fill the pans slightly more than half full. Level the mix with a spatula. Sprinkle the top with chopped pecans and cinnamon sugar. Bake at 365°F. When baked and still slightly warm, cut into about 2 in. squares or in oblong shape and serve with other breakfast items.

Cinnamon Nut Layers These are made by filling layer cake pans of varying sizes that have been greased and lined with a parchment paper liner about ½ full. The top of the cakes are then sprinkled liberally with streusel topping and baked at 360°F. The size of the layer will be determined by the number of people to be served at one table. Larger cakes may be made for large table groups. The layers may also be filled ¼ full and the batter sprinkled well with a blend of cinnamon sugar. The filling is then covered with additional batter so that the layer pans are half full. The tops may be sprinkled with chopped nuts and cinnamon sugar.

Marble Cakes and Layer Cakes These are made by pouring melted sweet chocolate over the top of the batter and giving just a few light turns from the bottom of the kettle to the top. The batter is then deposited into pans of varying sizes. The batter may also be separated so that a layer of yellow batter is followed by a layer of chocolate batter, and then covered with a layer of yellow batter. These cakes may be striped with sweet chocolate piped in circles or criss-cross effect before baking. The small layers may be garnished with a spiral effect made with jam or jelly over a garnish of streusel topping before baking.

Chocolate Cake

This cake batter may be used for cupcakes, sheet cakes, layers, and a variety of loaf and ring-type cakes. A variety of cupcakes may be made from the chocolate cupcakes when baked.

Chocolate Cake   (*Creaming Method*)

Ingredients	lb	oz	Mixing procedure
Sugar	6		Cream all the ingredients until soft and
Salt		1½	light. Scrape the sides of the kettle period-
Nonfat dry milk		10	ically
Butter	1		
Hydrogenated shortening	2		
Fudge base [1]	1	8	
Egg yolks	2		Add the eggs in 4 stages and cream well
Whole eggs	2	8	after each addition
Water	4	8	Dissolve the baking soda in the water.
Baking soda		2	Add the vanilla. Sift the cake flour and
Vanilla		2	baking powder. Add the water and flour
Cake flour	6		alternately and mix smooth
Baking powder		2½	

Deposit the batter into prepared pans. Pans should be greased and lined with parchment paper liners or cupcake liners.

Larger units such as loaf cakes, ring-type cakes, and sheet cakes are baked at 360–365°F. Cupcakes are baked at 375°F. These cakes have good volume and pans should be filled about half full. Test the cakes for proper bake by touching the centers very gently. If the cake springs back to the touch gently, it is baked.

Yield: Approx. 4 to 5 sheet cakes

---

[1]To replace the fudge base with cocoa, use 14 oz of cocoa and add 6 oz of shortening to the mix. If bitter chocolate is used to replace the fudge base, use an equal amount of chocolate as fudge base. Melt the chocolate and add with the sugar and shortening in the first stage of mixing. Be sure to cream in well before adding the eggs. This will avoid the formation of lumps of chocolate during mixing.

7.13
Finished cupcake

Chocolate Cupcakes   These may be finished in a variety of ways. As for the yellow cupcakes, they may be iced with fondant icing, fudge icing, buttercream variations, whipped cream varieties, and buttercream inserted into the centers as for the Yankee Doodle variety (Fig. 7.13).

Chocolate Layer Cakes   These may be finished as if they would be used for the chocolate sponge or chiffon cakes for a variety of gateaux or layers.

Chocolate Sheet Cakes   These may be finished with buttercream variations for large volume feeding. The portions may be garnished with buttercream or fudge rosette with any of a number of appropriate garnishes. Whipped cream or marshmallow icings may be used with excellent effect to finish the chocolate sheet cakes. Special loaf cakes may have buttercream injected into the loaf through the top by using a pastry bag and a small plain tube. A jelly or custard pump may also be used for this purpose. The tops of the loaves may then be iced with a chocolate fudge icing (Fig. 7.14).

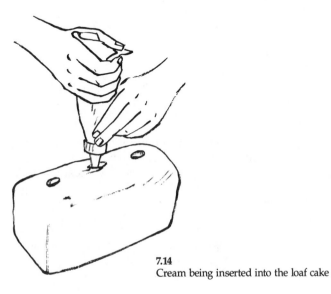

7.14
Cream being inserted into the loaf cake

Sunshine Cakes

This cake mix is a combination of several variables. The batter contains a variety of shortenings and butter. Because of the variations in fat content, it is best to mix this cake batter with the creaming method. The resulting cake is used for many purposes. Because it has a smooth, close grain and velvety texture, pastry chefs often use this recipe to replace the pound cake mix. Sunshine cake can be used for sheet cakes, layer cakes, loaf cakes, and special tube cakes.

Sunshine or Malibu Cakes

Ingredients	lb	oz	Mixing procedure
Sugar	7		Sift the dry ingredients. Add the butter
Salt		1½	and shortening and cream well until soft
Nonfat dry milk		6	and light. Scrape the sides and bottom of
Cake flour		8	the kettle
Butter	1	8	
Emulsified shortening	2		
Hydrogenated shortening	1	8	
Egg yolks	3		Add the eggs in 4 or 5 stages and cream in
Whole eggs	3		well after each addition. Scrape the kettle often
Water	3		Blend the vanilla and the rind or flavoring
Vanilla		1	with the water
Rind of 2 lemons and 1 orange (a blend of orange and lemon flavoring may be used to replace the rind)			
Cake flour	6	12	Sift the flour and baking powder together.
Baking powder		3½	Add the flour and water alternately and mix smooth

Deposit the batter into parchment paper-lined pans. The layer and loaf cakes are filled slightly more than half full. Sheet cakes are scaled approximately 5½–6 lb. Loaf cakes and thicker layer cakes are baked at 350–355°F. Sheet cakes are baked at 360°F. The loaf cakes may be baked plain and served as a pound cake slice. For large institutional feeding, pastry chefs will bake the sheets in deeper pans and then finish the tops of the sheets with a variety of icings. A chocolate fudge makes for an excellent contrast. A variety of buttercreams may be used. The cakes are usually sliced into squares and served.
Yield: 4 to 5 sheet cakes

Marble Sunshine Loaves Loaf cakes may be made into marble loaves by mixing part of the batter with chocolate and making alternate layers. Sweet chocolate that has been melted may be striped through the batter and then deposited into pans. The batter may also be striped with chocolate before baking.

Almond or Nut Rings These are often made from the sunshine cake mix. The pans are the scalloped, angel cake type pans, often called Turk head pans. The pans are well greased with butter and then the sides of the pans are sprinkled with sliced almonds. The bottom of the pan is sprinkled with almonds and cinnamon sugar. The cakes are removed from the pans as soon as they are baked. Turn the pans over on parchment paper-lined sheet pans. Tap them gently if they tend to stick.

Brownies

Brownies are a very popular cake and dessert. There are several recipes and several methods of mixing that may be used. The mix may be made with the creaming method, single stage blending method, or the whipping method for a sponge type of brownie. In addition, the chocolate color and flavor may be obtained with the use of cocoa, fudge base, bitter chocolate, or a combination of these. Brownies are usually covered with a chocolate fudge icing after baking and then cut into squares or oblongs. The sponge-type brownie is often used for a candy or cookie type.

Brownies   *(Pound Cake Variety)*

Ingredients	lb	oz	Mixing procedure
Sugar	5		Cream all the ingredients together until
Salt		1	soft and light. Scrape the sides and bottom
Butter	2		of the kettle
Hydrogenated shortening	2		
Chocolate fudge base [1]	1	12	
Egg yolks	2		Add the eggs in 4 or 5 stages and cream in
Whole eggs	3		well after each addition. Add the vanilla
Vanilla		2	last
Cake flour	2	8	Sift the flours together. Add and mix into
Bread flour	1	8	the above until smooth. Mix in the nuts in
Chopped walnuts or pecan pieces (variable)	3		the final stages of mixing

[1]To replace the chocolate fudge base with cocoa, use 14 oz of natural cocoa and add 6 oz of shortening to the mix. Sift the cocoa with the flour. Reduce the cake flour to 2 lb. To replace the chocolate fudge base with bitter chocolate, use 1 lb 10 oz of melted bitter chocolate. Mix the melted chocolate in with the sugar and shortening and cream in well.

Deposit the batter into sheet pans that have been greased at the sides and lined with parchment paper liners. Fill the pans almost to the top. This pound cake brownie may be brushed with egg wash before baking. The top may also be sprinkled lightly with chopped walnuts or pecans. Bake at 360°F. The cake will spring back to the touch gently when baked. The cake may be iced with a fudge icing if the top has not been egg washed.

Yield: 2 to 3 sheets

Chocolate Brownies   *(Layer Cake Texture)*

Ingredients	lb	oz	Mixing procedure
Sugar	5		Cream these ingredients together until soft
Salt		1¼	and light. Scrape the sides of the kettle
Nonfat dry milk		8	
Corn syrup or glucose		8	
Butter	2		
Shortening (regular)	2		
Fudge base	1	12	
Egg yolks	1	8	Add the eggs in 4 stages and cream in well
Whole eggs	1	8	after each addition
Water	2	8	Dissolve the baking soda in the water.
Baking soda		½	Add the vanilla
Vanilla		1½	
Cake flour	4	12	Sift the flour and baking powder together.
Baking powder		½	Add alternately with the water and mix smooth
Walnut pieces and pecans	3		Add the nuts in the final stages of mixing. Scrape sides of kettle

If cocoa powder or bitter chocolate is used to replace the fudge base, follow the same procedures as presented with the pound cake chocolate brownie. Bake the brownie sheets at 360°F. The brownies are turned over and the paper removed. The cake is then iced with a warm chocolate fudge icing. The top of the fudge may be combed in a wave-like effect. Allow the fudge icing to dry and then cut into squares or finger-like oblongs. Brownies may be cut into small cubes for a cookie variety.

Yield: 2 sheets

Brownies   *(Sponge-Type)*

Ingredients	lb	oz	Mixing procedure
Butter	1	12	Melt the butter, shortening, and fudge
Regular shortening	1	6	base over a low flame
Fudge base	3	2	
Sugar	6	4	Warm the eggs, sugar, and salt in a warm
Salt		½	water bath. Whip to a fluffy consistency as
Whole eggs	4		for sponge cake
Bread flour	3	2	Sift the flour. Blend the ground or finely
Chopped or	3	2	chopped nuts with flour. Add the vanilla
ground walnuts			to the eggs and sugar. Fold in the flour
Vanilla		1	and nuts gently until the flour is com-
			pletely mixed into a smooth batter. Add
			the melted butter, shortening, and fudge
			base in a steady stream to the above and
			mix in gently until the batter is smooth
			and completely blended

Deposit the batter into parchment paper-lined sheet pans and spread evenly. Sprinkle the tops with chopped nuts and bake at 360°F. Bake until the brownies feel just slightly soft in the center. Remove from the oven. The cake will fully set as soon as removed from the oven. Cut these brownies in the pan while they are still warm. Separate the cuts when cool, and serve. These brownies will have a chewy characteristic. If bitter chocolate is used to replace the fudge base, use 2 lb 4 oz of melted bitter chocolate melted with the butter and shortening.
Yield: 3 to 4 sheets depending upon thickness

Brownies   *(Cookie-Type)*

These brownies are approximately ¼ in. thick when baked. They are quite crisp and chew very easily. These sheets are cut into squares while they are warm to avoid breakage and uneven cuts.

Ingredients	lb	oz	Mixing procedure
Sugar	4		Cream the ingredients in this stage until
Salt		1	soft and light
Butter	1		
Regular shortening	1		
Fudge base	1		
Vanilla		1	
Eggs	1	8	Add the eggs in 3 stages and cream well
			after each addition
Cake flour	2		Sift the flour, add and mix smooth. Add
Chopped walnuts	1	8	the nuts and blend in well
or pecans			

Deposit the batter into 4 sheet pans that have been greased on the sides and lined with parchment paper. Spread the batter evenly over the pan. Sprinkle the top of the sheet cake with additional chopped nuts. Bake at 365°F until the cake feels mildly soft and tender in the center. Remove from the oven and allow to cool down until warm. Cut the cookies into about 2 in. squares. When cool, remove from the pans and serve. The cookies may be cut into finger-shaped oblongs about 2 in. by 1 in. These cookies are displayed with other cookies. They are also used as a garnish or supplement for ice cream desserts.

Yield: Approx. 4 medium thin sheets

Brownies   *(Candy Variety)*

These brownies will have a soft, close grain and texture. They are moist and chewy. They have the advantage of retaining moisture and will have an extended shelf-life and freshness.

Ingredients	lb	oz	Mixing procedure
Butter	1	8	Melt the butter, shortening, and fudge
Shortening	1	8	base over a low flame
Fudge base	2		
Confectioners sugar	8		Sift the dry ingredients together. Add the
Cake flour	4		melted butter and fudge base and blend in
Salt		1½	well
Baking powder		½	
Whole eggs	4		Add the eggs in 3 or 4 stages and blend in
Vanilla		2	well. Add the vanilla and stir in
Finely chopped walnuts or pecans	3		Add the nuts and blend in well

Deposit the batter into two sheet pans that have been greased on the sides and lined with a parchment paper liner. Spread the batter evenly over the pan. Bake at 365–370°F until just done. The center of the cake or brownie will feel just tender. Remove from the oven and the brownie will set during the first stages of cooling.

The candy brownies may be left plain and cut into small squares or oblongs. They may also be turned over while slightly warm and the parchment paper removed. The brownies may then be iced with a chocolate fudge icing that is combed in a wave-like form. The fudge is allowed to dry and the brownies are then cut and served.

Yield: Approx. 2 sheet pans

Blond Brownies

These brownies are made without chocolate or cocoa. This may be a specialty pastry or cake for people who are allergic to chocolate. For prolonged freshness, the use of an emulsifier is included in the formulary.

Ingredients	lb	oz	Mixing procedure
Granulated sugar	1	8	Cream these ingredients together until soft
Brown sugar	1		and smooth
Salt		1	
Shortening	1		
Butter or margarine	1		
Emulsifier		2	
Cake flour		8	
Eggs	1	12	Add in 3 stages and cream in well
Glucose or corn syrup	1	12	Add and stir in lightly
Water		12	
Vanilla		1	
Cake flour	3	4	Sift the flour and baking powder. Add and
Baking pwoder		2	mix smooth
Chopped walnuts or pecans (variable)	2		Add and mix in lightly

Desposit the batter in two sheet pans that have been lined with parchment paper or have been well greased and dusted with flour. Bake at 370°F. for about 30 min. The center of the cake should spring back lightly to the touch. When cool, the cakes are turned over and covered with a fudge icing. Color and flavor are optional. Chopped walnuts or pecans may be sprinkled over the top before the fudge icing dries.

Sour Cream Cake and Topping

Sour Cream Cake

Ingredients	lb	oz	Mixing procedure
Sugar	4		Cream these ingredients together until soft
Salt		1	and light. Scrape the sides and bottom of
Nonfat dry milk		4	the kettle
Butter	2		
Emulsified shortening	1		
Regular shortening	1		
Egg yolks	2		Add the eggs in 4 or 5 stages and cream
Whole eggs	2		well after each addition
Sour cream	4		Add the sour cream and stir in lightly
Water		8	Dissolve the baking soda in the water and
Baking soda		¾	stir into the above. Add the vanilla
Vanilla		1	
Cake flour	6	6	Sift the flour and baking powder together.
Baking powder		1½	Add and mix to a smooth consistency

Deposit the batter into sheet pans that have been greased and lined with a parchment paper liner. The sheet cakes may be garnished with a special topping made with sour cream. Loaf cakes may be filled with the same topping and garnished on top as well with the same topping. Special form cakes may be made with this batter and filled and garnished with the special topping. Chocolate striped or marbled cakes may be made by adding melted sweet chocolate or a special chocolate filling. Recipes for the special topping and the chocolate filling follow.

Sour Cream Filling or Topping

This filling is used extensively for yeast-raised cakes and babkas, as well as for the sour cream cakes made from the preceding recipe.

Ingredients	lb	oz	Mixing procedure
Brown sugar	1	8	Blend all the ingredients together lightly
Granulated sugar	1	8	and then rub together to form small lumps
Salt		½	as for streusel topping. If the topping is
Sour cream	2		too moist, add additional cake crumbs. If
Toasted, chopped nuts (walnuts, pecans, filberts)	1	8	too dry, add melted butter to soften
Chocolate chips	1		
Cocoa		1½	
Cinnamon		1	
Cake crumbs (variable	2		

The topping should have a slight crumbly feel and appearance. It should sprinkle as streusel topping. When used for a filling, the texture (feel) may be slightly finer and drier. Additional cake crumbs may be added. The loaf cakes or larger cakes may be filled ¼ full and then sprinkled with the filling. The filling is then covered with additional cake mix so that the loaf pans are slightly more than half full. The tops are then garnished liberally with the topping. The large sheet pans may be filled and topped with the special topping and baked as large-type French coffee cakes. These cakes are sliced and served when cool. Sheet cakes may be sprinkled with apple slices (canned, solid pack variety) and then sprinkled with added cinnamon sugar and topping before baking. Pastry chefs may serve the cut squares as a special breakfast item. Loaf cakes and larger cakes may be striped with sweet chocolate that has been melted or lightly folded into the batter and then deposited as for a marble cake effect. The following chocolate filling or smear may be used to replace the sweet chocolate:

Chocolate Filling and Smear

Ingredients	lb	oz	Mixing procedure
Confectioners sugar	9		Sift the sugar and cocoa together
Cocoa (natural)	5		
Fudge base or melted biter chocolate (liquor)	1		Add the softened fudge base and vegetable oil and mix lightly
Vegetable oil	2		
Hot water	4		Add the hot water in 2 or 3 stages and blend in well
Vanilla		2	

This chocolate filling base may be mixed with the cake batter for any of the cakes requiring a marbled or chocolate effect. The filling may also be used as a smear on yeast-raised coffee cake or babka specialties in place of melted sweet chocolate.

The filling or topping may be prepared in advance and kept in closed containers under refrigeration. It is advisable to warm the filling or topping in a warm water bath to soften before using.

Large Creamed-Type Cakes

There are a number of cake specialties that are baked in large, deep pans. These are sliced and served after they have been cooled. These cake slices are often mixed with a variety of cake slices made from other cakes. The slices are assembled in a variety form on special cake platters for special occasions. Slices of cake are often mixed with cakes that are cut into squares. French coffee cake, sponge cake, chiffon cakes, and pound cakes have been covered. These are only some of the cakes that are used for special display and service. The following are recipes for coconut cake and nut cake which are quite popular with pastry chefs.

Coconut Cake

Ingredients	lb	oz	Mixing procedure
Sugar	3		Cream all ingredients to a soft, light consistency. Scrape the sides of the kettle. The fruits will be well distributed
Salt		1	
Nonfat dry milk		4	
Butter	1	8	
Regular shortening	2		
Candied orange peel		12	
Glazed cherries		12	

Use the sugar or short dough to line the bottom of two sheet pans with a thin dough bottom. Bake the bottoms lightly. When cool, the bottoms may be smeared lightly with jam or jelly.

Ingredients	lb	oz	Mixing procedure
Egg yolks	1		Add the eggs in 4 or 5 stages and cream in
Whole eggs	1	8	well after each addition
Water	2		Add the water and flavoring alternately
Vanilla		1	with the flour and coconut
Orange flavoring		½	
Yellow coloring (few drops)	(as required)		
Macaroon coconut (unsweetened)	5		Sift the flours and baking powder together. Add the coconut and blend. Add
Cake flour	1	4	to the above alternately with the water
Bread flour	1		
Baking powder		½	

The cake mix is ready for depositing at this point. If a slightly lighter grain and texture is desired, add the following:

	lb	oz	
Egg whites	2		Whip to a medium peak and fold into the
Sugar		8	above

Bake at 350°F.
Yield: 2 full sheet pans

Nut Cake   (*With Cake Crumbs and Nuts*)

The sheet pans should have prebaked bottoms made from the sugar or short dough. Bake the bottoms lightly. Smear the bottoms with raspberry jelly or jam. If baked on paper liners, the sheets are put together.

Ingredients	lb	oz	Mixing procedure
Sugar	3		Blend the almond paste with a small
Salt		1¼	amount of eggs to a smooth paste. Add
Nonfat dry milk		4	the other ingredients and cream until
Glucose or corn syrup		12	light. Scrape the sides of the kettle.
Almond paste or macaroon paste	1		
Butter	1	8	
Shortening (regular)	1	8	
Egg yolks	1	8	Add the eggs in 4 or 5 stages and cream
Whole eggs	1	8	well after each addition
Water	1		Add the water alternately with the flour
Almond flavoring		½	and cake crumbs
Ground walnuts, cashews, filberts (lightly toasted)	2	12	Sift the cake flour and baking powder. Blend well with the nuts and cake crumbs. Add to the above alternately with the
Cake crumbs (toast lightly if crumbs are moist)	2	12	water and flavoring
Cake flour	1		
Baking powder		½	

The cake mix may be deposited into the pans at this point. If a lighter grain and texture is desired, add the following:

	lb	oz	
Egg whites	1	8	Whip to a medium peak and fold into the
Sugar		10	above

Deposit into the prepared pans (lightly baked bottoms smeared with jam) and level the batter. The pans should be filled almost to the top. Bake the cakes at 350–355°F. Pans that are lined with parchment and then filled are finished by combining two layers together. These pans are filled slightly more than half full. When baked, they are about 1 in. thick. Turn one sheet cake over on a cake board. If made in layer cake form, the layers are turned over on a cardboard with a doily or serving liner. Fill the turned cake with jam or jelly. A raspberry jam is preferred. Place the other layer cake on top and press down gently. Cover the top layer with a thin cover of the same jam. An apricot jam may be used as a contrasting jam for the top or center. The top is then sprinkled with lightly toasted walnuts. The nuts may be blended with lightly toasted sponge cake crumbs. Before serving, dust the cake slices lightly with confectioners sugar.

Yield: 2 full sheet pans

Upside Down Cakes

Upside down cakes are usually made with well drained sliced pineapple. The pans are well greased and lined with a sugar, honey or jelly, and shortening blend. The fruits are placed into the pans with a formal design or planned layout. This is necessary since the cakes are turned over as soon as removed from the oven and the bottom of the cake becomes the top. The partially glazed fruits and cherries are then glazed with an apricot coating or syrup and apricot jam blend. Peach slices or halves may be used. Fruits must be well drained. For the large pans, the pineapple slices are cut into quarters and laid out in lines or patterns that will make cutting into portions easy and equal.

Pan Preparation for Upside Down cake

Ingredients	lb	oz	Mixing procedure
Sugar	1		Cream these ingredients together until
Brown sugar	1	8	light and soft. A small amount of water
Honey [1]		10	may be added to make the spread easier to
Shortening (regular)	1		apply
Butter		12	

Grease the pans with shortening first and then apply a thick coating of the special pan preparation to the bottom of the pan. The sides of the pans may be greased a little lighter, but must be well covered to prevent the cakes from sticking when turned over after baking.

---

[1] A currant or raspberry jelly may be used in place of honey.

Upside Down Cake Mix

Ingredients	lb	oz	Mixing procedure
Sugar	3		Cream all the ingredients together until
Salt		1	soft and light. Scrape the sides of the ket-
Nonfat dry milk		4	tle periodically
Butter	1		
Regular shortening	1		
Glucose or		6	
corn syrup			
Cake flour		8	
Egg yolks	1		Add the eggs in 4 stages and cream in well
Whole eggs	1		after each addition
Water	2		Add the water and flavoring alternately
Vanilla		1	with the flour
Rind of 2 lemons		½	
or lemon flavor-			
ing			
Cake flour	3	8	Sift the flour and baking powder and add
Baking powder		2	alternately with the water. Mix until
			smooth

Deposit the batter in the prepared layer cake or sheet cake pans. Be sure the pineapple slices or pieces and cherries have been spaced evenly. Deposit the batter in sections over the cake. This will make spreading the cake mix easier and will avoid the possible movement of the fruits from the placed position. Bake the cakes at 365–375°F. The cake should spring back readily when touched in the center. Turn the cakes over as soon as removed from the oven. Use oven pads or cloths to avoid burning the hands. Deposit the pans in soaking water immediately. Glaze the top of the cake with hot syrup and apricot coating. Allow the cakes to cool before cutting and serving. Fruit pieces that may tend to stick to the pan should be removed with a spatula and placed in the vacant spaces on the cake. Do this before glazing the top of the cake. (Figs. 7.15 through 7.17.) **Yield:** Approx. 2 sheet pans

7.15
Grease pans heavily

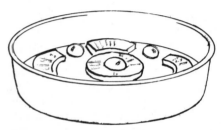

7.16
Place pineapple slices and cherries in pan

7.17
After cake is baked and turned, glaze with
hot syrup

Other Cake Varieties

Checkerboard Cake

Use the same recipe for the checkerboard layers or sheets as the one used for making upside down cake. Be sure the mix is creamed well and mixed to a smooth consistency. The pans are prepared by greasing the sides and lining the bottoms with parchment paper liners. If no liners are used, grease and dust the pans with bread flour. Remove the excess flour. The mix is deposited in a pastry bag with a plain tube. Sheet pans will require a slightly larger tube than a 10-in. layer pan. For the sheet pans, fill the bag with mix and bag out yellow cake lines spaced about 1 in. apart. Be sure the lines are of equal thickness. Two pans should be started with a yellow stripe at each side. The center pan should have the chocolate lines on the outside.

For the layer cakes, have two layers with yellow circles on the outside. Space the inner circles about three-quarter in. apart and of equal thickness. The center layer will have the chocolate circle starting on the outside. Half the mix should be made chocolate by adding the chocolate filling or melted sweet chocolate to the mix. Bake the layers and pans at 370–375°F (Fig. 7.18).

After the cakes have been baked, assemble the cakes in alternate layers. The bottom and top layers should have the same stripe at each end. The center layer should have the alternate stripe. If the stripes are bagged out evenly and spaced evenly, the cake will have alternate checkers or stripes showing. The layers may be filled with a layer of white or yellow buttercream icing and a layer of chocolate buttercream or soft fudge icing. Compress the layers well so that they do not move. The top layer may be iced with a chocolate fondant icing or chocolate fudge icing. The large cakes are sliced into oblong or square cuts. The layer cakes are cut into wedges and served. Thin slices are usually placed so that they are lying down on the plate and the checkerboard effect is obvious.
Yield: Approx. 3 sheet cakes

7.18
Bagged out strips of alternate yellow and
chocolate cake mix

Almond Fruit Cake

Ingredients	lb	oz	Mixing procedure
Sugar	2		Mix the almond paste with a small amount
Salt		½	of the eggs to a smooth paste. Add the rest
Almond paste		12	of the ingredients and cream to light and
Glucose or corn syrup		4	soft consistency
Clover honey		4	
Butter	1		
Regular shortening	1		
Egg yolks	1		Add the eggs in 4 stages and cream in well
Whole eggs	1	8	after each addition. Scrape the kettle often

Ingredients	lb	oz	Mixing procedure
Cake flour	1	2	Sift the flours together. Add to the above
Bread flour	1	4	and mix until smooth
Glazed cherries	1		Dust the fruits lightly with bread flour.
Mixed diced fruits	1		Sift to remove the excess flour. Mix with
Raisins	2		the nuts and then fold into the cake mix.
Walnut pieces	1	8	Mix until evenly distributed
Glazed orange peel		8	

Note: An unbaked bottom of sugar or short dough is required for the bottom of the sheet pan. This bottom should be quite thin and will bake through with the cake mix.

Deposit the mix into the sheet pan and spread evenly. The mix should be almost level with the top of the pan. The top may be washed with egg wash and then lightly criss-crossed with the tines of a fork for a design. The top of the cake may be left plain and later covered with the almond smear and chopped nuts and then lightly browned in the oven. Bake the cake at 350°F for almost 1 hr. Test by touching the center of the cake lightly. If it springs back to the touch, it is baked. Allow the cake to cool and then apply a thin coating of French macaroon mix (see cookie section) over the top of the cake. Sprinkle with chopped walnuts and return to the oven and bake at 400°F for about 8–9 min to allow the macaroon filling to brown lightly. Remove from the oven and cool. This cake is usually cut into 2 in. by 1 in. slices and served with other cake slices. Pastry chefs will also slice these cakes into 1 in. cubes and serve on a mixed platter or display of cookies. These slices are also used in Passover cookie-type display. The sheet is cut into 1½ in. strips and the strips are then thinly sliced as a special cookie.

Yield: 1 full sheet pan

Ginger Cake   (Creaming Method of Mixing)

Ingredients	lb	oz	Mixing procedure
Sugar	1		Cream the ingredients until soft and light
Salt		½	
Nonfat dry milk		6	
Shortening	1		
Eggs	1		Add the eggs in 3 stages and cream after each addition
Molasses	2	12	Add and stir in lightly. Add the spices
Ginger		½	and stir in
Cinnamon		½	
Water	2	8	Dissolve the baking soda in the water.
Baking soda		2	Add alternately with the flour
Cake flour	4	4	Sift the flour. Add alternately with the water

This batter or mix may be used for cupcakes, sheet cakes, or layer cakes. The sheet pans should be lined with a parchment paper liner. Layer cake pans may have a liner or be dusted with bread flour after greasing. Cupcakes are baked in the usual paper cupcake liners. Fill the pans approximately ½ full. Bake at 375–380°F. The sheet cakes are filled with a chocolate fudge icing or a maple flavored buttercream icing. The top of the cakes are iced with chocolate fudge icing and then combed. The layer cakes may be iced with a variety of buttercream and fudge icings. Chopped pecans or walnuts may be sprinkled over the icing.
Yield: Approx. 2 sheet cakes

Spice Cake

Spice cake recipes will vary from those made with molasses with a stronger spice blend to those made without molasses and mildly spiced. Spice cakes are often made with cake crumbs as a supplement and a filler. Cake crumbs are those made from leftover cakes and have become somewhat dry. This is a rather good outlet for the pastry chef in large institutions where the possibility of leftovers does exist. Spice cakes may be served in a single layer cut or double layer effect. A chocolate icing or a light boiled icing may be used.

Ingredients	lb	oz	Mixing procedure
Brown sugar	1		Cream together until soft and smooth.
Salt		½	Scrape the sides of the kettle
Nonfat dry milk		5	
Shortening (regular)	1		
Cinnamon		¼	
Nutmeg		¼	
Allspice		¼	
Cloves		¼	
Eggs		12	Add in 2 stages and cream in
Molasses	1	8	Add and stir in lightly
Water	2		Dissolve the baking soda in the water and
Baking soda		1½	add alternately with the flour and crumbs
Cake crumbs	1	8	Sift the flour. Combine with the crumbs.
Cake flour	2	6	Add alternately with the water and mix smooth

Deposit in sheet pans lined with parchment paper liners. Bake at 375°F.
Yield: Approx. 2 sheet pans (Layers will vary with size)

Dark Fruitcake

Dark fruitcakes are special cakes usually prepared for holiday seasons. The cakes are often prepared in advance and stored for later service. The freshness or shelf-life of the cakes is prolonged by the high percentage of dried fruits which have been soaked in rum or brandy. A blend of syrup and rum may be used for soaking the fruit. The amount of fruit used will depend upon the type of fruitcake the pastry chef will make. The greater the percentage of fruit, the heavier the cake will be. However, most pastry chefs will use an equal amount of fruit and cake batter.

The selection of fruits to be used will be controlled by the cost factor. A moderate fruit blend will contain approximately 25% raisins and currants. The remaining fruits will be composed of red glaze cherries, green glaze cherries, diced citron, glazed orange and lemon peel, pitted and chopped dates and figs. The fruits are washed in warm water to remove any foreign particles and the excess sugar is dissolved from the glazed fruits. The fruits are then steeped or soaked in syrup with or without honey or molasses. A blend of syrup may be made with rum or brandy. For the more discriminate chef, a fifth of rum or brandy may be used. For the pastry chef who prepares the fruitcake for schools and younger children, a warm syrup and honey with rum flavoring will do well for soaking the fruits overnight. The fruits are drained well before they are incorporated into the cake batter. Most dark fruitcakes will also contain nuts. Walnuts and pecans are often used. The amount may vary depending upon the cake desired and the costs involved. The nut pieces are incorporated into the batter before fruits are folded in. The following fruit and nut blend is suggested.

Dark Fruitcake

Fruit Preparation

Ingredients	lb	oz	Mixing procedure	
Seeded raisins	10		Wash the fruits well in warm water to remove the excess sugar	
Currants	5			
Red glaze cherries	2	8		
Green glaze cherries	2	8	Soak in syrup preparation composed of the following:	
Diced citron	2	8	Simple syrup	1 quart
Orange peel (glazed-chopped)	2	8	Honey	½ quart
			Rum flavoring	2 oz
Lemon peel (glazed-chopped)	2	8		
Chopped dates and figs	5			

A fifth of rum or brandy may be used for soaking the fruits. Soak the fruits overnight and then drain well before using.

Dark Fruitcake Mix

Ingredients	lb	oz	Mixing procedure
Almond paste or macaroon paste	2		Mix the almond paste and eggs to a smooth paste
Eggs		8	

Brown sugar	3		Add the ingredients in this stage to the
Granulated sugar	3		above and cream well. Scrape the sides of
Salt		1½	the kettle often
Butter	2		
Regular shortening	2		
Emulsified shortening	2		
Bread flour	1		
Eggs	6		Add the eggs in 5 stages and cream well after each addition
Molasses	1	4	Add the molasses and cream in lightly
Cinnamon		1	Add the spices and blend in
Cloves		¼	
Nutmeg		½	
Bread flour	2	8	Sift the flour and baking powder. Add and
Cake flour	3		mix smooth
Baking powder		½	
Mixed nuts (walnuts, pecans, almonds) (variable)	3		Fold the nuts into the above

Fold the fruit mixture into the above and mix until the fruits are completely and evenly distributed. Deposit the batter into paper-lined loaf pans. The size of the loaf pan and the height will determine the weight of the batter to be deposited. Most fruitcakes are filled approximately three-quarters full. Fruitcakes are baked slowly so that the cakes are baked through thoroughly. The average 2–3 lb fruitcake is baked at 345°F for approximately 2 hr. Test for doneness by touching the cake gently in the center. The cake should feel mildly firm and should spring back to the touch.

Baked and cooled fruitcakes are usually finished with an apricot coating glaze put on hot, and then garnished with slices of fruit and nuts in various designs. The fruits are glazed after placement on the cake. A special glaze made with gum arabic may be used.

Yield: Variable with the size of the pan

Fruitcake glaze

Glucose or corn syrup	1 quart	Boil the water and glucose. Add the gum
Water	1 quart	arabic and boil for about 5 min. Apply the
Gum arabic	1 oz	syrup while hot

Jewish Honey Cake

Ingredients	lb	oz	Mixing procedure
Light brown sugar	2		Place all ingredients in this stage in the
Salt		½	mixing machine and mix at slow speed
Eggs	1	12	until well blended. If the honey is firm
Oil (vegetable)	1		and crusted, warm in a hot water bath be-
Honey (dark, buckwheat honey preferred) 2 qts	6		fore adding to the mix
Cinnamon		¼	
Cloves		⅛	
Allspice		⅛	
Nutmeg		⅛	
Water	2		Dissolve the baking soda in the water and
Baking soda		2	mix into the above
Nut pieces (walnuts and filberts)	2		Add the nuts and fruits to the above and blend in
Chopped orange peel	1		
Mixed, diced fruits	1		
Rye flour	6	4	Sift the rye flour. Add and mix at slow speed for about 5 min until the mix is smooth and flows smoothly

Yield: Variable with size and shape of the pans

Note: The batter is quite soft and has the consistency of a thick gravy.

Deposit into loaf pans that have been lined with special parchment paper loaf cake liners. Fill the pans about half full or slightly less. Garnish the tops with almond halves spaced evenly over the cake batter. Bake at 340°F for smaller loaves. Larger loaves and square pans are baked at 330°F. Bake on double pans to avoid a heavy bottom crust.

The Blending Method of Cake Production

Cakes made from the blending method are distinctly different from the foam- or sponge-type cakes, as well as from the cakes made using the creaming method of mixing. Blending means to mix a number of ingredients together to a uniform state. In a recipe made with the blending method, the ingredients may be mixed all at once or in several stages. However, it also means that the ingredients are uniformly mixed in a shorter time than the added mixing that takes place in the creaming method. Thus, there is not much aeration of the batter resulting from adding mixing or whipping that takes place in creaming and whipping methods. Cakes made with the blending method of mixing have made great advances in the area of prepared mixes and have replaced many of the creamed and combination method cakes.

Note has been made of the rapid rise in the use of prepared cake mixes by pastry chefs and bakers. Greater varieties are being developed. The pastry chef in large institutions and those who must keep a sharp eye on portion costs and controls are presently using these prepared mixes to produce the cakes and pastries for the menus. Quality cakes and cakes that lend themselves well to refrigeration and freezing can be made from the prepared mixes. These mixes can be easily and successfully prepared by assistants to the pastry chef with careful supervision. The pastry chef adds the finishing touches which make these cakes appear the same as those made from "scratch." Pastry chefs often add a little extra in the way of ingredients (eggs, milk, and so forth) to supplement the basic prepared mix after they have experimented with it. However, there are decided advantages in their use. In fact, pastry chefs who make their cake mixes and recipes often keep prepared mixes in reserve for special emergencies where the need for quick mixing and rapid production are required.

The high ratio types of cakes are the basic or principal cakes made with the blending method of mixing. The term "high ratio" refers to the high percentage of sugar and liquid used in the recipes as compared with the amount of flour used. The cakes made with these recipes are usually moist, tender, of fine grain and texture, and have excellent keeping qualities or shelf-life. Most prepared cake mixes use the blending method of mixing, if not specified as the foam type of cake. A brief analysis of the construction of the recipes and ingredients used follows:

1. The weight of the sugar equals or exceeds the weight of the flour. Since sugar is a tenderizer, it follows that the increase will provide the sweetness, as well as the moist tenderness of the cake. The sugar, when dissolved, becomes a syrup and provides for a smoothness in the batter which makes for easy flow and filling of the pans.
2. In order to retain the high percentage of sugar and liquid without forming a curdling effect, an emulsified shortening, commonly called "high-ratio shortening," is used. The special emulsifying fat (lecithin, glycerides) makes possible the formation of the water-in-fat emulsion when the recipe is properly mixed. Prepared mixes usually have added emulsifiers to retain the smooth flowing characteristics of the cake batter.
3. The flour used for the high ratio cakes is a fine cake flour composed of fine starch particles and a low protein content. The starch components of the flour will readily absorb and retain the liquid and help to form the even, smooth grain and structure of the body of the cake. A low protein (gluten-forming) content is important. A high protein flour will tend to form a gluten that will provide toughness and stringiness in the batter when mixed. The low or moderate protein will provide the necessary characteristics for structure building in the cake.

4. Eggs are considered binders and tougheners. The protein of the egg has a binding effect. This is partially counteracted by the natural fat present in the yolk of the egg in the form of the emulsifying fat, lecithin. The eggs absorb and retain air cells when whipped and tend to absorb air cells when mixed in a blending method of mixing. The eggs expand during baking and have a direct leavening effect upon the cake batter. They also contribute to the color of the cake as well as providing essential food value in the form of nutrients. The amount and type of eggs will vary with each recipe, and in accordance with the judgment of the pastry chef.

5. Milk provides the source of liquid necessary for dissolving the dry ingredients and forming a uniform solution of all ingredients in the blending process. Of course, the liquid in the eggs (approximately 75% of the eggs are composed of moisture) provides additional liquid and supplements the liquid of the milk. Many pastry chefs have started to use skim milk powder for reconstitution into liquid milk. The milk solids add the food value. The proteins and milk sugar also provide for an improved crust color. Milk powder is usually added in dry form to the mix and the powder is hydrated during the mixing process.

6. As indicated, the blending method of mixing does not allow for added mixing to incorporate air and the extensive formation of numerous air cells, as in the creaming or whipping method of mixing. Therefore, it is necessary to increase the amount of chemical leavening to provide the light, delicate structure of the cake. Baking powder is the basic leavening used in most cakes. A double acting baking powder is considered best. It releases most of its gas (carbon dioxide) when in the oven and little when mixed in the batter. There are variables in the use of baking powder and other chemical leavening agents such as bicarbonate of soda. When the percentage of eggs (whole eggs, yolks, and whites) is increased in the cake batter, a lesser amount of chemical leavening is required. This is also true when making cakes with a closer grain and smooth texture, as in the case of pound cakes and special cakes for weddings and for petits fours. When the cake contains ingredients such as cocoa and natural syrups such as honey and molasses, the natural acidity (lower pH) is higher. To counteract the effect of the increased acidity, bicarbonate of soda is used in conjunction with the baking powder. The bicarbonate of soda reacts with the natural acids and neutralizes the degree of acidity. This action also has a leavening effect in that carbon dioxide gas is released in the process.

A well balanced high ratio type of cake recipe that is made with the blending method of mixing has the following basic composition:

1. As mentioned in the introduction, the weight of the sugar will equal or exceed the weight of the flour. In most cases the sugar will exceed the weight of the flour. It may often reach as high as 140% of the weight of the flour.

2. The weight of the eggs will exceed the weight of the shortening.
3. The weight of the shortening (emulsified or high ratio) is less than the weight of the eggs.
4. The weight of the milk and eggs is greater than the weight of the sugar in most cases. There may be a variable in special types of close-grained pound cakes.

There are many recipes for high ratio type cakes available. The recipes that follow have been tested and found to meet special needs of the pastry chef who prefers to make the cakes from "scratch."

High Ratio Basic Yellow Layer Cake

Ingredients	lb	oz	Mixing procedure
Sugar	6	10	Sift the dry ingredients together. Add the
Salt		2	water and mix to a smooth consistency at
Cake flour (high ratio)	6		medium speed. Scrape the sides of the kettle. Mix approximately 4 min
Skim milk powder		8	
Emulsified shortening (high ratio)	3	6	
Baking powder		5	
Water	2		
Whole Eggs	2		Add the eggs in 3 or 4 stages and blend in
Egg yolks	2		well after each addition. Scrape the sides and bottom of the kettle
Water	2		Add the water in 2 stages and blend in
Vanilla		2	well
Rind of 2 lemons (optional)			

When properly mixed, the batter should have the consistency of a medium thick gravy and pour easily. The batter may also be picked up in the palm of the hand and dropped out as for cupcakes. This batter may be used for sheet cakes, layer cakes, cupcakes, special loaf cakes, and ring-type cakes.

Pans should be greased on the sides and lined with parchment paper liners. Unlined pans should be greased and then dusted with bread flour. Remove excess flour after dusting. Layer cake and loaf pans are filled to half full or slightly more. Bake the larger and thicker cake units at 365°F. Thinner cakes such as sheets are baked at 375°F. Cakes that are properly baked will have a golden brown crust color and spring back gently to the touch.

Yield: Approx. 4 to 5 sheet cakes, 18 x 24 in.

High Ratio Basic White Cake

Ingredients	lb	oz	Mixing procedure
Sugar	6		Sift the dry ingredients together. Add the shortening and water and mix at medium or slow speed until the batter is of smooth consistency. Scrape the sides of the kettle periodically
Salt		2	
Nonfat dry milk		8	
Cake flour (high ratio)	5	4	
Emulsified shortening (high ratio)	2	8	
Water	3		
Baking powder		5	
Egg whites	3	8	Blend the egg whites, water, and flavoring together. Add in 3 or 4 stages and blend in well after each addition. Mix at slow or medium speed and scrape sides and bottom of the kettle frequently to ensure uniform mixing and blending of all ingredients. The lemon juice will provide a better flavor to the baked cake
Water	1	8	
Vanilla		1	
Almond flavoring (optional)		½	
Lemon juice (optional)		1	

This batter may be used for sheet cakes, layer cakes, cupcakes, and cakes baked in special pans. Prepare the pans as for yellow cake. Larger cakes are baked at 365°F. Smaller or thinner units are baked at 375°F.

Layer cakes and pastries made from sheet cakes can be finished in many different varieties. Buttercream icings, marshmallow icings, and chocolate fudge icings may be used as fillers to sandwich the layers. The same icings may be used for finishing the tops of the cakes. Many of the cakes and pastries made with a sponge cake base may be made from the white cake and the yellow layer cake.

Yield: Approx. 4 sheet cakes, 1 to 1¼ in. thick

High Ratio Chocolate Layer Cake

Ingredients	lb	oz	Mixing procedure
Sugar	6	12	Sift the dry ingredients together. Add the shortening and water and blend at medium speed until a soft, smooth consistency is obtained. Scrape the sides and bottom of the kettle. Mix at medium speed
Salt		2	
Nonfat dry milk		12	
Cocoa (natural)	1	2	
Cake flour (high ratio)	6		
Emulsified shortening (high ratio)	2	8	
Water	4		
Water	2		Dissolve the baking soda in the water and blend into the above
Baking soda		1	

	lb	oz	
Eggs	1	8	Add the baking powder and blend in.
Egg yolks	1	8	Add the eggs in 3 stages with the vanilla
Vanilla		2	and blend in well after each addition
Baking powder		4	

Be sure to scrape the sides and bottom of the kettle periodically to ensure complete distribution and blending of all ingredients. This cake batter may be used for layer cakes, sheet cakes, cupcakes, and special form cakes. Bake the larger units at 360–365°F. Smaller units are baked at 375°F.

Cakes to be finished with the use of whipped cream and pastry custard cream should be chilled before using. In warm weather, these cakes may be finished with marshmallow icing. A variety of combination fudge-type icings and buttercreams may be used. Chocolate and yellow cakes may be combined for variety layers.

Yield: Approx. 5 sheet cakes

High Ratio Devil's Food Cake

Ingredients	lb	oz	Mixing procedure
Sugar	7		Sift all the dry ingredients together to
Salt		2	blend properly. Add the shortening and
Nonfat dry milk		12	water and blend well. Mix at slow or me-
Cake flour (high ratio)	5	4	dium speed until the batter is of smooth consistency. Scrape the sides of the kettle
Cocoa	1	2	periodically
Baking powder		3	
Baking soda		1½	
Emulsified shortening (high ratio)	2	12	
Water	4		
Egg yolks	1	8	Combine the water and the eggs. Add to
Whole eggs	2		the above in 3 stages and blend in well at
Vanilla		2	medium speed. Use slow speed on a high
Water	3		speed mixer

Deposit the batter into prepared pans. The mix can be used for sheet cakes, layer cakes, cupcakes, and specialty loaf and pan sizes. Bake the larger units at 365°F. Smaller units are baked at 375°F. These cakes lend themselves well to finishing with a variety of icings. For example, the cupcakes may be filled with a buttercream or marshmallow icing that resembles a specialty type of cupcake. The layers and sheets may be filled with the same icings and covered with icings that are marbled lightly with chocolate. A variety of fudge-type icings and buttercreams may be used for a variety of finishes.

Note: Cinnamon may be added as a supplementary flavoring. If used, add approximately ½–1 oz. Blend in with the flour.

High Ratio White Pound Cake

Ingredients	lb	oz	Mixing procedure
Cake flour (high ratio)	5	4	Sift all dry ingredients for proper blending and distribution. Add the shortening and water and mix at medium speed to a soft, smooth blend. Scrape the sides of the kettle periodically
Sugar	6	2	
Salt		1½	
Nonfat dry milk		4	
Baking powder		2½	
Cream of tartar		¼	
Emulsified shortening (high ratio)	3	4	
Water	3		
Egg whites	4		Add the egg whites in 4 stages and blend in well after each addition. Use a medium speed. Scrape the bottom and the sides of kettle periodically to avoid lumps
Vanilla		1	
Almond flavoring (optional)		½	

Deposit the batter into prepared sheet pans, layer pans, or loaf-type pans. Bake the larger units at approximately 340°F. Smaller units, such as sheet cakes, are baked at 355°F.

The loaf cakes may be marbled by streaking melted sweet chocolate lightly through the batter and then depositing the batter gently into the loaf pans. Part of the batter (approximately 6 lb) may be mixed with 4 oz of natural-type cocoa, 6 oz of granulated sugar, 4–5 oz of water, and approximately ¼ oz of baking soda. Mix well and form a layer of the chocolate batter over the bottom layer of white mix in the loaf pan. Cover the chocolate layer with a cover of white cake mix. The pans should be a little more than half full, depending upon the height of the pan.

Yield: Approx. 4 sheet cakes, 1 in. thick.

High Ratio Golden Pound Cake

Ingredients	lb	oz	Mixing procedure
Sugar	9		Sift all dry ingredients to blend properly and evenly. Add the shortening and water and blend at slow to medium speed until a soft, smooth consistency is obtained. Scrape the bottom and sides of the kettle frequently
Salt		3	
Nonfat dry milk		10	
Cake flour (high ratio)	7	12	
Baking powder		1½	
Emulsified shortening (high ratio)	5		
Water	3		
Whole eggs	4		Blend the eggs, water and flavoring. Add in 4 stages and blend in well after each addition. Mix at slow to medium speed
Egg yolks	2		
Water	1		
Vanilla		2	

Deposit the batter into prepared pans lined with parchment paper liners. Pans that have no paper liners should be greased and dusted with bread flour. It may be advisable to bake large units that have no paper liners on double pans. Bake the large or deep units at 345°F. Sheet cakes are baked at 350–355°F. This cake mix may be used for special layer cakes, birthday cakes, wedding cakes, and the sheets may be used for French pastry and petits fours. It is advisable to chill the sheets before filling and cutting.

For marble pound cake varieties, mix part of the cake batter with the same preparation as for the white pound cake. The batter may also be striped through with melted sweet chocolate and then deposited in loaf pans.

Yield: 5 to 6 sheet cakes (Loaf cakes filled almost two-thirds full. Fill layer cakes a little more than half full)

High Ratio Banana Cake

Ingredients	lb	oz	Mixing procedure
Ripe bananas	5		Blend the ripe bananas (peeled) with the
Cake flour	2		flour to a smooth consistency
Brown sugar	4		Add the sugar, salt, milk, and shortening
Granulated sugar	2		to the above and blend at medium speed
Salt		2½	to a soft, smooth consistency (6–7 min).
Nonfat dry milk		8	Scrape the sides and bottom of the kettle
Emulsified shorten- ing (high ratio)	2	12	
Egg yolks	1	8	Add the eggs in 3 stages and blend in well
Whole eggs	1	8	after each addition
Water	4		Dissolve the baking soda in the water.
Vanilla		2	Add the vanilla and stir. Sift the cake flour
Banana flavoring		1	and baking powder together. Add the
Cake flour	4	4	water and flour alternately in 2 or 3 stages.
Baking powder		2	Blend at slow speed. Scrape the kettle after
Baking soda		2½	each addition to remove lumps

Deposit the batter in sheet pans that have been greased at the sides and the bottom of the pan lined with a parchment paper liner. Layer cake pans may be greased and dusted with bread flour if no paper liners are available. Fill the layer pans no more than ⅓ to ½ full. It is better to combine two thinner layers than to bake one thick layer and cut into sections after baking. Bake the sheets at 365–370°F. Thicker layers may be baked at 350°F. Special ring pans such as angel food pans and oval-shaped pans may be used for these cakes. Fill these pans about ½ full and bake at 350°F.

Yield: Approx. 4 sheet pans, 1 to 1¼ in. thick

Finishing of Banana Cakes Banana cakes should be finished with a special type of banana fudge icing. Pastry chefs may fill the sheets with the fudge icing, and the layer cakes as well, and then garnish the tops with a whipped cream rosette with a slice of banana glazed with an apricot coating. The loaves and ring cakes may be iced on top with the banana fudge icing and then sprinkled lightly with chopped walnuts. There are other variations in finishing and the creative pastry chef will use them.

Banana Fudge Icing

Ingredients	lb	oz	Mixing procedure
Confectioners sugar	6		Sift the dry ingredients together
Salt		1/4	
Nonfat dry milk		8	
Emulsified shortening (high ratio)	2		Add the bananas and shortening to the above and blend well until smooth and slightly creamy in appearance
Ripe bananas (peeled)	1		
Water		8	Add the water and flavoring in 2 stages and blend in well after each addition. Scrape the sides of the kettle
Vanilla		1	
Banana flavoring		1/2	

Finish the cakes when cool with freshly made fudge icing. Keep the fudge icing covered with a moist cloth when not in use. The icing will form a very thin crust after standing for awhile.

High Ratio Cinnamon Apple Cake

These cakes are usually baked in sheet pans although layer cake pans may be used. The pans are usually lined with parchment paper for both the sheet cakes or the layer cakes. In view of the tenderness of the cake, some pastry chefs will prefer to use a thin, partially baked sugar or short dough bottom for the sheet cakes. Smaller layer cakes will require the parchment paper liner.

Ingredients	lb	oz	Mixing procedure
Granulated sugar	3	4	Sift all dry ingredients together to blend properly. Add the shortening and water and blend for about 7 min to slow to medium speed until soft and smooth
Brown sugar	1	4	
Salt		1½	
Nonfat dry milk		4	
Cake flour	5	8	
Baking powder		1½	
Cinnamon		½	
Emulsified shortening (high ratio)	1	8	
Water	1	8	
Whole eggs	1	4	Add the eggs in 2 stages and blend in well

Water	8	Dissolve the baking soda in the water and
Vanilla	1	vanilla and add. Blend in well
Baking soda	1½	
Canned apples (solid pack preferred) 1 No. 10 can		Add the apples and fold in gently

Deposit the batter into sheet pans or other types of pans and sprinkle the tops with a blend of cinnamon sugar and chopped pecan pieces. Bake at 365–370°F. A lemon cream sauce may be served with each portion.
Yield: Approx. 3 sheet pans

Dutch Apple Cake

These cakes are most often baked in ring-shaped pans similar to those used for angel cakes. Turk-head pans may also be used although they are difficult to prepare because the fluted ridges are not easily greased. Dutch apple cakes are also baked in regular layer cake pans or in large sheet pans. The apples used in this formula are solid pack apples in number #10 cans. The approximate weight of apples and juice is 6 lb. If apple chunks are large, it may be desirable to chop them slightly.

Ingredients	lb	oz	Mixing procedure
Almond paste or macaroon paste	1		Blend together to a smooth paste
Whole eggs		8	
Sugar	3		Blend all ingredients including the almond
Brown sugar	1	8	or macaroon paste to a smooth consis-
Salt		1¼	tency. Mix in second speed until slightly
Nonfat dry milk		5	creamed and aerated.
Cake flour	6	4	
Baking powder		2	
Emulsified shortening	2		
Emulsifier		2	
Water	1	8	
Cinnamon		½	
Egg yolks		12	Add the eggs in 2 stages and blend in well
Whole eggs		12	
Water		8	Dissolve the soda in the water. Lightly
Baking soda		1	blend into the above with the flavorings
Vanilla		1	
Lemon flavoring		½	
Canned apples (1 No. 10 can)			Add the apples and raisins and blend in lightly
Raisins (optional)	2		

Pan Preparation Grease the pans heavily with softened shortening. Combine equal amounts of sifted cake crumbs and chopped pecans. Line the bottom and sides of the pans with the cake-nut preparation. Add a little extra to the bottom of the pan. This will help support the cake batter and prevent sticking after the cakes have been baked. Fill the pans slightly more than half full. Sprinkle the top of the cake batter with Streusel crumb topping and pecan pieces. Sprinkle cinnamon sugar over the topping. Chocolate bits may also be added to the topping for variety.

Bake the cakes at 360°F. until the center of the cake feels slightly firm and springs back gently to the touch. Larger cakes are baked at lower temperatures for a longer period. Remove the cakes from the pans while still mildly warm on to a cardboard liner. Stripe the cakes with warm fondant icing or sweet roll icing. The tops of the cakes may be left plain and later dusted lightly with confectioners sugar.

When baked in large sheet pans, it is advisable to line the bottom of the pan with a thin short dough. Bake the bottom lightly before placing the batter into the pan. Layer cake pans may be lined with parchment paper liners. The sides of the pan are greased and lined with the cake crumb and pecan preparation.

Cakes Made by Combined Methods

Pastry chefs often combine the creaming and whipping methods of mixing old-fashioned pound cakes. Maximum leavening is obtained through the incorporation and retention of air cells in the creaming and whipping methods. For example, old-fashioned pound cake requires creaming the butter and shortening with the flour. The eggs and sugar are whipped as for sponge cake. The whipped eggs and sugar are then folded into the creamed flour and shortening. Most batters made in this manner require little or no chemical leavening. Recipes that include added moisture in the form of water, milk, or other liquids will require chemical leavening to raise the cake and provide the necessary grain, texture, and structure. An example of this was indicated in the recipes for the nut cake and the coconut cake. The use of whipped egg whites and sugar was optional for further aeration. A small amount of baking powder was used to aerate the added milk (nonfat dry milk and water).

Cakes made with this method will follow the regular method as for the creamed cakes, except for the fact that additional egg whites are whipped with sugar and then folded into the creamed batter. Pastry chefs will often separate the whites from the yolks of whole, fresh eggs. The yolks are creamed into the batter with the sugar and shortening. The egg whites are whipped separately with some of the sugar and then folded in. The cake structure is usually more delicate, has a closer grain, and a slightly smoother texture than cakes made with the creaming method. Care must be used in whipping the egg whites to a medium soft peak for easy folding in and distribution. Improperly distributed whipped egg whites are often the cause of large air pockets or holes and uneven grain. The recipes that follow are examples of some of the popular cake varieties made from the combination method of mixing.

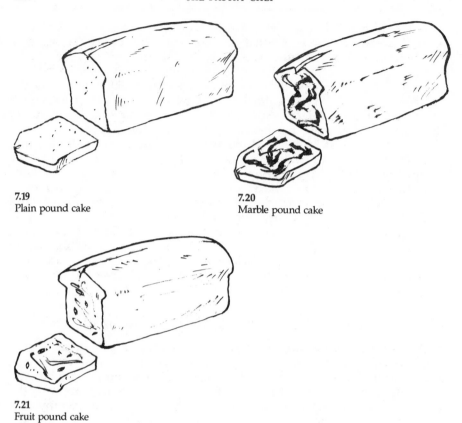

7.19
Plain pound cake

7.20
Marble pound cake

7.21
Fruit pound cake

Old-Fashioned Pound Cake

Ingredients	lb	oz	Mixing procedure
Cake flour	2		Sift the flours. Add the butter and short-
Bread flour	1		ening and cream until light. Scrape the
Butter	1	8	sides of the kettle
Shortening (regular)	1	8	
Sugar	3		Whip the eggs and sugar as for sponge
Salt		½	cake. Fold in the vanilla. Fold the whipped
Egg yolks	1		eggs into the above. Mix until fully
Whole eggs	2		blended.
Vanilla		1	

Deposit the batter into sheet pans that have been lined with parchment paper liners. These sheets are often used for petits fours glaces and for special cakes. Bake the sheet cakes at 360°F. For loaf-type pound cakes, fill parchment paper-lined loaf pans about two-thirds full (Fig. 7.19).
Yield: 2 full sheets (variable with size of loaf pans used)

Marble Pound Cakes Add some chocolate filling or sweet chocolate to ⅓ of the batter. Fill the pans with a layer of yellow. Follow with a layer of chocolate. Cover with another layer of yellow (Fig. 7.20).

Fruit Pound Cake Loaves Increase the bread flour to 2 lb and reduce the cake flour to 1 lb. Add approx. 5 lb of mixed fruits and nut pieces to the batter and fold in gently to distribute evenly. Bake the pound cakes at 345°F (Fig. 7.21).

Chocolate Marble Cake

This cake is marbled or striped through with melted sweet chocolate and is often called Wonder Cake by bakers and pastry chefs. It may be made in loaf form, as for pound cakes, or in large, deep pans.

Ingredients	lb	oz	Mixing procedure
Almond paste or macaroon paste		12	Mix the almond paste and eggs to a smooth consistency
Eggs		4	
Sugar	2	8	Combine these ingredients with the al-
Salt		1	mond paste and cream well until soft and
Nonfat dry milk		2	light. Scrape the sides of the kettle
Bread flour		8	
Butter	1	4	
Regular shortening	1		
Egg yolks	1	8	Add the eggs in 4 or 5 stages and cream in
Whole eggs	1	8	well after each addition. Scrape the kettle
Water		8	after each addition of eggs. Stir the water
Vanilla		1	and flavoring in lightly
Cake flour	2	12	Sift the flour and baking powder. Add and
Baking powder		1	mix into the above until smooth
Egg whites	2		Whip the egg whites and sugar to a me-
Granulated sugar		8	dium soft peak. Fold into the above
Melted sweet chocolate (variable)	2	8	

Pour the melted sweet chocolate over the entire batter in the mixing bowl. Fold the batter over from the bottom to the top about 3 or 4 turns. This will stripe the chocolate through the batter. Deposit the batter in large handfulls into the prepared loaf cake pans that have been lined with parchment paper liners, or into the large deep pan whose sides have been greased and the bottom lined with a paper liner. Avoid smearing the chocolate in order to maintain the marbled effect. Loaf pans should be filled about two-thirds full. The tops of the batters in pans may be striped with sweet chocolate before baking. Bake at 360°F for the loaf pans. Large pans are baked at 350°F. The cakes are sliced as for pound cakes when served. Large cakes may be turned over and the bottom of the cake iced with a chocolate fudge icing and then cut into portions of varying sizes and shapes.

Yield: Approx. 1 large deep pan ($16 \times 24 \times 3\frac{1}{2}$)

Yellow Layer Cake   (*Combination Method of Mixing*)

Ingredients	lb	oz	Mixing procedure
Sugar	3	8	Cream the ingredients in this stage until
Salt		1	soft and light
Nonfat dry milk		8	
Butter	1		
Regular shortening	1	4	
Cake flour	5	4	Sift the cake flour and baking powder.
Baking powder		2¼	Add alternately with the water and blend
Water	4		smooth. Add the juice and rind of the
Vanilla		1	lemons and blend in
Juice and rind of 2 fresh lemons			
Egg yolks	1	8	Whip the eggs and sugar as for sponge
Whole eggs	1		cake and then fold into the above
Sugar		2	

Deposit the batter into sheet pans lined with paper or prepared layer cake pans. Fill the pans slightly more than half full. Bake at 370°F. These cakes will have a tender, springy feel when baked. Finish the sheets or layer cakes in a variety of ways as for regular layer cakes made from the high ratio or chiffon-type cake mixes.

Yield: Approx. 4 sheet cakes

Gold Pound Cake

Ingredients	lb	oz	Mixing procedure
Cake flour	3	8	Sift the cake flour. Cream the flour, butter,
Nonfat dry milk		6	and shortening to a soft, smooth consis-
Butter	1	8	tency
Regular shortening	2		
Sugar	4	8	Whip the eggs and sugar as for sponge
Salt		1½	cake. Fold gently into the above
Egg yolks	1	8	
Whole eggs	1	12	
Water	2		Dissolve the sugar in the water with the
Vanilla		1	vanilla. Add alternately with the remain-
Sugar	1		ing flour and baking powder
Cake flour	2		Sift the flour and baking powder and add
Baking powder		2	alternately with the water. Mix at slow speed to avoid overmixing and reducing the volume of air cells

Deposit into loaf pans or ring pans as for angel cake. Bake at 355°F. Sheet pans are baked at 365°F.

Yield: Approx. 4 sheet pans (Loaf cakes will vary with size)

Special Variety Cakes and Pastries

Many of the Continental style pastries and cakes are made from various types of sponge or foam cakes. The recipes for the popular varieties have been presented. The choice of recipe will largely depend upon the dessert or pastry to be made and the judgment of the pastry chef. Many of the desserts have a fundamental American title or name and still retain the same name even when slightly changed. Changes in filling, covering, garnish, and design are simply variations that pastry chefs in this country will make to provide variety. However, this is not altogether the practice followed in other countries. Many European chefs have a different name for each variation. Thus, it should be understood that many pastries with differing names are basically similar except for minor changes in filling or cover. For example, a chocolate roll, Swiss roll, Fedora roll, or a Marquise roll are all made from a chocolate sponge cake batter. The filling and finish of each is varied.

Jelly Rolls and Filled Rolls

Jelly rolls may be made from a variety of the sponge recipes presented. The basic sponge cake may be used for the rolls that are filled with jam or jelly. The chiffon cake recipe may be used as well. Many pastry chefs prefer the chiffon cake recipes because of the flexibility of the baked cake and its longer shelf-life or freshness.

There are basic procedures to be followed when making the jelly rolls and other types of filled cake rolls. The sponge cake batters are usually slightly softer than the sponges for larger sponge-type cakes and spread easily when placed in sheet pans. Sheet pans are usually lined with parchment paper liners. If no paper liners are used, pans are greased and then dusted with bread flour. The cake batter is spread quickly and evenly over the surface of the pan. Even thickness and distribution of the batter is important in order to have an even sheet cake and an even roll when the cake is rolled (Fig. 7.22). Sheet cakes for jelly rolls should be baked immediately.

7.22
Spread sponge mix evenly over pan

7.23
Turn baked sheets on floured or sugar-dusted cloths and roll up

Proper baking temperature will vary with the sponge or chiffon cake used and the thickness of the cake. Very thin sheets for miniature rolls (Swiss pastries) require a higher baking temperature for a quicker bake. Baking temperatures will vary from 400°–425°F. Sponge cake rolls will bake faster than the chiffon-type cake rolls. The additional oil and beaten egg whites will require a slightly longer baking time. The structure of the cake must be fully set for the chiffon to avoid shrinking and to prevent collapse of the cake after baking. Avoid baking sheets for sponge-type jelly or other filled rolls in ovens that are not hot enough. This tends to overbake or dry the cake which, when rolled, would tend to crack. Overbaking at proper temperature will also have the same effect. A thin sheet cake will continue to bake slightly for the first minute or so after the cakes have been removed from the oven.

Making Up or Finishing Jelly Rolls

1. Sponge cake sheets should be turned over onto dusted cloths or parchment paper sheets. The cloths or sheets may be dusted with fine granulated sugar before turning over the sheet cakes. Some pastry chefs will use a light dusting of bread flour. Allow the pans to remain over the turned sheets. This will retain most of the moisture in the cake (Fig. 7.23).
2. When the sheet cakes are still warm, not hot, roll up loosely in the bottom cloth or parchment paper with the cloth or paper acting as a temporary filler or separator of the cake layers formed in rolling. This procedure sets the structure and shape of the cake and will prevent the sheet cake from cracking or breaking when filled and then rolled. This method also avoids possible tearing or flattening of the sponge sheet cake when the jelly, jam, or other filling is applied while the cake is hot or warm. It is especially helpful when the cake has to be filled with a buttercream type of icing or whipped cream and then rolled. The cakes must be cool before filling and rolling.

Note: Sheets made with the chiffon cake recipe may be left in the pans to cool. They may or may not be turned over when removed from the oven. Thin sheets, as for seven-layer cakes, do not have to be turned if

7.24
Spread jam or other filling over sheet

baked properly. Chiffon cakes, as indicated, have the vegetable oil and the chiffon-sponge structure provided by the whipped egg whites to provide the flexible rolling qualities not present to the same degree in ordinary sponge batters. However, the French type of sponge cake with the whipped egg whites will perform as well as the chiffon cake. In addition, the recipe for the chocolate roll or Swiss roll has a high percentage of liquid and sugar which will also allow the sheet cakes to cool and then be rolled without any difficulty.

When preparing the filling for the jelly roll, the jelly or jam should be soft and smooth. Lumps in the jelly or jam are removed by working the jelly in a bowl with a wooden spoon. A small amount of simple syrup may be added to soften the jelly or jam if too stiff. Jelly prepared to a soft, smooth texture will result in even distribution, use of less jelly to cover the cake surface, and will take less time to apply. Unroll the roll if it is made from a sponge cake type recipe. You will note that the cake will tend to curl slightly as if to roll up again. This is desirable. Chiffon cake sheets are simply turned over on a cloth or parchment paper sheet dusted with sugar for filling and rolling. Deposit the required amount of jelly or jam (this may be measured or weighed for portion control) on the sheet cake and spread evenly with a spatula (Fig. 7.24). Grasp the upper end of the cloth or parchment paper liner and roll the sheet cake up with a firm pressure so that the cake sticks to the jelly or jam (Fig. 7.25). When completely rolled, roll up again in the cloth or paper to keep the roll in place and to set. The jelly roll may then be refrigerated or placed in the

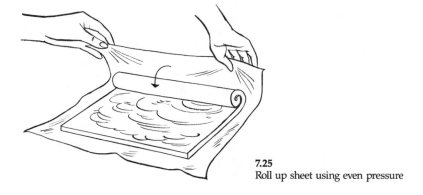

7.25
Roll up sheet using even pressure

7.26
Finish the roll with jelly and coconut or
other method of finishing

freezer for finish as required. When the rolls have set for about 30 min, unroll and then finish in any of the following methods:

1. Dust with confectioners sugar and slice into portions. *Dip the knife in hot water when slicing to obtain smooth, even slices.*
2. Cover the top and sides of the roll with a thin cover of the same jam or jelly used for the filling and then roll in medium shred coconut. Sponge cake crumbs may be used as a topping. Dust with confectioners sugar and slice.
3. The tops of the cakes may be covered with a buttercream type of icing and rolled in a variety of toasted nuts or commercially prepared crunchies.
4. The roll may be decorated for special occasion cakes in log or roll form (Fig. 7.26).

Swiss Rolls

Swiss roll varieties are largely made from the chocolate sponge or chocolate Swiss roll recipes. The chocolate chiffon recipe is used extensively by many pastry chefs. Note is made of the fact that Swiss rolls are often mixed with other French pastry varieties when made in smaller thicknesses and slightly wider slices. A yellow or plain type of sponge cake recipe may also be used for the Swiss roll made with this recipe. The French-type sponge cake recipe is used for this type of Swiss roll. The sheets for the Swiss roll are thinner than those made for the regular jelly rolls. This allows for a thinner spiral of cake and filling in the roll.

Swiss Chocolate Roll Fill the sponge sheet (either the yellow French sponge or yellow chiffon cake may be used) with an even filling of chocolate buttercream. Roll up firmly and chill the roll before finishing. The top of the roll may be covered with chocolate buttercream and then combed for a rough log effect. The top may also be finished with a pastry bag and tube design. Special log cakes may be made from the roll with special lengths cut from the log. Thin rolls are cut into slices and placed into cups for French pastry.

Pistachio Swiss Roll (Fedora Roll) Fill the chocolate sheet with a layer of pistachio colored and flavored buttercream. Chopped pistachio nuts may be mixed into the buttercream before the cream filling is placed into the roll. Refrigerate the roll and cover the top of the roll when chilled with a covering of pink buttercream or pink fondant icing. Slice and place into paper cups. Thin rolls may be cut slightly wider. Thicker rolls are cut thinner. Be sure to dip the knife in hot water when slicing to prevent smearing the buttercream or the icing when slicing.

Swiss Fudge Roll (Marquise Roll) Fill the chocolate sheet with a thin spread of warm chocolate fudge icing. For the more expensive variety, use Aganasse or Ganache cream as the filler. Chill the rolls and then cover the tops with chocolate fudge icing. The tops may also be garnished with sliced almonds. The fudge icing may be combed while still warm and before garnishing.

Mocha Swiss Roll Fill either a yellow sponge or chiffon sheet, or a chocolate sheet with a mocha or coffee flavored buttercream and roll up. Chill the roll and cover the top with a thin cover of mocha buttercream. Use a pastry bag and tube to decorate the top in a variety of designs made with a French tube or star tube. Chill and then cut into slices.

Walnut Roll (Marguerite Roll) A nut sponge cake sheet that has been baked thin, as for a jelly roll, may be used for this pastry specialty. A chocolate sheet or yellow sheet may be used since the filling and finish provide for the special appearance and flavor. Fill the sheet with a layer of coffee or mocha buttercream icing. Roll up and chill. When chilled, cover the top with mocha or coffee buttercream and garnish the top with chopped walnuts. Chill and then slice into pastry slices.

Miniature Swiss Chocolate Rolls Thin chocolate sheets are required for this special pastry. Some pastry chefs will use the regular chocolate roll and then cut the sheet in half horizontally to form two separate sheet halves. Each half is filled with a chocolate buttercream and then rolled up tightly and chilled. The tops of the rolls are then finished with melted sweet chocolate or a warm fudge icing that is spread rather thin but covering the top and sides of the roll. Chill the roll when the chocolate or icing has set and dried. Slice and serve for French pastry with other forms of French pastry (Figs. 7.27 and 7.28).

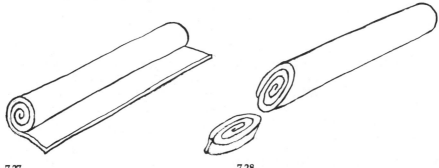

7.27
Buttercream-filled miniature cake roll

7.28
Miniature cake roll cut at an angle

Whipped Cream Rolls   These are not the Swiss rolls but are listed as a roll type of pastry or dessert. Sponge cake or chocolate sponge cake, or chiffon sheet cakes may be used for these specialties. The whipped cream is spread evenly over the sheet and the sheet rolled up with just enough pressure to make the cake adhere to the cream without forcing the whipped cream out of the sides of the roll. Roll up the cake in cloths or parchment paper liners and chill. Finish the tops with whipped cream using a pastry bag and tube. The tops or individual slices may be garnished with nuts, fruits, shaved chocolate, or other garnish selected by the pastry chef. The center of the roll may be filled with bananas so that the banana slice shows with each individual cut or slice. The cream may also be sprinkled with sliced strawberries and the tops garnished with whole or half strawberries when finished.

In warm weather, the pastry chef may use a boiled icing or marshmallow icing for the filler. Chocolate sheets may be filled with marshmallow icing and rolled. The tops are also finished with marshmallow and a design made with the edge of the spatula for a rough finish. The top of the roll is then sprinkled with chocolate cake crumbs or a chocolate crunchie. Chocolate sprinkles or chocolate shavings may be used as a garnish for the chocolate rolls.

Specialty Log Cakes   These may be made from any of the rolls. The design and inscription will depend upon the occasion. Small cakes for individual table service or large cakes may be made and assembled for special design and display (Fig. 7.29).

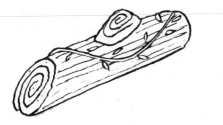

7.29
Log-type cakes

Gateaux

The variety of cakes presented in this section are those that are made with a sponge-type cake base. The plain sponge, almond sponge, nut sponge, butter sponge, and French sponge are some of the sponge-type cakes that will be suggested for use in order to make the cake specialties. Pastry chefs will usually pattern the cake after the recipe and name given the cake or gateau. Gateaux are cakes made with sponge-type cake base and the names for each of the cakes vary with the Continental source. They also vary with names derived from former pastry chefs and chefs who embellished the recipes for the cake. Many of the gateaux have names of places in various European countries. Others may have the names assigned in honor of particular people.

Basically, the pastry chef will vary the menu with the impressive gateaux names and adjust the contents and finish of the cake to the various factors related to cost and production. In large-scale feeding and serving, gateaux names are often replaced by the American or home-made title associated with the cake or dessert. A strawberry shortcake will be made with either a sponge cake base or layers of sponge cake, or it may be home-made American style on a light biscuit and served in a special deep dish. In any case, the pastry chef will determine the type of cake, the methods of production, and the time and effort required for the particular method of finishing the cake.

Note is also made that pastry chefs frequently differ in the exactness of the filling and finishing or decorating the cake. In fact, the detail, finish, and time for these factors is also controlled by the establishment and feeding requirements. It is still the masterful skill required by haute cuisine that allows for time and expression of the skills in decorating fine cakes and pastries. The demands of modern dining and larger numbers of diners have been responsible for the changes in the production of many cakes, pastries, and desserts. The changes are equally reflected in service to the diner. The cakes that follow are a selected group that are popular as gateaux with Continental names and either identical or similar cakes with American names or titles.

Shadow Layer—Gateau Javanaise

A round layer or oval-shaped deep pan may be used for the cake. A basic sponge cake or butter sponge may be used. The cake should be about 3 in. high. When the cake has cooled and been chilled, slice the cake into 3 layers of equal thickness. Fill the layers with a mocha or coffee buttercream. Two different buttercreams may be used such as a chocolate buttercream and a coffee buttercream for variety of color and taste. Cover the layer with a thin or prime cover of chocolate buttercream and chill the cake. When chilled, cover the top with chocolate fondant icing. The icing may cover the entire side of the cake or small strips of icing may be drawn or piped down from the top surface of the cake. The cake may also be covered with pistachio buttercream and chilled slightly. The top may then be covered with chocolate fondant icing or spread with melted sweet chocolate with streaks or drip lines of the icing or chocolate drawn down the sides. The top of the cake may be decorated with small rosettes of pistachio buttercream garnished with a pistachio nut in the center. The serving slice will depend upon the size of the layer cake or oval-shaped pan.

Strawberry Sponge Layer—Gateau Alhambra

An almond sponge or a regular sponge cake may be used for this cake. It is usually baked in a square or rectangular pan about 3 in. thick. Slice the cake into 3 or 4 layers and fill each layer with a strawberry buttercream. This buttercream may be made by blending strawberry jam and crushed fresh strawberries or cooked strawberry filling with basic buttercream icing. A few drops of red coloring and some strawberry flavoring may be added to the buttercream. Press the layers together gently and then cover the entire surface of the cake (top and sides) with a thin layer of buttercream to seal all exposed openings around the sides and the top. Chill the cake and then cover the top and sides with a pink (strawberry flavored) fondant icing. When the fondant dries, decorate the top with small rosettes or rosebuds made from buttercream or rose paste icing.

Mocha-Eclair Surprise—Gateau Ecossaiss

This fine pastry dessert is quite impressive in appearance both in the whole cake form and in the individual portion served. The cake is very useful for serving large numbers of diners. It may be made in large baking sheet pans or in deep square or rectangular pans. A sponge cake or butter sponge may be used for the cake. Some pastry chefs will use a chocolate sponge for blending two different sponge layers when finishing the cake. The baked cake should be about 2½–3 in. thick. If separate sheet pans are used, the sheets should be about three-quarters to 1 in. thick when baked. Slice the baked sponge cake into 3 layers or assemble 3 baked sheet cakes. Fill the layers or sheets with mocha or coffee buttercream. Cover the top of the cake with a thin layer of coffee or mocha buttercream to fill in any unevenness. Chill the cake and then cover the top with a mocha or coffee fondant icing.

Prepare enough miniature eclairs (about 2 in. long and ½–¾ in. wide). Fill with pastry cream custard and ice with chocolate fondant icing. The eclairs may be iced with a coffee or mocha icing and then striped with fine chocolate fondant or sweet chocolate across the tops. The square or rectangular sponge cake, or the sheet cakes which have been put together as a large sponge cake, should be marked off carefully for portion size. In the center of each serving or portion a rosette of mocha or coffee buttercream is made. Place a finished eclair in the center of each rosette and press in gently.

Kirsch or Cherry Layer—Gateaux Supremes

A basic sponge cake or butter sponge cake may be used for this cake. Bake the cakes in layer cake pans about 3 in. high. Slice the cake into 3 or 4 layers. Cakes with thicker fillings will require 3 layers. Fill the layers with a cherry buttercream. This is made with basic buttercream that has chopped glazed cherries mixed into it with added red coloring and cherry flavoring. A kirsch flavoring may be added. Regular kirsch may be added to the buttercream with a slight increase in confectioners sugar to absorb some of the kirsch. Cover the top and sides with buttercream and garnish the sides of the cake with chopped walnuts. The top is finished with a design made with a spatula and garnished with chopped cherries and candied (diced) fruits. Dip the knife in hot water when slicing the cake.

Mocha Chocolate Layer—Gateau Milka

The cake is made from a chocolate sponge cake recipe. It is baked in round or rectangular pans. Large sheet pans are advisable for service to large groups of diners. Slice the layer cakes into 3 or 4 layers if the cake is about 3 in. thick. If sheet cakes are used, use 3 or 4 sheet cakes depending upon the thickness of the sheets. Fill the layers with mocha buttercream icing and press gently together. Cover the top of the cake and the sides with a thin covering of mocha buttercream and chill the cake. When cold and firm, cover the top with chocolate fondant icing. The sides of the round layers may be garnished with chocolate sprinkles, chocolate cake crumbs, or chocolate crunchies. Mark off the cake portions to be sliced and garnish each slice or portion with a design made with mocha buttercream. Garnish with chocolate shavings or small diamond shapes cut out of thin sheets of sweet chocolate.

Orange Sponge Cake—Gateau Portugaise

Use a plain sugar or butter sponge for the round layer cakes. The cakes may be made in sheet cake form. An orange chiffon cake batter may be used very nicely for this cake. Bake the layer cakes about 2½ to 3 in. thick. Three sheet cakes may be used if large numbers are to be served. Slice the baked and cooled layer cakes into 3 layers. Fill the layers or sheet cakes with orange buttercream. A blend of buttercream and orange pastry cream may be used. It may be advisable to smear each layer very thinly with an orange jam or marmalade and then add the orange buttercream. For added color, take a small part of the basic buttercream and mix it with yellow and a few drops of red coloring to form an orange buttercream. Add this to the basic buttercream with some added orange flavoring. Concentrated orange juice may be added to the buttercream for a more natural flavor. Cover the cake with orange buttercream. The sides may be garnished with sponge cake crumbs or sliced almonds which have been lightly toasted. Each portion may be garnished with a rosette of buttercream and a slice of mandarin orange placed on top.

Pineapple Suprise Layer—Gateau Ananas

Layer cakes or sheet cakes may be made from a basic sponge cake or French sponge cake. A chiffon layer cake made with lemon and orange may also be used. Flavor the sponge cakes with the added rind of fresh lemons. Cut the layer cakes into 3 layers or use three sheet cakes that have been baked and are about three-quarters in. thick. Prepare a pineapple buttercream by combining pineapple filling (cooked or canned) with the buttercream. Additional coloring may be added to the buttercream. The layers may first be smeared lightly with pineapple filling before adding the buttercream. Cover the top and sides with the pineapple buttercream. The sides of the round layers may be garnished with sponge cake crumbs or sliced almonds. Mark off the portions of the cake and then garnish each portion with a quarter slice of canned pineapple that has been brushed lightly with hot apricot glaze. Pastry chefs may use a light yellow buttercream and make a rosette or other design with a pastry bag and tube. The center of the design may then be filled with a small amount of pineapple filling. The center of the filling may have a half of a glazed cherry placed in the center for further color.

Dobos Cake or Dobos Torte

This is a Hungarian dessert cake that has achieved popularity in many European countries and in the United States. It is similar to seven-layer cake. In most instances the Dobos torte is usually composed of eight thin sponge-like cakes or sheets. Pastry chefs have the choice of using a butter sponge or an almond sponge cake mix. Some chefs will use the chiffon cake flavored with almond flavoring. Round layer pans of the same size are used and 7 or 8 thin layers are baked. One pan is used for each of the layer cakes. If sheet pans are used, the batter is spread thinly over the pans as for the seven-layer cakes. The sheets are baked in a hot oven (435°F). The following is a special recipe for the pastry chef who wishes to prepare the sheets or layers from this Dobos torte recipe:

Dobos Torte Cake

Ingredients	lb	oz	Mixing procedure
Sugar	1	10	Warm the egg yolks and sugar in a double
Salt		¼	boiler. Whip until thick
Yolks	2		
Heavy cream	1		Add the cream and fold in gently until
Vanilla (optional)		1	distributed
Bread flour	2		Sift the flour and fold in gently
Egg whites	2	8	Whip egg whites to a medium stiff consistency and fold into the above

Deposit into layer pans that have been greased and dusted with bread flour. Spread the mix evenly but thinly over the bottom with a flexible spatula. Divide the batter evenly over the 7 or 8 sheet pans that have been lined with a parchment paper liner. Bake at 425–435°F until just done and remove from the oven. Allow the sheets to cool. The thin layers may be removed from the layer pans while still warm. Fill or sandwich the layers or sheets together with chocolate buttercream. The top layer of the round pans may be iced or covered with a caramel icing or caramel sugar. The top layer is then cut into sections to equal the number of servings to be cut from each of the round layer cakes. To prepare the caramel sugar cover, proceed as follows:

Ingredients	lb	oz	Mixing procedure
Sugar	2		Place in a sauce pan and mix continuously
Butter		3	over a low flame until the sugar has melted and takes on a light brown color

Spread with a spatula over the top of the cake while hot. Cut the layers into slices to equal the number or portions. It is advisable to dip the knife in vegetable oil or brush the blade lightly with butter to prevent the caramel sugar from sticking to the knife.

The tops of the cakes may also be covered with sweet chocolate or Aganasse cream. A chocolate fudge icing may also be used. For the round layer top that has been covered with caramel sugar and cut into slices, after compressing 6 or 7 of the layers, place a small rosette of chocolate buttercream under each of the slices of caramel covered cake sections so that they stand up as separate blades of a fan. The large sheet cake put together with 7 or 8 sheets filled with chocolate buttercream should be compressed and then chilled before finishing. The full sheet is cut into strips that will vary from 3 to 4 in. wide. The strips are then covered with sweet chocolate or the cookie dip chocolate and then combed with a slight wavy effect for design. Place the strips of cake on an icing grate so that excess chocolate or icing may run off onto the marble table top or the pan under the grate. This makes collecting the excess icing or chocolate easier and eliminates waste. The strips are then cut to size for the portions required. This preparation is similar to that to be followed for the preparation of seven-layer cake.

Chocolate Rum Layer—Gateau Jamia
A chocolate sponge cake or chocolate chiffon cake mix may be used for this cake. Bake the cake in layer cake pans or sheet cake pans. The layer cakes should be about 3 in. high. Chill the baked layers before slicing. Slice into 4 layers. Fill the layers with a rum flavored icing. The cake layers and the sheets may be brushed lightly with a rum syrup before applying the buttercream. This will increase the flavor of the cake as well as moistening the cake. Cover the entire layer cake with a thin coating of rum buttercream and chill. Sheet cakes may be put together (4 thin chocolate sheet cakes) the same way. When the cakes are chilled, cover the tops and sides with a light pink fondant icing. The tops or marked off portions are decorated with rum flavored buttercream. The rosette effect and long spiral effect is impressive. Use a small to medium size French tube with a pastry bag for decorating.

Coffee Mocha Layer—Gateau Mocha
A plain sponge or coffee flavored chiffon layer cake mix may be used for the layers or sheet cakes. Slice the baked layer cakes into 3 or 4 layers and fill them with a mocha or coffee buttercream. The cakes may be finished with mocha buttercream using a spatula and garnished with thin stripes of sweet chocolate. The cake may also be covered with a light covering of buttercream, chilled, and then iced with a mocha flavored fondant icing (Figs. 7.30 and 7.31.).

7.30
Cutting and filling the layers

7.31
Icing and finishing the layers

Chocolate Fudge Layer—Gateau Fedora

A chocolate sponge or chocolate chiffon layer is required for this cake. Pastry chefs may also use the high ratio type of cake batter to prepare the layers or the sheet cakes. The layer cakes are cut into 3 or 4 thin layer slices. Thin sheets may be used for the larger cakes. Fill the layers with chocolate fudge icing or Aganasse cream. The tops of the cakes are also finished with chocolate fudge icing or Aganasse cream. The sides of the cakes are garnished with chocolate cake crumbs or chocolate sprinkles. The individual portions may be garnished with rosettes of fudge or Aganasse cream and sprinkled lightly with chopped pistachio nuts or walnuts.

Chocolate Harlequin Layer

A vanilla or plain sponge cake may be used for the cover layers. Slice the sponge layer in half or use two slices about ½ in. thick. Cut a chocolate sponge sheet cake or layer (any other type of chocolate cake may be used) into small cubes. If the cake is dry, brush the top with simple syrup that has been heated and allow to dry slightly before cutting into cubes. Mix the chocolate cake cubes with soft buttercream. Mix the buttercream with a little syrup to soften and make smooth. The buttercream may also be warmed in warm water bath to soften. Fill the layers with this filling about 1½ in. high and press down gently when the top layer is in position. Chill the layers and then cover with a chocolate fondant or chocolate fudge icing. Some pastry chefs may use a white fondant icing and stripe the top with chocolate fudge or sweet chocolate. Draw the knife through the chocolate stripes to form a herring bone or cross-hatch effect.

Seven-Layer Cake

Seven-layer cakes are made with thin sheets of sponge or chiffon cake mix. A plain sponge or chiffon, or the chocolate variety may be used. When both types are made, they are usually mixed with other types of French pastry. Seven-layer cakes may also be made in miniature form and served with petits fours. Pastry chefs often prepare the seven-layer cakes up to the point of final finishing or decorating. The assembled sheets are refrigerated or kept in the freezer for use when required. The following sponge-type recipe is suggested for seven-sheet cakes to be assembled for the seven-layer cake.

Seven-Layer Cake—Sponge Sheets

Ingredients	lb	oz	Mixing procedure
Sugar	3		Warm the eggs and sugar to approximately
Salt		1	105°F. Whip until light and fluffy
Egg yolks	3		
Whole eggs	3		
Glucose or corn syrup		8	
Rind of 1 lemon and 1 orange			Fold in the fruit rind gently
Cake flour	3		Sift and add gradually and fold in gently

Deposit into sheet pans that have been lined with parchment paper liners. Grease the sides of the pans lightly. Bake at 410°F until just done. Fill the sheets with chocolate buttercream when using the sponge sheets. If chocolate sheets are used, a white buttercream and pistachio flavored and colored buttercream may be alternated with the white buttercream for colorful variety. Distribute the buttercream evenly to be sure that the layers formed are straight and even. It is important to compress the layers so that the layers and the buttercream fillings are bound together well. Chill the sheets that have been sandwiched together.

To finish the seven layers, the sheet may be cut into strips from 3 to 4 in. wide. Place the strips on icing grates about 4 in. apart. Cover the top and sides with warm chocolate fudge icing or melted sweet chocolate. A chocolate couverture or special cookie dip may be used. Comb the sides and top of the strip before the fudge or chocolate starts to set. This provides for a more attractive appearance. Chopped pistachio nuts may be

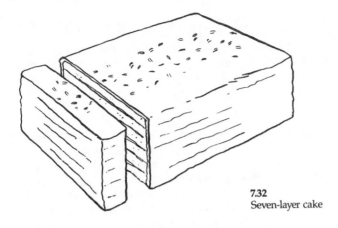

7.32
Seven-layer cake

sprinkled over the fudge or chocolate before the fudge or chocolate dries. Slice with a knife dipped in hot water to obtain a smooth cut (Fig. 7.32).

Apricot-Almond Sponge Layer—Gateau Alcazar

Slice an almond sponge or regular sponge layer into 3 slices. Fill each layer with apricot jam that has been thinned slightly. Place a filling of rum flavored buttercream over the apricot jam and cover the fillings with the layer cakes. Cover the sides of the layer cake with a thin cover of apricot jam and garnish with toasted, sliced almonds. With a pastry bag and star or French tube bag out a criss-cross design or diamond shape design with French macaroon mix (see cookie section) and border. Bake and brown in the oven at 415°F. When brown, glaze with apricot syrup and fill in the squares with apricot jam.

Chocolate-Cherry Cake—Black Forest Cherry Torte

A chocolate sponge layer or chocolate chiffon layer may be used for this special cake. Use black Bing cherries for the filling when fresh cherries are available. Canned Bing cherries may also be used and are cooked as a prepared fruit filling for pies and fruit cakes or flans. This dessert may be made in sheet cake form as well as in the layer cake form. The layer cake does have a more attractive appearance, especially in the triangular service of the cake or torte.

Cut the layer cake in two or use two chocolate cake sheets for large volume service. Brush the bottom layer with a cherry-flavored syrup or a syrup that has been mixed with kirsch. Of course, straight kirsch is most desired but expense must be considered. For the layer cake, bag out 3 or 4 rings of white buttercream about 1 in. apart on the bottom layer. For the sheets, bag out straight lines spaced about 1 in. apart. The ring of buttercream should be about 1/2–3/4 in. high. Fill in the spaces between the buttercream on the cake with black Bing cherry filling. Fresh Bing cherries that have been pitted may also be placed at intervals with the filling. Place the layer over the top and press down gently. Cover the top layer with whipped cream that has been mildly flavored with kirsch.

Cover the sides with whipped cream and garnish the top of the layer and the sides with chocolate shavings. Chocolate cake crumbs may be used to replace the chocolate shavings. Dust the top of the cake lightly with confectioners sugar. The large sheet cake may be cut into squares for service rather than triangular wedges as cut from the round layer cake. The squares from the large sheet may be garnished with a whipped cream rosette and a Bing cherry placed in the center of the rosette.

Cakes and Pastries Made with Whipped Cream

Pastry chefs will use sponge- or foam-type cakes mostly when preparing cakes and pastries finished with whipped cream. It is fitting that a light cream be used in conjunction with a whipped type of cake to maintain the compatibility of cake and cream topping. The pastry chef will vary the types of cakes and the shapes of the cakes and pastries at will. The names given to the Continental types of pastries made with whipped cream apply as they do for the gateaux. The ingenuity of the pastry chef will be reflected in the wide variety of cream desserts. Many of the cakes and fancy cake rolls may be filled with whipped cream and complemented with fruits, nuts, chocolate, and other garnishes appropriate to the type of dessert.

Sponge Shortcakes

Shortcakes, as they are known in the United States, are made with a wide variety of seasonal fruits. When strawberries are in season, for instance, the strawberry shortcake is quite popular. Of course, strawberries may be obtained on a year round basis, as are so many other fruits. Bananas are equally popular and are used in many shortcakes and special whipped cream-filled cake rolls. Canned fruits are often combined as a fruit filling with fresh fruits and used in whipped cream desserts. This is the case with the Black Forest Cherry Torte and also the many peach shortcakes and similar fruit shortcakes. Shortcakes are made in layer cake form, strip form as for French pastries, and sheet cake form for large volume feeding. They may also be made in a pie form when the sponge or other form cakes are baked in pie pans as for a Boston cream pie. Incidentally, the sponge cake pie form can be used for pastry cream custard in conjunction with the whipped cream. Thus, it is evident that the pastry chef has a wide latitude in creating whipped cream desserts from the many types and shapes of whipped cakes. (Figs. 7.33 through 7.35.)

Sponge or chiffon cakes are chilled before using for whipped cream fillings. This maintains a cool temperature and helps control the body of the whipped cream. Fruits and fruit fillings should be cooled before using. Fresh fruits are usually brushed with an apricot or other gel glaze to maintain their appearance and luster before they are used as a garnish for the cake or dessert.

The pastry chef who makes quality products makes whipped cream from heavy cream with a butterfat content of approximately 40%. Where portion control and costs require a lighter cream of approximately 18% butterfat, the pastry chef will use a stabilizer to ensure proper whipping, volume, and maintenance of the body of the whipped cream. Some pas-

7.33
Finished strawberry, or other fruit, shortcake

7.34
Cream-topped fruit pie

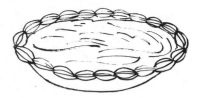

7.35
Cream-topped custard pie

try chefs will blend the whipped cream with cool meringue such as the Italian meringue. This will provide additional body as well as reduce costs. Whipped toppings that do not contain any of the dairy products or butterfats are quite popular. These are usually purchased in 10- or 30-lb cans. The toppings contain the sweetening, flavoring and stabilizers necessary for whipping. Pastry chefs will often use a blend of whipped topping and whipped cream. Each is whipped separately and then combined. The pastry chef may also whip the topping first and, when almost fully whipped, add the heavy cream and whip it directly into the whipped topping. The stabilizer in the topping will sustain the unwhipped cream and continue to aerate it in whipping.

The addition of chocolate to whipped cream should be done in the final stages and should be added while mixing at slow speed. The chocolate should be almost completely cool but sufficiently soft to be easily distributed without lumping. Pastry chefs will use a chocolate syrup with a stabilizer to prepare the chocolate whipped cream. It is advisable for the pastry chef to follow the instructions of the manufacturer when using a dry or powdered stabilizer for whipping cream. Approximately 3 to 4 oz of sugar are used for each quart of heavy cream to sweeten the cream. A fine granulated sugar will go into immediate and quick solution. Some pastry chefs sift and add confectioners sugar when the cream has started to aerate. Stabilizers in powdered form are usually sifted and blended with the sugar.

Flavoring should be used sparingly in whipped cream, especially when whipped cream is blended with a topping already containing flavoring. Vanilla, of course, is the basic flavoring.

When making the fruit shortcakes and other whipped cream desserts, it is advisable to whip the cream in mixing kettles that have been chilled. Place the kettle in the refrigerator or place ice cubes in the kettle before using. After the cream has been whipped keep it in the kettle and place it in the refrigerator. Some will place the kettle in a bowl with ice cubes or chopped ice while using the whipped cream.

Layer cakes or sheet cakes to be made into shortcakes are usually cut in half. Where combination layers (plain and chocolate) are used, two layers of one variety are combined with one of the other. The single layer is usually placed in the center. The bottom layer may be smeared with a fruit filling or jam before applying the whipped cream. The fruits are then placed over the cream. Fresh fruits or pieces of fruits are distributed evenly throughout the whipped cream. Place the top layer or second layer gently over the filling and fill again. The tops of shortcakes are usually finished with a smooth layer of whipped cream and then decorated with a pastry bag and tube in many designs. Slices or whole fruits are then placed on each portion to be served. Fresh strawberries are usually used either whole or cut in half. Canned fruit slices or sections are used as a garnish. Bananas are sliced or small quarter sections are placed on each portion. As a reminder, the fruits are often glazed lightly before placing on the cream. Whipped cream cakes and desserts must be kept under refrigeration until they are served.

Pastry cream custards, Bavarian creams, chocolate custards, and similar fillings are often used in conjunction with whipped cream. These cream or custard-type fillings are used as fillings for the layers of cake. The layers are filled and then chilled. The whipped cream is then used for finishing the tops and sides of the cakes. Some of the layer cakes may have both the cream filling and whipped cream in the center or between the layers for a special filling. The pastry chef will use his own judgment in this respect. Boston cream pies are often made with a cream custard, and whipped cream as the border for the filling. The top may then be garnished with whipped cream. Very often, a plain sponge or chiffon layer is combined with a slice of chocolate chiffon or sponge cake in a pie form similar to that of a Boston cream pie. The centers may have sliced bananas and other fruits such as strawberries. When sliced into portions, the fruits and custard fillings will show. This makes for an attractive dessert.

Whipped Cream Rolls

Plain or chocolate sponge sheets or chiffon sheets are often filled with whipped cream and then rolled up into a whipped cream roll. The pastry chef may lay out bananas or other fresh fruits in slices in the cream at the very top of the sheet cake before rolling. When rolled and sliced, the fruits will show in the center of the roll. Strawberries and small chunks of pineapple are often distributed throughout the roll.

When rolled up and then sliced, the fruits are exposed and present an attractive appearance. The tops of the rolls are usually covered with whipped cream. The sides are usually garnished with sponge cake crumbs or lightly toasted filberts or almonds. Chocolate rolls are usually combed

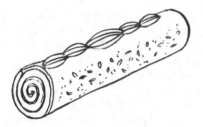

7.36
Cream-filled roll

and then decorated with rosettes of whipped cream. The tops may also be striped with sweet chocolate. Squares, diamonds, or small basket weaves made from sweet chocolate or couverture are often used to decorate chocolate rolls or chocolate sponge cakes filled and covered with whipped cream. (Fig. 7.36.)

Swiss Triangles
Swiss Triangles are made much like the buttercream-filled French pastries. A long strip of sponge cake or chiffon cake about 4 in. wide is laid on a pan. A full stripe of whipped cream is piped down the center of the strip. A strip of chocolate cake about 1 in. wide and 1½ in. high is placed into the whipped cream. The sides are now filled in with whipped cream using the bag and tube. Level the cream to form a smooth triangle on each side. Cover the sides of the triangle with a thin strip of yellow or chocolate cake and press in gently. Cover with whipped cream and garnish the sides with chocolate cake crumbs. Chill and then slice into triangular slices. The tops may be dusted lightly with confectioners sugar (Fig. 7.37).

Charlotte Whipped Cream Layers
These layers are made from any variety of the sponge or chiffon-type cakes. A combination of layers may be made so that the yellow sponge and chocolate sponge or chiffon cakes may be alternated when the layers of cake are assembled. The sides of the cake are well covered with whipped cream and then Lady Fingers are pressed against the sides of the cake. Pastry chefs will often use a finger-shaped spritz cookie. For a combination effect, a vanilla and chocolate spritz cookie may be alternated when pressed against the sides of the cake. The top of the cake is garnished with a design (bag and tube) with the whipped cream. If choc-

7.37
Swiss triangle

olate finger cookies are used, the top of the cake is usually striped or garnished with sweet chocolate.

Lady Fingers

Ingredients	lb	oz	Mixing procedure
Sugar		12	Warm the sugar and eggs in a warm water
Salt		¼	bath. Whip until light and fluffy
Glucose or corn syrup		4	
Yolks		12	
Whole eggs		12	
Rind of 1 lemon and juice			Fold in the juice and rind. Sift the flour and fold in gently
Cake flour	1		
Bread flour		8	
Egg whites	1	8	Whip the whites to a froth. Add the sugar
Sugar		12	gradually and whip to a medium peak. Fold into the above gently

Use a pastry bag and medium sized plain tube. Fill the bag and bag out the mix on parchment paper-lined pans. The fingers should be about 3 in. long. They may be made shorter and narrower by using a smaller size plain tube. The fingers will tend to spread slightly on the paper. Dust the tops of the fingers lightly with fine granulated sugar as soon as the fingers are bagged out. This will form a light syrup formation. Dust the fingers again with confectioners sugar and then remove the excess sugar from the paper.

Bake the Lady Fingers at 400°F. It may be necessary to bake the fingers on double pans if the bottom of the oven has a strong heat. The double pan will also prevent the formation of a deep brown crust color. The bottom of the Lady Fingers should be soft and somewhat moist after baking. Test for proper bake by gently touching the fingers in the center. If there is a mild springy feeling, the fingers are baked. Do not wait until the sugar starts to caramelize to a deep brown crust color.

The Lady Fingers may be left as single cookies when removed from the pan. If the Lady Fingers tend to stick to the paper (this may be the result of overbaking) turn over the paper with the fingers and brush the paper lightly with water. Wait 2 or 3 min and then turn the paper over. The fingers should release themselves without sticking. Very often, Lady Fingers are placed together so that an oval-shaped form or finger is made. Pastry chefs will serve them with other desserts as an extra garnish. They are left in single form for the charlotte layers with the flat surface of the Lady Finger pressed into the whipped cream around the sides of the layer cake. The very tips of the Lady Fingers may be dipped slightly into chocolate and allowed to dry. These are then pressed into the sides of the cake with the chocolate tips extending slightly above the top of the layer cake.

Cake and Pastry Icings

In view of the fact that many of the Continental pastries (French, Viennese, and so forth) use a foam or whipped cake as the base or body for the pastry, it is fitting that variety icings be introduced at this point. Icings with Continental names are many and varied by virtue of the type of flavoring, coloring, and the added ingredient or two that may be incorporated into a basic icing. For example, the pastry chef will usually limit himself to several basic icings which can readily be changed to produce specific types of pastries. A basic buttercream, usually termed "Crème au Beurre," can be made into a wide variety of icings. A fondant icing that is usually purchased in large cans is now used as a base for many other types of flat or simple icing. Fudge icing bases may be purchased and converted to a variety of fudge-type icings with the addition of flavorings, colorings, and other distinguishing ingredients. There is little time for the pastry chef with mass and rapid feeding requirements to be able to prepare an individual icing for each type of pastry. This section will stress the basic types of icings and suggest several basic recipes for each of the varieties.

Icings may be classified as creamed, boiled or whipped, flat or fondant, and combination icings that employ the whipping and creaming methods. In most instances, the icings are either a buttercream, a fudge-type, or simple or flat-type. With regard to the buttercream icings, the amount and type of fat used, and the method of preparation are the important factors. A quality buttercream icing will have lightness, dissolve easily when tasted and eaten, and handle well when being applied. The amount of butter or shortening may vary from amounts equal to the weight of the sugar, to as little as 15% based upon the weight of the sugar. The butter used to prepare buttercream icing should be sweet and of good quality. Large percentages of butter are used to prepare the Continental type of buttercream. Usually, these buttercreams are simple blends of creamed butter which has been softened and then combined with an equal amount of confectioners sugar or fondant icing. This is very costly and very perishable. In addition, it may become greasy when left standing because of the low melting point of the butter. Most pastry chefs will combine sweet butter with a hydrogenated shortening or with an emulsified shortening depending upon the amount of water or syrup used to prepare the buttercream. The use of the shortening will allow for greater volume in the creaming process and greater stability after the buttercream has been made.

It is a recognized fact that buttercream icings are usually masked or dominated by the flavorings and colorings added to them. The buttercream made with all sweet butter loses some of its buttery taste when mixed with other flavorings and ingredients. For example, a fine quality sweet or medium chocolate will prevail as the dominating color and flavor when added to a basic, white buttercream flavored with a small amount of vanilla. This is also true of fruits and fruit flavorings that may be added. The type of cake used for the pastry will often determine the type of icing and buttercream to be used. Buttercreams are also vehicles for carrying other types of fillings. For example, a buttercream may be blended with a cream custard for a cake specialty. It is important that the basic buttercream be able to accept the addition of added ingredients and not curdle or separate. Warming the buttercream in a double boiler and mixing briskly will remove the curdle from a good basic buttercream icing. The slight melting of the fat will tend to absorb or emulsify the separated liquid and restore the original smoothness of the icing.

Buttercream Icings

Basic Buttercream I

This buttercream may be used to prepare a wide variety of other types of buttercream. It has the characteristics of the French type of Crème au Beurre and lightness and workability. The combination method of mixing is used to prepare the buttercream. Fondant is used in conjunction with egg whites for whipping. The fondant may be replaced by boiling granulated sugar, glucose, and water to approximately 232–234°F and adding to the whipping egg whites. A commercial type of egg white stabilizer may be used to ensure maximum whipping capacity and aeration of the egg whites, and to avoid the possible weeping of moisture.

Ingredients	lb	oz	Mixing procedure
Fondant icing	8		Place in a double boiler and heat to ap-
Egg whites	2		proximately 110°F. Place in mixing machine and whip to light peak
Confectioners sugar	3		Sift the sugar and salt. Add the shortening
Salt		½	and butter and cream lightly. Scrape the
Butter (plastic condition)	4		sides of the kettle from time to time to ensure a proper blend and uniform distribu-
Emulsified shortening	6		tion of all ingredients. Use second speed during the creaming process.
Vanilla		2	

Add the whipped egg whites and fondant to the creamed butter-shortening-sugar and mix at slow speed until completely blended. The buttercream should be refrigerated when not used. It is good practice to cream the buttercream at medium speed when removing from the refrigerator. It is a good idea to add a little simple syrup to the chilled buttercream when mixing again. This will give a light sheen to the buttercream.

Chocolate Buttercream Add sufficient sweet chocolate that has been melted to produce the desired taste and color. A blend of sweet and bitter chocolate (chocolate liqueur) may be used to increase the color depth and the flavor of the chocolate. Pastry chefs will also soften commercially prepared fudge base and add it to the buttercream to prepare the chocolate butter. The fudge base may be combined with the sweet chocolate and then added. It is important that the buttercream be creamed light and soft so that the chocolate can be readily absorbed and distributed. Chocolate that is not properly heated and dissolved when added to a cool or refrigerated buttercream will tend to firm up into small pieces. This will cause a lumpy appearance and uneven distribution. Because chocolate tends to firm up when cool, it may be advisable to add some simple syrup in the final stages of mixing to obtain the desired consistency for spreading with the spatula or bagging out with a pastry bag and tube.

Coffee or Maple Buttercream Dissolve sufficient dried coffee crystals in a small amount of water and then blend in with a small amount of simple syrup. Add this slowly to the buttercream and blend in well. Further coffee or mocha coloring and flavoring may be obtained with the use of flavoring and coloring concentrates.

Fruit flavoring, natural fruit rind, and fruit coloring may be added to prepare special buttercream icings. A lemon or orange concentrate may be added with some syrup to provide color and flavor. Fruit-filled buttercreams are also made by combining cooked fruit fillings with the buttercream and then using the special cream for fruit-cream desserts.

Basic Buttercream II

This is a straight method of mixing a buttercream icing. It does not require a second whipping, allowing for rapid preparation.

Ingredients	lb	oz	Mixing procedure
Confectioners sugar	10		Sift the sugar, salt and milk powder together. Add the hot water and blend to a smooth consistency
Salt		½	
Hot water (variable)	1	8	
Skim milk powder		4	
Butter	4		Add the butter and shortening and cream until soft and light. Scrape the sides of the kettle periodically
Emulsified short-ening	5		
Egg whites		12	Add the egg whites gradually and cream well after each addition. Be sure to scrape the bottom and sides of the mixing kettle
Vanilla		2	

Continental-type buttercreams are usually made by combining egg yolks and milk or cream with sweet butter and flavoring. The sugar is heated with the milk or cream, or may be warmed and then blended with the butter. Egg whites and sugar may also be heated and then whipped. The butter is then creamed and combined with the beaten egg whites.
Note: For added richness, color, and emulsifying properties, 12 oz of egg yolks may be added after the shortening has been creamed in with the butter. This will provide for a richer, yellow color to the buttercream. Refrigerate the buttercream when not in use.

French Buttercream   (*Crème au Beurre*)

Ingredients	lb	oz	Mixing procedure
Granulated sugar	9		Boil the sugar and glucose dissolved in the
Water	5	8	water to approx. 238°F
Glucose or corn syrup	1	8	
Egg yolks	3		Whip the egg yolks until thick. Add the boiled sugar to the egg yolks in a very slow steady stream and whip until light. (Be sure to add the syrup slowly to avoid congealing the egg yolks)
Sweet butter	6		Blend the butter until smooth and plastic.
Emulsified short-ening	3		Add the shortening and cream lightly. Add the egg yolks and syrup slowly to the creamed butter and shortening and cream up well until light and soft. The buttercream should be smooth for application

The flavoring to be added is optional. A neutral vanilla may be used as the basic flavoring. Additional flavoring may be added in accordance with the use of the buttercream for the special cake to be made.

Note: The emulsified shortening will help to absorb and retain the liquid in the yolks and syrup, and allow for smooth remixing of the buttercream when refrigerated and softened again for application and use. The shortening may be replaced with sweet butter entirely. If all butter is used, it is advisable to add a small amount of confectioners sugar to the butter when working the butter from the hard, chilled state to a creamy light state. The butter may tend to exude some of its natural liquid. The sugar will absorb and retain it.

Hungarian Style Buttercream

The Hungarian type of buttercream may be made by two separate methods. One is very simple to prepare. The pastry chef combines an equal amount of butter which has been softened and creamed with an equal amount of fondant icing. The fondant and sweet butter are then creamed until light. A vanilla flavoring is added as the basic flavor. Additional flavorings, colorings, and selected ingredients may be added.

The second type of Hungarian buttercream is prepared by boiling sugar and water to a temperature of approximately 238°F. This is then added to whipped egg whites as for a marshmallow icing (without the use of gelatin or gum). The whipped whites are then added to butter and/or emulsified shortening for completion of the buttercream.

Ingredients	lb	oz	Mixing procedure
Sugar (granulated)	6		Boil to 238°F. (This is almost the soft ball stage in boiling of sugar)
Water	4		
Glucose	1		
Egg Whites	3		Whip to a soft peak and add the syrup in a slow, steady stream and whip until light and fluffy
Sweet butter	4		Soften the butter to a plastic state. Add the shortening and cream until light. Add the vanilla and blend in. Add the whipped egg whites in several stages and blend in well at medium speed. A wire whip may be used for the final blending and whipping of the buttercream. This will tend to increase the amount of air whipped into the buttercream and provide for additional smoothness. Additional flavorings, colorings, and other ingredients may be added to meet the special requirements of the pastry or cake
Emulsified short- ening	2	8	
Vanilla		1	

English and Belgian Style Buttercreams

These buttercreams are made with a base formed from a cooked custard. The contemporary pastry chef must carefully consider the cost as well as the time required to prepare this type of buttercream. A custard made from a prepared custard mix or powder could serve well and be less costly.

Ingredients	lb	oz	Mixing procedure
Water	6		Dissolve the sugar, salt, and milk powder in the water. Bring to a slow boil, stirring occasionally
Sugar	1	12	
Salt		¼	
Milk powder	1		
Water	1		Dissolve the cornstarch in the water. Add the egg yolks and whip in lightly. Add a small amount of the boiling milk to the starch-yolk solution and whip slightly. Add the starch-yolk solution to the boiling milk in a slow, steady stream, stirring constantly, and bring to a boil again. Remove from the fire and add the vanilla and butter and stir in well. Allow the custard to cool and then chill in the refrigerator.
Cornstarch		8	
Egg yolks	1	8	
Vanilla		1	
Sweet butter		6	
Sweet butter	4		Cream the butter and shortening and sugar until soft and light. Add the chilled custard in 4 stages and mix in well
Emulsified short- ening	2		
Confectioners sugar	3		

Chocolate Cream Type Icings and Fillings

As indicated previously, chocolate icings and cream-type fillings are very popular. The basic buttercream or Continental style buttercreams may be flavored and colored with chocolate, chocolate fudge, cocoa, or a combination of chocolate-type ingredients. Buttercream flavored chocolate is used most often to fill and hold together the several layers of a cake. It is quick, light, and easy to handle. In fact, pastry chefs will often have their assistants assemble the body of the cakes for the final finishing by the pastry chef. However, there are requests for special chocolate-type fillings and covers for cakes that resemble chocolate creams and custard-type creams. Once again, these may vary from the expensive Continental style creams to the more practical and economical varieties. For example, a Ganache Cream or Aganasse Cream are two Continental chocolate creams that are quite expensive but very delicate and tasty.

Ganache Cream or Aganasse Cream

Ingredients	lb	oz	Mixing procedure
Sugar (granulated)	2	4	Dissolve the sugar in the cream and bring
Heavy whipping cream	4		to a slow boil. Stir to prevent catching or scorching
Sweet chocolate	5		Add the chocolate and stir well to dissolve
Bitter chocolate (liqueur)	2		the chocolate and get a smooth consistency
Heavy whipping cream	2		Add the heavy cream slowly and continue to whip until all the cream has been blended in with the melted chocolate

When cool or chilled, whip for additional creaminess. If all sweet chocolate is used, the sugar may be eliminated or reduced. A fine vanilla flavoring and rum flavoring may be added.

Chocolate Cream Icing and Filling

This chocolate cream filling may be used to assemble cakes and to cover many cakes and pastries. It is a custard type of cream filling and is quite economical in preparation and use.

Ingredients	lb	oz	Mixing procedure
Sugar (granulated)	6	4	Dissolve the sugar and salt in the water
Salt		½	Add the butter and bring to a boil.
Water	6		Stir occasionally
Butter	1	8	
Water	1	8	Dissolve the starch in the water and add to
Cornstarch		14	the above in a slow, steady stream, stir-
Vanilla		1	ring constantly, and bring to a boil once
Cocoa		8	again

Remove from the fire and stir in the vanilla. The cream may be poured into baking sheet pans to cool more rapidly. Stir the cream occasionally to prevent a crust formation. When the chocolate cream has cooled, it may be used for filling the cakes and pastries. If it is to be used for finishing or garnishing the tops of cakes, as for the Blackout layer cake, it should be cooled first. This cake is made with chocolate layers or sheet cakes. The layers are filled with the chocolate cream and covered with the chocolate cream. The tops are garnished with chocolate cake crumbs made from the same cake used for the base. The chocolate cream icing or filling may also be used as a base for special tarts or chocolate sponge pies. These are cakes baked in pie pans and then finished as for a Boston cream pie.

Fondant, Fudge, and Whipping Icings

Flat or fondant icings are used extensively to cover cakes, French pastries, petits fours, and for the finishing of many types of cookies. The pastry chef usually purchases prepared fondant icing that is ready to use by merely warming in a double boiler to approximately 98–100°F. Fondants and other simple flat icings are made thicker and thinner with the use of added simple syrup or the addition of binding agents such as cocoa, gelatin, and agar-agar. Prepared fudge bases (basic white and chocolate) are available for purchase and ready for immediate use. The pastry chef will most often use these bases for large volume preparation as well as for the economy in use and control of product uniformity. Fudge bases vary in richness. The principal ingredient that determines richness is the amount of fat in the fudge. The fat may be emulsified or the natural fat found in the chocolate may be the enriching factor. Whipped icings, such as boiled icings and marshmallow icings, may also be made from prepared powders containing the proteins, albumen, and stabilizers for aeration and whipping. Boiled icings are light, fluffy icings that are used for special cakes and pastries that require delicate icing. There is little difference in the ordinary white, boiled icing and the marshmallow icing except for the addition of gelatin and stabilizer. The boiled icing may be used as a base for added flavoring and coloring. Marshmallow icing is often used for specialty cakes. It is popular with younger dishes because of its candy-like taste and appearance. It is also used as a blend with other icings, as well as with whipped creams. Pastry chefs will often use prepared marshmallow powder bases, requiring only the addition of water and sugar and the icing is whipped directly on the machine to the desired consistency. Stabilizers in the powder preparation help keep the icing in a fixed condition after the icing is prepared. For the pastry chefs who wish to prepare their own icings from "scratch" the following recipes will cover the basic icings in each of the categories. These recipes may be varied by controlling the viscosity or thickness as well as making variations by adding supplementary flavorings and special ingredients.

Fondant Icing

Ingredients	lb	oz	Mixing procedure
Granulated sugar	15		Dissolve the sugar and cream of tartar in
Water	4		the water and corn syrup. Bring to a boil
Corn syrup	2		and boil to 240°F
or glucose			
Cream of tartar		2	

Wash the sides of the kettle with a brush dipped in cool water. This will prevent the formation of sugar crystals on the sides of the kettle. Prepare the marble table by brushing lightly with vegetable oil and then pour the boiled syrup over the marble. Allow the syrup to cool down to approximately 120°F and then place in the mixing machine. Run the machine at slow speed with the paddle beater. The fondant is ready when it turns white, smooth, and creamy in appearance. The fondant should not be mixed or agitated when the syrup is still hot or warm, as this will cause the grainy effect of sugar crystallization. It is advisable to allow the fondant to age or mellow for a few days before using. Fondant may then be thinned down with simple syrup if too thick. It is also advisable to cover fondant icing in cans with a film of simple syrup when not in use. This will prevent the formation of sugar crustation. It is well to remember that fondant icing and simple icings are best warmed in a double boiler and kept at a slightly warm temperature. Overheating will cause the fondant or simple icing to lose the shine when cool. There may also tend to be a partial crystallization of the icing after cooling. This may cause the icing to flake and peel.

Simple Icing   (Flat-Type)

Ingredients	lb	oz	Mixing procedure
Confectioners sugar	15		Sift the sugar and place into a bowl or
Hot water	2		large pot. Add the hot water and glucose
Glucose or	1		and mix smooth
corn syrup			
Salt		(pinch)	
Vanilla		1	Add the vanilla and egg whites and mix
Egg whites		6	smooth
(optional)			

This icing should be of smooth consistency and have the same thickness as regular fondant icing. If cool, the icing is warmed in a double boiler.

Vanilla Fudge Icing

Ingredients	lb	oz	Mixing procedure
Confectioners sugar	10		Sift the sugar. Blend well with the other
Salt		½	ingredients
Glucose	1		
Emulsified short- ening	1	10	
Water	1	6	Dissolve the milk in the water. Heat to ap-
Milk powder (optional)		4	proximately 140°F. Add gradually to the above and blend in well. Add the vanilla
Vanilla		1	last

Use the vanilla fudge while it is warm. If it stiffens, place in a double boiler to warm. A little simple syrup may be added to further soften the fudge icing.

Chocolate Fudge Icing

When using a prepared fudge base, the following basic recipe may be prepared for the chocolate fudge-type icing:

Ingredients	lb	oz	Mixing procedure
Chocolate fudge base	3	8	Sift the sugar and place in a bowl. Add the fudge base and glucose and part of the
Confectioners sugar	10		hot water. Mix to a smooth, stiff paste.
Glucose (optional)		8	Add the remaining water and vanilla in 2
Hot water (variable)	4		or 3 stages and blend in well after each
Vanilla		2	addition

The chocolate fudge base should be mildly warm, and have a creamy appearance when used. If the fudge base is stiff, warm in a double boiler and add simple syrup to further soften the fudge icing if necessary. Use the fudge icing while warm. Pastry chefs will often add syrup and melted sweet chocolate to further enrich and firm up the fudge icing.

Chocolate Fudge Icing   (Made with Cocoa Powder)

Ingredients	lb	oz	Mixing procedure
Confectioners sugar	10		Sift the sugar and cocoa
Cocoa		12	
Salt		½	Add the salt, glucose, and hot water and
Glucose or corn syrup		8	mix smooth. Add the melted butter and shortening and blend in well. Add the va-
Water (hot)	2		nilla and mix to a smooth, creamy state.
Vanilla		2	Use while warm. Keep in a double boiler
Melted butter		8	while in use
Melted shortening		6	

Chocolate Fudge Icing   *(Made with Bitter Chocolate)*

The pastry chef may wish to use a blend of bitter chocolate (liqueur) and semisweet chocolate. The added sweetness and butterfat may add to the taste and finished color of the fudge icing. The use of a straight bitter chocolate will provide for a darker, chocolaty color and taste.

Ingredients	lb	oz	Mixing procedure
Confectioners sugar	5		Sift the dry ingredients. Add the shorten-
Emulsified short-ening	1	10	ing and mix to a soft, smooth blend
Salt		½	
Skim milk powder		6	
Glucose or corn syrup		14	Add to the above and blend in
Melted bitter chocolate	1	12	Add to the above gradually and blend in well
Confectioners sugar	5		Sift the sugar and add to the above. Add
Hot water (variable)	2		the water in 3 stages and blend in well
Vanilla		1	after each addition. Mix in the vanilla

If the fudge icing is too stiff, add some simple syrup. If the icing is soft, add additional melted chocolate. A sweet chocolate may be used. Keep the fudge icing in a double boiler while in use. A warm fudge will have a luster when applied. The fudge should dry on the cake or pastry with just a thin crust while the interior should be soft and moist. For a cream type of icing, pastry chefs will add heavy cream to replace the hot water. The cream is to be heated almost to a boil (avoid scorching) and then added gradually to the sugar-chocolate-shortening blend. This type of fudge icing is mildly similar to the Ganache or Aganasse cream.

White Boiled Icing

Ingredients	lb	oz	Mixing procedure
Granulated sugar	10	8	Combine all ingredients to dissolve and
Glucose or corn syrup	1	10	boil to 240°F or soft ball stage. Wash the sides of the kettle with a brush dipped in
Cream of tartar		½	water during cooking
Water	4		
Egg whites	3	12	Whip the egg whites to a wet peak and
Salt		½	then add the hot syrup in a slow, steady
Vanilla		½	stream to the egg whites. Continue to whip until the icing is soft and light. The icing should show white, soft peaks that tend to form a pillowlike effect. Add the vanilla in the final stages of mixing

Note: In the summer weather, pastry chefs will often add some of this icing to whipped cream and combine both gently at slow speed. The icing provides greater stability to the whipped cream and increases volume considerably. It also reduces the cost factor of finishing desserts.

Marshmallow Icing

Ingredients	lb	oz	Mixing procedure
Granulated sugar	9		Boil the sugar, water, and glucose to 242°F
Water	3		(soft ball stage)
Glucose or corn syrup	1		
Gelatin powder		1½	Dissolve the gelatin in the water
Water		8	
Egg whites	3		Whip the egg whites and sugar to a wet
Sugar		12	peak. Add the hot syrup in a slow, steady
Vanilla		1	stream and whip light and fluffy. Add the gelatin and whip in well. Add the vanilla and whip in gently

It is best to use the marshmallow when it is freshly made. The icing will tend to firm up as it stands because of the binding effect of the gelatin. Marshmallow icing is used extensively in warm or hot weather to finish a wide variety of cakes and pastries.

8

Dough Conditioners and Softeners

Commercial bakers have been using additives and dough improvers to increase bread softness and extend the shelf life of yeast-raised products for some time. Retail bakers and pastry chefs have recently begun using dough improvers to meet the special production requirements related to the retarding, freezing, and makeup of doughs that have been frozen and defrosted, and the improvement in quality of products that are heated in microwave ovens immediately prior to serving. All additives must be approved by the Food and Drug Administration before distribution. In addition, there are mandatory guidelines for safe quantity and use for the consumer.

Dough conditioners improve the volume of the bread loaf, the grain and texture, eating qualities, and extend the shelf life of the loaf. They often increase the gluten strength and improve the stability of the dough. The development time of weaker flours may be increased with a resulting increase in product volume due to the ability of the dough to withstand the strain of makeup and proofing.

Dough improvers and additives in the form of surfactants fall into the categories of various monoglycerides, polysorbate 60, sodium stearoyl-2 lactylate, calcium stearoyl-2-lactylate and others. These are now in powder form and hydrate easily. Dough improvers are identified by bakers and pastry chefs by their trade names. Such products as EMPLEX* or PATCO 3 are primarily composed of SSL or CSL, or a combination of both. Others, in a paste form, are also known by trade name. Selection

*C. J. Patterson Company

and use depends upon the baker. The dry forms are usually added directly with the flour and are readily hydrated during the mixing of the doughs. They are used in doughs made by the sponge dough, straight dough, or continuous mix methods. It is advisable for the baker and pastry chef to read and adhere to the instructions carefully. Amounts to use will vary with the product. For example, CSL or SSL is used in the range from 0.2 percent to 0.4 percent for bread and roll varieties and up to 0.5 percent for sweet yeast goods and doughnuts. This percentage is based on the weight of the flour. The range may vary from 3 oz to 8 oz for bread and rolls and as much as 8–10 oz for sweet yeast goods for each 100 lb of flour used in the dough. Accuracy in scaling is important; increased amounts will not improve the product. New product development will have the recipes listed in percentage and weight form and will indicate a specific dough conditioner and surfactant. Where this is not indicated, the baker should inquire about the type to use. Adjustments may be required in dough mixing and development, water absorption, and in the total conditioning of the dough.

Emulsifiers

Emulsifiers are used primarily in cake batter including batter-type muffins and cake-type doughnuts. Emulsifiers are used in conjunction with dough improvers and other additives in yeast-raised doughs to increase shelf life and freshness. Emulsifiers are used in special shortenings for cakes containing high percentages of sugar and liquid. They assist in the formation of an emulsion of fat and water. They make possible the use of basic fats, oils, or compounds of fats and oils in the production of cakes and other products. Emulsifiers are used in cakes, such as sponge cakes, made with the whipping method of mixing. Emulsifiers used properly produce a better cake made at a lesser cost. It is often possible to reduce the amount of eggs and to use quality vegetable oil in place of shortening. Pastry chefs and bakers are probably familiar with special powder preparations and plastic-type emulsions for special products. They are often used as whipping supplements for sponge-type cakes to speed production and to insure maximum incorporation of air cells in the whipping process. Emulsifiers, like dough conditioners, vary in composition. They may be in the form of glycerol monostearate, polysorbate 60, mono and diglycerides, propylene glycol, and others. Emulsifiers may contain a combination of several types of emulsifiers in a hydrated blend. Instructions for use will indicate the amounts and when they should be added. In creamed and blended types of cakes, emulsifiers are usually added with the fat; in sponge cakes they are added with the eggs and liquid; in single blend cakes and batters, all ingredients are added at one time. It is important that the emulsifiers are thoroughly blended in order to be effective in the mixing process. When adding emulsifiers to the pastry chef's own recipes, adjustments in quantity may be necessary. For example, one popular emulsifier, a blend of several components, suggests the use of 3–4% based on flour weight for sponge cake. For cakes made with an emulsified shortening 1–2% is used as compared with 3–4% emulsifier for batters made with oil or shortening that is not emulsified. For bakers in countries where a variety of shortenings and other fats are limited, emulsifiers can be very useful. As indicated, the reduction in eggs and fats may permit a quality product to be made at a lesser cost. In countries where only one or two types of flour are available, neither of which is a special cake flour, emulsifiers will help to produce cakes that are tender, with a uniform grain and texture.

Chemical Additives and Dough Mixing Processes

Changes in dough mixing methods and dough development mean an increase in the use of oxidants and reducing agents. Retail bakers and pastry chefs are not fully affected by these radical changes. There are bases for sour-type and sponge-type doughs that eliminate the time required for sponge dough maturation or even the preparation of sour doughs. There are special dough bases or mixes that require very short resting periods before makeup into bread or roll units. Still others use high speed and high energy input for dough mixing. In some countries where the available flour is milled from a single type of wheat or wheat of lesser quality, no-time doughs are made so that the strain of long fermentation and dough conditioning is avoided. These doughs are chemically developed for immediate use. The following are some of the methods of special dough mixing and the customary chemical additives that act as oxidants and reducing agents.

Activated dough development (ADD) is one process in which low-speed mixing equipment is used. In this process, reducing agents such as L-cysteine and oxidizing agents such as bromate and/or ascorbic acid are used in the dough. The doughs are developed during mixing as a result of the action of the chemical additives. This method of mixing is used in many developing countries and in countries where modern mixing equipment is not available. The chemical additives are often too loosely measured and added to the dough, rather than scaled carefully, producing a distinct aftertaste and odor in the baked bread. Doughs made this way are fully developed by passing large chunks of the dough through dough brakes as many as twenty or more times. Reducing and oxidizing agents allow for little gluten resistance. This method is used largely because the quality of the flour is not good. Flours with high gluten content of excellent quality would tend to become bucky or resist immediate dough brake treatment unless higher percentages of reducing and oxidizing agents were used. Breads produced with this method do not have the usual fine qualities of bread made with quality American wheat and flour.

The Chorleywood Bread Process is based upon high speed, mechanical dough development in conjunction with the use of chemical additives. A very high input of energy is required together with a combination of oxidants such as potassium bromate and ascorbic acid. The combination may usually contain approximately 20 ppm of potassium iodate (rapid acting oxidant) 45 ppm of potassium bromate for later oxidation during the proofing and baking period and approximately 75 ppm ascorbic acid.

The Brimec process is an Australian development. It requires a high input of energy similar to the Chorleywood process with a high percentage of potassium iodate for rapid acting oxidation of the dough. A pressure lid is often lowered into the mixing chamber of the machine to further speed the dough development.

Before using any of these methods, it is advisable to read the labels on the cartons of chemical additives and to examine the contents of dough bases and preferment preparations. The following chemicals are most likely present and a brief description of their function follows:

1. Potassium iodate is a rapid acting oxidant providing immediate oxidation during the dough-mixing process. The level of 10 to 20 ppm is commonly used in mixes of additives.
2. Potassium bromate is a delayed acting oxidant that provides oxidation during the proofing and baking stages. It is usually used at levels of 45 to 55 ppm.
3. Ascorbic acid, while not as rapid acting as potassium iodate, is found to be more effective when used in combination with potassium bromate. It is often used at levels of 75 ppm and can be used with most flours. L-cysteine is used for reducing action. This has a softening and relaxing action on the gluten. It is necessary for high speed mixing for dough development as well as for the chemical activation method of dough development.
4. Azodicarbonomide (ADA) is a more recent oxidizing agent and is used at levels not to exceed 45 ppm. This powdered material becomes active in the flour only in the presence of water, as in a dough. The actions of ADA and bromate are complimentary and a ratio of one part bromate to two parts ADA is quite effective.
5. Yeast foods are combinations of chemicals that provide nutrients for yeast and promote vigorous yeast activity. Yeast activity during fermentation requires nitrogen, phosphorus, and other inorganic ions. The presence of ammonium salts in yeast foods supplements the nutrients present in flour. They tend to increase yeast activity during the fermentation and proofing period. While the flour may provide sufficient nutrients, the added yeast food will increase the rate of fermentation. For bakers and pastry chefs who prepare yeast-raised doughs for retarding and freezing, the added yeast food may be helpful in maintaining a good rate of yeast activity during the final dough conditioning during makeup of the products and the final proofing of the makeup units.
6. Minerals and buffers are used to reduce the dough pH and the use of monocalcium phosphate is especially valuable when water that is alkaline in nature is used for the dough. Fermentation is slowed or reduced when the pH is too high (pH refers to degree of acidity in the dough). Where the water is soft, the use of calcium salts is essential. Calcium carbonate is often included in most yeast foods. It has a strengthening effect on the gluten of the dough which may be soft-

ened by the nature of the water used. Yeast foods may be prepared to meet special needs of bread production as well as the type of flour and other materials used.

The formulas that follow are representative of popular bakery products that contain dough conditioners and/or emulsifiers. The yeast-raised products are specialty products which can readily be produced by the baker and pastry chef. Cake products and specialties contain emulsifiers to illustrate the wide use of these additives. These are included in the formulas. Ingredient weights in the formulas will be listed in pounds and ounces as well as in percentage form for bakers using the metric system. Specialty grains and flours may be adjusted to meet special requirements. For example, bran flour or flakes and soy flour, if unavailable, may be increased or eliminated entirely. The baker must use judgement in making the adjustments in formulas.

Country Farm Bread

Ingredients	lb	oz	%	Mixing procedure
Yeast (variable)		5½	5.5	Dissolve the yeast and set aside
Water	1		15.0	
Sugar		4	4.0	Dissolve all ingredients in the
Salt		2	2.0	water and blend in well
Nonfat dry milk		2	2.0	
Molasses		2	2.0	
Soy flour (defatted)		2	2.0	
Wheat germ		2	2.0	
Dough conditioner		¼	0.2	
Water (variable)	3	8	52.0	
Whole wheat flour	1	4	20.0	Sift and add the flour and stir
Bread flour	5		80.0	slightly. Add the yeast and mix
(13 to 14% protein)				to a dough
Shortening		2	2.0	Add the shortening and develop to a smooth dough

Allow the dough to rise well and punch. Relax for 15 min and then scale and round the units. Give the units slightly less than full proof before baking.

Note: The dough consistency should be checked before final development. It should be slightly stiffer than regular white pan bread dough. If additional whole wheat flour or bran is added, or if high-protein flour is used, the water should be slightly increased to allow for increased absorption. If instant dry yeast is used, use approximately 2 oz and add with the flour. The dough conditioner, such as cs1 (Emplex) or ss1 (Patco 3), may be added with the flour.

Cheese Bread

Ingredients	lb	oz	%	Mixing procedure
Yeast (variable)		5	5.0	Dissolve the yeast and set aside
Water	1		16.0	
Sugar		4½	4.5	Dissolve in the water. Blend well
Salt		2	2.0	
Nonfat dry milk		2½	2.5	
Soy flour (defatted)		2	2.0	
Wheat germ		1	1.0	
Dough conditioner		¼	0.2	
Water	3		48.0	
Bread flour (13% protein)	6	4	100.0	Sift and add. Mix slightly. Add yeast and mix to a dough
Shortening		3	3.0	Add and develop the dough
Grated cheddar cheese (variable)		10	10.0	Add the cheese in the final stage of dough development

Keep the dough temperature cool (78–80° out of the mixer). Allow the dough to rise well and then punch (fold over to remove gas). Relax the dough for about 15–20 min and then scale and round the dough units. Allow the units to relax (preliminary proofing) about 12 min and shape or mold into bread loaves. Give the units three-quarter proof and then brush the top lightly with water or egg wash. Sprinkle with grated cheese. The center may be cut for a split top effect. Bake at 410–415° F. with mild steam in the oven.

Note: A grated hard cheese is preferable. Soft cheese will smear and streak the dough when mixed in. Do not use hard, dry granular cheese. Add the cheese during the last minute of dough development for equal distribution throughout the dough.

Egg Bread and Rolls   (*Commercial Type*)

Refer to pages 30–37 for varieties and illustrations in makeup.

Ingredients	lb	oz	%	Mixing procedure
Yeast (variable)		8	4.0	Dissolve the yeast and set aside
Water	2		16.0	
Sugar		12	6.0	Dissolve dry ingredients and
Salt		4	2.0	blend well
Nonfat dry milk		6	3.0	
Egg yolks		6	3.0	
Whole eggs		6	3.0	
Dough conditioner		½	0.3	
Water (variable)	5		40.0	

	lb	oz	%	
Bread flour (14%) (High gluten)	12	8	100.0	Sift, add and mix to a dough. Check consistency
Shortening		8	4.0	Add shortening and develop the dough

Allow the dough to rise well and then punch. Relax the dough for 15 min and then scale and round the dough units. Dough units that are to be retarded (refrigerated or frozen) should be made from a dough that is not fully conditioned or young—to prevent the dough from becoming old or overconditioned.

Note: A strong bread flour should be used. This dough is quite stiff and firm when compared with white pan bread dough. Egg content may be increased if desired. Egg shade may be used in areas where this is permissible. This may allow for a reduction in eggs. It will also result in a decrease in volume.

Egg Bagel Varieties

These bagels do not have to be boiled like plain bagels. By varying the toppings or garnishes, a variety of bagels may be made and served on the premises. The bagels may be hand shaped or made with an automatic bagel shaping machine.

Ingredients	lb	oz	%	Mixing procedure
Yeast (variable)		8	4.0	Dissolve the yeast and set aside
Water	1	4	10.0	
Sugar		13	6.5	Dissolve ingredients. Blend well
Salt		3	1.5	
Whole eggs		8	4.0	
Egg yolks (optional)		10	5.0	
Vegetable oil		13	6.5	
Dough conditioner		½	0.25	
Water (variable)	4	8	36.0	
Bread flour (14% protein)	12	8	100.0	Sift and add the flour. Mix lightly and add yeast. Mix well to develop

Allow the dough to rise. Scale the dough into presses weighing approximately 4 lb 8 oz and round. Divide the press after relaxing it for 15 min into 36 equal units. Make up into evenly shaped rings. Place on lightly greased pans or pans lined with parchment paper. Give the bagels three-quarter proof and brush lightly with egg wash. Garnish with poppy seeds, sesame seeds, chopped onion preparation, garlic and onion mix, celery, or other topping for variety. Give full proof and bake at 415–420° F.

Note: This dough is quite stiff. If a weaker flour is used, increase the amount of flour for proper consistency. If egg yolks are not used, slightly increase the water. Egg shade may be used where permissible.

Plain Bagels   (*Boiled Variety*)

Ingredients	lb	oz	%	Mixing procedure
Yeast (variable)		8	4.0	Dissolve the yeast and set aside
Water	1	8	12.0	
Sugar		9	4.5	Dissolve ingredients and blend
Salt		3	1.5	well
Malt syrup (optional)		4	2.0	
Vegetable oil		4	2.0	
Dough conditioner		½	0.25	
Water (variable)	4	8	36.0	
Bread flour (high gluten-14% protein)	12	8	100.0	Sift, add and mix lightly. Add yeast and develop the dough

Boil water in a large open bowl or vat and keep at a simmer. A small amount of caustic (sodium hydroxide) and malt syrup may be added to the water. Place the bagels that are about three-quarter proof into the water for 1 to 2 min. Bagels will rise to the surface. This is a form of parboiling and produces the hard, shiny outer crust when the bagels are baked. Place on parchment paper-lined pans and garnish with a variety of toppings. Bake at 435° F. Units may be placed on canvas covered boards (bagel boards) that have been moistened with water. When bagels have risen and started to color in the oven the boards are turned and bagels bake on the oven hearth.

Note: This dough should be quite stiff or firm. No dusting flour is used in the makeup or shaping of the bagels. Allow the dough to rise for about 1 to 1½ hr depending upon the conditions in which the dough is allowed to ferment. Scale the dough into 4½ to 5 lb presses and round up. Relax the dough about 20 min and press out. Roll out and shape the bagels.

Onion Bread and Rolls

These are specialty breads and rolls that are open-grained, soft, and a bit chewy. They may be made in several forms and are usually served or merchandised while still warm. These products can be quickly frozen and promptly restored to warm freshness in a microwave oven.

Ingredients	lb	oz	%	Mixing procedure
Yeast (variable)		8	4.0	Dissolve the yeast and set aside
Water	2	8	20.0	
Sugar		5	2.5	Dissolve dry ingredients and
Salt		4	2.0	blend well
Malt syrup (optional)		3	1.5	

Ingredients	lb	oz	%	Mixing procedure
Dough conditioner		¼	0.2	
Water	5	8	44.0	
Bread flour (13 to 14% protein)	12	8	100.0	Sift and add flour. Stir slightly, add yeast and mix to a dough
Shortening		2	1.0	Add and develop dough

Allow the dough to rise well. First punch about 1½ hr. Relax the dough about 15 min and scale as follows: For the small mini breads: 6 oz. For the flat-type onion rolls: 3 lb 8 oz. Round up the units and allow to relax for 10 min. Prepare chopped onions mixed with a small amount of vegetable oil, salt, pepper, and garlic powder. Poppy seeds may be added to the onions. Flatten the bread or roll units and dip into the onions. Roll up the units into small French bread size. Rolls are rolled out flat or may be rolled up to enclose the onions. Proof and bake on pans.

Note: The dough is slightly softer than white pan bread dough. If malt is not used, increase sugar by 2 oz. Dough should be cool after final development (temperature 78–80° F.)

Sour Rye Bread   (*Made With Sour Rye Culture*)

Ingredients	lb	oz	%	Mixing procedure
Yeast (variable)		10	5.0	Dissolve the yeast and set aside
Water	2	8	20.0	
Salt		2	1.0	Dissolve and blend
Molasses		4	2.0	
Water (variable)	5	8	44.0	
Dough conditioner		½	0.2	Sift flours and dry ingredients to blend. Add and mix lightly. Add yeast and mix to a dough
Sour culture *(Heart O Rye)		12	6.0	
Rye flour	2	8	16.0	
Bread flour or clear flour	10		84.0	
Shortening (optional) Caraway seeds (optional) quantity as desired.		2	1.0	Add and develop dough

Maintain a cool dough temperature by using ice water if necessary. Dough temperature out of mixer should be about 78–80° F. Allow dough to rise for about one hr. Punch or fold the dough and relax for about 20 min. Scale the units for the desired loaf size. Large sandwich loaves may be scaled 3 lb. Smaller mini loaves may be scaled about 7 oz. Round up the scaled units and relax for about 10 min. Shape the loaves as desired. The flattened dough units may be dipped or sprinkled with caraway seeds before final molding. Give the units slightly less than full proof. Bread may be cut with a sharp knife about ½ in. deep and brushed with water. Bake with steam injected into the oven before loading. Continue steam until oven spring is complete and the loaves start to show a slight crust color. Bake at 420° F.

Note: *(Heart O Rye is a sour culture made by Caravan Products Co.) There are a number of culture preparations available.

American Rye Bread

This is also known as light rye bread because of its even, midly open grain and soft texture. The taste, flavor, and color of the bread is obtained by the use of rye flour, an optional amount of rye culture, and molasses and some sugar color in the dough.

Ingredients	lb	oz	%	Mixing procedure
Yeast (variable)		8	5.0	Dissolve the yeast and set aside
Water	2		20.0	
Salt		3	1.9	Dissolve dry ingredients and
Malt (nondiastatic)		2	1.2	blend well
Molasses (dark)		2	1.2	
Sugar color (optional)				
Caraway seeds (optional)		3	1.9	
Water	4		60.0	
Dough conditioner		½	0.25	Sift flours, add and mix lightly.
Rye flour	2		20.0	Add yeast and mix to a dough
Bread flour or clear flour	8		80.0	
Sour rye culture (optional)		4½	3.0	
Shortening		3	1.9	Add the shortening and develop the dough

Dough temperature should be kept cool. (78–80° F.) Scale the dough and shape as for the sour rye bread. The dough units may also be placed in regular bread pans and baked as for a sandwich type bread. The units may be baked directly on the hearth or on parchment paper-lined pans. Bake with steam at 420° F. Reduce oven heat slightly after a light crust color has formed.

Note: If sour rye culture is used, reduce the salt content to 2½ oz. The culture usually contains salt. If culture is used, reduce conditioning time to about one hour. If no culture is used, allow dough to rise for about 1½ hr. Punch the dough and allow to relax before scaling.

English Muffins

Ingredients	lb	oz	%	Mixing procedure
Yeast (variable)		3½	2.0	Dissolve the yeast and set aside
Water	1		10.0	
Sugar		4	2.4	Dissolve the dry ingredients and
Salt		3½	2.0	blend well
Water (cold)	6	8	65.0	
Dough conditioner		¼	0.2	
Mold inhibitor, if used (Sodium or calcium propionate)		¼	0.2	
Wheat gluten		1½	1.0	Sift the flour. Add and stir
Bread flour	10		100.0	slightly. Add the yeast and mix to a dough
Shortening		1½	1.0	Add the shortening and develop the dough well

Allow the dough to rise well for approximately 1½ hr. The exact time will vary with the amount of yeast used, the temperature of the water, and the conditions under which the dough is conditioned or fermented. Scale the dough into presses weighing 4½ lb. The size of the press depends upon the size of the muffin pan used. Relax the presses for about 10 min and divide into 36 equal pieces. Round the pieces by hand or in an automatic divider. Place the pieces into a large pan lined with yellow or white corn meal. After 10 min, flatten slightly and turn the muffins over so that both sides are dusted with corn meal. Place the muffins into the special corn muffin pans and cover with the sliding top. Leave the last muffin section slightly open so that the degree of proof may be checked. The units are given approximately three-quarter proof (they will feel quite soft to the touch). Cover the muffins completely now. Be careful to avoid dragging units that have risen above the level of the tin. Bake the muffins at 390–400° F. for about 9–10 min. Check for complete bake by pressing lightly in the center of the muffin. The muffin should spring back firmly to the touch. If the muffins are baked on a griddle, check the heat of the griddle to avoid flash heat. Bake on one side for about 4–5 min and then turn the pans over and bake for another 4–5 min. Remove from the pans soon after baking.

Note: This dough requires extensive development to impart an open, porous grain in the baked muffin. The dough is quite soft and should be kept cool. If possible, ice should be added to the water. If the dough is too soft, depending upon the type of flour used, additional flour should be added to make handling easier. For handmade muffins, increase the flour to 10 lb 12 oz. The wheat gluten increases gluten extensibility and allows for maximum expansion during the baking process. The amount of gluten flour may be increased slightly if desired.

Pita Bread   (*Pocket Bread*)

This type of pocket bread can be made in most any type of oven. The baker and pastry chef can regulate the size, shape, and degree of thickness to meet special production needs. For catering purposes, smaller units can be made for special fillings. The pita bread may also be specially flavored with condiments.

Ingredients	lb	oz	%	Mixing procedure
Yeast (variable)		6	3.4	Dissolve the yeast and set aside
Water (cool)	2		20.0	
Sugar		2	1.3	Dissolve the ingredients and
Salt		3	1.8	blend well
Malt syrup (optional)		1	0.6	
Dough conditioner		½	0.3	
Mold inhibitor, if used		¼	0.15	
Water	4		40.0	
Bread flour	10		100.0	Sift and add the flour. Mix lightly and add the yeast. Mix to a dough
Shortening (optional)		2	1.2	Add and develop dough

Allow the dough to rise well before punching. Punch the dough and relax for about 15 min. Doughs made with weaker flour should not be punched but scaled out soon after the dough has risen. Scale the dough into presses that produce the desired unit size. The popular package size has units weighing 3–4 oz. For small, specialty pocket bread, scale dough into presses weighing approximately 4 lb. Allow the rounded presses to relax for about 12 min and divide and round the units of dough. Relax the rounded units for 12 min, or until soft and gassy.

Roll out the relaxed units to about ¼ in. or slightly thinner. The units may be rolled into round or oval shape. Place the rolled out units on pans or oven peels that have been dusted with a blend of flour and corn meal. This will allow for easy peeling into the oven when the units are ready for baking. Allow the units to relax until soft and slightly gassy. This may take 20–30 min depending upon proofing conditions. Oven temperature for baking should be 450–460° F. The thin units of dough require rapid baking. The heat of the oven will cause rapid expansion of the gas, and the yeast will cause further gas activity. Rapid moisture evaporation also causes expansion. The gas is trapped in the dough causing a large pocket to form. Baking on the hearth of the oven provides immediate, necessary transfer of heat to the dough. Bake the units for 7 min. The actual baking time will depend upon the size and thickness of the dough units. The large, balloon-like pockets will flatten when the pita bread is removed from the oven. The pockets can be opened and filled when the bread has cooled. Breads may be stored for later use by sealing in poly bags. They can be frozen rapidly and later reheated in microwave ovens. **Note:** The dough should be developed until gluten extensibility is at its maximum. The dough should be slightly softer than white pan bread dough. The type of flour used will determine water absorption and degree of dough development. For bakers who do not have strong bread flour, it would be advisable to add approximately 1–1½ percent wheat gluten for extensibility. Dough temperature out of the machine should be about 78–80° F. Use ice water to make the dough.

Indigenous Breads of India

These bread specialties can readily be duplicated by bakers and pastry chefs. The following is a brief overview of the characteristics of the various breads, their composition, and the conditions relative to their production.

The indigenous or native breads of India are thin, flat, small sheets of dough similar in some respects to Middle East bread. They are representative of the types of wheat, grains, and flour varieties native to India. The availability of limited raw materials in outlying areas and the lack of modern baking equipment were the major factors in the development and acceptance of these bread varieties. These native breads, such as Nan, and several similar breads, are always present when dining at home and often compose the major part of any meal. When dining out, these breads are ordered almost immediately and are served hot since they are prepared very quickly from the ever-present doughs. Since these breads are rather small and flat and often 50–60 grams in weight (about 2 oz), individual orders are easily met.

The Nan-type bread is most convenient to bake because of the flour used and the manner in which the bread is baked. The indigenous flour of India is rather low in protein content and will vary considerably in quality and quantity from one milling of wheat to another. The addition of other grains that are blended with the wheat allow the production of variety breads. The average bread flour used may vary from 7–10 percent in protein content with accompanying quality variables in the protein. Thus, the gluten capacities of the flour blends are equally varied. Since the breads are thin and flat, they are not processed with the same production requirements as for the regular white pan bread.

For the commercial or retail production of Indian type breads such as Nan, Chappati, or Roti, it is advisable to use a softer Western White wheat with a blend of Hard Red Winter wheat. The proportions would be approximately 30 percent Western White and 70 percent Hard Red Winter. There will be variations, but high gluten bread flours might cause excessive expansion and blistering during the baking process. Actually, the pastry chef and baker may use a blend of 50 percent pastry flour and 50 percent bread flour for the doughs. These flours should be sifted together to insure a proper blend.

The dough for these breads is rather lean, so it is important to enrich and strengthen it. Since these breads are often the basic food staple, adding a variety of natural native grains and flours is a valuable practice. The addition of protein-added grains and dough supplements results in new and varied products. Formulas that follow include a number of grains and flours with dough conditioners. The method of dough conditioning in India for the native breads follows a simulated sponge dough method. A selected piece of leftover dough from the previous day is used as a base for the mixing of a fresh dough. It is similar to a sour dough preparation. The sponge dough can be controlled for readiness by controlling the rate of sponge conditioning. Because of the lower protein content of the flour, a shorter sponge dough time is suggested. The final dough should be given a short resting period of 15 min before being processed. The dough is divided into large units or presses and rounded. These units are relaxed for 10 min and then sent through the bun divider and rounder. Presses may be scaled 5 lb or more. Individual dough units weighing 4 oz may be scaled and rounded. The rounded units are then given the usual resting period (preliminary proofing) of 10–12 min. It is important not to overextend this period because of the nature of the flour. The units are sent through the sheeter or are rolled out with a rolling pin to a thin, even thickness (about $1/16$ in.). The shape may be round or oval. The Nan is customarily round while the Chappati and Roti may be round or oval. After sheeting, the round units may be slightly stretched to form the oval shape. Due to the softness of the dough, there may be some dusting flour remaining on the surface. If you wish to, brushing or spraying lightly with water may reduce the surface flour although its presence is quite common on the baked bread. The units are docked or stippled before baking. The stippling will prevent excessive blister formation. Small air pockets are desirable and these pocket surfaces will tend to be darker in spots to provide the homemade appearance.

The units are relaxed for 10 min on pans or peels lightly dusted with flour. The baking process is very rapid. A travelling band oven may be best since the units are deposited directly on the band or hearth of the oven. Units may also be peeled directly on to the hearth of the oven. Oven temperature is hot. Usually, units are baked at about 500° F. for about 3–4 min for the smaller units. Larger units, while of equal thickness may take an extra minute. Note is made of the inclusion of dough conditioners, softeners, mold inhibitors, and oxidizers such as potassium bromate in the formulas. The author found these additives essential for the commercial production of these breads in India. The Nan-type of bread is often made with added spices for flavor variety.

Nan Bread

Ingredients	lb	oz	%	Mixing procedure
Sponge Dough				
Yeast (variable)		6	3.0	Dissolve the yeast. Add the sugar
Malt or sugar		2	1.0	and malt and dissolve. Add flour
Water	5		40.0	and conditioner and mix to a
Dough conditioner		¼	0.2	smooth dough. Allow dough to
Flour	7	8	60.0	rise until it starts to settle. (Approximately 2 hr)

Final Dough

	lb	oz	%	
Sugar		2	1.0	Place the sponge dough into the
Salt		4	2.0	mixer. Add the dry ingredients
Soy flour (defatted)		4	2.0	and water; mix to dissolve and
Wheat germ (toasted)		2	1.0	break up the sponge dough. Add
Ground nut (peanut)		2	1.0	the flour and mix to a dough.
flour (if available)				Add the shortening and develop
Mold inhibitor (if		¼	0.2	the dough. Check development
necessary)				of the dough with a gluten exten-
Water (variable)	2	8	20.0	sibility check
Flour	5		40.0	
Shortening		3	1.5	

Note: Use cold water for the final dough. This dough will require less mixing time for dough development because of the flour quality. Relax dough for 20 min and take to the divider and rounder.

Chappati Bread   (*Made with 75% whole wheat flour*)

Ingredients	lb	oz	%	Mixing procedure
Sponge Dough				
Yeast (variable)		6	3.0	Dissolve the yeast in the water
Water	5	10	45.0	and sugar. Add the flour and de-
Sugar		2	1.0	velop to a smooth dough. Allow
Whole wheat flour	4	6	35.0	the sponge to rise until it starts
Bread flour	3	2	25.0	to settle
Dough conditioner		¼	0.2	
Final Dough				
Sugar		2	1.0	Place the sponge dough into the
Salt		4	2.0	mixer. Add the water and dry in-
Molasses or honey		2	1.0	gredients and mix well to break
Soy flour (defatted)		2	1.0	up the sponge. Add the flour and
Wheat germ		2	1.0	mix to a dough. Add the short-
Mold inhibitor		¼	0.2	ening and develop the dough
(optional)				
Wheat bran		4	2.0	
Water (variable)	2	8	20.0	
Whole wheat flour	5		40.0	
Shortening		3	1.5	

Use same dough processing procedure as for Nan bread.
Note: The amount of water will vary with the quality of the flour. In this formula, regular bread flour should be used to provide support for the high percentage of whole wheat flour. This dough is slightly softer than regular white pan break dough. The dough will tend to firm slightly because of the delayed absorption of the whole wheat flour.

Roti Bread   (Made with 30% corn meal)

Ingredients	lb	oz	%	Mixing procedure
Sponge dough				
Yeast (variable)		6	3.0	Follow the same procedure as for
Water	5		40.0	the Nan and Chappati
Sugar		2	1.0	
Flour	7	8	60.0	
Dough conditioner		¼	0.2	
Final dough				
Sugar		2	1.0	Follow the same procedure as for
Salt		4	2.0	Nan and Chappati dough
Malt or honey		2	1.0	
Soy flour (defatted)		4	2.0	
Wheat germ		2	1.0	
Yellow corn meal (Coarse type)	3	12	30.0	
Water (variable)	2	8	20.0	
Bread flour	1	4	10.0	
Shortening		3	1.5	

Note: A coarse corn meal will provide a grainy effect which is typical of the native Roti bread. As previously indicated, all doughs should be relaxed for about 15 min before sending to the divider and rounder. Stippling of the rolled out units should be close and spaced evenly to allow for an even, slight blistering effect during baking. When cool, these breads should have a soft flexibility and be easily rolled. If overbaked, the units will be brittle and break sharply. This may be desirable for variety. Frozen units should be in poly bags and reheated quickly before serving.

Topping for Dutch Bread

This special topping is made with rice flour which is starchy and composed of very fine starch particles. It will feel sandy to the touch. Flour with gluten-forming protein should not be used because the topping contains yeast and the resulting doughy effect would make application of the topping difficult and create a doughy, blistered effect.

Ingredients	lb	oz	%	Mixing procedure
Yeast		2	8.0	Dissolve the sugar and yeast in
Water	1	8	100.0	the water
Sugar		2	8.0	
Rice flour	1	8	100.0	Add the flour, salt and melted
Salt		½	2.0	shortening and mix well
Melted shortening		2	8.0	

Mix the topping and apply quickly to the half-proofed bread units. The dough will be firm enough to withstand the handling. Cover the top of the dough completely and then form the box design using a round edged stick or even a small spatula. As the dough continues to rise to full proof, the topping will spread. The yeast will be active and create a slight rise in the topping as well. Bake the bread at 410–415° F. Fill the oven chamber with steam before baking to prevent rapid crust formation of the topping and to allow the bread to have even oven spring during the first 5–7 min of baking. When the crust color forms reduce the oven temperature slightly to develop a crisp loaf.

Combination Sweet Yeast Dough

The baker and pastry chef may have scrap dough left from the makeup of Danish pastry, coffee cake dough, sweet roll dough, or doughnut dough. The accumulation of scrap dough is used as the base for the combination sweet yeast dough. Some bakers plan to have extra sweet yeast dough prepared to serve as the base because of the popularity of the products that are made from this dough. The products made are similar to those made from Danish pastry dough. The madeup units are usually brushed with melted butter or margarine rather than egg wash. A variety of fillings and toppings are used for these products.

Ingredients	lb	oz	%	Mixing procedure
Yeast (variable)		6	6.0	Dissolve the yeast and set aside
Water	1		16.0	
Sugar	2	4	36.0	Blend all ingredients together
Salt		1½	1.5	well to break up the dough
Scrap dough (sweet yeast dough, Danish, etc.)	6		100.0	scraps and mix to a smooth consistency. The cheese is optional. When used, it provides for a rich
Nonfat dry milk		4	4.0	taste and flavor
Honey or glucose syrup		8	8.0	
Butter or shortening	2		32.0	
Margarine	1	12	28.0	
Dough conditioner		½	0.5	
Bakers cheese (cottage or cream cheese) (optional)	1		16.0	
Vanilla (variable)		1	1.0	
Whole eggs	1		16.0	Add the eggs in 2 stages and
Egg yolks	1		16.0	blend in well
Add the yeast solution and mix in lightly.				
Bread flour (variable)	4	4	68.0	Sift the flour and baking powder. Add and mix to a smooth dough
Baking powder		2¼	2.25	

Divide the dough into two equal pieces of about 11 to 12 lb each and form into a smooth rectangular shape. Give each piece of dough two rolls of three-fold as for the rolling in of Danish pastry. No additional fat is to be rolled in. Allow the dough to relax for about 15 min in the refrigerator between rolls. It is best to refrigerate the doughs for 12–24 hr before makeup. Refer to the chapter on Danish pastry for the makeup of variety units. Units are brushed with melted butter or margarine and topped with streussel or chopped nuts. Units baked without topping are usually dusted lightly with confectioners sugar when the products are baked and cooled. A chocolate smear and almond filling are often used in combination for the makeup of butter horns, snecks, and cigar shapes. Long sticks or stongen may be made and later sliced into portions after baking.

Special Chocolate Smear

Ingredients	lb	oz	g	Mixing procedure
Confectioners sugar	2	2	1000	Sift the sugar, salt, cocoa to-
Salt		1/8	3	gether. Add the oil and hot water
Cocoa powder		12	350	and mix smooth
Vegetable oil		6	170	
Hot water (160° F)	2		900	
Melted margarine		10	270	Add the melted margarine and
Vanilla		1	30	vanilla and blend in. Add the
Chocolate liquor melted (bitter chocolate) (optional)		3	80	melted chocolate and mix smooth

The melted chocolate will tend to firm the smear. This may be necessary. To soften the smear for spreading, if too thick, add a small amount of simple syrup. The smear should be covered when not in use. It tends to form a mild crust when exposed to the air for any length of time. When applying the smear, it is advisable to brush the rolled out dough with melted butter or margarine. This will make for easy smear of the filling. The smear may be blended with almond smear (recipe to follow) by first applying the almond smear and then the chocolate smear. This combination has been very appealing to consumers.

Basic Almond Smear   (Using Cake Crumbs)

Ingredients	lb	oz	%	Mixing procedure
Almond or macaroon paste (kernel paste may be used in a blend)	2		100.0	Blend the almond paste and egg whites to a smooth blend
Egg whites		8	25.0	

Sugar	2		100.0	Add the dry ingredients and
Salt		½	1.5	shortening to the above and
Shortening	2		100.0	blend in. Add the egg whites in
Cinnamon		1	3.0	2 stages and cream to a soft,
Egg whites		8	25.0	smooth consistency
Water	2		100.0	Add the water and dry cake
Cake crumbs (variable)	4		200.0	crumbs and blend

These units freeze well and may be kept for extended periods. The baked units have the characteristics of a rich, yeast-raised cake-like product. Shelf life is longer than sweet yeast dough products.

Note: Very dry or toasted cake crumbs will absorb more liquid. Additional water may be necessary. If the almond smear is to be used with the chocolate smear as a blend, it is best to apply the almond smear first and then the chocolate smear. Additional cake crumbs, toasted, chopped nuts, and cinnamon sugar may be sprinkled on top of the smears.

9

Prepared Mixes

A great majority of bakers and pastry chefs are using prepared mixes of various types for various purposes. In fact, prepared mixes extend beyond the baking industry into all areas of food preparation and food service. Originally intended primarily for home use, prepared mixes have gone beyond the confines of the home and the homemaker. The original self-rising flour and early biscuit preparations have been technically developed so that mixes for the areas of yeast-raised products, cakes, cookies, pies, doughnuts, and related bakery foods are now readily available. For the retail and wholesale baker prepared mixes play an important role in the daily production of bakery foods. They offer variety products, quality control, more efficient operation, consistency in product production, and very importantly, they help to overcome the problems attendant with unskilled bakers. Basic products are now produced with prepared mixes and with the services of semi-skilled and partially trained personnel.

This chapter is directed to bakers who are presently using or are seriously considering using prepared mixes. It is not the intent of the author to persuade bakers and pastry chefs to use these prepared mixes but rather to provide fundamental information relating to their content and preparation. A number of basic prepared mix formulations are also presented. There are many varieties of prepared mixes, some of better quality than others because of the ingredients used. Selecting the appropriate prepared mix will depend on factors controlling production and merchandising. The baker and pastry chef who prepare their own baked goods from scratch may have reservations about using prepared mixes feeling that the prepared mix undermines the quality of their finished products. After trying some basic prepared mixes and comparing the resulting products with those made from scratch, many bakers have found that prepared mixes do have decided advantages. For example, most cake-type and variety doughnuts are made with prepared mixes. Time, quality control, product consistency and training of personnel are factors considered when making specific basic products. One readily recognizes the growth of special doughnut shops as a part of the fast food industry. Many bakers are using prepared flour and multi-grain blends for specialty breads. The emphasis on nutrition and bread enrichment has led to the use of the prepared flour blends by bakers. Thus, basic products in the form of prepared mixes that are not very expensive to produce are quite acceptable to many bakers. The special products, cakes and pastries, and many bakery food varieties are still being made from scratch—specialties of the skilled baker and pastry chef. In some instances, basic mixes may be used with special improvements and modified by the baker to improve the finished quality.

It may well be that bakers and pastry chefs may wish to prepare mixes in part. They may wish to maintain complete control of the content and quality of their products and still provide for the easy mixing of semi-skilled or partially trained personnel. They may not wish to purchase in bulk but rather to prepare their own mixes for a short period of one week. In some instances, purchasable prepared mixes may not be available for one reason or another and a chef may have to prepare his own mixes. For bakers who may wish to make adjustments in purchased prepared mixes this chapter will provide basic information to allow for the necessary adjustments. For example, the addition of eggs will require an adjustment of the formula. Mixing procedures and baking of mixed batters may have to be adjusted to meet the equipment used for production. In some instances, as for specialty breads, bakers may wish to increase the amount of honey or molasses or introduce natural syrups to bread specialties. The baker must understand the required adjustments.

Most prepared mixes are fundamentally similar in ingredient content. The mixes will contain the essential ingredients necessary for an average quality product with the addition of the liquids and other recommended ingredients and following the instructions on the package. Very often, the instructions may indicate options and suggestions for the baker or pastry chef to further improve the quality of the product by adding eggs, milk, butter, and other enriching ingredients. Many bakers do so. This chapter will provide a brief review of the basic ingredients contained in most prepared mixes, the blending of the ingredients, and suggestions for variables that may arise in production. The suggested prepared-mix formulas that follow have been tested under regular bakeshop conditions by the author and have proven to be highly satisfactory. These formulas may be adjusted to meet specific needs and production requirements.

Mixing and Blending of Basic Ingredients
For Prepared Mixes

Formulas for special bakery foods are often not available as a prepared mix. As previously indicated, the more sophisticated cakes, pastries, and other specialties are usually created by bakers and pastry chefs. To meet production needs, quality control and so forth bakers often make their own preparations in the form of a prepared mix. For example, a short dough or special pie crust may be prepared for the final addition of liquid by the baker's assistant or apprentice pastry chef. In larger plants, this may be done by the mixer with mixing instructions provided in short training programs. Understanding the dry ingredients used, sifting and blending the dry ingredients, and blending these ingredients with the fats and powdered eggs and chemical leavening agents are the fundamental factors. While large manufacturers of prepared mixes use the most sophisticated equipment in scaling, measurng, and final blending, the average baker can make preparations with the current available mixers, scaling and measuring equipment, and the variety of sieves. The vertical mixer using a dough hook, a flat beater, a grinder and cutting attachments, can serve equally well to meet the special blends required for the preparation of the preliminary blends for the mixes. With an understanding of the ingredients used and the methods of blending the ingredients, and the shelf life of the prepared mixes, the skilled baker and production man can use the present equipment to maximum advantage. The technique of proper blending and control of mix consistency is related to the knowledge of the ingredients used, their composition, granular structure, and procedure for combining and blending. Ingredients that are similar in character are usually blended together. The dry ingredients of fine granulation, such as flour, sugar, salt, and similar ingredients, are usually sifted first and then blended together. Coarser dry ingredients, such as corn meal, bran, wheat germ, are blended and then added to the flour blend. Shortening and other fats are added in the final stages of blending. This topic will be discussed with fats.

Prepared mixes that are not purchased and are self-prepared in the bakeshop are usually made for short periods. Stock items such as pie crust mix, short dough mix, muffin mix, pancake and waffle mix, sweet yeast dough mixes, and specialty bread mixes, are usually prepared for about one week at a time. As a result, they do not create a storage problem and are not stored long enough to create a sanitation problem. Mixes should be stored in clean, covered containers and kept in a cool storage area. The same storeroom used for flour and similar ingredients can be quite satisfactory. New preparations and batches are made as the last mixes are depleted. The smaller batches allow for product and production control and adjustments can be made should the initial test indicate that they are necessary. Smaller batches make possible the control of infestation and reduce the possibility of rancidity in mixes with higher percentages of fat.

Basic Ingredients Used in Prepared Mixes

The ingredients that form the basis for prepared mixes are flour, sugar, milk (dried), eggs (dried), shortening, and leavening agents. The varieties of these products will be discussed briefly and specific information about uses and blends of the varieties for special products will be given. Ingredients, such as dried flavors and ground spices, will be discussed in terms of their use and addition to the formulas.

Flour in Prepared Mixes

Large manufacturers of prepared mixes often have the flour varieties for these mixes preblended at the mill before shipment to the plant for final blending. Still others will have the various flours tested in their own plants and then blend the flours at the plant. This approach insures that the flours meet the specifications required for the mix and the products to be made from the mix. For example, cake flours used for high-ratio cake mixes will be bleached while unbleached cake flour may be used for cookies, crackers, or a blend with other flours. Those bakers and pastry chefs who prepare their own mix bases will have to regard the flours available in terms of their own experience. In other words, the regular formula should be followed and the flours blended with other dry ingredients as though they were being scaled for a "scratch" mix. New flour shipments should be tested and note made regarding any necessary adjustments. In most instances, hard-type products such as hearth-baked French or Italian breads will use only a high-protein flour. Rye breads, on the other hand, will use a blend of rye flour with a high-gluten flour. For bakers who use a regular rye sour dough, there is little need for a prepared mix. Those using dry sour cultures may wish to blend the flours with the sour culture and the salt. The multi-grain breads are most popular in the field of enriched breads. The baker may prepare his own blend of various grains and flours and add these to the bread flour. Usually, the enriching grains and bran compose approximately 20–25 percent of the total flour blend. Some bakers prefer to blend only the special grain, bran and flours and these are proportionately added to the bread flour at the time of mixing. There are bakers who purchase the prepared multi-grain blend and add additional grains, raisins, nuts, and other enriching ingredients to make their own special product.

Sweet yeast goods and soft roll-type products often use a medium-strong flour (approximately 12.5 percent protein). This flour is often blended with a softer flour for special characteristics. This flour blend may also be enriched with the use of soy flour. Note is made of the use of additives such as extenders, softeners, mold inhibitors, and so forth which are often included in the prepared mix. The baker who makes his own mix or blend would do well to add these at the time of mixing. Because of their small quantity, often less than 0.2 percent based on the weight of the flour, it is difficult for the baker to get maximum diffusion of these products in the blend.

For short dough and pie crust doughs, a blend of pastry flour and short patent flour is used by most bakers and pastry chefs. The percentage of each will vary with the formula. For example, a high percentage of fat in a rich pie crust dough will require slightly more flour of 9.5 percent protein content in a blend with a softer pastry flour. Pie crust for fried pies using less fat will use almost total pastry flour. Flour blends for muffins, biscuits, special cakes and cookies require careful analysis of the present formula and the flours selected and blended for these mixes if they are to be in prepared mix form. The following tables provide an overview of the most commonly used flours and their uses in bakery foods production. The flours are categorized in terms of wheat source. The smaller baker and pastry chef can refer to the tables for guidance but will be limited to the basic flours available. These are usually the high-gluten flour, the medium-short patent flour, the pastry flour, and the high-ratio cake flour. Excellent flour blends for prepared mixes may be made from the basic flours available.

Sugar in Prepared Mixes

There are several basic types of sugar used by the baker and pastry chef. Of these, granulated sugar of a medium fine structure is the most widely

TABLE 9.1 COMPOSITION AND USES OF HARD SPRING WHEAT FLOURS*

Protein percent	Ash percent	Bakery products in which flour is used
12.5–12.8	0.42–0.44	White pan bread (both sponge and straight dough). Specialty and variety breads. Hamburger and Wiener rolls Yeast-raised sweet goods Soft rolls (Parker House type) Doughnuts, yeast-raised variety Hard rolls and hearth bread
12.8–13.1	0.46–0.48	White pan bread (both sponge and straight dough) Hard rolls and hearth bread Specialty and variety breads
13.5	0.48	Hard rolls and hearth bread Blender flour for coarse flour breads
15.0	0.48	High gluten flour for Kaiser rolls Italian, French and Jewish hearth breads
15.0–15.5	0.70–0.74	Carrier flour used in making whole wheat, rye specialty and variety breads Blender flour used in mixes with rye flour for rye bread

TABLE 9.2 COMPOSITION AND USES OF HARD WINTER WHEAT FLOURS*

Protein percent	Ash percent	Bakery products in which the flour is used
12.25–12.50	0.42–0.44	White pan bread (both sponge and straight dough) Hamburger and Weiner rolls Soft rolls (Parker House type) Specialty and variety breads Yeast-raised sweet goods and doughnuts
12.50–13.0	0.46–0.48	White pan bread (both sponge and straight dough) Blender flour in some variety and specialty breads and rolls Blender flour for chemically-leavened biscuits and muffin and waffle mixes Heavy fruit cake mixes
15.00–15.50	0.70–0.74	Carrier flour used in making rye, whole wheat, specialty and variety breads Blender flour for baking powder doughnuts, and muffin and waffle mixes

*Matz, *The Technology and Chemistry of Cereals as Food and Feed*

TABLE 9.3   COMPOSITION AND USES OF SOFT WHEAT FLOURS*

Protein percent	Ash percent	Bakery products in which the flour is used
7.5–8.0	0.32–0.35	Angel food cakes High ratio cakes and cookies (no spread) (Unbleached) High ratio cakes, spread-type cookies
8.0–8.5	0.35–0.38	Layer cakes and pound cakes Slightly rich wire cut cookies (no spread) (Unbleached) Cracker topping
9.0–9.5	0.39–0.42	Unbleached flour: General line of cookies Pie crust doughs Blender flour in yeast-raised fried goods Cracker doughs Blender flour in yeast-raised sweet goods Sugar cones Doughnuts Bleached: No spread ice box cookies Loaf cakes Low-ratio cup cakes Lunch box cake items
9.5–10.0	0.45–0.48	General purpose flour used much the same as the 0.39 to 0.42 ash flour

*Matz, *The Technology and Chemistry of Cereals as Food and Feed*

used for the production of variety bakery foods. Sugar plays a very important role in the preparation of prepared mixes. Large baked-goods producers will define the exact type of sugar and its granulation to the sugar refiner for final blending of the prepared mixes. The average baker and pastry chef has available fine granulated sugar, coarse grain sugar, dusting sugar, powdered sugar, and an icing sugar that is very fine in particle size. Special sugars such as light brown, dark brown, and yellow sugar are available along with syrups. The syrups reduced to powder form are available as dried honey, molasses, and corn sugar. Of these, corn sugar is the only sugar most bakers will use in prepared mixes for such special products as pancake mixes, waffle mixes, and icings. These syrup-reduced powders are difficult to include in prepared mixes because of their hygroscopic (moisture absorbing) properties. Malt syrup in dry, powder form is used sparingly in prepared mixes for the same reason. Thus, it is advisable for the average baker to indicate in his formula for a self-made prepared mix that the syrups be added along with the water and other liquids.

Sugars are used in small percentages in specialty breads made with prepared mixes. In sweet yeast goods, the sugar content may equal 20–25 percent based on the weight of the flour. Sugar is most important in the preparation of cake mixes. High-ratio cakes, with a sugar content often as high as 130–140 percent based on the weight of the flour, are quite popular for bakers, pastry chefs, and homemakers as well. Sugar in cakes, cookies, and other sugar-rich bakery products has the following functions:

1. the sweetness provides taste and flavor;
2. when dissolved in the liquid, the sugar becomes a syrup and provides a tenderizing effect on the product;
3. sugar provides a crust color formed by the exposed surface of the product to the heat of the oven;
4. a desirable grain and texture is developed in the baked product resulting from the blending and creaming of the sugar with the fat content and other ingredients in the mix;
5. keeping quality is improved and shelf life extended with the use of the sugar and its moisture-retaining properties;
6. nutritional values and enrichment are provided
7. in the case of yeast-raised products, sugars provide for a source of food for yeast

As previously indicated, fine granulated sugar is predominantly used in prepared mixes. The sugar or sugars are blended by sifting. They are then sifted and blended with the flour and other dry ingredients. The baker preparing his own mix would do well to use a very fine sieve for the powdered sugar and then blend that sugar with the more granular sugars before blending with other ingredients. This is most important for cake-type products. Where the prepared mix is to have extended mixing for preparation and for the formation of added air cells, the finer granulated sugar is most advisable—it creams well and provides better grain and texture. Powdered sugars will have a tightening effect and restrict the absorption of air cells in mixing. Because powder and icing sugars contain a small percentage of starch to prevent caking, they tend to restrict the spread of cookies during baking. These sugars are often used for ice-box cookie prepared mixes.

Milk in Prepared Mixes

It is obvious that prepared mixes containing milk use dried milk products. There are several varieties of milk powder such as whole milk powder, skim milk powder, those of flake variety, and those of fine powder variety. Dairy processors will manufacture milk powder in accordance with the specifications submitted by the manufacturer of prepared mixes. Most average bakers and pastry chefs will use dry skim milk powder that has been sufficiently heat treated to reduce the chemical activity of the whey proteins. The higher heat treatment of whey proteins in milk, called the denaturation of the proteins, reduces the negative chemical changes and action caused by whey proteins that have not been processed with the higher heat treatment. This is especially important in bread and roll production. Denaturation of the whey proteins has been found to be desirable for the preparation of prepared mixes for doughnuts. Since the baker uses regular dry skim milk powder, he may continue to use it to prepare his own dry or prepared mixes. However, it is noted that low-heat treated milk is used to advantage in the preparation of mixes for puddings, fillings, toppings, and special cream-type icings.

The use of milk powder will increase the nutritional value of the product, provide for product enrichment, produce a richer crust color, and very importantly, increase absorption. In yeast-raised doughs the milk powder will provide for improved dough conditioning and increased tolerance during the makeup and final proofing of the products. The milk powder should be sifted and then resifted and blended with the other dry ingredients for the prepared mix.

Shortenings and Other Fats in Prepared Mixes

The many different bakery products and prepared mixes to produce these products require modifications in the amount and type of fat or shortening. For example, the high-sugar and high-liquid content cakes known as high-ratio cakes require the use of a shortening with high emulsifying properties. On the other hand, the prepared mix for pie crusts and biscuits may use lard for the mix. The modifications are necessary to produce a finished product with the desired characteristics. A small percentage of fat is used in bread mixes when compared to pound cake prepared mixes. The variation extreme may extend from 1 percent of the total weight of the flour used for lean bread-type products to as much as 75 percent for special cake mixes. Shortenings and other fats provide the following characteristics and qualities in the baked product:

1.   Increased volume resulting from the incorporation and distribution of air cells during the mixing process
2.   A soft product resulting from the tenderizing effect of the fats used. The higher the percentage the softer the product, depending on the properly balanced formula and mixing procedures.
3.   A fine grain and texture drived from the mixing process and formation of the air cells
4.   Improved shelf life and keeping quality, especially with cake mixes that have a high percentage of shortening and those that use emulsified shortenings or are supplemented with the use of glycerides, extenders, and softeners.

Since the average baker or pastry chef will prepare a premix or dry mix in a quantity that will not require extensive storage time, the problem of fat rancidity is minimal. There is no need to add antioxidants to the fats used in the mixes. A high quality shortening with good emulsifying properties should be used. Shortenings should be mixed with the dry ingredients without excessive clumping or lumping. Blending the milk powder with the shortening will tend to provide a drying effect and blending with other dry ingredients will therefore be more uniform. It is important to have this degree of shortening tolerance in prepared mixes with a high percentage of fat. The shortening should also allow for rapid aeration during the mixing. Some bakers add to the mix a small percentage of mono or diglycerides with other additives to assist in emulsifying the liquids. The baker producing his own prepared mixes should experiment with these emulsifiers and additives to establish the correct amounts and most advantageous types of emulsifiers to use for the mixes.

Regular shortening and plastic lard are often used for pie crust dough preparations. Because of the high percentage of fat required, bakers often blend a small percentage of flour with the fat to plasticize it. The fat is then mixed with the remaining flour and other dry ingredients to form the small fat-flour particles without causing a pasty effect. It is wise to chill the fat blend (butter-lard-shortening-margarine) and then blend with a small amount of flour. This preparation is then chopped before final blending. Flavor is one of the determining factors in the choice of fats to be used for pie crust. Most bakers prefer to use an odorless shortening and wish to avoid the special flavor of lard. However, there are those bakers who still prefer the mild flavor of lard in pie crusts. Slow speed mixing is essential to prevent the pasting or clumping of shortening and other fats. A chopper may be used to reduce fat-flour lumps and final blending may be done with a dough hook. If a flat beater is used on a vertical mixing machine, extreme care should be used to avoid the pasting effect.

For the preparation of prepared mixes for soft rolls, sweet rolls or buns, yeast-raised doughnuts, and other sweet-yeast dough products, it is advisable to use shortenings containing mono and diglycerides, usually about 1 percent of these emulsifiers based on the weight of the flour. A higher percentage is advisable if the percentage is based on the weight of the total shortening or fat used in the mix. The emulsifiers will provide increased tenderness and improved keeping qualities, reduce the dough conditioning time, and allow for more rapid production. The blend of flours used in the doughs also affects the keeping qualities and production time.

A regular hydrogenated shortening is most often used for cake-type doughnuts. Large manufacturers of these prepared mixes try to maintain the characteristics of good shape and doughnut symmetry as well as the desired tenderness. It is best to avoid the use of liquid fats or oils for doughnut premixes, although they do allow for easier frying and handling. While regular shortening is used in small amounts in doughnuts, the shortening provides a slight increase in fat absorption but with the added tenderness and keeping quality desired.

Eggs in Prepared Mixes

Manufacturers of variety prepared mixes are aware of the importance of eggs in the mixes, especially in the production of cake mixes, cookie mixes, and sweet yeast dough mixes. The amount and type of eggs are related to the type of prepared mix and the quality of the product to be produced. Thus, manufacturers of prepared mixes will have special dried egg blends prepared to meet special product needs. The smaller baker or pastry chef who prepares his own prepared mixes or premixes may blend only the dry ingredients and then add the eggs and other liquids when mixing. Eggs in dry form are used extensively in these mixes to eliminate the unnecessary addition of various liquids and to control the quality of the product. It is important that the baker understand the basic factors regarding the composition and use of eggs and the blending and treatment of eggs in the drying process. Dried eggs are processed into dried albumen or egg white, dried whole eggs with variations in treatment and composition, dried egg yolks with or without the addition of carbohy-drates, and special blends of whole eggs and egg yolks. Eggs in cakes and other bakery products

1. Provide a leavening effect due to the ability to absorb and hold air cells resulting from whipping or creaming and mixing. The natural expansion of the eggs in the presence of heat and moisture evapora-tion in the form of steam add to the leavening effect of the eggs.
2. Have a binding and toughening effect in that they aid in the absorp-tion of water and flour and the proteins of the eggs form a structure that adds to the structure of the baked product.
3. Provide color for the baked foods by the natural color of the yolk, making the product richer looking.
4. Provide taste and flavor. The larger the quantity of eggs used in the mix the more pronounced the taste and flavor.
5. Allow for greater distribution of the fats as well as the added emul-sifying properties because of the natural lecithin in the yolk. A more rapid emulsification of the liquid in the batter produces a more tender product with a longer shelf life.
6. Impart nutritional value. The egg is almost a complete food bearing most of the necessary nutritional needs.

The baker preparing his own mix must know the types of dried eggs available. Eggs are highly perishable. Stabilized whole eggs are often used to allow for longer storage time under normal conditions. Stabili-zation is possible by removing the natural glucose in the eggs before drying them. The dried whole eggs are reconstituted by mixing one part of the dried whole eggs with three parts water.

Enriched, or fortified whole eggs are prepared to meet production needs for special mixes for cakes, cookies, and similar products. These eggs are a special blend of approximately two-thirds whole eggs and one-third egg yolks before drying. After drying, the blend is composed of approxi-mately equal amounts of whole eggs and egg yolks with the balance in favor of the egg yolks. The shelf life of these eggs is extended with the use of stabilized whole eggs in the blend. This type of dried egg may be reconstituted by mixing one part egg with two parts water. There are special egg preparations available. In the liquid state, they are canned and the labels indicate a variable content of added sugar that extends from 10–30 percent. The sugar and other carbohydrates enables the egg to retain its whipping and leavening capacities. The eggs and sugar dis-solve quickly forcing the rapid formation of a solution. These eggs are used for sponge cakes and other cakes that require whipping or cream-ing. Frequently these eggs are a blend of whole eggs and egg yolks.

Egg yolk solids are widely used for special products. They are used extensively in the manufacture of doughnut prepared mixes. They are widely used in the production of egg breads and special Jewish breads known as challah. They are also used in richer cake mixes such as those for pound cake. The dried egg yolk does not whip very well and is not recommended for use in whipped cakes such as sponge cakes. However, they may be used for chiffon cakes where the eggs are blended with other ingredients. Egg yolks may be reconstituted by mixing one part dried egg yolk with one and one-quarter parts water.

Egg white powder or dried egg albumen is frequently used by all bakers of cakes, pies, cookies, and other special bakery foods. It is used for icings, toppings, meringues, as well as special cookies and garnishes. The quality of the egg whites used to make the dried albumen is of utmost importance to the baker. Poor quality egg whites or poor quality eggs from which the whites are removed will result in a product of poor quality. If the whites have some of the yolks mixed in with them, the whipping potential is reduced along with the ability of the cake to retain its structure and volume after baking. Several whip boosters or egg white improvers are available to bakers. They are used with quality egg white powders for further volume and rapid whipping. In some prepared albumen or egg white powders, these boosters may already be blended with the albumen. They constitute approximately 0.1 percent of the total weight of the dried egg albumen. The average egg white powder may be reconstituted by mixing one part egg white powder with approximately seven parts water.

As previously indicated, many smaller bakers who prepare their own premixes or prepared mixes will add the liquid eggs or yolks at the time of mixing. Many bakers feel that fresh whole egg, egg yolk, or egg white, is by far superior to dried eggs. This may be true if egg quality is controlled and maintained. However, it does mean that one must use either frozen canned eggs stirred properly for equal distribution or that the fresh eggs be broken and examined before use. The matter of storage and refrigeration must be carefully considered. It is important to use quality prepared mixes for basic bakery products. With the use of carefully selected dried eggs, prepared mixes can be used with excellent results. The dried eggs are blended with the other dry ingredients before the shortening and other fats are added. Since self-prepared mixes are made in limited quantities, the question of storage, sanitation, or shelf life do not present serious problems. The proper formulation and handling of the mix is necessary.

Leavening Agents in Prepared Mixes

Commercial prepared mixes have gone through extensive laboratory testing in order to establish the proper type and balance of chemical leavening agents. Mixes from the large manufacturers are reasonably well balanced and have good shelf life, particularly those that depend mainly on chemical leavening agents. From the first self-rising flours, baking soda (sodium bicarbonate) served as the base for a variety of acids which were blended with the flours and baking soda for later reaction during mixing and final baking. In fact, many retail bakers prepared their own blend of baking powder. Some experimented with varying proportions of acids (usually cream of tartar) and baking soda. Corn starch can be added as a buffer to prevent a too-rapid action when dissolving the acid in the liquid of the mix. Volatility and loss of action as a result of extended storage is another problem. The modern pastry chef uses well-

balanced, delayed-action baking powders and is not concerned with preparing leavening agents. A consistent release of carbon dioxide gas resulting from the action of acids with the baking soda in the presence of
moisture and heat, and producing quality baked goods are sufficient. In
the preparation of self-made prepared mixes, it is important for the baker
to understand the sources of leavening in chemically raised bakery products, for example the leavening effects of carbon dioxide resulting from
the action of acids in conjunction with the baking soda; the leavening
resulting from entrapped air resulting from whipped and foam cakes with
or without the addition of baking powder; water vapor in the form of
released steam resulting from the heat of baking; the homogenization of
cake batters with air and supplemented with baking powder. Since the
average baker and pastry chef rely on the standard, slow acting baking
powder that allows for maximum release of carbon dioxide gas during
the baking period, there is little need for special chemical leavening
preparation. Larger producers of prepared mixes are concerned with
storage and shelf life. Thus low moisture of the flour, the selection of the
proper acids, and the quantities of each to be used are the concern of
large producers.

The chemicals most widely used by the prepared mix industry are calcium and sodium phosphates. For low-sodium diets and special mixes
for diet-conscious consumers, sodium salts are replaced with potassium
salts. Few retail bakers prepare their own special preparation for angel
food cakes. Generally, those who do have a large volume of business.
Actually, this requires two separate preparations. One package will contain the dried egg white powder or albumen, whip booster if desired,
sugar, stabilizer and coagulant. The other package will contain the flour,
starch if used, and the minimal amount of chemical leavening if used.
The first package is mixed with the water and whipped. The second
package contents are gently folded into the whipping mix of the first
package. The salt and cream of tartar may be incorporated in either the
first or second package. For bakers who wish to prepare a special leavening blend for prepared mixes similar to those used in prepared mixes
commercially prepared for household and commercial use, the following
chart indicating the type of products and the specific acids which react
with sodium bicarbonate is presented.

Prepared mixes for yeast-raised bakery goods do not contain yeast.
They may have yeast foods, emulsifiers, extenders, softeners, surfactants,
and other supplements added and blended in with the dry ingredients.
The average baker preparing his own premix or total prepared mix will
not include the yeast, even in dry form. All the required dry ingredients
in the formula are blended together with specific amounts of yeast for
each batch of yeast-raised dough. Thus the baker is able to control dough
conditioning and production timing by adding the required yeast at the
time of mixing. Dried yeast and fresh yeast are dissolved in part of the
water and added when the dough is mixed. Instant dried yeast with a
high degree of solubility and dispersion is often added when the dry
ingredients are placed into the mixing machine.

TABLE 9.4   PREPARED MIXES*

	Acid Code[1]
A Self-rising products	
Self-rising flour	2, 3, 8
Self-rising corn meal whole ground and degermed	2
Self-rising corn meal mix (less than 15% wheat flour)	2
Self-rising pancake mix	2, 2+8
B Semi-sweet products	
Corn muffin mix (over 40% wheat flour)	2, 1
Biscuit mix (household)	2, 1
Biscuit mix (institutional)	3
Muffin mixes, specialty products (orange, raisin, etc.)	1
C Cake mixes	
White	1, 2, 3
Yellow	1, 2, 3
Devil's Food or chocolate	1, 2, 3
Spice	1, 3
Gingerbread	1, 3
Brownie or fudge	3, 6, 9
Cup cake	3
Specialty cake mixes	5, 9
Date bar	6,9
Specialty cookie mixes	6, 9

*Matz, *The Technology and Chemistry of Cereals as Food and Feed*

[1] Acid code (baking acids which react with sodium bicarbonate to furnish carbon dioxide gas CO_2).

1. Anhydrous monocalcium phosphate, coated + sodium acid pyrophosphate.
2. Anhydrous monocalcium phosphate, coated
3. Sodium acid pyrophosphate
4. Sodium acid pyrophosphate + monocalcium phosphate, monohydrate
5. Sodium aluminum phosphate (100 N.S.)
6. No baking acid
7. Dicalcium phosphate, dihydrate + anhydrous monocalcium phosphate, coated. (33 N.S.)
8. Monocalcium phosphate, monohydrate. (80 N.S.)
9. Sodium bicarbonate only.

For combination doughs that are leavened by both yeast and chemical leavening agents, the chemical leavening agents are blended with the flour as for other types of cake and doughnut mixes. The yeast is added as the dough is mixed. This method is applicable in the production of combination doughnuts, combination biscuits, and special remix doughs to which baking powder is added at the time of remixing. The premix or complete prepared mix is handled in much the same way as regular premixes for other yeast-raised doughs. Flavors and spices, determined by the baker or pastry chef, are traditionally added at the time of final mixing to prevent the loss of flavor and errors in scaling these essential ingredients by inexperienced bakers. Many bakers will package the flavors and spices separately.

There are specific guidelines to be followed for yeast-raised specialty breads and sweet goods.

TABLE 9.5   NEUTRALIZING STRENGTH OF BAKING ACIDS IN
COMMERCIAL USAGE*

Anhydrous monocalcium phosphate percent	Sodium acid pyrophosphate percent	Neutralizing[1] strength
100	—	83
90	10	83
80	20	81
70	30	78.5
60	40	76
50	50	73
40	60	70
30	70	70
20	80	70
10	90	70
—	100	72

*Matz, The Technology and Chemistry of Cereals as Food and Feed

[1]Pounds of bicarbonate which will be neutralized by 100 lb of acid. As indicated most bakers and pastry chefs will use the regular leavening agents ordinarily used in the regular formulary. The important point is to blend and distribute the chemical leavening thoroughly throughout the dry mix. Because of the shorter storage period before preparing the next batch, baking powder should be sifted several times with the flour or flour blend. Bicarbonate of soda may be of the fine powder variety since storage is short. For longer storage mixes, the granular and buffered type of bicarbonate should be used. The bicarbonate is also sifted with the flour and well blended. Prepared mixes should be in closed receptacles to eliminate moisture absorption. Mixes that are exposed to moisture and humidity for lengthy periods will lose a portion of the gassing power supplied by the chemical leavening agents.

1. The type of flour and flour blends normally used should be used in the premix preparation. Experimentation will determine any necessary adjustments. It is important to remember that water absorption will vary with the flour used. The addition of whole grains, bran, and other enrichment grains and seeds necessitates an increase in the water in the formula to allow for the increased absorption of these grains. Some bakers premix their own special blend of flours and variety grains to meet specific production standards. All other ingredients are added at the time of mixing. Some bakers add to prepared mixes purchased from commercial producers. It may be advisable for bakers to refer to the chart on the various wheat types and the general uses of flours with specific protein levels.

    When blending the flours, the fine grain flours are sifted and then blended together first. The coarser grains are then blended with the sifted finer grain. The other ingredients are added in a sequence related to their granular structure. For example, the sugar and salt are blended together and then blended in with the flours before adding other ingredients. As previously indicated, the use of several sieves of varying sizes will be helpful in preparing the final blend of all materials used.

2. It is good practice to blend the sugars and salt and then add the sifted milk solids. This mixture is then blended with the flour and other, grains. The egg solids, if used, are sifted and blended with the other ingredients.

3. The addition of shortening or other fats is very important. While the large manufacturer of prepared mixes has sophisticated equipment for adding fats, the average baker will use the regular mixing equipment. For formulas for bread and similar yeast-raised products using less than five percent fat, the fat should be melted or in semi-liquid form and added in a slow stream while the dry ingredients are being blended. Mixing at slow speed prevents clumping. Regular hydrogenated or emulsified shortenings are indicated in most formulas to prevent rancidity during the extended periods in which the prepared mix is not used. Butter or margarine is not recommended for use in prepared mixes unless the mix is kept under refrigeration. Some bakers still prefer to add the small percentage of fat in the final stages of dough development for bread doughs and other lean doughs. Emulsifiers and extenders, usually in paste form, are often blended with the fat and added to the premix—a common practice with formulas that have reasonably high percentages of fat.

4. Egg solids, both whole egg and egg yolk, are sifted (to remove lumps that may have formed in storage or through exposure to humidity) and then blended with other ingredients. The formulas list the percentage of egg solids and the amount of water necessary to reconstitute the egg solids. The required water for the dough or the mix will be listed in addition. The total water will represent the liquid eggs and milk (if milk powder is used) in the formula. Care must be taken in adding water to the various egg solids used.

5. Syrups such as honey, molasses, corn syrup, maple syrup, are best added at the time of mixing. There are dried syrup forms such as honey crystals but it is not advisable to include them in the premix because of their hygroscopic character. They tend to absorb moisture even over short periods, cause clumping and are often the cause of streaking doughs in the final mixing. Fruits, nuts, and seeds are best added in the final stages of dough mixing. Raisins and other dried fruits are usually presoaked to absorb lost moisture. Adding these to a premix will require added liquid and extensive mixing for absorption. It is best to add dried fruits at the time of mixing and after they have had a chance to plump. It is quite obvious that nuts and seeds are best added at the mixing stage of the final dough.

6. Commercial manufacturers of prepared mixes, whether for the home consumer or commercial baker, add the chemical additives to the mix before packaging. The emulsifiers, extenders, mold inhibitors, flavors in dry form, enrichment powders, and similar materials are blended in with the mix. It is best to have such additives carefully prescaled in tightly sealed small packs to be added at the time of mixing. If added with the flour and other dry ingredients, the minute amounts may not be evenly distributed. Chemical leavening agents are scaled, sifted, and then blended in with the flour and other dry ingredients. The type of leavening will depend on the type of product and the formula used. It is essential to keep prepared mixes in tightly closed packages and in a dry storage area to prevent the absorption of moisture causing a slight of the leavening agents.

The formulas that follow are rather small when compared to the large packages (100 lb or more) commercially prepared. The formulas and amounts will allow for smaller batches to be made and tested by the baker and pastry chef. Adjustments to meet special needs in either product character or production procedures may be necessary. The total amount of water and other ingredients are listed. The percentages are based on the weight of the total flour unless otherwise indicated. Icings are usually based on the weight of the sugar. Thus, a formula containing approximately 50 lb of flour may be halved to meet production requirements for a specialty bread. All other ingredients must be comparably scaled to be added at the time of mixing.

The balance of yeast and water temperature is essential to dough conditioning and the rate of production. Formulas presented are primarily for straight dough and the amount of yeast suggested is slightly higher than that used for sponge dough. Adjustment should be made to meet individual requirements. Water temperature, as well as other factors that affect fermentation, should be given careful consideration when mixing the doughs.

Country Style Bread—Premix

Ingredients	lb	oz	%	Preparation
Bread flour (12.5 to 13%)	50		100	Sift the flours separately and then sift together to blend
Potato flour	1	2	2.6	
Soy flour (defatted)	1	2	2.6	
Sugar	1	8	3.4	Sift the sugar, salt, and milk powder together and then blend with the flour
Salt	1		2.0	
Non fat dry milk	1	14	4.0	
Whole egg solids (optional)		10	1.4	Sift and add to the above
Shortening (melted or semi-liquid)	1	14	4.0	Add the melted fat in a slow stream to the above. Mix in slow speed

Add at the time of mixing

Water (variable)	27		54.0	Combine the honey with the water and add. Mix lightly in slow speed. Dissolve the yeast, add and develop the dough
Water (if egg solids are used)	1	12	3.6	
Honey (clover)	1	8	3.0	
Yeast (variable)	1	14	3.8	
Water	6		12.0	

This is a straight dough method of mixing.
Dough conditioning estimate: Dough temperature approximately 78°–80°F.
First punch: approximately 1½ hr
Second punch: approximately ½ hr
Relax dough about 10 min and take to bench or scaler-rounder.
Preliminary proofing time: Approximately 20 min. Take to molder or hand makeup.

Granola (Multi-Grain) Bread—Premix

Ingredients	lb	oz	%	Preparation
Bread flour (13.5 to 14% protein) [1]	36		86.2	Sift each flour separately and then blend together
Whole wheat flour [1]	5	12	13.8	
Potato flour	1	8	3.6	Sift these flours and blend with
Soy flour (defatted)	1	2	2.7	above
Bran flour or flakes	1		2.4	Blend these flours and grains to-
Rolled oats	3		7.2	gether and blend in with the
Yellow corn meal	2	4	5.4	above
Pumpernickel flour (Whole rye meal)	3		7.2	
Sugar	2	4	5.4	Sift together and blend in with
Salt	1		2.4	the above
Nonfat dry milk	1	8	3.6	
Shortening (melted)	2		4.8	Add in a slow stream while mixing the above in slow speed. Do Not Overmix

Add at the time of mixing

	lb	oz	%	
Water (variable	24		57.6	Mix the syrups with the water,
Malt (nondiastatic)		12	1.8	add to the above, and mix
Molasses	1	8	3.6	lightly
Yeast (variable)	2	2	5.0	Dissolve the yeast. Add the solu-
Water	9		21.6	tion to the above and develop the dough

Natural Wheat Bread—Premix

Ingredients	lb	oz	%	Preparation
Bread flour (13.5 to 14% protein)	37	8	71.5	Sift the flours separately and then blend together
Whole wheat flour	6		11.4	
Cracked wheat flour	9		17.1	
Sugar	1	2	2.1	Sift these ingredients together
Salt	1		1.9	and then blend with the above
Nonfat dry milk	1	2	2.1	
Shortening (melted)	1	14	3.6	Add in a slow stream to the above while blending in slow speed

[1] These flours together compose the 100% flour basis. Adjustment and variation in the type and amount of grains is at the discretion of the baker. Dough Conditioning: Dough temperature approximately 78–80° F.
First rise: approximately 1½ hr
Second rise approximately 30 min. Take to bench or divider-rounder.

Add at the time of mixing

Water (variable)	24		45.6	Mix the malt and molasses with
Malt (nondiastatic)		12	1.4	water and add to the above mix-
Molasses	1	8	2.9	ing lightly
Yeast (variable)	2		3.8	Dissolve the yeast. Add to the
Water	9		17.1	above and develop the dough
Raisins (optional)	12–18		24–36	Add to the dough in the final
presoaked and				stages of mixing
drained				

Straight dough method of mixing.
Dough conditioning: Dough temperature approximately 78–80°F.
First rise: approximately 1½ hr
Second rise: approximately 30 min. Take to bench or to the divider-rounder. Preliminary proofing time approximately 20 min and makeup.

Basic Sweet Roll Dough—Premix

Ingredients	lb	oz	%	Preparation
Bread flour (13%	40		80.0	Sift the flours separately and then
protein)				blend together
Cake flour (9%	10		20.0	
protein)				
Soy flour (defatted)	1		2.0	
Sugar	10		20.0	Sift these ingredients together
Salt	1		2.0	and then blend with the flour
Nonfat dry milk	2		4.0	blend
Whole egg solids	1	8	3.0	Sift the egg solids and blend
(variable)			3.0	with the above
Egg yolk solids	1	8		
Shortening	7	8	15.0	Blend in with the above while
Emulsifier (optional)		4	0.5	mixing in slow speed
(paste form)				

Add at time of mixing

Water (variable)	20		40.0	Add to the premix and mix
Water (for reconsti-	6	8	13.0	slightly
tuting dry egg				
solids)				
Yeast (variable)	2	8	5.0	Dissolve the yeast, add to the
Water	6		12.0	above and develop dough

Suggested flavors—vanilla, lemon, mace used individually or in a flavor blend. It is advisable to add the flavors at the time of mixing. Vanilla powder may be added with the milk powder and blended into the premix.

Dough Conditioning: Dough temperature approximately 78–80°F.
First rise: approximately 1½ to 2 hr. Take to bench for make up without punching. Doughs to be retarded are to be scaled sooner.
Note: If margarine or butter is used in conjunction with the shortening, it is advisable to keep the premix refrigerated to avoid rancidity.

Light Rye Bread—Premix

The use of additional, prepared sour rye culture in powder form is advisable to increase the rye taste and flavor in the bread. There are a number of prepared rye sour dough cultures available for purchase. They eliminate the need for the usual sour rye sponge dough that may be added for the same purpose. However, the use of either the prepared culture or regular rye sponge dough is optional.

Ingredients	lb	oz	%	Preparation
First clear flour (14%) or	40		80.0	Sift the flours separately and then blend together with culture
High gluten bread flour				
Rye flour (light or medium)	10		20.0	
Sour rye dry culture (optional)	2		4.0	
Salt		15	1.9	Blend the salt into the above
Shortening (melted)		15	1.9	Add slowly to the above while mixing slowly
Add at time of mixing				
Malt (nondiastatic)		10	1.2	Mix the malt and molasses with
Molasses		10	1.2	the water and add to the pre-mix
Water (variable)	20		40.0	and mix slightly
Sugar color (use and amount optional depending on color of crumb)				
Caraway seeds (optional)		15	1.9	Add with the water

Dough Conditioning: Dough temperature approximately 78–80°F.
First rise: approximately 1½ hr. If sour culture is used, 45 min to 1 hr for the first rise. Take to bench or divider-rounder after the first rise.
Note: If sour culture is used, reduce the amount of salt in the premix to 13 oz. The sour cultures contain additional salt in the preparation.

Coffee Cake Dough—Premix

Ingredients	lb	oz	%	Preparation
Bread flour (13%)	32	8	75.0	Sift the flours separately and then
Cake flour (9.5%)	11	4	25.0	blend together
Soy flour	1		2.27	
Sugar	10		22.8	Sift these ingredients together
Salt		12½	1.8	and blend with flours
Nonfat dry milk	2	8	5.6	
Whole egg solids	1	4	3.0	Sift the egg solids and blend
Egg yolk solids	2	8	6.0	with the above
Shortening	10		22.8	Add to the above and blend in
Emulsifier (optional) (paste form)		4	0.5	slow speed

Add at time of mixing

Water (variable)	10		22.8	Add water and flavors to the pre-
Water (for reconstituting egg solids)	7		16.0	mix and mix lightly

Vanilla, orange, lemon, spices (amount and types variable and optional)

Yeast (variable)	2	8	5.6	Dissolve the yeast, add to the
Water	10		22.8	above and develop dough

Dough Conditioning: Dough temperature approximately 78–80°F.
First rise: approximately 1 hour 45 min. Take to bench or divider after the first rise.
If butter or margarine are used in place of shortening, the premix should be refrigerated when not in use.
Note: Doughs for retarded, unbaked units, or freezer, unbaked units, should have a slightly higher percentage of yeast and the doughs should be taken to the bench for makeup slightly on the young or underfermented side.

Cake Doughnuts—Premix

Ingredients	lb	oz	%	Preparation
Flour[1] (9.5% protein)	61		100	Sift the flours separately and
Soy flour (defatted)	4		6.56	blend together with the baking
Potato flour		12	1.2	powder
Baking powder	2		3.28	

[1]The flour should be a blend of equal parts bread flour, cake flour, and pastry flour.

Sugar (fine granulation)	20		32.8	Sift these ingredients separately and then blend together. Add to the flours and blend
Dextrose (corn sugar)	2		3.28	
Salt	1		1.64	
Nonfat dry milk	3		4.92	
Egg yolk solids	3		4.92	Sift and blend with the above
Vanilla powder[1]		3	0.3	
Shortening (melted or semi-soft)	4		6.56	Add slowly to the above and blend in

Note: The sugar content may be increased by 1 or 2 lb (1.64% to 3.28%) to obtain a slightly darker crust color during the controlled frying period. For each 10 lb of the above dry mix add 4 lb to 4 lb 8 oz water and mix for approximately two minutes at medium speed. Allow the mix to stand for approximately 10 min before depositing into the frying fat. Fry the doughnuts at 380–385°F. for about 40 sec on each side.

The baking powder may be replaced by:

Sodium bicarbonate 12 oz (1.2%)

Sodium acid pyrophosphate 1 lb (1.64%)

Cake Doughnut Sugaring Mix

Ingredients	lb	oz	%	Preparation
Dextrose (corn sugar)	40		40	Sift these ingredients together several times for thorough distribution and uniformity.
Powder sugar	40		40	
Corn starch	11		11.0	
Nonfat dry milk	1		1.0	
Shortening (heat to 150°F. or 66°C.)	8		8.0	The melted fat is sprayed or poured slowly into the mixer or blender and mixed lightly with *only half the dry ingredients.* Add the balance of the dry ingredients and blend for about 2 min on slow speed. Mixing on high speed or for extended periods would cause the sugar mix to lump. Unused or leftover sugaring mix should be kept in a sealed or well-covered container for the prevention of excessive moisture absorption. Leftover sugar may be blended with fresh sugaring mix.

[1]Other flavors in dry form and spices finely ground may be added with the vanilla powder.

Combination Doughnut Premix

Ingredients	lb	oz	%	Preparation
Bread flour	33	8	67.0	Sift these ingredients separately
Cake flour	16	8	33.0	and then blend together
Baking powder		12	1.5	
Sugar	3	8	7.0	Sift these ingredients together
Salt		12	1.5	and blend in with the above
Nonfat dry milk	1	8	3.0	
Egg yolk solids	1	8	3.0	Sift and blend into the above
Vanilla powder [1]		4	0.5	
Shortening	5		10.0	Add and blend in with the above
Emulsifier (optional)		2	0.25	in slow speed

Add at the time of mixing

Water (variable)	16		34.0	Add to the above and mix
Water for reconstituting the egg yolk solids	2		4.0	slightly
Yeast (variable)	1	8	3.0	Dissolve the yeast. Add to the
Water	6		12.0	above and develop the dough

Dough conditioning: Dough temperature approximately 78–80° F.
Allow dough to rest 25–30 min and then roll out or send through the sheeter and cutter.
Allow units to relax to about ½ proof and fry at 385° F.

Old-Fashioned Crullers Premix

Ingredients	lb	oz	%	Preparation
Cake flour (9.0%)	5		25	Sift the flours separately and then
Bread flour (12% to 12.5% protein)	15		75.0	blend together with the baking powder
Baking powder		14½	4.4	
Sugar	4	9	23.0	Sift together and blend with the
Salt		4¼	1.6	above
Nonfat dry milk	1	4	6.0	
Egg yolk solids		13	3.9	Sift and blend into the above
Vanilla powder [2]		2	0.6	

[1] Additional flavors and spices in fine powder form may be added in conjunction with the vanilla flavor. Liquid flavors should be added at the time of final mixing of the dough.

[2] Additional powder flavors and finely ground spices may be added to the premix with the other dry ingredients.

Shortening	2	6	12.0	Add and blend into the above
Emulsifier (optional)		1	0.3	mixing in slow speed
(monoglyceride)				

Add at the time of mixing (optional):

The following conditioned yeast-raised or combination doughs may be added with the water. These fermented doughs provide added body

Sweet roll dough			Total scrap dough 4 lb 10 oz	
Yeast-raised doughnut dough scrap				
Soft roll dough	4	10	23.0	Add the scrap dough and water
Water (variable)	10		50.0	and mix to a smooth dough
Water for reconstitu-	1	8	7.5	
ting the egg yolk				
solids				

The type and amount of scrap dough (fermented) may require a slight increase in the water.

Allow the dough to relax for about ½ hr and then divide into dough presses. Round the presses of dough (scale 3½ to 4 lb per press) and allow them to relax about 10 min and divide. The units may be made into twist crullers, bow tie crullers, Long Johns, and so forth. The dough may be allowed to relax for 20 min after mixing and then rolled out or sent through the sheeter and made up into ring doughnuts for the old-fashioned doughnut variety.

Pie Crust Dough Premixes

Pie crust doughs are varied in content and use. The rich pie crust dough made by retail bakers and pastry chefs are rich in terms of the high percentage of fat they contain. The range of fat may vary from 50 to 75 percent based on the weight of the flour. The richer pie crust preparations require more care in the premix preparation. The method of adding the shortening to the flour and other dry ingredients will also influence the pie crust characteristics. For example, if the shortening and other hard type fats are melted slightly and then sprayed on the flour, a mealy pie crust dough will result. When firm or plastic shortening is cut or added in small lumps, there will be a flaky effect. The flour used for pie crust is usually a pastry flour of about 9 percent protein. Many bakers and pastry chefs will use a blend of short patent flour or a bread flour of about 12 percent protein and blend it with a cake flour of approximately 8.5 percent to approximate a pastry flour. This will require some experimenting to derive the desired flour blend. The important point is to avoid toughness at the time of mixing in the water with the prepared mix. Some bakers may use a blend of lard and shortening. Others may prefer to add some butter or margarine to the fat blend. If the butter or margarine is used, the prepared pie crust mix should be kept under refrigeration when not in use. In very warm climates, the prepared mix should be kept under refrigeration because of the high percentage of fat in the mix. The nonfat (skim) milk powder may be blended with the shortening to produce a drying effect and prevent excessive lumping or pasting.

Basic Pie Crust Premix

Ingredients	lb	oz	%	Preparation
Pastry flour [1]	50		100.0	Sift the dry ingredients sepa-
Sugar (optional) (Dextrose can be used)	1	4	2.5	rately and then blend together
Salt (variable)	1		2.0	
Nonfat milk solids [2]		10	1.25	
Shortening (variable)	37	8	75.0	If softened, add slowly or spray into the above. Mix in slow speed. Avoid overmixing

Add at time of mixing dough

Cold or ice water (variable)	17	8	35.0	Add and mix slowly until absorbed. Dough should be lumpy or mealy

Chill the dough before using.

Pie Crust for Soft-Filled Pies Premix

Pastry flour	37	8	100.0	Sift the dry ingredients sepa-
Sugar or dextrose	1	5	3.57	rately and then blend together
Salt		12	2.0	
Nonfat milk solids	1	4	3.4	
Shortening (softened)	12	8	33.4	Add gradually in a steady stream

Refrigerate the dough before using.

Add at time of mixing dough

Cold water (variable)	15		40.0	Add and mix smooth. Use slow speed

Prepared Mixes for Cakes

Most mixes prepared for bakers and home consumers are complete except for milk or water. The method of mixing these mixes is quite simple since most require a single stage of mixing in which the liquid is added all at once and the batter is mixed for a short period on slow or medium speed. This is a form of high-ratio cake mixing. The ingredients used for

---

[1] A blend of cake and bread flour may be used (60% cake flour, 40% bread flour)
[2] The milk powder may be blended with the shortening for a drying effect to prevent excessive lumping or pasting.

these prepared mixes require a brief explanation as a reminder to the baker and pastry chef who will prepare his or her own special premixes.

A fine cake flour with a protein content of 8 percent to 9 percent should be used. This type of flour has a soft gluten formation and the starch particles are fine and will readily absorb and retain moisture during the structure formation in the early stages of baking. Bleached cake flour is better than the unbleached variety because the starch particles are more highly absorbent. When unbleached flour is used, a slight addition of some short patent flour or gelatinized starch will be helpful.

Emulsified shortening allows for aeration during the mixing process. Monoglycerides and diglycerides are often added to ensure proper emulsification during the mixing stage. Suggested premixes for cakes that follow will contain small percentages of emulsifiers (approximately 0.5 percent based on the weight of the flour). The amount of water to be added includes that necessary to reconstitute the egg solids used in the mix. Some variation in water content may be necessary to meet changes in flour characteristics and other ingredient changes. The water added should be adjusted to meet the amount of mix used. If half the dry mix is used, then only half the water should be added.

Basic White Cake Premix

Ingredients	lb	oz	%	Preparation
Cake flour (8.5%) to (9.0%)	26	4	100.0	Sift these ingredients together several times for thorough blend
Baking powder	1	7	5.5	
Cream of tartar		2	0.5	
Sugar	30		114.0	Sift these ingredients together
Salt		10	2.4	and blend well with the above
Nonfat milk solids	2	8	9.6	
Vanilla (powder)		3	0.72	
Egg white solids (egg albumen)	2	4	8.64	Blend in well with the above
Shortening (emulsified)	12	8	47.5	Blend the emulsifier with the shortening. Blend into the above at slow speed
Emulsifier (mono or diglyceride)		2	0.5	

Add at the time of mixing batter

Water (variable)	38		144.4	Add the water in two or three stages and mix at slow speed for the first addition of water. Mix until the batter is smooth
Almond flavor (optional) other flavors as desired [1]		1½	0.36	

[1] Flavors in powder form may be added with the vanilla powder. Liquid flavors should be mixed with part of the water and added in the first stage of mixing.
The sides of the kettle should be scraped down with each addition of water and during the mixing process to eliminate lumping and insure even distribution of the mix.

Brownies Premix

Ingredients	lb	oz	%	Preparation
Cake flour	12		100.0	Sift the flour and cocoa separately
Cocoa	3	2	26.0	and then blend together with the
Baking powder		2½	1.3	baking powder and soda
Baking soda		1¼	0.65	
Sugar	12	8	105.0	Sift these ingredients together
Salt		2	0.3	several times for equal distribu-
Nonfat milk solids	1	4	10.5	tion and blend with the above
Vanilla (powder)		2½	1.3	
Whole egg solids	1	14	16.0	Sift and blend in with the above
Emulsified shorten-ing	10		84.0	Blend the emulsifier with the shortening and blend into the
Emulsifier		1	0.5	above

Add at the time of mixing the batter

Ingredients	lb	oz	%	Preparation
Water (variable)[1]	11	2	95.5	Add half the water to the above mix and mix for three minutes in slow speed. Add the remaining water in two stages and mix at slow speed for two min each time the water is added. Scrape the bottom and sides of the mixing kettle several times
Walnut pieces (variable)	7	8	63.0	Add and mix at slow speed for 1 to 2 min

Basic Yellow Cake Premix

Ingredients	lb	oz	%	Preparation
Cake flour	30		100.0	Sift the flour and baking powder
Baking powder	1	9	5.25	together
Sugar	33	2	110.1	Sift these ingredients together
Salt		10	2.1	several times and blend with the
Nonfat milk solids	2	8	8.32	above
Vanilla (powder)		3	0.63	
Whole egg solids	3	12	12.6	Sift and blend in well with the
Egg yolk solids	2	2	7.14	above

[1] The water includes the water required for reconstituting the whole egg solids. If liquid flavors are used, they should be added with the water.

Ingredients	lb	oz	%	Preparation
Shortening (emulsified)	16	14	56.2	Blend the emulsifier with the shortening and blend into the
Emulsifier (mono or diglycerides)		2½	0.5	above
Total weight	90	14½		

Add at time of mixing:

Water[1]	34	2		Add the water and flavor in 3 stages and blend in slow speed for approximately 3 to 4 min after each addition. Scrape the sides and bottom of the kettle to remove lumps
Liquid flavor (optional)				

For each 22 lb 12 oz of premix (¼ the total dry premix), add 8 lb 8 oz of water.

When not in use keep the premix in a closed container to prevent moisture absorption.

Note: The egg yolk solids may be replaced with whole egg solids. If so, increase the water approximately 14 oz to 1 lb.

Basic Chocolate Cake Premix

Ingredients	lb	oz	%	Preparation
Cake flour	30		100.0	Sift these ingredients together several times for complete blend
Cocoa	5	10	18.9	
Baking powder	1	4	4.2	
Baking soda		5	1.05	
Sugar	33	12	112.4	Sift these ingredients well for even blend. Blend in well with the above
Salt		10	2.1	
Nonfat milk solids	3	12	12.6	
Vanilla (powder)		3	0.6	
Whole egg solids	3	12	12.6	Blend in well with above
Shortening (emulsified)	12	8	41.6	Blend the emulsifier with the shortening and then blend in with the above
Emulsifier (mono or diglycerides)		2½	0.5	
Total weight	91	14½		

[1]The water content includes the water necessary to reconstitute the egg solids.

Add at time of mixing

Water [1]	41	4	137.4	Add in 3 stages and blend
Liquid flavor (optional)				

For ¼ mix (approximately 23 lb of dry premix) add 10 lb, 5 oz water. Keep the dry mix in a well-covered or sealed container when not in use. The type and amount of emulsifier may be varied to meet specific needs and production requirements.

Devil's Food Cake Premix

Ingredients	lb	oz	%	Preparation
Cake flour	26	4	100.0	Sift these ingredients together
Baking powder		15	3.6	well to insure an equal blend
Baking soda		7½	1.8	
Cocoa	5	10	21.4	
Sugar	35		133.0	Blend these ingredients together
Salt		10	2.4	well and blend into the above
Nonfat milk solids	3	12	14.3	
Vanilla (powder)		3	0.72	
Whole egg solids	2	13	10.7	Sift and blend together. Add and
Egg yolk solids	2	4	8.6	blend into the above
Shortening (emulsi- fied)	13	12	52.3	Blend the emulsifier with the shortening and blend into the
Emulsifier (mono or diglycerides)		2	0.5	above
Total weight	91	12½		

Add at the time of mixing:

Water [2]	46		174.8	Add the water and flavor to the
Liquid flavor (optional)				above in 3 stages and mix at slow speed for approximately 4 to 5 min after each addition. Scrape the sides and bottom of the mixing kettle after each addition to insure thorough distribution and smoothness. The added mixing time is necessary for complete hydration of dry ingredients and reconstitution of the egg solids

[1]The water content includes the water required for reconstituting the whole egg solids. The water is added in 3 stages and blended at slow speed for approximately 4 to 5 min after each addition. Scrape the sides and bottom of the mixing kettle and the beater to remove any lumps and to insure a smooth batter.

[2]The water includes that necessary to reconstitute the dry egg solids. For ¼ of the dry premix (approximately 23 lb 8 oz) add 11 lb 8 oz water.

Banana Cake Premix

Ingredients	lb	oz	%	Preparation
Cake flour	31	4	100.0	Sift these ingredients together
Baking powder		10	2.0	well for proper blend
Baking soda		12	2.4	
Granulated sugar	10		32.0	Sift these ingredients together
Brown sugar[1]	20		64.0	well and blend into the above
Salt		10	2.0	
Nonfat milk solids	2	8	9.0	
Vanilla (powder)		3	0.6	
Banana flakes (dried) or in powder form	8	4	26.4	Blend in to the above
Egg yolk solids	2	4	7.2	Blend the egg solids and then
Whole egg solids	2	8	9.0	blend into the above
Shortening (emulsified)	13	12	44.0	Blend the emulsifier with the shortening and blend into the
Emulsifier (mono or diglycerides)		3	0.6	above
Total weight	103	2		

Add at the time of mixing:

	lb	oz	%	
Water[2]	46	14	150.0	Add the water and flavor in 4
Liquid flavor (optional)				stages and blend for 4 or 5 min at slow to medium speed during the first 2 stages. Thereafter, use slow speed for mixing. The extended mixing time is necessary for thorough hydration of the ingredients

For ¼ mix (25 lb 12½ oz) add 11 lb 11½ oz water.

[1]The brown sugar may be replaced with granulated sugar if excessive moistness exists. A dry crystal form of brown sugar may be used.
[2]The water content includes that required for reconstitution of the banana flakes and the egg solids.

Golden Pound Cake Premix

Ingredients	lb	oz	%	Preparation
Cake flour	38	12	100.0	Sift together several times for
Baking powder		7½	1.2	proper blend
Sugar	45		116.1	Blend these ingredients together
Salt		10	1.6	well and blend with above ingre-
Nonfat milk solids	3	2	8.1	dients
Vanilla (powder)		3	0.48	
Whole egg solids	5		12.9	Sift and blend together and then
Egg yolk solids	4	7	11.4	blend in with the above ingredients
Shortening (emulsified)	25		64.5	Blend the emulsifier with the shortening and then blend with
Emulsifier (mono or diglycerides)		3	0.5	above
Total weight	123	1½		

Add at the time of mixing:

	lb	oz	%	
Water[1]	40	10	105.0	Add the water and flavor in 3 or
Liquid flavor (optional)				4 stages and mix for 4 or 5 min after each addition at slow speed. Scrape sides and bottom of the kettle after each addition and at final stage of mixing

For each ¼ of the dry premix (31 lbs) add 10 lb 3 oz water.

Note: If fruits and/or nuts are to be added, an adjustment in the type and amount of flour should be made to maintain the fruits and nuts in an evenly distributed manner in the baked cake. Replace approximately 20 percent of the cake flour with a 12 percent protein flour.

Reminder: It may be advisable to blend the milk solids with the shortening to make blending easier without excessive clumping.

White Pound Cake Premix

Ingredients	lb	oz	%	Preparation
Cake flour	26	4	100.0	Sift several times and blend to-
Baking powder		12½	3.0	gether well
Cream of tartar		1¼	0.3	

---

[1]The water total includes that required to reconstitute the egg solids.

Ingredient				Instructions
Sugar	30	10	116.7	Sift these ingredients together
Salt		7½	1.8	well and blend into the above
Nonfat milk solids	1	4½	4.9	
Vanilla (powder)		3	0.72	
Egg albumen (spray-dried)	2	8	9.5	Sift and blend in with the above ingredients
Shortening (emulsified)	16	4	61.9	Blend the emulsifier with the shortening and blend in with the
Emulsifier (mono or diglycerides)		2¼	0.54	above
Total weight	78			

Add at time of mixing:

Water[1]	32	8	123.8	Add the water and flavor in three stages and mix for approximately 4 to 5 min at slow speed (reduce mixing time if medium speed is used for mixing). Scrape the sides of kettle and beater after each addition to insure thorough mixing and complete blending of all ingredients
Liquid flavor (optional)				

For ¼ of the dry premix (19 lb 8 oz) add 8 lb 2 oz water.

Note: Be sure to use cool water to avoid possible coagulation of the egg albumen during mixing.

[1]The water includes the required amount of water to reconstitute the egg albumen.

10

Pancakes, Crepes, and Fritters

Most pastry chefs will take advantage of the prepared mixes for pancakes, crepes, and fritters. For example, frozen waffles and blintzes are ready for immediate use after a quick defrost in a microwave oven or slow defrost in the refrigerator. For large volume, quick service, these units are placed on large baking pans and placed in the oven for quick reheating or final cooking. For cafeteria-style institutional feeding, pans containing waffles and fried and baked blintzes are removed from the oven as required and are replaced with others to meet feeding requirements. For individual service, frozen waffles are placed into the toaster for quick defrost and further browning or crisping of the crust. As for blintzes, many chefs and pastry chefs anticipate orders depending upon the meal, menu, and time of day. Blintzes may be defrosted and partially baked. A quick exposure to the frying pan (greased with butter or margarine) will further brown the dough surface and the blintzes will be ready to serve in a few minutes. It is noteworthy that frozen blintzes are now available with a wide variety of fruit and cheese fillings.

As for the pancakes and fritter batters, there are many prepared mixes available for quick preparation with control of the quality. Pastry chefs are known to make some additions to further enrich the quality of the pancakes. Some pastry chefs will use a basic, prepared mix and add additional ingredients for a complete change. For example, for added protein enrichment, wheat germ, eggs, bran, and defatted soy flour may be added. This is especially so for the old-fashioned buckwheat and darker type of pancake. Pastry chefs will also use the basic pancake or waffle batters as a fritter batter. Additional eggs and milk will thin the batter where necessary. In fact, many pastry chefs will use the same batter for waffles and for pancakes. Thus, a pastry chef can increase productivity and maintain product quality with the use of prepared mixes requiring little mixing and preparation time, and with frozen-prepared products.

There are many pastry chefs who still prepare their own batters. The matters of quality and variety are important to them and they feel that the best way to control these factors is to prepare from the very beginning. There are specialties that cannot be made from a prepared mix. For example, yeast-raised buckwheat cakes require special attention and a special formula. They also require special handling and griddle completion. The use of fruits, both fresh and frozen, will also require special treatment. Formulas are presented for the pastry chef who wishes to make these specialties himself and for those who may not be able to avail themselves of the prepared or frozen products. We must remember the cost factor. Institutional feeding will often require stringent budget control. The self-made formula may be cheaper in preparation and still be of good quality, depending upon the skill and knowledge of the pastry chef.

Brief mention is made of the special requirements for griddle and iron preparation of foods. For example, the pancake varieties usually require clean, properly heated, and lightly greased griddles. Griddle heat is often not equally distributed and shifting is often necessary. The pastry chef must know the equipment he is using and train assistants who will use it. Waffle irons require careful attention for multiple production and use. The avoidance of leftover waffle scraps that may burn is only one of a number of factors. The cleanliness of the grid and the temperature control are other factors requiring attention. The amount of batter and batter consistency are additional factors. Timing of the waffles and their removal are the controls for waffle appearance. These are all factors to be considered in the preparation of waffles and in training the assistants to the pastry chef.

Safety and cleanliness are vital to a smooth system of production. They are to be stressed in all training and production of the specialties in this unit. Other important factors associated with each of the formulas and the products to be made from them will be emphasized at the proper time and place in the explanations.

Pancakes and Waffles

Basic Pancake and Waffle Batter

Ingredients	lb	oz	Mixing procedure
Sugar	1	12	Blend together
Salt		2½	
Bread flour (medium strength)	7	4	Sift the flour, baking powder, and skim milk powder together. Place in bowl or mixer
Baking powder		4	
Skim milk powder	1		

Water (variable)	8		Add the water slowly and mix at slow speed to avoid lumps
Eggs	4		Add the sugar and salt and blend in. Add the eggs and flavoring in a steady stream and blend. Add the butter last
Vanilla		2	
Melted butter or margarine	2		

1. Be sure to scrape the sides of the bowl or the mixing machine kettle to eliminate any lumps or caking on the sides. Continue mixing on slow or medium speed for complete hydration of all dry ingredients and to develop a smooth batter.
2. Allow the batter to rest for 1 to 1½ hr. This will relax the gluten structure of the batter and allow smooth depositing without any stringiness. It will also permit the batter to thicken slightly.
3. If the batter is too soft or runny, additional sifted flour may be added gradually and mixed in. If the batter is too thick, additional milk and eggs may be added to obtain the desired consistency.
4. The pancakes should be cooked on a hot griddle. Be sure the griddle surface is clean; wipe across with a cloth dipped in melted butter or oil.
5. The batter should be deposited in a pitcher with a pouring lip with a spigot effect to control the amount and size of the pancake. A measured dipper may be used for each pancake. This will help control uniformity of size.
6. It is advisable to check the heat of the griddle and the spread of the pancake, as well as the rate of browning and turning of the pancake, by pouring two or three pancakes in different parts of the griddle to determine evenness of heat distribution.
7. For waffles, the waffle iron should also be checked for cleanliness and heat. A trial waffle at the beginning for each waffle iron is in order to check temperature and timing. Gas-heated griddles may require adjustment of the gas flames at intervals. Electric griddles are usually well controlled by the thermostat and temperature controls.
8. Pancakes are usually ready to be turned with the formation of large gas bubbles on the surface. A brief check with the pancake turner will indicate color of the crust before turning.

Yield: 100–120 medium pancakes or waffles
Uses: Variety pancakes, breakfast items, menu specialties

Waffle and Pancake Varieties and Desserts

The basic waffle and pancake batter can be used for many varieties. For example, fresh blueberries that have been washed and drained may be added to the basic mix and used for blueberry waffles. Canned blueberries that have been drained may also be used. Carefully mix in the blueberries to avoid excessive discoloration of the batter. These waffles may be served with a blueberry filling or sauce.

Waffles are served in many ways. A variety of warm syrups are frequently served with the hot waffles. For cafeteria-style service, hot waffles are garnished with hot syrup, at the selection of the consumer, directly at the serving counter. For ice cream specialties, choice of ice cream is made by the customer or diner. A selection or combination of ice cream flavors may be placed on the waffles with an ice cream scoop. The size of the scoop depends upon service size, menu, and cost.

Pancake varieties made from the basic pancake batter are usually reflected in the size of the pancake as well as the varieties of syrup available for application. Pancakes may vary from the small silver dollar to the larger pancake. Butter, especially whipped, is served with the pancakes. For large volume service, pancakes are prepared in advance and placed in a bain-marie, or in a covered serving pan to maintain the moistness of the pancake and to keep them hot. It is not advisable to keep them in these pans for excessive lengths of time. Pancakes will lose their fluffiness and tend to stick after awhile. Where pancakes are a selected menu item for all diners, the griddles are kept going with a constant turnover of the pancakes for service. For individual service, some pancake specialties may be served with a variety of fruit fillings. Such pancakes covered with a cherry filling are quite popular. For basic breakfast or special dishes, pancakes are often served with eggs and meats. In this instance, pancakes are usually made somewhat smaller to allow for convenient placement of the eggs and/or meats on the same plate. In many instances, the pancakes may be served separately on a smaller plate.

Apple Waffles
Thin slices of cored and peeled fresh apples are added to the batter and stirred in gently. The apple slices may be dipped in a solution of apple juice and lemon juice to avoid oxidation and subsequent discoloration. Canned apples are also excellent. They are precooked and tender. Drain the apple and slice thinly and add to the batter. These waffles may be served with a blend of cinnamon sugar sprinkled liberally over the top.

Coffee or Maple Nut Waffles
Coffee waffles are made by adding instant coffee crystals to part of the water or milk and stirring well to dissolve before mixing into the batter. The amount and type of coffee will determine the strength of the flavor and the color of the batter. For maple nut waffles, add toasted and finely chopped nuts to the batter. Approximately 1 lb of these nuts is sufficient. In addition, maple flavoring is added to provide the flavor and the slight maple-like color. It may be necessary to add a small amount of milk because the nuts may tend to stiffen or thicken the consistency of the batter.

Fruit Juice Waffles
These are made by substituting concentrated fruit for an equal amount of water in the batter. For example, concentrated orange, pineapple or grapefruit juice, or a combination of any or all of these may be used. The frozen juice concentrate must be mixed or diluted with the water before adding to the batter. Be sure to stir the batter before cooking these pancakes. These waffles may be served with a fruit-flavored syrup and/or garnished with orange marmalade. If served with whipped cream or

whipped topping, the tops may be garnished with slices of fruit for color and appearance.

Note: Pancakes may also be made from this same batter.

Buckwheat Pancakes

Ingredients	lb	oz	Mixing procedure
Bread flour	3		Sift and blend all the dry ingredients
Buckwheat flour	3	8	
Bran flour [1]		4	
Wheat germ [1]		4	
Baking powder		4	
Nonfat dry milk		12	
Sugar	1	8	
Salt		3	
Water (variable)	8	8	Add the water in a slow, steady stream
Molasses		8	and mix at slow speed to a smooth consis-
Eggs	3		tency. Add the eggs in a steady stream
Vanilla		1	and blend. Add the melted butter and mix
Melted butter	1	12	to a smooth batter

Yield: 100–125 pancakes

Old-Fashioned (Yeast-Raised) Buckwheat Pancakes

Ingredients	lb	oz	Mixing procedure
Yeast (variable)		4	Dissolve the yeast
Water	2		
Buckwheat flour	2		Blend the flours together. Add the water
Bread flour	2		in a steady stream and mix smooth. Add
Bran flour		6	the yeast alternately with the sugar, salt,
Wheat germ		3	and molasses and mix smooth
Water (variable)	4	8	
Salt		2	
Molasses		4	
Sugar		3	
Eggs	1		Add the eggs gradually and mix smooth.
Melted butter	1	8	Add the melted butter and mix smooth

[1]The bran and wheat germ will enrich the batter with additional protein. The batter will tend to thicken as it stands due to whole grain or flakes of bran and the absorption qualities of the buckwheat flour. Additional water may be necessary to thin the batter. Allow the batter to rest for about ½–1 hr. Cook the same as for pancakes. Serve with maple syrup.

1. Check the consistency of the batter. It may be necessary to add additional water to bring to the desired consistency.
2. Allow the batter to rise for a period of 2–3 hr. There will be a thickening effect. Stir the batter well and then add more liquid if needed. The buckwheat flour and the bran flour will absorb liquid as the batter is being conditioned by the yeast.
3. Cook as for regular pancakes.

Yield: 100 pancakes

Bavarian Chiffon Pancakes

Ingredients	lb	oz	Mixing procedure
Sugar		8	Sift all dry ingredients together
Salt		½	
Cake flour	1	4	
Bread flour	1	4	
Nonfat dry milk		8	
Water	4		Add most of the water and vanilla in a
Vanilla		½	steady stream and mix smooth. Add the
Melted butter or margarine		12	melted butter and mix smooth
Egg yolks	1		Add the yolks and remaining water and mix smooth
Egg whites	1	8	Whip the whites to a medium stiff peak (wet peak). Fold into the above and mix gently until the batter is smooth

1. Heat a frying pan (about 10 in. in diamter) and add enough butter to coat the bottom surface.
2. Pour about ½ qt of the batter over the surface of the frying pan. Turn the pan rapidly to spread the batter evenly over the surface.
3. Cook to a golden brown on each side. The batter will rise and have a sponge-like texture.
4. Place the pancake in a hot oven for a few minutes to completely cook and set the pancake so that it does not fall back.
5. Place pancake on a cloth and spread with fruit filling.
6. Roll pancake up gently, as a jelly roll. Cut into portions depending on the size or number to be served. Dust top of roll with cinnamon sugar or confectioners sugar. For more elaborate service, cognac or another brandy may be lightly sprinkled over the surface.

Cornmeal Pancakes

Ingredients	lb	oz	Mixing procedure
Sugar		8	Sift and blend all the dry ingreidents to-
Salt		1½	gether
Nonfat dry milk		6	
Cornmeal [1]	1	8	
Cake flour	2		
Bread flour		8	
Baking powder		3½	
Honey (clover		4	Add the honey and eggs and blend
Eggs	1		smooth
Melted butter	1		Add the melted butter and blend. Add the
Water (variable)	3		water gradually and mix smooth

1. Allow the batter to rest or relax for about 1 hr.
2. The batter will thicken because of the added absorption of the cornmeal. Add more water to obtain the proper consistency for pouring.
3. If too soft, add additional cake flour.
4. Cook on a heated griddle that has been lightly greased.

Crepes and Blintzes

Crepes (French Pancakes)

Crepes, often called French pancakes, are very thin. They are thinner than regular pancakes and are much richer in eggs and melted butter. The batter is thinner than that used for pancakes and is cooked in small frying pans or skillets that are about 4 in. in diameter. The modern pastry chef will serve these with a variety of fillings and finishes. It is important to remember that the crepe is actually the carrier of a filling and garnish. It is equally important to know that the crepe must be made so that it can be stored for awhile if it is not to be served immediately. A hot sauce and a flambé effect will provide the required heat to a precooked and stored crepe.

There are many names for a great variety of crepes. Naturally, most have French names. It will be noted that different names do not always mean a great change in the preparation and service of the crepe. There are similar crepes that have different dessert names. This may be a choice of the chef, pastry chef or the "house." It may be that the crepe is filled and rolled rather than served with a fruit filler in the style of a sandwich. The skilled pastry chef will decide the manner for the proper service. For large volume service, the pastry chef will prepare the crepes in advance

[1] Either white or yellow cornmeal may be used. The yellow cornmeal will provide for mild yellow color and a bit more coarseness.

and then fill and serve as quickly as possible. For the special individual service, the more elaborate preparation and service will be followed.

The skilled pastry chef will use a number of frying pans at the same time. The pans are heated after they have been brushed or greased lightly with melted butter or margarine. A controlled heat or flame will enable the chef to time each of the crepes and turn them in sequence. Further explanation will follow with each variety.

Crepes or French Pancakes

Ingredients	lb	oz	Mixing procedure
Sugar		5	Sift the flours and other dry ingredients to
Salt		1	blend
Nonfat dry milk		8	
Cake flour	1		
Bread flour	1		
Whole eggs	1	8	Whip the eggs slightly to blend in the
Egg yolks	1		yolks. Add slowly and blend into the above.
Water (variable)	4		Add water slowly. Hold back about 1 lb to check consistency
Melted butter or margarine	1		Add slowly and blend in. Add with the melted butter
Cognac or similar brandy (optional)		2	

1. The batter must be sufficiently thin so that it spreads evenly and quickly in the frying pan.
2. If too thick, add water or eggs to thin, but only after the batter has been allowed to rest for about an hour. The batter may thicken slightly during that period.
3. Batter that is too thin will produce crepes with small air pockets or blisters which will form into small spaces or open pockets. Additional flour or eggs may be added to bind the batter.
4. Remember to heat the pan well before adding the batter while the pan is off the flame.
5. Quickly tilt the pan after depositing a small amount of the batter into the pan. Return to the flame or grid and allow to brown lightly. Turn the crepe over and lightly brown the other side.
6. Turn the crepes out on a cloth and repeat once again. The crepes may be placed on a plate and covered with a moist or wet cloth and stored in the refrigerator for later use. As indicated previously, the crepes may be reheated with a hot sauce before serving.

Yield: approx. 100 crepes

Crepes Suzette Spread the crepes with a hard sauce made by creaming equal parts of confectioners sugar and butter until soft and light. Add the outside, grated rind of an orange and the strained juice of the orange.

(Use approximately 1 orange for each pound of hard source.) Cream in the juice and rind. Finally, add a dash of curacao or Grand Marnier for flavor. The brandy or cordial is optional. Imitation flavoring may be used for large service and cost control. Fold each of the filled crepes into four turns and place on a serving platter. The crepes may be dusted with confectioners sugar and then quickly seared with an iron in a cross-hatch design.

The crepes may be individually dipped in the following preparation before folding each crepe in four:

Ingredients	lb	oz	Mixing procedure
Granulated sugar		12	Place in chafing dish and melt the sugar. Use a small flame to avoid burning the sugar
Juice of two oranges Juice of half a lemon Rind of the oranges and lemon (outside rind only)			Add the juice and rind and stir until golden brown. Add the juice and butter. Stir to blend well
Butter		8	
Cognac or other brandy (optional)		4	Place the crepes in the syrup singly and sprinkle lightly with sugar. A special syrup flavored with brandy may be used for flavoring only.

Fold the crepes into four folds. Add cognac and light for effect and further heating before service. Serve immediately. This will be enough sauce for about 12–16 servings.

Crepe Varieties

A variety of crepes may be made with different types of fruits, jams, jellies, or combinations of each of these. The following are representative of the more popular varieties:

Crepes Normande The crepes may be filled with hot or cold applesauce and then folded over into four folds. In another version, the crepes may be filled with thin, fresh apple slices that have been lightly sautéed in butter. The apples may be sprinkled lightly with a fine blend of cinnamon sugar before folding. The crepes may then be dusted with confectioners sugar and served. The crepes may be seared with a hot iron.

Crepes a la Russe These are made by filling two crepes with applesauce and serving with a special sauce in the form of a custard or Bavarian cream poured over the tops of the crepes when ready to serve.

Crepes Bonne Femme These are made by filling the crepes with applesauce and sprinkling with toasted sliced almonds. The crepes are covered with a rum flavored cream or sauce. The use of sauces is usually at the discretion of the chef or pastry chef.

Crepes Empire   These are filled with crushed pineapple filling. The filling may be flavored with a brandy or kirsch. Fold in four and serve plain, dusted with confectioners sugar, or with a pineapple sauce made from the drained juice of the canned pineapple.

Crepes Parisienne or Crepes Confiture   These are made by spreading the cooked crepes with jam or red currant jelly (Bar-le-Duc) and rolling up as for a jelly roll. The crepes are then dusted with confectioners sugar and seared or burned with a hot iron in a cross-hatch design.

Crepes Mirette   These are made by spreading the crepes with Bar-le-Duc (red or white currant jelly in which the berries are mostly whole) and then rolling up like a jelly roll. Finish by dusting with confectioners sugar and cross-hatching with a hot iron.

Crepes Georgette   These are filled with a spread of currant jelly with diced pineapple. The crepes are served with a pineapple sauce that is flavored with curacao.

Crepes Royale   The crepes are filled with apricot jam slightly softened with rum-flavored syrup or rum. The crepes are then folded in four and covered with meringue bagged out with a French or star tube. The meringue is lightly dusted with confectioners sugar and quickly browned. A rum-flavored sauce may be used to lightly garnish or cover the top.

Crepes Bonne Marie   The cooled crepes are covered with a vanilla pastry cream or custard. Sliced strawberries may be used with cream. The crepes are rolled up like a jelly roll. The tops are garnished with a custard or cream sauce that is blended with sliced strawberries. Pastry chefs may vary the toppings by using whipped cream, whipped topping, or a blend of both to garnish many of the crepes. This is quick and can be prepared in advance. This is especially useful in large volume production and service. The fruit, nut, cold or hot sauce may be used as a garnish and applied by the pastry chef's assistants before serving.

Blintzes

Blintzes are very thin, pancake-like, round skins, that are used to enrobe a variety of fillings. These are then folded and made into rectangular shape and fried in skillets or frying pans. The variety is increased by the variety of fillings and the manner in which they are served. Blintzes must be thin and flexible after they have cooked so that they may be rolled up and shaped with the filling in them. This is possible because of the large percentage of eggs used to make the batter. The second factor is the manner in which they are cooked. They are cooked quickly in a hot skillet in which butter or other fat is used to prevent sticking. They are cooked lightly on one side and then turned out of the skillet onto cloths. The blintz leaves are made in advance and can be stored in the refrigerator for use at a later time.

Prepared, frozen blintzes are available for purchase and need only to be cooked and served. These are available in a variety of fillings. However, pastry chefs and chefs often prepare their own fillings and prefer to prepare their own blintz leaves.

Blintz Batter

Ingredients	lb	oz	Mixing procedure
Cake flour		8	Sift the flour and salt together to blend
Bread flour		8	well
Salt		1	
Vegetable oil		7	Add the water and oil gradually and mix
Water		8	well until smooth. Whip the eggs slightly
Eggs (fresh shell eggs)	4	8	and add gradually. Blend well to a smooth batter

1. The batter must be quite thin so that it may be poured easily and spread quickly and easily in the skillet. The batter should have a thin consistency similar to that of coffee cream.
2. Several skillets of 5–6 in. diameter may be used. This is very much the same as the procedure for making crepes. It is important to control the flame or heating unit so that an equal temperature may be maintained and the timing of cooking the blintz leaves makes possible the use of several skillets at the same time.
3. The amount of batter should be sufficient to quickly cover the entire skillet and form a thin covering. The skillet is tilted to allow the batter to quickly cover the skillet surface. The skillet is then returned to the flame or heating unit and cooked until the batter has firmed, and then removed from the fire.
4. Turn the blintz leaf over on a cloth and lightly grease the skillet and refill the skillet once again. Allow the leaves to cool and then place on a platter and cover with a moist cloth if the leaves are not to be filled immediately.
5. Usually, the chef or pastry chef will have the fillings prepared in advance, and fill and shape or fold the blintzes as the leaves are cooked. The filled blintzes may then be fried after filling and shaping. Pastry chefs will often place the blintzes in the refrigerator or freezer to use as required.
6. Blintzes are fried in a large skillet that has been well buttered. Fry until golden brown on each side. Use a medium heat to cook the filling properly. Cooked blintzes may be placed in the freezer and then quickly reheated in microwave ovens for rapid service.
7. For large multiple service, the pastry chef may line the blintzes on large, greased baking pans and place them into the oven to cook. They may also be kept warm in the oven for cafeteria-style service.

Yield: Approx. 100 blintzes

Cheese Filling for the Blintzes

Ingredients	lb	oz	Mixing procedure
Bakers' cheese	10		Blend the cheeses and cornstarch together
Cream cheese	4		at slow speed on the mixer
(optional), replace			
with bakers cheese			
Cornstarch		5	
Sugar (variable)	1	4	Add to the above and blend in. Use slow
Salt		1	speed
Nonfat dry milk		4	
Egg yolks		8	Add the egg yolks and whole eggs gradu-
Whole eggs		8	ally and blend in
Water (variable)		8	Add the water and flavoring and blend
Vanilla		1	smooth
Rind and juice of			
2 lemons			
Raisins (optional)	2		Add and mix in gently
(presoaked)			

1. The cheese filling should be of medium stiff consistency. It may be necessary to soften with the addition of eggs.
2. Place the cheese filling in the refrigerator to firm before using.
3. If cottage cheese is used to replace the bakers' cheese, send the cheese through the fine grinder to reduce the lumpiness and curd to finer particles. For each pound of cottage cheese add 1½ oz of cornstarch to the cheese and blend in well. This will help to bind the cheese and retain the natural whey or moisture.
4. Spread the individual blintz leaves over a large cloth on the table. Deposit a generous amount of cheese filling or other filling in the upper center part of the round blintz leaf. A large spoonful can be used as a measure. (Fig. 10.1).

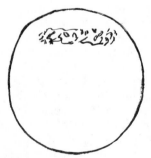

10.1
Filling deposited on blintz

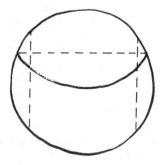

10.2
Method of folding blintz

5. Spread the filling a bit so that it forms a straight line of equal thickness but does not extend beyond the edges.
6. Fold the top of the blintz leaf over the filling so that it folds about halfway down and forms a semicircle. Press the ends gently to seal.
7. Fold the sides about 1 in. or so toward the center so that the ends of the fold are closed. (Fig. 10.2) Then fold the filled and covered part over twice to form a rectangular shape about 1½ in. wide and about 4 in. long.

Yield: Approx. 200 blintzes

Fruit-Filled Blintzes　For fruit-filled blintzes, apple, cherry, or blueberry pie filling may be used. The fillings may be slightly thickened by adding light cake crumbs to the filling. This will tighten the fruit filling. When preparing the filling, especially for blintzes, add a little more cornstarch or other thickening agent to the filling and cook well. Refer to the fruit fillings for pies listed in the unit on variety pies for formulas and methods of cooking the fruit fillings.

Note: Blintzes are customarily served with sour cream. Very often applesauce may be served with the blintzes for variety.

Variety Fritters

Fritters are selected foods, usually served in small quantites, that have been dipped in a special batter and then fried in deep hot fat. The pastry chef may be required to prepare such products as desserts or supplements to the total menu. However, the pastry chef usually prepares those fritters which contain fruits. Special choux paste (eclair and cream puff batter) desserts may also be fried, as are French crullers, and then filled with jam or special cream fillings before they are served. Very often, the pastry chef may wish to prepare a special fritter batter containing beer instead of milk. The beer will have a slight gassing or fermenting effect on the batter and will impart a special taste to the batter. This batter will have to be allowed to rest for several hours to create the slight fermenting activity.

There are a number of prepared fritter batter mixtures, in dry or powder form, which are available for quick preparation. These are commonly used for large scale production and for product uniformity. They also make preparation easy for those who are not quite as experienced as the skilled pastry chef. Pastry chefs may make additions to the prepared fritter preparations for further enrichment and special flavors.

A special note is made regarding the frying fat. Fritters are deep fried and the same care is necessary for this fat as for frying fat used to fry doughnuts. Fritters are usually dropped into a basket that has been submerged in the frying fat. One lifts the basket to remove the fried fritters from the fat. The frying fat should be clean and free from particles of other fried products. This requires straining after use and will help avoid foreign flavors and odors and burned food particles which often attach themselves to the new products being fried. The temperature of the frying fat for fritters may vary from 350–380°F. Foods that are large and raw will require a lower frying fat temperature in order to slow the cooking and allow the foods to be cooked through or softened. Fruits that are canned are precooked and, when used for fritters, require a higher frying fat temperature so that they are cooked for a lesser period. The size and contents of the fritter must be given careful consideration before frying in deep fat.

Basic Fritter Batter

Ingredients	lb	oz	Mixing procedure
Sugar		12	Sift all dry ingredients together and place
Salt		½	into the machine kettle or mixing bowl
Nonfat dry milk		4	
Cake flour	1	4	
Bread flour (variable)	1		
Baking powder		½	
Eggs	1	8	Beat the eggs slightly to blend the yolks
Vanilla		½	and whites. Add the flavoring and fruit
Rind of 1 lemon (outside of rind only)			rind and mix lightly. Add the eggs and water alternately and mix to a smooth batter
Rind of 1 orange (optional)			
Water (variable)	2		

Allow the batter to rest for about ½ hr before dipping. This will allow the batter to thicken slightly. If the batter is too soft, add some cake flour or eggs to bind.
Yield: Approx. 100 fritters

Beer-Type Fritter Batter

Ingredients	lb	oz	Mixing procedure
Sugar		8	Sift all dry ingredients together to blend
Salt		½	well
Nonfat dry milk		2	
Cake flour	1	2	
Bread flour	1		
Eggs (yolks preferred)	1		Blend the eggs and water. Add gradually
Water		6	and mix smooth. Add the melted butter
Melted butter or margarine		5	and mix smooth

Beer (not cold)	2	8	Add the beer gradually and mix smooth
Egg whites	1		Whip egg whites to a firm, wet peak. Fold into the batter after it has rested for the period designated. Fold in gently, but be sure the whites are well blended

1. The batter must be used immediately so that the leavening effect of the beaten egg whites is not reduced. The egg whites will make for a lighter batter structure with an airy, crisp fried batter cover.
2. Fritters made with this batter should be fried at about 360°F. The fritter batter should be poured into a shallow pan so that the fruits or other foods to be dipped can easily be placed into the batter and removed.

Yield: Approx. enough for 100 fritters

Fruit Fritters

Fruits to be used for fritters require special preparation before they are dipped into the fritter batter and fried. Fresh fruits are usually placed into the fritter directly without draining. Fruits dipped into sugar or liqueur or packed in syrup should be drained before dipping into the batter. The syrup or sugary coating often prevents the batter from sticking to or covering the fruit. This is obvious after frying. Parts of the fruit are not covered with fritter batter.

Apple Fritters Apple fritters are made with freshly peeled and cored apples. The slices may vary depending upon the size of the apple and the thickness desired. Apple slices are usually about ¼–½ in. thick. The slices are dipped into the fritter batter and then placed into the hot fat at about 370°F. The slices may be lifted out of the batter with tongs and then placed into the hot fat. If the fingers are used, it is important to be very careful not to splash the hot fat. A slotted spoon may also be used for placing the dipped fruit into the prepared frying fat. Do not overfill or crowd the fritters. They must have enough room to fry without sticking to each other. There should be sufficient room for turning fritters for complete frying. The pastry chef realizes that filling the frying basket to capacity will also lower the temperature of the frying fat which would extend the frying time and increase the absorption of fat.

Fry the apple fritters to a golden brown crust color. Remove and place the fritters on absorbent paper to drain. Allow the fritters to drain for a few seconds over the hot fat before removing. The apple fritters are usually sprinkled with cinnamon sugar while hot and then served. If canned apples are used, select the large slices for dipping and frying. These apples will not have the ring or doughnut shape as those made from the whole sliced, fresh apple. The canned apples will have the smaller, chunky effect. The apples are drained and then dipped into the batter. Fry and sprinkle with cinnamon sugar as for the fresh apples.

Pineapple Fritters These are made from either fresh or canned pineapple. Full ring slices are best used for fritters. However, half slices are often used for smaller fritter servings. The canned pineapple should be drained well before dipping. Fresh pineapple is cut into thin slices. The slices may be cut into halves or quarters and then dipped and fried. If the pineapple is sprinkled or dipped into sugar for a period of time, the pineapple should be drained of the excess syrup formed by the sugar before dipping and frying.

Fresh Peach or Apricot Fritters   These fruits are usually cut in half and the pits removed. The fruits may then be soaked in liqueur if desired, or dipped in a flavored syrup. These fruits are then drained before dipping and frying. The fritters, when cooled slightly, may be dusted with confectioners sugar before service. Canned peach or apricot halves packed in syrup are drained before dipping and drying. Finish and serve these as the fresh fruits.

Strawberry Fritters   These are best made from selected, large, firm, fresh strawberries. The strawberries are usually sprinkled well with sugar and liqueur for special flavor. The berries are allowed to set for about 2 hr to absorb some of the sweetness in the syrup formed. The strawberries are drained before they are dipped and fried. Orange slices may be prepared for fritters in much the same manner. If bananas are used for fritters, the bananas may be sliced in half and then into quarters. The size of the banana and the desired portion of the banana fritter will determine the size of the banana. Bananas cut horizontally into ½ in. slices are often used for smaller servings.

Choux Paste Fritters   These are often called Beignets Souffle and are small, round choux paste balls that are fried as you would fry the French crullers. For a crisper crust after frying, the fat content in the choux paste formula may be reduced by 25%. This will tend to reduce the tenderness of the crust formed and make handling easier after frying. The choux paste is bagged out into small balls on a well-greased parchment or freezer paper and then carefully placed into the hot fat, face down. The melted fat on the paper will release the beignets and the paper may be drained and removed for use once again. This is the same procedure as for French crullers. The beignets are fried at 360°F so that they are fully expanded and crisp. Some pastry chefs will drop the beignets directly from the pastry bag into the hot fat. This requires special skill and should be avoided by the inexperienced. The beignets are then sprinkled with cinnamon sugar and covered lightly with a vanilla or custard sauce and served hot. Larger sized beignets are bagged out the same as the smaller ones on greased papers for depositing into the frying fat. A small ice cream scoop may be used to deposit the choux paste into the hot fat. Be careful to avoid splashing. The larger beignets are fried at about 350–355°F. They require a longer frying period. The larger beignets are filled with a custard cream or fruit jam and then served with a confectioners sugar coating. They may also be served with a hot sauce over the surface. The variety of sauces will increase the varieties of beignets served.

11

Custards, Puddings, Mousses, and Souffles

Pastry chefs have changed their approach to the preparation of many desserts such as baked puddings, custards, and mousse due to changes in eating habits, mass feeding, quick food preparation, and the requirements of a moderately priced menu. The long, tedious preparation of desserts such as fancy souffles and Savarins is now the choice of a few expensive restaurants that cater to the gourmet diner. This chapter is largely devoted to the preparation of the most popular custards and puddings that may be quickly prepared at a moderate cost per portion, although the preparation of souffles is mentioned with accompanying recipes.

Preparation time for puddings and dessert custards has been reduced considerably with the use of prepared basic powders. The use of prepared gelatin dessert powders has simplified matters considerably. Pastry chefs in large institutions, such as schools, hospitals, and other mass feeding institutions, base much of their preparations on the use of quality dessert preparations. The advantages are rapid production, control of quality and cost, and the assignment of basic preparation to semiskilled assistants under the supervision of the pastry chef. As indicated in prior chapters on soft-filled pies and desserts, pastry chefs will often use a basic, prepared mix and improve upon it in the final preparation through the use of whipped creams, fruits, and other toppings. Speedy service, storing prepared desserts, and maintaining a fresh appearance are additional factors of concern to the modern pastry chef. The precooked puddings, whether they are made from the prepared pudding mixes or from scratch, have been covered in the section on pies. For example, a chocolate pudding used for the chocolate cream pie may also be used as the pudding to be poured into individual pudding cups or special serving dishes. The gelatins are also prepared and poured after mixing the prepared gelatin powders that have been sweetened, flavored, and colored. Precooked preparations make the preparation of these desserts simply a matter of mixing according to the directions provided on the package by the manufacturer and pouring into dessert dishes for individual service. Garnishing the desserts before service is a matter of judgment for the pastry chef. The varieties are many.

Baked Custards

While preparing baked custards and puddings is not much different than following a cake recipe and baking a cake, there are some basic fundamentals that apply to the preparation and baking of puddings. For example, the individual pudding cups are usually made of earthenware, although other baking cups may be used. The cups are usually prepared by lining the bottom and sides with melted butter or semisoft butter and sprinkling or dusting the sides and bottom with sugar. This will keep the pudding from sticking so that it can be unmolded and will also provide a syruplike cover for the custard or pudding when unmolded. Puddings that are consumed directly from the cup do not require the butter-sugar process for the interior of the baking cup.

The amount of eggs used for the baked custard is of importance. Increased egg content will provide a firmer baked pudding and make unmolding easier. Of course, it will increase costs. It is advisable to use fresh eggs for baked custards. They are more easily blended (yolk and white) and can be separated into yolk and white when necessary. In addition, straining the pudding before baking is easier to avoid lumps and strings in the baked custard due to uneven blending of the eggs and improper straining. If frozen eggs are used (10- or 30-lb cans), the eggs should be completely defrosted and whipped slightly and strained before using. The custard will be strained when completely mixed before pouring into the dishes for baking.

Custard and pudding cups are usually filled almost to the brim. The custards and puddings are baked in pans that have been partially filled with water so that approximately two-thirds of the outside of the cup is submerged in water. Baking temperature is usually about 375–380°F. The average custard cup takes approximately 35–40 min to bake; it is important not to overbake. If overbaking occurs, the custard will tend to curdle and a weeping or watery effect takes place. Custards can be checked for proper bake by inserting a paring knife into the center. If the knife blade comes out clean the custard may be considered baked. A slight firmness or sponginess in the center is another indication that the custard is baked.

Baked custards that are to be unmolded must be allowed to cool and then be chilled before unmolding. The cold temperature causes a mild congealing of the custard away from the sides and allows the syrup formed in baking to serve as a lubricant. The edge of the custard is freed by running the point of a knife around the edge. Place a plate, usually the serving dish, over the top of the custard. Shake the cup gently to loosen the edges and unmold.

Vanilla Cup Custard

Ingredients	lb	oz	Mixing procedure
Milk[1] Vanilla	20		Heat the milk with a natural vanilla bean to a light scald, stirring occasionally. Remove the bean when the milk is hot. If vanilla flavoring is used, it is added with the eggs and sugar in the final stages of mixing. Use a double boiler, if available, or a steam jacket
Fresh whole eggs	8		Whip the eggs and sugar slowly to blend
Granulated sugar	4	8	well. Do not whip to aerate the eggs

1. Add about 2 quarts of the hot milk slowly to the eggs and sugar, whipping constantly. This softens the eggs and provides a more uniform blend.
2. Now pour the remainder of the hot milk gradually into the egg blend and stir quickly while pouring. Strain the custard preparation before pouring into the custard cups.
3. The baking cups, earthenware preferred, should be buttered and dusted with granulated sugar. Fill the cups almost to the top. Use a pitcher with a spigot to avoid spilling and waste when pouring.
4. Place the cups in a baking pan about 3–4 in. high. Fill the pan with cool water about half full. Place the cups in the pan alongside each other. This will cause the water in the pan to rise so that about two-thirds of the cup is surrounded with water.
5. Place gently into the oven that has been preheated to 375°F. Bake for about 35 min.
6. Allow the custards to cool and then chill before unmolding and serving.

Yield: Approx. 100–120 servings

Chocolate Cup Custard

There are variables in the preparation of chocolate cup custard. Some pastry chefs will use bitter chocolate or chocolate liqueur for the color and flavor; others will use a blend of sweet and bitter chocolate in equal proportions. Still others may use a fine grade of cocoa dissolved in the

---

[1]Milk powder, if used, should first be dissolved in cool water by stirring briskly with a wire whip.

milk. In addition to the flavoring supplied by the vanilla or natural vanilla beans, the flavor of the chocolate may be supplemented by dissolving a small amount of instant coffee in the milk. These are variables which each pastry chef resolves by using his own judgment.

Ingredients	lb	oz	Mixing procedure
Milk [1]	20		Bring the milk and chocolate with the
Bitter chocolate	1	10	sugar to a slow boil. Stir occasionally to
Sugar	3		avoid scorching
Egg yolks	3	8	Whip the yolks and sugar on slow speed
Sugar	2		or with a wire hand whip to blend well.
Vanilla		2	Do not aerate
Instant coffee (optional)		½	

1. Add the boiling milk and chocolate to the eggs and sugar in a steady stream, stirring well to blend.
2. If instant coffee is used, dissolve in the hot milk before adding to the egg-sugar blend.
3. Strain and then pour into custard cups which have been buttered and sugared. Bake as for the vanilla cup custard.

Yield: Approx. 100–120 average cups

Note: Very often a foam (often termed a scum) will form on the tops of the chocolate cup custards after pouring. This should be removed to avoid a porous and uneven top. Pastry chefs often cover the tops of the custard cups with a pan or parchment paper liner to prevent too dark a crust color.

Coffee Cup Custard

A concentrate of instant coffee is used to provide the flavor of the custard. The concentrate is dissolved in part of the hot milk and then returned to the milk to be boiled. For special requests, a decaffeinated coffee may be used. The amount of coffee used will determine the strength of the flavor as well as the color of the custard. A light blend of vanilla and mocha flavoring may be added to supplement the coffee flavor.

Ingredients	lb	oz	Mixing procedure
Milk [2]	20		Bring the milk and sugar to a slow boil,
Sugar	3		with the dissolved coffee crystals

[1] If whole milk powder or skim milk powder is used, the powder should be dissolved in cool water before heating.

[2] If whole or skim milk powder is used, dissolve the milk powder in cool water. It is advisable to strain the reconstituted milk.

Instant coffee crystals (variable) (dissolve in part of the hot milk)	3		
Egg yolks	3	8	Blend the yolks and sugar together well. Add the hot milk and coffee to the yolks in a steady stream, stirring constantly to blend well. Strain and pour into the baking cups that have been buttered and sugared
Sugar	1		

Place the cups in a pan with water and bake as the vanilla cup custard. **Yield:** Approx. 100–120 cups

Baked Caramel Cup Custard

The bottoms of the custard baking cups are first covered with a cooked caramel sugar prepared by boiling 6 lb of sugar with 3 lb of water to a temperature of 320°F or until the sugar turns a golden brown. While cooking, wash the sides of the pot with a brush dipped in water. This will prevent sugar crystallization on the sides of the cooking kettle. As the sugar cools a little it will turn slightly darker. Fill the bottoms of approx. 100–120 custard cups about 2 in. high with the caramel sugar.

Ingredients	lb	oz	Mixing procedure
Milk[1]	18		Whip the eggs, sugar, and vanilla on slow
Whole eggs	7		speed to blend well. A hand wire whip
Sugar	3	8	may be used. Do not aerate. Add the milk
Vanilla		2	in a steady stream and stir constantly to blend well

1. Pour into the custard cups with the caramel at the bottom and fill almost to the top.
2. Place in large pans half-filled with water. Bake at 375–385°F. Test for doneness by inserting the point of a knife into the center. If the blade comes out clean the custard is baked.
3. Allow the custard cups to cool. Free the edges by running the point of a knife around the inside of the cup. Unmold by inverting on the serving dish.
4. Pastry chefs may add prepared caramel syrup before serving.

The caramel cup custard recipe may also be used for the *Vienna Cup Custard*. In this instance, the baking cups are buttered and sugared, and approximately 2 lb of the caramel sugar is added to the milk before it is poured into the cups. The caramel sugar may also be supplemented with additional coffee crystals dissolved in the milk.

[1]If whole or skim milk powder is used, dissolve the milk powder in the water and strain before using.

Orange Cup Custard

Ingredients	lb	oz	Mixing procedure
Milk [1]	20		Heat the milk and the orange rind and fla-
Rind of 12 oranges			voring together
Orange flavoring and coloring (variable, depending upon the concentrate)			
Eggs	8		Whip the eggs and sugar only to blend
Sugar	3	4	well. Do not aerate. Blend in the vanilla
Vanilla		2	

1. Add the heated milk to the eggs and sugar in a steady stream, stirring constantly to distribute evenly.
2. Prepare the custard cups by buttering and sugaring. Fill the cups almost to the top and bake as for the vanilla cup custard.
3. The orange cup custard is usually served with an orange sauce when cool. The cup custards are turned over into deeper dishes to contain the custard and the sauce.

Yield: Approx. 100–120 servings

Orange Sauce

This sauce is often called an Orange Mousseline sauce.

Ingredients	lb	oz	Mixing procedure
Orange juice [2]	8		Blend the sugar and juice and bring to a
Sugar	3	12	boil
Juice of 4 lemons			
Water	1		Dissolve the starch in the water. Add to
Cornstarch		4	the above in a steady stream, stirring constantly. Bring to a boil again and cook until clear

1. This sauce may be applied while hot to the cooled orange cup custard. The sauce may also be kept in a double boiler for a lengthy serving period to keep it flowing smoothly.
2. For a lighter mousseline effect, allow the sauce to cool completely and blend in ½ qt of lightly whipped heavy cream before serving.
3. For a more expensive dessert sauce, the pastry chef may add some brandy with the cream.

[1] If whole or skim milk powder is used, dissolve the milk powder thoroughly in the water before heating the milk.
[2] Use the juice of fresh oranges from which the rind was removed. If frozen orange juice concentrate is used, dilute as for regular orange juice. If dehydrated orange crystals are used, follow the instructions for reconstitution on the package.

For rapid preparation of sauces without cooking, to be used for large volume service, pastry chefs will use the prepared pudding fillings. This may be in the form of prepared lemon pie filling or an orange filling. The cold process vanilla custards may also be used. These fillings and custards are usually thinned down to sauce consistency by adding light cream for a mousseline effect. For a natural fruit sauce, the filling may be thinned with the use of hot or cold simple syrup. Additional flavoring and fruit juice may be added.

Baked Puddings

Puddings for large volume service, or where individual pudding cups are not feasible or available, are often baked in large, deep pans. The type of pan used has sides that are about 3–4 in. high and is prepared very much as the individual cup is prepared. Bread puddings, rice puddings, and cabinet puddings are some examples of the puddings that are baked in large pans very much like large cakes. The puddings are then dished out into individual portions after baking. Puddings may be served hot or cold. The sauces or cold creams used are placed over the puddings at the time of service.

Some puddings lend themselves well to being scooped out with a large ice cream scoop and maintain the half-circle shape when placed in the dish. Others may be scooped out for portion control, but flatten or run slightly when placed in the deep dish. They are then garnished while in the dish. Still other types of pudding may be firm enough to cut into portions while in the pan and then placed into dishes. Sauces are poured over the puddings in serving dishes. Puddings baked in large pans are usually baked on a double pan filled with water to prevent scorching the bottom and causing the pudding to stick. These puddings are baked at approximately 370–375°F. They are tested for proper bake in very much the same way as the cup custard is tested. Most pastry chefs will look at the crust color of the top and will also test the firmer type of pudding with a light touch of the fingers. Puddings are considered baked when they feel slightly firm in the center. Baked puddings are often placed in a bain marie or double boiler section of the steam table to keep them hot. The cold puddings are placed in the refrigerated section of the cafeteria-style serving setup.

Bread Pudding

Individual bread puddings are baked in regular custard baking cups. Oval shaped cups, if available, provide a more impressive appearance. In either case, the cups are buttered and sugared. In using the oval-shaped cups about 1½ in. deep, the whole, thin slice of bread dipped in melted butter is used to line the bottom and sides of the cup. If the regular custard cup is used, the thin slice of bread is cut in half and then dipped in melted butter. The half slices are then criss-crossed to cover the bottom and as much of the sides as is possible. If the large pan is used, it should be buttered well. The slices of bread dipped in butter (stale bread may be dipped in a blend of butter with a little milk to further soften the bread) are then spread evenly over the sides and bottom of the pan. The bread is then sprinkled well with seedless raisins if available. The larger Muscat raisins may be used. A blend of the regular raisins may be made with the larger Muscat variety. Fill the prepared cups or large pans with the following custard filling.

Custard Filling for Bread Pudding

Ingredients	lb	oz	Mixing procedure
Milk [1]	20		
Eggs	4	8	Whip the eggs and sugar slightly to blend
Sugar	4	8	well. Do not aerate. Blend in the vanilla
Vanilla		3	

1. Add the cool milk in a steady stream, stirring constantly. Pour over the bread and bake at approximately 390°F.
2. The puddings may be served either hot or cold. The cold custards are served with a soft vanilla cream custard or with a whipped cream garnish.
3. A regular vanilla custard may be cooked with 1 oz cornstarch and egg yolks rather than eggs for the English type of custard cream. The regular cream custard may be softened with the addition of a small amount of light cream or heavy cream to thin it down. Strain the custard cream before using.
4. The whipped cream may be garnished with half a glazed cherry for attractiveness.

Yield: 100–120 servings

Cabinet Pudding

Prepare the individual cups by buttering and sugaring the bottom and sides. Cut sponge cake sheets or layer cakes into small cubes. The pastry chef will often use leftover sponge cakes and other yellow cakes that have aged or staled for the cabinet pudding. The cakes are softened by the pudding filling during baking. For added variety, a combination of cake cubes may be used that contain both the vanilla (or yellow) with the chocolate types of cake. Cover the bottom of the custard cups with the small cake cubes. For the cabinet pudding baked in large pans, butter the pans and then line the entire bottom with the cubed cakes. Some pastry chefs will use an entire thin sheet cake to form a solid bottom liner for the pudding. They then sprinkle the cubes over the cake liner before adding the custard filling. Sprinkle the cake cubes with raisins before adding the custard filling.

---

[1]If whole or skim milk powder is used, dissolve the milk powder in cool water before using. It may be necessary to strain the milk.

Custard Filling for Cabinet Pudding

Ingredients	lb	oz	Mixing procedure
Milk	12		Blend the eggs and sugar well. Add the
Eggs	3	4	milk steadily and stir constantly to blend.
Sugar	2	4	Strain and pour into cups or large pans
Vanilla		1	

1. Bake the individual cups in a pan half-filled with water. The large pan may be placed in a baking sheet pan with water poured into the pan after placing into the oven. Water may have to be added during the baking of the large pan due to evaporation in baking.
2. Bake at 385°F until the puddings are done. The large pan will take longer to bake and may be checked as for the bread pudding for doneness.
3. The individual cups may be turned over while still warm and garnished with the hot vanilla cream sauce. Portions may be served directly from the large pudding pan either hot or cold. The same vanilla sauce or English cream sauce may be used. Whipped cream may also be used as the garnish for the cold cabinet pudding.

Yield: Approx. 100 servings.

Rice Pudding

There are several methods of preparing a baked rice pudding. For example, you might have the rice prepared in advance and kept under refrigeration, and add to the custard filling for the final baking. There are a variety of rice types and these require consideration for cooking. Pastry chefs will cook the rice in the milk. Others may partially cook the rice in boiling water and then strain it. It is then mixed with milk for completion of the cooking. Rice must be handled carefully during the cooking to prevent formation of lumps and breaking of the rice kernels. In addition, rice is to be stirred carefully with a wooden spoon and not with a wire whip. It is advisable to place the rice and milk, after the rice has been partially cooked in water and strained, in a shallow pan with the milk and allow it to actually steam through in the oven until the rice is tender. This makes for more rapid cooking since the rice and milk are spread over a larger surface. The rice-milk combination may be placed on a double pan in the oven.

Rice Pudding

Ingredients	lb	oz	Mixing procedure
Rice (long grain)	3	8	Wash the rice carefully. Boil in water for
Milk [1]	30		about 5–6 min. and drain

[1] If whole or skim milk powder is used, mix the powder well with cool water. Strain to remove possible lumps.

Combine the rice and milk and boil
slowly in a steam jacket cooker, or place
in large shallow pans and place in a
400°F oven. Stir occasionally and slowly
to prevent sticking. Cook until the rice
is just tender. The rind of an orange
may be cooked in with the rice and milk
until the rice is completely cooked

Egg yolks	2		Blend the egg yolks well with the sugar.
Sugar	4		Add the vanilla and the light cream and
Vanilla		2	blend well. Do not aerate the yolks
Light cream	7		

1. Fill the individual custard cups that have been buttered and sugared
   and bake in a pan with hot water until a light golden crust is formed.
2. The individual custards may be served with a hot sauce.
3. The rice and pudding custard may be returned to the large, deep
   pans (similar to cheese cake pans made of stainless steel) and returned to the oven for about 7–8 min at 400°F. Stir occasionally until
   the pudding thickens. Remove from the oven and place into individual cups.
4. The pudding may be portioned into deep dishes and served cool or
   hot.
5. If the rice pudding is served while hot, it is usually garnished with
   a mild dusting of cinnamon sugar. A hot orange sauce may be served.
6. If the rice pudding is served cold, it may be garnished with whipped
   cream and a glazed cherry for decoration.

Yield: 100–120 servings

Rice Puddings With Fruits Individual pudding dishes may be layered
or partially filled with a variety of fruits before the pudding is poured
into the cups for final baking. The fruits are usually precooked or poached.
For example, peeled and cored fresh apples may be poached in a light
syrup of 2 lb water and 1 lb granulated sugar. The juice of 1 or 2 lemons
is added to the syrup before it is boiled. More syrup will be required for
a larger quantity of apples. The apples are boiled for about 4–6 min ,
depending upon their hardness. The apples are then allowed to simmer
until they feel just tender. They are cooled and then sliced or quartered.

Large pan rice pudding may also be lined with a variety of fruit combinations. When a thicker or firmer rice pudding base is required for
special molds or shapes, a special rice preparation is made and poured
into molds. This is usually known as a rice condé.

Rice Condé

Ingredients	lb	oz	Mixing procedure
Milk [1]	8		Cook the rice as for rice pudding
Sugar	2		
Rice	1	8	
Egg yolks	2		
Vanilla		2	

1. Pour the condé into a mold or large deep pan that has been oiled.
2. Allow the condé or pudding base to cool and then garnish with the desired fruits. Apples that have been sliced may be layered over the condé. Apricots that have been neatly layered and glazed with apricot coating and syrup are often used. Fresh strawberries may be used when in season.
3. The various fruits may then be garnished with whipped cream before serving.

Tapioca Pudding

Tapioca is a starchy substance that is derived from the cassava root. It comes in several forms. The pastry chef will probably use the quick-cooking variety which softens and binds in a few minutes. If the regular pearl tapioca is used, it is soaked in cold water for about 1 hr and drained. It is then cooked in with the milk until tender. Tapioca pudding is quite tender. It requires care in the addition of the yolks and in the final addition of the whipped egg whites.

Tapioca Pudding

Ingredients	lb	oz	Mixing procedure
Milk [2]	20		Bring the milk to a mild boil. Add the tapioca and cook at a simmer until the tapioca is tender. Remove from heat
Tapioca (minute or quick cooking)	1	8	
Egg yolks	1	8	Blend the yolks, sugar, and salt together and add gradually to the tapioca and milk
Sugar	2		
Salt		1	
Vanilla		2	
Egg whites	2	12	Whip the egg whites to a firm peak and fold gently into the tapioca pudding
Sugar	1	6	

[1] If milk powder is used be sure to dissolve the powder in cool water and then strain before cooking.
[2] If milk powder is used, dissolve the powder in cool water first.

1. Ingredients may vary in the making of tapioca pudding. For example, if pearl tapioca is used, it will require longer soaking and cooking. There may be an increase in the amount of egg whites or egg yolks. Cost is always a factor in recipe development.
2. Care should be taken to prevent the beaten egg whites from curdling while folding them into the pudding.
3. The prepared tapioca pudding is poured into the serving dishes and allowed to cool.
4. A fresh strawberry sauce may be used. Cook the strawberries as for a strawberry pie filling and use a reduced amount of cornstarch. The filling may be thinned with simple syrup if too thick. A strawberry jam that has been thinned with simple syrup to which a little red coloring has been added may be used.
5. A whipped cream topping is often used to garnish the tops of the tapioca pudding.

Yield: 100–200 servings

Chiffon Custards (Pots de Crème)

These baked custards have a lighter texture and a luster induced by the eggs. A light cream, rather than milk, is often used to make these custards. However, milk is primarily used by modern pastry chefs who are cost conscious. Another choice to reduce costs might be a blend of light cream and milk. When milk is used as the base for these custards slightly increase the amount of eggs to form the gel texture. The custard cups for pots de crème are lined with butter and sugar as the regular baked custards. They are baked at a slightly lower temperature in a pan filled with water. Care must be used to avoid overbaking. Foam on the surface of the custard should be removed in order to obtain the fine, shiny luster on the top surface.

Vanilla Chiffon Custard (Pots de Crème)

Ingredients	lb	oz	Mixing procedure
Milk	8		Bring the milk and cream to a light simmer or scald. Use a double boiler or steam jacketed cooker to avoid scorching.
Light cream	8		
Egg yolks	2		Whip the eggs and sugar, salt, and vanilla at slow speed to blend well. Do not aerate.
Whole eggs	4		
Granulated sugar	3	8	Add the hot milk and cream in a steady
Salt		¼	stream, stirring constantly
Vanilla		2	

1. Strain the custard and pour into the prepared custard cups. Fill the cups almost full and bake at 355–365°F in a pan half full of water.
2. The custard cups may be covered with aluminum foil or a baking pan to prevent a dark and heavy crust from forming. The average cup custard should take abut 25–30 min. to bake. Avoid overbaking which may cause cracking and weeping. The puddings should be

removed from the oven when they show signs of mild setting in the center. A very light touch will indicate the slight firming.

3. The puddings will continue to cook after they have been removed from the oven or heat. The eggs will firm up the pudding to a tender smoothness. Overbaking will cause excessive binding of the eggs with a loss of the custard structure. These custards are usually served in the cups because of their delicacy.

Yield: 100–120 servings

Chocolate Chiffon Custard (Pots de Crème)

Chocolate or cocoa powder may be used to flavor and color the basic custard. If all bitter chocolate (chocolate liqueur or cocoa powder) is used, an increase in the amount of sugar will be necessary. It should be noted that all cocoa powder will have a slight thickening effect on the consistency of the baked custard. A blend of chocolate and cocoa is often used.

Ingredients	lb	oz	Mixing procedure
Milk	8		Dissolve the cocoa in part of the cool milk before mixing with the milk and light cream. Add the melted sweet chocolate and bring all to a light simmer or scald. Use a double boiler or steam jacketed cooker for large quantities to avoid scorching
Light cream	8		
Sweet chocolate (shaved and melted)	2		
Cocoa powder	1	2	
Egg yolks	2	8	Whip the yolks, sugar, salt, whole eggs, and vanilla on slow speed to blend well. Do not aerate. Add the hot chocolate milk and cream in a steady stream, stirring constantly to ensure an even blend
Whole eggs	2	4	
Sugar	3		
Salt		1	
Vanilla		2	

1. Strain the custard and pour into custard cups that have been buttered and sugared.
2. Remove any foam on the surface of the custard before baking. Bake as for the vanilla pots de crème.
3. The cooled chocolate pots de crème may be garnished with whipped cream.

Bavarois or Bavarian Puddings

Bavarois or Bavarian puddings are practically the same in that the basic binding is caused by gelatin. Pastry chefs will have differing opinions and different methods of producing these puddings. For example, the Bavarois will use egg yolks as a supportive binding and tenderizing ingredient. The yolks will also supply the added richness of the natural lecithin fats which have an emulsifying effect, as well as providing the rich, yellow color desired by many pastry chefs for the Bavarois. The

Bavarian pudding may contain both egg yolks and egg whites. Some are made without the use of the egg yolks and will use only the egg whites in whipped form to be added after the whipped cream has been folded into the cooled pudding filling.

A combination of both of these methods is present in the preparation of the whipped cream pie fillings (Bavarians) in the section on variety pies. These recipes use egg yolks, whole eggs, and gelatin for the basic custard, followed by the addition of whipped cream and whipped egg whites. These recipes may be used to good advantage in the preparation of individual Bavarois or the larger molds. The recipes that follow will introduce both methods for the Bavarois and the Bavarians. A separate basic recipe for each will be listed.

For individual service, the prepared Bavarian or Bavarois puddings may be poured directly into individual dishes, which are the same or similar to the dishes used for variety gelatin desserts. The individual desserts are garnished with whipped cream and other fruit toppings and served. For larger molds, the pans are oiled before the Bavarois is added. After the filling has chilled, the pan mold is dipped into warm water and then quickly turned over onto the dish in which it will be served. The dish or plate should have the special liner placed on it before the mold is turned over. When turned on the dish and the napkin, the mold is then decorated with whipped cream using a pastry bag and tube. Fresh or specially prepared fruits, such as candied fruits, are often used as garnish with the cream. Special sauces of the mousseline variety are often served with these desserts. Charlottes are desserts which are prepared in deep molds or pans having straight sides. The sides are usually lined with Lady Fingers, filled eclair shells that have been iced or left plain, a border of sponge cake, or another form of liner made of special cake or cookies, such as cat tongues or lace-type cookies.

Vanilla Bavarian Pudding

Ingredients	lb	oz	Mixing procedure
Milk [1]	10		Boil the milk and sugar
Gelatin		9	Dissolve the gelatin in the milk. When the
Milk	2		milk and sugar have boiled, remove from
Sugar	2		heat, add the gelatin and then strain. Allow the basic custard to cool and gel
Heavy cream for whipping	3		Whip the cream with the sugar to a medium peak. Fold into the cool basic custard
Sugar (confectioners)		5	

[1] If milk powder is used, dissolve the powder in cool water and strain.

Egg whites	3	Whip the whites to a froth. Gradually add
Granulated sugar	1	the sugar and whip to a medium dry peak. Fold into the custard gently. Be sure the whites are fully mixed in and evenly distributed. Pour into the individual cups or large molds and chill

Yield: Approx. 100 servings

Vanilla Bavarois Pudding

Ingredients	lb	oz	Mixing procedure
Gelatin		9	Dissolve the gelatin in the milk
Cool milk	4		
Milk [1]	12		Bring the milk to a light boil
Egg yolks	3	8	Whip the yolks and sugar together until
Sugar	3		quite thick and light as for a sponge-type
Vanilla (variable)		2	cake. Fold in the vanilla flavoring

Pour the hot milk into the beaten eggs and sugar in a steady stream, stirring constantly until all the milk has been added and blended. Add the dissolved gelatin and stir in well to an even blend.
Yield: Approx. 100–120 servings

Whipped Cream

---

1. Whip 2 qt of heavy cream to a froth. Add 6–8 oz of sugar and whip to a medium peak. Approximately 1/2–1 qt of cold milk may be added to the heavy cream when using a whipped cream stabilizer (about 1½ oz).
2. Fold the whipped cream into the cooled custard. The custard may be cooled by placing in a large bowl that has been set into another bowl of ice. Stir periodically to cool.
3. The custard may be placed in the refrigerator to cool quickly. The custard should be stirred from time to time.
4. Pour the Bavarois mixture into prepared serving dishes or molds and chill. The individual servings may be garnished with whipped cream and fruits of the fresh, canned, or candied variety.
Yield: Approx. 6–7 full qt

[1] If milk powder is used, dissolve the powder in cool water and then strain before cooking.

Variety Bavarois or Bavarian Puddings

The basic Bavarian or Bavarois pudding (vanilla) may be used to make a variety of similar puddings. The addition of a new ingredient such as chocolate or cocoa will change the vanilla to a chocolate Bavarian or Bavarois. The addition of other natural ingredients and fruits will develop another variety. Each of the puddings may use a different sauce. It is necessary to prepare the serving dishes as for the basic vanilla Bavarois. For the large molds, it is important to remember to oil the mold with a vegetable oil to make unmolding neat and smooth.

Chocolate Bavarian or Bavarois Pudding   If using the Bavarian or the Bavarois pudding recipe, add 2 lb of shaved and melted bitter chocolate (chocolate liqueur) to the milk at the time of boiling. Stir well to distribute the chocolate and to prevent scorching. Remove from the fire and then mix in the gelatin. Strain before cooling the pudding. The whipped cream and whipped egg whites are added as for the vanilla Bavarian. Some pastry chefs prefer to use a blend of sweet chocolate and bitter chocolate for the chocolate Bavarian or Bavarois. If all bitter chocolate is used, it is advisable to increase the sugar an additional pound. If sweet chocolate is used, approximately 3 lb of sweet chocolate is necessary without any increase in the sugar content of the recipe. If cocoa is used in conjunction with the chocolate, a slight increase in the amount of milk will be necessary to compensate for the binding effect of the cocoa. The cocoa should be dissolved in part of the cool milk and then added to the milk before it boils. A chocolate sauce, cold or hot, may be served with the chocolate Bavarian or Bavarois. These sauces are available in prepared form in cans. The pastry chef may prepare the hot fudge or chocolate sauce himself.

Hot Chocolate Sauce

Ingredients	lb	oz	Mixing procedure
Granulated sugar	9	8	Bring the sugar and glucose dissolved in
Water	6	4	the water to a rolling boil
Glucose or corn syrup	3		
Bitter chocolate (dissolved)	4	8	Add the chocolate and bring to boil, stirring constantly

1. Remove from the fire and strain before using. The sauce may be stored and reheated as required.
2. For large volume service, the chocolate sauce may be kept in a double boiler during service to maintain the heat of the sauce.
3. For a cold sauce, the water may be replaced with milk, or half milk and water may be used. The hot sauce may also be reduced with the addition of a small amount of light cream and served as a cold chocolate sauce. Use as desired.

Chocolate Mousseline Sauce   Partially whip 1 qt of heavy cream and mix into the cold chocolate sauce and serve.

Coffee Bavarian or Bavarois Pudding   Dissolve approximately 2 oz of instant coffee in the milk before boiling. Some caramel coloring and mocha flavoring may be added for additional color and flavor. The Bavarois or Bavarian pudding may be served with a coffee sauce. The vanilla cream custard may be thinned slightly with some light cream or milk in which some instant coffee has been dissolved.

Fruit Bavarois or Bavarian Puddings
The fruit-type Bavarois or Bavarian puddings may be made with a cooked process that contains milk with the natural fruit pulp and juices added after the gelatin has been mixed in with the boiled milk and sugar. This will avoid curdling of the milk when in direct contact with the natural acids of the fruit.

The puddings may also be made with a cold process where no cooking is necessary, but without the use of milk. The whipped cream is folded in after the water or juice of the fruits has been combined with the cooked syrup (plain, simple syrup) and the gelatin has been added. Pastry chefs will use prepared gelatin dessert powders in commercial packages for large volume preparation and service. Part of the water used for gelatin dessert is replaced by the natural fruit juice and fruit pulp. Additional fruits are added after the gelatin has been cooled and the whipped cream has been folded into the gel.

Fruit Bavarian

Ingredients	lb	oz	Mixing procedure
Gelatin		9	Dissolve the gelatin in the milk
Milk	2		
Milk	7		Dissolve the sugar in the milk and bring
Sugar	2	8	to a boil. Add the gelatin and strain. Add
Crushed and strained fruit and juice	6		the fruit and juice and blend in
Heavy cream for whipping	3		When cool, add the whipped cream and fold in. Add the whites whipped to a me-
Egg whites	3		dium peak and fold in gently
Sugar	1		

1.   Fill the individual serving dishes or larger molds and allow the pudding to be chilled. This makes unmolding easier.
2.   A strawberry or other fruit sauce may be served separately.
3.   A basic fruit sauce may be made by heating neutral apricot coating (prepared in cans) with an equal amount of fruit and juice that has been strained. Additional coloring and flavoring of the fruit may be added. Fruit pieces may also be added.

4. Bring the ingredients to a boil stirring constantly.
5. To make the individual fruit sauces, such as a strawberry sauce, see the next section, on pudding sauces.

Note: A variety of fruits may be used for the fruit Bavarian pudding. Strawberries (fresh, or frozen and defrosted) make excellent desserts. This is even more attractive when the individual or large servings are garnished with whipped cream and fresh strawbberies. Peaches, apricots, raspberries, and similar fruits may be used. While the fruits are strained, pastry chefs will add fruit pieces to the pudding when the pudding is almost cool.

Yield: Approx. 100–120 servings

Pudding Sauces

Strawberry Sauce   (*hot or cold*)

Ingredients	*lb*	*oz*	*Mixing procedure*
Fresh or frozen strawberries	4	(2 qt)	Use 3 qt of fresh strawberries and strain to reduce the pulp and to obtain the natural
Sugar (variable)[1]	2–3		juices. Add enough water to make the required amount
Juice of 3 lemons			Bring the juice, strained fruit, and sugar to a boil. Stir frequently to dissolve well
Cornstarch (variable)		3	Dissolve the starch in the water. Add to the boiling fruit and juice in a steady
Water		2	stream, stirring constantly
Strawberry flavoring			
Red coloring			

1. Add the strawberry flavoring and a few drops of red coloring to meet the requirements of the sauce. The sauce may be served hot or cool.
2. The consistency of the hot sauce may be controlled by the amount of starch used to thicken the sauce. A sauce that thickens considerably when cool may be thinned or reduced by adding some simple syrup.
3. The recipe for the strawberry sauce may be used to prepare other fruit sauces such as raspberry, apricot, loganberry, and others.

Lemon and orange sauces may be made by thinning the regular lemon or orange custard or pie filling by adding simple syrup. If the fillings are to be served hot, then it is best to prepare them as separate sauces.

---

[1]Depending upon the sugar in the canned or frozen strawberries. Fresh strawberries will require more sugar

Lemon Custard Sauce

Ingredients	lb	oz	Mixing procedure
Milk [1]	6		Bring to a boil, stirring to prevent scorching
Sugar	2	4	
Salt		¼	
Water	2		Dissolve the starch in the water. Add the yolks and blend in well. Add ½ qt of the hot milk and blend in. Pour the starch and egg yolk solution slowly into the boiling milk in a steady stream, stirring constantly, and bring to a boil
Cornstarch		5	
Egg yolks	1	4	
Egg whites		12	Beat to a medium stiff peak
Juice of 4 to 6 lemons; rind of 3 lemons			Fold into the above. Add the juice and rind and mix in well

It is advisable to strain the hot sauce before serving. A few drops of yellow coloring may be necessary. An orange sauce may be made from the same recipe as the hot lemon custard sauce by adding 5–6 oranges (juice and the rind of 2 oranges) and 2 lemons in place of the lemons.

A Melba sauce is often used in hot or cold form for many of the puddings. It is simply made by combining several selected jams and fruit juices and boiling. The selection may vary. For example, a raspberry jam may be combined with a current jelly and a fruit juice as a base for the Melba sauce. Strawberries that have been mashed and strained to obtain a natural fruit juice may be combined with currant jelly. The following is a recipe for Melba Sauce.

Melba Sauce

Ingredients	lb.	oz	Mixing (cooking) procedure
Strawberry fruit and juice (approximately 2 qt)	4		Stir well to dissolve the sugar and blend the jelly, fruit pulp and juice. Bring to a boil
Currant or raspberry jelly			
Sugar (variable)	1	8	
Water		8	
Cornstarch		1½	Dissolve the starch in the water and add to the above in a slow, steady stream and bring to a boil. Cook until clear
Water		8	

Strain the sauce for smoothness and serve hot. The sauce may also be served when cold. If the sauce thickens slightly, thin with a simple syrup.

[1] If milk powder is used, dissolve the milk powder in cool water and strain.

Hard Sauce

This sauce is used as a garnish for hot or cold puddings, and is made simply.

Ingredients	lb	oz	Mixing procedure
Confectioners sugar	2		Blend the butter with the sugar and then
Butter (sweet)	2		continue to cream until soft and light
Vanilla or rum flavoring		1	

The sauce may be bagged out into rosettes and refrigerated for use. Each rosette may be garnished with a glazed cherry, nut, or sprinkles.

Basic Vanilla Sauce

A basic vanilla sauce is often prepared for a variety of puddings. The richness of the sauce will determine the method by which it is to be prepared. A more economical vanilla sauce (one using less egg yolks) will require the addition of a thickener such as cornstarch. A sauce that is rich (thickened entirely with the use of added egg yolks) requires no added thickening agent and must be heated very carefully to avoid curdling or separation. The hot vanilla sauce is often called by a French or other foreign name. Some may call the richer sauces, served hot, a French sauce. Others may call the vanilla sauce a Vanilla Sauce a L'Anglaise or something similar.

Basic Hot Vanilla Custard Sauce

Ingredients	lb	oz	Mixing procedure
Milk	5	8	Boil the milk and sugar. Stir occasionally
Sugar	1	8	to prevent scorching
Salt		(pinch)	
Cornstarch		2½	Dissolve the starch in the milk. Add the
Milk		8	yolks and blend in well. Add a small
Egg yolks	1		amount of the hot milk to the starch-egg
Vanilla		1	solution and blend in well. Add the egg-starch solution to the boiling milk in a slow, steady stream and bring to a boil, stirring constantly. Remove from the fire. Add the vanilla and strain. Serve hot

By adding whipped egg whites and sugar, a hot mousseline sauce may be made using the above basic custard sauce. (Whip 1 lb of egg whites with 1 lb of sugar to a meringue consistency and fold into the hot sauce.) For a cold mousseline sauce, allow the basic vanilla sauce to cool and fold in ½ qt of heavy cream that has been whipped to a medium peak.

Some of the finer and more delicate sauces are often made with a white wine for special desserts. These require special care in preparation since these sauces are heated but are never boiled.

White Wine Sauce or Sabayon Sauce

Ingredients	lb	oz	Mixing procedure
White wine (1 gal.)	8		Place the yolks and sugar in a bowl and
Fine granulated	2		set over a double boiler at moderate heat.
sugar			Whip the eggs and sugar until light
Egg yolks	2		

Add the wine and continue to whip until reasonably thick. The mixture or sauce will stick to the whip or will coat a spoon when tested. Do not allow the sauce to boil. Remove from the fire and serve. A small amount of fine rum may be added to further flavor the sauce. Pour the sauce into champagne glasses and serve. Some pastry chefs will sprinkle a trace of nutmeg over the sauce served hot. The hot sauce may be placed into a large sauce bowl and served.

The wine sauce may also be served cold. The sauce is placed over a large bowl containing chopped ice and chilled. Stir occasionally. For a thicker consistency to be served in a chilled form, dissolve 2 oz of gelatin in a small amount of water (½ qt) and add to the heated sauce. Pour into the glasses and chill or refrigerate before serving. The firmer body will allow the use of a variety of garnishes—whipped cream, for example.

Charlotte Puddings and Blanc Mange Pudding

Charlotte puddings are made in special molds to contain the filling and to provide the special shape desired. Most molds are round and are about 5 in. high. Where the special molds are not available, deep layer cake pans may be used. These may vary in size from the 6 in. to the large 16-in. pan. The size of the mold and the height of the charlotte will determine the number of portions.

The charlotte pans are usually lined with Lady Fingers, sponge or chiffon cake slices, filled eclairs that have been iced with a variety of fondant-type icings, a sponge or chiffon cake that has been baked and cooled with the center part removed, or with bread slices that have been dipped in melted butter. All of these liners are used to shape and contain the contents of the mold. The contents may vary with the type of charlotte and the filling. They may be filled with a vanilla Bavarois or Bavarian pudding, or filled with a variety of ice creams. The charlottes are chilled and then unmolded on the serving dish or tray. After unmolding, the charlottes are decorated. Decoration may be in the form of whipped cream, candied fruits, special fruit fillings, or fresh fruits used in conjunction with whipped cream. The pastry chef will usually decide the appropriate finish and sauce to be served. With each variety of charlotte there is usually a change of name. This accounts for the many varieties of charlottes and the many impressive names given to them.

Charlotte Glacés
The charlotte glacé is made by lining the mold with Lady Fingers placed close together. The mold center is then filled with a single type of ice cream or a combination of several types of ice cream. When the charlotte has been chilled (frozen) it is unmolded and garnished with whipped cream. The choice of sauce will depend upon the charlotte. The charlotte glacé may also be made with a combination of Bavarois pudding and ice cream.

Charlotte Russe
The fundamental approach for the Charlotte Russe is the complete lining of the mold with Lady Fingers. The bottom of the mold is also lined with the Lady Fingers placed closely together. The mold is then filled with Bavarois or Bavarian pudding and chilled. The pudding may be vanilla, chocolate, or other variety. The charlotte is then finished with whipped cream after unmolding. The garnish is usually based upon the type of filling used. Fresh fruits may be used for special charlottes as part of the filling as well as the garnish.

Charlotte Eclair (Pompadour)
Line the molds with eclairs that have been filled with custard cream. These are miniature eclairs. They actually replace the Lady Fingers. The eclairs may be iced with several different colored and flavored icings. Fill the mold with Bavarois or Bavarian vanilla cream. Chill and then unmold the charlotte. The charlotte is then finished with whipped cream. A Melba sauce or fruit sauce may be served with this charlotte.

Charlotte Sponge
A round mold or deep layer pan may be used for this charlotte, often called Phyllis or another name. Bake a sponge cake in the pan or mold. When the cake has cooled or chilled, cut out the center and leave a ring of sponge cake about 2 in. thick. Some pastry chefs will use tube or Turk head pans to bake the sponge cake or chiffon cake. The baked ring is then place on the serving tray and filled with Bavarois pudding, whipped cream, or a combination of both. The cream or Bavarois may be blended with candied and fresh fruits. The top of the charlotte is usually garnished with whipped cream. A sauce may be served with the charlotte.

Pinwheel Charlotte
This charlotte is called a Royale or similar name because of the jelly roll slices used to line the sides of the mold. The slices are thin and are about 3 to 4 in. in diameter. Overlay the slices as the mold is lined. The center may be filled with whipped cream into which fresh fruits may have been mixed. A Bavarois or Bavarian pudding may be used with the whipped cream. When unmolded, garnish the top with whipped cream and fruits.

Apple Charlotte

These are usually made in molds that are shaped like bread pans or loaf cake pans. In fact, these pans may be used for making the apple charlotte. The pans are lined with thin bread slices that have been dipped in melted butter. It is advisable to overlay the slices to contain the apple filling. The bottom of the pan is lined as well as the sides. The apples are peeled, cored, and sliced thin. The apple slices should be sautéed in butter to soften. The apples are sweetened in accordance with the natural sweetness or tartness of the apples. A blend of cinnamon sugar may be used. The apples are mixed with some light bread crumbs to tighten the mixture. Fill the molds about 1½ to 2 in. high. If desired, raisins may be blended in with the apples. Cover the apple-filled molds with a sheet pan and bake at about 390–400°F. The bread crusts will show a light brown crust color. The charlotte may be served with a variety of sauces.

Blanc Mange Pudding

The term "blanc mange" is usually applied to many varieties of white puddings or foods similar to a pudding. In most instances, the pudding is primarily made with a whipped cream and placed into a mold or serving dish. It is garnished in a manner suited to the pastry chef. A whipped cream garnish and a sauce may be used in conjunction with each other.

Ingredients	lb	oz	Mixing procedure
Gelatin		7	Dissolve the gelatin in the milk
Milk	2		
Milk powder[1]	1	12	
Water	10		
Almond or macaroon paste (variable)	1	8	Work the almond paste to a smooth cream by mixing with a small amount of milk.
Sugar	2	8	Work in slowly
			Bring the milk, sugar, and the softened almond or macaroon paste to a slow boil. Remove from the fire and add the gelatin. Place in the refrigerator to cool, stirring occasionally, or place in a large bowl over another bowl filled with ice for a more rapid cooling.
Heavy cream for whipping	4	(2 qt)	Whip the cream to a froth. Add the sugar gradually and whip to a medium peak
Sugar		6	
Vanilla		1	

Fold the vanilla into the whipped cream and then gently mix the whipped cream into the pudding that is thickening. Pour into dessert dishes. **Yield:** Approx. 100–120 servings

[1]Dissolve the powder in cool water first and then strain to remove any possible lumps.

Steamed Puddings

Steamed puddings are similar in many respects to cakes made from medium soft batters which are placed in molds or pans and steamed rather than baked directly on the shelf or hearth of the oven. Large producers of steamed puddings will place them in steam kettles and cook under controlled pressures. For the average pastry chef who will produce limited amounts of steamed puddings, the puddings are placed into special pudding molds with covers. Then the molds are placed into pans with water, and then into the oven. The actual steaming takes place by the release of moisture in the pudding, and is contained in the covered mold. The steam in the oven surrounding the molds is created by the evaporation of the water in the baking pans. For puddings that are steamed for several hours, the pans of water may have to be refilled.

Puddings of the steamed variety may be made in advance. For example, a plum pudding may be made and stored in the refrigerator until service is required. The puddings may be reheated in the oven and then sliced and served, or placed directly on serving dishes and reheated in a microwave oven. The firm or hard puddings are usually garnished with a hard sauce flavored with rum or brandy.

Pastry chefs will often serve the pudding by pouring brandy into the serving tray and flaming the pudding slightly. A custard cream sauce flavored with rum or brandy may also be used with a hard type of pudding such as plum pudding. The softer pudding varieties are often made with whipped eggs or egg whites and have souffle characteristics. These are served with a variety of custard or fruit sauces.

Blueberry Pudding

Ingredients	lb	oz	Mixing procedure
Sugar (granulated)	6		Blend well and then cream to a light con-
Salt		1	sistency
Milk powder[1]		10	
Butter or margarine	3		
Egg whites	4		Add the egg whites in 4 stages and cream well after each addition
Water	3	8	Add half the water and vanilla and stir
Vanilla		1	slightly
Cake flour	6	4	Sift the flour, baking powder, and cinna-
Baking powder		3½	mon together. Add alternately with the
Cinnamon		½	water and mix to smooth batter
Fresh blueberries (variable) (washed, cleaned, and drained)		4 qt	Fold in the blueberries gently

[1]For added richness, pastry chefs may blend whole milk with a light cream.

Deposit the pudding batter into molds that have been buttered. Steam for approximately 1½ to 2 hr. *It is important to have the pudding molds covered. If covers are not available, the tops of the molds may be covered tightly with aluminum foil and a baking pan placed over the tops.*

The amount of blueberries may be increased or decreased. Unmold the puddings while still warm. Serve with a choice of a vanilla custard cream sauce, a lemon cream sauce, or a hard sauce.

Yield: Approx. 100 servings

Steamed Apple Pudding *(Pudding Normande)*

Fresh apples, frozen apple slices, canned solid pack apples, or a combination of these may be used. Bread crumbs, cake crumbs, or toasted bread or cake cubes may be used to bind the apples and act as an extender or filler.

Ingredients	lb	oz	Mixing procedure
Fresh apples (peeled, cored and sliced)	15		Blend the apples with the sugar, cinnamon, and lemon rind. Do this in a large bowl
or			
Frozen apple slices	(12 to 15 lb)		
or			
Solid pack canned apples	(3 No. 10 cans)		
Granulated sugar (variable, depending on the apples used)	3	4	
Cinnamon		1	
Rind of 3 lemons			
Eggs	3		Whip the eggs slightly to blend. Add the eggs, milk, and crumbs gradually and fold in. Allow the mixed apple pudding to set for about ½ hr and check on the consistency. If too soft, add additional crumbs. Bread crumbs will absorb and retain more moisture than the cake crumbs. If cake crumbs are used, a lesser amount of sugar will be required. If only canned apples are used, additional crumbs may be necessary to absorb the liquid
Milk	6		
Bread crumbs (light)	(4 to 5 lb)		
or	(variable)		
Cake crumbs (light)			

Place the mixture into well-buttered molds and fill about three-quarters full. Cover the molds with the covers or with aluminum foil and steam for approximately 2 hr depending upon the size and depth of the mold. Serve warm or cold with a hot fruit sauce. Apricot, lemon, or other fruit sauce may be used.

Yield: Approx. 100 servings

Steamed Coconut Macaroon Pudding

Ingredients	lb	oz	Mixing procedure
Almond or macaroon paste	2		Add the eggs slowly to the macaroon paste and mix smooth
Eggs	1		
Sugar	5		Cream the sugar, salt, and butter until
Salt		1	smooth and soft. Add the macaroon paste
Butter	2	8	and cream light
Eggs	1	8	Combine the eggs and whites and blend.
Egg whites	1	8	Add to the above in 4 stages and blend in well
Macaroon coconut	3	8	Add the coconut and blend in
Milk	1		Add the milk and candied fruits with the
Rind of 2 oranges			orange rind and blend
Candied orange peel and glazed cherries	2		
Cake flour	4	12	Sift the cake flour and baking powder to-
Baking powder		2½	gether. Add to the above and mix smooth
Egg whites	1	8	Whip the whites to a wet peak and fold in gently

Deposit into well buttered molds. Fill three-quarters full and cover with mold covers or with aluminum foil. Steam for about 1½–2 hr depending upon the size and depth of the mold. Serve either cold or hot with a fruit sauce or a vanilla, cream custard sauce.
Yield: Approx. 100–120 servings

Plum Pudding

Plum pudding may be made in a manner similar to that of making an old-fashioned fruit cake. The fruits are steeped in a syrup of brandy or rum and then mixed into a cake batter resembling the old-fashioned pound cake. The batter is then placed in molds and steamed. This pudding may be stored, when wrapped well, for a lengthy period and served when required.

Ingredients	lb	oz	Mixing procedure
Currant raisins	2	8	Soak the fruits in the rum-brandy-syrup
Sultana raisins	2		blend overnight
Chopped glazed cherries	2		
Chopped, candied orange and lemon peel	2		

Citron peel	1	
Melon peel	1	
Rum		2
Brandy		2
Simple syrup	1	

Sugar	5		Cream the sugar, salt, and butter until soft
Salt		1	and light
Butter	3		
Shortening	2		
Eggs	5		Add the eggs gradually and cream in well
Bread flour	5		Sift and mix in well

Fold in the drained fruits and place into well buttered molds. Cover and steam for about 3 hr depending upon the size and depth of the mold. Serve warm with a hard sauce or rum-flavored custard cream sauce.
Yield: Approx. 100 servings

Mousses

Mousses are soft, light, and airy desserts similar to the Bavarians and the Bavarois. They are usually served in individual serving cups or champagne glasses. It is quite popular to place a large bowl filled with a mousse on a special dessert table where the diners may help themselves. The mousses may be made with a variety of strained fruits and the natural juices of the fruits. In some instances, gelatin may be used to firm the consistency of the mousse. This is especially so in the preparation of the fruit type of mousse.

Chocolate Mousse

Ingredients	lb	oz	Mixing procedure
Sweet chocolate (shaved and melted in a double boiler)	9		Combine the melted chocolate and the cream and milk, and cool
Light cream	1		
Milk	1	8	
Egg yolks	3		Whip the eggs and sugar slightly and
Sugar	1	8	blend in with the chocolate, milk, and cream
Egg whites	4		Whip the egg whites to a froth. Add the
Sugar	1	8	sugar and whip to a wet peak
Heavy cream (1 qt)	2		Whip the heavy cream to a medium peak.
Sugar		3	Fold in half the egg whites and the
Vanilla		1	whipped cream. Now fold in the remaining egg whites followed by the remaining whipped cream

Pour into the individual serving dishes or glasses. Chill well and serve.
The chocolate mousse may be garnished with whipped cream.
Yield: Approx. 100–120 servings

Basic Vanilla Mousse

Ingredients	lb	oz	Mixing procedure
Plain gelatin		5	Dissolve the gelatin in the water and set
Water	2		aside
Milk [1]	7		Bring the milk and sugar to a boil, stirring
Sugar	1	8	occasionally
Egg yolks	2	8	Whip the eggs and sugar to light, thick
Sugar	1		consistency as for a sponge cake

Pour some of the hot milk into the egg-sugar froth in a slow, steady
stream, stirring consistently. Add the egg mixture to the simmering milk
in a steady stream, stirring constantly, and allow the custard to thicken.
Do not boil. Add the gelatin and mix in well. Cool the custard by placing
in a bowl set over ice cubes in another large bowl. Stir every so often to
cool more rapidly. When cool and almost set, fold in the following:

	lb	oz	
Heavy cream (1 qt)	2		Whip to a medium peak and fold into the
Sugar		3	above gently
Vanilla		½	

Mashed and strained fruits, such as bananas and strawberries, may be
folded in with the whipped cream. Pour into serving dishes and chill.
The mousse may be garnished with whipped cream and slices of banana,
whole strawberries, or with just a large rosette of whipped cream.
Yield: Approx. 100–120 servings

Variety Fruit-Type Mousses

Pastry chefs will often use fruit gelatin dessert preparations as the base
for a fruit type of mousse. For example, strawberry or other fruit gelatin
may be prepared using the natural juices of the fruits that have been
mashed and strained to replace part of the water. When canned fruits are
used, the light syrup or the juice from the water pack is drained and
used in place of the water to prepare the gelatin. The amount of sugar
used will have to be adjusted to allow for the natural sweetness of the
canned syrups. To extend the yield, pastry chefs often add natural gelatin
powder and additional water with the fruit juices. The egg whites that
are whipped and folded into the gelling dessert are whipped to a medium firm peak with part of the sugar and then folded into the gelatin
for the mousse effect. In the case of strawberries, the mashed strawberries and sugar may be whipped with dissolving gelatin and egg whites

[1] If milk powder, whole or skim, is used, dissolve the milk powder in the cool water and
then strain to remove any lumps.

into a mousse and placed directly into the serving glasses. The strawberries have a natural pectin and gelling capacity which enables the strawberries to be whipped. For most fruit or juice types of mousse, lemon juice is added to provide a tang for an otherwise bland or flat taste.

Orange or lemon mousse is made with the natural juice of the fruits with some of the rind added to enhance the flavor. A prepared gelatin dessert powder is very often used and is supplemented with additional natural juice. To this, the pastry chef will add additional gelatin to firm up the mousse because of the high acidity of the fresh lemons and oranges. Frozen juice concentrates may be used after they have been reconstituted. If powdered lemon or orange crystals are used, follow the instructions for reconstitution provided on the package.

Fruit Mousse Varieties

Ingredients	lb	oz	Mixing procedure
Gelatin (variable, depending upon the acidity)		12	Dissolve the gelatin in part of the water
Water or fruit juice	12		
Fruit pulp of fresh or canned druits equivalent of 2 to 3 Number 10 cans of fruit and juice. Mash and strain the fruit into pulp	(5–6 qt)		Mash and drain the fruit into pulp. Blend the fruit pulp and lemon juice. Add the dissolved gelatin and blend well. Allow the preparation to start to gel
Sugar (variable) (less if a prepared gelatin base is used)	3		
Lemon juice	(4–6 oz)		
Egg whites	4		Whip egg whites to a firm peak. Fold into the above and blend in for even distribution
Sugar	1	8	

Fill the dessert cups or special dessert glasses and place in the refrigerator to firm up. When chilled and firm, decorate the tops with whipped cream. Garnish with the fruit variety used. A whole strawberry, a peach slice, an orange slice, or a fresh raspberry, are some of the fruits that may be used.
Yield: Approx. 100 servings

Prune Whip Mousse

The selection of prunes is important for the prune whip. The California prune is quite sweet and pulpy. The Oregon prune is tart and will require sugar to be added to the prunes. Prunes should be soaked for several hours or overnight before being cooked to soften the outer skin and enable some of the moisture to be absorbed. The prunes should be washed and drained before soaking. The juice from the prunes may well be used for a special serving of prune juice, after the prunes have been cooked and drained from the juice.

Ingredients	lb	oz	Mixing procedure
Prunes	8		Soak the prunes overnight. Cook at a slow simmer until tender. Drain the prunes and remove the pits. Strain the prunes
Sugar (variable, depending upon the prunes used)	3	8	Add the sugar and lemon juice and blend in
Lemon juice		(3–4 oz)	
Egg whites	3		Whip the egg whites to a froth. Add the sugar gradually and whip to a firm peak. (Not dry)
Sugar	1		

The strained prunes may be added to the egg whites while the machine is running at slow speed. A blend of the juice from the prunes may be gelled with the addition of powdered gelatin to the juice. Dissolve 2 oz of gelatin in each quart of prune juice used. Allow the juice to gel and then add the blend of drained prunes and meringue to the juice. Fold in gently and pour into the dessert dishes or glasses. Chill before serving. The chilled prune whip may be garnished with a rosette of whipped cream. Apricots will also serve well to make an apricot mousse or whip. Apricots when cooked and strained may be whipped in with the egg whites if a small amount of dissolved gelatin is added with the apricot pulp.

Yield: Approx. 100 servings

Souffles

Souffles are light and airy preparations that are served as soon after they are baked as possible. Since the souffles are largely leavened by the expansion of the yolks and whipped egg whites during baking, delay in service will often cause the souffles to lose their delicate structure. In fact,when a short delay occurs in service, souffles are placed in hot water baths to maintain the heat necessary to keep the structure of the souffle at the same consistency during baking. A souffle that has collapsed is partially raw or soggy in the interior and also becomes somewhat tough.

The pastry chef is aware of the importance of the timing between the preparation of the souffle, the baking time, and the immediate service. Souffles are prepared to order and never in large bulk for mass service. This eliminates the preparation of souffles for large institutional feeding, in most instances. In addition to the difficulty of preparation and service, there is the cost factor to be considered.

Souffles are usually prepared in dishes that have been well buttered and dusted with sugar. Some pastry chefs prefer the use of sifted confectioners sugar for dusting the dishes rather than fine granulated sugar. The feeling is that the syrup formation makes the souffle easier to serve when using confectioners sugar. The tops of the souffles are often dusted with confectioners sugar to provide a deep brown crust on the souffle resulting from the caramelization of the sugar during baking. The souffle is usually placed in a pan that contains hot or boiling water and baked. This prevents burning the bottom of the souffle or the formation of a heavy crust at the bottom. The baking temperatue for souffles will vary from 380–420°F depending on the timing for the service as well as the size of the souffle.

Souffles are usually prepared for small groups, from 4 to 12 diners. While the souffle batters are made for individual orders, pastry chefs will save time by preparing a base for the souffle. A blend of flour, butter and sugar in equal amounts is made into a paste form and kept ready for expected souffle requests. The basic mixture may be kept in the refrigerator for use as demand requires. The mixture may be left at kitchen temperature to soften if souffles are part of the menu for the dining service. A mixture composed of the following may be made in advance to make enough individual souffles for approximately 100 servings (approximately 8 souffles, approx. 12 servings each).

Souffle Base

Ingredients	lb	oz	Mixing procedure
Sugar	1	8	Blend together to a smooth paste and re-
Butter	1	8	frigerate if the base is not to be used at
Bread flour	1	8	the same time as it is mixed

The paste may be scaled into separate units of 9 oz each and used for each souffle to serve approximately 12 servings. It is advisable to mix the basic paste to soften. This will make the addition of the hot milk easier.

Pastry chefs will also prepare a separate mixture for each variety of souffle containing a lesser amount of thickening-binder than the flour present in the basic mixture. Where a lesser amount of flour or starch is used, there is an increase in the amount of egg yolks and egg whites to provide for the structure of the souffle. This makes the souffle more delicate, requires immediate service to prevent settling of the souffle, and adds to the cost of preparation. Souffles are usually served with a sauce that will complement them. The type of sauce will depend largely upon the judgment of the pastry chef.

Vanilla Souffle

Ingredients	lb	oz	Mixing procedure
Milk (1 qt)	2		Bring the milk to a boil. Add the vanilla
Vanilla		1	and remove from the fire
			Place 2 units of basic mixture each weighing 9 oz (1 lb 2 oz) into the hot milk and mix well to a smooth consistency. Return to the fire and bring to a mild boil.
Egg yolks		14	Add the egg yolks slowly and mix in well after each addition
Egg whites	1	6	Whip the whites to a froth. Add the sugar
Granulated sugar		8	gradually and whip to a medium soft peak

Fold the beaten whites into the yolk-base mixture gently. Use a folding motion with a large wooden spoon to avoid breakdown of the air cells in the egg whites. Deposit the souffle into two separate dishes that have been well buttered and lined with sugar. Fill the dishes almost to the top, depending upon the height of the dish. Dust the tops of the souffles with confectioners sugar and bake in a pan with hot water at 415°F. It will take about 25–30 min to bake. Serve at once. A vanilla sauce may be served with this souffle. A fruit sauce made with fresh fruits in season is equally appropriate.
Yield: 2 souffles of 12 servings each

Chocolate Souffle   Follow the procedure used for the vanilla souffle with the following additions:

1. Sweet chocolate that has been melted (approx. 6 oz) should be added to the mixture after the egg yolks have been incorporated and before the egg whites are folded in. A blend of sweet and bitter chocolate may be used (2 oz of bitter chocolate and 2 oz of sweet chocolate). If cocoa is used, dissolve the cocoa (2½ oz) in the milk before boiling to eliminate any lumps. The milk may be strained.
2. The chocolate or cocoa will have a tendency to thicken or bind the souffle. This will be noticed when the egg yolks are added. It is advisable to increase the egg yolks slightly to soften the mixture.
3. If the mixture tends to bind slightly before the egg whites are folded in, a slight increase in egg whites will be helpful. A small amount of light cream or milk may be used to soften the mixture before the beaten egg whites are added.
4. Bake the chocolate souffle as the vanilla souffle. Serve hot with a vanilla cream custard sauce. The regular cream custard may be softened with some light cream and used as a vanilla sauce.

Coffee Souffle   This may be made from the vanilla souffle preparation by dissolving 3 heaping tablespoons of instant coffee in the milk before adding the yolks to the mixture and proceeding as for the regular souffle preparation. A vanilla sauce flavored with coffee may be used.

Combination Souffle   This is often called a Harlequin Souffle. It is made by preparing a vanilla souffle and a chocolate souffle and combining half of each in the same souffle dish. A vanilla sauce is often served with this souffle.

Lemon and Orange Souffles   These may be made from the basic vanilla souffle by adding the grated rind of 3 lemons or oranges, depending upon the flavor desired, to the hot milk and proceeding as for the vanilla souffle preparation. The souffle may be garnished with a few slices of orange or lemon and then baked. A lemon or orange sauce is served with the souffle.

Souffle Palmyre or Souffle Royale   These are made by using Lady Fingers to form layers. A jam may be used with the Lady Fingers for variety and taste. Fill the bottom of the buttered and sugared souffle dish with a layer of vanilla souffle mixture. Place a layer of Lady Fingers smeared with apricot or other jam over the souffle mixture. Cover the Lady Fingers with another layer of souffle mixture. Place another layer of Lady Fingers over this. Three separate layers may be made. Bake as for the vanilla souffle.

Cheese Souffle

Ingredients	lb	oz	Mixing procedure
Milk (2 qt)	4		Boil the milk. Melt the butter in a sauce-pan. Add the flour and cook slowly as for a roux. Do not brown or darken the souffle Remove the souffle from the fire and add the hot milk gradually and stir well to a smooth consistency. Salt and pepper may be added for taste. Return to the fire and bring to a slow boil, stirring constantly. Remove from the fire and add the egg yolks.
Bread flour		7	
Butter or margarine		12	
Egg yolks	1	12	Add a few yolks at a time and mix well after each addition
Grated cheese [1]	1		
Egg whites	2	8	Whip the egg whites to a medium stiff consistency. Fold the whites into the cheese preparation.

[1] A combination of cheeses may be used. Gruyere cheese, Swiss cheese and Parmesan cheese may be used. Stir the grated cheese into the egg yolk mixture.

The molds or dishes for the cheese souffle are well buttered. They may then be dredged with flour or sprinkled well with grated cheese. Fill the souffle dishes about 1½ in. from the top to allow for the expansion of the eggs and the spreading effect of the melted cheese. Bake the cheese souffles at 375–385°F for approx. 15 min. Serve as soon as removed from the oven. Keep in a double boiler pan with very hot water if delayed in service.

Quiche Lorraine

Quiche Lorraine is often prepared and served as hot hors d'oeuvres. For large quantity service the quiche is baked in regular baking sheet pans and then cut into small squares or cubes. The quiche is usually prepared in advance and then heated and served.

Ingredients	lb	oz	Mixing procedure
Salt		1	Mix the cream, salt, pepper, and egg yolks
Pepper (black or white)		(pinch)	together. Dissolve the flour in the milk and add to the above. Mix well
Light cream	7		
Milk	1	8	
Cake flour		12	
Egg yolks	2	8	
Swiss cheese (grated)	2		Sprinkle evenly over the bottom crust
Parmesan cheese		8	
Well-browned bacon chopped into fine pieces	1	4	

Line the bottom of a baking sheet pan with a thin bottom crust made from either puff pastry dough or rich pie crust dough. Allow the dough bottom to relax. Stipple or puncture the dough with a fork. Partially bake the dough. Fill in the dough edges with thin strips of dough if there is shrinkage in baking. Sprinkle the bottom crust with the cheese and bacon. Pour the prepared custard into the pan. Chopped chives may be sprinkled over the top before baking.

Bake the quiche at 415°F (a reasonably hot oven). This will form a crust. Reduce the heat to about 375°F and bake until the custard is set. Test with the point of a knife. If the blade comes out clean, it is done. It will also have a mild gel feel in the center. Allow the quiche to cool before cutting into desired shapes and portions for service.

Yield: Approx. 1 full sheet pan

12

French Pastries

French pastries include a wide variety of small cakes that are served individually. A considerable number of varieties have been mentioned and described in previous chapters. For example, there are the various French pastries made from cream puff and eclair mix (often called choux paste) and those made from puff pastry dough. These are finished with a variety of pastry custard creams, whipped cream, and a blend of several icings, fillings, and creams. There are others to be made with fruits and special doughs. However, the greatest number of continental style French pastries are made with a selected sponge or chiffon-type cake base. These sponge cakes include the almond and nut sponge varieties. In addition, these French pastries can be filled with special creams and fillings such as frangipane, pastry creams, and an assortment of buttercreams mixed with toasted, ground nuts. Many of the French pastries are given individual continental names because of the difference in finish. They are impressive in both name and appearance.

The pastry chef is very often compelled to mass produce French pastries. French pastries requiring detailed, individual attention are almost an impossibility when large groups are to be served. However, display trays are important to the caterer, and in fine hotel dining rooms and restraurants French pastry displays play a prominent role. This section on French pastry will stress the use of more rapid techniques of producing the pastries and will emphasize the use of the variety sponge cakes

(Genoise) and short dough bases for their production. The pastry chef will refer to the recipes for the sponges as well as the other types of cake mixes used for preparing sheet cakes. The high-ratio mixes may be used. However, the characteristic light cake base for French pastry is the most accepted form and pastry chefs are partial to the sponge cake varieties. The sponge cakes most widely used are of the butter sponge type. These may be the hot milk and butter variety, the straight melted butter variety, or the chiffon cake variety.

While many French pastries start with baking individual cakes in special tart pans or cupcake forms, as well as the oval flan type of pan, individual servings are also made from the basic sheet cakes. The sheets are chilled and then assembled in two or more layers. This will depend upon the type of pastry to be made. Most French pastries are seldom more than 2 in. high at the base although they may be slightly higher as a result of the finish. Pastry chefs assemble the baked sheets with special fillings and have them ready for finishing long in advance. They are kept under refrigeration or in the freezer. The fillings are often the specialty of the pastry chef. Some have developed their own special icings, and creams. These may be blends of creams mixed with toasted nuts, fruits, and cake crumbs. Still others are partial to the natural flavor and taste of creams laced with special liqueurs. Still others favor many decorations made with a variety of chocolate discs, slices, and other forms cut from sweet chocolate that has been melted and formed into thin sheets for the cut-outs.

Emphasis is placed upon the neatness of workmanship and finish. Delicate designs are made with pastry tubes and fine line piping. The selection of colors and flavors for the creams and icings is equally important. The blending of colors and the final garnish and finish will determine the attractiveness of the French pastry. These are dependent upon the skill and judgment of the pastry chef as well as the production requirements. The following French pastries are some of the fundamental varieties which may readily be supplemented by the pastry chef.

French Pastry Fillings, Toppings and Molds

There are fundamental creams and fillings as well as covers that are used by pastry chefs in the production of variety French pastries. Those made with a short or sugar dough base, as for tartlets, will often be filled with a frangipane filling and baked. The frangipane filling may also be mixed with diced fruits and then baked. After baking, the French pastry is finished. As indicated previously, many of the pastries are garnished with a variety of cut-outs made from a sweet chocolate sheet. The handling and tempering of sweet chocolate and the formation of chocolate shells or molds requires explanation to avoid loss of bloom as well as breakage. Marzipan covers are used for many other French pastry varieties as well as for other decorative garnishes. The following are basic formulas for the aforementioned:

Frangipane Filling

Ingredients	lb	oz	Mixing procedure
Almond paste	5		Add the eggs gradually to the almond
Whole eggs	1		paste and mix to a soft, smooth consistency
Sugar	5		Add the sugar and butter with a part of
Butter	5		the egg yolks and mix smooth. Add the
Egg yolks	2		remaining eggs gradually and mix smooth.
Whole eggs	2	8	Scrape kettle often
Cake flour	2		Sift the flours together. Add and mix
Bread flour	2		smooth. Add the flavorings in the final
Vanilla		1	stage of mixing
Rum flavoring		1	

1. This frangipane cream filling may be stored in the refrigerator and used as required.
2. When used in individual tartlet or oval patty pans, the pans are first lined with a thin short or sugar dough bottom. This dough is always prepared in advance and stored in the refrigerator for use as required. The dough is rolled out on a flour-dusted cloth to about ⅛ in. thick.
3. The small pans are lined up close together on a separate section of the bench. The rolled out dough is then rolled up on a rolling pin about 1 in. in diameter. Be sure to dust the short dough lightly with bread flour to prevent sticking when rolling up the dough.
4. Lift the rolling pin with the dough directly over the lined up tart or oval patty pans. (Figs. 12.1 and 12.2.) Unroll the short dough loosely over the tart pans so that part of the dough tends to settle into the center of the pan. Be sure all the pans are covered.
5. Form a ball of short dough about the size of the inside of the tart or oval pan. Dip the ball or oval of dough into bread flour and gently press the dough to the bottom and sides of the pan.
6. Roll the rolling pin over the tops of the pans to cut the dough from the edges of the pans. Press the top of each pan with the palm of the

12.1
Tart shell

12.2
Placing rolled-out dough on shells

hand to remove any excess dough. Cracks or small, uncovered spaces may be filled in with the pieces of rolled out dough removed from the pans.

7. Place the tarts on sheet pans. It is customary to pipe a dot of raspberry or apricot jam in the center of the tart or oval pan before filling with frangipane filling.

8. Fill the tartlets about two-thirds full and bake at 375–380°F. The filling will crack slightly in the center and have a light, golden color when properly baked. After cooling, the basic tartlets or oval pattys are finished in accordance with the particular French pastry to be made.

Yield: Approx. 200–225 small tarts or ovals

Marzipan For Covers and Discs

Marzipan is used extensively for covering sheet cake bases to be used for French pastries. It provides a smooth or decorative cover as well as a variety of flavor. A variety of discs or shapes may be cut out from the sheeted marzipan and used as garnishes or decorative pieces for the French pastry.

Ingredients	lb	oz	Mixing procedure
Almond paste	5		Work the almond paste with part of the
Glucose or		8	egg whites until smooth. Sift the sugar
corn syrup			and starch together. Add with the glucose
Confectioners sugar	5	8	and remaining egg whites and mix
Cornstarch		2	smooth. Blend in the flavorings
Egg whites (variable)		8	
Vanilla		½	
Rum flavoring		¼	

1. Marzipan is quite firm and can be molded by hand or rolled out with a rolling pin. When rolling out, dust the bench or marble with sifted confectioners sugar.
2. Scalloped discs and other shapes may be cut out of the rolled out marzipan.
3. Marzipan may be prepared in advance and stored in a crockery jar or stainless pot and covered. The top may also be covered with a moist cloth or wax paper and aluminum foil to prevent crustation. Cut-outs made from marzipan should be kept in a cool place and covered.

Chocolate for French Pastries

Pastry chefs often keep a supply of various cut-outs or shapes made from melted sweet chocolate to garnish French pastries of various types. Chocolate is very popular as a candy and is very attractive when used in contrast with pastel colors. Many pastries are made with a base of chocolate by pouring melted chocolate into selected molds. Still others, such as square-shaped pastries, have the sides made from square discs cut from a sheet of sweet chocolate. The cut-outs and variety shapes are further supplemented with the use of chocolate shavings and swirls. All of the chocolate garnishes may be prepared in advance and kept in a cool place for use when required.

Chocolate or couverture requires understanding and careful handling in order to achieve the desired results. The rules for handling are few, but must be adhered to when chocolate is being prepared. Sweet chocolate has a rather low melting point and dissolves readily. However, chocolate must be melted at a moderate temperature (not over 90°F) and slowly. Application of excessive heat will cause the separation of the cocoa butter and cause the whitening often known as "blooming." A controlled water bath is advisable. A chocolate warmer may be purchased which has a controlled heat thermostat. The chocolate is broken into small pieces and then placed in the warmer. Some pastry chefs keep a pot of chocolate in some warm place close to the oven but not in direct contact with the heat of the oven. The chocolate is stirred during melting for equal distribution of heat and more rapid solution of the softened lumps of chocolate. The temperature of the melted chocolate is approximately 85°F. Pastry chefs will often add some shaved chocolate to melted chocolate to check for proper temperature. The shavings will soften and melt readily when stirred into the melted chocolate. This technique also tempers melted chocolate that may be just a bit too warm.

Chocolate for cut-outs of various sizes and shapes are made by pouring the melted chocolate on a sheet of parchment paper placed in a sheet pan or left on the bench. (Figs. 12.3 and 12.4.) Work the chocolate with a spatula to a thin sheet that is spread evenly. As the chocolate sets or cools in the cool work area (finishing room if available at a temperature of approximately 65°F) cut into a variety of discs, circles, circles with the holes cut out, square shapes about 2 in. square, rectangles about 1½ × 3 in., and triangles made by cutting diagonally across the squares or the rectangles. The various shapes are then kept in a cool place for use as required in the formation or finishing of the French pastries. Avoid using the hands when mixing or handling chocolate because the temperature of the body and the natural oils or moisture of the hands may cause discoloration in the chocolate. Leftover chocolate pieces may be chopped into smaller shavings or pieces or be returned to the chocolate warmer.

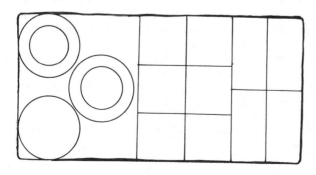

12.3
Shapes drawn on melted
chocolate spread on paper

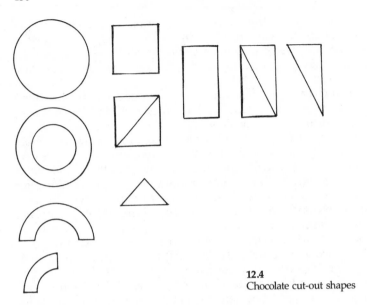

12.4
Chocolate cut-out shapes

Chocolate that thickens readily, even after warming, may be softened or thinned with the use of melted cocoa butter. For warm or hot climates, a small amount of melted wax (1 oz of wax to each 1 lb or 1½ lb of chocolate used) may be added.

Chocolate Molds

As mentioned previously, molds or bases for French pastry are often made from chocolate. These may be purchased from a manufacturer or purveyor of chocolate specialties and filled and finished by the pastry chef. Where these molds are not available for purchase, the pastry chef will use special molds made of tin or plastic. These molds are to be maintained carefully and not used for other purposes other than the preparation of the chocolate molds. A scratch or rough finish such as a scrape or cut will prevent the molds from being released. The tins are to be kept clean and smooth by polishing. This will keep the metal pores closed or sealed and prevent the chocolate from sticking. Molds for chocolate come in various sizes and shapes. For individual French pastry service, the molds may be in round shape as a muffin, slightly flanged, oval shaped as a boat, half-moon shaped, and other special shapes.

To make the chocolate molds, warm the chocolate carefully to the proper temperature (approximately 85°F) and fill the clean, polished molds to the very top with a ladle. Place the molds in a cool place. When a crust starts to form on the surface of the chocolate and around the rim of the mold, pour the contents of the mold back into the pot or warmer. Remove the excess chocolate at the top edge with a knife. Allow the molds to remain for 1–2 hr and then release by turning the molds over. It may be necessary to squeeze the sides of the mold slightly to release the chocolate mold or base. These are stored for later use or used as soon as the molds are firm. Clean the tins or plastics after use.

French Pastry Varieties

French pastry varieties are made in large quantities from sheet cakes that have been put together and chilled. They are easier to handle and cover much more rapidly than the individual pastry bases. The pastry chef will select the special cake formula to be used for preparing the sheet cakes. As indicated, the butter sponge or Genoise is quite popular with many pastry chefs for preparing French pastries. Sheet cakes are often mixed so that a special pastry may have a blend of yellow sponge, chocolate sponge, nut or almond sponge, or chiffon-type sheet cakes. Where several sheets are combined for the base, the sheets are about ½ in. thick so that they are not too high. Where two sheets are combined, the sheets are thicker (three-quarters to 1 in. thick). Where two or more fillings are used to assemble the sheet cakes, the fillings are not very thick in order to avoid excessive height.

Sheet cakes to be used for French pastries are usually placed on large cake boards with the bottom sheet sprinkled liberally with finely chopped nuts or toasted cake crumbs to prevent the cake from sticking. The buttercreams, jams, and jellies are applied evenly and thinly over the entire surface to be sure that each sheet sticks to the next. Sheets should be leveled if uneven by filling in with added cream fillings and then compressing the sheets when assembled. Contrasting cake sheets should be alternated and the cream fillings should highlight the contrast. The chilled sheets are then cut into strips about 3 in. wide. The strips are covered with a thin coating of buttercream and chilled if they are to be covered with a poured fondant icing. (See Figs. 12.5–12.7)

French pastries that are to be covered with a poured fondant icing may be decorated with a center design (spiral or rosette) of colored buttercream and then chilled. The fondant is poured after the buttercream has been firmed. Individual glace-type pastries may be made by cutting the chilled sheets into a variety of shapes (squares, oblongs, diamonds, triangles, and so forth) approximately 2 in. overall. The actual size and shape will be determined by the pastry chef. The cut units may then be garnished with a variety of buttercreams and special fillings, and chilled. The units are then placed on screens and covered with poured fondant icing. The fondant may be colored in various pastel colors. When the units have dried, the pastries may then be decorated with fine line piping designs made with piping gel, chocolate, and other icings.

12.5
Two sheets with one filling of jam or buttercream

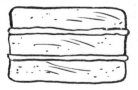

12.6
Three sheets with two fillings

12.7
Two sheets with one heavy filling of chocolate or rum filling

Marzipan Strips

Combine two selected sheets of either the same cake mix or a combination of chocolate and yellow cake. Chill the sheet cakes and then cut into strips about 3 in. wide. Cover the top and sides of the strips with a thin coating of either raspberry or apricot jam. Roll out the prepared marzipan to approximately ⅛ in. thickness, slightly larger than the length of each strip. The tops may be rolled with a grooved or corrugated rolling pin for a special lined design on the marzipan. The marzipan may be left plain. Brush the tops of the marzipan lightly to remove excess confectioners sugar used for rolling. Roll up the marzipan on a narrow rolling pin and unroll over the tops and sides of the strips of cakes. Press the marzipan firmly against the top and sides to be sure that it sticks to the jam. Brush the top of the marzipan with simple syrup to create a shine on the strips. Cut the strips into slices about 2 in. wide. Cut each strip across diagonally to form two triangular-shaped units. With a fine French or star tube and pastry bag, pipe a rosette of buttercream at the wide end of the triangle. Now pipe some pear-shaped buttercream drops toward the point. Fill the center of the rosette with apricot or raspberry jam. (See Figs. 12.8, 12.9)

Chocolate Marzipan Cuts

Add some melted sweet chocolate to the marzipan to color it. The marzipan may firm up slightly. If there is the tendency to crack or dry while rolling, add a small amount of simple syrup to the marzipan and work in. Follow the same procedure as for the plain marzipan cover. The tops may be finished with a chocolate buttercream and garnished with a chocolate disc or semicircle. The pear-shaped drops may be striped lightly with sweet chocolate piped across each of the drops.

Marzipan-Nut Pastry

A sponge nut cake should be used to prepare the sheet cakes. The sheet cakes are slightly thinner because three sheets are usually used to form the sheet cake base. Put the three sheets together with two fillings of buttercream filled with chopped, toasted filberts. Spread the filling evenly when applying and then compress and chill the sheets. When chilled, cut the sheets into strips about 2½ in. wide. Roll out the marzipan to

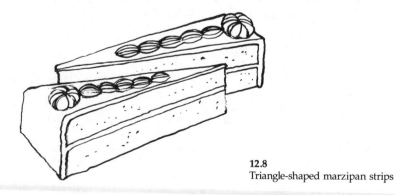

12.8
Triangle-shaped marzipan strips

12.9
Bar-shaped marzipan strips

about ⅛ in. thick. A serrated or corrugated rolling pin may be used to make the fine line design in the marzipan. Remove the excess sugar and then turn the marzipan sheet over by rolling up on a rolling pin and then unrolling on the opposite side. Cover the marzipan with a thin film of jam and place the strip of cake at the edge of the marzipan. Roll the strip in the marzipan until the strip is covered on all sides. The same method of covering only three sides may be used as for the regular marzipan strips. Brush the marzipan with simple syrup to remove the excess sugar and to promote a shine or luster on the surface. The strips are then cut into slices about three-quarters to 1 in. wide. Garnish each slice with a rosette of buttercream in the center. A pecan or walnut half may be placed in the center of each slice.

The strips may be varied by covering them with chocolate marzipan. After covering the strips with marzipan, form a long strip of chocolate marzipan about ½ in. thick and the length of the strip. Brush the strip with simple syrup and then roll the strip in chocolate sprinkles. Pipe a ½ in. strip of chocolate buttercream down the center of the strip with a plain tube. Place the marzipan strip in the center of the buttercream and press in slightly. Cut the strip into slices as for plain marzipan. These are called Chocolate Nut Pastries.

Boat Pastries

The name implies the shape of the pastry. (Fig. 12.10). The special boat-shaped pans are used for these pastries. Short or sugar dough is rolled out as for the tarts and the boat-shaped pans are filled with the dough. The centers of the boat may be filled with any of a number of fillings. A frangipane or almond filling may be used and baked as an almond or frangipane-filled tart. The centers may also be filled with a vanilla or chocolate pastry cream and baked. A small amount of fruit filling may also be used as the basic filling. Once the boat bases are baked, finishing then becomes the option of the pastry chef. The frangipane-filled boats

12.10
Pastry boat

may be filled with a line of mocha or chocolate buttercream drawn down the center with a plain tube. Each side of the center line of buttercream may be filled in with a meringue type of icing or light buttercream. Vanilla may be placed on one side and pink on the other. Level the sides so that a smooth triangular effect is obtained. The boat may be garnished with chocolate shavings or chocolate sprinkles at the very tip. A small chocolate quarter disc may be inserted at one end for greater effect. Boat pastries may also be effectively finished with whipped cream piped in a spiral design over the top of the boat surface. A raised center can also be made with the whipped cream. If the boat is fruit-filled, the top of the cream may be garnished with a slice of the fruit or a whole fruit such as a strawberry brushed with colored apricot coating or currant jelly.

Grape-Type Boats
These may be filled much the same as other boat pastries. The finish in the form of glazed grapes is made with a marshmallow type of icing piped in the form of grapes. Use a medium plain tube to pipe the circles resembling the grapes. Be sure the center is built up before piping the grape drops to give the effect of a grape bunch. The boats may then be chilled and covered with a thin coating of chocolate fondant icing. Place the boats on icing grates set into sheet pans before pouring the icing. When using fresh grapes, use a frangipane base or a custard cream filling. Build up the grapes by placing them into the marshmallow icing close together. Cover the grapes with a boiled apricot coating and allow to cool. (See Fig. 12.11)

French Pastry Oblongs
A variety of French pastries may be made from this basic form or shape. Two or three sheets of butter sponge, chiffon cake, or almond-nut sponge may be used. The sheets are about ½ in. thick. The fillings used to assemble the sheet cakes may vary. Usually, a combination of buttercream and jam or jelly is used. The buttercream flavor and color may be varied, depending upon the finish and overall appearance of the French pastry. However, the shape is basically the same. After the sheets have been chilled, cut into strips about 2½–3 in. wide. Cover the sides of the strip with a buttercream and then garnish suitably for the French pastry. For example, for fruit flavored and colored buttercreams, toasted, chopped filberts or other nuts can be used for the sides. Chocolate-filled and buttercream-decorated pastries will often use chocolate sprinkles as a garnish. Flowered finishes may be made attractive with light sponge cake crumbs around the sides. Cut the strip into slices about 1 in. wide. Lift the unit and hold between the thumb and the fingers. Ice the exposed sides with the same buttercream and garnish with the same garnish as the other two sides originally covered before cutting into slices.

12.11
Grape boat

12.12
Oblong strawberry mallow

Strawberry Mallow Pastry

This is made from the oblongs that have been prepared. The oblongs may be basically formed and refrigerated for finishing as required. Pipe pink colored boiled meringue or marshmallow in a spiral effect with a plain tube down the center of the oblong. Glaze the top with either red piping gel that has been thinned slightly with syrup or with colored apricot coating. Pipe a fine border of yellow buttercream around the edge of the pastry. Pink or other colored icing may be used. The variations are many. (Fig. 12.12)

Chocolate Delights (Delice)

Made by combining the sheets with a chocolate buttercream and an apricot jam for flavor variety. After the oblongs have been cut, ice or cover them with chocolate buttercream and roll the top and sides in chocolate sprinkles. Chill the units in the refrigerator. Remove and cut a slice into the top of the oblong at a slight angle to form a flap that can be lifted or folded. With a French or star tube, pipe a border of yellow or pink buttercream into the flap so that the buttercream design shows clearly. The top may be garnished with a rosette. (Fig. 12.13.)

Floral French Pastries Made from Pastry Oblongs

The oblongs are usually covered with a vanilla buttercream and garnished on the sides with toasted chopped nuts, or lightly toasted sponge cake crumbs. The flowers and stems are piped directly onto the pastry top. Half roses are quite customary, or sprays of buds. The colors may vary from a light pink to a pastel yellow. Stems are usually made with a green buttercream and chocolate piping gel combination. The leaves may be made from the same combination. Pastry chefs will often keep a quantity of prepared flowers for this very purpose. The flowers are usu-

12.13
Chocolate delice

ally made from a rose paste or flower paste and stored in a cool dry place for use. A mild crust will form on the flowers but the centers will remain soft. The following formula is suggested for the rose or flower paste:

Rose Paste or Flower Paste

Ingredients	lb	oz	Mixing procedure
Confectioners sugar	5		Sift the sugar. Add the shortening and
Salt		¼	blend to a medium soft consistency. Add
Emulsified shortening	2	8	the water a little at a time and blend smooth. Add the flavoring and blend in.
Water (variable) or egg whites		(4–6)	Keep the icing covered with a damp cloth when in use
Vanilla		1	

This icing may be made slightly softer and used for wedding cakes and other specialty cakes in addition to the making of variety flowers.

Basket-Type French Pastry

These can be made from baked frangipane-filled tarts or from a combination of baked cuts made from short dough or sugar dough. The tarts may be filled with pastry cream filling and baked. The tarts may be made from the shells cut or shaped from tart shell machines in large numbers. The shells are then filled with a variety of fillings and finished with a whipped cream spiral, marshmallow-type icing, small meringue tart, or finished with a butterfly, basket effect. For the basket variety, use the following procedure:

1. Cover the tart pans with the short dough or special tart or shell dough used for cream-filled pies.
2. A thick sheet cake (about 1 in. thick) made of pound cake may be used. Cut out circles about 2½ in. round.
3. Cut out short dough cookies about 2½ in. round for the tops of the tarts or cake circles. Cut out and bake an equal number of circles with the centers cut out. The cookie circles are covered with apricot jam and dipped in chocolate sprinkles. The baked circles are cut in half after baking to form a basket handle.
4. Pipe a border of green or pink buttercream down the center top of the cake or tart. Cut the chocolate sprinkled top in half and insert halves into the buttercream so that they stand out as wings. Under each wing pipe a border of pink buttercream. Insert the half ring into the center to form the handle of the basket. The ends of the handle may have a small star or rosette inserted where the end of the handle meets the top of the basket. Color arrangements and covering for the wings may be replaced with other types of garnish such as finely chopped or macaroon-type coconut that has been lightly toasted. (Fig. 12.14.)

12.14
Cream basket

Metropolitan (Cup-Shape) French Pastries

These desserts or French pastries are made from a cupcake base made from sponge cake or high-ratio type cake batters. As the cake batters vary, so do the varieties of French pastry made from them. This means that yellow, chocolate, mocha, white, or devil's food cakes can be made into cupcake form and used as the base for the pastries. The muffin or cupcake pans (fluted or tart pans may be used) are greased and dusted lightly with bread flour. Fill the pans half full and bake as for regular metropolitans. Cover the sides and top with a thin covering of jam, jelly, or apricot coating that is heated. Then coat the sides with toasted, chopped filberts. (Figs. 12.15 through 12.18.) For the mocha dessert (Fig. 12.19), pipe a rosette of mocha buttercream in the center. A dot of mocha jam may be placed in the center. For variety, cover the sides with chocolate sprinkles and ice the top with chocolate fondant. A rosette of chocolate buttercream or fudge may be used to garnish the center. A strawberry or raspberry pastry is made by covering the sides and top with raspberry jam and rolling the sides in sponge cake crumbs or chopped nuts. The centers may be decorated with a rosette of pink or yellow buttercream. The centers may also have a dot of raspberry or apricot jam placed in the center.

French Pastry Glace Varieties

These are usually made from the tart pan forms. The scalloped edges enhance the appearance. The plain cupcakes may also be used. The baked tart cakes or cupcakes are often filled by cutting them in half and filling with a jam or jelly, or buttercream. Very often, the buttercream is mixed with some of the selected jam or jelly for a special blend. The tops are replaced and pressed gently. At this point, the tops may be decorated with a rosette or round drop effect, or a pear-shaped drop extended from the center to the edge of the inverted cupcake base. The cakes are then chilled. The chilled cakes are placed on icing grates set into sheet pans and covered with a fondant icing so that the entire surface of each cake is covered. A variety of iced cakes may be made. Starting with vanilla fondant, the fondant may be warmed and colored in small amounts to cover a specific number of pastries. The colors of pastel yellow, pink, green, orange, are used. The icing drippings are collected and made into a chocolate fondant icing for coverage of the remainder of the pastries to be glazed. The units are allowed to dry and then may be garnished with a fine star tube or French tube decoration. Pastries with a buttercream

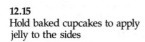

12.15
Hold baked cupcakes to apply
jelly to the sides

12.16
Roll cupcakes in coconut, covering sides
completely

12.17
Fill pastry bag with butter cream to make
border around rim of cupcake

12.18
Finished metropolitan with jelly center

12.19
Mocha dessert

design before coverage with fondant will have a special effect after coverage.

Tart-Shaped French Pastries

These are made by making a variety of tarts filled with either frangipane or almond tart filling (see almond tarts) and baked. The tart pans may be filled with special sponge cake or high ratio cake mix and baked for the base of the pastry. The pans are greased and dusted with flour. The tarts are decorated with the top facing up, providing a larger area for decorating. These pastries may also be made by putting two sponge or special sponge sheets together with jam or jelly. The sheets are chilled and are then cut out into circles about 2½ in. in diameter. The sides may be covered with jam and garnished with sponge cake crumbs made from the leftovers of the cut-out discs. Toasted cake crumbs or nuts may be used for the baked tart cake bases. The tops of the cakes are iced with a white, yellow, or pink fondant icing.

The cherry tart (Fig. 12.20) is made by dipping two glazed whole cherries in hot apricot jam or coating that has been colored red. The twig effect is made with chocolate piping gel. The leaves are made with green buttercream blended with chocolate piping gel.

The rose tart (Fig. 12.21) is made by icing the top of the baked tart or cut out cake circle with a chocolate fondant. When dry, a pink or yellow tea rose is piped directly on the cake. Pastry chefs will often prepare the flowers in quantity and have them ready for immediate placement. The flower is surrounded by wide pale green leaves.

Filled Cup-Type French Pastries

Cupcakes made with a fine sponge or chiffon cake mix are often the base for the filled cup-type French pastries. For example, the butterfly cupcake is often used for a French pastry when filled with whipped cream. The high ratio mixes can be used with equally fine results. These cupcakes are often baked in paper liners and served as they would be for the butterfly variety. The French pastries made from cup-type cakes that have no paper liners usually have the sides covered with a buttercream icing or jam, and then are garnished with a variety of garnishes suited to the particular pastry. The filled cup varieties have the centers cut out in a deeper cone shape, rather than the flat top removed as for butterfly pas-

12.20
Cherry tart

12.21
Rose tart

12.22
Baked cupcake

12.23
Top cut off the cupcake

12.24
Cream bagged on top of
the cupcake

12.25
Cone effect upon removal of cupcake center

12.26
Finished filled cup-type French pastry

try. The baked cupcakes (Fig. 12.22) are cut into the top with a sharp, pointed knife (paring knife) at a 45° angle to form the cone shape (Fig. 12.23). The tops are removed and the hollow centers are filled with a variety of creams and other fillings. The cone tops are inverted when replaced to form a round cone shape. The cones may be dipped in hot apricot jam that has been colored or into hot currant jelly for effect. They may be covered with a buttercream and then further decorated with a French or star tube after being placed on top of the filling. The tops are then garnished with a suitable garnish. Each of the pastries that follow are made in this manner. (Fig. 12.22 through 12.26.)

Lemon Mocha Cup French Pastry

The cupcake base for this pastry may be baked with a paper liner or left plain. If left plain, the sides are usually covered with mocha buttercream and then rolled in chopped walnuts or lightly toasted cake crumbs. Cut the center out in a cone shape. Fill the hollow with a lemon cream filling. A vanilla or chocolate cream may be used and the name of the pastry changed to suit the filling. Replace the cut-out top with the pointed side facing up. Press down quite firmly to be sure the base of the cone sticks to the filling. Be careful not to force the filling over the sides of the cup.

With a medium star tube cover the entire top with mocha buttercream so that there is a spiral effect. A similar effect may be obtained by covering the cone with mocha buttercream using a spatula. Using a pastry comb, go around the buttercream lightly to create the grooved effect. The top may be garnished with a sprinkle of chopped walnuts or pecans.

Chinese French Pastry

Remove the centers of the baked cups. Be sure to form a cone-shaped effect. Fill the hollow in the center with chocolate buttercream. A spatula or pastry bag and tube may be used to fill the centers. The sides may be covered with chocolate buttercream and garnished with chocolate cake crumbs or chocolate sprinkles. Replace the top by pressing the round base well into the buttercream to be sure it sticks. The top may be covered with red piping gel applied with a spatula. The top may be dipped into hot apricot coating that has been colored red. Be careful when dipping. A blend of currant jelly and apricot jam may be used for the dip. A thin border of crumbs or sprinkles may be placed around the edge of the pastry.

Chocolate Cream French Pastry

A chocolate sponge cake or high ratio cake mix may be used to make the base. For the finer desserts, a tart shell filled with chocolate pastry cream may be used. If using the cupcake as a base, cut the centers out in a cone shape. Fill the hollow with chocolate pastry cream or a chocolate buttercream to which toasted, ground filberts and chopped pecans have been added. Chopped walnuts may be used in addition to the other nutmeats. Replace the top of the cupcake with the base of the cake cone pressed gently into the filling to cause it to stick. Cover the top with chocolate buttercream applied with either a spatula or pastry bag and star tube. The top is garnished with chocolate cake crumbs or chocolate shavings. The top is then dusted lightly with confectioners sugar. If the tart form is used, cover the top with chocolate buttercream applied with a star tube in a cone-shaped form. Garnish with chocolate cake crumbs or chocolate sprinkles and dust lightly with confectioners sugar.

Mushrooms

These French pastries are also filled pastries and the centers are cut out and used for a mushroom effect. The centers are not cut quite as deeply. A variety of cake mixes can be used for the base. This pastry can be made quickly and in large volume. Cut the centers out and place to one side. Fill the cupcakes with any desired filling, such as a flavored and colored buttercream, various fruit fillings, whipped cream, marshmallow icing, boiled icing, or a blend of two icings. Replace the top over the well filled centers which are about 1/4–1/2 in. above the level of the cupcake. Be sure the smooth side faces up. Dust the top with confectioners sugar. The tops may be garnished with a rosette of the icing or cream used for the center.

Savarins and Babas

Savarins and babas are made from a rich, yeast-raised dough that is well mixed for maximum gluten development. The savarins are leavened by the fermenting action of the yeast and also by the high percentage of eggs and egg yolks used to make the dough. The baked babas are light and quite porous. This is a necessary characteristic in that the babas are dipped in a hot rum syrup to absorb some of the syrup as a sponge and maintain their structure. While a yeast-raised baba dough that has been properly conditioned may be converted to a savarin dough by the addition of added eggs to form the semiliquid dough, the pastry is better when made from the regular dough.

Savarin Dough

Ingredients	lb	oz	Mixing procedure
Yeast (variable)		(6–8)	Dissolve the yeast and sugar in the water.
Water	1	8	Add the flour and mix to a soft sponge
Sugar		2	dough. Allow the sponge dough to rise
Bread flour	1	8	until it starts to settle
Sugar		10	Add the sugar, salt, milk, and the egg
Salt		1½	yolks and blend with the sponge dough.
Nonfat dry milk		8	Add the bread flour and mix to a dough.
Egg yolks	1		Add the remaining eggs gradually while
Whole eggs	2	8	running machine at second speed. When
Vanilla or rum flavoring		1	smooth, add the melted butter gradually while machine is running and develop
Bread flour	4	8	dough
Melted butter	3		
Raisins or currants (if used for babas)	1	8	

1. The finished dough is a very soft, semiliquid dough. Allow the dough to reach final conditioning by almost doubling in size. The kettle for the dough should be greased with melted butter for ease in removing the dough and to prevent sticking. Placing the dough in a warm place will speed up the final conditioning of the dough.
2. Note is made of the fact that raisins or currants are used for the individual babas if desired. The babas are like firm-bodied cupcakes.
3. Savarins, large or small, are baked in special ring forms for either the small individual Savarin pastry or the Savarin baked in large ring pans with the scalloped sides. These do not contain raisins or currants. The pans are well greased with melted butter. The conditioned dough is usually placed into a pastry bag with a large plain tube. The dough is then bagged into the small baba pans (similar to tart pans or deeper pans with grooved or scalloped sides) or special small ring pans for the savarins. Fill the pans about one third to slightly less than half full. Large pans are filled in the same manner.

The dough may be dropped out by hand for the large pans.
4. The pans are placed in the proof box or other warm place and the dough is allowed to rise until it has about doubled in size.
5. Place the pans into the oven carefully. Small units are baked on large sheet pans. Large units may also be baked on double pans. Bake at 385–395°F. Larger units are baked at slightly lower temperatures. When properly baked, the babas or savarins will feel firmly spongy to the touch. Larger units should be baked through thoroughly to maintain the open, sponge-like grain and texture after baking.
6. Allow the baked units to cool and then dip in the following special rum syrup:

Yield: Approx. 100–120 small babas or savarins

Dipping Syrup for Baba and Savarin

Ingredients	lb	oz	Mixing procedure
Water	5		Dissolve the sugar in the water. Add the
Granulated sugar	6		oranges and lemon and bring to a rolling
Sliced oranges (2)			boil. Remove any film or foam with a
Sliced lemon (1)			skimmer. Remove the fruits and add rum
Glucose	1		or kirsch. Rum flavoring is used if a non-
Rum flavoring		2	alcoholic syrup is desired

Note: If rum or kirsch is used for syrup, add from 1 pt to 1 qt of either after the syrup has been boiled and removed from the fire.

Finishing the Babas

Dip the individual babas in the hot syrup and then place on a wire grate set in a sheet pan to contain the draining hot syrup. After draining, brush the babas with hot apricot jam or apricot coating. A blend of jam and apricot coating may be used. If the syrup glaze is too thick, add some simple syrup to it. Babas may be garnished with a cherry on top and leaves made with green piping gel or marzipan. The cherry and marzipan may be brushed lightly with hot apricot jam. The individual or large babas may be cut in half after glazing and then filled with whipped cream for Baba Chantilly.

Oval or boat-shaped babas are sliced partially at the top after they are dipped and glazed. The lid is then spread and filled with whipped cream. This dessert is called Marignan. Large babas are finished in the same manner as the individual units. These may be cut into portions and kept together to serve groups at a table.

Savarins are baked in small, individual molds or in larger ring pans. The savarins are dipped into the hot dipping syrup and allowed to drain as were the babas. The savarins are then glazed with the hot apricot coating or apricot jam. Small or single servings are garnished on the sides with chopped, toasted nuts. Filberts may be used. The individual servings are then placed in paper cups or on serving dishes with a bottom doily. The centers are filled with whipped cream. The cream is piped in a rosette form and the center of the cream is slightly higher than the level of the savarin. It has a resemblance to a glazed ring doughnut with the hollow center filled with whipped cream.

Savarin Creme   Slice the glazed savarin in half. Fill the center with pastry cream custard bagged out with a plain tube. A Bavarian cream may be used for the filling. The tops may be garnished with glazed cherries placed in a rosette of whipped cream.

Savarin Chantilly   This is made by cutting the savarin in half and filling the center with cream and mixed, diced fruits. The fruits may be soaked in hot syrup flavored with kirsch and then drained before placing into the savarin. The savarins are then garnished with whipped cream in the center or the top may have some rosettes of whipped cream on top.

French pastries are often garnished with crushed or powdered croquante or nougat. Very often, powder croquante will be added to special dough bases used for making French pastry. While croquante and praline may be purchased, some pastry chefs may wish to make these garnishes. They may be stored in closed containers for use as required.

Croquante or Nougat

Ingredients	lb	oz	Mixing procedure
Almonds	3		Roast carefully in the oven and cool. Chop or grind the almonds coarsely
Water	2		Boil the sugar and water to a soft ball
Sugar	4		stage (240°F). Skim any foam or impurities
Cream of tartar		½	from the surface. Wash the sides of the kettle with a brush dipped in water. Boil to a light caramel (gold) color and remove from fire

Add the almonds and stir in well. Pour the mixture on an oiled section of a marble-top table. Sheet pans that have been oiled may be used. Allow the croquante to cool, then break into pieces. The croquante may be crushed by rolling with a large rolling pin to form smaller pieces. These pieces may also be ground to a finer, powder state. If cut-outs of various forms are to be made from the nougat, cut the forms or roll up on a thin, oiled rolling pin while the nougat is still warm.

Praline Paste

Ingredients	lb	oz	Mixing procedure
Sugar	3		Place these ingredients in a saucepan over
Filberts or hazelnuts	2		a small flame and stir constantly until the
Almonds (toasted)	1		sugar melts and starts to take on a light yellow or gold color

Pour on an oiled marble table or oiled pan. When cool, break into small pieces with a rolling pin. Grind to a fine, powder-like consistency. Store in containers and use as required.

Quick French Pastry Specialties

The following are French pastries that may be made rather quickly and are quite impressive when finished properly and neatly. They are listed with their continental names. Where feasible and appropriate, an American name will be listed.

Cardinals (Fruit-Filled Pastries)
Sandwich two sponge sheets, or butter sponge sheets, together with a filling composed of apricot jam mixed with crushed pineapple. Pineapple pie filling may be used as a blend with the jam. Other fruit fillings in which the fruits are chopped finely may be used. Press the sheets together well and chill. After chilling, cut the sheet into 2 in. squares. Cover the sides with a thin currant jelly. A mixture of currant jelly and buttercream may be used for the sides since this will handle easier than plain currant jelly. Garnish the sides with chopped almonds by dipping the sides directly into the chopped almonds. Brush the tops of the squares with hot apricot jam or coating. Place 2 quarter slices of pineapple (cut full slices of pineapple into quarters) in the center with the hollows forming a center. Place a glace cherry in the center and brush with hot apricot jam.

Glorieux (Fruited Frangipane Tart)
Use the scalloped tart pans for these French pastries. Line the pans with short dough or sugar dough. Place a dot of raspberry or currant jam in the center. Fill the tart with frangipane filling (almond filling) and bake at 345°F. When cool, remove the tarts from the pans. Cover the tops of the tarts with a film of hot apricot jam. Sprinkle the tops with mixed, diced fruits that have been soaked in a hot rum or kirsch syrup and drained. Brush the fruits lightly with the hot apricot jam and sprinkle lightly with chopped pistachio nuts.

Noisetier (Walnut French Pastry)
An almond sponge or a nut sponge may be used for the base. Use three sheets of cake about ½ in. thick for each sheet. Combine a mocha or walnut-flavored buttercream with some chopped walnuts. Sandwich the sheets together with this buttercream. Press down firmly to be sure the sheets stick together. Refrigerate the sheets. Cut the sheets when chilled into 2 in. squares. Place a small rosette of coffee buttercream in the center of each square. Place the squares on an icing grate placed on a sheet pan and cover the squares by pouring coffee-flavored fondant icing over the squares. When dry, place a half walnut in the center.

Sans Souci (Praline French Pastry)

Use a nut sponge or mocha chiffon cake for the sheet cakes. Prepare three sheet cakes about ½ in. thick. Mix buttercream with mocha flavoring and praline of fine consistency. Press the sheets together and refrigerate until chilled thoroughly. This will make cutting easier. Cut into 2 in. squares. Use a sharp French knife and dip knife into hot water at intervals to obtain a smooth cut. Cover the sides and top with mocha buttercream. Garnish the sides and top with crushed praline. Dust the tops lightly with confectioners sugar before serving. If praline is not available, use a croquante that has been finely crushed.

Castillon (Coffee-Nougat French Pastry)

Prepare three sheets made from almond sponge or mocha flavored chiffon cake. Sandwich the sheet cakes with a nougat or caramel flavored buttercream. Refrigerate the sheet cakes and then cut out with a 1½–2 in. round cutter. Cut closely to avoid excessive leftovers. Spread the cake leftovers from sheet cake on the bench and chop finely. Mix the chopped cake crumbs with mocha or caramel buttercream to form a medium thick paste. Form the paste into round balls and refrigerate. The round balls should be no more than 1 in. in diameter. When the cake circles and the balls have been chilled, press out a rosette of buttercream in the center of the circles and press the round ball into the rosette. Place the pastries on an icing grate set into a sheet pan. Cover the pastries with warm, coffee-flavored fondant. The center wall may be decorated with a fine spiral of chocolate mixed with piping gel. The center may also be decorated with a chocolate disc.

Pistachio Squares

Prepare three sheets from a genoise or butter sponge cake. The sheets should be about ½ in. thick when baked. Sandwich the sheets with a chocolate-mocha buttercream and then refrigerate. Chill the sheets and then cut into 2 in. squares. Using a well flavored, pistachio buttercream (add some green coloring to the buttercream for added color) cover the sides and top of the squares. Dip the sides in finely chopped pistachio nuts to cover the sides. Garnish the top with a fine rosette made with pistachio buttercream and place a pistachio nut in the center of the rosette. These pastries may also be made in round or oval form with a slight change in the decoration shape placed on the top. Use a center rosette with pear-shaped drops extending from the rosette.

Esperance (Lemon-Apricot Triangles)

Use a butter sponge that is flavored with added lemon rind and lemon juice. A lemon chiffon cake mix may also be used for the sheets. Prepare three sheets about ½ in. thick when baked. Fill the sheets with a smooth apricot jam. If the jam is too thick, thin with some simple syrup. A blend of apricot jam and buttercream may be used for the filling. Press the sheets together well and chill in the refrigerator. When chilled, cut into even strips about 3 in. wide. Cover with a thin coating of pistachio flavored and colored buttercream and chill. When chilled cover the entire strip with pistachio flavored and colored fondant icing. Allow the icing to dry and then cut into strips about 2½ in. wide. Now cut each strip diagonally across to form triangular wedges. Decorate the center with a small rosette of pistachio buttercream. Form two pear-shaped drops on either side of the rosette. Place a pistachio nut in the center of the rosette.

Marjolaine (Custard-Sponge Pastry)

Prepare three sheets about ½ in. thick using a butter sponge or orange chiffon cake mix. Use a custard pastry cream for the filling. The custard may be frenched by adding 2 qt of prepared, vanilla buttercream to the pastry cream and blending together. Chill the sandwiched sheet cakes and then cut the sheet into 2 in. squares. Cover the squares with the frenched custard cream and dip the sides and top into sponge cake crumbs which have been very lightly toasted. A blend of chocolate and plain sponge cake crumbs may be used if chocolate cake is available. Dust the tops of the pastries lightly with confectioners sugar before serving.

Potato French Pastry

This type of pastry enables the pastry chef to use almost all leftover cake pieces which remain from the cut-out type of French pastry. Usually, mocha, nut, almond, and coffee flavored and colored sponge or other types of cake are used for this purpose. The cakes, layered or plain, that have been left over have usually been refrigerated for this purpose by the pastry chef. Mix all the leftover pieces of cake in a bowl with a rum syrup to moisten. Add more syrup if the cakes are very dry. A pure rum may be used, if cost is not a factor. Combine the cakes with sufficient buttercream to form a medium firm texture. Do not compress to a solid paste. The body of the potato must be reasonably light and quite edible. Mold the pieces removed from the mixture into potato shapes of almost equal size. The shapes may be varied slightly. Refrigerate the shaped potatoes in the refrigerator to firm them up. It may be advisable to freeze them for a few minutes before enrobing them.

Marzipan paste is used to enrobe the shaped potatoes. Roll out the marzipan on a canvas cloth or table top. Use confectioners sugar that has been sifted for dusting purposes. Pastry chefs will often use cornstarch or a blend of cornstarch and confectioners sugar for rolling out the marzipan. This will eliminate stickiness during rolling. The marzipan should be quite thin (less than ⅛ in. thick.) Divide the marzipan into squares large enough to enrobe the entire potato cake shape. The ends of the marzipan may be moistened slightly with egg white or water to seal the ends. Remove any excess marzipan but be sure the entire potato is covered. Roll the potato into a chocolate powder (a blend of confectioners sugar and cocoa that has been sifted several times to form a pale brown color may be used). Eyes and slight creases may be made in the potato with a modeling tool. The eyes may be further accentuated with a dot made with sweet chocolate or cookie dip that dries rapidly. The potatoes are usually displayed with an assortment of other French pastries.

Florentin (Orange French Pastry)

Make three sheets about ½ in. thick from a butter sponge, Genoise, or orange chiffon layer cake mix. Sandwich the three layers together with orange flavored buttercream. A blend of buttercream may be combined with an orange custard cream for increased flavor. Chill the compressed sheets in the refrigerator. Trim the edges of the sheet cake and then cut into strips about 3 in. wide. Cover the sides and top of the strips with orange flavored and colored buttercream. The orange flavoring usually contains the orange color. Where this is lacking, add yellow coloring with a few drops of red coloring to obtain the orange color. Garnish the sides of the strips with toasted chopped almonds or chopped walnuts. The top may be combed with a comb in a wavelike effect. After 1¼ in. spaces have been marked off for cutting into portions, decorate centers with rosettes of orange buttercream. The center may be garnished with an orange slice that has been brushed with hot apricot jam. Mandarin orange segments are often used for the garnish.

Supremes (Round Pistachio Pastries)

Use a butter sponge, genoise, or almond sponge cake to prepare the sheets for this pastry. The sheets are sandwiched with a pistachio flavored and colored buttercream and refrigerated. The chilled sheets are then cut into round shapes with a 2-in. round cutter. Use three sheets, each about ½ in. thick, for assembling into the one large sheet. Many pastry chefs will use muffin pans that have been greased and dusted with bread flour to prepare the cake bases for this pastry. This avoids the cutting of shapes and the accumulation of cake scraps. The round cakes are cut in half and filled individually with the pistachio buttercream. The round pastry bases are placed on an icing grate placed in a pan. The pastries are covered with pistachio fondant on top and sides. The tops of the centers may first be garnished with a rosette of pistachio buttercream and chilled before pouring the fondant. The pastries are then garnished with a half pistachio nut.

Sevilles (Apricot French Pastry)

These pastries may be made into a round or a bar shape. Use a butter sponge flavored with the rind of fresh lemons. A lemon flavored chiffon cake may be used for the preparation of three sheet cakes about ½ in. thick. Assemble the baked and cooled sheets with smooth apricot jam. The jam may be combined with vanilla buttercream for easier spread and variety. Compress the sheets and chill in the refrigerator. For round shapes, cut out with a 2-in. round cutter. For bar shapes or rectangular shapes, cut into strips 2½ in. wide. Cover the tops of the rounds or the strips with fine apricot jam. Place an apricot half in the center of each pastry with smooth surface facing up. Brush the tops of the apricot and the surface of the pastry top with hot apricot coating and jam. The sides may be covered with apricot buttercream and garnished with toasted, sliced almonds.

13

Petits Fours and Cookies

Petits fours and cookies are widely used as the finishing touch to a meal where dining is reasonably formal and somewhat sumptuous. Caterers will most often present diners with trays filled with a variety of petits fours and cookies. Displays, which may be considered an introduction to the pastries and desserts available in the dining establishment, are often placed in prominent places for the diner to observe the workmanship of the pastry chef. Pastry chefs will usually extend themselves in the preparation of the petits fours and cookies. However, due to the factors of cost, time, volume of production, and service, it is quite understandable that a pastry chef will use the fastest production methods to meet the requirements of institutional, large-volume feeding. The pastry chef must also limit the amount of time spent in decorating petits fours. Thus, the finer techniques of production may have to be blended with the more rapid production methods.

Petits Fours Glaces

Petits fours glaces are small cakes, almost bite-size, that are covered with a fondant-type icing. The cakes are cut into various shapes before they are covered with warm fondant. The tops of the individual cakes may be garnished with a buttercream design and chilled before covering. Others may have a rosette or similar design piped on the petit four and a nut or fruit inserted before covering with fondant. The iced units may then be further decorated with fine line piping, small floral displays, or gar-

449

nished with a variety of nuts and small fruits. Other petits fours may be shaped in special molds with a marzipan cover before they are covered with the fondant. The following are basic procedures for the production of petits fours glaces.

Glace refers to the covering of the small cake with a smooth type of poured icing such as fondant icing. In order to have a smooth surface after pouring the icing, the units must be made from a cake that is close-grained and reasonably firm. These characteristics apply to cakes that are made from a pound cake batter. They may also be made from cake mixes that will provide for similar characteristics. The close grain and smooth texture allows for easier handling and a reasonably smooth surface to which the poured fondant will adhere.

Petits fours glaces made from softer or sponge-type batters are usually bagged out into various shapes and forms and then two units are sandwiched together to provide for a smooth surface. This is like putting two Lady Fingers together to obtain an oval, finger shape with a smooth top surface. For the sponge-type cake base for petits fours glaces, commonly known as Othellos, the Lady Finger recipe may be used, or the following recipe may be used for bagging out the individual shapes and forms.

Othello Petits Fours Base

Ingredients	lb	oz	Mixing procedure
Sugar	1	2	Warm the sugar and yolks slightly. Add
Salt		¼	the glucose and whip until quite thick.
Glucose or		4	Fold in the lemon rind
corn syrup			
Egg yolks	3		
Rind of 2 lemons			
Egg whites	3		Whip to a soft peak and gently fold into
Sugar	1		the yolks
Cake flour	3		Sift the flour and gently fold into the
			above. Do not overmix

1. Bag out the batter with a pastry bag and plain tube. The tube should be about ½ in. in diameter. This provides an easy flow and less compression of the cake mix. Bag out the variety of shapes (round, oval, crescent, finger, and so forth) on parchment paper-lined pans.
2. Bake the Othellos as soon as they are bagged out, at a temperature of 400°F. Test for proper bake by pressing or touching the units gently. They should feel soft and springy. Remove from the oven when just done. The units will continue to bake or dry after removal from the oven. The various units are sandwiched together with selected jams or fudge-type icings.
3. Similar shapes may be cut from prepared sheet cakes. Two thin sheet cakes may be filled with a variety of jams or jellies and sandwiched together. The sheets are then chilled before cutting into var-

ious shapes and sizes. Pound cake sheets, or cakes made from batters similar to pound cake, are usually made about 1 in. thick if they are not to be sandwiched.

4. The sheets, single or sandwiched, are usually covered with a light covering of apricot jam. They are then covered with a thin layer of marzipan. Roll out the marzipan on a canvas cloth or table top using confectioners sugar or cornstarch for dusting purposes, and then trim to the size of the sheet cake. A sheet pan lightly placed on the rolled out marzipan can be used as a guide. Then lightly dust the marzipan with sugar and starch and roll up on a thin rolling pin to be unrolled on top of the cake. Roll the marzipan gently with the rolling pin to ensure good adherence and then trim the excess from the edges. Chill the sheets before cutting. When chilled, cut into various shapes. A long ruler may be used as a guide for the knife and as a straight edge to get even cuts and units of equal size.

5. At this point, the cut-out shapes may be garnished with a rosette or other design made with buttercream. A nut or small glazed fruit piece may be inserted into the buttercream. These units are placed on grates, set in sheet pans, and carefully placed into the refrigerator to chill the buttercream.

6. Those that are left with a plain surface top are placed on the icing grates about 1–2 in. apart. The fondant icing, prepared in advance, is usually ready for pouring. The temperature of the fondant is mildly warm, not over 110°F. It may be necessary to add simple syrup to the fondant to achieve the smooth-flowing consistency. Petits fours need uniform icing coverage to be attractive.

7. The fondant is used in its white state for petits fours that are to be covered with white fondant. Other pastel shades are mixed as required in small pots which should have pouring spouts to control the amount and coverage of the fondant icing. Where these pots are not available, fill pastry bags with ¼ in. plain tubes and pour the fondant through the tubes over the petits fours. Cover the units evenly and fully to avoid overicing.

8. When all the petits fours are covered with the lighter, pastel shades of icing, the icing accumulated in the sheet pans is gathered together and mixed into one pot to be used for the chocolate fondant to cover the petits fours. It is usually necessary to soften the chocolate fondant with simple syrup because of the binding effect of the chocolate or fudge base used to make the fondant chocolate.

9. Care is necessary when covering the units with buttercream designs on top. Avoid smearing the tops and allow the fondant to fully cover the designs and then permit it to cover the sides of the unit fully.

10. Units that are to be decorated with fine line designs on top are usually placed on sheet pans lined with parchment paper. Fondant used for fine line designs should be smooth and somewhat firmer or stiffer than the icing used for pouring. Pastry chefs may often add a small amount of white fudge base to the pastel shades of fondant used for piping. This provides for control of the piping and

prevents the design from running or spreading over the dry coverage of the petits fours. Pastry chefs will also use colored piping gel for the fine line designs. Melted chocolate will firm up the fondant, as will chocolate fudge base. A blend of chocolate and piping gel is often used for fine line designs made with chocolate.

Small paper decorating cones made from parchment paper or special wax paper are used for the final petits fours decoration. Be sure the hole is small to provide a fine line. When making flower and spray designs on petits fours, leaves and stems are often made with a blend of green buttercream with one side of the cone streaked with a chocolate piping gel. The contrast is effective. Small leaves made of marzipan may also be used. The small buds or drop flowers (daisies, dahlias, violets, carnations, lilies of the valley, sweet peas, apple blossoms, geraniums, and so forth) are usually made in advance from royal icing and kept for this purpose. Refer to the illustrations for guidance and choice in finishing the petits fours glace. (See Figs. 13.1 and 13.2.)

Petits fours glaces are very attractive when arranged properly on trays that have been lined with special liners or doilies. Very often the colorful pieces, floral decorated units, are centered and then surrounded with other petits fours or a variety of cookies.

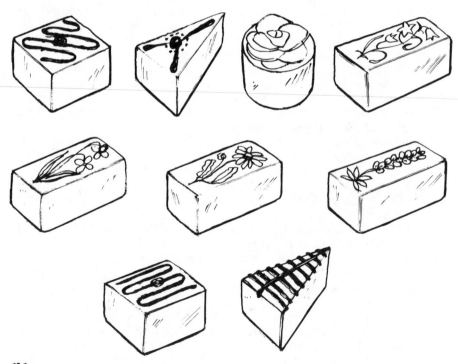

13.1
Fondant-iced petits fours with fondant-made
designs

Royal icing is used for making the small flowers to decorate the petits fours glace. The following recipe for royal icing will serve the purpose well. This icing may also be used for larger flowers. When thinned down with egg whites, this icing can also be used to cover the layers for wedding cakes and special cakes where a hard, dry surface is desired.

Royal Icing

Ingredients	lb	oz	Mixing procedure
Confectioners sugar	5		Sift the sugar and cream of tartar. Add approximately two-thirds of the sugar to the egg whites and whip at medium speed until blended. Add the remaining sugar and whip to a thick peak
Cream of tartar		½	
Egg whites (variable)	1		

1. This icing tends to dry rapidly when exposed to the air. Keep it covered with a damp cloth at all times.
2. Bag out or shape the variety of drop flowers on parchment paper.
3. Allow to dry and store for later use. Use colors carefully and mix in well to avoid streaks.

13.2
Decorated petits fours

Eclair and cream puff paste (choux paste) is often used for the preparation of petits fours glaces. (See the chapter on eclairs and cream puffs.) The cream puffs are dropped out the size of a quarter and baked. When baked, they are about 1¼ in. in diameter. Eclairs are bagged out about ¼ in. thick and about 1½–2 in. in length and baked until golden brown and crisp. The shells are then filled with a variety of pastry creams or custards and then dipped in a variety of fondant icings. Chocolate and coffee are the most popular. They are striped when dry.

Marzipan Fruits

Marzipan fruits are often included in a select variety of petits fours. Their variety, colorful appearance, miniature size, and attractive finish are impressive. To achieve all of this, the pastry chef must make the marzipan fruits genuinely resemble real fruits. Pictures of the fruits or vegetables in natural color are very helpful to the beginner. Refer to the marzipan recipe for the preparation of the marzipan base. For uniformity of size, the marzipan units may be scaled into small pieces weighing from ½–1 oz each. Larger fruits, such as apples and bananas, will require more marzipan. In addition to the fruits, small green leaves may be molded from the marzipan. Small brown twigs may also be prepared in advance. Many fruits may first be shaped with the hands. Modeling tools are very helpful in making the final indentations and creases in the fruits and vegetables to make them more realistic. When shaped, the marzipan fruits and vegetables are placed on clean pans or parchment paper and allowed to dry overnight to form a slight crust and make handling and coloring of the marzipan fruits easier.

Colors for most fruits and vegetables are most often subdued or pastel. In some instances, a deeper color is required as in the case of the deep redness of an apple that gradually shades off to a light yellow green. Paste or powder colors are used effectively when dissolved in pure alcohol. A syrup solution may be prepared for coloring in which the color is dissolved in separate little trays and then applied with a brush or spray applicator. Applicators may be obtained readily since these are available for many different purposes. When using a brush, it is advisable to have a stiff brush for firm application and a softer brush for the mild or delicate touches to be made with the color.

13.3
Peach

13.4
Pear

13.5
Apple

13.6
Banana

Syrup Solution for Coloring

Ingredients	lb	oz	Mixing procedure
Sugar	1		Boil the sugar, glucose, and water for
Glucose or corn syrup	1		about 3 min. Remove any foam or impurities
Water	1	8	ties
Alcohol (pure)		4	Allow the syrup to cool and mix in the alcohol. The alcohol has a drying effect when the coloring is placed on the marzipan fruits or vegetables

The procedures for shaping marzipan petits fours in the form of fruits and vegetables varies as seen in the following examples.

Marzipan Peaches Shape the peach fruits by hand and make the center crease. Allow the peaches to dry. Color the peaches light yellow. Brush one side of the peach a light red from the top almost to the very bottom. A few tiny spots of red may be applied to the other side. For the fuzz effect, roll in cornstarch and blow off the excess. A small brown stem is inserted at one end with a small leaf adjacent to it. The yellow coloring may be applied with the applicator and the red with the brush. (Fig. 13.3.)

Pears The marzipan should be colored a pale yellow. Shape the marzipan units into pear shapes and allow them to dry. Color the center of one side a pink-red color that shades off to a light pink. Some brown dots or spots may be applied with a fine brush or toothbrush. A brown stem and small leaf may be inserted at the top. A small brown stem piece may be attached at the bottom of the pear. The top leading toward the center may be accentuated with a few thin lines. (Fig. 13.4.)

Apples The apples may be colored a very pale yellow green. Shape the marzipan units into apple form and allow to dry. The yellow variety may be shaded a slightly darker yellow with fine lines of brown drawn near the stem and base. The red apples are shaded a deep red, spreading to a pale reddish color. A shading of yellow green may be placed at either end. Place a marzipan brown stem and small green leaf at the top. (Fig. 13.5.)

Bananas Color the marzipan pale yellow. Shape the bananas and allow to dry. Color the bananas a deeper yellow from the center out. Use a fine brush to form the fine brown lines running down the banana. Spots of brown may be placed on the outside with a fine, pointed brush or a firm toothbrush. The ends should be shaded a light to deep green. The brown base at each end may be made with a small round piece of brown marzipan slightly wrapped around each end of the banana. (Fig. 13.6.)

13.7
Potato

13.8
Cherry

13.9
Strawberry

Potatoes Shape the potatoes from the marzipan using several varying oval and round shapes. The potatoes may be rolled immediately after shaping in a blend of cocoa, confectioners sugar and cornstarch that has been sifted several times and well blended. A very light brown spray may be used in place of the cocoa blend. Slight creases and eyes may be made with a fine brush using a chocolate or deep brown color. Small pieces of brown marzipan may be inserted for larger eyes. (Fig. 13.7).

Cherries Smaller units are scaled from the marzipan base. The base for cherries may be colored red before shaping. Individual cherries may be shaded a deeper red in the center. Place a brown stem of marzipan at the top of the cherries. Cherries may have a slightly oval shape and a very fine crease made down the center with a knife or the sharp edge of a modeling tool. (Fig. 13.8)

Strawberries These are small units scaled from the marzipan. The marzipan may be colored yellow before dividing and shaping into strawberries. Shape the fruits and then make the small indentations with a toothpick or other sharp instrument. Color the berries red to a lighter shade of red. Roll the strawberries in coarse granulated sugar if desired. Place the green stem at the top of the strawberries. A small green leaf may be placed at the top as well for added effect. The stems are made from marzipan. (Fig. 13.9)

Carrots Color the marzipan yellow. The units for carrots are slightly larger than other fruits. Shape the carrots in an irregular and tapered form. Make slight creases to accentuate slight lumps or unevenness. Very fine root filaments may be formed at the very bottom and tip of the carrot. A green, stalk-like stem is made from the marzipan and inserted at the top. (Fig. 13.10)

13.10
Carrot

13.11
Green peas in pod

Green Peas in a Pod Color the marzipan green. Form an oval cylinder by rolling out or shaping in the palm of the hand and then lengthen to form slightly pointed ends. Hollow the center slightly with a modeling tool. Form a number of small green balls of varying sizes. Place the balls in the pod, with the larger peas in the center and smaller peas tapering toward the end of the pod. The peas may vary in color from light to a darker green. (Fig. 13.11)

Cookies

While there are many commercial suppliers of cookies for caterers and restaurants, most pastry chefs prefer to produce their own. It permits the maintenance of high standards of quality as well as the professional touch of the pastry chef. The uniformity of appearance of the machine-made cookies is identifiable by the discriminating consumer. These cookies may be purchased and kept to meet an emergency, or they may be mixed with those made by the pastry chef. Since cookies are supplements to a great variety of desserts, the commercial varieties may be used extensively. For example, a dry biscuit is often served with frozen desserts. They may be used to decorate the ice cream desserts. These same cookies are often served with hot chocolate and tea. The modern pastry chef may have to use some of the commercial cookies because of cost as well as the time to produce a fine variety of high quality cookies. This section on cookies will provide a number of cookie recipes that ranges from the more elaborate and expensive to the rapidly produced and less expensive varieties.

Equipment used for cookie production is important. The pastry chef who produces a large volume of cookies uses automatic equipment. This may be in the form of cookie droppers that deposit the cookies on pans, equally spaced and of even size. These automatic droppers have die changes to alter the size and shape of the cookie. Wire cut cookie machines are also available for a variety of soft or dough-type cookie batters. These cookies have straight or plain tops after baking. These varieties do save the pastry chef the time and effort required for bagging out the individual cookies with a pastry bag and tube. Cookie machines may have a sheeter attachment for rolling out stiffer cookie doughs such as sugar dough or short dough. The sheeted doughs are then cut and stamped with a design set by the die-cutter. All of this assists the pastry chef who must produce large quantities of assorted cookies.

The production of cookies may create problems for the pastry chef who does not have a basic understanding of the ingredients and their functions. Some common problems are: toughness in the baked cookies, cookies that crumble easily after baking, cookies that spread too much during baking, others that do not spread enough, cookies that tend to stale or dry out quickly, and those that have lost the design made by either machine or pastry bag and tube during baking. These are some of the major cookie faults. A brief examination of the basic ingredients used in making cookies and their function is important.

Sugar

Sugar imparts sweetness, taste, tenderness, and, to a large extent, spread. High percentages of sugar tend to produce greater spread. Some of the sugar is often replaced with syrups to reduce sweetness and increase shelf-life and tenderness of the cookies. Natural syrups such as honey and molasses will further increase the tenderness and moisture retention of the cookies. These syrups are used in special cookies that derive a special taste, color, and other characteristics from the natural syrups. Coarse or granular sugar will tend to cause a greater spread than fine or confectioners sugar. Confectioners sugar will tend to create a closer grain and texture, and may be dissolved in part of the liquid before adding to the mix. Unless otherwise specified, a fine granulated sugar is used for cookie production in addition to other sweeteners called for.

Shortenings

Shortening and other fats are used extensively in cookie production. Short dough cookies and bag-out French-type cookies are very rich and may contain as much as 60–70 percent fat based upon the weight of the flour. The bagged out cookie varieties are most often creamed very lightly. Hydrogenated shortening or a blend of hydrogenated shortening with other fats produces a blend that is easy to cream well.

Quality cookies will contain a good percentage of butter. The butter is blended with the hydrogenated shortening and then creamed. The use of all butter limits the amount of creaming and the absorption and retention of air cells. Pastry chefs will often add a small part of the flour with the fats, especially when a higher percentage of butter or margarine is used. This will aid in the absorption of the liquid in the eggs added for further creaming, and will avoid a curdling effect.

Where cost is an important factor, cookies of reasonably good quality can be made with the use of regular hydrogenated shortening only. This is especially so in the production of the larger cookies and the crisp snap-type cookies, and bar cookie varieties. It is important to remember that increased amounts of fat in a cookie batter or dough promotes shortness and tenderness in the baked cookie when mixed in properly. It is equally important to understand that hydrogenated shortening has a higher melting point than butter and will improve the handling of cookie doughs during the makeup of the cookies when they are hand-rolled or machined for makeup.

Eggs

Eggs serve as structure builders and leaveners, and also as tougheners or driers in cookie production. As in cakes, they aid in the further creaming of the mix for the incorporation of additional air cells. In cookie mixes where the egg whites are whipped and folded in, they add additional structure and leavening. This is especially demonstrated in the production of the kisses type of cookie. Eggs at room temperature will function best during the creaming process. For other whipped batters, as for sponge zweibach, the eggs may be warmed with the sugar before whipping.

Flour

Flour provides the basic structure for most cookies. In most instances, commercially produced cookies are made with a soft flour milled from soft red winter wheat or white wheat. The cookies rich in sugar and fat content are often made with a blend of soft cake flour and a stronger bread flour. The bread flour helps to maintain the shape of the cookie and prevents excessive spreading during baking. Cookies made with egg whites, either in the creaming process or in a whipped form, are often made with a soft flour since the protein of the egg whites provide structure-building characteristics. This is usually the case in the production of wafer-type cookies. It is important to sift the flour, or blend of flours, before folding or mixing into the batter.

Supplementary Ingredients

Supplementary ingredients such as leavening agents, milk in powder or liquid form, cocoa, and similar ingredients often act as tougheners and structure builders. These are most often added after the batter has been creamed and the liquid added alternately with the flour. The milk powder is usually creamed in with the fat and sugar. Dry ingredients such as cocoa are usually sifted with the flour.

Mixing

Mixing of cookie doughs and batters requires care and understanding. In most cases, the toughness in cookies and other common faults are due to improper mixing. Most bagged cookies or drop out cookies are usually creamed well. The sugar, shortening, dry milk, and a small part of the flour may be creamed soft and light. The eggs are added gradually and creamed in well after each addition. The flour is then mixed in lightly or folded in gently to avoid overmixing and gluten development. When gluten development occurs, the dough or batter becomes tough and somewhat rubbery or stringy. This causes toughness in the cookies. Short doughs or sugar doughs are often mixed in a single stage procedure. The sugar, shortening, and liquids are blended together to form small particles. The flour and other dry ingredients are added and mixed only until a dough is formed and the flour is fully absorbed. The short doughs are worked smooth during the rolling and handling of the cookies, and during makeup and cutting or stamping. In the case of the whipped egg and sugar varieties, eggs are usually whipped as for sponge cake and the flour then folded in gently. Egg whites are whipped to a medium soft peak and then folded in gently.

Baking

Baking the cookies properly is very important. The finest cookies mixed with the best of ingredients may be spoiled because of improper baking. Most cookies are deposited on parchment paper-lined pans. This protects the bottom of the cookie from excessive color and heavy crust formation. Cookies that are rich in sugar and quite lean in fat will tend to spread due to the added leavening required. These cookies are baked at lower oven temperatures than those that are rich in fat content and lower in sugar content. This is evident in short dough and icebox cookies. Cookies are baked to a just-done stage because they continue to bake for a few minutes after removal from the oven.

Shortbread or Short Dough Varieties

As we have seen, sugar dough or short dough is used in the production of a variety of products. The dough used as bottoms for cakes may well be used for a variety of short dough cookies. The pastry chef will generally store selected short doughs and cookie doughs in the refrigerator ready for makeup. Cost will often determine the type of cookie dough the pastry chef will prepare. The larger cut-out cookies used for children may well be made without butter. Many of these cookies are garnished with a variety of toppings. Still others are dipped in chocolate or icings. The added sweetness and flavors will satisfy the tastes of young consumers. There are many recipes for short dough and shortbread cookies; several basic formulas using different mixing methods follow.

All Purpose Short Dough

Ingredients	lb	oz	Mixing procedure
Sugar	4	8	Mix all ingredients at slow speed to dis-
Salt		1	solve and blend well
Nonfat dry milk		2	
Glucose or corn syrup		4	
Water	1		
Eggs	1		
Vanilla		1	
Shortening	6		Add the shortening and blend
Cake flour	4	8	Sift the flours. Add and mix slowly until a
Bread flour	4	8	dough is formed. Do not overmix

The dough will be medium soft and should be refrigerated before using. This dough may be used for a variety of cut-out cookies both large and small. It is also useful for cake bottoms and can be mixed with other doughs such as pie crust for special pie shells.

All Purpose Sugar Dough

Ingredients	lb	oz	Mixing procedure
Sugar	2	8	Blend well until smooth. It is not neces-
Salt		1	sary to cream these ingredients
Nonfat dry milk		2	
Corn syrup or glucose		6	
Shortening	2	8	

Eggs	1		Add in 2 stages and blend in
Water		8	Add the water and vanilla and stir in
Vanilla		1	lightly
Cake flour	2	8	Sift the flours and baking powder to-
Bread flour	2	8	gether. Add and mix lightly to a dough.
Baking powder		½	Do not overmix

Chill the dough before using to make handling and rolling easier. This dough may be used for various purposes including large cut-out cookies and the bottoms for various cakes, for specialty cookies and cookie bases. These will be explained in the makeup of shortbread and cut-out cookies. For the richer and more expensive shortbread-type cookies, the following recipe is recommended.

Shortbread Cookies

Ingredients	lb	oz	Mixing procedure
Sugar	3		Mix the ingredients in this stage until soft
Salt		1½	and smooth. Be sure the butter is not hard
Butter	3		and brittle before mixing. If it is, work
Shortening	3		smooth with a small amount of flour
Glucose or corn syrup		10	
Egg yolk	1		Add the eggs in 3 stages and blend in well
Whole eggs		12	after each addition. Add the vanilla and
Vanilla		1½	stir
Cake flour	4	8	Sift the flours. Add and mix lightly to a
Bread flour	4	8	dough. Do not overmix

1. It is advisable to chill the dough in the refrigerator before using to firm the high percentage of fat and make rolling and handling easier.
2. There are basic practices and procedures to follow when making a variety of cookies from the various short doughs and shortbread dough. The chilled dough to be rolled out should be worked lightly with the hands in very little dusting flour to get the dough smooth and ready for rolling. A canvas cloth dusted lightly with bread flour is advisable. The cloth absorbs the flour and keeps the dough from sticking. Use enough dusting flour to keep the rolling pin from sticking. Finally, be sure the dough is rolled out evenly for even cookie thickness.
3. Where automatic cookie equipment is used (hopper and sheeter) the necessary adjustments will be made for sheeting and cutting.

Variety Cut-Out Cookies These cookies may be made with large or small cookie cutters. Large cookies are usually cut out with 2½–3 in. diameter cookie cutters. A plain or scalloped edge may be used. Specialty cookies with a variety of shapes and figures can also be made in the shape of animals, trees, diamonds, and so forth. The cut-out cookies are placed on parchment paper-lined pans and spaced about ½ in. apart. The cookies are left plain if they are to be dipped and garnished after baking. Other cookies are brushed lightly with water or mild egg wash and then dipped in a variety of toppings before baking. Such toppings may be chocolate sprinkles, chopped nuts, coconut, sugar, or a blend of sugar and nuts. The garnish may be a drop of jam or jelly or a nut or fruit. Square, diamond, or rectangular cookies may be garnished before cutting since very little scrap dough remains. A pastry wheel is used and regular hand or die cutters may be used for cutting closely. Scrap cookie dough is to be gently worked into the next piece of fresh dough to be rolled out for cookies. Bake at 385–395°F until golden brown. (See Figs. 13.12 through 13.22.)

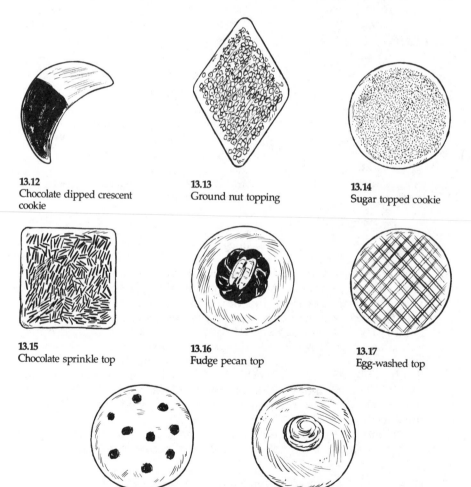

13.12
Chocolate dipped crescent
cookie

13.13
Ground nut topping

13.14
Sugar topped cookie

13.15
Chocolate sprinkle top

13.16
Fudge pecan top

13.17
Egg-washed top

13.18
Chocolate chip top

13.19
Cookie with jam center

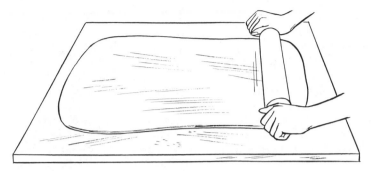

13.20
Roll dough evenly to ⅛ in. thickness

13.21
Cut out cookies. Avoid excess scrap dough

13.22
Place cookies on pan evenly spaced

Chocolate shortbread cookies may be made from the same shortbread dough, making the following adjustments in the recipe. Add 4 oz of water with ¼ oz of baking soda dissolved in it after the eggs have been added. Reduce the bread flour by 8 oz to 4 lb. Add 8 oz of natural cocoa which has been sifted with the flour. Some pastry chefs simply add some melted fudge base or bitter chocolate (approximately 1 lb of either) to the mix during the final stages of mixing. This may tend to tighten or stiffen the dough slightly. The amount of fudge base or chocolate may be varied to achieve the desired color and chocolate taste. For a marble effect in the cookies, chocolate and vanilla dough may be mixed slightly and then rolled or melted sweet chocolate may be added and lightly mixed into the dough.

For the nut-filled and fruit-filled varieties, add the nut pieces (slightly toasted) to the dough in the final stages of mixing. Chocolate sprinkles or chocolate drops may also be added for a varied effect. The larger cut-out cookies are often finished in this way and accompany a frozen dessert, such as ice cream, or a small dish of canned or fresh fruit served as dessert.

Cookies to be dipped in chocolate are baked to a golden brown color and allowed to cool. There should be contrast between the chocolate and the crust color of the cookie. The chocolate used is most often the special cookie dip specially treated to dry quickly, maintain its shine, and with a slightly higher melting point than regular sweet chocolate. Handling and serving is made easier because of this special dipping chocolate.

Short Dough or Shortbread Cookie Specialties
There are a number of cookie specialities that require the use of a short dough or shortbread cookie dough. The cookie dough is either used as the base for the top of the cookie or is used as the enrobing dough for specialty fillings.

Hamantash or Triangle Cookie   These cookies are made for special holiday occasions. They are made from either the short dough or shortbread cookie dough. The dough is rolled out to about ⅛ in. thickness and then cut out with a round cookie cutter. The size for larger cookies is about 3–3½ in. in diameter. Extra-large cut-outs may be made for larger servings. These are commonly used in cafeteria or restaurant service and are a la carte dessert items. The smaller, miniature varieties are cut out about 1½–2 in. round. A plain or scalloped-edge cookie cutter may be used. The center of each cookie is filled with a filling of prune, poppy seed, apricot and ground nut, or other similar variations. The edges of the cookie dough are then squeezed to form the sides of the triangle. The remaining side is then squeezed to close the entire triangle. The center may be left slightly open so that the filling is visible. The seams formed should be of equal size to maintain even sides of the triangle. Be sure the edges are completely shut. Place the hamantash cookies on parchment paper-lined pans and bake at 385°F. The tops of the cookies may be brushed lightly with egg wash and garnished lightly with poppy seeds, sugar, or chopped nuts. The garnish will indicate the type of filling if the cookies are completely sealed. (Figs. 13.23 and 13.24.)

French Sables or Linzer Tarts   A shortbread cookie dough is best suited for quality cookies. These cookies are often made in large form and served as an individual dessert. For the smaller cookie variety, roll out the short dough or shortbread dough about ⅛ in. thick. Cut out round cookie

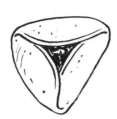

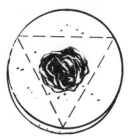

13.23
Circle of cookie dough with
prune, poppy, or other
filling

13.24
Edges of dough pressed
together with filling
showing

circles about 1½ in. in diameter and place on parchment paper-lined
pans. Cut out an equal number of cookie circles as on the pan and then
cut the centers out of the circle with a small round cookie cutter leaving
a three-quarter-inch center hole. Bake the cookies at 390°F until light,
golden brown. When cool, turn the cookie bottoms (no hole in center)
over to obtain a smooth surface. Place a large drop of smooth apricot or
currant jelly or jam in the center. Dust the ring-shaped tops with confectioners sugar, and place over the bottoms so that the jelly filling shows
through the center and the bottom and top stick together. (Figs. 13.25
and 13.26.)

Christmas Cookie Cut-Outs Roll out the shortbread dough to approximately ⅛ in. thick. Remove the excess flour and cut out into shapes such
as stars, trees, crescents, circles and small Santas or men similar to gin-
germen. The cookies may be garnished with red- and green-colored sugar
before baking. They may also be decorated with simple designs piped
on with currant or apricot jam. Cookies left plain may be decorated with
royal icing after baking. Soften the royal icing so that the icing flows
evenly and covers the entire cookie before decorating. These cookies may
also be brushed with egg yolks and then criss-crossed with a fork to form
a fine line design when baked. Before baking, these cookies may be garnished with a half red or green cherry. Slice each glazed cherry carefully
in half and place the cut side down on the washed cookie before the egg
wash dries.

13.25
Cut out equal number of bottoms
and tops. Tops have centers cut
out

13.26
Assembling tops and bottoms

Royal Icing Shortbread Cookies   Roll out the dough slightly more than 1/8 in. thick. Remove the excess flour from the surface of the dough. Deposit freshly made royal icing in spots over the dough and then level with a spatula so that the entire dough is covered with a film of royal icing about 1/16 in. thick (the dough surface should not be visible). It may be necessary to soften the royal icing with a little egg white so that it is easier to spread and distribute evenly. Allow the royal icing to dry for about 15–20 min. and cut into squares, rectangles, or diamonds with a French knife or pastry wheel. Bake at approximately 310°F (cool oven) until the cookies are fully baked and crisp. Check the bottoms by lifting a cookie from the center of the pan with a spatula.

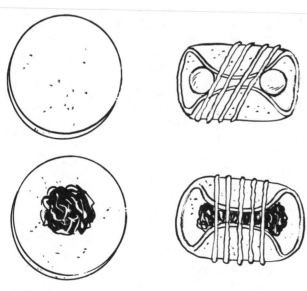

13.27
Shortbread bow tie cookies

Shortbread Bow Tie Cookies The shortbread or the short dough cookie dough may be used for these cookies. They are made small and add to the variety because of their shape and the variety of fillings and icings that may be used for finishing the cookies.

Roll out the cookie dough to an even ⅛ in. thick. Remove the excess flour and then cut out round cookie circles with a plain or scalloped cutter about 1½ in. in diameter. Remove the scrap dough and place to one side. Place the cut-outs side by side on the bench and fill with a small amount of apricot or other selected jam or jelly. Raise opposite sides and pinch together to form a bow tie shape. Place on a parchment paper-lined pan and bake at 390–400°F. The cookies may be pinched together to form the bow tie shape without the filling. After pinching together, place the cookies on the pan. With a pastry bag and small plain tube, a small amount of jam is piped at either side of the bow tie shape. A half cherry or other dried fruit may be used in place of the jam. After baking and cooling, the cookies may be striped with vanilla icing or sweet chocolate. (Fig. 13.27.)

Large Cut-Out Type Cookies

These cookies are less costly to make than the richer cookies made from a shortbread or short dough cookie mix containing butter and egg yolks, or whole eggs. There are many varieties and a selected group of these will be presented in this section. Most pastry chefs will have their own favorite recipes. However, the recipes that follow may add to the variety of the cookies that may be made at a lesser cost and with less production time.

Sugar Cookies

Ingredients	lb	oz	Mixing procedure
Sugar	3		Cream the ingredients to a soft, smooth
Salt		1	consistency. Scrape the sides of the kettle
Nonfat dry milk		4	
Glucose or corn syrup		6	
Shortening	2	4	
Eggs		12	Add the eggs in 2 stages and cream in
Water	1	2	well. Add the water and vanilla and stir in
Vanilla		1½	lightly
Cake flour	6	4	Sift the flour and baking powder. Add and
Baking powder		3	mix until the flour is absorbed and a smooth dough is formed

1. Place the slightly soft and sticky dough on a floured pan and form into a rectangular shape. Chill before using. Work the dough lightly in a little dusting flour to obtain smoothness. Place the dough on a

13.28
Roll dough to ¼ in. thickness on flour-
dusted cloth

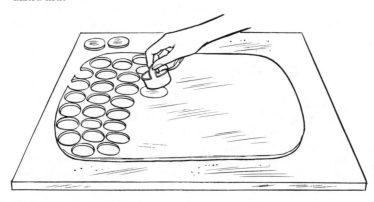

13.29
Cut out cookies as close as possible

flour-dusted cloth and roll out to slightly less than ¼ in. thick (Fig. 13.28). Check for even thickness. A small rolling pin may be used for the final rolling and to obtain even thickness throughout.

2.   Remove any excess flour and brush the top of the dough lightly with water or milk. Sprinkle the top with granulated sugar and cut out into various shapes (Fig. 13.29). For minimum scrap, the cookies may be cut into squares, rectangles and diamond shapes. Round cookies may be cut out without washing and then dipped into a pan containing sugar. Coarse or crystal sugar may be used.

3.   The cookies are panned and spaced about 1 in. apart (Fig. 13.30). The tops of the cookies may be garnished with a drop of jam or jelly. Other toppings and garnishes such as chopped nuts, cinnamon sugar, macaroon coconut, and so forth, may be used for variety. Work the scrap dough into fresh dough when rolling the cookie dough again.

4.   Bake the cookies at 390°F until golden brown.

5.   Plain cookies may be decorated with a fudge-type icing after baking. They may also be striped with a fondant type of icing. A variety of colors and flavors may be added to the fondant for striping.

Yield: Approx. 250 to 300 cookies (2½–3 in.)

13.30
Place on paper-lined sheet pans in
evenly spaced rows

Chocolate Sugar Cookies   These require the following changes in the
basic sugar cookie recipe:

Add 8 oz of natural cocoa (sift the cocoa with the cake flour)
Reduce the cake flour to 5 lb 12 oz.
Add ½ oz of baking soda (dissolve in the water and add with vanilla).
Reduce the baking powder to 2¼ oz.
Chill the dough and make up as the basic sugar cookies.

Chocolate-Nut Cookies   (*Richer type*)

Ingredients	lb	oz	Mixing procedure
Sugar	3		Blend these ingredients to a soft, smooth
Salt		1	consistency. Scrape the sides of the kettle
Nonfat dry milk		2	
Butter	1		
Shortening	2		
Glucose or corn syrup		4	
Egg yolks		12	Add the eggs in 2 stages and cream in.
Water		6	Dissolve the soda in the water and stir
Baking soda		¼	into the above
Toasted ground filberts or walnuts	2		Add the nuts and stir in
Cake flour	3	4	Sift the flour, cocoa, and baking powder
Cocoa		8	together. Add to the above and mix lightly
Baking powder		½	until the flour is absorbed

1. Chill the dough and then roll out to ¼ in. thickness. Sprinkle the
    top with toasted, chopped nuts and cut into 2½ in. round cookies.
2. Bake these cookies at 385–395°F. Check for proper bake and avoid
    overbaking.
3. The cookies may be left plain and then garnished with a fudge icing
    when cool. The center of the fudge rosette may be further garnished
    with a nut piece.
Yield: 200 2½-in. cookies

Ginger Cookies

Ingredients	lb	oz	Mixing procedure
Sugar	1		Cream the sugar and shortening and other
Brown sugar		10	ingredients until smooth and soft
Salt		1/2	
Shortening	2		
Nonfat dry milk		2	
Ground ginger (variable)		1/2	
Water		8	Dissolve the soda in the water and stir
Baking soda		1	into the above
Molasses (light)	2	12	Sift the flour. Add alternately with the
Cake flour	4	8	molasses and mix to smooth dough

The dough will feel somewhat soft and slightly sticky. Place on a flour-dusted pan and chill well before using. Roll out on a flour-dusted cloth to slightly more than 1/8 in. thick. The cookies may be cut into various shapes and sizes. Gingerbread men may be garnished with raisins, nuts, and fruits before baking. Bake at 385°F. When cool, the cookies may be iced with a softened royal icing or fondant icing.
Yield: Variable with the size and shape of the cookies to be made (120 gingerbread men)

Coconut-Honey Cookies

These cookies are made with unsweetened macaroon coconut. They are moist and chewy after baking and keep well for extended periods.

Ingredients	lb	oz	Mixing procedure
Sugar	3		Cream these ingredients until soft and
Salt		1	smooth. Scrape the sides of the kettle
Nonfat dry milk		2	
Ammonium bicarbonate		1/8	
Shortening	2		
Eggs		12	Add in 2 stages and cream
Honey (clover)	1	2	Add the honey and blend in. Dissolve the
Water		8	soda in the water and add with the vanilla.
Baking soda		3/4	Stir slightly
Vanilla		1/2	
Macaroon coconut	1	8	Sift the cake flour. Blend with the maca-
Cake flour	4		roon coconut. Add and mix to a smooth dough

1. Chill the dough and then roll out on a flour-dusted cloth to slightly more than ⅛ in. thick.
2. Cut out the cookies with a round cutter and place on parchment paper-lined pans.
3. Egg wash the tops lightly and bake at 390–400°F. The cookies should have a golden brown crust color. If ammonium carbonate is not available, increase the baking soda to 1 oz.
4. The tops of the cookies may be garnished with macaroon coconut before baking. A dot of jelly may be placed in the center.

Yield: 200 2½–3-in. cookies

Poppy Seed Cookies

These cookies are specialties for specific groups of consumers. In most cases, the cookies are cut into diamond shapes or squares for ease in make-up and to avoid excessive scrap dough.

Ingredients	lb	oz	Mixing procedure
Sugar	2		Cream these ingredients until soft and
Salt		¾	smooth
Glucose or corn syrup		8	
Honey (dark)	1		
Shortening	1		
Nonfat dry milk		3	
Eggs	1		Add the eggs in 3 stages and cream in
Water	1		well. Add the water and poppy seeds with
Baking soda		1	the dissolved soda and stir slightly
Poppy seeds		8	
Cake flour	2		Sift the flours together. Add and mix to a
Bread flour	3	12	smooth dough

1. Chill the dough before rolling out. Work the dough lightly into a rectangular shape and roll out on a flour-dusted cloth to about ¼ in. thickness.
2. Cut into triangular shape or square shape. Remove the excess flour and lift the cookies with a spatula and place on parchment paper-lined pans. Egg wash the tops of the cookies and sprinkle lightly with poppy seeds.
3. Bake at 400°F until light brown. Check the bottoms of the center cookies for proper bake.

Yield: 150 large cookies

Icebox Cookie Varieties

Most cookies made from chilled doughs are categorized as icebox cookies. Actually, most of these cookies are made from cookie doughs that are similar to the shortbread cookie. They are rich in fat content and are medium soft and somewhat sticky when first mixed. By chilling the doughs, the fat in the cookie dough becomes firm. This makes handling easier, an important factor in forming the shapes, colors, and designs of the cookies. The checkerboard cookie and other similar cookies may have designs formed by combining two or more different colored cookie doughs into a specific design. Still other cookies may have chopped nuts and fruits added to the dough. By chilling these doughs, clean, even slices may be made with a sharp knife such as a French knife. This also prevents the smearing of different colors into each other and allows a clear and distinct pattern or design in the baked cookie.

Icebox-type cookies may have to be handled more than once before the final cookie is completed and ready for baking. It may be necessary to form layers or designs of different colored cookie doughs and chill these before they may again be processed into the finished form. This is true of checkerboard cookies where layers are assembled and then chilled before forming the checkerboard effect. Round cookies are shaped into cylinder form varying from 1–2 in. in diameter and rolled in parchment or waxed paper before refrigerating. The paper will help to maintain the round shape of the cookies. Pastry chefs will often prepare a variety of icebox cookies in unbaked roll form and place them in the freezer for use as required. The dough is defrosted at room temperature for about 20 min. and then sliced with a sharp knife. In most cases, they will be transferred from the freezer to the refrigerator for slow defrost and still maintain the firmness necessary for proper slicing.

Icebox Cookie Dough

Ingredients	lb	oz	Mixing procedure
Granulated sugar (fine)	1	4	Cream the ingredients in this stage to a soft, smooth consistency
Confectioners sugar	1		
Salt		3/4	
Glucose or corn syrup		4	
Butter	2		
Shortening	2	4	
Egg yolks	1		Add in 3 stages and cream in. Add the vanilla and stir in
Vanilla		1½	
Cake flour	3	6	Sift the flour. Add and mix to a smooth consistency
Bread flour	3	6	

After the dough has been mixed, it may be divided into sections and coloring and flavoring added for various types of icebox cookies. Melted sweet chocolate could be added to color and flavor the dough for chocolate icebox cookies or to serve as the contrasting color for checkerboard or other mixed color cookies. A blend of chocolate fudge base and sweet chocolate may be used. For the stronger and darker color of chocolate, melted bitter chocolate may be used. This will provide a bittersweet chocolate flavor. When adding other colors such as red, green or yellow, care must be used not to make the color effect too deep or too strong. The colors should be worked in evenly to avoid streaking the dough. After the dough sections have been colored, form them into rectangular shape and refrigerate or freeze them for later use. Pastry chefs will often prepare a separate dough for the chocolate icebox cookie variety, one that will spread a little more and will not be as rich in fat content.

Yield: Variable with size of the cookie

Chocolate Icebox Cookie Dough

Ingredients	lb	oz	Mixing procedure
Granulated sugar (fine)	2		Cream these ingredients together until soft and smooth. Scrape sides of the kettle
Confectioners sugar	1		
Salt		¾	
Nonfat dry milk		2	
Glucose or corn syrup		4	
Butter	1	8	
Shortening	1	12	
Eggs	1	8	Add the eggs in 3 stages and cream in
Water		8	well. Dissolve the soda in the water. Add
Baking soda		½	with the vanilla and stir in
Vanilla		1	
Cake flour	3	4	Sift the flour and baking powder together
Bread flour	3		with the cocoa. Add and mix to a smooth
Cocoa (natural, dark)		12	dough

The dough may be divided into smaller units and formed into a square or rectangle and refrigerated for later use. You may add finely chopped nuts or chocolate bits to it in the final stages of mixing. When these additions are made, the dough is scaled into small units and rolled up into cylinders which are then rolled in waxed or parchment paper and then refrigerated for later slicing and baking.

Yield: Variable

13.31
Roll up the dough on a thin rolling pin

Checkerboard Cookies

1. Use the preceding recipes for Icebox Cookie Dough and Chocolate Icebox Cookie Dough.
2. Use a flour-dusted cloth to roll out pieces of dough of even weight (approx. 3 lb) to ¼ in. thickness. Be sure the doughs are of even thickness all over. Either a vanilla or a chocolate dough layer may be first. Roll up the dough on a thin rolling pin (pie pin) and unroll again on a flour-dusted cloth or parchment paper placed on a sheet pan (Fig. 13.31).
3. Egg wash the top of the unrolled dough with egg whites blended with some water. This solution will make the layers of dough stick together.
4. The second layer of dough should be of the contrasting color (Fig. 13.32). Roll up this layer of dough and unroll evenly over the first. There should now be two layers, one vanilla and one chocolate. This procedure is to be repeated until 4 layers are put together (2 vanilla and 2 chocolate).
5. Square off the edges by pressing gently against the sides with the flat blade of a bench scraper or large spatula. Roll the top surface gently to even the thickness if necessary. Chill this dough in the freezer for about 15 min.
6. Gather any scrap dough and combine with a fresh piece of the chocolate or vanilla icebox cookie dough. Roll out the dough to approximately ¹/₁₆ in. thickness in a rectangular shape equal to the overall length of the four-layered dough in the refrigerator.
7. Remove the excess flour and brush the surface with the egg white and water wash. Slice the chilled combination of contrasting cookie layers into slices about ¼ in. thick with a sharp French knife (Fig. 13.33).
8. Place the first slice on the washed surface of the dough. Wash this layer with the water-egg white solution. Place the second layer over the first so that the chocolate section now faces the vanilla. Alternate the next two layers in the same manner thereby forming 4 layers in a checkerboard effect (Fig. 13.34).

13.32
Use contrasting dough for the second layer

13.33
Slice the layers

13.34
Checkerboard effect

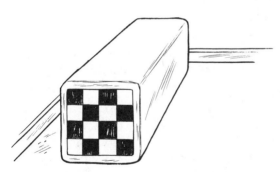

13.35
Contrasting dough is used for enrobing

9. Wash the base dough with egg white and water and roll the square formed over the dough so that the square is now completely enrobed (Fig. 13.35). Cut the dough and remove the covered square to a pan. Follow the same procedure with the remaining dough.
10. Contrasting doughs for enrobing may be used for variety. Freeze the strips and then slice with a sharp knife into cookies about ¼ in. thick. Bake on parchment paper pans at 380°F.

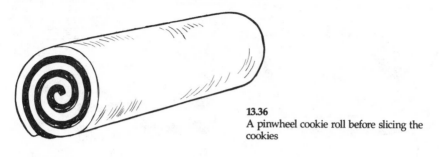

13.36
A pinwheel cookie roll before slicing the cookies

Pinwheel Icebox Cookies

These may be made with a combination of 2 or 3 contrasting colored cookie doughs. Chill the sections of dough that have been colored. Roll out the first dough to about ¼ in. thick. Roll up and unroll this dough on a floured cloth or parchment paper-lined pan and wash with egg white and water mixture. Roll the second and third sections the same way and unroll after washing the lower layer so that the layers stick. Wash the top surface of the last layer and then roll up into rolls about 1½ in. in diameter. Cut the dough through at the base and continue to roll so that additional rolls are formed. Roll out the cylinders to about 1–1¼ in. diameter and place on a pan. Chill or freeze the rolls of dough and then slice into ¼ in. slices. Pan and bake as for the checkerboard cookies. (Fig. 13.36.)

Bull's Eye or Target Icebox Cookies

Divide the dough into two sections. Color one chocolate or other color. Leave one plain or yellow. Roll out one piece into a rectangular shape about ¼ in. thick. Wash with egg whites. Form the other dough into rolls or cylinders about ¾ in. in diameter. Place on the washed surface of the rolled out dough. Cover the cylinder and cut the edge of the dough. Continue until the entire base dough has been used to cover the cylinders. The doughs may be reversed for contrast and variety. Chill the rolls and then cut into slices about ¼ in. thick. Bake as for checkerboard cookies. (Fig. 13.37.)

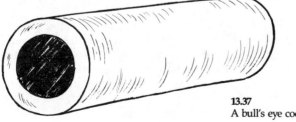

13.37
A bull's eye cookie roll before slicing

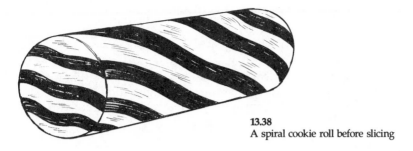

13.38
A spiral cookie roll before slicing

Spiral Icebox Cookies

Have 3 separate colored dough sections of equal size. Divide them into units of 1 lb each. Roll each unit into round strip about ½ in. in diameter. Place 3 contrasting strips alongside each other. Braid the 3 strips together loosely. Roll into a cylinder form about 1 in. in diameter. Roll out a separate piece of dough about ¹/₁₆ in. thick for enrobing the cylinder of contrasting doughs. Wash the rolled out dough with egg white wash. Place the cylinder on the rolled out dough and cover the cylinder. Do this until all cylinders are made. Chill or freeze the cookie rolls. When chilled, slice ¼ in. thick and bake as for checkerboard. (Fig. 13.38.)

Icebox cookies are often made in square or rectangular shape. These doughs have chopped nuts or nut pieces, or diced fruits added to the dough in the final stages of mixing. The doughs are then placed into square or rectangular pans and flattened evenly so that the dough is approximately 1 in. thick. The dough is then chilled and strips are then cut about 1¼–1½ in. wide. The strips are then sliced into ⅛ in. or slightly thicker slices. The slices are placed on parchment paper-lined sheet pans. The cookies are baked at 385–390°F.

Pecan Icebox Cookies

Add approximately 2 lb of pecan pieces to each 10 lb of icebox cookie dough. Pecan or maple flavoring may be added with the nuts to provide additional color and flavor. Place the dough into a rectangular or square pan and chill. Follow the procedure listed above.

Fruited Icebox Cookies

Add 2 lb of mixed diced fruits to each 10 lb of icebox cookie dough. Some chopped nuts may be added for contrast and variety. Follow the same procedure as for the pecan icebox cookies. Be sure the fruits are diced rather finely. Large fruit pieces will be difficult to slice even after the dough has been chilled.

Icebox-type cookies are made from cookie doughs that require chilling so that they may be sliced into a round form. Separate recipes are used to meet the desired characteristics of these cookies. Many of the filled types (nuts, fruits) of cookies are shaped into cylinders and then rolled into a variety of garnishes for covering the dough cylinders. When sliced, the cookies have a special, distinguishing covering around the sides. The recipes that follow are selected for their popularity and variety.

Walnut Icebox Cookies

Ingredients	lb	oz	Mixing procedure
Granulated sugar	2		Cream these ingedients together until soft
Brown sugar	2		and light
Salt		1	
Butter	1		
Shortening	1		
Baking soda		½	
Egg yolks		12	Add the eggs in 3 stages and cream well
Whole eggs		12	after adding
Vanilla		1	Add the flavorings and blend in
Maple or mocha flavoring		1	
Cake flour	5		Sift the flour and mix into the above. Add
Chopped walnuts	2		the walnuts in the final stages of mixing

1. The dough should be chilled for about 15 min. before scaling into units weighing about 1½ lb.
2. Shape the units into round cylinders about 1½ in. in diameter. Use just enough dusting flour to prevent the dough from sticking when rolling.
3. Roll the cylinders in finely chopped or ground walnuts. Granulated sugar may be mixed with the nuts.
4. Roll the cylinders in waxed or parchment paper to maintain the round shape. Chill the units in the feezer for about 1 hr.
5. Slice into cookies about ¼ in. thick. Place on parchment paper-lined pans and bake at 380°F. Space the cookies about 1 in. apart on the pan. This will allow for a mild spread of the cookies during baking.

Cherry Icebox Cookies

Ingredients	lb	oz	Mixing procedure
Almond or macaroon paste	2	8	Mix the almond paste and eggs to form a smooth paste
Eggs		8	

Sugar	2	8	Add the sugar, salt, shortening, and butter
Salt		½	to the above and blend in well
Butter	1	4	
Shortening	1	4	
Egg yolks		10	Add the yolks and blend in well
Maraschino cherries (chopped fine)	2		Add the juice and cherries with the flavoring and mix lightly. Use coloring carefully
Vanilla		1	
Red coloring (few drops)			
Cake flour	2	8	Sift the flour and add. Mix to a smooth
Bread flour	2	8	dough

1. Chill the dough for about 1 hr before taking to the bench for makeup. Scale the dough into units weighing 1½–2 lb.
2. Roll out the units to about 1¼ in. in diameter and then roll the cylinders in granulated sugar. Roll up the cylinders in parchment paper and place in the freezer.
3. Slice into ¼-in. slices and place on parchment paper-lined pans. Space the cookies about 1 in. apart.
4. Bake at 375–380°F. Be careful not to overbake the cookies, as this will cause a brown crust to be formed. This will eliminate the pink color of the chopped cherries. Check the bottoms of the center cookies. If they have a light brown crust color at the bottom, remove from the oven.

Chinese Almond Cookies

Ingredients	lb	oz	Mixing procedure
Brown sugar	1	8	Blend the sugar, almond paste, and eggs
Almond paste	2		to a smooth consistency
Eggs		8	
Granulated sugar	2		Add these ingredients to the above and
Salt		1	cream in
Butter	1	8	
Shortening	2		
Baking soda		¾	
Eggs		8	Add and blend in well. Add the vanilla
Vanilla		1	and stir in. Sift the flours. Add and mix
Bread flour	1		lightly to a smooth dough
Cake flour	4	4	

1. Scale the dough into units weighing about 1½–2 lb.
2. Melted sweet chocolate may be striped over the dough and folded in gently to form a marbled effect (Fig. 13.39).

13.39
Part of the dough may be colored and mixed in

3. Form the units into cylinders about 1½ in. in diameter. Roll the cylinders in sliced almonds and roll up in parchment or wax paper (Fig. 13.40).
4. Chill the cylinders and then slice into ¼ in. slices (Fig. 13.41). Place on parchment paper-lined sheet pans and space 1½ in. apart (Fig. 13.42).
5. Bake at 375°F.
6. The cookies are baked until crisp around the edges. They will feel slightly soft in the center. These cookies will dry and firm up after removal from the oven.
7. When cool, the cookies may be garnished with a center drop of chocolate fondant icing or chocolate fudge icing (Fig. 13.43). A fudge rosette with a sliced almond placed on top is the usual method of finishing these cookies.

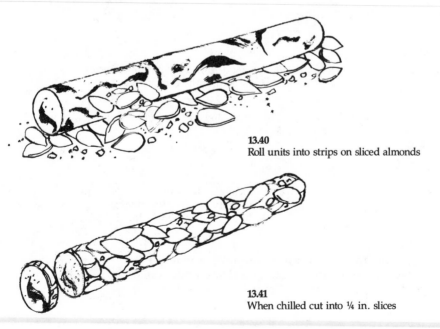

13.40
Roll units into strips on sliced almonds

13.41
When chilled cut into ¼ in. slices

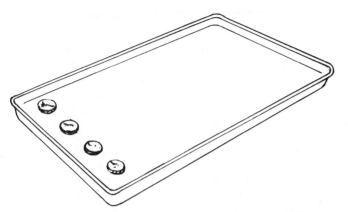

13.42
Space cookies so that they do not touch
when baked

13.43
Chinese cookie garnished
with chocolate fudge in
center

Butterscotch Cookies

Ingredients	lb	oz	Mixing procedure
Brown sugar	1	8	Cream all the ingedients in this stage to a
Granulated sugar	2		smooth, soft consistency
Salt		1	
Butter	1		
Shortening	1		
Molasses		6	
Baking soda		¼	
Eggs	1	12	Add the eggs in 3 stages and cream in.
Vanilla		1	Add the flavoring and blend in well
Cinnamon (optional)		¼	
Cake flour	5	6	Sift, add, and mix to a smooth dough

1. Scale the dough into units weighing 1½–2 lb.
2. Shape into round strips or cylinders about 1½ in. in diameter. Roll the cylinders in parchment or waxed paper and freeze or refrigerate.
3. When chilled, cut into slices about ¼ in. thick.
4. Bake at 375–380°F. These cookies may be garnished with a mocha fondant icing.

Bagged or Spritz Cookie Varieties

The term "spritz" cookies refers to cookies that are bagged out with a pastry bag and star tube or French tube. The grooved designs made with the tube and the shapes are usually retained after baking. These cookies are also made automatically with a cookie dropping machine and various dies for shaping the cookies. The cookies are usually garnished with a variety of toppings or garnishes before baking and are also finished after baking by dipping in chocolate or other forms of garnish.

There are many recipes for various spritz cookie varieties. Pastry chefs usually have their own favorite recipes. A large percentage of fat, consisting of butter, margarine, and shortening, is contained in most recipes. These recipes use the creaming method of mixing to obtain maximum aeration and distribution of the fat particles.

Both bread flour and cake flour are used for these cookies. The bread flour will maintain the shapes and prevent excessive spreading during baking. Very often, egg whites will be used rather than whole eggs in order to provide added protein and reduced cookie spread. Of major importance is the understanding that the flour is to be mixed in very lightly to avoid the development of gluten. Overmixing is the major cause of toughness in the cookie mix. The cookie dough is further mixed when deposited into the pastry bag or into the machine hopper. This mixing effect continues while the cookies are being compressed through the tubes or the machine dies and deposited on pans. Uniformity of size and shape of the cookies is also important. A pastry chef is judged on the neatness of the workmanship displayed by the finished cookies. The recipes that follow are selected for the quality and variety they provide.

Butter Spritz Cookies

Ingredients	lb	oz	Mixing procedure
Almond or macaroon paste	1	4	Mix the almond paste and egg whites to a smooth consistency
Egg whites		8	
Sugar	2		Add these ingredients to the above and cream until soft and light. Scrape the sides of the mixing kettle
Salt		1	
Butter	2		
Shortening	2		
Cake flour		8	
Egg whites	2		Add the eggs in 4 stages and cream in well after each addition. Scrape the sides of kettle. Add the vanilla and stir in
Vanilla		2	
Cake flour	2	8	Sift the flours together. Add to the above and mix in lightly
Bread flour	3		

13.44
Heart-shaped French
cookie

13.45
Pear-shaped French cookie

13.46
Wing-shaped French cookie

13.47
Drop-shaped French cookie

13.48
Bar-shaped French cookie

1. Mix batches of this size in the machine and then fold the flour in lightly by hand to avoid overmixing.
2. Larger batches are mixed on slow speed after adding the flour. Mixing stops as soon as the flour is completely blended into the batter. This will avoid overmixing and resulting toughness.
3. Cookies are bagged out with either a French tube (#4 or #5) or a star tube on parchment paper-lined pans. The cookies are formed into a variety of shapes such as the plain drop, star shape, pear shape, bar shape, heart shape, wing shape, crescent shape, small ring shape, "S" shape, and "U" shape. (See Figs. 13.44 through 13.48.)
4. The cookies may be garnished with half a glazed cherry or a nut piece or diced fruit in the center. Cookies may also be garnished with ground hazel nuts or chopped pecans. Remove the excess nuts after sprinkling the cookies.
5. Ungarnished cookies are finished after baking by dipping in chocolate, filling centers with chocolate, making rosettes in the center with chocolate fudge icing, and striping with chocolate. Various colored fondant icings may be used to fill the centers. A circle of chocolate fudge or French chocolate may be piped around the edge of round cookies and the center filled with fondant icing. (Figs. 13.49 through 13.51.)

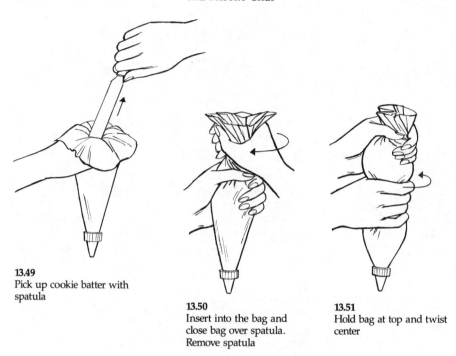

13.49
Pick up cookie batter with spatula

13.50
Insert into the bag and close bag over spatula. Remove spatula

13.51
Hold bag at top and twist center

French Chocolate for Dipping and Garnishing

Ingredients	lb	oz	Mixing procedure
Evaporated milk (1 can)		15	Bring to a boil over a low flame. Stir to prevent scorching. Remove from fire when boiling
Butter		4	
Shortening		4	
Granulated sugar	1		
Salt		¼	
Vanilla		½	Add to the boiled mixture and mix in well
Melted sweet chocolate	1		
Melted bitter chocolate	1		
Evaporated milk		8	Add and blend in well

1. Use the French chocolate preparation while it is warm.
2. Place the various designs on the cookies and allow to firm up and dry. The rosettes may be garnished with a walnut or pecan piece.
3. If large quantities of cookies are to be finished, keep the chocolate in a double boiler of warm water to maintain the medium soft consistency.

French Almond Butter Cookies

Ingredients	lb	oz	Mixing procedure
Almond paste	4		Blend the almond paste and egg whites
Egg whites		12	smooth
Sugar	2		Add the ingredients in this stage and
Salt		1	cream in well. Scrape the sides of the ket-
Butter	3		tle frequently
Shortening	3		
Egg whites	2		Add the egg whites in 4 stages and cream
Vanilla		1	in well after each addition. Add the vanilla
Bread flour	6		Sift the flours and fold into the above
Cake flour	1		lightly. Do not overmix

Jumble Cookies

Jumble cookies are large size cookies that are bagged out into various shapes, with combinations of colors and flavors added to the basic cookie mix. This cookie mix is cheaper to make than the richer spritz cookies. These large cookies are excellent for children.

Ingredients	lb	oz	Mixing procedure
Almond paste or macaroon paste		12	Mix the almond paste and eggs to a soft, smooth consistency
Eggs		8	
Sugar	2	4	Add these ingredients to the above and
Salt		1	cream in well. Scrape the sides of the ket-
Nonfat dry milk		4	tle
Glucose or corn syrup		4	
Butter	1		
Shortening	1		
Eggs	1	8	Add the eggs in 3 stages and cream in well
Water		12	Add to the above and stir in lightly
Vanilla		2	
Cake flour	4	14	Sift the flour and baking powder. Add and
Baking powder		2¼	mix in lightly until the batter is smooth

To convert the basic vanilla jumbles to chocolate, add the following:

Ingredients	lb	oz	Mixing procedure
Cocoa		8	Sift with flour
Water		8	Dissolve the baking soda in the water.
Baking soda		¼	Add with the vanilla

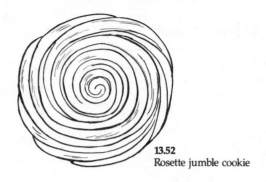

13.52
Rosette jumble cookie

13.53
"S" shaped cookie

13.54
Ring-shaped cookie

1. Jumble cookies are bagged out with a pastry bag and tube with a large French or star tube.
2. Deposit the cookies on parchment paper-lined pans or pans that have been lightly greased. Cookies are shaped into large rosettes (Fig. 13.52), "S" shapes (Fig. 13.53), ring shapes (Fig. 13.54), heart shapes, combination sticks, sticks with contrasting rosettes at the end of the stick, and other varieties.
3. Space the cookies about 1½ in. apart to allow for spread during baking. Bake the jumbles at 385°F.
4. Cookies are usually garnished before baking with glazed cherries, chopped nuts or nut pieces, chocolate sprinkles, and other garnishes before baking. Plain cookies are usually finished after baking by striping with sweet chocolate or fudge icing, filling the cookie centers with variety fondant icings, or dipping the cookies in fondant icing or cookie coating.

Yield: Approx. 200 large cookies

To make chocolate cookies similar to the vanilla jumbles and to make jumble cookies that are a combination of chocolate and vanilla, the following recipe is recommended.

Chocolate Jumble Cookie

Ingredients	lb	oz	Mixing procedure
Sugar	2	4	Cream these ingredients to a soft and
Salt		1	smooth consistency. Scrape the sides of
Nonfat dry milk		4	the kettle periodically
Butter	1		
Shortening	1		
Glucose or corn syrup		4	
Eggs	1	8	Add the eggs in 3 stages and cream well after each addition
Water		12	Dissolve the soda in the water. Add with
Baking soda		½	the vanilla and stir in lightly
Vanilla		1½	
Cake flour	4	4	Sift the flour, cocoa, and baking powder
Cocoa		8	together. Add to the above and mix to a
Baking powder		1½	smooth consistency. Do not overmix

1. These cookies may be bagged out in the same shape as the vanilla jumbles.
2. The vanilla jumble may be bagged into a stick form. The chocolate mix may be used to bag a stick of the same size right alongside to make a *combination jumble* (Fig. 13.55).
3. Single vanilla sticks may have a chocolate rosette bagged at the very end of the stick for a shovel effect. This type is often made for ice cream and other frozen desserts.
4. Vanilla rosette jumbles may be garnished with a smaller chocolate rosette in the center.

Pastry chefs will often offer a plain cookie selection. That is, there will be no almond paste or nuts, or fruit flavors in the cookies. They may use a recipe for both the spritz and the button or sandwich variety. The following recipe meets these qualifications.

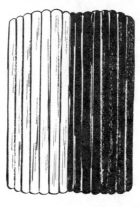

13.55
Black and white combination jumble cookie

Butter Rosette Cookies

Ingredients	lb	oz	Mixing procedure
Sugar	3		Cream these ingredients until soft and
Salt		1½	light. Scrape the sides of the kettle fre-
Butter	3		quently
Shortening	3		
Vanilla		1½	
Egg whites	2	4	Add the egg whites in 4 stages and cream in well
Cake flour	4	8	Sift the flours and fold into the above until
Bread flour	3	12	the flour is evenly blended in

1. These cookies may be bagged out with a French tube, star tube, or a plain tube. They will maintain their shapes and will have a slight spread during baking.
2. The cookies may be garnished in the same manner as the butter spritz variety of cookies containing almond paste.
3. The pastry bags are filled carefully and handled without excessive twisting and squeezing to bag out the cookies.
4. Bake the cookies at 375°F. The plain cookies are often sandwiched together after baking.

Tea Cookies

Ingredients	lb	oz	Mixing procedure
Cake flour	1	12	Cream these ingredients together until soft
Bread flour	2		and light. Scrape sides of the kettle
Butter	1	4	
Shortening	1	4	
Confectioners sugar	1	12	Sift the sugar. Add with the salt to the
Salt		½	above and cream in well
Egg whites	1	2	Add to the above in 4 stages and cream in
Vanilla		1	well after each addition

1. These cookies will be quite crisp when baked and have a closer grain than the regular butter spritz type of cookie.
2. The mix is bagged out into a variety of shapes with a number 4 or 5 French tube.
3. Bake at 385°F.
4. The cookies may be garnished before baking or finished after they are baked.

Praline Butter Nugget Cookies Increase the egg whites to 1 lb 8 oz. Add 1 lb finely ground toasted hazelnuts or filberts and ¼ oz cinnamon in the final stages of mixing and fold in gently. Bag these cookies out with a star tube, rather than a French tube, to avoid clogging the fine teeth of the French tube and smearing the designs of the cookies. A plain tube may be used and the plain round or stick shape cookies may be garnished with chopped nuts or with a sliced almond before baking.

French Chocolate Spritz Cookies

Ingredients	lb	oz	Mixing procedure
Granulated sugar	1	4	Cream these ingredients together until soft
Confectioners sugar	1	4	and light. Scrape sides of the kettle fre-
Salt		½	quently
Butter	1		
Shortening	1		
Chocolate fudge base [1]		8	
Heavy cream	2		Add the cream in 4 or 5 stages and cream
Vanilla		1	in well after each addition
Cake flour	2		Sift the flour and then fold lightly into the
Bread flour	2		above

Filbert Spritz Cookies

Ingredients	lb	oz	Mixing procedure
Sugar	2	8	Cream these ingredients together until soft
Salt		½	and light. Scrape the sides of the kettle
Butter	2		
Shortening	2	8	
Finely ground, toasted filberts	1	8	
Egg yolks	1	4	Add in 3 stages and cream in well. Add
Vanilla		1	the vanilla and mix in
Cake flour	2	8	Sift and add the flour. Fold the flour in
Bread flour	3	8	gently. Avoid overmixing

1. These cookies are usually bagged out with a star tube into stick or finger shapes and rosette shapes on parchment paper-lined pans.
2. Bake at 375°F.

[1] Bitter chocolate (melted), 12 oz, may be substituted for the fudge base. Bag out and bake as for the regular butter spritz cookies and garnish in much the same manner as the vanilla butter spritz cookies.

3. When cool, the finger cookies are dipped at each end. This may be done as single cookies or they may be sandwiched together with a chocolate fudge and then dipped.

4. The rosettes may be dipped almost half way into the chocolate or chocolate cookie dip as a single cookie or sandwiched first before dipping.

Almond Dessert Cookies

Ingredients	lb	oz	Mixing procedure
Sugar	2		Cream these ingredients together well.
Salt		1	Scrape the sides of the kettle frequently
Butter	1	8	
Shortening	2		
Almond paste	1	2	Blend the almond paste and eggs to a
Egg yolks	1		smooth, soft paste. Add in 3 stages to the
Rum flavoring		½	creamed sugar and shortening and cream
Vanilla		1	in well. Add the flavorings
Cake flour	2		Sift the flour and fold into the above. Mix
Bread flour	2	12	until the flour is completely blended. Do not overmix

The cookies are bagged out into various shapes with a French tube or a star tube.

Figure "S" Cookies These are baked and then dipped in chocolate dip or regular sweet chocolate. The French chocolate cookie dip may be used as well.

Chocolate or Caramel Glace Cookies These may be made by bagging out rosettes just slightly higher than usual. The baked rosette cookies are then dipped in warm fondant icing that is colored and flavored with mocha or caramel. The fondant should be sufficiently thin so that the cookies are covered and the ridges of the tube show through the icing. The cookies are then placed on screens. The cookies may be garnished with chopped, roasted filberts. The same procedure is followed for the chocolate covered rosettes.

Tart-Like Cookies Use the very small muffin tins that are about 1¼ to 1½ in. in diameter. Bag the mix around the bottom and the sides of the tin and bake at 385°F. When baked, the cookies are thicker at the outside and have a slightly depressed center. Fill the cookies with a currant jam or jelly, apricot or raspberry jam. If muffin tins are not available, bag the rosettes slightly higher in the center and then with fingers lightly moistened with oil depress the centers of the cookies before baking. Fill the hollow with a small dot of jam before baking. After baking and cooling, the cookies are lightly dusted with confectioners sugar and the centers completely filled with selected jam or jelly.

Sandwich-Type Cookies

There are a number of cookies that can be sandwiched together after baking. For example, the Lady Finger sponge-type cookie may be left as a single cookie or doubled without a filling for sandwiching. Spritz-type cookies, when made thin or small, are often sandwiched. Cookies made with whipped egg whites such as kisses, nut-filled cookies, as well as the wafer-type cookies are often sandwiched together after baking. The popular button type or other shaped cookies made from a basic sandwich type of cookie mix are often colored (usually yellow, pink, green, or chocolate) and then baked.

Fillings used to sandwich cookies together vary with the type of cookie. Chocolate is probably the most popular. The chocolate may be French chocolate filling, fudge fillings made with either a fudge or chocolate base, or a chocolate fondant. Jams and jellies are also popular. They are often used with cookies that are made with almond paste either as a filling or as a garnish.

Finishing sandwich-type cookies is very important. The cookies must be of equal size and shape since uneven cookies, when sandwiched together, detract from a neat appearance. Dipping and striping the cookies requires care, neatness, and an organized approach. Cookies should be neatly lined up before they are striped, and the striping pattern or design neat. Dipping should be even and excess chocolate dip should be removed. Cookies that are garnished after dipping should be dipped into the garnish carefully so that equal amounts are applied to equal parts of the dipped and garnished cookies.

Basic Sandwich Cookies

Ingredients	lb	oz	Mixing procedure
Sugar	3		Cream the ingredients in this stage until
Salt		1	soft and light. Scrape the sides of the ket-
Butter	1	8	tle periodically
Shortening	1	8	
Cake flour		8	
Egg yolks	1	8	Add the eggs in 4 or 5 stages and cream
Whole eggs	1	8	well after each addition. Add the vanilla
Vanilla		1	last
Cake flour	4		Sift the flour, add and fold in lightly until smooth

1. The batter may be divided and colored for various cookies. A part of the batter may be colored, or melted chocolate or fudge added for a chocolate sandwich cookie.
2. The cookies are bagged out with a pastry bag with a medium to small plain tube. Cookies may be round (buttons), made into stick or small finger form, horseshoe or crescent form, and other designs.

3. When placed into the hopper of the cookie depositor, check the dies and depositor for an even cookie size.
4. Cookies are deposited on parchment paper-lined pans and backed at 380–385°F. Remove the cookies from the oven when a slight crust has formed around the edge and they feel spongy in the center. Check the cookies in the center of the pan; if the bottom shows a slight crust color and feels tender, remove them from the oven. The cookies will continue to dry for a short period after they have been taken from the oven.
5. Upon cooling, the cookies of the same shape are divided in half. One half is spread in the filling and the other placed on top. Cookies to be filled are lined up close to each other. Place the tops on with a small amount of pressure to ensure sticking. Avoid excessive filling; it will run out when the tops are placed on the filling. Jam or jelly should be smoothed and deposited.
6. Cookies to be striped are usually lined up close together to avoid excessive use of striping chocolate. Thin stripes are best for neatness. They should be spaced evenly. Where they are criss-crossed, the design and spacing should be done neatly and without excessive striping.
7. Cookies that are dipped must be dipped evenly. Sticks and crescents are dipped about ½ in. in either a straight dip or a diagonal dip. Round cookies are usually dipped about ¼ of the area on top. If garnish is applied after dipping, dip immediately into the garnish after removing excess chocolate or other covering. Keep the garnish loose and separate to avoid lumps. (Figs. 13.56 through 13.61.)

13.56
Sandwich-type cookie bagged out with plain tube

13.57
Turn baked cookie and fill

13.58
Sandwich cookies together

13.59
Dip ⅛ to ½ the cookie into sweet chocolate or cookie dip

13.60
Short stick-type cookie bagged out with plain tube

13.61
Turn baked cookie and fill

13.62
Sandwich cookies

13.63
Dip ¼ into sweet chocolate or cookie dip

13.64
Dipping and striping cookies

French Button Cookies   (*Sandwich varieties*)

Ingredients	lb	oz	Mixing procedure
Almond paste or macaroon paste	2		Mix the almond paste and eggs to a smooth consistency
Eggs		8	
Confectioners sugar	2		Add these ingredients to the above and cream well. Scrape the sides of the kettle periodically
Salt		1	
Butter	2		
Shortening	2		
Eggs	1	12	Add to the above in 4 stages and cream well. Add vanilla last
Vanilla		1	
Cake flour	3		Sift the flours and fold in lightly until smooth. Do not overmix
Bread flour	1	8	

1. These cookies will have less spread during baking and will have a closer grain and texture. They will have the added richness and flavor supplied by the increased amount of butter and shortening and the almond paste.
2. These cookies may be made into various colors by coloring the batter before bagging out.
3. The same cookie variety may be made as from the basic sandwich cookies. After bagging out, the cookies may be garnished with finely ground nuts. Remove the excess nuts before baking.
4. The cookies are sandwiched with a variety of fillings and then finished in the same manner indicated for the basic sandwich cookies.
5. For chocolate cookies, add melted sweet chocolate or melted chocolate liqueur to the mix. A small amount of baking soda dissolved in a small amount of water may be added at the same time to ensure equal spread. The soda and water are optional in view of the higher percentage of fat in the cookie mix.

Button (Bouton) Cookies   (*Rich Variety*)

Ingredients	lb	oz	Mixing procedure
Confectioners sugar	2	4	Sift the sugar. Add the fat and cream
Salt		1	lightly. Scrape the sides of the kettle
Butter	2		
Shortening	2	8	
Egg yolks	3		Add the yolks in 4 stages and cream in
Vanilla		1	well after each addition. Add the vanilla
Rind of 3 fresh lemons			and lemon rind and stir in
Cake flour	4	8	Sift the flour and mix to a smooth consistency

Make up as for the cookies made from the basic sandwich cookie mix.

Cinnamon Crescent Sandwich Cookies

Ingredients	lb	oz	Mixing procedure
Almond paste or macaroon paste	2		Mix the almond paste and egg whites to a smooth paste
Egg whites		8	
Sugar	1	6	Add these ingredients to the above and
Salt		½	cream in well. Scrape sides of the kettle
Butter	1		
Shortening	1		
Egg whites		12	Add in 3 stages and cream in well. Add
Rind of 2 lemons			the rind last with the cinnamon and blend
Cinnamon		¼	in
Bread flour	2		Sift the flour and fold into the above until
Cake flour		12	smooth

1. Bag out the cookies with a plain tube in a crescent shaped form.
2. Bag out on parchment paper-lined pans. A star tube may be used (#4).
3. Space the cookies about three-quarters in. apart to allow for spread during baking.
4. Bake the cookies at 375°F.
5. Allow the cookies to cool and then fill with smooth apricot jam and sandwich together. The cookies may then be dipped in fine cinnamon sugar or they may be iced with a fine chocolate stripe.

Lady Fingers

Ingredients	lb	oz	Mixing procedure
Sugar	1	8	Warm the sugar and salt dissolved in the
Salt		¼	egg yolks in a warm water bath. Place in
Egg yolks	2		machine and whip thick
Cake flour	2	6	Sift and fold in lightly
Rind and juice of 2 lemons			Fold in with the flour
Egg whites	2		Whip the egg whites and sugar until me-
Sugar		12	dium stiff. Fold into the above

1. Bag out on parchment paper-lined pans with a pastry bag and plain tube (medium) into strips or sticks about 2½ in. in length. Use a light, even pressure on the pastry bag to maintain even size and shape.
2. Space the fingers about 1 in. apart.
3. Sprinkle the fingers lightly with granulated sugar and allow to stand for about 1 min. for the sugar to dissolve partially.
4. Dust the tops with confectioners sugar and remove the excess from the pans by lifting and shaking the pans gently.
5. Bake the cookies at 410°F. until the cookies feel spongy and springy to the touch. Avoid browning the sugar on top of the cookies. The cookies may be baked on double pans to avoid a brown crust color on the bottom of the fingers.
7. Allow the Lady Fingers to cool and remove from the pans. The Lady Fingers are placed together in a sandwich form as soon as they are removed. Fingers that do not easily release from the paper liners may be removed by turning the papers over with the sticking cookies and moistening the paper lightly with water. Allow the paper to moisten slightly and then remove the cookies. (See Figs. 13.65, 13.66.)

Yield: Approx. 100 to 120 double fingers

13.65
Dust lady fingers before baking

13.66
Sandwiched lady fingers

Lemon Stick Sandwiches

Ingredients	lb	oz	Mixing procedure
Confectioners sugar	1		Sift the confectioners sugar. Combine all
Granulated sugar	1		ingredients and cream soft and light
Salt		1/2	
Butter	1		
Shortening	1		
Egg whites	1	6	Add the whites in 3 or 4 stages and cream
Rind of 4 lemons			in well. Add the rind and flavoring in the
Lemon flavoring		1	last stage
Bread flour	2	10	Sift and fold gently into the above and mix smooth

Bag out on parchment paper-lined pans with a medium plain tube. Bake at 385°F. When cool, sandwich the finger-shaped cookies together with apricot or raspberry jam. The cookies may be striped with a lemon fondant icing.

Rajahs   (Chocolate Sprinkle Sandwich)

Ingredients	lb	oz	Mixing procedure
Almond or macaroon paste	1	4	Mix the almond paste and eggs to a smooth paste
Eggs		4	
Confectioners sugar	2		Sift the sugar. Add the ingredients to the
Salt		1/2	above and cream in well. Scrape the sides
Butter	1	8	of the kettle
Shortening	1	8	
Eggs		12	Add in 2 stages and cream in. Add the fla-
Vanilla		1/2	vorings and blend in
Coffee or mocha flavoring		1	
Cake flour	1	12	Sift the flours together and mix into the
Bread flour	2		above until smooth

1. Bag out on parchment paper-lined pans with a pastry bag and medium star tube. Form into wavy fingers about 2 in. long.
2. Sprinkle the tops of the cookies with chocolate sprinkles and remove the excess by tilting the pan while holding the paper. Then lift the paper and shake the sprinkles from the paper.
3. Bake the cookies at 380°F. These cookies have a slight spread and tend to hold their shape.
4. When cool, sandwich the cookies with chocolate fudge icing, French chocolate, or a smooth jam.

5. These cookies may also be made in round form. Bag out as for the button-type cookie. Fill with chocolate fudge after baking and then make the sandwich. If you have skipped the chocolate sprinkles, dip the cookies now into a chocolate dip and then into chocolate sprinkles as a garnish.

Rainbow Cookies

These cookies are made from sheets of special cookie or cake mix that are sandwiched together after baking. As the name of the cookie implies, the sheets are made of various colors and the finished cookie reflects layers of different colors. Variety is achieved in the combination of colors to be used for the sheets, the nature of the fillings used, the covering of the cookie sheets or strips, and the final application of the chocolate or couverture. In some instances, the chocolate may also be covered with chopped nuts. The pastry chef will use his own combinations.

Ingredients	lb	oz	Mixing procedure
Almond paste or macaroon paste	2	8	Mix the eggs and almond paste to a smooth consistency
Eggs		12	
Sugar	2	8	Add these ingredients to the almond paste
Salt		1	and cream until soft and light
Butter	1	4	
Shortening	1	4	
Eggs	1	12	Add the eggs in 4 stages and cream in.
Vanilla		1	Add the vanilla last
Cake flour	2	8	Sift and mix into the above until smooth

1. Divide the batter evenly into 4 or 5 equal parts. The parts may then be colored yellow, pink, green, chocolate, and the natural vanilla color of the mix. Spread the colored parts evenly on parchment paper-lined sheet pans.
2. Bake the sheets at 375–380°F. The sheets are rather thin and should be baked lightly. After about 10 min. in the oven, check the centers of the sheets. When they spring back gently to the touch the sheets should be removed. They will continue to dry or bake for a short period after removal from the oven. Try to maintain the color of the sheets by avoiding a dark crust formation.
3. While still warm, wash the tops of the sheet cakes lightly with hot apricot jam or apricot coating mixed with apricot jam. Allow the sheets to dry before assembling.
4. Assemble with apricot jam and press the sheets firmly together. Pastry chefs will often store the sandwiched sheets in the refrigerator with weights on the covering pan to cause the jam to stick. When chilled, the top of the sheet is covered with a thin film of apricot jam or heated apricot coating.

5. Cover the top with a thin cover of marzipan rolled out about $1/16$ in. thick. Roll up on a thin rolling pin and unroll over the apricot jam. When fully covered, roll in lightly with the rolling pin to ensure sticking. Trim off the excess marzipan.

6. Turn the sheet over and remove the parchment paper liner. Cover this side as the other with jam and marzipan.

7. Cover the top with melted sweet chocolate, cookie dip chocolate, or French chocolate. Comb with a metal comb before the chocolate sets. Use a slight wavy motion when combing the chocolate. (See Fig. 13.67 through 13.72.) Allow the chocolate to dry and turn the sheet over and coat with chocolate as on the other side. Allow the chocolate to dry well before cutting.

8. Cut the sheet into strips about $1\frac{1}{2}$ in. wide. Then cut into slices about $1/2$ in. wide. These cookies are displayed with a variety of others.

9. The sheets may be finished by chilling and then cutting into strips about $1\frac{1}{2}$ in. wide. Roll out the marzipan about $1/16$ in. thick.

10. Cover the strips with a thin covering of warm apricot jam or apricot coating mixed with jam. Place the strip on the marzipan and roll up until the strip is covered completely.

11. Pastry chefs will often cover the marzipan that has been rolled out with hot apricot jam and then place the strip on the jam and roll up until the entire strip is covered.

12. After covering with marzipan, cover the strip with melted sweet chocolate or other chocolate covering. When dry, cut into slices about $1/4$ to $1/2$ in. thick.

13. The rainbow cookie mix may be used as the base for petits fours glaces. Prepare two thicker or three thinner sheets of the same or different colors and bake. When baked, sandwich with apricot jam and then cover the top with marzipan as above. Chill the sheet and then cut into various sizes and shapes as for the regular petits fours.

14. The rainbow sandwich cookies may be made with a colored marzipan filling. Use two almond sponge cake sheets as the outside covers. Prepare a chocolate marzipan filling by adding melted sweet chocolate to the prepared marzipan. Coat one almond sponge sheet with apricot jam. Cover the marzipan with apricot jam and place the other almond sponge sheet over it. Chill the sheet and proceed as for the rainbow cookies.

Yield: 4 sheets

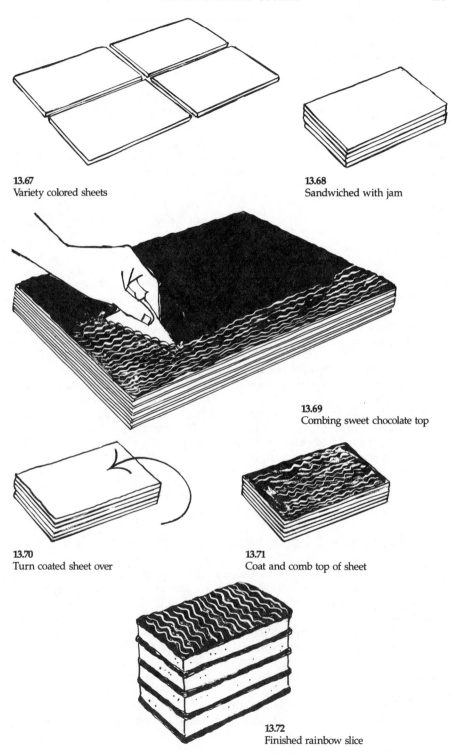

13.67
Variety colored sheets

13.68
Sandwiched with jam

13.69
Combing sweet chocolate top

13.70
Turn coated sheet over

13.71
Coat and comb top of sheet

13.72
Finished rainbow slice

Frangipane Rainbow Cookies

Ingredients	lb	oz	Mixing procedure
Almond paste or macaroon paste	4		Mix the almond paste and eggs to a smooth consistency
Eggs	1		
Sugar	4		Add these ingredients to the above and cream in well. Scrape the sides of the kettle from time to time
Salt		½	
Butter	2		
Shortening	2		
Eggs	3		Add the eggs in stages and cream in well. Add the flavorings and blend in
Vanilla		1	
Rum flavoring		1	
Cake flour	1	12	Sift the flour. Add and mix smooth

1. The pastry chef has the option of forming 2, 3, or 4 sheets of different colors for these cookies. Naturally, two sheets will mean thicker sheets.
2. The variance in colors is optional but each sheet should be of a different color.
3. Bake the sheets carefully, so as not to overbake, at 375–380°F until the sheets feel slightly springy to the touch.
4. When cool, sandwich the sheets with apricot jam to which some rum or rum flavoring has been added. Compress the sheets well.
5. Cover the sheets with melted sweet chocolate, chocolate cookie dip, chocolate fudge icing, or French chocolate couverture.
6. The top of the chocolate may be sprinkled with toasted ground filberts, pecan pieces, or walnut pieces before the chocolate has dried.
7. Cut the sheet into squares about 1–1½ in. square. Dip the French knife in hot water periodically to get a smooth cut.

Yield: 1 full sheet

Wafer and Lace-Type Sandwich Cookies

There are many wafer cookie varieties and many recipes for them, many simply changing the flavor or adding nuts and fruits. Most pastry chefs will use a separate recipe for each of these thin cookies. Most wafers are usually sandwiched after they are baked and then garnished or dipped. A number of them are garnished before baking and left as single cookies after baking. The important factor to remember is that wafer cookies have considerable spread during baking, are baked crisp, and usually bake quickly. Wafer cookies are also bagged out with a plain tube on lightly greased pans and spaced so that there is enough room for the cookies to spread. Wafer cookies are ready when they have just a slight crust color formation around the very edge of the cookie. Wafers continue to dry and bake for a few moments after they have been removed from the oven.

Lace-type cookies are very thin and porous. They are more candylike than the wafer cookies. They can be made with a heated process wherein all the ingredients are cooked or boiled, or they can be made with a cold process. The cookies are bagged out on greased pans or parchment paper-lined pans. Allow sufficient space for spreading. These cookies are often filled or sandwiched together after baking. Still others are placed over thin rolling pins for special shapes while they are still hot. Others may be rolled up and then filled with chocolate or fudge, as for cigarette-type cookies. The recipes that follow are quite popular and provide sufficient variety for the pastry chef's production of variety cookies.

Vanilla Wafers

Ingredients	lb	oz	Mixing procedure
Sugar	3		Blend these ingredients together until soft
Salt		1	and smooth
Nonfat dry milk		4	
Butter		12	
Shortening		11	
Honey		4	
Baking soda		½	
Eggs		12	Add in 2 stages and cream
Water	1	8	Dissolve the ammonium bicarbonate in
Ammonium bicarbonate[1]		¼	the water. Add the water and flavoring alternately with the sifted flour. Mix to a
Vanilla		1	smooth consistency
Rind of 1 fresh lemon			
Cake flour	3	12	

1. Bag out with a plain tube into round drops about the size of a nickel on parchment paper-lined pans, spaced about 1½ in. apart.
2. The wafers may be dusted or sprinkled with chocolate sprinkles or finely chopped or ground nuts. Remove the excess garnish before baking.
3. Bake the wafers at 375°F. When cool, turn half the cookies over and fill with a desired filling.

[1]If ammonium bicarbonate is not available, substitute ½ oz of baking powder which has been sifted with the cake flour.

13.73
Wafer cookie

13.74
Wafer cookie turned over and filled

13.75
Sandwiched wafer cookie

4. The sandwiched cookies may be dipped in chocolate or striped if they have not been garnished before baking. (See Figs. 13.73 through 13.75.)

Orange Wafers

Ingredients	lb	oz	Mixing procedure
Sugar	2		Cream these ingredients together until soft
Salt		½	and smooth
Butter		12	
Shortening		12	
Eggs	1		Add the eggs in 3 stages and cream well
Light cream		8	Add the cream and fruit rind and stir in
Rind of 3 oranges			lightly
Rind of 2 lemons			
Bread flour	2		Sift the flour, add and mix until smooth. Do not overmix

1. Additional orange flavoring may be added with a few drops of yellow coloring mixed with a drop or two of red.
2. Drop these cookies out with a small plain tube about the size of a penny or nickel. Space them about 2 in. apart on the parchment paper-lined pans.
3. Bake at 375–380°F until the cookies have a light crust formation around the edges. Remove from the oven and allow to cool.
4. The orange wafers may be sandwiched together and finished as other sandwich-type cookies.
5. The wafers may be turned over and covered with sweet chocolate, cookie dip, or French chocolate. The chocolate is combed before drying.
6. The cookies may be further garnished with a rosette of chocolate fudge or French chocolate and a half cherry or walnut piece placed into the rosette. The nut or cherry will stick as the chocolate rosette dries.

Lemon Wafers

Ingredients	lb	oz	Mixing procedure
Sugar	2	8	Blend these ingredients well until soft and
Salt		½	smooth. It is not necessary to cream very
Butter	1		lightly
Shortening	1		
Egg whites	1		Add the egg whites in 3 stages and blend
Rind of 4 lemons			in well. Add the lemon rind and flavoring
Lemon flavoring		½	last
Cake flour	2	12	Sift the cake flour. Add and mix smooth

1. Bag out the cookies on parchment paper-lined pans. Space them about 2 in. apart. An evenly greased pan may be used for slightly more spread during baking.
2. Single cookies are usually garnished with a pecan half or nut piece before baking.
3. Bake at 380°F until the cookies show a light brown crust around the edge. Remove from the oven at this point.
4. Cookies may also be filled when cool and sandwiched. These may be finished by dipping or striping the tops of the cookies.

Nut Wafers

Ingredients	lb	oz	Mixing procedure
Sugar	2		Cream these ingredients together until soft
Salt		¾	and light
Butter	1		
Shortening	1		
Egg whites	1		Add the egg whites in 4 stages and cream
Vanilla		1	in well. Add the vanilla last
Toasted, finely ground nuts (hazelnuts or filberts)	4		Sift the flour and blend with the nuts. Add to the above and mix lightly until smooth
Bread flour		8	

1. Bag out on parchment paper-lined pans or lightly greased pans about the size of a quarter or slightly smaller. Space the wafers about 2 in. apart to allow for spread during baking.
2. Bake at 360°F until the cookies have spread and the outer edge of the cookies takes on a light brown crust color.
3. Allow the cookies to cool and then sandwich together with jam, fudge, sweet chocolate (French chocolate), and so forth. These cookies may be striped with chocolate or dipped into the chocolate. The nut wafers may be made in round or finger-shaped form.

Lace Cookies   (*Cold process*)

Ingredients	lb	oz	Mixing procedure
Brown sugar	2		Blend these ingredients well until soft and smooth
Salt		½	
Butter		12	
Honey		4	
Cake flour		8	
Nonfat dry milk		1	
Water		8	Add the water in 2 stages and blend in well
Cake flour		8	Sift the flour. Blend with the nuts and cinnamon. Add and mix smooth
Toasted, finely ground nuts (hazelnuts or filberts)	1		
Cinnamon		¼	

1. Bag out the cookies with a small, plain tube about the size of a penny. Space the cookies about 2 in. apart to allow for spread. These cookies will spread considerably during baking and will have an open, lacelike appearance.
2. Bake at 355°F until the cookies take on a medium brown crust color with a slight crust formation at the ends. Remove from the oven and cool before sandwiching.
3. Fill with fudge, apricot or raspberry jam, or other selected filling. Sandwich and then stripe the cookies with melted sweet chocolate or cookie dip. The cookies may also be dipped.
4. For making cigarette cookies from this wafer mix, lift the cookies individually while warm and roll in a dowel or thin round stick about ¼ in. in diameter. If the cookies cool and become brittle, return to the oven for a few seconds and continue to roll up and remove from the dowel or stick. The cigarettes are filled with chocolate fudge, French chocolate, or Ganache cream. The ends are then dipped lightly in sweet chocolate or cookie dip. (See Figs. 13.76 through 13.79.)

13.76
Lace cookie

13.77
Sandwiched and striped lace cookie

13.78
Lace cookie dipped one-third into chocolate

13.79
Rolled and filled lace-type cookie

Ganache Cream

Ingredients	lb	oz	Mixing procedure
Heavy cream	2		Bring to a light boil over a slow fire
Sweet chocolate	2	8	Chop the chocolate into small pieces. Add to the boiling cream and mix well to dissolve. Place in a bowl of ice cubes and continue to mix until smooth. Use while warm

Lace Cookies   (*Cooked process*)

Ingredients	lb	oz	Mixing procedure
Sugar	2		Boil these ingredients over a low flame.
Salt		½	Stir constantly to keep from scorching
Butter	1		
Shortening		8	
Honey		8	
Water		8	Add the water and boil
Finely ground, toasted nuts (filberts or hazelnuts)	2		Sift the flour and blend in well with the nuts and cinnamon. Add and stir in well
Bread flour		11	
Cinnamon		¼	

Allow the batter to cool down to about 130°F and then bag out as for the cold process lace cookies. Finish in a similar manner.

Florentine Lace Cookies   (*Cold process*)

Ingredients	lb	oz	Mixing procedure
Confectioners sugar	2		Blend the sugars and the butter to a soft,
Granulated sugar		12	smooth consistency
Butter	1		
Salt		½	
Heavy cream	1	8	Add in 3 stages and blend in
Finely ground, toasted filberts	2	4	Sift the flour. Blend with the nuts and fruits. Add and mix smooth
Diced fruits (candied) (chopped finely)	2	4	
Bread flour		12	

1. Bag these cookies out on lightly greased pans with a medium-large plain tube to avoid blocking the tube. Drop the cookies out about

the size of a nickel. Space the cookies about 2 in. apart to allow for spread.
2. Bake the cookies at 385°F. The cookies will have a brown crust around the edges when properly baked. Do not overbake.
3. When cool, the cookies may be finished by striping with melted sweet chocolate or cookie dip. The cookies may also be sandwiched with French chocolate or chocolate fudge.

Almond Shell Cookies

Ingredients	lb	oz	Mixing procedure
Sugar	3	4	Blend these ingredients together
Salt		¼	
Cake flour		11	
Sliced almonds	1	12	
Eggs	1	4	Add the eggs and blend in
Egg whites		14	Whip the whites slightly and mix into the above until smooth

1. Drop out on greased and flour-dusted pans. These cookies may be dropped out by hand or with a spoon to about the size of a quarter. Flatten slightly by dipping the hands in some water and flattening the cookies.
2. Bake at 380°F until a light brown crust color forms around the edge of the cookies.
3. Place the hot cookies over a small rolling pin to form a half circle or shell-like appearance.
4. If cookies cool too fast, return to the oven for a few seconds to reheat and continue to form shells.

Macaroon Cookie Varieties

Macaroon cookies may be divided into two varieties. The major variety is one in which most cookies are made with almond paste, macaroon paste, or kernel paste (cheapest). The paste is mixed with the sugar and egg whites to a smooth consistency. Some mixes for cookies are quite stiff and are warmed or heated in a double boiler to soften before bagging out. Pastry chefs avoid this procedure by adding additional egg whites and bagging out the cookies. It is a matter of opinion how to get the cracking effect. It may be obtained by lightly spraying a fine mist over the cookies before baking or by using a damp cloth to moisten the macaroons.

The stiffer macaroon mixes are bagged out with French or star tubes to make special designs and to increase macaroon varieties. Still other macaroon varieties are made from stiff batter consistencies so that they may be formed and shaped as for icebox cookies. These are usually made in a bar or slice form. The mix may be colored and even filled with nuts and fruits for further variety. Pastry chefs will often fill small or miniature tart pans with a special short dough and then fill the pans for miniature almond tarts to be mixed with a cookie variety.

Coconut macaroons are made with *unsweetened*, fine shred coconut. Almond or macaroon paste is usually combined with the coconut for a better tasting and better quality coconut macaroon. The mixture is usually heated and then bagged out while quite warm. The macaroons are allowed to dry to form a crust which helps to maintain the shape and avoid excessive spread. Coconut macaroons are usually left plain but may be garnished with a cherry or other fruit before baking. Special macaroons may be dipped in sweet chocolate or cookie dip after baking and cooling.

French Almond Macaroons

Ingredients	lb	oz	Mixing procedure
Almond paste or macaroon paste	4		Break the almond paste up into small pieces. Add the egg whites and mix to a
Egg whites		8	smooth consistency
Granulated sugar	1	8	Add the sugar and blend in. Add the egg
Confectioners sugar	1	4	whites in 3 stages and blend well after
Egg whites (variable) [1]		12	each addition. Scrape sides of kettle

1. The machine should be allowed to run at medium speed so that the ingredients are thoroughly blended and a mild aeration of the mix takes place. The mix will turn from a light grayish color to a lighter color. Adding whites in a hurry will often cause the mix to soften too much to bag out into shapes.
2. Bag out the macaroons into various shapes with a pastry bag and French or star tube. Moisten the bag with water if the bag is made from canvas. This will prevent seepage through the pastry bag.
3. Bag out into stars, rosettes, pear shapes, heart shapes, bar shapes, wing shapes, and so on.
4. The cookies may be garnished with glazed cherries, nut pieces, diced fruits, or left plain.
5. Allow the cookies to dry for several hours or overnight. Use parchment paper liners on the pans. The paper will prevent excessive spreading during baking. It will allow for a better cracking effect.
6. Bake the cookies at 385–390°F. If ovens have a strong bottom heat, it is advisable to bake the cookies on double pans. Bake the cookies to a golden brown crust color.
7. Wash the cookies gently with hot apricot coating or jam that has been mixed with an equal amount of simple syrup. Apply while the syrup is hot. (See Figs. 13.80 through 13.85.)

Yield: Approx. 200 cookies

[1] If a stiff batter is desired because the mix will be heated in a hot water bath, use approximately 1 lb of egg whites. If the mix is to be bagged out immediately after mixing and without heating, add enough egg whites to form a medium stiff batter.

13.80
Heart-shaped French
macaroon

13.81
Pear-shaped French
macaroon

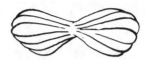

13.82
Wing-shaped French
macaroon

13.83
Drop-shaped French macaroon

13.84
Bar-shaped French macaroon

13.85
French macaroon varieties

Chocolate French Almond Macaroons   Add 6 oz of natural cocoa to the
mix. Increase the egg whites about 4–8 oz to compensate for the binding
effect of the cocoa.

Plain Almond Macaroons

Ingredients	lb	oz	Mixing procedure
Almond or macaroon paste	3	12	Mix to a smooth paste
Egg whites		8	
Sugar	3	12	Add the sugar and blend in. Add the egg
Salt		1/2	whites gradually and mix well after each
Egg whites (variable)		8–12	addition. Scrape the sides of the kettle

1.   If a stiff cookie mix is desired, warm the cookies in a double boiler
to soften and then bag out with a medium plain tube on parchment
paper-lined pans. Greased and flour dusted pans may be used.

2. To eliminate warming the mix, add additional egg whites to form a medium stiff consistency that will not run or spread after bagging out on pans.
3. Space the cookies about 1½ in. apart. Flatten the peaks on the cookies by placing a damp cloth over the entire pan and lightly touching the cookies to depress any points.
4. The cookies may be sprinkled lightly with granulated sugar before baking. Remove the excess sugar from the pans.
5. Bake the cookies until golden brown at 360°F. Allow the cookies to cool before removing from the pans. If cookies stick to the paper, turn the paper over with the cookies and moisten the underside with water. Allow to stay for about a minute or so and then turn over. The cookies will come off easily.

Yield: Approx. 200 cookies

Chocolate Almond Macaroons

Ingredients	lb	oz	Mixing procedure
Almond or macaroon paste	3	12	Mix to a smooth consistency
Egg whites		8	
Sugar	3	12	Add the dry ingredients to the above with
Salt		½	part of the egg whites and mix smooth.
Egg whites (variable)		12	Add the remaining egg whites and mix
Confectioners sugar	1	4	smooth. Scrape the sides of the kettle
Cocoa		8	
Vanilla (optional)		1	

1. Place the mix in a double boiler and heat to approximately 125°F. Stir well to avoid overheating in parts.
2. Bag out on parchment paper-lined pans with a medium plain tube and pastry bag about the size of a quarter.
3. Allow these cookies to dry for several hours or overnight before baking.
4. Bake at 375°F until they have risen and cracked in the oven and have deepened the chocolate color slightly. Check the bottoms of the center cookies with a spatula for bottom crust formation. Do not overbake. Remove from the paper when cooled.

Yield: About 250 large cookies

Vienna Macaroon Mirrors

These are similar to French sable cookies except that they may be made entirely out of a macaroon mix or a combination of macaroon mixes. The base for these cookies may also be made from the shortbread cookie dough. This recipe is for the macaroon bottom.

Ingredients	lb	oz	Mixing procedure
Almond or macaroon paste	3	12	Mix the almond paste and eggs to a smooth paste. Use slow speed for mixing
Eggs		8	
Sugar		14	Add the sugar, salt, and flour to the above
Salt		¼	and blend in. Add the eggs slowly and
Cake flour		4	mix to a smooth, *stiff* consistency
Eggs		4	

1. Roll out the almond wafer mix very thin on a cloth dusted with flour or cornstarch.
2. Cut out the bottoms with a round cutter about 1½ in. in diameter and place on a greased pan. Space the round bottoms about 1½ in. apart. Use the basic French almond macaroon mix to make the circles around the edge of the bottoms. Use a small star or French tube and bag a circle around the edge of each bottom.
3. Allow the cookies to dry for about 2 hours until a light crust has formed.
4. Bake the cookies at 390°F until the macaroon circles are golden brown on top. Remove from the oven and brush the almond circles lightly with hot apricot jam and apricot coating mixed with some simple syrup.
5. When the cookies have cooled, fill the centers with apricot or raspberry jam. The centers may be sprinkled lightly with chopped pistachio nuts.

Miniature Almond Tarts

These tarts may also be made in regulation size tart pans and served as a special individual dessert rather than as part of a cookie or petits fours display. Use a short dough or sugar dough for the bottoms. Roll out the dough on a flour dusted cloth about ⅛ in. thick. Remove the uneven edges of the dough. Dust the dough lightly with bread flour and roll up on a small rolling pin (pie pin). Line up the tart pans close together in straight rows equal to the width of the rolling pin. Unroll the dough over the tart pans loosely. (See Figs. 13.86 and 13.87.) Form a ball of dough made from the excess or scrap dough about the size of the small tart pan. Dip the ball of dough into some bread flour and gently depress the dough in the individual tart pans. Cracks in the dough may be filled in with small dough scraps from the rolled out scrap dough. Place the tart pans on a sheet pan and pipe a dot of jam or jelly at the bottom of the tart. Fill the tart with almond filling.

13.86
Tart shell

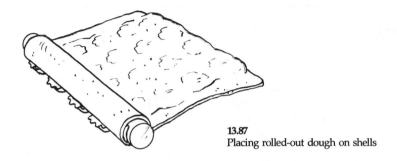

13.87
Placing rolled-out dough on shells

Almond Tart Filling

Ingredients	lb	oz	Mixing procedure
Almond or macaroon paste	3	12	Mix the almond paste and egg whites to a smooth paste
Egg whites		10	
Sugar	3	8	Add the sugar, salt, and cake flour and
Salt		¼	blend in. Add the egg whites gradually
Cake flour		3	and blend in well after each addition
Egg whites	1	4	

1. Fill the tart pans with the almond filling almost to the very top or rim.
2. Spray the surface of the top with a fine mist of water before baking. This will cause cracking over the top surface during baking.
3. The top may be designed with two narrow strips of short dough placed across the top of the tart before baking.
4. Bake at 370°F until the tops have cracked and have turned golden brown and feel quite firm when touched lightly. (Fig. 13.88).

Yield: 100 to 120 small tartlets

Railroad Almond Cookies

These cookies are made in bar form and then sliced into individual cookie slices. A variety may be made from the basic cookie bar since the fillings and icings used will make for colorful variations. Roll out the short dough or shortbread dough on a floured cloth about ¼ in. thick and roll up on

13.88
Almond tart with cookie dough cross on top

a rolling pin. Unroll the dough on a pan lined with a parchment paper liner. Remove the excess dough. With a French knife or pastry wheel cut strips about 2 in. wide and leave the cut strips in the pan. Bake the cookie dough strips slightly until very light brown. When cool, place the dough strips on pans spaced about 2 in. apart. Using the basic French Almond Macaroon mix, bag out a spiral shaped border design down the length of each side of the cookie strip. Use a small to medium sized star tube. Allow the macaroon mix to dry for several hours or overnight and then bake at 390°F until the macaroon borders are light brown. Remove from the oven and wash the macaroon borders with hot apricot coating or apricot jam mixed with simple syrup. When cool, fill the centers with apricot jam, raspberry jam, and cover with a thin, pink fondant icing. Additional varieties may be made by piping a center border (pear shaped) with the French almond macaroon mix before baking. This will allow for two separate jams or other fillings to be used. Garnish the tops with a light sprinkling of chopped pistachio nuts.

Almond Crescents and Other Shaped Cookies

These cookies may be made with a variety of shapes and toppings. When a different nut or topping is used, the name of the cookie may be changed to a glorified continental name appropriate to the cookie. The following is a basic recipe and method of handling these cookies.

Ingredients	lb	oz	Mixing procedure
Almond or macaroon paste	4		Blend the egg whites and almond paste to a smooth consistency
Egg whites		8	
Sugar	2		Add the sugar and part of the egg whites
Egg whites (variable)		8	and mix smooth. Add the rest of the whites and mix to a smooth paste

This mix should be quite stiff and should be easily molded or shaped by hand. Place the mix on sliced almonds and form into strips about ½ in. in diameter. Cut the strips into small, equal sections and drop into the almond slices on a part of the workbench.

Almond Crescent or Horns   Roll out to about 2 in. in length in the almond slices and form into horns or crescents. If the almond mixture is dry and stiff, dip the cookie units into egg whites and then roll in the almond slices. Place the crescents on parchment paper-lined pans and space about 1¼ in. apart. Allow to dry for about 2 hr and bake at 380°F. Bake to a golden brown and wash with hot apricot coating or jam mixed with simple syrup. (See Figs. 13.89 through 13.91.)

Apricot Ovals   These similarly made units are shaped into small oval or finger forms. Place on pans and depress the centers slightly. Place a half glazed cherry or a good-sized dot of raspberry or apricot jam in the center. Bake as the horns and wash as soon as removed from the oven.

13.89
Almond horn

13.90
Almond horn made into a finger shape (jelly or cherry in center)

13.91
Almond horn mix made into a round shape (jelly or cherry in center)

Almond Rounds These are shaped into round balls and then dipped into egg whites before rolling in sliced almonds. Place on parchment paper-lined sheet pans and space about 2 in. apart. Flatten the units slightly and then depress the center. The centers may be filled with jam, jelly, or fruit pieces. The depressions may be left unfilled until after baking. Bake as for the horns or ovals and then fill with additional jam or jelly. The centers may also be filled with French chocolate, or colored fondant icing.

Raspberry Macaroons Add a few drops of red coloring and raspberry flavoring to the basic almond crescent mix. Form strips about 1¼ in. in diameter and roll in chopped filberts. The strips may be washed with egg whites before rolling in the nuts. Divide the strips into small units and round up. Roll the balls in ground filberts and place on a parchment paper-lined pan. Flatten the balls slightly and make a depression in the center. The depression is filled with raspberry paste made by mixing the following ingredients:

Raspberry Paste

Ingredients	lb	oz	Mixing procedure
Almond paste	1		Add part of the jam to the almond paste
Raspberry jam	1		and mix smooth. Add the remaining jam
Rum flavoring		¼	and flavoring and mix smooth

If the paste is too soft, a small amount of sponge cake crumbs or toasted chopped filberts may be added to tighten the filling. Fill the centers of the raspberry macaroons with the paste and bake at 370°F. When baked, wash the top of the cookies with a syrup made with equal parts of glucose and apricot coating.

Pignolia Macaroons   These are made with the almond crescent basic mix. Roll out the mix into strips. Divide into small units and round up into small balls. Brush the balls with egg whites and roll in pignolia nuts. Round up in the palms of hands to press the nuts into the almond mix. Shape into small ovals and place on parchment paper-lined pans. Allow the cookies to dry for about 1–2 hr and bake at 365°F. Wash with hot apricot coating or jam when removed from the oven.

Cherry Macaroons

To the basic crescent almond mix add the following ingredients:

Ingredients	lb	oz	Mixing procedure
Chopped maraschino cherries (with the syrup added)		12	Add the cherries and syrup and blend into the mix. Add the nuts and flour and blend in well. If the mix is a bit soft, add some cake crumbs
Toasted, ground filberts	1		
Cake flour		2	
Red coloring (as desired)			

1. Form the mix into strips about 1¼ in. in diameter.
2. Cut into individual units or cookies and round up.
3. Brush the balls lightly with egg whites and roll in granulated sugar.
4. Place the units on parchment paper-lined pans and flatten slightly. Make a depression in the center and press a glazed half cherry in the center of the cookie.
5. Allow the cookies to dry for about 2 to 3 hr and bake at 365°F. Wash with apricot wash after baking.

Pecan Macaroons   Add 1 lb 8 oz of chopped pecans to the basic almond crescent mix and mix in well. From into individual balls and roll into chopped pecan pieces. Place on pans and flatten slightly. Place a pecan half in the center. Bake and finish as for the cherry macaroons.

Parisian Macaroons

Ingredients	lb	oz	Mixing procedure
Almond paste	2		Mix the almond paste and yolks to a smooth consistency
Egg yolks		12	
Sugar	2		Add the sugar, nuts, and crumbs and blend in. Add the flavoring and blend in. If too stiff, add a little egg yolks
Ground, toasted filberts	1	8	
Sponge cake crumbs	1	4	
Rum flavoring		1	

1. Line a cake board with a sheet of parchment paper. Dust the board with sugar and roll the dough out about three-eighths in. thick into a rectangular shape. Square off the edges with a bench scraper or spatula. Allow to dry for an hour or so.
2. Prepare a batch of royal icing (enough to cover the top surface of the rolled out cookie dough) and flavor it with coffee or mocha flavoring. Soften the royal icing with egg white so that it smears evenly and easily.
3. Allow the royal icing to dry somewhat and then sprinkle the top of the icing with chopped filberts. The icing should be sufficiently moist for the filberts to stick.
4. Allow the sheet to dry overnight. Cut out with a round cookie cutter into crescent-shaped cookies.
5. Place on parchment paper-lined pans and bake at 365°F to a light color. The cookies should feel tender when baked. They will continue to dry after baking.

Coconut Macaroons

Ingredients	lb	oz	Mixing procedure
Macaroon or almond paste	2		Blend the almond paste and egg whites to a smooth paste
Egg whites		8	
Sugar	3	8	Add the sugar, salt, and egg whites and mix smooth. Place in a double boiler and heat to about 140°F. Add the coconut and sifted confectioners sugar and mix in well. Add vanilla last
Salt		1	
Egg whites	1	8	
Unsweetened, macaroon coconut	3		
Confectioners sugar			
Vanilla		1	

1. Bag out on paper-lined (parchment paper) pans with a medium plain tube. Space the cookies about 2 in. apart. The macaroons are usually left plain and allowed to dry for an hour to form a crust. The macaroons may be garnished with pieces of glazed cherry before baking.
2. Bake the macaroons at 380°F until golden brown. Do not overbake.

Yield: 200 large macaroons (variable with small cookies)

Chocolate Coconut Macaroons These may be made from the same coconut macaroon mix by adding the following: cocoa, 4 oz and egg whites, 4 oz and mix in well in the final stages of mixing.

Coconut Macaroons   (Without Almond Paste)

Ingredients	lb	oz	Mixing procedure
Sugar	4		Place these ingredients over a low flame
Salt		½	and heat to about 110°F
Glucose or corn syrup		8	
Egg whites	2		
Macaroon coconut	4		Blend the coconut and flour. Add to the
Cake flour		4	above and heat to approximately 135–
Vanilla		1	140°F. Stir constantly

Make up as for the coconut macaroons made with almond paste.

Chocolate Coconut Macaroons   (Cold Process)

Ingredients	lb	oz	Mixing procedure
Sugar	2		Sift the sugar. Blend all the dry ingredi-
Confectioners sugar	2		ents together
Salt		½	
Cocoa		10	
Cake flour		12	
Macaroon coconut	3	8	
Egg whites	2	8	Whip the egg whites to a froth. Add the
Glucose or honey		5	glucose or honey gradually and whip the
Vanilla		1	egg whites until stiff
Red coloring (option-al) (few drops)			

1. Add the dry ingredients in a slow, steady stream and fold in gently but thoroughly.
2. Bag out on parchment paper-lined pans.
3. Allow to dry for about 20 min. and bake at 375–380°F.

Coconut Kisses

Ingredients	lb	oz	Mixing procedure
Macaroon coconuts	3		Place all ingredients in a double boiler and
Sugar	1	8	heat to 135°F. Stir constantly for even heat-
Salt		½	ing
Butter		6	
Glucose or corn syrup	1	8	
Egg whites	2	8	
Vanilla		1	

1. Bag out the macaroons with a pastry bag and plain tube (#5) on paper-lined pans or pans that have been greased and dusted with flour. Remove the excess flour. Bag out the cookies about the size of a quarter and about 1¼ in. high, coming to a point at the top.
2. Allow the cookies to dry for about 1 hr and then bake at 390–400°F. Use double pans if the bottom heat of the oven is strong.
3. When cool, remove the cookies and dip the bottoms in chocolate dip or cookie coating. Some pastry chefs prefer to dip the tops of the cookies in chocolate for a coconut peak effect.

Macaroon Cups

Ingredients	lb	oz	Mixing procedure
Egg whites	3		Whip the whites to a soft peak. Add the
Sugar	2	4	sugar and salt gradually and whip to a
Salt		¼	medium stiff peak
Vanilla		1	Fold in the vanilla
Macaroon coconut	3	6	Blend the coconut, sugar, and flour
Sugar	3		together and fold gently into the beaten
Cake flour		4	egg whites

1. Drop the mix into paper-lined cupcake pans. Fill the pans about ¾ full.
2. Bake at 375°F until golden brown at the top and the cupcakes feel slightly firm in the center.

Yield: Approx. 140 cups of cupcake size

Stencil-Type Almond Paste Cookies

Stencil cookie mix is medium soft and spreads easily when smeared with a spatula or bowl knife. Stencil forms with which to make the shapes are made in various sizes and shapes and can be purchased from baker equipment and supply houses. The most popular stencils are those for leaves and square forms for making into cigarette or wafer types that are rolled up while warm. It is also practical to purchase stencil sheet forms that cover an entire sheet pan for more rapid production of large quantity cookies. The prepared mix is applied over the surface of the pan and the stencil sheet lifted. The cookies remain on the pan and the excess is removed and returned to the mix. Should the mix stiffen, add some egg white or milk to soften.

Almond Cigarettes

Ingredients	lb	oz	Mixing procedure
Almond paste	1	8	Mix the almond paste and egg whites to a
Egg whites		6	smooth paste
Confectioners sugar	2	4	Sift these ingredients together and blend
Salt		¼	into the above
Cake flour		6	
Bread flour		6	
Egg whites		12	Add to the above in 3 stages and blend in
(variable)			well after each addition. Scrape the kettle

1. The mix should be medium soft and able to be picked up with the point of the spatula or bowl knife and smeared evenly.
2. Pans for the cigarettes are lined with parchment paper or greased and dusted with bread flour. Remove the excess flour.
3. Place the stencil (usually two cut-outs to each hand stencil) at the corner of the pan and cover the squares evenly with the cookie mix. (Fig. 13.92). Remove the excess with the spatula and lift the stencil form cleanly so as not to smear the squares formed.
4. Remove the excess from the surface of the stencil and return to the bowl. Place the stencil about 1 in. away, and in the same line, and repeat until the pan is full.
5. Bake one pan at a time at 385°F until the squares show a slight brown color at the very edges of the square. Remove from the oven and with a spatula lift each square and place over a small wooden dowel or very thin rolling pin and roll up (Fig. 13.93). If the cookies tend to crack because they are cool, return the pan to the oven for a few seconds to reheat.
6. The cookies will retain their cigarette shape when cool. These cookies may be stored for finishing as required.
7. In the hollow form, these cigarette cookies may be used to garnish other desserts such as ice desserts (bombes and sundaes).

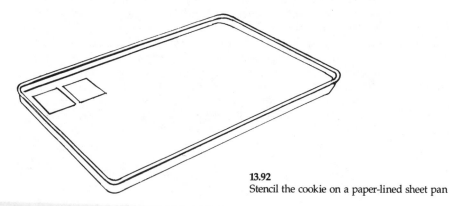

13.92
Stencil the cookie on a paper-lined sheet pan

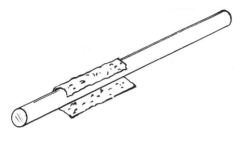

13.93
Roll the cookies on a thin rolling pin or stick

13.94
Fill the end of the cookie with chocolate or
fudge

13.95
Dip one end into the chocolate

13.96
Dip chocolate end into toasted ground nuts

13.97
Finished cigarette cookie

8. To finish the cigarettes, fill them with chocolate fudge or French
   chocolate. Use a pastry bag and small plain tube (Fig. 13.94).
9. Dip the ends in cookie dip, sweet chocolate, or a thinned and warmed
   chocolate fudge or fondant (Fig. 13.95). The ends may be left as they
   are with a chocolate cover or they may be dipped in finely ground
   toasted nuts (Fig. 13.96). One end of the cookie may be dipped or
   both ends may be dipped. (Fig. 13.97).

Note: Where a stencil for these cookies is not available, clean the back of
the sheet pans very well. Grease them lightly. Spread the mix over the
back of the pan evenly and thinly. Bake at 375°F until a slight brown
crust color appears. Remove from the oven and cut into squares or rectangles about 2½ in. × 1¾ in. Roll the cut squares while they are still
very warm. If the cookies dry or break, reheat by returning the pan to
the oven. Bake one pan at a time. It is important to have even pans for
even spread of the cookie mix.

Chocolate Almond Leaves

Ingredients	lb	oz	Mixing procedure
Almond paste	1	8	Mix the almond paste and egg whites to a
Egg whites		4	smooth paste
Sugar	1		Add these ingredients to the above and
Salt		¼	blend in well
Butter		2	
Bread flour		6	
Egg whites (variable)		8	Add the egg whites in 2 stages and blend in well. Scrape the sides of the kettle

1. The batter should be similar to a thick gravy and be able to be picked up with the spatula and smeared over the stencil.
2. If too thin, add a small amount of the batter to 4–6 oz of almond paste and 1 oz of bread flour and work smooth. Now, add this to the full batter and blend in well to thicken.
3. If too thick, add a small amount of egg whites.
4. The pans for the leaves should be lined with parchment paper liners.
5. Place the stencil (2 or 3 cut-outs depending upon size of the leaf) on the pan and cover with an even smear of the mix.
6. Lift the stencil quickly and evenly to prevent smearing. Remove the excess mix and return to the kettle. Be sure the underside of the stencil is clean to prevent sticking to the pan.
7. Bake the leaves at 375°F until they have a slightly brown crust color. Remove from the oven and cool (Fig. 13.98).
8. When cool, cover the flat or bottom side of the leaf with melted sweet chocolate or cookie coating (Fig. 13.99). Use a small spatula for this. The veins may be made by marking the chocolate with the edge of the spatula from the sides to the base of the leaf. Many pastry chefs will comb the chocolate with a fine comb drawn lightly across the chocolate after it has been applied (Fig. 13.100).

Yield: 150 to 200 cookies (depending upon size)

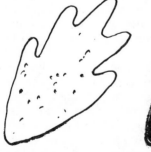

13.98
Baked leaf cookie

13.99
Coated leaf cookie ready to be combed

13.100
Finished chocolate leaf cookie

French Almond Roll Cookies

Ingredients	lb	oz	Mixing procedure
Almond or	6		Blend these ingredients together to a
macaroon paste			smooth, thick consistency. Mix on slow
Sugar	3		speed. Scrape sides of kettle
Salt		¼	
Egg whites	1		
Butter	1		Add to the above and blend in. Soften
Juice and rind of			butter before adding for ease in mixing
1 lemon			
Almond flavoring		1	Add and blend in
(optional)			
Cake flour		4	
Egg whites		8	Add and mix smooth. The mix should be quite firm and handle very much like an icebox cookie or short dough

1. Divide the batter into 3 or 4 sections and add color for variety. A combination of yellow, pink, green, chocolate, and neutral are often used to form these colorful bar-type cookies.
2. The cookies are usually made up as for the bull's eye icebox cookie. Roll out one colored section on a cloth dusted with cornstarch into a rectangular shape about ¼ in. thick. Remove the excess starch and brush the top surface with egg whites.
3. Roll out another colored section into a cylinder form about 1 in. in diameter and the length of the rolled-out strip. Place the cylinder near the edge of the washed strip and then roll up so that the entire cylinder is wrapped in the bottom strip.
4. Roll out the cylinder to about 1 in. in diameter. Measure pieces the width of a sheet pan and cut. Place the strip on a parchment paper-lined pan and flatten slightly.
5. Space the strips about 2½ in. apart on the pan. Wash the strips with egg yolks and allow to dry for several hours or overnight.
6. Wash the strips a second time with egg yolks and then bake at 360°F until a light brown crust color is formed and cracks appear in the cookie bar.
7. Remove from the oven and brush lightly with hot apricot coating or apricot jam mixed with simple syrup.
8. When cool, slice the cookies into 1-in. slices. The tops of the bars may be garnished with chopped nuts as soon as they are washed with the apricot coating. (See Fig. 13.101A–D.)

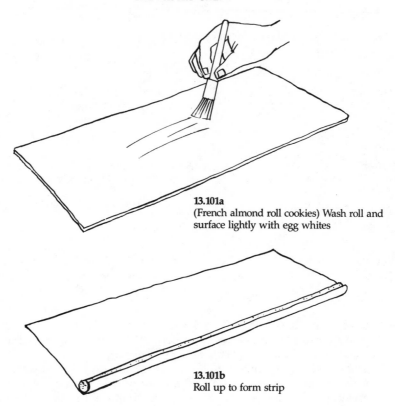

13.101a
(French almond roll cookies) Wash roll and
surface lightly with egg whites

13.101b
Roll up to form strip

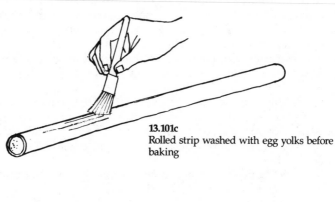

13.101c
Rolled strip washed with egg yolks before
baking

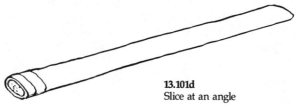

13.101d
Slice at an angle

Sponge and Meringue-Type Cookies

Sponge and meringue-type cookies are made with the whipping method of mixing. The eggs, egg yolks, and egg whites are whipped as for sponge, chiffon, or angel cake. These cookies may be made into a variety of shapes and forms such as Lady Fingers, anise drops, sponge zweibach, and a variation of meringue-type cookies such as kisses and others. In most instances, the cookies are baked as soon as they are bagged out on the pans. Bar-type cookies are sliced after baking and the slices are then toasted. Each of the methods and procedures will be explained with the appropriate cookie recipe.

Aniseed Sponge Cookies

Ingredients	lb	oz	Mixing procedure
Sugar	2		Warm the eggs and sugar in a double
Salt		¼	boiler until warm to the touch. Stir con-
Egg yolks		12	stantly. Whip light and thick as for sponge
Whole eggs		12	cake
Cake flour	1		Sift the flours and aniseed together. Fold
Bread flour	1		in lightly as for sponge cake
Ground aniseed		½	

1. Bag the cookies out with a pastry bag and small plain tube on parchment paper-lined pans or pans that have been greased and dusted with flour.
2. Remove the excess flour. Bag out the drops the size of a quarter. Space the cookies about 1½ in. apart to allow for a slight spread during baking.
3. Allow the cookies to dry overnight.
4. Bake the cookies at 375°F until light brown in crust color.

Yield: Approx. 5 pans, small size cookies

Hazelnut Cookies

Ingredients	lb	oz	Mixing procedure
Egg whites	2		Whip the whites to a froth. Add the sugar
Sugar	4	4	in a steady stream and whip to a medium peak
Hazelnuts or filberts (toasted and finely ground)	2		Sift the cake flour. Blend with the nuts and fold gently into the above. Do not overmix
Cake flour		7	

1. Bag out the cookies in round or finger shapes on parchment paper-lined pans. Space the cookies about three-fourths in. apart.

2. Bake at 370°F until the edges of the cookies show a light brown crust color. Avoid overbaking and excessively drying out these cookies.
3. Allow the cookies to cool and sandwich together with apricot jam, chocolate fudge, or French chocolate.
4. The sandwiched cookies may be striped with sweet chocolate or cookie coating (chocolate). The finger-shaped cookies may be dipped partially at the ends.

Yield: Approx. 150 cookies

Nut Kisses

Ingredients	lb	oz	Mixing procedure
Sugar	3	4	Whip the egg whites to a froth. Add the
Egg whites	1	8	sugar gradually and whip until medium stiff
Chopped sliced almonds	1	4	Be sure the almonds are finely chopped. Sift the flour and sugar and blend in with
Cake flour	1		the nuts. Fold into the egg whites gently.
Confectioners sugar	1	8	Do not overmix

1. Use a plain tube (medium size) and pastry bag and deposit the cookies on parchment paper-lined pans. The cookies should be about the size of a quarter and about 1 in. high. Space the cookies with 1¼ in. apart.
2. Sprinkle the tops of the cookies with sliced almonds and then remove the excess nuts from the pan.
3. These cookies may also be made in large individual form by bagging out with a pastry bag without a tube into 2 in. diameter and about 2 in. high.
4. Bake the cookies at 250°F (cool oven) until the cookies feel crisp to the touch. These cookies should not have a brown crust color.
5. Allow the cookies to cool and dry well for several hours after baking. The cookies may be left plain and in single form or they may be sandwiched together with apricot jam into a ball shape.

Yield: Approx. 150 medium cookies

Almond Kisses

Ingredients	lb	oz	Mixing procedure
Egg whites	2		Whip the egg whites to a froth. Add the
Granulated sugar	4		sugar in a slow, steady stream and whip to a medium stiff peak.
Sliced almonds	2	10	Fold the almonds into the beaten egg whites gently. Be sure they are evenly distributed

1. Drop out the cookies by hand or with a pastry bag without a tube and with a sufficiently large opening to prevent the mix from clogging the opening.
2. Bag out on parchment paper-lined pans or pans that have been greased and dusted with flour.
3. Bake at 250°F (cool oven) until crisp. Do not brown. Allow to cool and dry for several hours.

Yield: 200 medium-large cookies

Variety Kisses Cookies

Ingredients	lb	oz	Mixing procedure
Egg whites	2		Place the egg whites and sugar in the mix-
Sugar	4		ing bowl and set into a warm water bath
Salt		⅛	over a low flame. Heat to about 115°F, stir-
Vanilla (optional)		½	ring constantly

1. Place the egg whites and sugar in the machine and whip to stiff consistency. This should be an almost dry peak.
2. Bag out the cookies with a star tube (Fig. 13.102) for drop (Fig. 13.103), rosette, finger shape, and other varieties. For the plain round, mushroom (Fig. 13.104), and other shapes, use a plain tube. Bag the cookies on parchment paper-lined pans and space about 1–2 in. apart depending upon the size of the cookie.
3. If the cookies are to be garnished with colored sugar or nuts, the garnish is to be applied as soon as the cookies are bagged out and before a crust formation takes place.
4. Bake the cookies at 275°F (cool oven) until they are dry and crisp.
5. For variety, medium shred coconut may be added for making coconut kisses. These cookies are used for garnishing many other desserts and pastries.

Yield: Approx. 200 large cookies

13.102
Star tube and pastry bag for kisses

13.103
Drop-shaped kisses cookie

13.104
Mushroom-type kisses cookie

Sponge Zwieback

Ingredients	lb	oz	Mixing procedure
Almond paste	1		Blend the almond paste and eggs to a
Eggs		8	smooth paste
Sugar	3		Place the sugar, salt, and eggs in a bowl
Salt		1	and warm in a double boiler to about
Egg yolks	2	8	110°F stirring constantly. Place in machine
Whole eggs	1		and whip with the almond paste until
Vanilla (optional)		½	thick. Fold the flavorings in gently
Almond flavoring (optional)		¼	
Bread flour	3	8	Sift the flour and fold in gently
Walnut and filbert pieces (chop)	2		Blend the nuts and cherries and fold into the above
Glazed cherries (chopped)	1		

1. Bag out with a pastry bag with no tube into bars about 1½ in. wide on paper-lined pans (Fig. 13.105). Allow enough space for spread.
2. Bake at 390–400°F as soon as the mix is bagged out. The cookie bars will spring back gently to the touch when baked (Fig. 13.106).
3. Allow to cool, and slice strips into ½–¾ in. slices (Fig. 13.107).
4. Lay the slices with cut-side facing the pan and facing up and toast at 350°F until light brown (Fig. 13.108). Check the bottoms for even crust color.

Yield: Variable with size of strip and slice

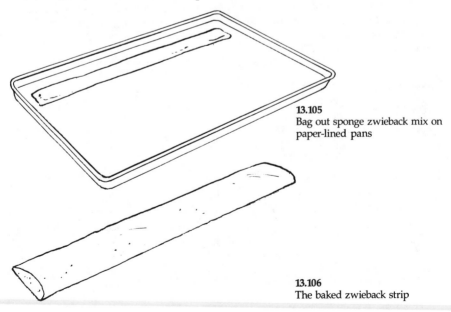

13.105
Bag out sponge zwieback mix on paper-lined pans

13.106
The baked zwieback strip

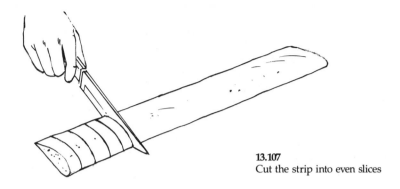

13.107
Cut the strip into even slices

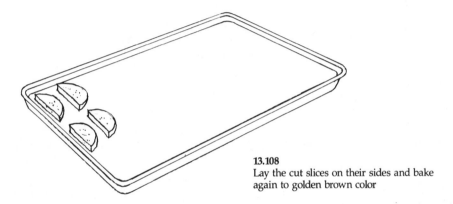

13.108
Lay the cut slices on their sides and bake
again to golden brown color

Bar-Type Cookies

Bar-type cookies are usually made from a stiff or firm mix. Very often, the pastry chef may use a batter that is slightly soft and then chill the dough before using. As to be expected, bar cookies are usually rolled out into long strips on sheet pans, egg washed or left plain, and baked. Some bar cookie varieties are iced with a fudge or fondant icing and then cut into slices after the icing has dried. A basic recipe may be used for making various bar-type cookies or a separate recipe may be used for each. Since these cookies are not expensive to make, and have good shelf life, pastry chefs will often make up a variety of these cookies and serve them for afternoon or tea snacks. Children also like them with milk during the day.

Some bar cookies are made into bar shapes after they are fully baked. For example, the candy type of brownie is a bar or square cookie. Others are made with a baked cookie bottom, and the cooked or heated filling is poured into the pan and allowed to dry. When dry, these sheets are cut into small bar form and then placed on pans for baking. Still others are made into the softer type cookie dough and then placed into a shallow pan and chilled. When chilled, the cookie dough is cut into strips and the strips cut into slices for individual cookies. The cookies are then panned and baked. There are many recipes for bar-type cookies. Several selected recipes are presented to illustrate the varieties. These may be further revised slightly with the addition of fruits, nuts, syrups, spices, colors, and flavors to produce additional bar-type cookies.

Basic Bar Cookie Mix

Ingredients	lb	oz	Mixing procedure
Almond or macaroon paste	1	4	Mix the eggs and almond paste until smooth
Eggs		4	
Sugar	3		Add these ingredients to the above and cream in well
Salt		1¼	
Nonfat dry milk		4	
Glucose or corn syrup		8	
Butter	1		
Shortening		12	
Egg yolks	1	4	Add the eggs in 4 stages and cream in well
Whole eggs		8	
Water	1		Add the rind and water and stir in slightly
Vanilla		1	
Rind of 2 lemons			
Cake flour	3		Sift the flours and baking powder and mix into the above until smooth
Bread flour	3		
Baking powder		2½	
Raisins	1	8	Add the fruits and nuts and mix in lightly. Be sure they are evenly distributed
Glazed cherries	1	8	
Diced, mixed fruits	1		
Filberts or walnuts	1	8	

1. Place the mix on a lightly floured portion of the bench. At this point part of the mix may be made chocolate by adding melted chocolate or melted fudge base to the mix and mixing in well. The cookie mix may be left in the original state and made up without the contrasting, marbling effect of the chocolate. Pastry chefs may simply add softened chocolate and stripe the soft chocolate through the mix for a marbling effect.
2. Scale the units into 1½-lb pieces and shape into bars about 1½–2 in. wide and about ½ in. thick. Place on parchment paper-lined pans or pans that have been greased and dusted with flour. Flatten the strips slightly.

13.109
Scaled units (12 oz –1 lb)

13.110
Chocolate placed into mix

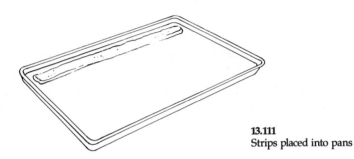

13.111
Strips placed into pans

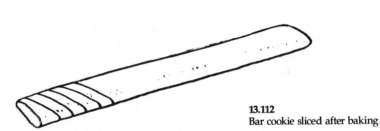

13.112
Bar cookie sliced after baking

3. The tops may be brushed with egg wash and garnished with chopped filberts or walnuts and sprinkled with sugar. The tops may be left plain and later iced with a chocolate fondant icing or fudge icing after baking.
4. The bars are then cut into slices about ½–¾ in. thick.
5. Scale the units into 12 oz–1 lb pieces (Fig. 13.109) and shape into an oval, loaf form.
6. For a marbled effect, place equal amounts of vanilla and chocolate cookie mix together, flatten slightly, and then roll up (Fig. 13.110). The mix may be made up into separate loaf units shaped in an oval form.
7. Place on pans about 3 in. apart (Fig. 13.111). Wash the tops with egg wash and sprinkle with chopped nuts and sugar.
8. Bake the strips or bars at 400°F. The larger loaves are baked at 380°F. Slice into bars when cool (Fig. 13.112).

Yield: Varies with the size of the cookie bar and the thickness of the slice

Nut-Crumb Bar Cookies

Ingredients	lb	oz	Mixing procedure
Almond or macaroon paste	1		Mix the almond paste and eggs to a smooth consistency
Eggs		4	
Sugar	1	8	Add these ingredients to the above and cream in
Salt		½	
Butter		8	
Shortening		8	
Honey		4	
Cinnamon		¼	
Egg yolks		12	Add the eggs in 3 stages and cream into the above
Eggs		8	
Toasted, ground filberts	1	4	Add the nuts and crumbs with the mixed fruit and mix in
Cake crumbs, slightly toasted	1	8	
Diced, mixed fruit	1		
Cake flour	1	4	Sift the flour and baking powder together
Bread flour	1	2	Add to the above and mix in well
Baking powder		1½	

1. Place the mix on a floured portion of the bench. Scale into units weighing about 1½ lb and form into bar shapes about the width of the baking pan.
2. Place on the pan and flatten slightly. Allow about 3 in. of space between each strip.
3. Egg wash the tops and sprinkle with chopped nuts and sugar.
4. Bake at 390–400°F.
5. When cool, slice into bar cookies at a slight diagonal cut.

Yield: Variable with size (average 6–8 bar strips)

Molasses Fruit Bars

Ingredients	lb	oz	Mixing procedure
Brown sugar	2		Blend the ingredients until soft and smooth
Salt		1	
Shortening	1	4	
Nonfat dry milk		2	
Cinnamon		1	
Baking soda		1	
Eggs		12	Add the eggs in 2 stages and cream in well
Molasses	1	8	Add the molasses and stir in
Water		8	Add the water and stir in

Cake flour	4	8	Sift the cake flour. Add and mix until smooth
Raisins	2		Add the raisins and walnuts and mix
Chopped walnuts	1	8	smooth

1. Place the mix on a floured portion of the bench and scale into units weighing 2 lb.
2. Shape the units into bar form as for the basic bar cookies. Place on parchment paper-lined pans or pans that have been greased and dusted with flour. Flatten slightly to about ½ in. thickness.
3. Bake at 390–400°F.
4. When baked and cooled, ice the cookies with a variety of fondant icings or with a chocolate fudge icing.
5. When the icings have dried, slice into bars with a sharp knife. Dip the knife in hot water periodically to maintain a smooth cut. These bar cookies are often used as part of Christmas cookie varieties.

Yield: Approx. 8 strips

Nut Bar Cookies

These cookies are made with a short dough or shortbread cookie dough base. Cover the bottom of a sheet pan with a cookie dough about ¼ in. thick. Stipple or puncture the dough with fork or docker to prevent the formation of slight blisters or air pockets in the cookie dough bottom. Bake the bottom lightly until just done. A slight tinge of brown will show as the crust color is formed at a baking temperature of 400°F. Allow the bottom to cool and then grease the sides with melted butter or shortening. Fill the baked bottom with a thin film of apricot jam or raspberry jam. Prepare the following filling for the cookies:

Nut Topping

Ingredients	lb	oz	Mixing procedure
Sugar	2	10	Place these ingredients into a cooking ket-
Egg whites		12	tle and bring to a boil over a low flame,
Toasted, ground filberts or hazelnuts	2		stirring constantly. Boil for about 2 min

1. Remove from the fire and pour immediately into the prepared pan with the baked cookie dough bottom.
2. Spread the nut topping evenly over the surface of the pan while the mix is still hot or warm.
3. When cool, the nut mix will firm up. Allow the mix to dry overnight at room temperature.
4. Place the pan into the oven to heat the bottom of the pan slightly and to melt the shortening around the sides of the pan. This will release the sheet easily.
5. Turn the sheet over on a cake board and then turn again on another board so that the short dough bottom is at the bottom. Cut the sheet

into bars of varying widths. Larger units served as an individual serving may be cut 2½–3 in. wide. Small bar cookies are cut about 1½ in. wide. Cut each of the bars into slices varying from 1–1¼ in. for the individual bars to ½ in. for the cookies.

6. Place the cut bars on parchment paper-lined pans about 1 in. apart to allow for a slight spread during baking. The egg white and nut mixture will spread very slightly over the surface of the cookie dough bottom.

7. Bake the cookies at 370°F until they are a light brown color.

Walnettos

Ingredients	lb	oz	Mixing procedure
Brown sugar	1	8	Blend these ingredients together until soft
Granulated sugar	1	8	and smooth
Salt		1	
Butter	1		
Shortening		10	
Baking soda		¼	
Honey		4	
Egg yolks		12	Add the eggs in 3 stages and cream in well
Whole eggs		8	
Vanilla		1	Add the flavorings and stir in
Walnut or maple flavoring		1	
Cake flour	3	12	Sift the flour and baking powder together.
Baking powder		¼	Add and mix smooth
Chopped walnuts	1	8	Add and mix smooth

1. Place the mix into a sheet pan lined with parchment paper. Dust lightly with flour and flatten until evenly distributed.

2. Roll the top of the cookie dough lightly with a rolling pin to even out the thickness.

3. Chill the cookies until the cookie dough is hard.

4. Cut strips of cookie dough about 1½ in. wide and place on a cake board. Cut the strips into small slices and place with cut side facing the pan.

5. Bake at 390°F until a slight brown crust forms around the edge.

Yield: One full sheet pan

Blitz Kuchen (*Almond Squares*)

These cookies are treated much the same as the candy-type brownie cookies. While the cookie sheet is still warm, the sheet is cut into small squares and allowed to cool. They will be crisp when cool.

Ingredients	lb	oz	Mixing procedure
Sugar	2	10	Cream the ingredients in this stage until
Salt		½	soft and light
Butter	1	8	
Shortening	1	8	
Egg yolks	1		Add the eggs slowly and cream well after
Whole eggs	1	4	each addition. Scrape sides of kettle
Cake flour	1	4	Sift the flours, add, and mix smooth
Bread flour	3	4	

1. Divide the batter evenly over 3 sheet pans that have been greased and dusted with flour, or lined with parchment paper.
2. Spread the batter evenly over each pan. Sprinkle the cookie mix liberally with sliced almonds and sprinkle the tops of the almonds with cinnamon sugar.
3. Bake at 375–380°F until just done.
4. Remove from the oven and cut into 2 in. squares while hot or still warm.

Yield: 3 sheets

Christmas Cookie Specialties

Pastry chefs always add cookie specialties for Christmas along with a variety of other cookies that have been finished with colorful decorations appropriate to the season. Ginger cookie dough (refer to the cut-out type of cookies) is often used to make a variety of Christmas cookies. A variety of bag-out type cookies are usually garnished with colored sugar or dipped in a variety of colorful fondant icings. To these are added some of the more traditional cookies made for the holiday season. The following are the cookies that fall into that caregory.

Lebkuchen

Ingredients	lb	oz	Mixing procedure
Clover honey (light color)	3		Place these ingredients over a low flame and heat well to blend ingredients to-
Sugar		10	gether. Allow to cool until slightly warm
Cinnamon		¼	
Allspice		¼	
Ground cardamom		¼	

Nonfat dry milk		4	Add the yolks and nonfat dry milk and stir
Egg yolks		8	in well. Dissolve the ammonium bicarbon-
Water	1	8	ate in the water and add. Stir lightly
Ammonium bicar- bonate [1]		1½	
Cake flour	3		Sift the flours together. Add and mix to a
Bread flour	5	12	smooth dough
Diced mixed fruits	3		Add and mix into the dough

1. Place the dough on a lightly floured pan, cover, and allow the dough to relax in a cool place or in the refrigerator overnight.
2. Roll out the dough on a floured cloth using enough dusting flour to prevent the dough from sticking to the rolling pin. The thickness may vary from ⅛–¼ in. thickness depending upon the size and shape of the cookies. For example, gingerbread men or clowns will require a slightly thicker dough than the smaller cookies cut into stars or trees.
3. Cut out the cookies and place them on parchment paper-lined pans or pans that have been greased and dusted with flour. Be sure to remove excess flour from the cookie dough before cutting out the cookies. Space the cookies about 1 in. apart on the pans.
4. Bake the cookies at 360°F. They will feel slightly tender when touched in the center and should spring back when touched.

Finishing Lebkuchen Cookies   (See Fig. 13.113)   These cookies may be covered with softened royal icing of various pastel colors, applied with a spatula or table knife. Allow the icing to dry and then decorate with stiffer royal icing used for piping various designs and decorations on the cookies. Colored sugar and decorations may be sprinkled on the royal

[1]If ammonium bicarbonate is not available, substitute 1 oz baking soda dissolved in the water and 1½ oz baking powder sifted with the flour. The dough will become slightly gaseous after resting and should roll easily. The dough should be of medium stiff consistency when mixed. It may be necessary to add liquid (eggs) if too stiff, or additional bread flour if too soft.

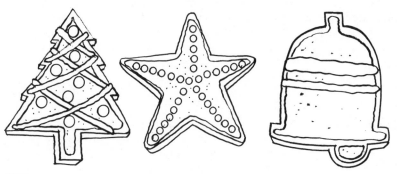

13.113
Decorate Lebkuchen cookies with royal icing

icing while it is still soft. The cookies may be left with the regular light brown crust color and the various icing designs piped on the cookies. The cookies may also be covered with a variety of fondant icings that have been colored.

Pfefferneusse   (*Spice drops*)

Ingredients	lb	oz	Mixing procedure
Honey	3		Warm the honey and sugar over a low
Brown sugar		8	flame to soften
Egg yolks		6	Add these ingredients to the above and
Salt		1	blend in well
Vegetable oil		4	
Cinnamon		1	
Allspice		¼	
Cloves		¼	
Ginger		¼	
Water		12	Dissolve the baking soda and ammonium
Baking soda		1	bicarbonate in the water. Add to the
Ammonium bi-carbonate		½	above and stir in well
Bread flour	2	8	Sift the flours. Add to the above and mix
Cake flour	2	8	to smooth dough

1. Place the dough, which is of medium stiff consistency, on a floured pan and refrigerate or place in a cool place for several hours or overnight.
2. Cut pieces of dough from the dough and roll out into strips about ½ in. in diameter. Cut the strip into pieces about ½ in. thick.
3. Round up the units into round balls in the palms of the hands. Use a little dusting flour to prevent the balls of dough from sticking. Place the balls on parchment paper-lined pans spacing them about 1 in. apart.
4. Bake the cookies at 365–370°F. The cookies will spread a bit during baking but will maintain their round, half-ball shape.
5. Allow the cookies to cool and then place them in a large bowl. Pour the following prepared syrup over them:

Yield: 300–400 cookies

Syrup for Pfefferneusse

Ingredients	lb	oz	Mixing procedure
Sugar	6		Boil the syrup to 240°F which is the soft
Water	1	8	ball stage
Glucose or corn syrup		4	

1. Pour the hot syrup over the cookies and stir with paddle or large ladle so that the cookies are covered with the syrup.
2. Remove the cookies in small amounts and roll them into a blend of:

Ingredients	lb	oz	Mixing procedure
Confectioners sugar	8		Sift the sugar and the starch together sev-
Cornstarch	2		eral times to obtain a good blend

The cookies will be covered with this mixture of sugar and starch. Remove and continue this process until all the cookies are covered. The sugar may be colored with a few drops of color for greater variety.

Springerle Cookies

These are special Christmas cookies made from a dough that is like a firm sponge cake mix. The eggs are whipped before the flour is added and mixed into a dough of medium stiff consistency. The various shapes and forms are obtained with the use of special forms containing sets of impressions. There may be as many as 12 square or other shaped impressions in each of the springerle forms. For added spice and flavor, finely ground aniseed may be used to dust the parchment paper-lined pans.

Ingredients	lb	oz	Mixing procedure
Confectioners sugar	3		Sift the sugar and salt. Whip the eggs
Salt		½	slightly and gradually add the sugar. Whip
Eggs	2		until thick
Cake flour	5		Add the flavorings and mix in. Sift the
Ammonium bi-carbonate		½	flour and ammonium bicarbonate. Add and mix to a smooth dough
Lemon flavoring		½	
Anise flavoring		½	

1. Form the dough into a smooth, rectangular shape. Place on a flour dusted cloth and roll out to approximately ¼ in. thick. The dough may be rolled slightly thicker if the form pans have deep impressions and the forms must be pressed into the dough deeper to get the impression on the cookies.
2. Dust the top of the rolled out dough lightly with sifted cornstarch or bread flour. This will prevent the form from sticking. Be sure to apply equal pressure over the entire form for even impressions.
3. With a pastry wheel or sharp French knife, cut the cookies out in the pattern lines separating each of the mold impressions.
4. Remove excess amounts of flour or starch with a soft bristled brush. Place the cookies on parchment paper-lined pans spaced about 1½ in. apart. As indicated previously, the paper on the pan may be dusted lightly with finely ground aniseed for additonal flavor.
5. Allow the cookies to dry overnight at room temperature.

6. Bake at 350°F until the cookies are baked through thoroughly and have a dry crust. Average cookie thickness will take about 30 min. to bake through thoroughly.

Yield: Variable with size and shape

Swiss Lackerli Cookies

Ingredients	lb	oz	Mixing procedure
Honey	3		Warm the honey and sugar. Use a low
Sugar	1	6	flame and stir while heating
Salt		½	
Ammonium bi-carbonate		1	Dissolve the ammonium bicarbonate and baking soda in the water and add to the
Baking soda		½	above
Water		8	
Allspice		¼	Blend the spices. Add to the above and
Cinnamon		½	mix in well
Nutmeg		¼	
Cloves		¼	
Bread flour	2	4	Sift the flours and add to the above. Add
Cake flour	1	4	the fruits and nuts and mix to a smooth
Diced, mixed fruits	2		dough. The dough should be of medium
Chopped walnuts and almonds	2		stiff consistency. It may be necessary to add some flour

1. Roll out the dough on a flour dusted cloth to about ¼ in. thickness.
2. Cut out cookies with a variety of cookie cutter shapes. The square and diamond shapes may be cut out by using a pastry wheel and straight edge or ruler to guide the wheel or the knife.
3. Place the cookies on parchment paper-lined pans spaced about 1 in. apart.
4. Bake the cookies at 370–375°F until just done.
5. Brush the cookie tops with a medium-thin simple icing using a brush and return to the oven for a few minutes to glaze the cookies. Do not overbake when glazing.

Yield: Approx. 200 large cookies

Egg Cookie Varieties (Kichel)

The egg cookies, commonly called kichel, are very popular with certain ethnic groups. For example, Jewish people have a preference for these cookies. However, because of their lightness, crispness, and bland taste, they are quite popular with many people. Caterers will often have pastry chefs prepare these cookies in rather large volume since they have long shelf life and do not stale readily. The preparation of these cookies does require special care. Some are baked with steam, others are baked without. Some cookie varieties are rolled in sugar and others are bagged out or rolled out in flour. The baking of these cookies requires a rather slow approach and moderate oven temperatures when the cookies are rolled in sugar. Those containing lesser amounts of sugar and rolled in flour as a dusting agent are baked at a higher temperature. It is important for the pastry chef to remember that egg cookies must be baked dry and crisp without developing a dark crust color.

Bow Tie Sugar Egg Cookies

Ingredients	lb	oz	Mixing procedure
Sugar		7	Blend all ingredients well
Salt		¾	
Vegetable oil	1		
Egg yolks	1	8	
Whole eggs	1	8	
Vanilla (optional)		½	
Rum flavoring (optional)		½	
Bread flour (variable)	3	12	Sift the flour. Add and mix to a smooth dough

1. The dough should be of medium stiff consistency and have a slight tendency to spread a little on the bench. Place the dough on a floured pan or bench and allow to relax for 20–30 min. The dough may be refrigerated for later use.
2. Brush the top surface of the dough with vegetable oil to prevent heavy crust formation.
3. To make up the bow ties, place the dough on a sugared part of the bench. Dust the top of the dough with granulated sugar and roll out to about ⅛–¼ in. thickness. Check the bottom of the dough when rolling.
4. Roll up on the rolling pin and spread additional sugar over the bench to prevent the dough from sticking. Dust the top of the dough with additional sugar. Allow the rolled out dough to relax for about 10 min.
5. Be sure the dough is of even thickness. Using a pastry wheel, cut the dough into small, three-quarter-in-wide rectangles about 1½ in. long. The size may vary for larger cookies.
6. Pick up each cookie and give it one turn to form the bow tie. Place the cookies on parchment paper-lined pans spaced about 1 in. apart. A pan that has been brushed with vegetable oil may be used.
7. Allow the cookies to relax for ½ hr and bake at 350°F until dry and crisp. (See Figs. 13.114 through 13.116.)

Yield: Approx. 300 cookies

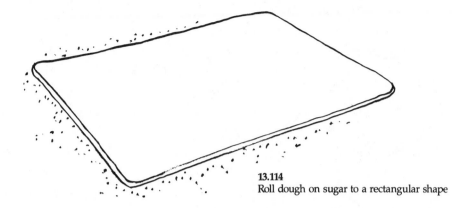

13.114
Roll dough on sugar to a rectangular shape

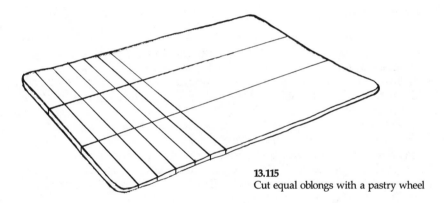

13.115
Cut equal oblongs with a pastry wheel

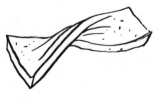

13.116
Twist to a bow tie shape

13.117
Place six kichel on a sheet pan

Sugar Egg Cookies   (*Kichel*)

The same dough may be used to make the larger, thinner, flakier type of cookie in a round form. These are usually served in a large unit about 6 in. in diameter.

1. They may also be rolled out into an oval form for variety. After the dough has been mixed and placed on the bench, scale the dough into presses in units of about 4–4½ lb per press.
2. Individual units of dough weighing about 2 oz each may be scaled and rounded up into ball shapes. Allow the rounded units to relax for about ½ hr.
3. Roll each unit in granulated sugar. Use bread flour to dust the top of the unit so that the rolling pin does not stick. Be sure to have enough sugar on the bench to prevent the dough from sticking.
4. Roll out the dough quite thin (1/16 in.) and evenly. Place the units on a pan that has been brushed with oil. Place about 6 rolled-out units on each pan. (Fig. 13.117.)
5. Allow the large kichel to relax for about ½ hr and then stipple or puncture about 2 in. apart with a fork. This will prevent excessive blistering during baking.
6. Bake these large egg cookies at 365°F until golden brown. Remove from the pans while still slightly warm. Handle gently to avoid breaking.
7. These units may be rolled out into a long oval as well as round shape. Cookie size may be controlled by scaling.

Saucer-Shaped Egg Cookies

These cookies are made from a soft egg dough batter that is bagged out on lightly oiled sheet pans. These cookies, when properly made, will expand during baking and form small saucer or cup shapes that have the appearance of mushroom caps.

Ingredients	lb	oz	Mixing procedure
Sugar		4	Sift all the dry ingredients together to
Salt		½	blend
Bread flour	1	8	
Ammonium bi- carbonate		¼	
Vegetable oil	1		Add the eggs and oil and mix for about 10
Eggs (fresh shell)	1		min. on 2nd speed until the oil shows signs of separating out
Eggs (fresh shell)	1		Add the eggs in 6 or 7 stages and mix well after each addition. Continue to mix for about 15 min. and the mix tears short when touched

1. Deposit the cookies on pans that have been lightly brushed with vegetable oil. Use a medium-size plain tube. Bag out the size of a quarter and give the tube a quick twist to tear the mix sharply away and prevent a stringlike streak of batter from following each bagged cookie.
2. Space the cookies about 1 in. apart or slightly more depending upon the size.
3. Bake at 410–415°F until the cookies have risen and expanded and have formed the saucer shape. Bake until golden brown, dry, and crisp.

Yield: Variable (250–300)

Honey-Type Cookies

Honey Salami Slices

Ingredients	lb	oz	Mixing procedure
Sugar	6		Boil the sugar and honey over a low flame
Honey	6		to a temperature of 275°F (soft crack)
Almond or macaroon paste	12		Add enough jam to form a smooth stiff paste out of the almond paste and red
Red coloring (enough to color the paste to medium dark red)			coloring. Add the boiled honey in a steady stream to the almond paste and mix at slow speed to a firm consistency
Apricot jam (variable)			
Ground filberts (toasted)	4		Add the nuts and mix smooth. When slightly warm, the mix should be medium
Walnut pieces	4		stiff and have a plastic feel for ease in
Filberts (whole or pieces)	2		molding

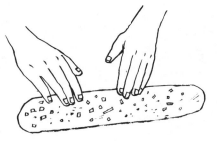

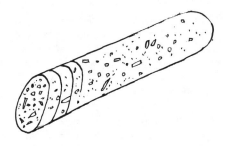

13.118
Honey salami slices

1. If the batter becomes too stiff, it may be softened by adding some apricot jam and mixing at slow speed.
2. Place the batter on a marble bench or workbench that has been lightly oiled. Shape the units into rolls about 2½ in. in diameter and roll up in light wax paper.
3. When cool and firm, slice at a diagonal. The exposed and sliced nuts will provide the appearance of salami. Use sufficient color to make the salami appear like a genuine salami slice.
4. The units may be rolled into smaller sizes and sliced for a smaller cookie appearance. (See Fig. 13.118.)

Yield: Variable with thickness of shaped rolls and slices that are cut

Honey Nuts

Honey nuts are made by combining baked, small, dough balls with a coating of boiled honey and sugar. In addition, glazed cherries and a variety of nut pieces are added in the final stages of preparation. The pastry chef will often serve these as individual servings in special paper cups or shape them into larger round balls or oval shapes placed on a doily and serving platter. The honey nuts are colorful and attractive and are especially prepared for special holidays and special requests.

Ingredients	lb	oz	Mixing procedure
Sugar		6	Blend these ingredients together until
Salt		1	evenly blended
Egg yolks	2		
Whole eggs	1		
Vegetable oil		12	
Vanilla		1	
Rum flavoring (optional)		½	
Bread flour	4	8	Add the flour and mix to a smooth dough

1. Place the dough on a floured portion of the bench and form into a rectangular shape. Allow the dough to rest for about 15 min.
2. The dough is scaled into units weighing about 12 oz–1 lb.
3. Round these units and allow to relax for 10 min.
4. Roll out the units into strips about ½ in. in diameter (Fig. 13.119). Several strips may be rolled out and dusted with flour.
5. The strips of dough are then lined up next to each other and then cut into units about ½ in. wide (Fig. 13.120).
6. Dust the cut pieces with flour and then separate them by lightly tossing on the bench. Place the cut units of dough into a coarse sieve and shake lightly to remove excess flour (Fig. 13.121).

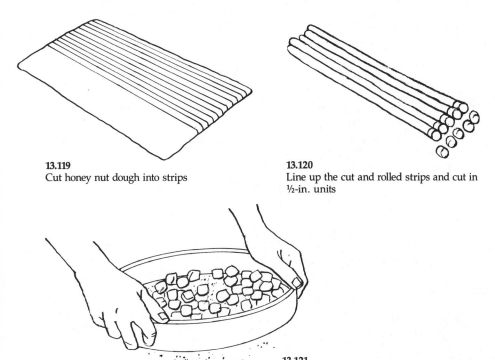

13.119
Cut honey nut dough into strips

13.120
Line up the cut and rolled strips and cut in ½-in. units

13.121
Place the baked units of dough into a coarse sieve. Shake to remove the excess flour

7. Place the pieces on a parchment paper-lined pan so that the surface of the pan is covered with the separated units. Use enough pans to avoid heaping units on top of each other.
8. Bake the units at 350°F until they have a light, golden brown color and feel crisp and firm to the touch. Place the baked units into a sieve after they have cooled and sift to remove excess flour attached to the baked dough units.

Yield: Variable with size and shape

Honey Coating for the Nuts

Ingredients	lb	oz	Mixing procedure
Honey	3		Place the ingredients into a bowl and cook
Sugar	1		over a low flame to 265°F. A drop of the
Cloves		⅛	boiled honey will tend to form a hard ball when dropped into cool water

Add the baked honey nuts and stir with a wooden paddle or large stirring paddle. When the nuts are coated add the following ingredients:

Ingredients	lb	oz	Mixing procedure
Glazed cherries	4–5		Add and mix gently with the paddle until
Hazelnuts or filberts	3		the cherries and nuts are coated
Walnut pieces	4		

1. Place the entire mix on a part of the bench which has been lightly oiled.
2. Moisten the hands with water and form the units into various shapes and sizes.
3. As indicated, small, individual servings may be made up into round ball shapes and placed in paper-lined cups.
4. Larger units may be shaped into large balls or mounds or into oval, loaf shapes. (See Figs. 13.122–13.125.)

13.122
Cook the honey to proper room temperature and add honey nuts, regular nuts, and fruits

13.123
Allow the mix to cool on bench

13.124
Scale into 8 oz balls

13.125
Place smaller units in cupcake liners

Large Snap-Type Cookies

These less expensive cookies are often served to children with milk, hot chocolate, or with an ice cream dessert. The pastry chef may often be required to produce a variety of these cookies if they are not purchased. The pastry chef may also prefer to make his own snap-type cookies. Very often, a wafer cookie mix may be bagged out in larger size and used for the "cookie and milk" break. Snap cookies are also made from thicker cookie batters that are chilled and then sliced as an icebox cookie. These cookies may be kept in dough form in the refrigerator for lengthy periods and then sliced and baked as required. The recipes that follow are those which are quite popular and used extensively. There are many other recipes and varieties which may be used.

Lemon Snaps

Ingredients	lb	oz	Mixing procedure
Sugar	5		Blend these ingredients to a smooth con-
Salt		1	sistency. It is not necessary to cream
Shortening	1	12	
Cake flour		12	
Baking soda		1½	
Cream of tartar		2	
Whole eggs	2		Add the eggs slowly and blend in well after each addition
Powdered lemon juice or		5	Add to the above and stir in well
Juice and outside rind of 6 lemons			
Cake flour [1]		5	Sift, add, and mix until a dough is formed. Do not overmix

[1]If the juice of 6 lemons is added, increase the flour by 8 oz.

1. Scale the dough into units weighing approximately 1½ lb. Form the dough into cylinders about 1½–2 in. in diameter.
2. Place the cylinders of dough on a flour-dusted pan and refrigerate. When chilled, slice into cookies about 1 oz each.
3. Dip the cookies into sugar and place on parchment paper-lined pans or pans that have been greased lightly. Space the cookies about 2 in. apart to allow for spread.
4. Bake the cookies at 355–365°F until light brown. The cookies will spread considerably during baking and feel soft when taken from the oven. The cookies will become crisp when cool.
5. If the cookies are not dipped in sugar before baking, they may be decorated with a good sized drop of lemon fondant icing when cool.

Chocolate Chip Cookies

Ingredients	lb	oz	Mixing procedure
Brown sugar	2		Cream these ingredients to a soft, light
Granulated sugar	1		consistency
Salt		1	
Nonfat dry milk		4	
Butter	1		
Shortening	1		
Eggs	1	8	Add the eggs in 4 stages and cream well after each addition
Water		10	Dissolve the baking soda in the water.
Baking soda		½	Add with the vanilla and stir in
Vanilla		1	
Cake flour	3	4	Sift the cake flour. Add and mix to a
Chocolate chips (variable)	3	8	smooth batter. Add the chocolate chips and mix until evenly distributed

1. Bag out the cookies with a pastry bag and large plain tube on parchment paper-lined pans or pans that have been lightly greased. Space the cookies about 1½ to 2 in. apart to allow for spread during baking. The size of the cookie should determine the space required.
2. Bake the cookies at 385°F until they have a brown crust color around the edge and feel just mildly soft in the center. These cookies will tend to firm up after they are removed from the oven.

Note: Pastry chefs may also add finely chopped nuts to the batter. Chopped walnuts or finely chopped pecan pieces may be added. It is advisable to reduce the amount of chocolate chips by a weight equal to the nuts added.

Yield: Approx. 250 cookies

Chocolate Drop Cookies

Ingredients	lb	oz	Mixing procedure
Sugar	2	4	Cream these ingredients until soft and
Salt		1	smooth
Nonfat dry milk		4	
Butter	1		
Shortening	1		
Eggs	1	8	Add the eggs in 3 stages and cream in well
Water		12	Dissolve the baking soda in the water and
Baking soda		½	add with the vanilla. Stir slightly
Vanilla		1	
Cake flour	4	2	Sift these ingredients together. Add to the
Cocoa		8	above and mix smooth
Cinnamon		¼	
Baking powder		1¼	

1. Bag out the cookies with a plain tube on parchment paper-lined pans or pans that have been lightly, but evenly greased. Deposit the cookies the size of a half-dollar for the larger size. The peaks on the cookies may be flattened with a moist cloth placed over the pan and gently flattened with the palms of the hands.
2. The cookies may be garnished with chocolate sprinkles, chopped nuts, cherries, or other garnish before baking.
3. Bake at 380–390°F until the cookies indicate a light crust around the edge and the centers feel slightly springy.
4. Cookies that were not garnished before baking may be iced with a chocolate fudge center or striped with fondant icing.

Yield: 250 large cookies

Macaroon Snap Cookies

Ingredients	lb	oz	Mixing procedure
Sugar	2	10	Cream these ingredients to a soft, smooth
Salt		1	consistency
Nonfat dry milk		3	
Butter		8	
Shortening	1	2	
Baking soda		½	
Eggs		10	Add the eggs in 2 stages and cream in well
Water	1	2	Add the water and flavorings and stir in
Vanilla		1	lightly
Orange flavoring (optional) or rind of 2 oranges		½	

Macaroon coconuts	2	8	Add the coconut and stir in
Cake flour	2	10	Sift the flour and baking powder together.
Baking powder		1/4	Add and mix to a smooth consistency

1. Bag out the cookies with a plain tube on parchment paper-lined pans or pans that have been lightly and evenly greased. The points may be flattened by dipping the palms of the hands in water or milk and gently flattening the points.
2. The cookies may be garnished with pieces of glazed cherries before baking.
3. Bake the cookies at 375°F until they have a golden brown crust color. The centers will feel slightly soft but will firm up and turn crisp when the cookies cool.
4. Plain cookies may be garnished with a drop of cookie coating in the center when cool.

Yield: Approx. 250 cookies

Oatmeal Cookies

Ingredients	lb	oz	Mixing procedure
Sugar	1	5	Cream these ingredients together until soft
Salt		1/2	and smooth
Nonfat dry milk		2	
Shortening	1	4	
Cinnamon		1/2	
Nutmeg		1/4	
Eggs		12	Add in 2 stages and cream in
Water		8	Dissolve the baking soda in the water and
Vanilla		1	add with the vanilla. Stir in slightly
Baking soda		1/2	
Molasses	2		Add and stir in
Ground raisins (optional)	1		Add the raisins, nuts, and rind and stir in well
Finely chopped walnuts	1		
Rind of 1 lemon and 1 orange			
Oatmeal	1	12	Add and blend in
Cake flour	1	6	Sift the flour and baking powder. Add and
Baking powder		3/4	mix well to a smooth dough or batter

1. This batter will be medium stiff. It may be bagged out with a large plain tube.
2. The dough may be formed into cylinders about 1 1/2 in. in diameter and chilled.
3. It is then cut into slices about 1/4 in. thick.

4. Place on parchment paper-lined pans. Bake at 400°F until mildly brown. The cookies will feel slightly soft in the center but will crisp up when cool.

Yield: Approx. 200 cookies

Peanut Butter Cookies

Ingredients	lb	oz	Mixing procedure
Sugar	3		Cream these ingredients until soft and
Brown sugar	3		light
Salt		1½	
Nonfat dry milk		4	
Shortening	2	8	
Peanut butter	3		
Eggs	1	8	Add the eggs in 4 stages and cream in well
Water	1		Dissolve the baking soda in the water.
Baking soda		1½	Add with the vanilla and stir in
Vanilla		1	
Cake flour	5		Sift, add, and mix to a smooth batter

1. The batter will be medium stiff. It will also become firmer as it stands because of the absorption of the peanut butter and flour.
2. Bag out with a plain tube on parchment paper-lined pans.
3. The batter may be chilled and made up into cylinders about 1½ in. in diameter. Smaller cylinders may be formed for smaller size cookies.
4. Chill the cookie cylinders and then cut into slices about ¼ in. thick.
5. Place on pans and bake at 400–410°F. The cookies will have considerable spread during baking and will feel tender when baked. These cookies will become crisp when they cool.

Yield: Approx. 300 large cookies

14

Variety Tarts (Flans), Fruit Cakes (Cobblers), and Strudel

This section will cover the production of the many varieties of tarts, fruit cakes and cobblers, and the various types of strudel the pastry chef is often required to make. Many related fruit-filled desserts such as pies and other desserts made from puff pastry have been covered in previous sections. There will be reference made to the recipes used for the different crusts and fruit fillings used in the prior sections. The recipes for pie crust, short dough, and so forth, will not be repeated in this section. However, they will be used for the production of the many desserts made from tarts and other pan forms.

The modern pastry chef may have available the equipment to automatically produce tart shells, pie shells, and other forms that relate to tart and fruit cake production. For example, Mary Ann pans for cakelike tart bases and for large flan-type cakes may be available. On the other hand, the pastry chef will also find that prebaked tart shells and other cake bottoms may be purchased in ready-made form. All that has to be done to complete the pastry or dessert is to fill and finish these purchased or prepared shells or cake shells. Production or purchase will depend in large measure upon the volume, menu, cost control, and facilities for production. In fact, prepared fruit and custard fillings, such as lemon filling, may be purchased for use as required. All of these factors are often efficiency methods for fast food operation and cost control. These shortcuts in production are most often used in fast food operations for large volume turnover. They are also used very often where the personnel lack the skills of the qualified pastry chef. They may also be used where a single pastry chef has to supervise a large staff in dispersed feeding operations. The following recipes, procedures, and dessert suggestions are for the skilled pastry chef and his assistants.

Variety Tarts (Flans)

Tart pans, tart shells, and other tart-shaped bases provide the pastry chef with the capacity to produce a great variety of desserts. Some desserts that are made with tart pans, such as the almond paste and frangipane-filled tarts, have been discussed previously. Fruit-filled, pastry cream and custard-filled tarts, and combination tarts (fruit- and custard-filled) will be covered in this chapter. The variety of tarts that may be made is only limited by the ability of the pastry chef to produce them. Fruit tarts and flans are most popular and are made throughout the year with either fresh, frozen, or canned fruits. The design and finish of the tarts provide the attractiveness and appeal to the diner or consumer.

Tarts are made with a shell or bottom as are pies. The most commonly used dough for pastry tarts is the short dough or the sugar dough. Pie crust is very often used, or a combination or half-and-half dough made with equal parts of pie crust and short dough. The shell dough for pies is used extensively. This dough is similar to the shell dough used for pie shells made automatically by machine. Tarts are made with the same equipment, but with smaller dies. The machine-made tart shells are pre-baked and used for various custard or pastry cream fillings. They may also be filled with precooked or prepared fruit fillings.

Handmade tarts are made with a short dough because of the delicate, cookie tenderness of the baked crust. They may also be made with the basic pie crust or combination dough. The doughs are rolled out on a floured cloth to ⅛ in. thickness, rolled up on a thin rolling pin, and then unrolled over the lined up tart pans. (Figs. 14.1 and 14.2) The insides are pressed in with a ball of the short dough or pie crust dipped in flour. The rolling pin is rolled over the tops of the tart pans to cut the dough. Each of the tart pans is then checked for complete coverage. The scrap pieces of dough are used to fill in uncovered areas of the tart pan. It may be necessary to fully press the dough to the very bottom of the tart pan when deep tart pans are used.

14.1
Tart shell

14.2
Placing rolled-out dough on shells

It is advisable to use a tart pan that is scalloped, has a depth of approximately 1½ in. and a top diameter of approximately 2¼–2½ in. Shallow tart pans do not allow for much filling and often make the dessert look skimpy. Where pie crust is used, it is necessary to allow the dough to fall loosely over the tart pans so that there is little shrinkage when the tops are cut with the rolling pin. It is also advisable to allow the dough to relax for a few minutes over the tart pans before cutting. Pastry chefs may prefer to remove small pieces of dough for making individual tarts. The dough is rounded up and then rolled out larger than the top of the tart pan so that provision is made for coverage of the bottom and sides. Excess dough is removed with the palms of the hands. Where puff pastry dough is used, the dough should be rolled out slightly thinner than the pie crust or short dough. The dough should be stippled or punctured with a fork to prevent excessive blistering during baking. It is very important to allow the rolled out puff pastry dough for the tarts to relax completely before covering the tart shells.

Tarts that are baked with fruit or other filling are usually filled about ½ to ¾ full. The filled tarts are placed on baking pans and baked at 400°F. Tart shells made with a cookie short dough will brown more rapidly than will the tart made with pie crust dough. This is due to the higher percentage of sugar in the dough. The tarts are considered baked when the rim or edge of the tart dough is browned. Pastry chefs may often select the center tart on the pan and turn it slightly on a wet, flat plate to check the bottom for proper bake. Tart shells are usually filled with a paper cupcake liner half filled with dried beans or rice. The tarts are then baked to retain their shape without the collapse of the sides of the tart during baking. The paper cups and beans may be used over and over for some time. The baking shells are stored in covered containers and used when required.

Tart pans made of aluminum foil are available and are disposable with service. These tart pans usually have straight sides and are flanged so that the top diameter is larger than the bottom. These tart pans are usually filled with a sponge or chiffon cake batter (approximately half-full), and baked. The tarts are then finished with added fruits, pastry creams, and other garnishes.

As previously indicated, Mary Ann pans provide the means for making the cake shells. The pans have raised centers and grooved sides. When the pans are half-filled with cake batter and baked, the entire pan is filled. The cakes are turned over with the center only half-filled with cake while the sides are the full size of the pan. Fill the centers and decorate the top and sides of the tart as desired. Some pastry tarts are made by cutting out round discs of cake from a cake sheet; the sides of the disc are then covered with buttercream or jam and garnished with a variety of coverings such as ground nuts, sliced almonds, sponge cake crumbs, or chocolate sprinkles.

These are supplements where there may be no tart pans available. Tart pans vary in size and include boat shapes or ovals. The same procedure is followed for making the shells for the ovals as for the round tarts. However, the oval or boat-shaped tarts are often shallow and require little filling when baking. Otherwise they will run over during baking.

When preparing tarts for finishing, a number of fillings and arrangements may be used. For example, the straight fruit-filled tart or flan may be filled with additional precooked fruit filling and the top may be garnished with fresh fruits and covered with a fruit glaze. Others may be partially filled with a pastry cream or custard and then covered with a fruit filling. Fresh fruit slices and glazing may follow for the final finish. Some tarts are baked with a small amount of fruit or custard filling which may then be covered with a thin slice of cake gently pressed over the baked filling. Additional fruits are added and the tart is then garnished with slices of fresh fruits and glazed.

Other tarts fall into the category of the meringue-topped tarts. Lemon or another cream-type filling is placed into the prebaked tart shells. The fillings are then covered with meringue and browned quickly in a hot oven. Still other tarts may be finished in Chantilly style with a whipped cream filling and decoration. These tarts may also be combined with Bavarois creams and finished with whipped cream. Very often, the pastry chef will combine fresh fruits or berries with whipped cream.

Some tart specialties will have the tart baked with a dry filling, such as an almond or frangipane filling. After baking, the tarts are inverted with the smaller diameter of the bottom facing up. The tarts are then finished with the desired topping. These tarts may also be made with a cupcake base from a sponge or chiffon mix. They may be served with heated brandy and lit as for flambé.

Fruit tarts or flans are most often finished by glazing the fruits or berries placed on the top of the tart. This provides a shine or luster, protects the fruit and prevents discoloration due to oxidation, and adds special taste to the finished tart. The glaze is important in that it must add to the taste and appearance rather than merely act as a gel. For a basic glaze, many pastry chefs prefer to use apricot coating mixed with apricot jam. The apricot coating has an amber or almost neutral color and can be used for glazing almost any type of fruit. However, additional taste as well as color is often desirable. Thus, equal parts of the apricot coating can be boiled with the apricot jam. If the glaze is slightly stiff or firm when cool and after it has been applied, a small amount of simple syrup will dilute the gel consistency. Pastry chefs will also add coloring to the glaze when it is being heated, to blend the glaze with the color of the fruit. For example, yellow coloring may be added for covering or glazing sliced bananas or peaches. A few drops of red coloring may be added to obtain orange.

For the red-colored glaze, currant jelly is often blended with apricot coating. The currant jelly or jam provides a reddish color as well as providing added sweetness and the tartness of its natural taste. Additional red coloring may be added where required. Thus, strawberry tarts, cherry tarts, raspberry tarts, and so forth, may be glazed with this mixture with excellent results. It is noteworthy to mention that glazed tarts are often garnished with toasted cake crumbs, chopped nuts, and similar garnishes around the very edges of the tart. This provides a cover for glaze that has run over slightly and also provides a contrast in color.

Apple Tarts

Line the tart pans with a short dough or half and half dough. Place a large dot of apricot jam at the bottom. Fill the tart with apple pie filling in which the apple pieces have been chopped to smaller pieces. Fill the tart pan about two-thirds full. Using small fresh apples that have been peeled and cored, slice the apple in half. With a sharp knife (paring knife or vegetable knife) cut slices about ⅛ in. thick but do not entirely separate the slices of apple. Place the sliced apple half over the top surface of the tart and spread the apple slices slightly so that the entire surface of the tart is covered. Bake the tarts at 415°F for approximately 30 min. The crust of the shell will have a brown crust color and the apples will feel soft to the touch. Allow the apple tarts to cool until warm and remove from the tart pans. Place the tarts on a sheet pan and then cover with the hot apricot glaze. The sides of the tart may be garnished with toasted chopped filberts or lightly toasted sponge cake crumbs.

Apple Cream Tarts

Round, scalloped tart pans or boat-shaped tart pans may be used for these tarts. Line the pans with short dough or tart dough used for the prebaked shells. Fill the tarts with vanilla custard pastry cream about two-thirds full. Place the sliced apples over the custard, separating the slices so that the entire surface of the tart is covered. Pastry chefs will use the frozen, cured apples that are peeled and cored. This saves considerable time and improves quality control as apple sizes are important factors. Bake these tarts at 415°F until the edges of the dough are light brown. Cool and cover with apricot glaze after the tarts have been removed from the tart pans. Place the tarts in paper liners for service and ease in handling.

Pineapple Tarts

There are two popular methods of preparing pineapple tarts. The first follows the usual procedure for making fruit-filled tarts. Line the tart pans with short dough about ⅛ in. thick. A pie crust or combination dough may be used for the tart bottoms. Fill the tarts about two-thirds full of pineapple pie filling. It is advisable to add some small pineapple chunks to the filling for a richer and more natural fruit filling. Bake the tarts at 415°F. The edge of the crust will develop a light brown color. When cool, place a full pineapple slice taken from sweetened, canned pineapple that has been well drained, over the top of the tart. If the pineapple slice is too large for a small diameter tart, cut the slice into quarters and place two quarters over the top leaving a space in the center. Place a glazed cherry in the center and glaze with apricot glaze. Pastry chefs will often use the syrup of the pineapple and blend it with the apricot coating for added flavor. The sweetened juice is boiled and thickened slightly with cornstarch and then combined with the hot apricot coating.

Pineapple Cream Tarts

Half-fill the tart shells with pineapple filling and bake. Allow the tarts to cool and fill the tarts with custard cream filling. Form a slight mound in the center and place a quarter slice of pineapple on each side of the mound of custard. Place a cherry in the center and glaze the tart top with hot apricot glaze or a glaze made with the sweetened syrup in which the pineapple was packed. Additional yellow coloring may be added to the syrup glaze. These tarts may also be made with a complete custard filling. This requires prebaked tart shells. Fill the shells completely with custard cream. Place some pineapple filling over the custard and then garnish with a slice of pineapple and a cherry. Glaze to finish.

Strawberry Tarts

These tarts are most attractive when made with fresh strawberries as a garnish. While fresh strawberries can usually be obtained, there may be times when only the frozen berries are available. In this case, use the whole strawberries that have been drained for the top of the tart. The tart bottoms may be half-filled with strawberry pie filling or a blend of strawberry jam and strawberry pieces, either fresh or frozen. Bake the shells until done, and cool. Prebaked tart shells are necessary for tarts to be filled entirely with a pastry custard. Fill the baked or the prebaked tart shells with custard almost to the very top. Cut discs of sponge cake or chiffon cake from a sheet that is about 1/4–1/2 in. thick. Place the discs on top of the custard and press in gently so that the cake adheres to the custard. Place some red colored glaze (apricot or apricot-currant) over the cake disc. Place selected strawberries (about 5 or 6 medium berries) around in a pyramid form. The center strawberry should be placed with the pointed end facing up. Glaze the strawberries with the red-colored glaze. Garnish the edge of the tart with fine sponge cake crumbs or ground filberts.

Strawberry Tart Chantilly

Fill the tart bottoms two-thirds full with strawberry pie filling and bake. When cool, garnish the top of the tart with a charlotte design made with whipped cream. A whipped topping or blend of topping and whipping cream may be used. Garnish the top of the cream with a fresh strawberry that has been dipped in red currant glaze. These tarts may also be decorated with a meringue and then quickly browned in a hot oven for a few minutes.

Almond Custard Tarts

These tarts are made in either boat or oval-shaped pans. The round, scalloped tart pans may also be used. The prebaked shells are filled with the following almond cream custard filling. The tarts may have a small amount of apricot filling placed in the tart pans and baked with the filling. Upon cooling, the tarts are then filled with the almond custard cream.

Ingredients	lb	oz	Mixing procedure
Almond paste		12	Mix the almond paste and eggs to a
Whole eggs		8	smooth, soft paste

Sugar	1	6	Dissolve the milk in the water. Add the
Salt		¼	sugar and salt and boil. Stir to prevent
Nonfat dry milk		12	scorching
Water	4		

Cornstarch		6	Dissolve the starch in the water. Add the
Water	2		egg yolks and whip slightly. Add the al-
Egg yolks	1		mond paste and blend in well. Add a
Butter		4	small amount of the boiling milk and
Vanilla		1	blend in. Add this to the boiling milk in a
			steady stream and bring to a boil stirring
			constantly. Add the butter and vanilla, re-
			move from the fire and mix smooth

1. Pour the custard through a strainer. Allow the custard to cool and then fill the prebaked tart shells or the shells baked with apricot filling.
2. With a pastry bag and large plain tube, pipe an oval shape of the custard over the boat-shaped tart shell. Be sure the center is higher and thicker than the ends. A spiral effect or design may be made.
3. If the round tart shells are used, pipe a round shape of the custard over the shell. The custard may have a charlotte effect with a point in the center.
4. Place the tarts in the refrigerator and chill well. Remove from the refrigerator and glaze the entire custard top with hot apricot glaze.
5. When the glaze has cooled and set, design the top by piping cross lines of red piping gel across the top. The round tarts may be garnished or decorated with red piping gel in a spiral form around the tart.

Yield: 100 tarts

Pecan Custard Tarts

The oval-shaped pans or boat tart pans are best suited for these tarts since they are shallow and require less baking time. Round tart pans may be used. A short dough bottom is best for these tart bottoms or shells. Line the tart pans with a thin short dough bottom as for almond tarts. Place a dot of red currant jelly or raspberry jam in the bottom of each tart pan. Fill the tarts slightly more than half full with almond filling or frangipane filling. Almond cream custard may be used. Bake the tarts at 370°F until properly baked. Bake the almond-filled tarts thoroughly. When cool, fill the tarts with a covering of almond cream custard so that the center has a slight mound that is higher than the edge of the tart. Place pecan halves over the custard so that the spacing forms a design. Chill and then glaze with hot apricot glaze. Garnish the edge of the tarts with finely ground filberts that have been lightly toasted.

Pignolia Tarts

The oval-shaped or round-shaped tart pans may be used for this tart. The short dough or thin puff pastry dough may be used for the tart shells. Be sure to allow the puff pastry dough to relax completely before covering the tart pans. Fill the tarts about one-half with frangipane filling or almond tart filling. Bake at 375°F until the filling is completely baked. When cool, fill the tarts with almond cream custard forming a slight mound in the center of the tart. Cover the top with pignolia nuts and chill in the refrigerator. When chilled, glaze the top with hot apricot glaze. The edges may be garnished with toasted, finely ground filberts or hazelnuts.

Banana Tarts
Oval or boat-shaped tart pans are best suited for these tarts. With these shapes, the sliced bananas may be laid out in a neat row for decoration and finishing. Line the boats or ovals with a thin short dough bottom. Fill the bottom about half full with a custard cream and bake in a hot oven. The shells may also be prebaked using the beans or rice in paper cups. Fill the cooled shells with custard cream almost to the top. Slice the bananas evenly and press them gently into the custard so that each banana slice overlays half of the preceding slice. Have the apricot glaze ready so that the banana slices are not exposed to the air for a lengthy period to cause the bananas to turn brown. Glaze the bananas with the hot apricot glaze. A little yellow color may be added to the glaze to enhance the appearance (Fig. 14.3).

Lemon Tarts
Lemon tarts are made in several varieties. For example, it may be baked with a short dough base and lemon pie filling, or prebaked shells may be used and then filled with the desired lemon filling. A Mary Ann cake shell may be used for the filling and for the final garnish. The selected method will depend upon the pastry chef and the production requirements. As for the finish of the tarts, a meringue top may be preferred. Other lemon tarts may be finished with whipped cream. Some pastry chefs may prefer to use the Mary Ann shell, garnish the edge with a fine border of lemon buttercream (a blend of buttercream with lemon pie filling) and fill the centers with lemon filling. Garnish for any of these tarts may be further enhanced with a lemon candy slice covered with sugar.

Lemon Meringue Tart
Use a short dough for the tart bottoms. Fill the tarts half full with lemon pie filling and bake at 400°F. When baked and cooled, fill the tart with lemon filling to the top. A thin slice of sponge or chiffon cake cut from a thin sheet may be placed over the lemon filling or custard. Using a French type of meringue, bag out a charlotte effect with a star tube or a pyramid

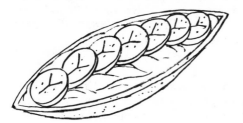

14.3
Banana cream boat

effect with a plain tube. Dust the meringue with confectioners sugar and brown in the oven at 425°F. A stabilizer may be used with the egg whites to prevent "weeping" after baking. The thin slice of cake placed over the filling will tend to absorb any "weeping" of the meringue.

Lemon Cream Tart
Use a prebaked tart shell for this tart, although the tart bases may be prepared as for the meringue-type tarts. Fill the shells with lemon custard cream or lemon pie filling. Chill and decorate with a spiral or charlotte effect made with whipped cream. Garnish with a sugared, candy lemon slice.

Mary Ann Lemon Tarts and Other Mary Ann Tart Varieties
A Mary Ann cake pan is required to make the cake shells for these and similar tarts made with a Mary Ann shell. The pastry chef will most often use a sponge cake or chiffon cake mix for these shells. A high ratio mix may also be used but they will not be as light. The centers of the baked shell are filled with the lemon custard cream after the shells have been baked and cooled. Other fillings of the fruit variety may also be used. The centers may then be garnished with whipped cream or buttercream that is finely piped across the top. The sides may be covered with cream or buttercream and then garnished with lightly toasted sponge cake crumbs or toasted hazel or filbert nuts. The top of the borders may be decorated with a finely piped pear-shape or spiral design made with selected cream to suit the tart. (See Figs. 14.4 and 14.5.)

Cherry Tarts
Line the tart pans with a short dough bottom. Fill the pans about two-thirds full with cherry pie filling and bake at 400°F. The edges of the tart bottom should be golden brown when baked. When cool, fill the tart to the top with cherry filling and then cover with either Royal Anne or black Bing cherries. Glaze with hot, red, apricot and currant glaze. The cherry tarts may be finished with a whipped cream top as for a tart Chantilly. The tarts may be decorated with a border of whipped cream and the centers have the glazed cherries exposed. The cherry tarts may also be finished with a meringue topping and browned in the oven. This is customary in warm or hot weather when whipped cream can be perishable or when sufficient refrigeration may not be available.

Pear Tarts
These tarts are made in round tart pans. A prebaked short dough tart shell is necessary. Fill the baked tart shell about two-thirds full with cus-

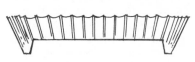

14.4
Mary Ann pan (cross-section)

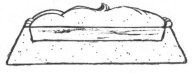

14.5
Lemon meringue tart (cross-section)

tard cream. Use drained pear halves to garnish the top. A thin disc of sponge cake may be placed over the custard before placing the fruit on the tart. The drained pear halves may be tinged with a light green color dissolved in syrup at one end. The other end may be lightly tinged with a pink shade. Cover the pear and the entire surface of the tart with hot apricot glaze. The edge of the tart may be garnished with lightly toasted sponge cake crumbs.

Peach Tarts

These tarts may be made the same as pear tarts. However, most pastry chefs will fill the short dough tart bottoms with peach pie filling and bake the tarts. After cooling, a thin layer of custard cream may be placed over the peach filling. A thin disc of sponge or chiffon cake may be placed over the custard if desired. Cover the top of the tart with a peach half that has been drained. The peach half may be finely sliced and then spread open over the top before adding hot apricot glaze. If sliced peaches are used, layer the slices over each other to form a neat layered design and glaze.

Grape Tarts

Use prebaked shells for these tarts. Fill the shells with custard cream filling. Place a disc of sponge cake or chiffon cake over the custard. Brush the top of the cake disc with hot apricot glaze and apricot jam. Cover the surface of the tart with drained, seedless, canned grapes. Glaze the grapes with hot apricot glaze. Garnish the sides with toasted sponge cake crumbs.

Apricot Tarts

Use a short dough bottom for these tarts. Fill the tarts about two-thirds full with apricot or peach filling used for pies. Bake the tarts at 400°F until the edges are golden brown. The cooled tarts may be filled with custard cream and covered with a thin disc of sponge or chiffon cake. Use well-drained, canned apricots for the tops. Layer the apricot halves slightly over the top and then glaze with hot apricot coating. These tarts may also be finished with whipped cream. The chilled, baked tarts are decorated with a spiral design made with whipped cream. The top of the cream may be garnished with a firm apricot half that has been dipped in apricot glaze and allowed to cool.

Frangipane Tarts

These tarts are made with a frangipane filling, similar to the almond filling used for almond tarts except that it contains butter, is firmer in consistency, and may be stored for use as required. In fact, pastry chefs will often thin the fragipane filling with milk or egg whites and use it as a smear for special almond fillings used for coffee cakes and other yeast-raised pastries. The frangipane cream is often mixed with nuts and diced fruits for special fillings for tarts. The following is a recipe for the basic frangipane filling.

Frangipane Filling

Ingredients	lb	oz	Mixing procedure
Almond paste	3		Mix the almond paste and eggs to a
Eggs	1		smooth consistency
Sugar	3		Add these ingredients to the above and
Salt		1	cream well until soft and light
Butter	2		
Shortening	1		
Eggs	2		Add the eggs in 4 or 5 stages and cream in
Rum		4	well after each addition. Add the flavoring and stir in
Rum flavoring may be substituted for the rum		1½	
Cake flour	1		Sift the flours. Add and mix to a smooth
Bread flour	1	6	consistency

Store the filling in a closed container under refrigeration. When needed, place desired amount in the machine and work smooth at medium speed until soft and creamy.

These tarts are usually combined with a variety of diced fruits and canned fruits that have been drained. Large fruit pieces are chopped into small pieces and combined with the frangipane. Equal amounts of fruits and frangipane are used. Fill the short dough tart pans about three-quarters full with the frangipane-fruit filling that has been flavored with rum flavoring. Bake the filling at 390°F for about 35 min. until the filling is quite firm in the center (springy to the touch). Allow the tarts to cool and garnish with a meringue topping, dust with confectioners sugar, and brown in a hot oven. If the tarts are to be finished with whipped cream, chill the baked tarts before applying the whipped cream. Decorate in a spiral form and place a glazed cherry on top. Mixed diced fruits dipped in rum may be used for garnish.

Almond Frangipane Tart

This tart is often called a Genova tart. The bottoms are made with a short dough and then a small drop of apricot or raspberry jam is placed in the center. Fill the tarts with frangipane cream or with the almond filling as for almond tarts. Bake the tarts at 380°F until the top is quite crisp and firm. Allow the tarts to cool and decorate with a praline or almond-flavored buttercream. Cover the entire top of the tart by making a round, spiral effect with a star tube. Garnish the top with whole almonds facing out from the center in a star form. The almonds may be dipped in sweet chocolate and allowed to dry before placing on the tarts.

Frangipane Boat Tarts

Use the oval or boat tart pans for these tarts. Line the pans with a thin short dough bottom. Pipe a line of apricot jam across the center bottom of the tart. Fill the tart with frangipane cream about two-thirds full. Bake at 385°F for approx. 25–30 min until done. When cool, finish by piping a walnut- or maple-flavored buttercream in a cone shape (similar to a cream roll) across the top. Chill and then cover one side with melted sweet chocolate and the other with pink fondant icing. Use a spatula or bowl knife to apply the icings.

Frangipane Duchess Tarts

Line the round, scalloped tart pans with a short dough bottom about ⅛ in. thick. Place a good-sized drop of apricot jam in the bottom center of the tart. Fill the tart about three-fourths full with frangipane cream and bake at 385°F for about 35 min. The center of the tart should feel almost firm. When cool, pipe a charlotte or spiral design on top of the tart with Italian meringue. A regular meringue with an egg white stabilizer may be used. Place the tarts in a cool oven (about 300°F) for about 12–15 min. to dry and firm the meringue top. When cool, the meringue tops are covered with melted sweet chocolate or cookie dip. A pastel colored fondant icing may also be used. The meringue may also be glazed with a hot apricot glaze.

Chantilly Tarts

Mention has been made about the finishing of fruit and cream-filled tarts with whipped cream. These tarts are often a combination of fruits and custard creams. The fruits include the smaller berries as well as the large-sized fruits. Tarts made with blueberries are first baked with blueberry pie filling and then finished with additional berries and whipped cream. These tarts may be covered with fresh blueberries that are lightly glazed with apricot glaze. The edge of the tart may be garnished with a border of whipped cream. Tarts that are completely covered on top with whipped cream usually have the identifying fruit placed on top of the cream to identify the finished tart. Note is made concerning the use of whipped cream or a blend of whipped cream and whipped topping. The topping is usually whipped first to a semifirm state. The heavy cream is then added and whipped together. Refrigerate all whipped-cream finished tarts until ready to serve.

Variety Fruit Cakes and Cobblers

Fruit cakes and cobblers are actually oversized pies baked in large pans. The pans may be round and varying in size from 8 in. to 14–15 in. in diameter and from 1–2 in. deep. The pans may also be rectangular or square and may vary from regular baking sheet pans to special pans. Large fruit cakes are often called cobblers, although a cobbler is usually a deep dish fruit pie or cake without a bottom crust. Pastry chefs much prefer to prepare the regular, large fruit cakes which have a bottom crust and a crust around the sides. This makes handling and serving easier. The cobbler requires special handling and is often difficult to serve. The large fruit cake replaces the individual tart or flan and is usually made for large volume service and production. It is much simpler to divide a large sheet fruit cake that has been finished into the desired number of portions and serve directly onto serving plates. In fact, pastry chefs will often divide the open-top fruit cake into servings and make the final decorations and garnishes (sauces) when the dessert is in the plate or special serving dish. For large institutional feeding the actual service may be made by the pastry chef's assistants.

Large fruit cakes are most often made with a short dough or sugar dough. This is the same dough that is used for so many other cake bottoms and for special cookies. It handles easily and bakes with a cookie-type shortness and crispness. The bottoms for the larger cakes are prebaked before the sides of the pan are lined with dough and the fruit filling deposited. Prebaking prevents the dough from becoming raw and soggy when filled with fruit and baked. Small layers, such as the 6 in. size, may have the bottom and sides of the shallow layer pan lined with raw dough, filled with fruit and baked. These cakes are baked directly on the hearth of the oven for direct exposure to the oven heat in order to ensure a properly baked bottom. These cakes are often shifted in the oven during baking to apply direct or fresh oven heat to the bottom.

Most pastry chefs will prebake the bottoms of all fruit cakes to be sure the bottoms are properly baked. A soggy or raw bottom cannot support the fruit filling and handling becomes difficult. Pie crust dough or a combination of pie crust and short dough is often used for large fruit cakes. When pie crust is used, the cake is treated the same as a pie. The dough is not prebaked. This holds true with the combination dough. However, pastry chefs may partially bake the bottoms for the combination doughs for fruit cakes. It is quite common for pastry chefs to sprinkle the bottom crusts made with pie dough with light cake crumbs before depositing the fruit filling. The crumbs will tend to absorb any excess liquid present in the filling during baking and act as a buffer so that the bottom crust may bake through completely. Puff pastry dough is often used for the top of large fruit cakes. The dough is rolled out very thin as for a napoleon sheet and stippled or punctured with a fork to prevent excessive blistering during baking. After the dough has been relaxed it is rolled up on a rolling pin and then unrolled over the top of the fruit cake. This dough provides a special flakiness as well as a contrast in doughs used for the fruit cakes.

The fillings used for fruit cakes or cobblers are the same as those used for regular pies. Fresh, frozen, canned, or even dried fruits may be used. A combination of two or more of these fruit types may be used. Pastry chefs will use the same recipes and perhaps increase the amount of thickening agents (cornstarch) to firm the fruit filling slightly. This makes handling and finishing easier, and makes serving the individual portions easier. As a reminder, fruits that are tart and require higher percentages of sugar for sweetening tend to spread during baking.

The fruit cakes are never filled to the very top, as this might cause overflowing of the filling during baking. A typical comparison is that of apple cake and blueberry or cherry cake. Fruit cakes are baked at temperatures that vary from 390–425°F. Those made with a short dough top are baked at a slightly lower temperature than those made with a pie crust top or combination dough top. Fruit cakes covered with a puff pastry top are also baked at a slightly lower baking temperature in order for the dough to bake through properly and develop the crisp, flaky characteristics of puff pastry dough. Fruit cakes made with a streusel topping are also baked at a slightly lower temperature to enable the topping to bake through with the desired crispness and color.

Making Large Fruit Cakes

When using a short or sugar dough for the bottom and sides, roll the short dough out on a floured cloth. For the large pan (sheet pan), roll the dough out about the size of the pan and slightly less than ¼ in. thick. Place the sheet pan over the dough and mark off the dimensions with a pastry wheel or knife. For the larger layer cake pans, roll out the dough the same as for the sheet pan and simply cut out the circles by inverting the pan over the dough and cutting out as for cookies.

For small layer pans, scale the dough into units and roll out to about ⅛ in. thick and slightly larger than the bottom and sides of the pan. Roll up the dough on the rolling pin and unroll directly over the pan. Lift the excess dough against the sides of the pan. Unfilled spaces or cracks may be filled in with the scrap dough. Roll the rolling pin over the top of the pan to remove the excess dough. Bake the bottoms of the large cakes at 400°F until golden brown. Be sure to stipple the dough before baking. When cool, roll out long strips of short dough and cover the sides of the pan. Remove the excess dough from the top or edge of the pan with knife or bench scraper. Fill the pans with fruit filling previously prepared and cooled. The edge of the crust may be brushed lightly with egg wash or water. Roll out the top crust on a floured cloth to about ⅛ in. thick. Roll up the dough on a large rolling pin and unroll over the top of the cake. This is similar to preparing a napoleon sheet. Using the rolling pin, roll over the edges of the pan to remove the excess dough. This will also seal the top dough to the washed edges of the dough lining the sides of the pan. Stipple or puncture the top dough with a fork. The top dough may be finished by washing well with egg wash. (See Figs. 14.6 through 14.11.)

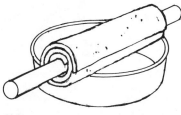

14.6
Roll up dough on rolling pin and unroll

14.7
Cover with a thin short dough top

14.8
Trim edge with rolling pin

14.9
Covered fruit cake

14.10
Lattice-top fruit cake

14.11
Streusel top

Allow the egg wash to dry and wash a second time with egg wash. Draw the tines of a fork over the top of the dough in diagonal lines spaced about 2 in. apart. Form a criss-cross effect. Bake the cake at 400°F until the crust has turned a medium brown color and the cross hatching design is clear. The crust should feel crisp. If a pie crust top is used or a combination pie crust short dough top is used, the top may be brushed with milk or left plain and baked. Be sure to stipple the top before baking. Bake at 410°F until the dough is crisp and has a light brown crust color. If the top is covered with a thin puff pastry dough top, be sure the dough top is stippled well and allow the top crust to relax on the fruit cake for at least 30 min before baking at 390°F. Fruit cakes may also be finished with a lattice-type effect. Roll the dough out on a floured cloth to about ⅛ in. thick.

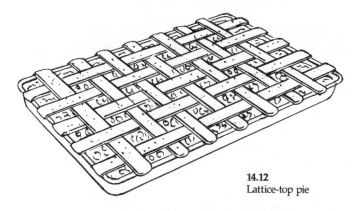

14.12
Lattice-top pie

Any of the doughs may be used for this purpose. However, it is advisable to use short dough or puff pastry dough when a short dough bottom and sides are used for the cake. Cut the dough into equal strips about ¼ in. wide (Fig. 14.12). Place the strips over the large round cake or the rectangular cake in a diagonal form so that diamond shapes are formed in the spaces between the strips. The dough strips may be washed with egg wash before placing on top of the cake. This produces a shiny brown crust when baked. Bake these cakes at a slightly higher baking temperature than the completely covered cake.

Large fruit cakes, round or rectangular, are often finished with a streusel topping, the same topping used for crumb buns, coffee cakes, and other specialties. The streusel is sprinkled over the entire surface of the cake so that the fruit filling is completely covered. It is important to have the fruit filling cold or chilled to prevent melting the fat in the streusel topping before the cake is placed in the oven. Bake these cakes at 400°F. The streusel lumps should have a golden brown color and feel quite dry when baked. Pastry chefs will often increase the amount of cinnamon in streusel topping to be used for apple or blueberry cakes to add to the taste of the cakes. When making the round cakes with a streusel topping, the pastry chef may place an inverted paper cupcake liner in the center before sprinkling the streusel on the cake. This is left there during baking and removed after baking. The result will be an even round space exposing the fruit filling. It adds to the appearance and also identifies the fruit filling in the cake.

Open-faced fruit cakes, both round and rectangular, are often finished with fresh fruits or fruit slices. For example, fresh blueberries may be sprinkled over the top of the cake and the cake baked in open form. These cakes are later finished again. This will be explained. Apple cakes may be layered with slices of frozen apples that are peeled and cored, and cured to prevent discoloration. The apples are sliced thinly and layered over each other as a covering for the cake. The cake is then baked as is. Other fresh and canned fruits may be sliced or placed over the top of the fruit filling and then baked. These cakes are baked at 415°F.

Methods of Finishing Large Fruit Cakes

Cakes that have been fully covered with a short dough and egg washed with a lattice design made with a fork, are allowed to cool completely. Pastry chefs will often chill all fruit cakes before attempting to remove them from the pans. When ready to remove, the cakes are placed in the oven for a few moments just to heat the bottom crust slightly. This will free the bottom of the cake from the pan. With a knife or spatula gently go around the sides of the pan to release the crust. Place a pan of equal size or a cake board over the cake and grasp the bottom of the pan and top firmly. With a quick motion, turn the cake over. Tap the pan gently and then remove the pan from the cake. It is advisable to lightly dust the bottom of the cake with some cake crumbs or finely ground and toasted filberts. Turn the cake over on another cake board or serving plate.

The plate may have a special doily (thin plastic, colorful doilies are now available to line the serving plate for round fruit cakes) before turning the cake over on the serving dish. The plain, egg-washed dough-covered cakes are then cut into portions. The rectangular cakes are usually cut into squares. The round cakes are cut into wedges. The same procedure is followed with cakes that have a lattice dough effect on top. It may be advisable to place a parchment paper liner that has been moistened with water over the cake before turning it over. This will prevent the fruit filling from sticking to the pan while it is being turned. The paper is removed easily after the cake has been turned over with the bottom facing the cutting board or the serving tray. The use of this technique also applies to the turning of open-faced fruit cake.

Cakes that have a streusel topping are turned and then cut into desired portions. The portions are then usually dusted lightly with confectioners sugar before serving. If there should be some small openings showing the fruit, these openings may be filled in with a blend of light cake crumbs mixed with chopped nuts to which a small amount of cinnamon sugar has been added. Sprinkle over the blank openings.

Cakes that have been covered with pie crust dough, combination pie crust and short dough, or puff pastry dough are often covered with a thin fondant icing after the cakes have been removed from the pans. When the icing has dried, the cakes are cut into portions for serving. Note is made of the fact that cakes are often covered with any of the dough tops that have been rolled out very thin and then sprinkled with streusel topping, or with a blend of ground nuts and cinnamon sugar. These cakes are also dusted lightly with confectioners sugar before serving.

Open-faced cakes are finished in a variety of ways. Cakes that have fruit slices such as apple, are usually glazed with hot apricot glaze after the cakes have been removed from the pans. When the glaze has dried, the cakes are then cut into portions for service. This procedure applies to peach cakes, apricot, pineapple, cherry, and so forth. In each cake type, additional fruits may be placed on the cakes before glazing. Pineapple cakes are usually decorated with half or quarter slices of canned pineapple. Cherry pieces or halves of glazed cherries are placed between the pineapple slices for added color and appearance before glazing. Blueberry cakes usually are brushed with a film of apricot glaze and additional fresh blueberries sprinkled over the surface. The blueberries may then be glazed or they may be dusted lightly with confectioners sugar before serving. Open-faced cakes may also be finished with a thin sheet of sponge cake or chiffon cake placed over the top of the cake after it has been cooled and turned out of the pan. The fruit is first glazed with apricot glaze and the sheet cake is placed over the glaze to make it stick. The top of the sheet is then covered with apricot glaze again. Fresh fruits, such as strawberries or peach slices, are neatly layered or placed over the top of the sheet cake. The fruits are then coated with apricot glaze or a blend of apricot glaze and currant jelly that has been further colored with a few drops of red coloring.

It is quite popular with pastry chefs to have fruit cake servings garnished with a whipped cream design. The square portions, whether open-faced or covered with a crust, usually have a charlotte effect with a slice of the appropriate fruit on top of the rosette or charlotte of whipped cream. Triangular slices made from the round fruit cakes usually have a cone-shaped design piped on the fruit cake wedge. The cream may also be garnished with fruit pieces or berries.

Combination Fruit Cakes
These are large fruit cakes made in round or sheet pan form. The baked bottoms and sides of the cake are prepared as for the other fruit cakes. The cakes are then half filled with fruit filling. Some may be filled higher, as with the apple filling. Still others may be filled three-quarters full depending upon the type of cake filling or topping used to cover the cake. The fruit filling is then covered with a soft cake batter. A sponge cake batter, high-ratio yellow cake batter, upside down cake batter, and similar cake batters may be used. The batter is best applied by filling a large pastry bag with a large plain tube and piping the cake batter across the fruit in lines close to each other. The batter is then easily smeared over the filling without discoloring the cake filling or smearing the fruit particles into the batter. The cake batter may be left plain or may be garnished with a streusel topping or a nut and sugar topping. The nuts should be coarsely ground and then blended with granulated sugar or cinnamon sugar. These may be striped over the cake in diagonal lines forming a diamond cross-hatch effect by allowing the nuts and sugar to slip out of the partially closed hand. These cakes are baked at 375–385°F until the cake springs back lightly to the touch when gently pressed in the center. These cakes are turned in the same manner as the fruit cakes. When cut into portions for service, they may be dusted lightly with confectioners sugar.

Cobblers
Cobblers are made with a variety of fruits. As indicated, they are deep dish fruit cakes made without a bottom. Round cakes are baked in deep dish Pyrex pans with a pie crust top. When ready to serve, the crust is cut into portions and the filling and crust are ladled out into deep serving

dishes similar to compote dishes. The tops may be garnished with a hard sauce or may be covered with a whipped cream rosette if the dessert is served chilled. For large quantity service on an individual basis, the fruit filling is prepared separately and kept warm. Pie crust tops are cut out of rolled out dough about ⅛ in. thick or slightly thinner. The dough discs are equal to the size of the custard cups or slightly smaller than the compote dishes used for service. The warm or hot filling is ladled into the cups or serving dishes and the prebaked crusts are then placed on top of the warm or hot fruit filling. This has the appearance of individually baked deep dish cobblers and makes serving much easier for large volume. Discs made from puff pastry may be used for a crisp, flaky specialty.

Variety Strudel

Strudel is the name of a continental type of pastry made with a special dough that is almost tissue paper thin when stretched. When this dough is filled with a variety of fillings, the most popular being apple, the resulting pastry is delectable and very desirable. Mention has been made of strudel-type pastries when making puff pastry products filled with variety fillings. Similar strudel pastries were indicated for use in making Danish pastry varieties. These pastries are made in either individual portions or in long strip form and later cut into portions. These pastries are not to be confused with the regular strudel presented in this unit.

The dough for strudel may be purchased in a ready-to-use condition. The dough leaves are packaged and layered so that they are kept slightly moist and do not dry until exposed to the air. The prepared leaves are about 3 ft × 2 ft and are simply placed on a floured cloth, filled with the desired filling, and then rolled up. This does save time for the busy pastry chef. The prepared strudel dough is of good quality and is readily available when required. This is an advantage. However, pastry chefs who wish to make a genuine type of Hungarian strudel will prepare their own strudel dough to provide for the special paperlike thinness as well as the flakiness characteristic of this type of strudel. There are other special strudel doughs that are used for other strudel varieties. For example, the fruit-nut strudel made with ground diced and sugared fruits, raisins, and nuts, requires a dough that is not quite as flaky but must have the characteristic of being able to be pulled or stretched until paper thin before applying the filling. The dough must also have durability on the floured cloth when pulled so as to avoid excessive cracking. In this unit both doughs will be presented, as well as the various fillings.

The dough for strudel is a rather soft dough made with a fine, high-gluten bread flour. This flour is necessary in that the quality and strength of the gluten formed in mixing the dough largely controls the degree to which the dough may be pulled without tearing. In addition, it is important that the dough be fully developed in the mixing machine so that it is smooth and elastic.

Strudel Dough—Basic Type

Ingredients	lb	oz	Mixing procedure
Sugar		4	Blend all ingredients together to dissolve
Salt		½	and blend well
Eggs		8	
Vegetable oil		10	
Water	2	8	
Bread flour (variable)	3	12	Sift the flour, add, and develop the dough for about 10 min. at medium speed

1. The dough will wrap itself around the dough beater when fully developed and smooth. In the early stages, it may be necessary to scrape the dough away from the beater and continue to mix in order to fully develop the gluten in the dough.
2. The dough should feel quite soft and tend to flatten when placed on a floured portion of the bench. Divide the dough into units depending upon the size of the table or bench on which the dough will be pulled or stretched. The average dough unit will vary from 1½–2 lb.
3. Form the dough units into rectangular shapes as though molding a loaf of bread. Place the units on a sheet pan that has been well oiled and brush the tops of the dough with vegetable oil. Pastry chefs often place the separate dough units in small loaf or bread pans that have been well oiled with vegetable oil. The tops of the dough units are oiled as well.
4. The dough must be allowed to relax before it can be pulled or stretched. The units are usually allowed to relax for about 1½–2 hr at room temperature before pulling.
5. Units of dough are often kept in the refrigerator for several days and used as required. For emergency and quick conditioning of the dough, a small amount of table vinegar or ½ oz of cream of tartar may be added to the dough when mixed. The increased acidity will have a more rapid softening and conditioning effect on the strudel dough and allow for easier and quicker pulling. However, excessive use may cause the dough to become overconditioned and the dough will tend to tear easily.

Yield: Variable with size of table used

Flaky Strudel Dough

Ingredients	lb	oz	Mixing procedure
Sugar		4	Blend all ingredients together well. Be sure
Salt		¾	dry ingredients are completely dissolved
Vegetable oil		8	
Nonfat dry milk		3	
Egg whites	2		
Water	2		

Bread flour (variable)	5	12	Sift, add the flour, and mix well for about 10 min. on second speed to develop

1. The dough should be quite soft and tend to flatten on the bench. If too soft, add a little bread flour. The degree of softness will depend upon the quality and strength of the bread flour used. However, dough made with a weak or poor grade of bread flour will not be stretched as easily as dough made with a fine, high-gluten bread flour. Relax the dough as for the basic strudel dough.
2. Place the floured cloth (a tablecloth may be used) over the bench or table. Be sure it is dusted well with bread flour. Lift the dough carefully from the pan and gently stretch in the hands before placing on the cloth.
3. Grasp the dough gently with the fingers near the center of the dough. Stretch gently in an outward fashion, pulling toward the end of the table. Move from the center of the dough out to the ends, stretching and pulling gently. If the dough tends to pull back or offer resistance, allow the dough to relax for 2 or 3 min and resume pulling and stretching. Return to the center edges of the dough and grasp the thick dough edge and stretch again holding the very edge of the dough between the tips of the fingers. Avoid the use of fingernails. This may cause the dough to tear.
4. It is advisable to stretch the dough so that the edges hang over the table slightly. This will prevent retraction of the dough while it relaxes. At this point, sprinkle or spray the dough with melted butter to prevent it from drying and cracking during the time it takes to add the filling. (See Figs. 14.13 through 14.15)

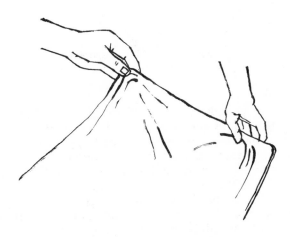

14.13
Stretching strudel dough

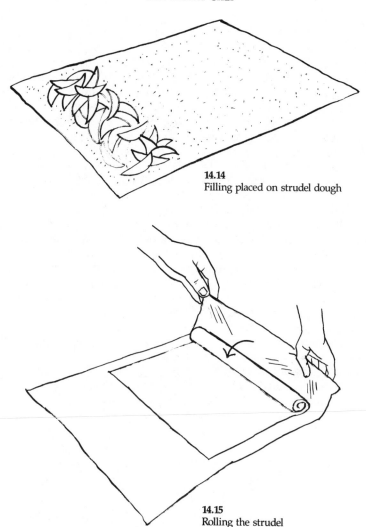

14.14
Filling placed on strudel dough

14.15
Rolling the strudel

Fillings For Strudel

Fillings are many and varied. Pastry chefs will often prepare their own blend or mixture of ingredients and fruits. For example, canned solid pack apples may be blended with frozen, cured apple slices. Some will use freshly peeled and cored apple slices. Still others will use an apple pie filling as a base and mix other apples in with it. Cake crumbs mixed with cinnamon and sugar are often added to bind the apple filling. Pastry chefs may often use melted butter directly mixed in with the apples. There are varying opinions and methods. In most instances, pastry chefs will use fresh, frozen apple slices. Where these are not available, canned apple slices will be used. A blend of both is advisable. However, a prepared, canned apple strudel mix can be purchased ready for use.

Apple Strudel Filling

Ingredients	lb	oz	Mixing procedure
Fresh frozen apple slices	10		Mix all these ingredients together lightly in a large mixing bowl before stretching the dough
Canned, solid pack apples	(2 No. 10 cans)		
Sugar (variable to taste and tartness of apples)	4		
Rind and juice of 2 fresh lemons			
Cinnamon		1	
Light cake crumbs (variable)	2		

1. Sprinkle the top 5 in. of the stretched strudel dough with light cake crumbs, or a blend of cake crumbs and toasted ground filberts.
2. Place the apples in a tight straight line of even thickness across the top of the strudel dough and directly over the layer of cake crumbs. The crumbs will absorb the syrup released by the apples. The top of the apples may be further sprinkled with cinnamon sugar if desired. Sprinkle the remaining dough lightly with cake crumbs to separate the layers of dough formed when rolling up the strudel. This allows for added flakiness.
3. Remove the excess dough at the edge of the table or bench by cutting with a pastry wheel or sharp knife. Fold the top edge of the dough over the apples.
4. Grasp the end of the floured cloth with both hands and roll the strudel dough by pulling the cloth firmly toward the opposite edge of the table. If the table is large, start at one end and pull down about 1/3 of the way. Then return to the other side and repeat the procedure. Do this until the dough is about 6 in. from the edge.
5. At this point, the rolled strudel may be lifted slightly and rolled up by stretching the dough slightly, and rolling the apple roll to tighten the dough. When the flaky type of dough is used, this is not often done since it will tend to bind the flaky layers formed in rolling.
6. Remove the excess dough at the bottom of the table edge. Even the thickness of the roll by pressing against the sides gently and stretching slightly or pushing thinner parts together.
7. Cut the strudel into individual portions at this time and then place them close together on a well oiled sheet pan. Strips the full length of the sheet pan may be cut and placed on the pan (these strips are cut after the strudel has been baked).
8. Tightly-rolled apple or other strudel made with the basic strudel dough may be brushed with melted butter as for the Hungarian type of strudel. Other types of apple strudel may be washed with egg wash before baking.

9. Wash the strudel with butter and bake at 430°F until the dough has a golden brown color. The egg-washed strudel dough will develop a shiny, brown crust color when baked. Lift a strudel slice with a knife to check the bottom for proper bake.
10. The butter-washed strudel is allowed to cool until warm and then sliced into portions. The strudel is dusted lightly with confectioners sugar and then served.
11. The Hungarian type of strudel may be baked in advance and the portions reheated slightly before serving.
12. Strudel that has been egg washed before baking is usually brushed with hot syrup and apricot glaze as soon as the strudel is removed from the oven. Pastry chefs will often boil honey over a low flame and then brush the hot strudel with the honey upon removal from the oven. The tops may be immediately sprinkled with coarsely chopped filberts or walnuts. These apple strudels may be warmed again before serving.

Note: The use of raisins for apple strudel is optional. Most pastry chefs will add raisins to the apple filling for Hungarian-type strudel. Still others will sprinkle the stretched strudel dough with raisins after the dough has been sprinkled with butter. Cake crumbs may be specially prepared for strudel by mixing the crumbs with cinnamon and sugar as well as ground nuts. The crumb mixture is then moistened with raspberry jam or apricot jam. The crumb combination is then rubbed together in the palms of the hand to form small, moist lumps. This blend is often used as a filling for apple and other types of strudel in addition to the fruits used.

Cheese Strudel

Bakers' cheese, cream cheese, or a combination of both cheeses may be used to prepare the filling for cheese strudel. Quality and cost are the determining factors. The following are two recipes for cheese strudel filling that are made with either bakers' cheese or cream cheese. A blend of equal parts of both cheeses may be used in either of the recipes. Be sure to blend both cheeses together before mixing.

Bakers' Cheese Strudel Filling

Ingredients	lb	oz	Mixing procedure
Bakers' cheese	7		Blend all these ingredients together to a
Sugar	2	4	smooth consistency
Salt		1	
Nonfat dry milk		4	
Cake flour		12	
Soft butter	1		
Egg yolks	1		Add the eggs in 3 stages and blend in
Whole eggs	1	8	after each addition. Do not cream

Ingredients	lb	oz	
Raisins (optional)	1	4	Add and blend until smooth
Vanilla		1	
Rind of 3 fresh lemons			

Refrigerate the cheese filling to firm up before using.

Cream Cheese Strudel Filling

Ingredients	lb	oz	Mixing procedure
Cream cheese	6		Blend these ingredients together until
Sugar	1	12	smooth
Salt		1/2	
Soft butter		12	
Cake flour		12	
Egg yolks	1	8	Add the yolks and blend in
Vanilla		1	Add the flavoring and lemon rind. Blend
Rind of 3 fresh lemons			in lightly
Sour cream		12	Add and blend in
Egg whites	1		Whip to a medium peak and fold into the cheese
Raisins (optional)	2		Fold in before adding the whipped egg whites. It is advisable to presoak and drain the raisins before adding

Chill the cheese filling before using. This will make handling easier.

1. Stretch the dough as for apple strudel. Sprinkle the entire surface of the stretched dough with melted butter.
2. Place a medium thick layer of light cake crumbs mixed with finely ground nuts over the top 5 in. of the stretched dough. Sprinkle the remainder of the dough lightly with cake crumbs and nuts. A mild sprinkling of cinammon sugar may be used with the cake crumbs and nuts.
3. Place handfuls of the cheese filling on a layer of nuts or cake crumbs on the bench or table and form into a cylinder about 1½ in. in diameter. The crumbs and nuts will keep the cheese from sticking. Lift each roll of cheese and place on the cake crumbs at the top of the stretched strudel dough until the entire dough is covered with a full strip of cheese filling.
4. Remove the excess strudel dough from around the edge of the table. Grasp the edge of the cloth and roll up the strudel as for the apple strudel. Check the thickness of the strip for evenness and adjust where necessary.

5. Cut the strip into individual serving sizes and place on a well oiled or parchment paper-lined pan close together. A strip may be cut the full length of the sheet pan and placed on the pan; the long strips may be cut into serving portions after baking. Brush the top crust of the strudel with melted butter and bake at 420°F until the crust is golden brown. Check the bottoms for proper bake.

Pineapple Cheese Strudel Place a thin strip of pineapple pie filling alongside the strip of cheese filling on the layer of cake crumbs and nuts. It may be advisable to make the layer of cake crumbs slightly thicker to absorb and retain the moisture of the fruit filling. The cheese strudel is usually served warm. If the strudel is prepared in advance, it should be kept under refrigeration. The portion slices are cut and then warmed by placing the entire pan into the oven for a few minutes. Dust the servings of strudel lightly with confectioners sugar. Individual servings may be heated by placing in a microwave oven for a few seconds on the serving plate.

Cherry and Blueberry Strudel   These are often prepared as an additional strudel variety. It is advisable to use a pie filling base for either of these fruit fillings. To each, add additional fruit and crumbs to bind the filling. For the cherry filling, add the drained cherries of one number 10 can of water-packed cherries to each can of cooked cherry pie filling. Additional sugar is required to sweeten. Pastry chefs may also add a pinch of cinnamon and approximately 2 oz of melted butter for each can of cherries used, and a few drops of red coloring. The cherry filling should be thicker than pie filling and thick enough to lay out on the cake crumbs placed on the strudel dough. Use enough cake crumbs to bind the cherries. Bake and serve as for the apple strudel.

For the blueberry filling, add an equal amount by volume of fresh blueberries. Sweeten accordingly with added sugar. Use ½ oz cinnamon for every three number 10 cans of blueberry filling used. Add sufficient cake crumbs to bind the filling. Pastry chefs may add pregelatinized cold process starch dissolved in a small amount of water to the mix to further thicken the filling.

Miniature Fruit Strudel
This type of fruit strudel is made with a special filling composed of raisins, diced mixed fruits, candied fruit peels and ground nuts. To these the pastry chef will often add cake crumbs and a variety of jams to soften and sweeten the taste of the filling. The strudels are small in size and are usually served with an assortment of cookies. They may also be made larger and served as individual servings.

Fruit Strudel Filling

Ingredients	lb	oz	Mixing procedure
Raisins	10		Grind all the fruit through a coarse
Glazed cherries	4		grinder. Grind the nuts after the fruit. Fi-
Mixed diced fruit	3		nally, grind some stale cake through the
Orange peel (candied)	1		grinder to remove all the fruits and nuts
Citron	1		
Filberts	2		
Walnuts	2		
Raspberry jam	1	8	Add the jams and mix in well. Additional
Apricot jam	1	8	cake crumbs may be added to firm up the fruit-nut mixture

1. Stretch the strudel dough as for regular strudel. Sprinkle the top of the dough lightly with ground nuts and cake crumbs.
2. Roll the fruit-nut filling in ground nuts or cake crumbs to form round strips about 1 in. in diameter. Place the strips across the dough and roll up about 4 or 5 times. Cut the dough and make another strip. As many as 3 or 4 strips of covered strudel may be made from one piece of stretched strudel dough.
3. Place the strips close together and cut into small units about 2 in. long. Place the cut units on well oiled or parchment paper-lined pans close together.
4. Egg wash the tops with eggs that have been beaten with a small amount of egg yolk for a deeper brown crust color after baking.
5. Bake the strudel at 400°F until the crust has the shiny brown crust color. Wash the strudel with hot apricot glaze or boiled honey.
6. The tops may be garnished with ground walnuts or filberts. Pastry chefs will sometimes egg wash the tops of the strudel and garnish with finely ground nuts and sugar across the tops of the strudel. There will be no need for further garnishing after baking.

15

Variety Cheese Cakes and Specialties

Cheese cakes are becoming increasingly popular as a dessert. In fact, many restaurants, hotel dining rooms, and other eating establishments are popular because of the cheese cake desserts served. Pastry chefs who produce these cheese cakes are justifiably proud of the variety they produce. It is important to understand the principles and practices of making the many varieties of cheese cake. For example, there are several basic cheeses that pastry chefs can use; bakers' cheese is the most common. It is also the most economical. Bakers' cheese is used for a great many varieties of cheese-filled desserts including Danish pastry, coffee cake varieties, and puff pastry. Variety cheeses are also used in cheese strudel. Cream cheese is rapidly assuming a more important role in the production of cream cheese cakes. Of course, it is more expensive than the bakers' cheese. Pastry chefs will often use a blend of bakers' cheese and cream cheese in their recipes. This reduces cost and yet makes a good quality cheese cake.

The quality of the cheese cake is dependent upon the type and quality and freshness of the cheese. The ability of the cheese to absorb and retain liquid (milk) is important because milk does add weight and moisture to the cake. The pastry chef who wisely uses the proper supporting flavors and fruits will produce cheese cakes of excellent quality that are visually attractive. There are prepared cheese cake mixes available in dry form. They require the addition of liquids (eggs, milk, and so forth) for reconstitution. The recipes and procedures that follow are for the pastry chef who produces his own cheese cakes from scratch. The selection and type of cheese cake from the recipes that follow will depend upon individual taste and the requirements of the menu such as cost controls.

Cheese cakes are very much like baked puddings. As a cake that is cut into portions and served, a supportive bottom is most often required. The support may be in the form of a baked short dough or sugar dough bottom, a cake crumb bottom, or a graham cracker type of bottom. The selection and use of the particular type of bottom will depend largely on the type of cheese cake made. For example, the large heavy or medium cheese cake baked in a large pan or large layer cake form will require a baked short dough bottom. Smaller or medium cheese cakes of the lighter variety are usually supported with a cake crumb lining. Cheese cakes made with a fruit filling at the bottom are usually supported with a pre-baked short dough bottom. For contrast and variety, the pastry chef may line the pans and bottoms with chocolate cake crumbs, especially for cheese cake that is marbled or striped with melted sweet chocolate.

The degree of lightness and consistency of the structure of the cheese cake is usually governed by the use of eggs and egg whites. Cheese cakes and cheese pies are often aerated with beaten or whipped egg whites. The egg whites may be combined with a boiled syrup, very much like a marshmallow type of icing, which is then folded into the cheese cake mix. The egg whites are whipped to a medium soft consistency so that they may be easily folded into the cheese batter. Generally, the greater the percentage of whipped egg whites added, the lighter the cheese cake. Thus, cheese cakes often range from a medium weight to the lightest, chiffon type.

The baking of cheese cakes is important. Those with prebaked bottoms are usually baked directly on the hearth of the oven if they are large. Smaller cheese cakes with a short dough bottom may be baked in a double pan or sheet pan. Cheese cakes with a cake crumb or graham cracker bottom are usually baked in pans partially filled with cold water. The water creates a steaming effect and prevents the direct contact of dry heat to the bottom and most of the sides of the cakes. This prevents burning and excessive drying of the cake crumbs. As for the graham cracker bottom (refer to the pie section for the recipe), these are usually prebaked or dried slightly and contain the added butter which provides for a short, cookielike taste and appearance.

The oven temperature for cheese cakes will vary with the type of cheese cake. For example, the French or California type of cheese cake is usually baked at a lower temperature than the heavier one. Cheese cakes are often baked in two stages. Cream cheese and other cakes are first baked at a high temperature so that the cheese cake rises above the pan and the top remains complete and without cracks. When the cakes have risen and formed a light brown crust around the edge they are removed from the oven and the sides gently cut around so that the cake settles evenly. The cakes are then returned to the oven at a lower temperature to complete the baking. At this point, note is made of the cheese cake mixes available that contain pregelatined, processed thickeners that do not require baking. The mix is prepared and poured into crumb-lined pans and placed in the refrigerator. When chilled, the cakes are removed from the pans and cut into portions for serving. The instructions on the package must be followed.

Fresh fruits and fruit fillings play an important role in the making and finishing of variety cheese cakes. Prebaked short dough bottoms are often lined with a layer of pineapple or other pie filling before adding the cheese cake mix. Fruit may be added to cheese cakes with cake crumb bottoms also. The center-bottom of the pan is lined a bit heavier with cake crumbs to support the fruit and to absorb the moisture released by the fruit during baking.

Most pastry chefs will usually finish baked cheese cakes by garnishing the tops. A thin base of fruit pie filling is first spread across the top of the cake, followed by a layer of fruit filling with added slices of fruit. For example, the pineapple filling may be decorated with half or quarter slices of drained canned pineapple. Fresh berries, such as strawberries and blueberries, are often used to decorate the tops of cheese cakes after they have been covered with fruit filling, which holds the fresh fruit in place. The final stage is brushing the fruits with apricot glaze or apricot-currant glaze to which a few drops of red coloring have been added.

Care must be taken to avoid damage or breakage when removing cheese cakes from their pans after baking. As indicated, cheese cakes are puddinglike in composition. The body or structure is formed by the natural proteins of the eggs, egg whites, and the cheese. Very little flour is used to help bind the cheese. The cheese cake should be trimmed around the sides promptly when removed from the oven so that the sides and top settle evenly. Allow the cake to cool completely so that there is firmness to the body. Place a board or the back of an equal-sized pan over the top. Layer cakes may use a cardboard liner. Turn the cake quickly. Remove the pan and dust the bottom with a light cover of ground nuts or cake crumbs. Place a board over the bottom and turn over again. Avoid excessive pressure when turning the cakes. If the cheese cakes have been left in the pans and have cooled or been chilled, it is advisable to place the cakes in the oven for a minute or so to heat the bottom and sides of the pan. This will release the bottoms and the cakes may be turned easily.

Before proceeding with the recipes, special emphasis is placed upon the *proper mixing of the cheese* in the batter. Some pastry chefs prefer to blend the flour or cornstarch with the cheese before mixing with other ingredients. This is a good practice when using bakers' cheese. It tends to bind the cheese as well as make the cheese smooth. It also enables the pastry chef to get the "feel" of the cheese to determine its "dryness" or absorption capacities. Cheese will vary from one shipment to another at times. Cheese cakes are mixed at slow or medium speeds to enable the moisture (eggs, milk, cream) to be absorbed without causing curdling or separating, particularly in the final stages of mixing. The recipes will indicate that the amount of milk added is variable. This is due to the fact that cheeses vary in the amount of liquid they can absorb and retain. A good quality bakers' cheese will retain more milk than a poorer quality. Where cottage cheese is the only cheese available, it is a good practice to add 1 oz of cornstarch to each pound of cottage cheese and blend until smooth. The cheese should be sent through a grinder to reduce the lumps or large curds. The cheese may then be used as regular bakers' cheese. If the cottage cheese is very soft or contains a lot of whey, the cornstarch should be increased to absorb and retain the whey. Most cheese cake batters will have the smooth consistency of a thick gravy or sauce when they are fully mixed. Those to which large amounts of whipped egg whites are added are usually thicker than the regular or heavier types of cheese cakes.

Variety Cheese Cakes

Cream Cheese Cake

Ingredients	lb	oz	Mixing procedure
Cream cheese	10		Blend the cream cheese and cornstarch to-
Cornstarch		5	gether on slow speed
Sugar	2	8	Add the sugar and salt and blend smooth
Salt		1/2	
Whole eggs	2		Add the eggs in 5 or 6 stages and blend at
Egg yolks	1	4	slow or medium speed. Scrape the sides of the kettle frequently
Light cream	1	4	Add the flavoring and stir in. Add the
Vanilla		1	cream gradually and blend in until smooth
Rind and juice of 2 lemons			

1. Cream cheese cakes are usually baked in layer cake pans. The pans may vary in size from 6 in. to 12 in. The pans may have a short dough bottom or they may have a cake crumb or Graham cracker bottom. It is advisable to prebake the short dough bottoms. Graham cracker bottoms should be partially baked and cooled before using.
2. For the short dough bottoms, roll out the short dough about 1/8 in. thick on a floured cloth. Using the layer pan as a cutter, press the tops of the pans into the rolled out dough. Place the cut-outs into the pans and stipple with a fork. Bake the bottoms until light brown. Allow the bottoms and pan to cool. Grease the sides of the cooled pans with butter.
3. Combine the scrap short dough with fresh dough and roll out into a square or rectangular shape. Cut into strips as wide as the height of the layer cake pans with the baked bottoms. Line the sides of the pans with the short dough, pressing the dough against the greased sides of the pans. Remove the excess dough with a knife. Fill the pans almost to the top of the layer pan, leaving about 1/4–1/2 in. from the top.
4. Place the pans on a sheet pan and bake at 400°F or slightly higher temperature. The cakes will rise to about 1/2–1 in. above the sides of the pan and the edge of the cake will have a light brown crust color. Remove the cakes from the oven and cut around the sides.

15.1
Cut out and prebake bottoms

15.2
Cut out strips of short dough

15.3
Line sides of pan with
short dough

15.4
Remove excess dough

15.5
Fill the pans almost full

5. Allow the cakes to settle for about 15 min. Return to the oven at a
    temperature of 365–375°F and bake until the center of the cake feels
    medium firm or springy to the touch.
6. Cakes made with a crumb bottom or Graham cracker bottom should
    be placed on sheet pans and filled with water to about 1 in. around
    the cheese cake layer pans. This will prevent excessive drying or
    burning of the cheese cake bottom during baking.
7. Allow the cheese cakes to cool before turning out of the pans. The
    cakes may be chilled before finishing with a variety of fruits and
    glazing, or they may be plain. (See Figs. 15.1 through 15.5.)

Yield: Approx. 6 10-in. layer cakes

Combination Cream Cheese Cake

This cheese cake is a combination of equal parts of cream cheese and bakers' cheese. It has the good quality of a fine cheese cake with a slightly reduced cost as a result of the use of bakers' cheese.

Ingredients	lb	oz	Mixing procedure
Cream cheese	5		Blend the cheese, cornstarch and flour together
Bakers' cheese	5		
Cornstarch		6	
Bread flour		3	
Sugar	4		Add the sugar and salt and blend in
Salt		1	
Egg yolks	2		Add the eggs in 5 or 6 stages and blend in well after each addition. Scrape the sides of the kettle frequently
Whole eggs	2		
Juice and rind of 3 lemons			Add the flavoring and blend in
Vanilla		1½	
Light cream (variable)	2		Add gradually and blend in until smooth. The batter should be of medium soft consistency

1. Deposit the batter into layers that have been prepared with either a short dough bottom or lined with cake crumbs. Fill and bake as for the regular cream cheese cake.
2. When cool, the cakes may be garnished with a thin, round slice of sponge cake. A chocolate sponge cake layer may be used for contrast. Place the fruit filling and fresh fruits on the sponge layer and then glaze with apricot or currant glaze.

Yield: 8 10-in. cakes

Medium Cream Cheese Cake

This cheese cake contains a blend of cream cheese and bakers' cheese and is made lighter with the addition of egg whites. The whipped egg whites are folded into the cheese batter last. The batter is baked in large, deep pans (3 in. deep) with a baked short dough bottom. The cakes are finished in the same manner as round cakes after baking.

Ingredients	lb	oz	Mixing procedure
Cream cheese	5		Blend the cheese and flour together until smooth. Use slow speed or mix by hand
Bakers' cheese	5		
Bread flour	1	2	

	lb	oz	
Sugar	1	12	Add the sugar, salt, and butter and blend
Salt		1	into the above at slow speed
Softened butter	1	10	
Egg yolks	1		Add to the above in 5 stages and blend in
Whole eggs	1	4	
Juice and rind of			Add the juice, rind, and flavoring and
3 fresh lemons			blend into the above
Vanilla		1	
Light cream	2		Add the cream gradually and blend in
(variable)			
Egg whites	1	8	Whip to a medium soft peak and fold into
Sugar	1	2	the above

1. Deposit into pans with prebaked short dough bottoms. Layer cake pans may be lined with cake crumbs.
2. The bottoms of the pans may be lined with pineapple or other fruit filling about ¼ in. thick. Place the batter over the fruit filling.
3. Bake at 380°F. The cakes will rise well and when baked will have a firm, springy feel when touched in the center.

Yield: 2 large pans 18 × 24 in.

Sour Cream-Cream Cheese Cake

Ingredients	lb	oz	Mixing procedure
Cream cheese	6	12	Blend the cheese and flour together until
Bread flour		8	evenly blended
Cake flour		3	
Sugar	1	12	Add the sugar and salt and blend in
Salt		½	
Egg yolks	1	8	Add the yolks in 4 stages and blend in well
Sour cream	4	8	Add the sour cream in 4 stages and blend
Rind and juice			well after each addition. Add the flavoring
of 3 lemons			and lemon last and blend in
Vanilla		1	
Egg whites	1	4	Whip to wet peak and fold into the above
Sugar	1		

1. The layer cake pans should be greased well with butter and lined with cake crumbs. Graham cracker bottoms may be used.
2. A pineapple or other fruit filling may be deposited at the bottom center of the pan before filling.
3. Fill the pans almost to the top. Place the layers in a large pan and fill half way with cold water.

4. Bake at 350°F. The cakes will rise above the top of the pan after about 25 min depending upon the size of the pan.
5. Remove from the oven and cut around the sides with a knife.
6. Allow the cakes to stand for about 15 min and return to the oven in a pan filled with water. Bake at 350°F for about 30 min or until the cakes feel springy to the touch.

Yield: 6 10-in. cakes

German Cheese Cake

This is a heavy type of cheese cake that is made without the use of whipped egg whites. A prebaked short dough bottom is necessary.

Ingredients	lb	oz	Mixing procedure
Bakers' cheese	10		Blend the cheese and flour together
Bread flour	1		
Cornstarch		4	
Sugar	4	8	Cream these ingredients together. When
Salt		1½	soft and smooth, add the cheese and blend
Nonfat dry milk		12	together until smooth. Use slow speed.
Butter	2		Scrape the sides of the kettle
Shortening	1		
Egg yolks	2		Add the eggs in 5 or 6 stages and blend in
Whole eggs	2		well
Vanilla		1	Add the flavoring and lemon and stir in
Rind and juice of 3 lemons			
Cold water (variable)[1]	4		Add the water in 5 stages and scrape the sides after each addition. The batter should be medium thick in consistency

Deposit the batter into the pans with the prebaked short dough bottoms. The bottoms may be covered with a thin layer of pineapple or other filling. Bake the large cakes at 390°F.

Yield: 2 large pans or 8 10-in. layers

Bakers' Cheese Cake   (*Medium light*)

Ingredients	lb	oz	Mixing procedure
Bakers' cheese	10		Blend the cheese, flour, and cornstarch to-
Bread flour	1		gether
Cornstarch		4	

[1]The quality of the cheese and its ability to absorb and retain the water (milk) will determine the amount of water (milk) to be added.

Sugar	4		Blend these ingredients together until soft
Salt		1½	and smooth. Add the cheese and blend in
Nonfat dry milk		10	well. Scrape the sides of the kettle
Butter	1	8	
Shortening	1	8	
Egg yolks	2		Add the eggs in 5 or 6 stages and blend in
Whole eggs	2		well. Scrape the sides of the kettle often
Vanilla		1½	Add the flavoring and lemon and blend in
Rind and juice of 3 lemons			
Water (variable)	3	8	Add the water slowly and blend in. Scrape the sides of the kettle. The batter should be quite thick
Egg whites	3		Whip the whites to a froth. Add the sugar
Sugar	1		gradually and whip to a medium soft peak. Fold into the above carefully

1. Deposit into pans containing a prebaked short dough bottom. The bottoms may be filled with a thin layer of fruit filling before depositing the batter.
2. Fill the pans about ½ in. from the top. The pans should be about 3 in. deep in order to obtain a cheese cake of reasonable height. The top of the cheese cake may be sprinkled with chopped filberts and cinnamon sugar before baking.
3. Bake the cheese cakes directly on the hearth of the oven. This cake does not have to be baked in a water-filled pan. Bake the cakes at 390°F for the first half hour.
4. The cakes will rise. Gently cut around the edge of the cheese cake and return to the oven. This may be done at the oven door without taking the cake out of the oven. Complete baking at 380°F until the cake has a light brown crust color and the center of the cake springs back or feels quite firm.
5. Upon removal from the oven, allow the cake to settle slightly and then push the sides toward the inside of the pan so that the cake settles evenly. This should be done for the layer cake cheese cakes as well. When cool, the cakes are turned out of the pans.
6. Cheese cakes that are plain on top may now be finished by covering the top with a fruit filling, or filling and fresh fruit or berries. Glaze the top with apricot glaze applied hot. When cool, cut into portions and serve.

Yield: 2 large pans or 10 10-in. pans

Cheese Tarts

Cheese tarts are usually made with a thin short dough bottom that does not have to be baked. The medium cheese cake filling or a regular cream cheese cake mix may be used. Fill the tart pans about three-quarters full with the cheese filling. Bake the tarts on double pans without any water in the pan. This will allow the short dough bottom to bake through.

When baked and cooled, remove the tarts from the pans. The tops are individually covered with a layer of fruit filling, garnished with fresh fruit or canned fruit and glazed with apricot or currant-apricot glaze. The sides of the tarts or the edges may be garnished with light sponge cake crumbs or finely ground hazelnuts or filberts. The cheese tarts may be baked in disposable aluminum foil tart pans. The pans do not require any bottoms or crumb lining. The cheese filling is deposited directly into the pans and baked in a pan that is partly filled with water. When cool, finish as the regular tarts.

French Cheese Cake

This cake is very light, as it is made with a large percentage of whipped egg whites. The cake also requires baking at a lower oven temperature so that it may rise fully, have an even top, and maintain a golden brown crust color.

Ingredients	lb	oz	Mixing procedure
Bakers' cheese	7	8	Blend the cheese and flour together
Bread flour	1		
Sugar	2		Blend these ingredients together well. Add
Salt		1	the cheese and blend at slow speed
Nonfat dry milk		8	
Butter	1	4	
Shortening	1		
Egg yolks	1	8	Add the eggs in 4 or 5 stages and blend
Whole eggs	1	8	well
Vanilla		1	Add the vanilla and lemon and blend in
Rind and juice of 4 fresh lemons			
Cold water (variable)	1	12	Add the water in 3 or 4 stages and blend in
Egg whites	4	8	Whip the whites to a froth. Add the sugar
Sugar	1	8	gradually and whip to a medium soft peak. Fold into the cheese batter until evenly distributed

1. Deposit the batter into pans with prebaked short dough bottoms. The bottoms may be covered with a layer of fruit filling before depositing the cheese batter. Fill the pans almost to the very top.
2. Place directly on the hearth of the oven or on double pans. No water is required in the double pan because of the prebaked bottom. Bake the cakes at 345–355°F. The cakes will rise quite high over the pan and the sides may be cut around slightly at the oven door after about 45 min of baking. Large pans should take about 70 min to bake. Layer pans will take less.

3. The depth of the pan and resulting height of the cake are also determining factors for baking time. If the cake should start to develop a deep brown crust before baking is completed, cover the top of the cake with a parchment paper pan liner. While the cake is settling slightly after baking, be sure to insert the outer edge of the cake inside the pan for a smooth top when the cake has cooled.
4. The French cheese cake is usually dusted lightly with confectioners sugar after it has been cut into portions and is ready to be served.
Yield: 2 large pans or 8 10-in. layers

California Cheese Cake

California-type cheese cakes are made with whipped egg whites to which a boiled syrup is added. This is a similar procedure to that for the preparation of boiled icings or marshmallow icing. This cake is lighter and somewhat dryer than the French type of cheese cake. The large pans are usually made with a prebaked short dough bottom. However, pastry chefs will often bake a thin sponge cake sheet to line the bottom of the pan. A chocolate sponge or a chiffon layer cake slice may be used. Prepared sheets are often made and kept in the freezer to be used as bottoms for the large size sheet cakes. For the layer cakes, prebaked 10-in. layers made with a variety of cake formulas are sliced about ¼–½ in. thick and placed in the bottoms of the pan for a bottom. The cake bottoms may be covered with a layer of fruit filling before depositing the batter into the pans.

Ingredients	lb	oz	Mixing procedure
Bakers' cheese	6		Blend the cheese and flour together
Bread flour		10	
Sugar		8	Blend these ingredients together. Add the
Salt		1	cheese and blend in well
Nonfat dry milk		6	
Soft butter		12	
Egg yolks	1		Add the eggs in 4 stages and blend in well
Whole eggs	1		
Vanilla		1	Add the flavoring and lemon and blend
Juice and rind of			in. Add the water in 4 stages and blend
2 fresh lemons			in. The batter should be medium soft. The
Cold water	2		consistency should be that of a medium
(variable)			thick gravy
Sugar	2		Dissolve the sugar and boil for about 2
Water	1		min to 220°F (thread stage)
Egg whites	2		Whip the egg whites to a soft peak. Add the sugar syrup in a slow, steady stream and whip to a soft peak again. Fold into the cheese mix

1. Fill the layer pans almost to the top. For large cakes, the same procedure applies.
2. Bake these cakes on double pans that are partially filled with cold water. Bake at 370°F for the large cakes. Bake the smaller layers at 375°F. The cakes will rise considerably over the edge of the pan.
3. The sides may be cut around after the cakes have fully risen and a light brown crust starts to form. Allow the cakes to bake until they feel quite firm in the center when touched.
4. Upon removal from the oven, allow the cakes to settle slightly and then gently push the edges of the cake into the pan so that the top settles evenly and the edges of the cake do not crumble.

Yield: 1 extra large pan or 8 10-in. layers

Marbled Cheese Cake

Melted sweet chocolate is lightly streaked over the top of the cheese cake mix when completed. The streaks are marbled into the cake with a few turns of the hand, lifting from the bottom to the top. The batter is then gently deposited into the pans. Stripe sweet chocolate across the top before baking.

Chiffon Cheese Cake Layers

These layers are quite light and tender. They have a special delicacy similar to that of an angel cake. The pans for these layers are lined with cake crumbs and the bottoms may be filled with variety fruit filling before depositing the batter.

Ingredients	lb	oz	Mixing procedure
Bakers' cheese	6		Blend together
Bread flour	1	1	
Sugar	1	8	Blend these ingredients together until soft
Salt		1	and smooth. Add the cheese and blend in
Nonfat dry milk		6	well
Butter	1	2	
Egg yolks	1	8	Add in 4 stages and blend in. Scrape the sides of the kettle
Vanilla		1	Add the vanilla and lemon and blend in.
Rind and juice of 3 fresh lemons			Add the water in 4 stages and blend in. Scrape the sides of the kettle. The batter is
Cold water (variable)	2		quite thick
Egg whites	2		Whip the whites to a froth. Add the sugar
Sugar	1	12	gradually and whip to a soft peak. Fold the whites into the cheese batter

1. Line the layer cake pans with sponge cake crumbs. Chocolate cake crumbs may be used for variety. Be sure the bottom and sides are well greased with soft butter so that the crumbs stick.
2. Fill the pans almost to the very top. Place the layers on sheet pans partially filled with cold water.
3. Bake at 435°F. This is a high temperature but the crust which forms will rise evenly without cracking as the cheese cake layers rise.
4. When the cakes have risen, cut around the sides and return to the oven for final baking at 400°F. These cakes will settle evenly when baked.

Yield: Approx. 7–8 10-in. layers

Cheese Cake Roll

These cakes are made very much the same as jelly rolls. The batter is made from a cheese cake mix especially constructed so that it may be rolled after it is baked and cooled. There is a wide variety of finishes and the pastry chef will develop an assortment of deserts to be made from the variety of fruit fillings and jams.

Ingredients	lb	oz	Mixing procedure
Bakers' cheese	2		Blend all these ingredients together to a
Cream cheese	2		smooth blend. Use slow or medium speed
Salt		½	
Sugar		6	
Soft butter		8	
Bread flour		6½	
Egg yolks	2		Add the yolks in 4 stages and blend in.
Vanilla		½	Add the vanilla and lemon and blend in.
Rind and juice of 2 fresh lemons			Scrape the sides of the kettle
Egg whites	4		Whip the egg whites to a froth. Blend the
Sugar	1	4	sugar and cream of tartar. Add in a slow,
Cream of tartar		½	steady stream and whip to a soft peak. Fold in gently with the cheese filling

1. Divide the batter equally over three sheet pans that have been lightly greased and lined with a parchment paper liner. Bake at 375°F until the cheese sheet has a golden brown color and is quite firm to the touch. Avoid underbaking. This will result in a sheet cake that is too tender and may not be able to be rolled up.
2. When the sheets are baked, turn them over carefully on a flour-dusted cloth as for a jelly roll.
3. When the sheets have cooled, spread lightly with a selected fruit filling such as pineapple, blueberry, strawberry, or a raspberry or apricot jam. The choice of filling is at the discretion of the pastry chef, who will probably name the cheese roll after the fruit filling.
4. Roll up the sheet with the cloth rather tightly and refrigerate the roll wrapped in the cloth or in a cover of parchment paper.

5. When chilled, finish the tops with the desired fruit filling applied over the top half of the roll. The sides may be lightly garnished at the edge of the filling with light cake crumbs or finely chopped nuts. As an example of variety, a cherry cheese roll may be finished with a thin layer of raspberry jam over the top and smeared lightly with a warm, thin, fondant icing. Allow to dry and then slice in portions and serve. An additional fruit sauce may be served separately.

Yield: 3 sheet pan rolls

Hungarian Cheese Cake

This cheese cake is somewhat similar to the German one. In this cake, a blend of bakers' cheese and cream cheese is used, as well as sour cream for further tang and enrichment. Raisins are optional but they are usually associated with Hungarian cheese cake. This cake is usually baked in deep, large sheet pans. The sides of the pan are usually about 2½ to 3 in. high. Frames are often placed into regular sheet pans where the deep-sided pans are not available. A prebaked bottom crust made from short dough is used to support the cheese cake, especially when fruit fillings are placed on the bottom crust before depositing the cheese cake filling. The use of fruit filling is optional since Hungarian cheese cake is often made without it.

Ingredients	lb	oz	Mixing procedure
Bakers' cheese	5		Blend the cheeses with the flour and corn
Cream cheese	5		starch
Bread flour		14	
Corn starch		4	
Sugar	4	8	Add to the cheese and flour blend and mix
Salt		1½	to a smooth consistency. Use slow speed
Nonfat dry milk		8	when mixing. Scrape the sides and bottom
Shortening	1	8	of the kettle
Butter or margarine	2		
Egg yolks	2		Add the eggs in 3 or 4 stages and blend in
Whole eggs	2		well
Sour cream	2		Add the sour cream and blend in
*Water (variable)	2		Add the water in 3 stages and blend. The batter should be quite thick. Add the rais-
Vanilla		2	ins and blend in
Rind of 2 fresh lemons or lemon flavor		1	
Raisins (presoaked)	3		

*Bakers' cheese and cream cheese will vary in consistency and quality. This will be reflected in the ability of the batter to absorb the water. Should the batter become slightly thin, do not add remaining water. Should the consistency be quite thick, add additional water or milk.

If fruit filling is used, place the filling on top of the baked short dough bottom. Keep the filling away from the edges of the bottom. Fill the pan about ½ in. from the top. It is advisable to grease the sides of the pan so that the cheese cake batter will rise evenly and avoid sticking to the sides and excessive cracking of the top of the cheese cake. The top of the cake may be sprinkled with a blend of light cake crumbs and toasted chopped nuts before baking. Thin strips of plain sugar or cinnamon sugar may be dressed over the nut-crumb topping for further design. This may be a criss-cross or lattice design. Bake at 365–370°F until the cake feels springy to the touch and a light brown crust color has been formed. The cake will rise above the level of the sides of the pan and will settle somewhat after baking. Run a knife around the sides of the cake soon after removal from the oven to allow the cake to settle evenly. Lightly dust the top of the cake with confectioners sugar when cool.

Icebox or Cold Process Cheese Cakes and Pie

As has been previously indicated, there are prepared cheese cake mixes available for purchase from a distributor of bakery supplies. One must only add eggs, egg whites, and milk to reconstitute the mix. The instructions for preparation and baking are on the package and should be scrupulously followed. In addition, there are many cheese cake desserts, made in a cold process, that are similar in preparation to Bavarois or Bavarian fillings. These desserts are poured into special dessert pans of various sizes and shapes and chilled. After chilling they are easily unmolded by dipping the mold in warm or hot water and turning over. Molds may also be prepared with a Graham cracker crust that is lightly browned in the oven before use. The recipe for the Graham cracker crust has been listed in the section on pies. Cheese pies are listed in this section on pies. The Graham cracker crust is best used for pans that have flat bottoms and can be baked. Scalloped and special pan molds as well as the small tart pans are best greased well with soft butter for easy unmolding.

Cream Cheese Icebox Cake

Ingredients	lb	oz	Mixing procedure
Gelatin		4	Dissolve the gelatin in the water and set
Water	1	8	aside
Cream cheese	6		Add the lemon juice to the cream cheese
Lemon juice		6	and blend in. Add the yolks in 3 or 4
Egg yolks	1	2	stages and blend in well. Add the lemon
Rind of 3 lemons			rind and blend in
Egg whites	1	8	Whip the whites to a froth. Add the sugar
Sugar		14	and whip to a soft peak. Fold the egg
Whipped cream	(1 quart)		whites and whipped cream alternately into the cheese *after the gelatin has been mixed into the cheese filling*

Pour the cheese mixture into the prepared molds and refrigerate until firm. Place the molds in hot water for a few moments and unmold directly on the serving plate. A fruit sauce may be served with the dessert.
Yield: Approx. 6 10-in. pans

Fruit-Filled Icebox Cream Cheese Cake   The flat molds may be lined with a Graham cracker crust that has baked for about 10 min at 350°F. Special shaped or scalloped molds may be buttered and lined with sponge cake crumbs at the bottom. Place the drained fruits or the fresh fruit pieces in the mold. Cover with the cheese filling and refrigerate. When chilled, dip in hot water for a few moments and unmold directly on the serving dish. These molds may be further garnished with a sauce. Pastry chefs may often decorate the tops of the molds or the tarts with whipped cream and a slice of fruit or sauce.

Cottage Cheese Icebox Cake

Ingredients	lb	oz	Mixing procedure
Gelatin		5	Dissolve the gelatin in the water
Water	2		
Cottage cheese (strained)	7	8	Blend the strained cheese and the starch, or blend the cheese and the starch first
Cornstarch		2	and then strain. Be sure to use the whey in the mix
Nonfat dry milk		4	Add these ingredients to the cheese and
Sugar	1	6	blend in well until smooth
Salt		¼	
Egg yolks	1		
Lemon juice		4	
Rind of 3 fresh lemons			
Water and gelatin blend			Add the water in 3 stages and blend in
Egg whites	2		Whip the whites to a froth. Add the sugar
Sugar	1	2	gradually and whip to a wet peak
Sour cream	2		Fold the egg whites and sour cream into the cheese mix alternately until well blended

Proceed with this batter as for the Cream Cheese Icebox Cake.
Yield: 6 10-in. layers

Cream Cheese Chiffon Pie

This is a cold process procedure and prebaked pie shells are required. The shells may be made from the special pie shell dough, combination short dough and pie crust, or from the regular pie crust. The pie shells may be lined with fruit filling varieties before depositing the batter into the shells. The pies may be made plain.

Ingredients	lb	oz	Mixing procedure
Gelatin		3	Dissolve the gelatin in the water and set
Water		12	aside
Cream cheese	4	8	Blend the cream cheese with the eggs.
Eggs		12	Add the lemon rind and blend in. Add the
Rind of 3 lemons			gelatin and blend in well. Refrigerate until the cheese starts to set
Egg whites	3		Whip the whites to a froth. Gradually add
Sugar	2		the sugar and whip to a medium stiff peak

1. Fold the egg whites into the almost set cheese mixture in three stages.
2. Be sure the egg whites are completely and evenly distributed. Deposit the mixture into the pie shells.
3. The centers of the filling or pie may be made in a mound-like form in the pie.
4. The top of the pie may be garnished with light sponge cake crumbs and the pie chilled before serving. Pastry chefs will often garnish these pies with a whipped cream design. Pieces of fruit or berries can be placed on top of the pie before chilling or after the pies have been chilled and completely set.

Yield: Approx. 8 10-in. pies

Baked Cheese Pie

Rich Cheese Pie

It is advisable to have a very lightly baked pie shell ready in advance for depositing the batter. Fruit filling may be placed in the shell.

Ingredients	lb	oz	Mixing procedure
Cream cheese	4		Blend the cheeses with the flour and the
Bakers' cheese	5		cornstarch
Bread flour		6	
Cornstarch		2	
Sugar	1	4	Blend well until soft and smooth. Add the
Salt		½	cheese and blend in
Soft butter	1		

Egg yolks	1	Add the eggs in 3 stages and blend in well
Whole eggs	1	at slow or medium speed. Add the lemon
Rind of 3 fresh lemons and the juice		
Light cream	1	Add in 3 stages and blend in
Egg whites	14	Whip the egg whites to a froth. Add the
Sugar	12	sugar and whip to a medium stiff peak. Fold into the cheese batter

1. Deposit the batter into the prebaked shells (with or without the fruit filling on the bottom of the pie shell) and fill almost to the very top. The edges of the pie may be garnished with sponge cake crumbs.
2. Place the pies on double pans and bake at 375–385°F. The pies will tend to brown around the edges and the centers will have an almost white appearance. The centers will feel springy to the touch when fully baked.
3. When cooled, these pies may also be covered with a thin disc of sponge cake.
4. The top is then covered with a fruit filling and fresh or canned fruits, or fresh berries. The top is then glazed with an apricot or currant glaze when cherries or strawberries are used as a fruit garnish. The edges of the pie may be garnished with finely ground filberts.

Yield: Approx. 10 10-in. pies (variable with depth of the pie pan)

Cream Cheese Miniatures

These miniatures are similar to the miniature varieties made from Danish pastry dough. The units are small, fashioned in a similar manner, and are often used to mix with cookies, petits fours, and other small tea cakes. Caterers will often use these miniatures as a specialty product and serve them for special occasions. The units have excellent keeping qualities because of their richness. The special flavor provided by the cheese and the flakiness of the dough makes them a popular asset to the menu.

Dough for Cream Cheese Miniatures

Ingredients	lb	oz	Mixing procedure
Cream cheese	4	8	Work the butter with a little flour to a
Butter	4	8	smooth, plastic state. Blend with the cream cheese until smooth and evenly distributed
Confectioners sugar	1		Sift the sugar and salt. Add with the va-
Salt		1¼	nilla to the above and mix in well
Vanilla		1½	
Bread flour	4	8	Sift the flour. Add and mix to a smooth dough. Do not develop

1. Place the dough on the bench that has been dusted with bread flour. Form the dough into a rectangular shape and allow the dough to rest for about 15 min.
2. Roll the dough out lightly with the rolling pin into a rectangular shape about three-eighths in. thick. Remove the excess flour and give the dough a three-fold turn. (This is similar to the procedure used for rolling in the dough for Danish pastry or puff pastry.)
3. Cover the dough with a cloth and allow to relax for about ½ hr in the refrigerator. Roll the dough a second time to about ¼ in. thick and give the dough a four-fold turn.
4. Cover the dough with cloth and refrigerate the dough overnight. This will allow the dough to condition or mellow so that it may be rolled easily and handle without tearing.
5. The miniature units are made up much the same way as for miniature Danish pastry. The varieties are small open pockets filled with cheese, apricot jam, prune jam, or other filling, Rugelach, snecks, and miniature horns. The makeup for each of these follows.

Open Pocket Varieties Roll out the dough into rectangular shape about ⅛ in. thick. Cut into 1½–2 in. squares. Deposit the desired filling (apricot jam, prune filling, and cheese filling are most popular) with a pastry bag and plain tube in the center of each square of dough (Fig. 15.6). Grasp the diagonally opposite corners of the square, and fold one edge or point over the other and seal the overlapping point. This will form a diamond-shaped effect with the filling showing at either side. (Fig. 15.7.)

Rugelach (Cinnamon-Nut Swirls) Roll out the dough into rectangular form about ⅛ in. thick (Fig. 15.8). Brush the top of the dough with melted

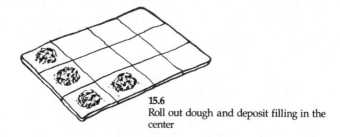

15.6
Roll out dough and deposit filling in the center

15.7
Fold end of one side over the filling. Fold other end over and seal

15.8
Roll out the dough ⅛ in. thick

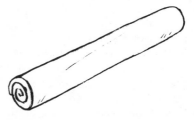

15.9
Brush dough with oil or melted fat and
sprinkle with raisins, cake crumbs, and
cinnamon sugar

15.10
Roll the dough up tightly and seal the edge

butter. Sprinkle the top with chopped nuts (walnuts, pecans, filberts), raisins, light cake crumbs, and cinnamon sugar (Fig. 15.9). Roll the filling in gently with the rolling pin so that the filling sticks to the dough. Roll the dough tightly into rolls about 1 in. in diameter (similar to the cinnamon bun) (Fig. 15.10). Cut the strips into 1 in. pieces (Fig 15.11). Several strips of dough may be lined up close to each other and the strips cut into units with a bench scraper or knife. Flatten the units slightly and brush the tops with melted butter and sprinkle with nuts and sugar.

Snecks   Follow the same procedure as for the Rugelach up to the point where the dough is rolled up. The roll should be slightly thicker (1¼ in. in diameter). Cut the strips into slices about ⅜–½ in. thick (Fig. 15.12). Place the units on pans with the open face (rolls of dough and filling) facing up (Fig 15.13.)

Miniature Cream Cheese Horns   Roll the dough out into a rectangular shape about ⅛ in. thick. Brush the dough with melted butter and sprinkle with chopped nuts, raisins (if desired), cake crumbs, and cinnamon sugar. Roll in the filling lightly with the rolling pin. With a pastry wheel or knife, cut the dough into strips about 2½ in. wide lengthwise. Then cut the strips into triangular shapes about 1¼ in. wide at the base (Fig. 15.14). Roll up each unit into a horn shape, flatten slightly, and place each unit next to one another on the bench (Fig. 15.15). When completely made up, flatten slightly with the palms of the hand and brush with melted butter. The tops may be sprinkled with finely chopped or ground nuts. Additional cinnamon sugar may be sprinkled over the tops of the horns (Fig. 15.16).

The miniatures are placed on parchment paper-lined pans and spaced about ½ in. apart. Larger units are spaced about 1 in. apart. Allow the units to relax on the pans for approximately 30 min and bake at 350°F until light brown and quite crisp. Rapid baking at a higher temperature will cause the units to feel soggy and have a raw appearance in the center. These miniatures are rich in butterfat provided by the butter and the fat in the cream cheese and must be baked out until crisp and dry. The units may be stored in the refrigerator or freezer for use as required. They may be defrosted and reheated quickly. They may be dusted lightly with confectioners sugar before they are served.

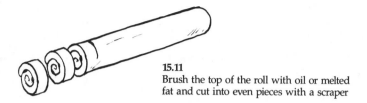

15.11
Brush the top of the roll with oil or melted
fat and cut into even pieces with a scraper

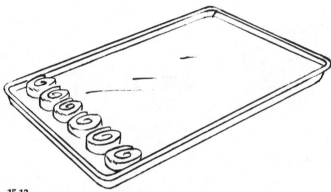

15.12
Pecan rolls made in sheet pans

15.13
Cut dough into triangular shape, apply
filling, and roll base of triangle toward the
point

15.14
Finished plain Danish horn

16

Frozen Desserts

Frozen desserts encompass all desserts that are subjected to freezing during the process of manufacture or after the products have been made. This would include desserts containing ice cream, either the French or American types, dietary types of ice cream such as ice milk, sherbet varieties, water ices, or any combination of any of these frozen desserts. The pastry chef is involved in making most of the frozen desserts, if not all of them. The pastry chef may be confined to only serving portions of ice cream. This service may be enhanced with the preparation and offering of a variety of cookies, petits fours, sauces, and special preparations that are flamed while being served. On the other hand, the pastry chef may still be in the position of preparing elaborate bombes, parfaits, coupes, and special ice cream desserts made to order. These specialties may be in the form of special ice cream cakes, ice cream rolls, ice cream or sherbet tarts, and a multitude of other frozen desserts. However, the trend is toward the purchase of prepared ice creams, sherbets, and other types of frozen preparations which are fully finished and ready for service. There is also the trend toward the purchase of equipment and prepared mixes for the quick-frozen specialties that are inexpensive, such as the frozen soft creams or frozen custards. This equipment is now being used by pastry chefs in large food service establishments where the unit cost of desserts is an important menu factor.

There are other factors which have appeared in the food industry which have made the preparation of frozen desserts a simpler matter for the pastry chef. There are specialized manufacturers of frozen desserts who supply a complete variety of frozen desserts in plastic, disposable serving dishes. For example, parfaits, coupes, or special champagne desserts may be ordered and they will be prepared and delivered frozen and ready-to-serve. Partially finished desserts may be ordered and the pastry chef will add the finishing touches. Whipped cream, fruit garnish, fruit sauces, syrups, glazed fruits, liqueurs and other alcoholic beverages are all in the domain of the pastry chef for completion and service of the desserts.

To all of this is added the value of desserts using ice cream or other frozen preparations as supportive adjuncts (for example, pie a la mode, cherries jubilee, baked Alaska, and similar desserts that combine a baked product with a frozen preparation). Ice cream tarts are now equally popular because of the individual service and the many varieties. Also, the use of cream puff and eclair shells to enrobe a variety of frozen desserts is popular with many pastry chefs.

There are times when caterers may be called upon to meet the requirements of Jewish orthodoxy in meal preparation and the serving of desserts. This is a specialized area of food service which requires different preparations. The pastry chef who is involved in this type of food preparation will use whipped toppings that contain no dairy products, as well as ice creams and sherbets made without dairy products. For the appearance and finish to be the same as for regular frozen desserts, a knowledge of the availability and use of these products is necessary.

There are many types of frozen desserts and the continental names given to them vary, yet the preparations of many of them are almost identical. Pastry chefs will often identify their own dessert specialties with some of these names. They often become "house" specialties and assume the name of the restaurant or hotel in which they are served. This unit on frozen desserts will not cover the actual manufacture of the basic ice creams or sherbets, but will discuss their composition and what the pastry chef should expect when purchasing the basic frozen desserts. The unit will also cover the more popular specialties which many pastry chefs prefer to make themselves. The shortcuts in preparation will be indicated where they may be of value and assistance to the pastry chef.

Ice Cream Cakes and Ice Cream Rolls

There are two basic types of ice cream. The French type is rarely used in this country because of its richness and expense. Actually, French ice cream may be classified as a partially cooked or heated custard. It is made with cream, milk, eggs, sugar, and flavorings. Special fruit and chocolate creams are made with additional ingredients. The ingredients are treated almost like a pastry cream or custard, in that they are heated to approximately 180°F and then cooled before freezing. The French ice cream is richer in butterfat content and eggs. Because of its richness, it is smoother and handles easier than some of the more economical types of American ice creams.

American ice creams vary with the manufacturer. The cream, milk, sugar, and flavorings are mixed together and usually allowed to stand for a period of about 24 hr to ripen or age before freezing. This applies to the finer grades of American ice cream. The more economical and the diet types of American ice creams contain lesser amounts of cream or creams containing less butterfat. These ice creams are gelled with the use of various binding ingredients and often use synthetic flavorings and colorings. The pastry chef will select the ice cream purveyor who will provide the best quality ice cream to meet the production needs and the budget. It is important to recognize the fact that the ice cream is the base for the dessert. The addition of fruits, sauces, whipped cream, icings, nuts, and other garnishes which enhance taste and appearance usually overshadow the basic ice cream. It is for that reason that a more economical grade of ice cream may be used for many desserts. For the plain ice cream dessert, it is advisable to use a fine grade of ice cream.

Sherbets and water ices are often used for many desserts. These are often served in an almost plain or ungarnished form. The water ices may be made into various shapes or forms by placing the basic mix into a mold and freezing. Decoration takes place after the ice is unmolded and ready to be served. As with ice cream, there are variables in the production of water ices and sherbet. The ices are usually mixed with fruit and colorings as well as whipped cream and egg whites when the basic ice is almost frozen. Sherbets are usually mixed with a variety of wines, liqueurs, fruits, and special flavorings. The pastry chef will order sherbets and ices from a manufacturer and use the basic sherbet or ice to prepare the dessert. Additional fruits, wines, and other garnishes and flavorings will be added at the last minute or at the time of service. In this instance, the quality of the products is important. A smooth, creamy sherbet is necessary and should be flavored naturally whenever possible. A cheaper quality may prove to be grainy and have the aftertaste of synthetic ingredients used for flavoring and gelling. Sherbet desserts are often served in conjunction with a variety of cookies and petits fours. Individual sherbets are often garnished and enhanced with dipped cookies or Lady Fingers.

Ice cream cakes are very popular desserts and are used widely by pastry chefs for feeding large groups and for special occasions. Catered affairs may require an individual ice cream cake with a special decoration for each table of guests. This may often run into as many as 100 or more tables requiring individual cakes. The pastry chef prepares in advance for this service. Special birthday and occasion cakes are made with an ice cream cake base. The base may be kept in the freezer and decorated as required. Thus, a stock of ice cream cakes should be kept on hand for immediate use when required. This holds true for ice cream cake rolls. These rolls are very much like jelly or cream rolls except that they are filled with ice cream. The ice cream center or roll may be a combination of several different flavored ice creams.

There are specialized purveyors who cater to the direct needs of pastry chefs in the preparation of ice cream combinations in layer or sheet form. These may be purchased in disc form ready for use for a 10-in. or other sized layer cake. The flavors and combinations are available or can be made to order. The same holds true for the sheets of ice cream for ice cream rolls. The time spent in cutting layers from a large round container, or even a large brick of ice cream, is saved for the pastry chef. In addition, there is a reduction in waste that usually occurs with large volume preparation. Very often ice cream surfaces will melt and the smeared ice cream may not be saved and refrozen for use as a filler for ice cream cakes and rolls. The assembling and rolling of cake rolls and layer cakes becomes an efficient operation with prepared ice cream layers and sheets. This is important where there is no chill room or refrigerated space in which these desserts may be prepared.

Cakes used for ice cream layers or ice cream rolls are usually made from sponge cake or chiffon cake mixes. However, a high ratio type of cake mix may be used. The sponge cakes will absorb ice cream, which will soften and tend to run during the makeup of the cake. This applies to the cake used for the ice cream roll. Pastry chefs will usually have a stock of such layers on hand in the freezer for special use when required. If large containers are used and the ice cream cut and shaped by the pastry chef, the ice cream should be placed on stainless steel sheet pans and cut on the pans. The melted cream may be poured into a separate container for refreezing. The large ice cream discs (2½–5 gal.) should be cut in half with an ice cream knife. The ice cream knife is actually a two-handled knife that is grasped with both hands and forced through the ice cream. This will allow for greater pressure and leverage in cutting the ice cream into desired size and shape. A large French knife dipped in hot water may also be used.

The cakes to be filled and/or rolled should be ready for application of the ice cream. The layer cakes should be sliced into three layers. A 2 in. high layer cake is sufficient. Unless the cake is a special cake size, most pastry chefs will use a 6–8 in. layer for table service. The layers are filled with two layers of ice cream about three-quarters in. thick and often different flavors unless otherwise specified. Remove excess ice cream around the sides and fill in any spaces. (See Figs. 16.1 and 16.2.)

Place the filled ice cream layers in the freezer. When frozen, cover the sides and top of the layer with whipped cream that has been prepared in advance. The cakes may be partially decorated with a border design and basic decoration and returned to the freezer. The final finishing or decoration is done before the cakes are served. At this time, the inscription may be applied and the flowers and other decorations which were

16.1
Layers of cake filled with ice cream

16.2
Finished ice cream layer with whipped cream topping

prepared in advance placed on the cake. Very often, the pastry chef may serve a special sauce in a separate sauce dish to accompany the cake. The cake slices may be covered with the special sauce.

When finishing ice cream rolls, a thin sheet cake is used. The sheet cake may be cut in half if a thin roll is to be made by using a thin layer of ice cream. A half sheet may also be used if a prepared roll of ice cream is used. These ice cream rolls may be purchased as individually prepared units or in long form. In either case, allow about 1 in. of cake at the top to be folded over the ice cream when starting to roll and 1 in. at the bottom to cover and seal in the ice cream filling. When cutting ice cream from a large brick or disc, cut into ½-in. slices and lay out on the cake roll. Flatten evenly with a spatula or special ice cream ladle. Be sure to fill in any uneven spaces. The sheet cake should be placed on a sheet of parchment paper or special cloth used for ice cream rolls. Grasp the edge of the paper or cloth and roll up as for a jelly roll, and return to the freezer to harden. (See Figs. 16.3 through 16.7.)

Ice cream rolls may be filled with a variety of fruit as well as a variety of ice creams. For example, with vanilla ice cream, a thin layer of pine-apple, strawberry, or blueberry filling may be placed near the top of the sheet after the ice cream has been layered on the sheet. Roll up and freeze. The fruit filling will show when the roll is cut into slices and served. The sugar in the fruit filling will tend to keep the filling soft. Avoid using

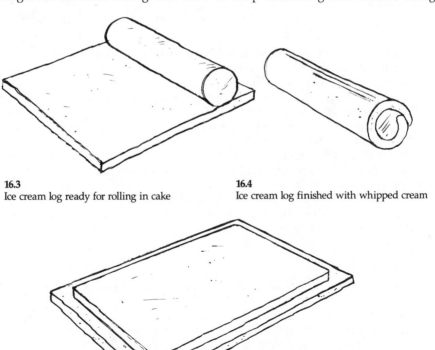

16.3
Ice cream log ready for rolling in cake

16.4
Ice cream log finished with whipped cream

16.5
Layer of ice cream on thin sheet of cake ready for rolling up

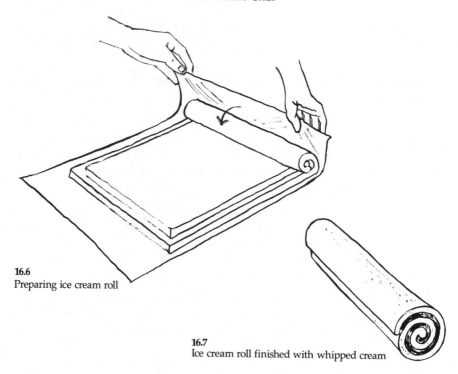

16.6
Preparing ice cream roll

16.7
Ice cream roll finished with whipped cream

fresh fruits and berries. These will freeze and remain hard long after the ice cream has softened or even melted.

The ice cream rolls are usually finished with whipped cream that is lightly applied over the top and sides of the roll. The roll is then covered with additional whipped cream piped on in varying designs with a pastry bag and tube. The roll may be made in the form of a log by striping the top with a star tube or combing with a heavier application of whipped cream that has been used to cover the outside of the roll. The rolls may be cut into 6–8 in. sections and frozen. These units are later decorated for special occasions as an ice cream layer cake. The tops may be garnished with special discs of sweet chocolate or the sides lightly garnished with chocolate shavings before serving. The cakes are sliced for service. Special fruit or other sauces may be served with the sliced ice cream roll.

Ice Cream Tarts and Specialties

Ice cream tarts may be made in a variety of ways. The term "tart" implies an individual dessert, one usually made in a prebaked tart shell. The tarts may also be baked with a small amount of special filling. For example, tarts partially filled with pineapple fruit filling may be baked. When cool and then chilled, the tarts may have a thin disc of sponge or chiffon cake placed over the fruit. The cake may have a ball of ice cream or sherbet (pineapple-flavored) placed on top. The ice cream or sherbet may then be garnished with a rosette of whipped cream and then garnished with a fruit sauce or a quarter slice of drained canned pineapple. This is but one instance of how the prebaked tart shells may be used. The same shell may also be filled with a custard cream and then covered with ice cream or sherbet. The finish is optional and the pastry chef will use a suitable method for decoration.

Prebaked Mary Ann tart cakes or shells may be used for frozen tarts. The shells are filled with a cream or fruit filling if desired. The centers may be filled with two different flavored ice creams or a combination of ice cream and sherbet. The top edge of the tart may be decorated with whipped cream, and a whipped cream charlotte placed in the very center. The top may be garnished with a special sauce. These tarts are usually placed in serving dishes before completely finished and kept in the freezer until ready to be served.

Discs may be cut from a chocolate sponge or chiffon sheet cake. The discs are then placed into paper cups, disposable plastic dessert dishes, or regular dishes. The top of the cake is covered with a ball of ice cream. Two smaller balls may be used when the balls are placed on top of each other for height. The top of the ice cream is garnished with whipped cream and a variety of sauces may be used for final garnishing of these individual tartlike servings. Whipped toppings or a combination of whipped cream and whipped topping may be used for garnishing. The preparation of these toppings has been explained. In the summer or extremely hot weather, a marshmallow topping may be used to replace the whipped cream.

Cake batters baked in tart pans or in regular cupcake pans are often used as the base for the individual frozen tarts. The pastry chef may select any of a number of recipes to be used for these cupcakes. Provision for greater cake variety is now possible. The baked cupcakes or tart cakes are chilled before they are finished. The centers of the cake are cut out and set aside. The cakes are filled with ice cream or sherbet. The outside edge of the cake may be decorated with a ring of whipped cream. The cake cut-out is replaced on the ice cream or sherbet and garnished with a rosette of whipped cream. The cream may be sprinkled with chocolate sprinkles, chopped nuts, or decorated with a special chocolate disc or cut-out.

Frozen Eclairs and Cream Puffs

The eclair or cream puff shells make excellent containers or bases for frozen desserts. The shells may be left plain or they may be dipped in a variety of fondant icings of differing pastel colors and allowed to dry. The tops are then cut from the cream puffs and eclair shells. The cream puffs that are to be filled with a fruit filling may have a small disc of cake placed in the bottom center of the shell to support the fruit filling and to absorb any syrup from the fruit filling The cream puff shells are then filled with a ball of ice cream, or a combination of 2 or more small balls. The ice cream may then be covered with a rosette of whipped cream and the iced top of the cream puff placed on top. Plain tops may be dusted

16.8
Ice cream placed in a tart shell

16.9
Ice cream tart finished with whipped cream

16.10
Ice cream-filled eclair

16.11
Ice cream-filled cream puff

with confectioners sugar before serving.

The eclairs are sliced along the top and the iced top removed. The centers of the eclairs are filled using a special ice cream scoop that is finger shaped, and the long scoop of ice cream or sherbet is deposited in the shell. Two or even three small round balls of ice cream, or a combination of ice cream and sherbet, may be placed along the length of the eclair shell. The ice cream may be garnished with a strip of whipped cream and the top replaced. Un-iced tops may be garnished with a spiral design made with whipped cream. The top may be striped with melted sweet chocolate.

Swan-shaped cream puffs or ovals may be filled with a variety of ice creams or sherbets and decorated accordingly. (See Figs. 16.8 through 16.11)

Baked Alaska

Baked Alaska may be made in different forms and shapes. Different types of ice cream or sherbet may be used. In addition, fresh fruits may be added to the ice cream or sherbet for variety. The cake coverings may be moistened and flavored with brandy and liqueurs of special choosing before the meringue is applied. The actual shape of the baked Alaska may vary with the shape of the ice cream and the formation of the strip. The strip may be in square, triangular, or oval or round shape. It is quite apparent that the pastry chef has wide latitude in preparing the baked Alaska. The cake used for the base and the sides or cover for the ice cream or sherbet is usually made from a sponge cake or chiffon cake. The base is usually thicker than the cake used for the sides or top. Pastry chefs will usually use a single sheet of average thickness. A thickness of one-half to three-quarters of an inch is sufficient.

Baked Alaska may be served on serving trays to be sliced and served at the table, or it may also be made and served in individual portions. Baked Alaska is often served flambé style. The serving trays are used directly for the preparation of larger units. The ice cream for the baked Alaska may be in brick or round form as prepared for ice cream rolls. A 4 in. square brick of combination-flavored ice cream or ice cream and sherbet may be used for the square or triangular-shaped dessert. The round ice cream roll may be cut to the size of the cake base.

For the larger table service, place the sponge cake bottom in the center of the serving tray. The strip of cake should be approximately 3½–4 in. wide. There should be about 1½–2 in. from each side of the strip of cake to the very edge of the serving tray. This space is necessary for the covering of the cake and application of the meringue. Place the brick of ice cream that has been cut to size and shape in the center of the cake base. The round cylinder of ice cream should be placed the same way. Cover the sides of the ice cream with strips of sponge cake cut to size. For a triangular effect only two sides are formed that come to a point. For the square shape, cover both sides and the top with three separate strips of sponge cake. For the round shape, place a single strip of cake over the ice cream so that the entire roll is covered. Press the strips of cake gently

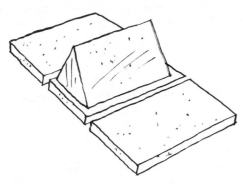

16.12
Cake sheet cut into three equal strips with ice cream on center strip

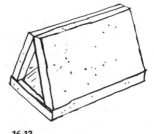

16.13
Cake strips placed against sides of ice cream to form triangle or "A" shape

16.14
Meringue topping placed on cake and ready for quick browning

against the ice cream. Use the prepared French meringue or the boiled meringue and cover the cakes with a thick cover (about 1 in.). (See Figs. 16.12 through 16.14) The bottom edges and the top may be decorated with a pastry bag and tube. Designs may vary. Dust the meringue with confectioners sugar and brown in a hot oven (425–435°F). The browned baked Alaska should be served immediately. It may be presented to the diners in flambé style by dipping sugar cubes in heated brandy or rum. Ignite the sugar. Place the heated brandy or rum in small cups, ignited, and bring to the diners. Special sauces, if desired, may be served separately.

As previously indicated, sherbet or a combination of sherbet and ice cream may be used. Additionally, fresh fruits may be added to the sherbet or ice cream and then the baked Alaska is completed and served. With each such change in cream, sherbet, or fruit, the pastry chef will probably change the name of the dessert. The modern pastry chef may wish to adopt some of these continental names for the desserts.

Cherry Baked Alaska　Prepare black Bing or Royal Ann cherries by mixing them with a small amount of apricot jam so that they stick together. Spread them over the ice cream or sherbet and then cover with meringue. The meringue may be garnished with glazed cherries before browning in the oven. The sponge cake covers may be sprinkled with kirsch or other liqueur before applying the meringue. A special cherry sauce flavored with cherry brandy may be served in separate sauce dishes, if desired.

Sherbet Alaska　Use orange or lemon sherbet for the interior. The pastry chef will have to prepare this dessert faster than those made with ice cream because sherbet melts faster than ice cream. The tray may be garnished with candied orange and lemon slices or marmalade candies or slices. An orange or lemon sauce may be used with the dessert.

Strawberry Alaska　Follow the same procedure as for the cherry Alaska and serve with a strawberry sauce. Frozen strawberries may be used for the sauce. They may also be prepared in a thick filling and added with the ice cream if a vanilla ice cream is used as a base.

Individual Baked Alaska

Individual servings of baked Alaska may be prepared by using tart shells baked in advance. The shells may be baked with a small amount of selected fruit or special custard cream fillings. The tart shells are filled with balls of ice cream or sherbet, or combinations of both. The tops are then covered with a charlotte design made with the prepared meringue and browned in the oven. The individual servings may be served with a special sauce. The tops may be slightly indented and a small amount of heated brandy applied and then lit to be served flambé.

The Mary Ann tart cakes or shells may be used for the same purpose. The centers are filled with the ice cream or sherbet. The tops and sides are covered with the prepared meringue and the units placed on sheet pans about 2 in. apart. The entire pan is then placed in a hot oven (435°F) and the meringue browned. Each tart is then placed on a separate serving dish. A small amount of warm brandy may be poured into the plate and lit for flambé service. A special fruit or thinned custard sauce may be served with these tarts in baked Alaska form.

The individual tarts may also be made from cut-out discs of sponge cake. A sponge cake sheet about 1 in. thick should be used. Cut out 3-in. discs with a plain cookie cutter. Place them on clean pans or parchment paper-lined pans and space them about 3–4 in. apart. Place a full scoop of round or pyramid-shaped ice cream or sherbet in the center of the sponge cake disc. Cover the entire cake and ice cream center with meringue using a pastry bag and large star tube. Form into a charlotte effect or design. Brown in the oven after dusting with confectioners sugar. Serve flambé style. A separate sauce may be served.

Fruit-Based Ice Cream Desserts

Pie a la mode is a typical American fruit and ice cream dessert. Large fruit cakes that have been cut into portions are equally popular when served with ice cream. This is especially effective when the fruit cakes are open and the fresh fruit has been glazed. An appropriate ice cream may be served, one that is compatible with the type of fruit used in the cake. Fruit tarts have been stressed as an excellent vehicle for an ice cream dessert. The tarts are usually filled almost three-quarters of the way and the chilled tart is garnished with a ball of ice cream. Fruit sauces have also been widely used in frozen desserts. These desserts are known as rapid service desserts and are satisfying to most diners. For the more discriminating and gourmet diner, pastry chefs will prepare the more elaborate continental type of desserts. These require special care and attention. They are also quite time-consuming. However, there are effective shortcuts to mass produce some of these desserts. The more popular and efficiently prepared and served desserts are presented. There are numerous other desserts in this category that may be made but do require additional time and added cost. These may be made at the discretion of the pastry chef.

Cherries Jubilee

Americans serve cherries jubilee with ice cream, usually vanilla or cherry ice cream. Canned black Bing cherries are used to prepare the cherry base or jubilee.

Ingredients	lb	oz	Mixing procedure
2 No. 10 cans of black Bing cherries			Drain the fruit. Measure the syrup and check for sweetness

Drained syrup	4		Bring the sugar and syrup to a boil
Sugar	1	8	
Lemon juice		2	
Cornstarch		3	Dissolve the starch in the water or leftover syrup. Add to the above in a steady stream and bring to a boil. Stir constantly and boil until clear. Remove from fire
Syrup or water		12	
Red coloring (few drops)			Add the coloring and mix in well

Allow the filling to cool a bit and then place into the serving dishes while still warm. The cherries are usually flamed in the dining room and served with balls of ice cream which have been portioned out on a separate serving tray.
Yield: Approx. 100 servings

The continental method of making cherries jubilee does not require the use of ice cream. The large, selected, black Bing cherries are pitted carefully and then lightly cooked or poached in simple syrup. Approximately 20 such cherries are cooked in ½–¾ qt of simple syrup. The syrup is thickened with approximately 1 oz of cornstarch dissolved in a little cool water (4 oz) and brought to a boil. Red coloring is added to highlight the sauce formed. The syrup and cherries are blended together, placed in a serving dish, and sprinkled with kirsch or other liqueur or brandy. Kirsch, a cherry brandy, is the most frequently used. The brandy is ignited and the cherries jubilee is served flambé.

Peach Melba

The peaches used for this dessert should be fresh, washed and lightly poached in syrup until softened. The syrup is flavored with kirsch and may be thickened with a little cornstarch and used to prepare the sauce. The peaches are placed over serving dishes that have a ball of vanilla ice cream and then garnished with a Melba sauce.

Ingredients	lb	oz	Mixing procedure
Currant jelly	3		Combine these ingredients and bring to a boil
Raspberry, strawberry juice (mashed and strained fruits)[1]	3		
Sugar	3		
Water	1		

[1]Cranberry juice may be used.

| Cornstarch or arrowroot | 5 | Dissolve the starch or arrowroot in the water and add to the above and bring to a |
| Water | 12 | boil. Cook until thickened slightly and clear |

Sprinkle the top with some sliced almonds and garnish lightly with a charlotte design of whipped cream. A glazed or maraschino cherry may be placed on top of the whipped cream.

A variety of other fruits may be used to make the Melba, such as strawberries, apricots, and pears. The ice cream flavors may be changed to suit the type of fruit that is used.

Banana-Type Frozen Desserts
Bananas are very popular for fruited frozen desserts. They are used extensively with a variety of ice creams and sherbets. The decoration and finish of the dessert, in conjunction with the fruit and ice cream, will often determine the name of the dessert. The variations are many and the names are equally varied and quite impressive. The popular American banana split often encompasses as many as 4 or 5 continental desserts made with bananas. If one visualizes the combination of three or more varieties of ice cream in one plate, served with sliced or quartered bananas, garnished generously with whipped cream, and covered with chocolate and other sauces and nuts, then it is likely that one American banana split may be the equivalent of several continental desserts combined. Some of the continental style banana desserts follow. These may be changed to meet specific needs and special requirements.

Chocolate-Banana (Banana Alexandria)
Place sliced bananas in the serving dishes. Fill almost half full with loosely placed banana slices. Place a large ball of vanilla ice cream over the top of the bananas. Cover the ice cream with chocolate sauce. A chocolate fudge poured warm or hot will be effective. A sauce mousseline may also be used. (For the sauce mousseline, add approximately ½ qt of whipped cream to each full quart of chocolate syrup.)

Pineapple-Banana (Banana Cardinal)
Place sliced bananas in serving dish and fill about half full. Cover the bananas with a portion of pineapple sherbet or pineapple ice cream. A small ball of each may be used. Cover the top of the ice cream or sherbet with Melba sauce. The top may also be garnished with a rosette of whipped cream.

Strawberry-Banana (Banana Fraisette)
A parfait or similar dish may be used for this dessert. Mix sliced bananas with Melba sauce and fill the glass dish about half full. Place a ball of strawberry ice cream on top of the bananas. Cover the ice cream with strawberry sauce and serve. The top may be garnished with whipped cream, and with a slice of banana and a strawberry which have been dipped in strawberry sauce.

Strawberry Sauce

Ingredients	lb	oz	Mixing procedure
Water	2		Boil the water and sugar. Add the lemon
Sugar	2	4	juice and strawberries and boil
Lemon juice		4	
Strawberries (2 qt) fresh, mashed and strained			
Arrowroot or cornstarch		1½	Add to the above in a steady stream and bring to a boil. Remove from fire and
Water		4	strain.
Red coloring (few drops)			Add the coloring and mix in

The sauce may be used warm or cold.

Orange-Banana (Banana Pompadour)

Place sliced bananas in the serving dish and fill half full. Place a ball of orange sherbet (a combination of orange and lemon sherbet may be used) over the bananas. Cover the sherbet with Melba sauce and serve. The sherbet may be replaced with ice cream (peach, orange, pineapple). The top may be garnished with a rosette of whipped cream and a small slice of fresh orange.

The modern pastry chef will use canned fruits extensively for many of the fruited frozen desserts. These fruits are not perishable and portions may be controlled. There is usually a count on the number of pieces of fruit contained in the can. The syrups in which the fruits are packed are very often used as the syrup base from which the fruit sauces are made, since they contain the natural flavor of the fruits. The degree of sugar and sweetness is taken into account and the pastry chef will usually add some fresh lemon juice and orange juice to enhance the tartness and flavor. For example, peach Melba may be made in various forms with half peaches. Peach halves may be placed on a disc of sponge cake in the serving dish. The hollow center is usually filled with a ball of vanilla ice cream and then covered with a sauce made with the syrup in the can mixed with a portion of currant jelly. The sauce is thickened with a small amount of arrowroot and cornstarch. The top of the ball of ice cream may be covered with another half peach and whipped cream. There are many variations which the chef may be using depending upon the volume of the service, the cost factor, and the facilities for production. Some additional continental-style peach desserts made with ice cream or sherbet follow.

Peach-Strawberry (Peach Fraisette)

Place a large ball of strawberry ice cream in the serving dish. Place one half of a canned or stewed fresh peach on top. Cover with strawberry sauce and serve. The sauce may be served in a separate serving dish. Whipped cream may be used to replace or accompany the sauce.

Peach Bar-le-Duc (Currant)
Place a scoop of vanilla ice cream in the serving dish. Place a peach half over the ice cream with the smooth round side facing up. Cover the top of the peach and ice cream with Bar-le-Duc sauce or Melba sauce. Garnish the top with fresh strawberries and serve.

Peach-Lemon (Peach Lily)
Place a good portion of lemon sherbet in the center of the dish. Place one half of a peach over the sherbet. Cover the top with a sauce made from the peach syrup blended with apricot jam and a small amount of currant jelly. Thicken lightly with arrowroot or cornstarch. Garnish the top with muscat or other grapes and then serve.

Raspberry-Peach (Pompoms)
Place a large ball of raspberry sherbet in the center of the serving dish. Place one half of a canned peach over the sherbet. Cover the peach with Melba sauce or a sauce made with the syrup of the canned peaches mixed with currant jelly and thickened lightly with arrowroot or cornstarch. Garnish the top with a rosette of whipped cream.

Strawberry Frozen Desserts
Fresh strawberries can be obtained almost all year round. However, when fresh berries are not available, canned or frozen strawberries thickened by cooking the syrup with some cornstarch and adding the drained frozen berries will suffice. There are many variables and combinations to be made using variety ice creams and sherbets in conjunction with fresh strawberries. There are also variables in desserts when strawberries are combined with other fruits and sauces. The following are some of the continental style desserts that may be made efficiently.

Strawberries Romanoff
This popular dessert may be served in large volume when fresh strawberries are in season and are reasonably priced. The dessert is prepared and served in almost the same manner as cherries jubilee.

Ingredients	qt	Mixing procedure
Fresh strawberries, washed and hulled	10	Extra large berries may be cut into smaller sections
Fresh orange juice	3	Add to the strawberries and stir gently. Chill well
Brandy	1	in the refrigerator
Curacao	1	

For the continental dessert and service, fill the special serving dishes or stainless steel cups (silver, if available) about three-quarters full. Garnish the tops with a charlotte of whipped cream and serve.

For more rapid dining room service, fill the serving dishes with the strawberries Romanoff and flame in the dining room. Dishes with balls of ice cream on a separate dish are prepared. The individual dishes are each filled with a ball of vanilla ice cream and then garnished with the strawberries. The amount of brandy and curacao may be reduced and replaced with more orange juice. Flame by sprinkling the strawberries with brandy and igniting.
Yield: 100 servings

Strawberries that are to be used with ice cream or sherbet are usually prepared in advance to develop flavor. The washed and hulled berries are dredged or well sprinkled with confectioners sugar and sprinkled lightly with curacao. The berries are then placed in shallow pans and refrigerated before using for desserts. This will maintain the shape and firmness of the fresh berries and allow the formation of a light syrup which enhances the color and the flavor of the strawberries.

Strawberry Devonshire
Fill the serving dish about half full with fresh strawberries. If there are any cut or very small berries, these should be used for the base and the larger berries used for the top garnish. Cover the berries with a ball of strawberry ice cream. Place a few large berries over the ice cream. Cover the dessert with Melba sauce and sprinkle the top lightly with chopped, roasted almonds.

Strawberry Bar-le-Duc
Mix the prepared strawberries with currant jelly (Bar-le-Duc) and place into parfait dishes about half full. Cover the berries with vanilla ice cream. Cover the top with strawberry sauce. The top may be garnished with whipped cream and a fresh strawberry on top.

Strawberry-Pineapple Sherbet (Medicis)
Fill the serving dish about half full with the prepared strawberries. Place a good sized portion of pineapple sherbet over the berries. Cover the top of the sherbet with a softened cover of orange marmalade or apricot marmalade. Thin the marmalade with simple syrup. Sprinkle the top with chopped pistachio nuts and then serve.

Strawberry Orloff
Place a ball of strawberry ice cream into the serving dish. Use the cone-shaped scoop if parfait glasses are used. Decorate the ice cream with a charlotte design made with whipped cream. Sprinkle the top with crushed praline or chopped walnuts. Pecans may also be used as a garnish.

Strawberry-Orange Sherbet (Wilhelmina)
Fill the serving dish half full with prepared strawberries. Place a ball of orange sherbet over the berries. Garnish with whipped cream and fresh strawberries and serve.

Coupes

Coupes are considered conglomerate desserts. That is, they are composed of a wide variety of ingredients. However, the most common ingredient is a fruit or combination of fruits. These may be fresh fruits that are sliced or left intact, such as strawberries, or they may be canned fruits packed in syrups, or they may be frozen fruits which have been defrosted and perhaps made into a sauce. In addition to the variety of fruits a variety of ice creams and sherbets are used for the different coupes. Very often a combination of ice cream and sherbet may be used with the fruits. To further embellish the coupes, a variety of liqueurs, syrups, and flavorings are often used. Finally, the top decoration may be made with whipped cream and additional fruits and nuts. Thus, it is evident that the pastry chef with imagination and a good sense of food and dessert balance can really produce a wide variety of coupes. In fact, the pastry chef may take advantage of seasonal fruits or special "buys" for other ingredients used for these desserts, and plan for large volume feeding.

Coupes may be served in large champagne glasses, silver dishes that are sufficiently large to contain the various ingredients of the coupe, or in special plastic dessert containers made specifically for the coupe type of dessert. Caterers will often purchase prepared bases for coupes and have the pastry chef decorate or finish the coupes just before they are to be served. At that time the pastry chef may add fresh fruits that have been lightly marinated in liqueurs or syrups, and add the whipped cream and other final touches to the coupes. Complete desserts may also be ordered to supplement those prepared by the pastry chef. The coupe desserts presented are selected for ease and practicality of production and service. Names of coupes are the specialty of the house and very often the names are selected from a prescribed long list, or they may be temporarily given in honor of some special individual for whom the dining service is prepared.

Pineapple-Raspberry Coupe (Coupe Cyrano)
Fill the coupe glasses or cups about half full with diced fresh pineapple. Canned pineapple may be used. The large slices may be cut or broken pieces may be used as well. Cover the fruit with raspberry sherbet and a ball of vanilla ice cream over the sherbet. A border of whipped cream may be placed around the edge of the glass with a pastry bag and star tube.

Strawberry Coupe (Coupe Marie-Louise)
Fill the coupe glasses or cups half full with strawberries that have been prepared with confectioners sugar and sprinkled with curacao. An orange sauce may be used to replace the curacao. Cover the strawberries with a ball of strawberry ice cream. A cone-shaped serving of ice cream may be placed on the strawberries for a pyramid effect. Cover the ice cream with whipped cream piped in a charlotte form. The cone-shaped

ice cream may be encircled with the whipped cream. Place a large, fresh strawberry on top and serve.

Banana-Peach Coupe (Coupe Mireille)

Fill the coupe glasses or cups half full with sliced peaches. These may be fresh or canned peaches that have been drained. The syrup may be thickened with a little arrowroot. Add a little peach brandy or sauce over the peach slices. Place a ball of banana and vanilla ice cream over the fruit. The ice cream may be garnished with a rosette of whipped cream and two or three slices of peach.

Orange Coupe (Coupe Valencia)

Fill the coupe glasses or dishes about two-thirds full of fresh orange slices (or canned orange slices). Canned mandarin orange slices will do quite well for this dessert. The syrup in the can may be cooked up and thickened lightly with arrowroot or cornstarch to prepare an orange sauce. Cover the orange slices with orange sherbet and then sprinkle the tops with curacao or the orange sauce. Garnish the top with a slice of orange and serve.

Fruit Salad Coupe (Coupe Thais)

This coupe is best prepared with a variety of slices and cubes of assorted fresh fruit. Peaches, pears, apples, cherries, oranges, pineapple, and other fresh fruits may be used. The fruits may be mixed with the natural juices that are mixed with a little simple syrup. Fill the glasses or dishes a little more than half full with the mixed fruit. If canned fruit salad is used, drain the fruit and use the syrup to prepare a light sauce mixed with currant jelly thickened with a small amount of arrowroot or cornstarch. Pour a small amount of the sauce over the fruit. Place a ball of lemon sherbet on top of the fruit. Decorate around the ball of sherbet with whipped cream and serve.

Coupe St. Jacques

Prepare the diced and sliced fruits (macedoine) as for the fruit salad coupe. Add sliced bananas and then add kirsch to the fruit for added color and flavor. Fill the glasses or cups half full with the fruit. Place a portion of lemon sherbet and strawberry ice cream on top of the fruit. The top may be garnished with sliced mandarin oranges and a little orange sauce.

Coupe Americana (Pineapple Coupe)

Use sweetened, crushed pineapple that has been cooked into a soft filling (slightly thinner than pineapple pie filling). Fill the coupe dishes or cups about half full with the filling. Place two almond macaroons over the pineapple filling. Place a ball of pineapple sherbet over the macaroons and garnish with a circle of whipped cream around the ball of sherbet. The top may be garnished with a spoonful of pineapple filling and a maraschino cherry.

Vanilla-Cherry Coupe

Use a cherry filling for the base. Place the filling in the glasses or cups to fill about one quarter of the glass. Place a large ball of vanilla ice cream over the cherries. Decorate the ice cream with a large rosette of whipped cream. Garnish the whipped cream with a cherry-flavored sauce and a glazed cherry.

Peach Coupe

Place a large ball of vanilla ice cream in the coupe dish or glass. Cover the ice cream with drained, canned, sliced peaches. Fresh peaches in season may also be used. Sprinkle the peaches with Grand Marnier and garnish the top with whipped cream in charlotte form.

Pineapple-Rum Coupe

Fill the glasses or cups about two-thirds full with a pineapple sherbet or lemon sherbet that has been mixed with pineapple chunks. Sprinkle the top with a fine rum or a syrup that has been laced with rum. Garnish the top with a rosette of whipped cream. Place an almond macaroon on top of the whipped cream.

Parfaits

Parfaits are a very popular frozen dessert. They are prepared in tall, rather narrow glasses or plastic disposable dishes for large groups. Parfaits are also a combination of a variety of ice creams and sauces, with occasional fruited varieties. Most parfaits are decorated with whipped cream on top and garnished with a fruit, nut, or syrup. Parfaits made primarily with ice cream can be made long in advance and kept in the freezer. When ready to be served, they are garnished with the whipped cream and syrup or other topping. These desserts may be ordered from a specialty ice cream manufacturer and custom-prepared according to specifications. The final decoration may be made by the pastry chef. When the pastry chef is ready to fill the combinations in the parfait glasses, the ice creams, fruits, and sauces are made ready and the glasses lined up. This is usually done with the help of assistants and follows an automatic system of filling. The ice creams are lightly softened so that they may be dropped into the glasses and will level themselves somewhat before the next filling or flavor is added. It is quite customary to fill the bottom of the glass with a syrup or sauce and then proceed to fill the glass with an alternating variety of ice creams. Sherbet varieties may also be combined with the ice creams. The colorful arrangements are usually decided upon by the pastry chef. Special color and filling arrangements may be made to meet the needs of special occasions.

Parfaits were originally made in a mousse form that was partially frozen. The finer parfaits are still made in a form similar to a mousse. The ice cream is softened and then carefully blended with whipped cream and then placed into parfait glasses. A blend of these mousse ice cream preparations is combined for colorful and flavorful desserts. The parfait recipes and arrangements that follow are quite popular and can be efficiently produced. They will also provide a measure of guidance should the parfaits be ordered from the ice cream specialty manufacturer serving the caterer of large groups.

Mousse-Type Parfaits
If the continental type of parfait is desired for smaller parties or special occasions, the ice cream is blended with almost equal parts of heavy, whipped cream with added confectioners sugar. A straight ice cream may be used for large-scale production.

Vanilla Parfait

Ingredients	lb	oz	Mixing procedure
Vanilla ice cream (French ice cream preferred)	(10 qt) (2½ gal)		Blend ice cream on slow speed to soften slightly and maintain smoothness. Whip the cream lightly
Whipped cream made with 3 quarts heavy cream	6		
Confectioners sugar	1		Gradually add the sifted sugar and whip
Vanilla		1	medium thick. Add the vanilla and blend in

With a wire whip, blend the cream and ice cream together. Pour into the parfait glasses and freeze. When ready to be served, garnish the tops with a rosette of whipped cream and a maraschino or glazed cherry.
Yield: Approx. 100 servings

Strawberry Parfait
Add to the basic vanilla parfait 4 qt of cleaned and hulled fresh strawberries that have been crushed and folded in after the whipped cream has been blended with the ice cream. This will provide for a mousse type of parfait. A regular strawberry ice cream may be used. The bottom of the parfait glass may be partially filled with a strawberry sauce before filling with the ice cream. Garnish the tops of the parfait with whipped cream and place one or two whole, fresh strawberries on top.

Chocolate Parfait (Mousse Style)
To the basic chocolate parfait mousse style, add 1–1½ qt of regular chocolate syrup to the chocolate ice cream before folding in the whipped cream. It is better to use the prepared chocolate paste or chocolate appareil for flavor and texture.

Chocolate Paste or Appareil

The appareil may be used for a wide variety of frozen desserts and is usually kept in stock for use when required.

Ingredients	lb	oz	Mixing procedure
Milk	6		Bring the milk, cream, and sugar to a boil
Cream (heavy)	6		over a low to moderate flame. Stir well to
Sugar	3		prevent scorching. When boiling, remove
Chocolate liqueur	4	8	from the fire and add the chocolate. Strain
(bitter chocolate)			and pour into a container
softened			

When cool, place in the refrigerator. The paste may be added where required for frozen desserts. It blends in easily. Add approximately 3 qt of the chocolate paste or appareil to the basic chocolate parfait (mousse style).

Ingredients	lb	oz	Mixing procedure
Chocolate ice cream,			Mix the same as for the mousse-type va-
2½ gal.			nilla parfait
Heavy cream (3 qt)	6		
Confectioners sugar	1		
Vanilla		1	

Chocolate Parfait—Mousse Style
Fill the parfait glasses with the chocolate parfait filling as soon as prepared. A chocolate syrup may be placed at the bottom of the glass before filling with the ice cream preparation. Freeze the parfaits and then decorate the tops with whipped cream and garnish with a dash of chocolate syrup, chocolate sprinkles, or chocolate discs. The mousse-style parfaits are lighter in texture and have a softer, creamier feel and taste when consumed. More ice cream is required when using the straight ice cream to make the parfaits.

Coffee Parfait—Mousse Style

Ingredients	lb	oz	Mixing procedure
Coffee ice cream,			Mix as for the basic vanilla mousse parfait
2½ gal.			
Heavy cream (3 qt)	6		
Confectioners sugar	1		
Coffee flavoring		1	

Fill the parfait glasses and freeze. Garnish the tops of the parfait with whipped cream when frozen. A coffee-flavored sauce may be used to garnish the whipped cream. A syrup of chopped walnuts may be used for the garnish.

The following are selected parfaits that are quite popular and reflect the combinations of ice creams, fruits, and syrups that may be used in the preparation of parfaits. The ice creams used are the regular type of ice cream. The fruits, syrups, sauces and garnishes used may vary with the preference of the pastry chef. The combinations may be varied and the names assigned to the parfaits are optional.
Yield: 100 servings

Orange Parfait

Place two or three teaspoons of orange syrup (simple syrup flavored with orange rind and orange flavoring) in each parfait glass. Turn the glasses to line the sides with the syrup. Fill the glasses about two-thirds full with vanilla ice cream and add a little of the orange syrup to the top of the ice cream. Decorate the top with whipped cream in a large rosette form or design. Garnish the top with a mandarin orange slice that has been dipped in hot apricot glaze.

Strawberry-Banana Parfait

Slice bananas in thin slices and pour some curacao over the bananas. Fill the parfait glasses one third full with lemon sherbet. Place sliced bananas over the sherbet. Place a filling of strawberry ice cream over the bananas. The tops are decorated with whipped cream and a few slices of banana that have been brushed with hot apricot glaze.

Fruit Salad Parfait

Fill the parfait glasses with separate layers of strawberry ice cream, vanilla ice cream, and fruit salad. Be sure to drain the fruit. The syrup of the canned fruit may be used to prepare a syrup or sauce which may be used as an added garnish. The syrup may be thickened with arrowroot and flavored lightly with strawberry flavoring. Decorate the top of the parfait with whipped cream and special strawberry sauce.

Melba Parfait

Pour a small amount of Melba sauce into the parfait glasses. Turn the glasses to line the sides of the glass with the sauce. Fill the parfait glasses with vanilla ice cream. Decorate the top with whipped cream and pour a small amount of Melba sauce over the cream.

Bar-le-Duc (Currant) Parfait

Pour a small amount of Bar-le-Duc or softened currant jelly into the parfait glasses. (Use simple syrup to soften the currant jelly.) Rotate the glasses to cover the sides of the glass. Fill the glasses with layers of vanilla ice cream and a thin layer of currant jelly between them. Cherry ice cream may be alternated with the vanilla ice cream. The top of the parfait is decorated with whipped cream and garnished with a glazed cherry.

Praline Parfait

Combine vanilla or walnut ice cream with crushed praline. Place about 1 tablespoon of walnuts in syrup at the bottom of the parfait glass. Fill the glass with vanilla ice cream and praline-filled or walnut ice cream. Decorate the top with whipped cream and crushed praline topping. Chopped walnut pieces may be used as a garnish.

Gelatin Parfaits

Pastry chefs will often combine a gelatin dessert with ice cream in a parfait glass. The desired gelatin or combination of gelatin and fruit is placed into the parfait glass and chilled so that it is set. The desired ice cream combination is placed on top of the gelatin and frozen. The tops are usually garnished with whipped cream and a sauce. The sauce is usually served separately in a gooseneck serving dish.

Bombes

Bombes are a form of frozen dessert prepared for larger groupings at a table rather than for individual service. The bombes, after presentation and display, are cut into individual portions and then served. The bombe may be accompanied by a special sauce which is usually placed in a gooseneck serving dish for pouring or ladling. The bombe is usually in a spherical, round, rectangular or square shape. These may vary in size from a depth of 4–6 in. to a diameter or cross-section of 5–6 in. The forms, shapes, and designs vary. They are obtainable at the better restaurant and hotel supply houses. For the pastry chef who must prepare for large groups seated at a number of dining tables, it is advisable to have sufficient bombe molds of the same size and design available. The bombes may be prepared, frozen, and turned out of the molds and returned to the freezer again so that the molds may be used to produce enough bombes.

It is quite common today for the pastry chef or caterer to order prepared bombes from the ice cream or frozen dessert manufacturer who services the hotel and catering industry. The design, ice cream, sherbet, and the filling (paté à bombe) may be specified and these bombes are prepared to order. Upon delivery, the pastry chef will do the final decorating and finishing. Most bombes are usually finished with a whipped cream design around the base of the bombe and over the surface of the bombe. The appropriate sauce is also prepared by the pastry chef and is served separately with the bombe for table service. For the pastry chef who still prepares the bombes from scratch, the following procedures should be followed. The selected bombe varieties are those that are quite popular and lend themselves to rapid, large-quantity production.

To prepare the bombes, the molds are oiled lightly and completely with a neutral, fine vegetable oil. This will make release of the frozen bombe easier. Bombes are usually coated or masked with ice cream about 1–1½ in. thick. The bombe molds should be chilled before masking. In fact, it may be advisable to have the molds arranged in a large bowl or deep pan with ice cubes. This will keep the ice cream from smearing when applied to the metal of the mold. When two or more layers of different ice cream are used, apply a three-quarter-in. thick layer with firm ice cream. Be sure the ice cream is pressed in properly so that fluted designs or grooves are completely filled. The second layer of ice cream is then applied to a thickness of about one-half to three-quarters in. A third ice cream variety may be applied which may completely fill the mold. Ice creams may be alternated with a firm sherbet of a different color and flavor. Bombes may have special fruits and liqueurs added to the ice cream and placed in toward the center of the mold. In most instances, pastry chefs will fill the center of the mold with a special filling. This mixture or paté is prepared in advance and then made into a mousse form with the combination of the mousse base with whipped cream. The mousse may be filled with fruits of various types. The fruits are often steeped in a variety of liqueurs or brandy before using. Upon filling the bombes completely, freeze them for at least several hours unless quick-freezing equipment is available. To unmold the bombes, dip the mold in warm water or hot water for a few seconds and quickly turn upside down on a prepared serving tray lined with a napkin.

As mentioned previously, bombes are generally filled with a mousse preparation in the center before being frozen. The fillings or center mixtures may vary with the different bombes to be made. A pastry chef may prefer to prepare a separate mousse for each variety. Most pastry chefs will prepare a basic mixture for the bombes called paté à bombe. The mixture is made and kept under refrigeration to be used as required.

Paté à Bombe   (Bombe mixture)

Ingredients	lb	oz	Mixing procedure
Sugar	4	8	Dissolve the sugar in the water and bring
Water	1	8	to a boil. Boil to approx. 240°F (soft ball stage)
Egg yolks	2		Whip the egg yolks until light and thick. Add the hot syrup to the egg yolks in a slow, steady stream and whip at medium speed until cool

Place the bombe mixture in a container and refrigerate. To use the bombe mixture or paté à bombe, whip 1 qt of heavy cream to a medium-firm consistency and fold into 1 lb 4 oz of prepared paté or basic bombe mixture. Be sure to have the bombe mold filled with ice cream mask and place the mixture into the center. The mixture may have fruits that have been soaked in liqueur added to it and placed into the bombe center. It is advisable to have the prepared sauces or syrups ready as well as other garnishes handy when putting the final decorations on the bombe.

Banana-Strawberry Bombe (Bombe Cyrano)
Coat the bombe mold with banana ice cream or vanilla ice cream layered with sliced bananas. Fill the center with basic bombe mixture to which strawberries have been added. Soak the strawberries lightly in kirsch before adding to the mixture. When frozen, remove from the mold and

decorate with whipped cream. A strawberry sauce may be served with the bombe. The whipped cream may be garnished with fresh strawberries.

Coffee-Rum Bombe
Mask or coat the bombe mold with coffee ice cream about 1 in. thick. Flavor the basic mixture of mousse base with rum and coffee flavoring. A maple or mocha flavoring and coloring may be used. Freeze and then unmold. Decorate the bombe with whipped cream and decorate with chocolate coffee beans or chocolate swirls.

Raspberry-Vanilla Bombe
Coat the mold with a vanilla ice cream. Place a second filling of raspberry sherbet over the ice cream. Flavor the basic paté mixture with strawberry flavoring and fresh strawberries and fill in the center. When frozen, decorate with whipped cream and garnish with a fresh strawberry. The center may also be flavored with currant jelly for a Bar-le-Duc effect. The bombe may be served with Melba sauce.

Coffee-Macaroon Bombe
Mask or coat the mold with coffee ice cream. Flavor the basic paté mixture with crushed praline and fill the center. When frozen, decorate with whipped cream and garnish with small French macaroons.

Pistachio-Praline Bombe (Bombe Pacifique)
Coat or mask the mold with pistachio ice cream about 1 in. thick. Place a filling of praline or walnut ice cream over the pistachio ice cream about ½ in. thick. Fill the center with praline flavored paté or bombe mixture. Freeze and then unmold. Decorate with whipped cream and garnish with pistachio nuts.

Chocolate-Rum Bombe (Bombe Sapho)
Coat the bombe mold with chocolate ice cream about 1 in. thick. Fill the center with the basic paté mixture that has been mixed with candied fruits mixed with rum and rum flavoring. Freeze and unmold. Decorate with whipped cream and garnish lightly with mixed, diced fruits that have been steeped slightly in rum and drained. Hot mousseline sauce may be served in separate gooseneck serving dishes.

Mousseline Sauce

Ingredients	lb	oz	Mixing procedure
Sugar	1	2	Mix all ingredients together well in a
Heavy cream	4		bowl. Place over another bowl with hot
Egg yolks	1		water (double boiler) and whip until thick.
Vanilla		1	The sauce will adhere to the wire

Vanilla-Chocolate Bombe
Coat the bombe mold with vanilla ice cream about 1 in thick. Place a coating of chocolate ice cream over the vanilla about ½ in. thick. Fill the

center with vanilla-flavored basic paté mixture and freeze. When frozen, unmold and decorate with whipped cream. Garnish the top lightly with chocolate swirls. Chocolate sauce may be served separately.

Orange-Strawberry Bombe (Bombe Americana)

Mask the bombe mold with strawberry ice cream about 1 in. thick. Combine the basic bombe paté mixture with sliced, fresh oranges. Canned mandarin orange slices may be used. Drain the orange slices. Fill the bombe center and freeze. When frozen, unmold and garnish with whipped cream and serve with a Melba sauce.

Vanilla-Anisette Bombe

Mask the bombe mold with vanilla ice cream about 1 in. thick. Fill the center with basic bombe paté mixture that has been flavored with anisette. Decorate the base and top with whipped cream and serve with a vanilla sauce. Vanilla pastry cream may be lightly thinned with some light cream for the sauce.

Orange Sherbet Bombe

Coat the bombe mold with orange sherbet about 1¼ in. thick. Flavor the paté bombe mixture with rum and rum flavoring. Fill the center and freeze. When frozen, unmold and serve with a Sabayon sauce.

Sabayon Sauce

Ingredients	lb	oz	Mixing procedure
Sugar	1	8	Combine the sugar and egg yolks in a
Egg yolks	1	4	bowl. Place over a hot water double boiler and whip until light and thick
Marsala wine or similar dark, sweet wine	1¼	qt	Add the wine in a slow, steady stream and whip over the hot water until thick. The sauce will adhere to the wire whip

The sauce may be served either hot or chilled.

Biscuit Glaces

Biscuit glaces are frozen specialties that are prepared in special glace paper cups. The cups are attractively colored and provide a desirable background for the contents. The glace is placed in the cup, frozen, and then garnished before serving with whipped cream or other garnish. The biscuit Tortoni is the most famous of these glaces. The biscuit glaces may be purchased in paper cups ready to serve. The pastry chef may add the finishing touch to the glace before service. For those who prepare the biscuit glace from scratch, there are two methods to use. The most efficient is to use the prepared paté à bombe as a base. To the base are added the necessary whipped cream, fruits if required for the glace, and chocolate paste or appareil. The other method is to prepare the glace from the original formula. The following is a recipe for the popular biscuit Tortoni.

Biscuit Tortoni

Ingredients	lb	oz	Mixing procedure
Sugar	1	12	Whip the yolks and sugar until thick
Egg yolks	2		
Heavy cream (5 qt)	10		Whip the cream with the sugar until medium stiff. Fold into egg yolks and sugar
Confectioners sugar	1		
Brandy or rum (rum flavoring may be substituted)		1 pt	Add the rum or brandy and stir in gently. Add the macaroons and fold in gently
French macaroons (crushed and sifted) (variable)			
Egg whites	2	8	Beat the egg whites and sugar to a medium stiff consistency and fold into the above
Sugar	2	4	

Fill the paper cups with the prepared tortoni mixture using a pastry bag and a large plain tube. Crush additional macaroons and sprinkle the tops of the tortoni and freeze. When frozen, garnish the tops of the biscuit Tortoni with a rosette of whipped cream. Garnish the top of the cream with a maraschino cherry or a glazed cherry.
Yield: Approx. 100 servings in special cups

Biscuit Tortoni Made with the Paté à Bombe Base

Ingredients	lb	oz	Mixing procedure
Paté à bombe base (1 full qt)			Blend the base to a smooth consistency
Heavy cream (5 qt)	10		Sift the confectioners sugar. Whip the cream lightly. Add the sugar and whip to a medium-firm consistency. Blend gently with the paté à bombe
Confectioners sugar	1		
Crushed macaroons (French)	2		Fold the macaroons and rum or brandy into the above
Rum or brandy		2	
Rum flavoring		1	

Deposit the batter into fancy paper cups. Garnish with crushed macaroons and freeze. Then garnish with whipped cream and place a maraschino or glazed cherry on top.

Note: For added volume and lightness, whip 2 lb egg whites and 1 lb 4 oz sugar to a medium stiff peak and fold into the above. This will provide for a lighter and more delicate structure.

If the heavy cream is partially diluted with cold milk, a whipped cream stabilizer should be used to maintain the gel and proper consistency. Approximately 1 oz of stabilizer is used for each quart of heavy cream blended with 12 oz of cold milk.

Macaroon-Chocolate Biscuit Glace

This glace is made in much the same manner as the biscuit Tortoni and similar procedures are followed using the paté à bombe as a base.

Ingredients	lb	oz	Mixing procedure
Chocolate paste (appareil) (approximately 1¼ qt)	2	12	Blend the chocolate paste and paté à bombe together gently
Paté à bombe (approximately 1 qt)	2	4	
Heavy cream (5 qt)	10		Whip the cream and sugar to a medium
Confectioners sugar		12	firm consistency. Add the vanilla and fold
Vanilla		1½	into the above gently

Deposit the batter into the fancy paper cups with a pastry bag and large plain tube. Fill the cups about three-quarters full. Garnish the tops with the following preparation:
Yield: 100 servings

Garnish

Ingredients	lb	oz	Mixing procedure
Paté à bombe (¾ qt)	1	4	Blend smooth
Heavy cream (2½ qt)	5		Whip the cream and the sugar until medium thick. Add the vanilla and blend
Confectioners sugar		8	into the above. Fold in the macaroons
Vanilla		1	gently
Finely ground and sifted French macaroons		6	

Bag out this mixture with a pastry bag and star tube into a rosette design on the tops of the filled cups. Sprinkle lightly with chocolate sprinkles or chopped chocolate swirls. Freeze and serve. About 1 oz of rum, or some rum flavoring, may be added to the garnish.

Strawberry Biscuit Glace

Ingredients	lb	oz	Mixing procedure
Paté à bombe (1 qt)	2	4	Blend smooth
Strawberries (fresh) (3 qt)			Wash and hull the berries. Crush the berries. Fold into the paté à bombe
Heavy cream (5 qt)	10		Sift the confectioners sugar. Whip the
Confectioners sugar	2		cream lightly. Add the sugar gradually and
Vanilla		1½	whip to a medium thick consistency. Add the vanilla and fold in

Bag out with a pastry bag and large plain tube into the fancy paper cups or special biscuit liners. Garnish the top with a rosette of whipped cream. Freeze and then garnish with a fresh strawberry before serving.
Yield: 100 servings

Chocolate Biscuit Glace

Ingredients	lb	oz	Mixing procedure
Chocolate paste (appareil) (approximately 1¼ qt)	2	12	Blend the chocolate paste and paté à bombe together gently
Paté à bombe (approximately ¾ qt)	1	4	
Heavy cream (5 qt)	10		Whip the cream until light. Add the sugar
Confectioners sugar	1		gradually and whip to a medium thick
Vanilla		1½	consistency. Add the vanilla and blend in. Fold into the above gently

Fill the cups about three-quarters full. Garnish with whipped cream that has been blended with chocolate paste, forming chocolate cream rosettes. Garnish the tops with chocolate swirls that have been chopped. Freeze and serve.
Yield: 100 servings

Souffle Glaces or Iced Souffles

Souffle glaces are frozen desserts that require special attention in their preparation. Souffles that are baked are served while they are above the level of the souffle dish. The iced souffle must have the same appearance when served. This requires placing a special liner on the inside of the souffle dish or cup so that the filling to be frozen extends above the level of the dish or cup by at least 1 in. When the souffle is frozen, it is dipped quickly in hot water for a moment to enable the paper liner or aluminum foil to be removed. The souffle is then returned to the original souffle dish and usually dusted lightly with a blend of cocoa and confectioners sugar. This is then scored or criss-crossed to resemble the appearance of a baked souffle when served. A basic vanilla and chocolate souffle mix can be prepared. These can then be changed into a variety of different souffles. Fruit-filled souffles are usually served with a fruit sauce or other sauce appropriate to the souffle and is served in separate goosenecks or sauce serving dishes. Where large numbers of souffles are prepared, they may be prepared in advance and frozen. The final finishing is done at the time of service. Pastry chefs will often add some gelatin to the souffle preparation to maintain the shape and consistency of the souffle.

Pastry chefs will vary in their approach to the preparation of the souffle glace. Some will use the paté à bombe and the chocolate paste (appareil) as the base. Others will prepare the souffle from scratch which is similar to the preparation of the paté à bombe with the addition of the whipped cream, ice cream, and the beaten egg whites. This is a matter of choice. However, it is advisable to prepare from scratch for assured consistency and better control.

Vanilla Souffle Glace

Ingredients	lb	oz	Mixing procedure
Confectioners sugar	1	10	Sift the sugar and combine with the egg
Egg yolks	1	12	yolks. Place in double boiler over a low
Gelatin		3	flame and whip until warm. Add the dissolved gelatin and whip in well until quite
Warm water	2	4	warm. Remove from fire and continue to mix until cool
Vanilla ice cream (soften the ice cream until smooth)		1 gal.	Add the yolks and gelatin to the ice cream and blend smooth
Heavy cream (2 qt)	4		Whip the cream until thick and fold into the above. Place the entire mixture in the refrigerator while whipping the egg whites
Egg whites (3 qt)	6		Whip the egg whites and sugar to a medium-thick consistency and fold into the
Sugar	1	12	refrigerated mix. Do this gently

1. Parchment paper or aluminum foil may be used to line the souffle cups or molds. Measure the depth of the cup or mold. Cut the parchment paper into widths that extend the paper liner about 2–2½ in. above the cup or souffle mold. Measure the length of the entire perimeter (outside) of the cup or mold. Cut the paper about 1–1½ in. longer so that the ends will overlap when placed inside the cup.
2. Grease the cups well with melted or softened butter. Line the sides of the cup or mold with the paper cut-outs. The overlapping ends

may be attached with a piece of Scotch tape.
3. Fill the cups or mold with the prepared vanilla souffle mix to the very top and freeze.
4. When ready to be served, unmold by dipping the glace in hot water quickly and then remove the paper liner.
5. Return the glace to the original souffle cup or mold. Dust the top with the cocoa and confectioners sugar blend and mark off a criss-cross or lattice design with a knife for the baked appearance.
6. Crushed macaroons or lightly browned crunchie topping may be used in place of the cocoa powder and sugar. If a sauce is served, it should be served in a separate serving dish.

Yield: Approx. 100 individual servings

Chocolate Souffle Glace

Ingredients	lb	oz	Mixing procedure
Sweet chocolate	3	8	Melt the chocolate to a soft, liquid-like
Bitter chocolate	1		state
Gelatin		5	Soften the gelatin in the water
Water	2		
Egg yolks	2	8	Sift the sugar and whip with the yolks un-
Confectioners sugar	3		til light and quite thick
Milk (fresh)	2		Combine the milk and yolks gently. Add these ingredients to the melted chocolate over a hot water bath in a double boiler and whip until well blended
Rum	(1 pt)		Add the rum and gelatin dissolved in the water and blend in gently but well for even distribution. Allow the mixture to cool
Heavy cream (2 qt)	4		Whip the cream until thick
Egg whites	3	8	Whip the egg whites and sugar until me-
Sugar	1	4	dium thick. When the chocolate mix is cool, fold in the whipped egg whites and the whipped cream gently but thoroughly

1. Fill the prepared cups or molds to the very top so that the frozen souffle will be about 2–3 in. above the top of the souffle cup or mold when the paper liner is removed after freezing.
2. Decorate the tops of the individual cups or molds with whipped cream. Dust the tops lightly with cocoa and confectioners sugar blended together in equal parts.
3. The souffles may be served with a vanilla sauce made by thinning the vanilla pastry cream with a little light cream. A chocolate sauce or syrup may also be served.

4. The basic souffle may be changed into another variety by simply changing the flavor of the ice cream. For example, coffee ice cream may be used for a mocha souffle with the addition of coffee or mocha flavoring.
5. Diced, mixed fruits may be soaked in brandy or rum and the drained fruit may be added to the basic vanilla souffle glace mix for a mixed fruit or a tutti-frutti variety.

Yield: Approx. 100 servings

Fruit Souffle Glace

Fruit souffles are made without the use of ice cream. They are made with a base similar to the Italian meringue in which the sugar and water are boiled almost to a hard ball stage (260°F) and then added to the whipped egg whites. The fruits are usually crushed or pureed and then added to the cool meringue. This is followed by the addition of whipped cream. The following is a recipe for a basic fruit souffle glace mix to which a variety of fruits may be added for variety fruit glaces.

Ingredients	lb	oz	Mixing procedure
Granulated sugar	8		Boil to approximately 260°F
Water	4		
Egg whites	5		Whip the egg whites until quite firm. Add the syrup in a slow, steady stream and whip until cool. Use medium speed after the syrup has been added
Fruit puree (selection of fruit is optional) (4 qt)	8		The fruit is crushed and pureed finely and combined with the lemon juice. Add gradually to the whipped whites and syrup
Lemon juice of fresh lemons preferred	1	4	
Heavy cream (2 qt)	4		Whip the cream to a medium stiff consistency and fold gently into the above. Avoid overmixing

The various fruit souffle glaces are usually served with a special sauce made with a similar or compatible fruit base. The sauces are served separately. Note is made of the fact that a knife dipped in hot water is best for cutting the frozen souffle glaces into portions. The hot blade makes a smooth cut and prevents smearing of the souffle.

Yield: 100 servings

Strawberry Souffle Glace

Wash and hull the fresh strawberries and then pass them through a sieve to puree the berries. A pint of kirsch may be added to improve the taste and flavor of the berries. Add to the fruit glace as indicated in the basic recipe for fruit souffle glace. Frozen strawberries may be used to replace the fresh strawberries. Follow the same procedure. Add some fresh whole or sliced strawberries when folding in the whipped cream. When frozen, garnish the tops with a rosette of whipped cream. Larger souffle glaces may be decorated with whipped cream around the base and sides. A strawberry sauce is served separately with the souffle.

Similar procedures may be followed with other fruits. The fruits used may be canned fruits that have been drained from the syrups. However, the drained syrup may be used for the base from which to prepare the fruit sauce to be served with the fruit souffle glace.

Spooms and Ice Mousses

A spoom is a chilled or partially frozen dessert that is usually served in champagne glasses. It is composed of two parts of Italian (boiled) meringue mixed with 1–1½ parts of sherbet. The sherbet is softened slightly and the cooled, whipped meringue is folded into the sherbet gradually. The sherbet may be added gradually to the whipped meringue and blended at medium speed on the machine. It should be poured immediately into the champagne glasses and served.

Ice mousses are a form of chilled or frozen gelatin based desserts. They are similar to the regular mousse desserts. A basic mousse is usually made which can be used to produce a variety of iced mousses.

Basic Vanilla Mousse

Ingredients	lb	oz	Mixing procedure
Fresh milk (nonfat dry milk and 12 oz and 6 lb of water may be used to replace the fresh milk)	6		Place in a large bowl and bring to a boil over a moderate flame
Vanilla		2	Add and remove milk from fire
Egg yolks	4		Whip the egg yolks and sugar until light.
Sugar	3	8	Add the hot milk and vanilla in a steady
Gelatin		12	stream, the egg yolks and sugar and blend
Water	4	8	in well. Return to the bowl, place on the
Heavy cream (whipped thick)	2	8	fire and heat until thick, stirring constantly. Remove from fire and strain. Al-
Italian meringue (whipped)		(4½ qt)	low to cool slightly and add the gelatin dissolved in the water. Cool and fold in the whipped cream and the prepared Italian meringue

Pour into champagne glasses or other special dishes and chill. Garnish with whipped cream and serve. Melted sweet chocolate, fruits, coffee, and other ingredients can be used for a variety of ice mousses.
Yield: Approx. 100 servings

17

Cake Decorating and Finishing

It is important to remember that not all pastry chefs are gifted with artistic ability and many will produce a fine line of pastries and desserts without unusual flair and first prize achievement. However, there are several major areas of work that must be considered. The fancy cake specialist and maker of showpieces may not be able to produce the great variety of breads, rolls and sweet yeast-raised goods so basic to the daily menu. There are pastry chefs who excel in making these and the many other baked products that are actually the backbone of the menu and supportive of the entire meal. In view of all the variables, and with an awareness of change in the industry toward greater productivity, the pastry chef is also a specialist in his field and in specific areas. Artistic development is a matter of degree and fundamentally based upon innate artistic ability. The unit on decorating is presented primarily for the apprentice pastry chef, the assistants to the pastry chef, and the pastry chef who is also training others to develop the special skills and knowledge related to cake and pastry making.

There are a number of texts and schools available for young pastry chefs who wish to develop the skills of the art of showpiece making. Recipes for a wide variety of icings have been listed in this text. These well serve the basic needs for cake decoration and pastry making and finishing. The illustrations following this chapter, presented with the basic explanation of procedure, are sufficient to start the young apprentice and assistant toward the development of decorating skills. The suggestions made are further enhanced by the skill and knowledge to be gained with practice and application under the guidance of a skilled pastry chef and a knowledgeable instructor.

Assembling the Cake

The cake recipe used is often determined by the type, size, and shape of the cake. A regular, single layer birthday cake may use most any type of cake mix or batter for the layer. In the case of the large, multi-layered wedding cake, or special cake of specific size and shape, the type of cake is more important. A firm cake usually a pound cake or similar cake with a fine, close grain able to support added weight is required for many-layered cakes or special, large shapes. The bottom layers of large cakes have dowels inserted into them at intervals to support the upper layers and the separate decorations between layers. In addition, the cake must be such that it may hold the icing applied without crumbling or settling. Layers for cakes are usually cut into two or more thinner layers and filled with required fillings. Fillings should be such that they do not make the cake heavy or create a problem when cut and served. Fillings should be applied so that they do not run down the sides of the cake. The cake should be of equal thickness throughout and level at the top unless otherwise indicated for a special design and shape.

Most cakes are usually primed with a thinner icing to fill in any layer separations and unevenness that may exist around the sides or at the top of the cake. The initial icing cover is either chilled or allowed to dry as for a royal icing primer. Still other cakes may be masked with a thin covering of jelly or jam and then covered with a thin covering of marzipan around the bottom and sides of the cake. The priming icing is important in that poured icings, such as fondant, may be poured and spread evenly over the surface with a smooth finish. It is also important to be sure the cakes are evenly cut.

Icing Coloring

Coordinating the color scheme of the cake with the floral and other decorations and designs is very important. The icings are colored in advance and the blending of colors is very important. In most instances, the colors are pastel or light in shade, an important consideration when blending two colors in the same decorating bag or conefill. The liquid vegetable dyes are easier to blend than the paste variety. In fact, it is advisable to dissolve the paste in a small amount of warm or hot water and then to keep it in containers for use as required.

When adding coloring to icings, it is necessary to add the coloring gradually since some colors may be stronger than others. In addition, some icings will tend to spread coloring much more readily than others. This is quite noticeable when coloring icings such as fondant, as compared with the coloring of rose paste or a thicker buttercream. While color shades of various types may be available, the pastry chef usually blends his own color shades from the basic colors such as red, green, blue and yellow. Of course, the green may be made by combining the blue and yellow, but its wide use in decorating makes it advisable to have the ready-made green coloring. Further basic combinations are: yellow and red to obtain orange, red and green to obtain brown, and blue and red to obtain purple or lavender. The degree of color or depth of color will vary with the specifics of the cake decoration.

Cake Inscriptions

Cake inscriptions and fine-line decorations are usually made with a parchment paper cone or a very fine, plain tube. Most pastry chefs prefer the special cone made of parchment paper or fine wax, decorating paper. The paper cones are usually made in advance and stored for ready use. To make the paper cones, the parchment paper is cut into squares of varying size. The squares are then folded into triangles and the paper cut along the base to form separate, triangular sheets. The ends of the base of the paper are formed into a point and then wrapped into a cone shape. The outside point of the cone is then folded into the cone and is well creased to prevent the cone from unraveling. The cones are then filled with the smooth icing or piping gel and the tops are folded over so that the icing cannot come out when squeezed from the top. The top folds are folded over so that the icing is squeezed down completely toward the point. With a scissors cut a small hole at the point evenly across. An uneven cut will cause the icing to curl when pressure is applied. The small cone is held between the forefinger and the middle finger as a cigar. The pressure is applied at the top with the thumb. Pressure must be applied evenly to maintain a smooth flow of the icing and to decorate with an even design. (Fig. 17.1)

The inscription on the cake is of central attention and importance. It is the first thing that is looked at. Neatness and clarity are essential. The type of inscription will vary. It may be in the form of script, printed block letters, scroll, or Gothic lettering. Whatever the method, it must be uniform and consistent in size and pattern. The pastry chef will decide which type to use if no type is specified. The inscription should conform to the size of the cake and the space alloted. A large cake may have a larger inscription over a wider area but may also be limited if the inscription is on a plaque or scroll made with marzipan, gum paste, or other preparation. The inscriptions illustrated are in simple written or script form and in a printed form with even lettering. The even pressure and control of the cone containing the icing will determine the result. It is perhaps easier for the apprentice pastry chef or decorating beginner to start with the printed inscription and then proceed to the continued flow of the written or script. It is advisable to make a test off the cake before placing it on the cake. (Fig. 17.2)

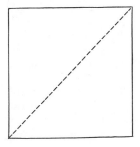
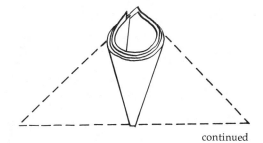

continued

17.1
Making a decorating cone for inscriptions

Cake Border Designs

First the inscription is placed on the cake, then the designs. Fine line decorations are usual for cake borders as well as for small petit fours glaces. The pattern or design should be uniform around the entire cake. A test pattern may be tried off the cake and then placed on the cake.

Control of the pressure on the icing cone is necessary. Changes in pressure will cause a change in the speed or even flow of the icing. It is advisable to hold the point of the cone about 1/2 to 1 in. above the surface of the cake. This will allow for better control of the icing or piping gel and for even movement to form the various designs. The illustrations provide some of the simple fine line designs. The formation of the basic spray design is also illustrated since this design may be used around the edge of the cake as well as at the center or side of the cake for a floral design and effect.

Pastry chefs have their own sets of decorating tubes, pastry bags and other decorating tools. The tubes will vary from the French, star, and plain as well as in the different sizes. Special tubes or nibs are used for making flowers which are piped directly on the cake or made separately

17.2
Designs which may be made with the plain cone

and kept in stock. Roses are usually formed on rose nails or on marzipan bases held in the hand while the petals are shaped into a flower. Special tubes are used for making leaves and other garland designs. These may also be made with a parchment paper cone that has been cut evenly on both sides of the point. The size of the cut will control the size of the leaf.

The designs to be made are controlled by the type of the tube and the size. The border designs are often similar to the designs made when bagging out a variety of spritz-type cookie. The star, the pear-shape, the "C," the rosette, the loop, and many others are used singly or combined for a more attractive design. The simple illustrations are those for the apprentice. The more elaborate tube designs will be found in the special books and courses on cake decorating. Once again, even pressure on the pastry bag is important for these designs.

Flower Designs

The simpler flowers used for sprays and spray designs are often drop-type or flat-type flowers made directly on the cake after the spray design has been made. There are special tubes with the base filled in with a slotted design and a closed center. These are often used for small drop flowers similar to a daisy. Still others are made with a small, curved rose petal tube. The small rose bud, sweet pea (three-petal flower), the apple blossom (five-petal flower) and the orange blossom (six-petal flower), are some of the flat-type flowers made directly on the cake. (Fig. 17.3)

A turntable is very useful when decorating the cake and turning the cake for the petals. These same flowers may be made of rose paste or royal icing and placed on parchment paper discs for use as required. The very small rosebuds may also be made without a rose tube by simply cutting one side of the parchment paper cone in a diagonal manner. A small cut is necessary to avoid large, thick blobs of icing from coming out. When the floral design is completed, the leaves are added to complete the design. Leaves may be made adjacent to the flowers or placed in an even pattern on the spray effect.

With the development of skill through training and practice, the pastry chef establishes a pattern or production method for the cakes to be made. When time permits, the decorating or finishing will be supplemented by preparing a wide variety of small and large flowers in advance. This is

17.3
Blossom designs

effective at times when a large group is to be served with a number of similarly decorated cakes for a special occasion or event. The cakes are lined up after covering and icing and the inscriptions placed on all the cakes at one time. The inscriptions may be placed on small scrolls made of marzipan in advance to speed up the preparation. The spray and floral decorations are then added and the final borders and touches are added. For the larger centerpiece and display piece, the pastry chef may spend many hours and days in the preparation of the showpiece. The masterful art and skill of the pastry chef is then on exhibit.

Cake Decorating Ideas

The illustrations that follow offer a variety of special occasion and holiday designs. These may be revised by the pastry chef to reflect his own artistic tastes and innovations.

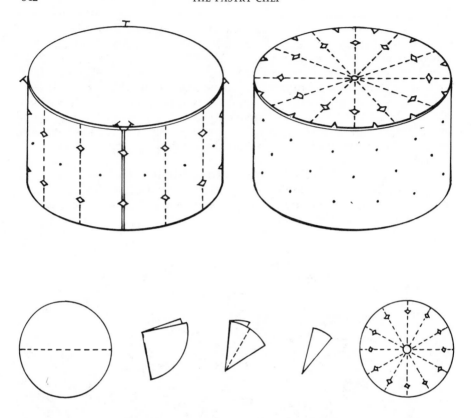

How to measure and mark a round cake

Intricate cake decorating is easier if you plan ahead. For the 10 in. cake
shown on the opposite page, cut a 10 in. circle from parchment or wax
paper. Fold the circle in half, then into quarters. Open the circle and fold
each quarter into thirds since we are using a division of 12 (there are 12
symmetrical designs on the cake). Now refold the circle in fan fashion
and crease sharply. From outer cut edge, measure in 1½ in. and cut a
notch on both sides of the fan. Make a tiny cut at the pointed tip of the
fan. Cut a notch on the curved edge of fan midway between two folded
sides. Open the circle and gently smooth it over cake top. Line up the
folds with the center marks on side of cake. Pin in place. With a
toothpick, mark all notches and cake-top center. Remove pattern, set
cake on serving tray, and decorate using marks as guide.

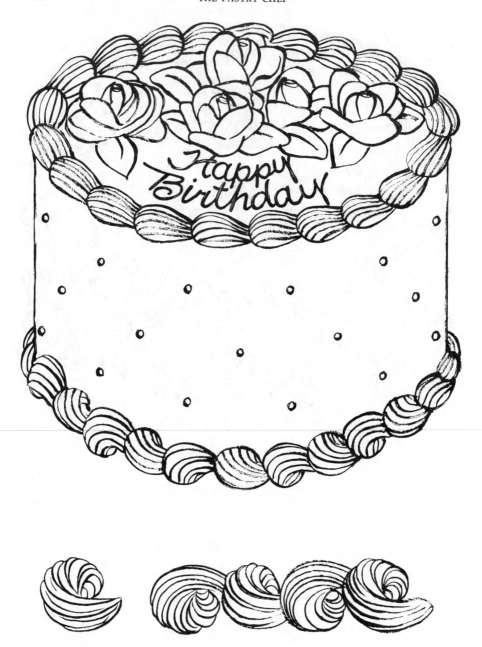

Appendix

Approximate Baking Temperature for Bakery Products and Desserts

Product	Temperature, °F
Variety Breads and Rolls	
White bread (homestyle)	400–410
Egg breads (challah)	350–360
French and Italian bread	410–420
Raisin bread	385–395
Granola bread	400
Cinnamon-tea loaves	385–390
Sourdough bread	400–415
Grandmother's loaf	350–360
Hard-type rolls	400–410
Soft rolls	400
Quickbreads	
Biscuits	400–420
Popovers	410–420
Muffins	375–390
Variety quickbreads	365–385
Sweet Yeast-Raised Dough Product	
Sweet rolls and buns	385–400
Danish pastries	380–400
Large Danish strips	355–370
Savarins and Babas	355–380
Puff pastry varieties	385–400

Note: Variables in temperature are controlled by the size of the product, degree of richness, and degree of crispness required after the product is baked. Miniatures are baked at higher temperatures.

Cakes

Sponge Cakes and Chiffon Cakes

Layer cakes (10 in.)	350–365
Sheet cakes	370–380
Loaves	350–365
Jelly rolls	390–400
Cups (tart forms)	385–390
Large pans (3–4 in. deep)	350

High-ratio Cakes

Layers (variable)	365–375
Sheet cakes	370–380
Loaves (specialties)	365–375
Cupcakes	380–390

Creamed-type Cakes

Layer cakes (10 in.)	365–375
Sheet cakes	370–385
Loaf cakes (variable)	360–370
Cupcakes	375–385
Large cakes (pans 3–4 in. deep)	350–365
Honey cakes and molasses-type cakes	345–360

Angel Cakes

Small tube variety	370–380
Large tube variety	360–365

Pound Cakes

Plain (small loaves)	365–370
Plain (large loaves)	355–365
High-ratio types	360–365
Fruitcake varieties (small)	350
Fruitcake vaieties (large)	340–350

Cheese Cakes

Cream cheese (10 in., variable)	410–370(reduced)
Combination cheese cakes (cream and bakers' cheese)	385–390
Medium cheese cake (large pan)	375–390
German (heavy-type) cheese cake	385–395
French cheese cake	370–380
Cheese tarts	390–400
Chiffon-type cheese layers	400–410
Cheese roll	390–400

Pies, Strudel, and Tarts

Fruit-filled pies	415–430
Fruit pies (open variety)	410–420
Fruit tarts	400–410
Cheese pies	390–400
Custard pies (baked)	385–400
Pie shells (prebaked shells)	400–410
Fruit-filled strudel (apple, etc.)	415–425
Cheese-filled strudel	400–410
Miniature strudel (mixed fruit)	400–410

Note: Variables in pan size and depth, richness of the cakes, consistency of the batter, and type of leavening are factors to be considered in making baking temperature judgments.

Variety Cookies

Sugar or short dough cookies	390–400
Large cut-out cookies	400–410
Bar-type cookies	390–400
Molasses and Christmas cookies	385–395
Large drop cookies (snaps)	385–395
Macaroons (coconut)	385–390
French macaroons	380–390
Spritz-type cookies	395–405
Lace-type cookies	380–385
Stencil-type cookies	385–390
Kisses	240–250
Sandwich-type cookies	390–400
Marzipan or frangipane-type sheets	375–380
Wafer cookies	385–390
Egg-white cookes (kichel)	365–375
Icebox cookie varieties	385–395
Filled cookies (Hamantash)	375–385

Note: Cookies will vary in size and shape. Other types of cookies may have to be baked twice such as the railroad type of cookie. Still others may require baking on double pans depending upon the type of oven and the baking efficiency of the oven. Judgments will have to be made in accordance with the variety of cookie and the method of finishing the baked cookies.

Weights and Measures

Weights and Metric Equivalent

1 ounce = 28.35 grams	1 gram = .04 ounces
1 pound = 0.45 kilograms	1 kilogram = 2.20 pounds
1 ton = 0.91 metric ton	1 metric ton = 1.10 ton

Liquid Measures and Metric Equivalents

1 pint = 0.47 liter	1 liter = 2.11 pints
1 quart = 0.95 liter	1 liter = 1.06 **quarts**
1 gallon = 3.79 liter	1 liter = 0.26 gallon

Lengths and Metric Equivalents

1 inch = 2.54 centimeters	1 centimeter = 0.39 inch
1 foot = 0.30 meter	1 meter = 3.28 feet
1 yard = 0.91 meter	1 meter = 1.09 yards
1 mile = 1.61 kilometer	1 kilometer = 0.62 mile

Avoirdupois Weight

1 grain	=	0.0648 gram	=	
1 dram	=	27.34 grains	=	1.77 grams
1 ounce	=	16 drams	=	28.35 grams
1 pound	=	16 ounces	=	453.59 grams

Ingredient Conversion Tables, Can Sizes and Temperature Conversions

Ingredient Conversion Table

16 oz = 1 pound
1 ounce = 28.35 grams
1 gram = 0.04 ounces
1 kilogram = 2.20 pounds

Ingredient	lb	oz
Whole eggs, 10	1	
Egg whites, 16	1	
Egg yolks, 25	1	
Whole eggs, 1 quart	2	
Egg whites, 1 quart	2	
Egg yolks, 1 quart	2	
Water, 1 quart	2	
Vegetable oil, 1 quart	2	
Buttermilk, 1 quart	2	
Honey, 1 quart	2	12
Invert sugar, 1 quart	2	12
Molasses, 1 quart	2	14
Malt syrup, 1 quart	2	15
Glucose, 1 quart	2	14

Conversion Table for Smaller Measurements
Equivalent Measurements and Weights

3 teaspoons (tsp) = 1 tablespoon (tbsp)
4 tablespoons = ¼ cup
5 tablespoons + 1 teaspoon = ⅓ cup
8 ounces (oz) liquid = 1 cup
2 cups = 1 pint (pt)
2 pints = 1 quart (qt)
4 quarts = 1 gallon (gal.)

Ingredient	Weight	Measurement
Apples, fresh (about 3 apples)	1 lb	3 cups sliced
Baking powder	1 oz	2½ tbsp
Baking soda	1 oz	2 tbsp
Bananas	1 lb	2½ cups (sliced)
Berries (strawberries, blueberries, raspberries)	1 qt	3½ cups (cleaned)
Butter or margarine	¼ lb bar	½ cup
Cake crumbs	3 oz	1 cup
Cardamom, ground	1 oz	5 tbsp
Cheese (hard-type) grated	4 oz	1 cup
Chocolate, grated	1 oz	4 tbsp
Cinnamon, ground	1 oz	4½ tbsp
Cocoa, sifted	1 lb	4¼ cups
Cornstarch	1 oz	2¼ tbsps
Cream of tartar	1 oz	3 tbsp
Eggs, fresh	4–5	1 cup

Egg whites	8–10	1 cup
Egg yolks	12–14	1 cup
Flour, bread or all-purpose	1 lb	4 cups
Flour, cake (sifted)	1 lb	4½ cups
Flour, whole wheat	1 lb	3½ cups
Gelatin	1 oz	4 tbsp
Honey	12 oz	1 cup
Lemon juice	1 oz	2 tbsp
Lemon rind	1 oz	4 tbsp
Mace, ground	1 oz	4 tbsp
Milk, liquid	8 oz	1 cup
Milk, powdered	1 lb	4 cups
Nuts, sliced	4 oz	1 cup
Nuts, ground	3½ oz	1 cup
Oil, vegetable	8 oz	1 cup
Orange rind	1 oz	4 tbsp
Peanut butter	1 lb	1¾ cups
Raisins	6 oz	1 cup
Rice	1 lb	2 cups
Salt	1 oz	2 tbsp
Shelled nuts (walnuts, pecans, almonds)	4 oz	1 cup
Shortening	1 lb	2½ cups
Sugar, brown	1 lb	3 cups
Sugar, granulated	1 lb	2¼ cups
Sugar, confectioners	1 lb	3½ cups
Vanilla	1 oz	2 tbsp
Yeast, fresh compressed	½ oz	1 small cake
Yeast, dried		½ oz compressed yeast equals 1 package dissolved dried yeast

Common Can Sizes
No. 1 (#1) can (tall) = 16 oz
No. 303 = 16 oz
No. 2 = 1 lb 4 oz
No. 2½ = 1 lb 12 oz
No. 3 = 2 lb 1 oz
No. 5 = 3 lb 8 oz
No. 10 = 6 lb 10 oz

Comparison of Can Sizes
1 No. 10 can equals 7 No. 1 tall cans
1 No. 10 can equals 5 No. 2 cans
1 No. 10 can equals 4 No. 2½ cans
1 No. 10 can equals 3 No. 3 cans
1 No. 10 can equals 2 No. 5 cans

Conversion of Fahrenheit and Centigrade Temperatures

F		C
32°F	Freezing Point of Water	0°C
212°F	Boiling Point of Water	100°C

To convert from Fahrenheit to Centigrade, subtract 32 from the Fahrenheit temperature and multiply by 5/9.

Example: Temperature 68°F $68 - 32 = 36$
Convert to Centigrade $36 \times 5/9 = 20°C$

Example: Temperature 20°C
Convert to Fahrenheit: Multiply the Centigrade temperature by 9/5 and add 32.
Step #1—$20 \times 9/5 = 36$
Step #2—$36 + 32 = 68°F$

Factors Concerning the Cooking of Sugar

Sugar in its various forms serves as the basis for most desserts, with special emphasis upon the vast variety of icings and fillings used by the pastry chef. While there are many ready-to-use preparations, some of which do cut production time, most pastry chefs will cook sugar for their special needs. Of course, there are basic preparations such as fondant and stabilizing supplements which assure good icing yield and stability that pastry chefs use in fast food, mass production situations. Still, there are the pastry chefs who prefer to cook the sugar syrups as required for the show-pieces, as well as for the pastries and icings made with cooked sugar.

The boiling and cooking of sugar requires a fundamental understanding of the principles involved. Simply put, with continued cooking of sugar syrups or sugar concentrates, the concentration of sugar becomes greater as more of the water is boiled or evaporated out with cooking. This also means that the temperature of the sugar syrup becomes higher with the increased concentration of the sugar. The varying degrees of the syrups will designate the condition of the syrup and what the pastry chef may do with the sugar concentrate at any given temperature. Thus, a sugar concentrate or syrup that reaches a temperature of approximately 240°F is ready for further processing into a fondant icing. At other stages, other uses are made for various products. The temperature of the sugar should be measured accurately with a sugar thermometer. Pastry chefs will often use other methods which require that droplets of the boiling sugar be immersed in cold water for the feel and the action. The concentration of the sugar is also determined by the proportion of sugar to water used for the basic cooking. It is good practice to use approximately 2½–3 lb of granulated sugar for each pound of water used to place the sugar into solution.

Glucose, cream of tartar, lemon juice, and other acid-type ingredients are often added to cooked syrups. The acid maintains the syrup in its cooked liquid or paste form without granulation of the sugar to its original state. These substances are used in cream-type icings and fillings used for candies and special bonbons and petits fours. The acid or cream of tartar is also used in egg whites to be whipped for aerated icings, to which boiled or cooked sugar syrups are added as the egg whites are being whipped. This is quite evident in the preparation of marshmallow-type icing. The kettle for cooking the syrup has traditionally been made of copper because of its excellent heat absorption and distribution capacities. Stainless steel has become popular. Kettles and other vessels used for the cooking of sugar should be clean and free of impurities.

During the early stages of cooking, the sugar is stirred gently to ensure complete and thorough solution to prevent early scorching. As the sugar starts to boil, the sides of the kettle are usually brushed with cool water to dissolve sugar crystals that form and tend to adhere to the sides of the kettle. The heat may be increased once the sugar has started to boil and the sides have been washed down. When boiling begins, and for a few minutes thereafter, a film or foam of impurities will surface on the syrup. This is to be removed with a slotted skimmer. The skimmer is washed with water and then returned to remove any further foam or scum surface. The sugar should be checked by a thermometer to get the accurate temperature. When the desired temperature has been reached, a coloring may be added and gently stirred in. The sugar syrup will continue to boil and increase in temperature even when removed from the fire. It is advisable to place the kettle with the sugar in another kettle containing cool water, or even set the kettle on a bed of ice to remove the heat immediately after removal from the fire. This will maintain the characteristic of the syrup at that temperature.

As previously indicated, sugar gradually changes its character as a syrup concentrate as it increases in temperature due to cooking. The stages for each temperature level are indicated and explained below:

220°F This is the approximate boiling point of the average simple syrup, and is called the simple syrup stage.

222–225°F This is the thread stage. A fork or small, slotted spoon or skimmer dipped into the syrup will show threads of the syrup extending from one tong to the other.

228°F The syrup on the fork or skimmer will form long threads when the droplets of syrup are blown with a deep breath.

232–235°F This is known as the blow stage or sugar bubble stage. The droplets of sugar syrup when blown will tend to blow out in the form of bubbles of sugar.

242–245°F A droplet of the boiling sugar when placed in a glass or cup of cold water will tend to form a soft ball when rolled between the fingers.

255–260°F This is known as the hard ball stage. A drop of the cooked syrup at this temperature will tend to form into a firm ball when molded between the fingers.

280°F This is known as the soft crack stage. A few drops of syrup will tend to crack when compressed with the fingers after dropping into cool water.

312°F This is known as the hard crack stage. The syrup will tend to crack readily when compressed after it has been cooled.

350°F This is known as the caramel stage. The sugar syrup will have turned dark brown and will eventually turn very dark or black into a burned sugar. At this point, the sugar is removed from the flame and water added to it to dilute the sugar and form a caramel color. This is used to darken bread such as pumpernickel. It is also used in the kitchen to color or darken gravies and sauces.

Note is made of the fact that pastry chefs will still test the temperature of boiling sugar by dipping fingers into ice water, quickly dipping the fingers into the boiling syrup, and returning them to the ice water. The consistency of the sugar is tested with the fingers. Very often pastry chefs will use their teeth to test the cracking or hard ball stages of cooking. These practices are hazardous and greater reliability should be placed upon the readings of the sugar thermometer.

Adjustments for High Altitude Baking

The important factor for bakers to remember is that as altitude increases atmospheric pressure decreases. This means that at high altitudes there is less resistance to the rising and expansion of chemically leavened cakes. Yeast-raised products react similarly but they are more readily controlled by reducing the yeast and slightly increasing the flour to make the dough firmer. This helps to maintain structure during final proofing and the initial stages of baking. For sweet yeast-raised goods, eggs are often increased to provide increased protein and for retention of volume during and after baking.

The greatest impact of altitude change is upon the production of cakes. The pure sponge cakes leavened solely with eggs are not affected much because of the structure formation of the egg protein. The cakes that are made with the creaming method of mixing and the high-ratio cakes made with the blending method of mixing require careful attention and adjustment of formulary. The following are factors and suggestions for bakers and pastry chefs to consider.

Leavening Agents and Ingredients that Function with Leavening Agents Baking powder, baking soda, cream of tartar, and other chemicals that have a leavening effect upon cakes are reduced with increased altitude. The higher the altitude the greater reduction beginning at 2000 feet elevation (making a 15% reduction at this level). The following reduction levels for chemical leavening agents are suggested:

Elevation	Percentage of Reduction
2000 feet	15
3000 feet	23
4000 feet	30
5000 feet	38
6000 feet	45
7000 feet	52
8000 feet	60

For each additional 1000 feet above the 8000 feet level, reduce the chemical leavening agent amount by 8%.

In darker cakes using buttermilk, molasses, honey, and other syrups, it is necessary to reduce the baking soda and baking powder proportionately. If yellow or white cakes contain buttermilk in the formulary, it may be advisable to replace the buttermilk with regular milk and replace the baking soda with a lesser percentage of baking powder. This eliminates the reaction of the baking soda with the acidity of the buttermilk and thus reduces the amount of chemical leavening.

When making creamed types of cake batter, it is important not to overcream the batter. Excessive creaming will incorporate large amounts of air cells some of which may overexpand and rupture during baking. A reduction in creaming will prevent the crumbling effect of open and porous grain and texture. Emulsifiers maintain keeping quality of cakes baked at high altitudes.

Eggs Beginning at 2500 feet elevation above sea level, add 2½% more whole eggs or egg whites in order to increase protein and structure building properties. Gradually increase the egg content as the elevation increases until at 7500 feet 15% more eggs are used. By increasing the eggs, more liquid is added to the cake mix. Eggs normally contain approximately 75% water, so the liquid content must be reduced accordingly.

Flour As previously indicated, yeast-raised dough should be made slightly firmer at higher altitudes than at sea level. This is especially important with rich sweet yeast dough in order to obtain proper proof and maximum volume. In cakes, beginning at 3500 feet elevation, increase the flour by 2½% and gradually increase the amount to approximately 10% at 8000 feet elevation.

Additional Suggestions Cake pans should be greased and dusted well if cake pan liners are not used. Beginning at 3500 feet elevation, increase the oven temperature approximately 10 to 15 degrees to avoid overbaking and drying out the cakes. At higher elevations there is more rapid evaporation of moisture during baking.

Where egg yolks are used in the recipe, egg adjustments at higher altitudes should be made with whole eggs or egg white additions. These egg varieties contain more moisture than do the egg yolks. Slightly less whipping of the eggs is required for sponge cakes and angel food cakes. Chemical leavenings used in cakes made with the foam or whipping method should be reduced as indicated for other cake varieties, especially when water or milk is folded into the whipped batter that is also leavened with baking powder or baking soda.

Glossary

Cake And Pastry Terms

Acidity   The degree or proportion of acid in a substance.

Agar-agar   A substance obtained primarily from seaweed that has a gelatinous effect when combined with liquids. It is used as a thickening agent in sauces, fillings, jellies, etc.

"A la"   In the style or fashion of a country or mode, such as "à la Francaise," meaning French style.

Albumen   A protein that is typical of egg whites.

Ammonium bicarbonate   A rapid-acting chemical leavening agent used in special bakery products and cookies.

Ananas   The French word for pineapple.

Angelica   Candied stalks of an aromatic plant that are used to decorate cakes and pastries.

Aniseed   The fruit of the anise plant that is quite fragrant. It is primarily used in finely ground form.

Arrowroot   A starch obtained from a tropical plant that is used as a thickening agent for sauces and fillings.

Baba   A yeast-raised cake that is rich in eggs and usually dipped in rum before serving.

Bag out   To press or squeeze a mix, icing, or topping out of a cone-shaped bag with or without a pastry tube.

Bain-Marie   A double boiler or one vessel containing hot or warm water into which another, smaller vessel is placed.

Bande Aux Pommes   A French pastry strip made with apples.

Bar-le-Duc   A jam made from currants and often in jelly-like form.

Bavarois (Bavarian)   A creamy dessert that is thickened with gelatin and which contains whipped cream.

Beat or whip   To whip air into a liquid mass such as eggs, heavy cream, or gelatin solution to a desired lightness.

Beignets   A light pastry usually fried in deep fat such as fritters.

Beurre   The French word for butter.

Beurre Noisette   Butter that has been melted and heated until brown.

Blend   To fold or mix two or more materials together to obtain equal distribution.

Biscuit Glace   A frozen dessert composed of a mixture of paté à bombe, whipped cream, and flavoring blended with ice cream.

Blanch   To remove the skin of various nuts by scalding in water.

Blinis   Small buckwheat cakes similar to pancakes.

Bonbons   Candies that are usually dipped in fondant and containing a variety of center fillings.

Bouchees   Small, delicate puff pastry patties.

Bombe   A round or oval-shaped frozen dessert made with a cover of ice cream or sherbet and usually containing a mousse center.

Brandy   A strong liquor that is distilled from wine or other fermented fruit juices.

Breaking down   Overcreaming of ingredients, causing weakened products which collapse.

Brioche   A sweet yeast-raised cake or bun that is rich in egg yolks and eggs and baked in single pans similar to a tart.

Canapés   A hot or cold type of hors d'oeuvres.

Candied fruits   Blanched fruits that have been soaked in syrup.

Caramel   Sugar syrup or sugar that has been boiled or heated to a light brown color.

Caramelization   The burning of sugar.

Caraway seeds   Seeds from the parsley herb that are used for flavoring and in variety breads.

Cardamom   The aromatic seeds of an Asian plant of the ginger family used especially for flavoring in rich, yeast-raised sweet yeast goods.

Cassia A coarse bark obtained from the cassia tree and the source of finely ground cinnamon.

Cassis The French word for black currants.

Chapelure Sifted bread crumbs.

Charlotte A sweet dessert usually lined with Lady Fingers.

Chausson French name for turnovers.

Chocolate The solid material or substance obtained from the crushing and refining of the cacao bean to which other ingredients are added for variations in types of chocolates.

Choux Chantilly A cream puff usually filled or garnished with whipped cream.

Choux paste Paste used for the production of cream puff and eclair shells.

Clarify To remove any impurities from a liquid such as fillings, juices, and jellies to establish a transparent condition.

Clove The bud of the clove tree that is usually ground for use in cakes or pastries.

Coagulate To clot or curdle.

Cocoa The finely ground and processed bean of the cacao tree.

Cognac A brandy usually distilled from wine.

Compote Stewed and chilled fruit or fruits served in combination.

Confiture A sweet preserve or jam.

Corbeille A basket-shaped form made from ice, sugar, or other material.

Cornet A cone-shaped paper used for decorating or a cone-shaped food used for canapés or hors d'oeuvres.

Coupe A chilled dessert usually served in a champagne glass, and most often composed of fresh fruits and ice cream or sherbet.

Couverture A chocolate used for filling and finishing of cakes, cookies, and pastries.

Cream To mix sugar, shortening, butter, and other ingredients to incorporate air into the mix or batter.

Cream Aganasse A Hungarian chocolate cream variety.

Creme Au Beurre A light buttercream used for cake fillings and cake finishing.

Crepes Very thin French-type pancakes.

Croissant A rich type of sweet yeast dough that is rolled up into a crescent shape.

Croquante A preparation composed of caramel sugar mixed with almonds used for cakes and special cake showpieces.

Croquembouche Small profiteroles (miniature cream puffs slightly larger than soup nuts) that may or may not be filled, and then coated with a caramel sugar and piled into a cone or pyramid shape.

Croustade The French name for a patty shell.

Cuisine The French term for cooking or kitchen.

Culinaire The term is applicable to the art of cooking and baking.

Currants A type of seedless raisin that is used for making jelly or jam.

Dariole A puff pastry type of cake that is made in special molds not much larger than the average drinking glass in size, and usually filled with a variety of selected cream fillings.

Dartois A puff pastry usually made into individual servings and often filled with an almond filling.

Decorating The art of inscribing fancy inscriptions or designs on cakes and pastries.

Divorson A French pastry usually composed of two colors.

Dry A condition present in a baked product resulting from a low liquid content or the degree to which the product was baked.

Dumplings A small mass of dough that may be filled and is usually placed in a boiling liquid for cooking or baked as for a biscuit.

Eclair A long, finger-shaped pastry made from a choux paste and filled with a pastry cream or whipped cream.

Entremets A dessert and often a vegetable that is served after the main course.

Feuilletage Refers to puff pastry.

Flan A French name for a tart filled with either a custard or fruit filling.

Fleurons A variety of small shapes cut from a puff pastry dough and often used as a serving garnish with meat, soup, or fish dishes.

Folding The act of gently incorporating flour or some other whipped and aerated mixture into a batter.

Fourres   Refers to bonbons.

Francaise (a la)   In the French style or manner.

Friandises   The French name for small cakes such as petits fours.

Frosting   Icings used for cakes and pastries.

Fry   To cook in hot fat.

Gateaux   Layer cakes, usually sponge-type cakes, filed with a variety of different fillings and iced or masked with buttercreams.

Gelatin   A dried protein extracted from bones and tendons of animals and used as a thickening or binding agent for a variety of fillings and aspics.

Gelatinize   To convert into a jelly-like substance.

Glace   Refers to frozen or iced cakes and desserts.

Glucose   A syrup manufactured from cornstarch that is quite thick and transparent.

Gourmet   A person who is a connoisseur of fine foods and is often called an epicure.

Gradually   The act of proceeding in stages.

Graining   Generally refers to sugar which has returned to a crystalline state after it has been boiled.

Greasing   The act of applying a soft or melted shortening or butter to a pan to prevent the cake or batter from sticking.

Guava   A tropical fruit that is used for jelly making.

Gugelhof   A light cake made from a sweet yeast-raised dough.

Guimauve   The French term for marshmallow.

Hericart   Refers to desserts made with strawberries or served with strawberries.

Ice   The act of applying a variety of icings to various cakes and pastries.

Icing   A frosting made with sugar and other ingredients that is applied to a variety of cakes and pastries.

Italienne   In the Italian style or manner.

Jalstroff   Refers to desserts made with raspberries or served with raspberries.

Kirsch   A liqueur made from fermented black cherries and often mixed with other fruits.

Kugelhof   The same as gugelhof.

Leavening   A substance, organic or inorganic, that will produce aeration before or during baking. It creates a gas which is released when coming in contact with liquid and heat.

Light and firm   That degree of lightness and stability usually applied to the whipping of eggs and sugar.

Lime   A fruit of the citrus group that is green in color and is used for flavoring.

Line   Applies to the placement of a dough around the bottom and sides of a pan to contain the batter or filling.

Mace   The berry of the nutmeg tree that is ground to a fine powder.

Macedoine   A mixture of fruits or vegetables.

Mango   A tropical fruit with a slight acid taste; it is often used in conjunction with other fruits or desserts.

Marignan   A yeast-raised pastry made in the shape of an oval or small boat.

Marrons   The French word for chestnuts.

Mask   To ice or cover cakes or molds with icings or ice creams, as well as sauces.

Marsala   A wine originally from Marsala, Italy, used in the preparation of Sabayon sauce.

Marzipan   A special confection in a paste form that is primarily made of almond paste and sugar; it contains some egg whites, other ingredients are optional.

Melba   Generally refers to a dessert served with a Melba sauce.

Menu   The bill of fare.

Mignardises   Another French term for petits fours.

Millefeuilles   Meaning one-thousand leaves and refers to puff pastries.

Mirette   A dessert that is made with a currant jelly or jam or Bar-le-Duc.

Moist   A product's ability to hold moisture which keeps the product fresher longer.

Montmorency   Refers to a dessert made with cherries.

Mousse   French term for any preparation that is whipped to a light consistency such as a frozen dessert made with whipped cream, paté à bombe, and other ingredients.

Nesselrode   A pudding or filling that is made with rum and diced fruits and combined with a special pastry filling.

Noisette   The French word for hazelnut.

Nougat   A French candy made with cooked honey, sugar, and a variety of nuts.

Paillettes au Parmesan   The French name for cheese straws.

Pain   The French word for bread.

Pain a la Mecque   An oval-shaped cream puff filled with cream.

Palmier   A puff pastry made in the form of a palm leaf by rolling the dough in sugar and folding into layers before baking.

Panache   A mixture of two or more types of fruits and/or ice creams.

Parfait   A frozen dessert made with a combination of a mousse and an ice cream and served in special glasses.

Parmesan   A hard cheese that originated in Parma, Italy.

Pastillage   A gum paste used for making a variety of candies, flowers, and cake specialities for exhibit.

Paté   A paste.

Paté à bombe   A special preparation made from egg yolks and boiled sugar used in ice cream bombes and similar desserts.

Patisserie   Refers to pastry varieties.

Pectin   A substance derived from fruits and used as a thickener for various fillings.

Petits fours   Small iced cakes of various shapes and designs.

Petits pains   Small rolls of various types.

Pomme   The French word for apple.

Pote Creme   A custard that is baked and served in a cup.

Praline   A paste made from boiled sugar, almonds, and other types of nuts and used as a flavoring and garnish in cakes and pastries.

Profiteroles   Small puffs that are made from choux paste or eclair and cream puff paste.

Punch   A drink or dessert, sometimes in a semifrozen state, that is made from fruit juices, sugar, water, and/or spirits.

Puree   Ingredients or foods passed through a fine sieve and made into a smooth pulp.

Quiche   A cheese-custard type of tart that is also made in large pan form and then cut into portions.

Rock sugar   A candy-type of sugar that is used for making show pieces and also for special garnishes.

Sabayon   A special sweet sauce made with Marsala wine, eggs, and sugar.

Sacher cake   A special chocolate cake originated by a pastry chef named Sacher.

Savarin   A sweet yeast-raised cake similar to the Baba.

Score   To make cuts or designs that are cross-hatch or lattice-like in design on cakes and desserts.

Scrape down   To scrape the batter from the sides of the kettle to form a uniform blend.

Sherbet or Sorbet   A water-ice dessert flavored with fruit juices and spirits.

Shrinking   The act of contracting as in a dough that has been rolled out and not allowed to relax.

Soggy   A condition in which the cake or pastry has an excessive amount of liquid or moisture, often causing doughs to be raw or not completely baked.

Souffle   A light baked or steamed pudding or dessert.

Souffle Glace   A light dessert made with ice cream or sherbet, whipped cream, and paté à bombe and frozen.

Sponge   A preliminary dough preparation in which the yeast is activated for the base dough upon which the final dough is made.

Stiff meringue   Egg whites and sugar whipped to a light, firm mass.

Stirring   The act of agitating a liquid or soft batter.

Streaky   A baked dough condition in which discolored, narrow bands appear.

Tapioca   A starchy substance obtained from the cassava root and used as a thickening agent for desserts and fillings.

Texture   The inside grain and degree of smoothness in a product.

Torte   A tart that is baked in a shallow tart pan or ring.

Tragacanth   A gum that is specially used for the preparation of gum paste and marzipan.

Turban   A cake or dessert made in a turban-shaped mold or pan.

Tutti-frutti   A term that refers to a mixture of a variety of fruits that are dried and sugared and often used in conjunction with ice cream desserts.

Valencia   A name usually applied to a dessert made with oranges.

Vol au Vent   Patty shells made from puff pastry dough and filled with a variety of fillings for different purposes and desserts.

Volume   That degree of size obtained by the mixture or dough upon being baked.
Washing   The act of applying a liquid over a product with a brush before or after baking.
Wet peak   Refers to a mixture of sugar and other ingredients such as eggs, egg whites, meringue powders, and heavy cream or topping, wherein the mixture forms a wet peak after being whipped.
Whip   The act of beating or whipping eggs, cream, and other ingredients with a wire hand whip or the wire beater of a mixing machine.

Bread Baking Terms

Absorption   The ability of a flour to absorb water, measured by the quantity of water absorbed, to produce the proper consistency.
Adding   The process of increasing.
Blending flours   The process of mixing flours for the purpose of obtaining the desired flour characteristics.
Bread box   A square wooden box 40 × 40 × 4 in. in which the rounded dough or molded loaves of bread are allowed to proof.
Cleave or round   To shape a piece of dough into a smooth, special form.
Cutting   The act of cutting the top crust of the loaf to allow the gas to escape while baking.
Developing dough   The act of mixing the dough to a smoother state by added mixing.
Dissolving   The act of liquefying.
Dusting   The act of spraying flour or corn meal.
Fermentation   The chemical reaction of the ingredients used in making the dough which causes the forming of a gas, carbon dioxide, in the dough which in turn causes the dough to expand.
Folding or punching   The act of forcing gas out of dough by folding one part of the dough over the other.
Gluten   The rubbery, elastic substance found in flour when water is added.
Humidity   The water vapor or water content of the air.
Hygroscopic   The ability to draw moisture from the air.
Incorporating   The act of mixing or blending one ingredient with another.
Knead   To work into a mass or to develop dough by added mixing.
Leavening   A substance which will produce gas to cause aeration within a product (in bread, yeast).
Measuring   The act of determining the amount of liquid ingredient.
Mixing   The act of blending into one mass.
Molding   The act of forming the loaf of bread.
Peel   A flat board fastened to the end of a long or short pole and used for placing bakery products in the oven and taking them out again.
Peeling   The act of putting bread or bakery products in the oven by means of a peel.
Pouring   To empty, as a liquid, out a vessel or kettle.
Preliminary proofing   A short period of fermentation after the dough has been scaled or rounded.
Press out   To divide a piece of dough into a specified number of pieces by means of a press machine.
Proof   The last stage of fermentation before baking.
Roll box   The same type of box as the bread box but with half the height. Used for molded rolls or doughnuts.
Scaling   The act of weighing ingredients.
Sifting   Running material through a sieve.
Steaming   The act of injecting steam into the oven while baking.
Stippling or docking   Piercing the loaf by means of a straight piece of heavy wire for the purpose of letting the gas escape while being baked.
Stirring   The act of agitation, used in dissolving.
Temperature   The degree of heat or coldness.
Tempering   To modify or regulate the temperature of the water to meet requirements.

Index